INVESTIGATION OF
THE ASSASSINATION OF PRESIDENT JOHN F. KENNEDY

HEARINGS

Before the President's Commission
on the Assassination
of President Kennedy

PURSUANT TO EXECUTIVE ORDER 11130, an Executive order creating a
Commission to ascertain, evaluate, and report upon the facts relating
to the assassination of the late President John F. Kennedy and the
subsequent violent death of the man charged with the assassination
and S.J. RES. 137, 88TH CONGRESS, a concurrent resolution conferring
upon the Commission the power to administer oaths and affirmations,
examine witnesses, receive evidence, and issue subpenas

Volume

II

UNITED STATES GOVERNMENT PRINTING OFFICE
WASHINGTON, D.C.

Reprinted by Michigan Legal Publishing Ltd.
www.michlp.com
ISBN: 978-1-942842-22-4

PRESIDENT'S COMMISSION
ON THE
ASSASSINATION OF PRESIDENT KENNEDY

CHIEF JUSTICE EARL WARREN, *Chairman*

SENATOR RICHARD B. RUSSELL
SENATOR JOHN SHERMAN COOPER
REPRESENTATIVE HALE BOGGS

REPRESENTATIVE GERALD R. FORD
MR. ALLEN W. DULLES
MR. JOHN J. McCLOY

J. LEE RANKIN, *General Counsel*

Assistant Counsel

FRANCIS W. H. ADAMS
JOSEPH A. BALL
DAVID W. BELIN
WILLIAM T. COLEMAN, Jr.
MELVIN ARON EISENBERG
BURT W. GRIFFIN
LEON D. HUBERT, Jr.

ALBERT E. JENNER, Jr.
WESLEY J. LIEBELER
NORMAN REDLICH
W. DAVID SLAWSON
ARLEN SPECTER
SAMUEL A. STERN
HOWARD P. WILLENS*

Staff Members

PHILLIP BARSON
EDWARD A. CONROY
JOHN HART ELY
ALFRED GOLDBERG
MURRAY J. LAULICHT
ARTHUR MARMOR
RICHARD M. MOSK
JOHN J. O'BRIEN
STUART POLLAK
ALFREDDA SCOBEY
CHARLES N. SHAFFER, Jr.

Biographical information on the Commissioners and the staff can be found in the Commission's *Report*.

*Mr. Willens also acted as liaison between the Commission and the Department of Justice.

Preface

The testimony of the following witnesses is contained in volume II: James Herbert Martin, who acted for a brief period as the business manager of Mrs. Marina Oswald; Mark Lane, a New York attorney; William Robert Greer, who was driving the President's car at the time of the assassination; Roy H. Kellerman, a Secret Service agent who sat to the right of Greer; Clinton J. Hill, a Secret Service agent who was in the car behind the President's car; Rufus Wayne Youngblood, a Secret Service agent who rode in the car with then Vice President Johnson; Robert Hill Jackson, a newspaper photographer who rode in a car at the end of the motorcade; Arnold Louis Rowland, James Richard Worrell, Jr., and Amos Lee Euins, who were present at the assassination scene; Buell Wesley Frazier, who drove Lee Harvey Oswald home on the evening of November 21, and back to work on the morning of November 22; Linnie Mae Randle, Buell Wesley Frazier's sister; Cortlandt Cunningham, a firearms identification expert with the Federal Bureau of Investigation; William Wayne Whaley, a taxicab driver, and Cecil J. McWatters, a busdriver, who testified concerning Oswald's movements following the assassination; Mrs. Katherine Ford, Declan P. Ford, and Peter Paul Gregory, acquaintances of Lee Harvey Oswald and his wife; Comdr. James J. Humes, Comdr. J. Thornton Boswell, and Lt. Col. Pierre A. Finck, who performed the autopsy on the President at Bethesda Naval Hospital; and Michael R. Paine and Ruth Hyde Paine, acquaintances of Lee Harvey Oswald and his wife.

Contents

COMMISSION EXHIBITS INTRODUCED

Hearings Before the President's Commission
on the
Assassination of President Kennedy

TESTIMONY OF JAMES HERBERT MARTIN RESUMED

The President's Commission reconvened at 3 p.m.

Mr. DULLES. Gentlemen, the Commission will come to order.

Are you ready to continue the testimony, Mr. Martin?

Mr. MARTIN. Yes, sir.

Mr. DULLES. Will you carry forward, Mr. Redlich?

Mr. REDLICH. Mr. Martin, I would like to hand you a group of newspaper clippings which have not as yet been introduced in evidence and I would ask you to look through them and to pick out any which you feel create an image of Mrs. Marina Oswald which you feel does not conform to the reality of her personality, as you know it, and ask you in regard to each one to tell us in what respect the facts as reported in each of these clippings do not conform to the real person as you know her.

Mr. DULLES. I assume we can avoid repetition, can't we?

Mr. REDLICH. Yes.

Mr. DULLES. Incidents here have been touched on in other papers and we don't need to touch them again.

Mr. REDLICH. Yes, Mr. Chairman.

During the intermission we have gone through all of the newspaper clippings and eliminated the duplicate stories and hope to eliminate duplicate facts as we go along.

Mr. MARTIN. Well, this one is inaccurate that it doesn't have anything to do with her image, so to speak. It says she spent Christmas——

Mr. REDLICH. For the sake of the record if we are going to have comment on them I would like to have them introduced as evidence because the record wouldn't state what they are about.

Are you going to make comment?

Mr. MARTIN. Do you want me to?

Mr. REDLICH. If you are going to make comment about it, if you feel there is some inaccuracy here then I would like to introduce that in evidence, since apparently you are.

Mr. MARTIN. It is inaccurate as far as the date in the article is concerned.

Mr. REDLICH. The witness has handed to us a newspaper story which we have marked as Commission Exhibit No. 328.

Mr. DULLES. Could we have the inaccuracy mentioned here?

Mr. REDLICH. Yes, the headline of which is "Mrs. Oswald Will Bare Life of Mate" and I request it be admitted in evidence.

Mr. DULLES. Any objection?

Mr. LEECH. No.

Mr. DULLES. It will be admitted.

(The document referred to was marked Commission's Exhibit No. 328 for identification and received in evidence.)

Mr. REDLICH. I show you Commission Exhibit No. 328 and ask you if there are any inaccuracies in that statement.

Mr. MARTIN. "Mrs. Oswald and Her Children Now Make Their Home at an

Undisclosed Hotel" which is inaccurate—"and it was in that motel room, somewhere in the Dallas-Fort Worth area that the youngest Oswald child spent her first Christmas. There was a tree, toys and even a visit from Mrs. Oswald's brother who lives 30 miles to the north in Denton, Tex."

That was the inaccuracy that she spent Christmas not in a motel but in our home.

Mr. DULLES. That is about from 3 o'clock in the afternoon as I recall until 7:30 in the evening.

Mr. MARTIN. No, sir; that was Thanksgiving.

Mr. DULLES. That was Thanksgiving. Spent the whole day of Christmas in your home?

Mr. MARTIN. Well, she lived there. She was at our home 24 hours a day.

This one—

Mr. REDLICH. The witness has produced before the Commission a newspaper story which we have labeled as Commission Exhibit No. 329, the headline of which reads, "Money Gifts to Tippit's Near $200,000 Mark."

Mr. Chairman, I request that Commission Exhibit No. 329 be admitted in evidence.

Mr. DULLES. Any objection?

Mr. LEECH. No.

Mr. DULLES. It shall be admitted.

(The document referred to was marked Commission Exhibit No. 329 for identification and received in evidence.)

Mr. REDLICH. Mr. Martin, I hand you Exhibit No. 329 and ask you if it is inaccurate in any respect.

Mr. MARTIN. The article states that Mrs. Shirley Williamson, a Fort Worth housewife, who felt compassion for the widow, Mrs. Oswald, and the two babies said the fund for the Russian-born widow had reached $76,000."

The fund that Mrs. Williamson collected amounted to some $2,600. That was her total. That is the inaccuracy there.

Mr. DULLES. Is she referring to the funds she collected or the whole collections?

Mr. MARTIN. Her funds. This has come up numerous times. We even called her about it one time. She had given out press releases that she had collected personally, I think, in excess of $8,000, whereas what she was doing was adding what she had collected to what had already been sent to Marina, and saying that she was holding that money.

Mr. DULLES. But even that total is exaggerated, is it not?

Mr. MARTIN. At that time, yes.

Mr. DULLES. The total collections?

Mr. MARTIN. At that time, yes.

Mr. REDLICH. Mr. Martin, this article also makes reference to the fund on behalf of the wife of Officer Tippit with which, of course, you have no connection.

I would like to ask you, however, whether at the time you extended the offer to Marina Oswald to live in your home you were aware of the fact that there were funds being raised for Officer Tippit's wife.

Mr. MARTIN. I was undoubtedly aware of it but I don't recall any conscious knowledge of it or thinking of it.

Mr. REDLICH. Do you recall whether you were aware at the time that there were any funds coming in on behalf of Mrs. Oswald?

Mr. MARTIN. No.

Mr. REDLICH. You were not aware?

Mr. MARTIN. Not aware, no.

Mr. REDLICH. The witness has offered to, has presented to, the Commission a newspaper story appearing in the Buffalo Evening News, December 7, 1963, headline of which reads, "Oswald's Widow Reported Hoping to be U.S. Citizen."

This story has been identified as Commission Exhibit No. 330 and I ask that it be introduced in evidence.

Mr. DULLES. Any objection?

Mr. LEECH. None.

Mr. DULLES. Accepted.

(The newspaper article referred to was marked Commission's Exhibit No. 330 for identification and received in evidence.)

Mr. REDLICH. Mr. Martin, I show you Commission's Exhibit No. 330 and ask you if it is inaccurate in any respect to the best of your knowledge?

Mr. MARTIN. In the second paragraph it says, "Mrs. Oswald, 23," which is inaccurate—"Russian-born Mother of Three—"

Mr. REDLICH. Will you state the inaccuracy?

Mr. MARTIN. The age is inaccurate. She is 22, "Russian-born Mother of Three" that is inaccurate. She is the mother of two, "burst into tears when she learned at least $7,700 had been sent to her by sympathetic Americans." There was no burst of tears.

Mr. REDLICH. Will you tell the Commission what the reaction was?

Mr. MARTIN. I would say of happiness rather than—she was glad that that was there, which is normal.

Mr. REDLICH. Do you recall anything she told you?

Mr. MARTIN. No. This was December 7. No, I have no recollection of anything that she said?

Mr. DULLES. Didn't you testify before, maybe it is with regard to another or similar clipping, that she had some reference to the silly Americans who were giving this money?

Mr. MARTIN. Well, it was a comment she had made at sometime or another. I don't know whether it was during this particular thing or not. I think it was further on.

Mr. DULLES. On a similar occasion?

Mr. MARTIN. A little later date, yes.

Mr. REDLICH. Mr. Martin, you have commented on the respects in which the newspaper clippings were at variance with the facts about Marina Oswald as you knew them.

Are there any other facts which perhaps were not reflected in these clippings but which you might be aware of in respect to which the public image of Marina Oswald differed from the true person that you knew on the basis of your contact with her?

Mr. MARTIN. No. Of course, she is not the least bit frugal. She spends money quite freely, which it is her money to spend, but it won't last very long at the rate it is going.

Mr. REDLICH. In connection with that did Marina Oswald ever discuss with you the financial difficulties she may have encountered while she was married to Lee Oswald?

Mr. MARTIN. Yes. She remarked one time that she had always wished for $500 just to do with as she wanted. She also mentioned that the small amount of money that it took them to live upon. She said it ran between $130 and $135 a month.

Representative FORD. Did she complain about this limited amount?

Mr. MARTIN. No. I asked her how she could live on that little and she said well, all they had was rent and food, and occasionally she would get a dress or get a pair of shoes. She said that she didn't object to it.

Representative FORD. But when more money became available she found ways and means of spending it?

Mr. MARTIN. Yes. Well, she mentioned one time to me that—I told her she was spending too much money, and she said, "Well, when it is all gone I will go to work." That is——

Mr. DULLES. That is a little Russian, may I say for the record.

Mr. REDLICH. Mr. Martin, this Commission has recovered information to the effect that the public announcements which you made concerning the amount of funds which had been collected on Marina Oswald's behalf actually reflected figures that were less than the amount which had actually been collected on her behalf.

Without getting into specific figures at this time, are these reports correct in your opinion?

Mr. MARTIN. Which report?

Mr. REDLICH. The report——

Mr. MARTIN. Oh, yes, we were obtaining a smaller figure, that is true.

Mr. REDLICH. That is true. Did you consult with Marina Oswald on this policy on reporting to the press a lesser figure than had actually been collected?

3

Mr. Martin. Yes.

Mr. Redlich. What was your reason for doing it?

Mr. Martin. To—well, the money she had collected was considerable, and most people in their life don't accumulate that much money in their entire lifetime.

What we were trying to do for her was to build enough of a—enough capital to furnish her from the interest a steady income. And by keeping the figure down figured it would increase.

Mr. Redlich. I don't want to put words in your mouth. Could you be a little more specific about your reason?

Mr. Martin. Well, so people would keep contributing to her cause.

Mr. Redlich. And she was in accord with this policy of keeping the public amount at a low figure so that people would contribute to her cause?

Mr. Martin. Yes.

Mr. Redlich. I would like to revert to a point that you made this morning to clear up the record. You said that you left your job at the Six Flags Inn Motel because of your obligations to Marina Oswald. Did you leave the job voluntarily or were you fired?

Mr. Martin. I left voluntarily. I actually left on the 15th of December, and I had a week's vacation coming, they gave me that which paid me to the 1st of January.

Mr. Redlich. When you met Mrs. Oswald in late November and in your conversations with her at that time, did she discuss with you the fact of her husband's trip to Mexico?

Mr. Martin. No.

Mr. Redlich. Are you now——

Mr. Martin. She did at a later date, sometime in January before she went to the Commission.

Mr. Redlich. When did you first learn of Lee Oswald's trip to Mexico?

Mr. Martin. I guess it was from newspaper accounts.

Mr. Redlich. When you read it in the newspapers did you ask Marina about it?

Mr. Martin. No.

Mr. Redlich. What prompted you to discuss with Marina in January the question of her knowledge about it?

Mr. Martin. Let's see—she told me when the FBI was questioning her one day, she told me that they had information that he had attempted suicide, and that particular day she didn't want to see the FBI at all, and she was a little bit unhappy with them and I just asked her what else did she learn.

Mr. Redlich. Who else was present at this conversation?

Mr. Martin. I don't think anybody.

Mr. Redlich. Just you and Mrs. Oswald?

Mr. Dulles. Who was this who had attempted suicide, I didn't catch that?

Mr. Martin. Lee Harvey Oswald.

Mr. Dulles. At what time?

Mr. Martin. That was in Russia sometime before, I think before he met her.

Mr. Dulles. And she said she had heard this from the FBI or the FBI had asked her about it?

Mr. Martin. The FBI had read, I think, in his manuscript that he had attempted suicide.

Mr. Dulles. And they asked her about it?

Mr. Martin. She didn't know that. Yes. And at that time I asked her if she learned anything else, and she said no, but that they still didn't know that she knew that he had gone to Mexico, and at that time we were talking about the Commission, that general area of time, and I mentioned to be sure to tell the truth to the Commission.

Mr. Redlich. Did you ask her why she had not revealed knowledge of her trip—of her knowledge of Lee Oswald's trip to Mexico?

Mr. Martin. I can't recall exactly whether I did or not.

Mr. Redlich. Did you ask her?

Mr. Martin. I have a recollection but I have no idea what was said.

4

Mr. REDLICH. Did you and she discuss the purpose of Lee Oswald's trip to Mexico?

Mr. MARTIN. No.

Mr. REDLICH. Do you say you advised her to tell this Commission about that trip to Mexico?

Mr. MARTIN. Yes.

Mr. REDLICH. When you were here and she testified did you inquire of her as to whether in fact she did tell this Commission about the trip to Mexico?

Mr. MARTIN. I inquired of John Thorne and he said that she had.

Mr. REDLICH. But in connection with the Nixon incident, you indicated earlier in your testimony that you had not inquired of her as to whether she had told this Commission about the Nixon incident.

Mr. MARTIN. Right.

Mr. REDLICH. Did you think that the Nixon incident was of less importance than the Mexican trip?

Mr. MARTIN. No, I didn't quite believe the Nixon incident.

Mr. REDLICH. Do you believe it now?

Mr. MARTIN. I don't know. I don't know if there is any corroboration other than her say so.

Mr. REDLICH. It was because you had doubts about the actual existence of the incident that you didn't pursue with her the question as to whether she should tell this Commission about it?

Mr. MARTIN. Yes. I didn't tell her not to say anything about it. I didn't mention it specifically at all. The only thing I told her to do was to tell the Commission the truth in all cases.

Mr. REDLICH. At the conclusion of each day's testimony while she was here before this Commission did you discuss the nature of her testimony with her?

Mr. MARTIN. No. I asked her how the day went. And she would tell me, "fine," and that was the end of it.

Mr. REDLICH. But you did inquire specifically about the Mexico trip?

Mr. MARTIN. Yes. Because I knew she lied about that to the FBI.

Mr. REDLICH. Are there any other incidents you knew she had lied about to the FBI?

Mr. MARTIN. No.

Mr. REDLICH. That is the only one?

Mr. MARTIN. Yes.

Mr. REDLICH. Did you and Marina Oswald ever discuss the question of her husband's rifle practice?

Mr. MARTIN. No. The only time I recall that ever being asked of her was at the press conference here in Washington, and I never specifically asked her at all, whether he practiced.

Mr. REDLICH. Did you ever discuss with her the question of Lee Oswald's ownership of a rifle?

Mr. MARTIN. No.

Mr. REDLICH. When you discussed the General Walker incident with her, did you discuss his ownership of a rifle?

Mr. MARTIN. No. The only thing, I think about the only thing I asked her about that was how he got there and how he got back.

Mr. REDLICH. What did she say?

Mr. MARTIN. She said he walked and took the bus.

Mr. REDLICH. And you didn't ask her what weapon he had shot at General Walker with?

Mr. MARTIN. No. That was in the newspaper, it was a rifle. And there were many things I didn't ask about because I was previously informed through the news or I thought I was anyway.

Mr. REDLICH. You specifically, with regard to the rifle, you are telling this Commission that you had no conversations with Marina Oswald concerning her husband's practice with the rifle either in Dallas or in New Orleans.

Mr. MARTIN. Let's see—I think I did discuss with her one time at the rifle range out in Grand Prairie was it, wherever it was, that the owner had seen Lee Harvey Oswald out there with a rifle, and he drove up in a car.

Mr. REDLICH. Who is "they"?

Mr. MARTIN. The owner of the rifle range.

Mr. REDLICH. You say they drove up in a car?

Mr. MARTIN. He drove up in a car.

Mr. REDLICH. The owner of the rifle range?

Mr. MARTIN. No; Lee Harvey Oswald.

Mr. REDLICH. Drove to the rifle range in a car?

Mr. MARTIN. Yes. And——

Mr. DULLES. Did he drive himself?

Mr. MARTIN. Well, this is a report from the rifle range owner who said he had seen Lee Harvey Oswald there on numerous occasions practicing, and that he drove up in a car by himself. He always came by himself, and I did ask her if he could drive and she said no, definitely.

Mr. REDLICH. Where did you read this report or where did you hear about it?

Mr. MARTIN. It was right after the start there, in the Dallas papers.

Mr. REDLICH. This was something you read. This was not a personal conversation you had with the owner of the rifle range?

Mr. MARTIN. No, it was a newspaper account.

Mr. REDLICH. Were there any other conversations you had with Mrs. Oswald concerning rifle practice?

Mr. MARTIN. No.

Mr. REDLICH. Did you have any conversations with her concerning Lee Oswald's ability as a rifleman?

Mr. MARTIN. No.

Mr. REDLICH. Did Mrs. Oswald ever discuss with you the fears that she claims to have had that Lee Oswald would attempt to kill a public figure as a result specifically of the Walker incident?

Mr. MARTIN. No, other than when she told me that she told him that if he tried anything similar to the Walker incident she would have him arrested. And she never mentioned to me a particular figure that he would do anything like that. She evidently had it though or she wouldn't have made the threat to him.

Mr. REDLICH. Other than the Nixon incident, and the Walker incident, Mrs. Oswald never related to you any other specific incident with regard to the attempt to take the life of anyone?

Mr. MARTIN. No.

Representative FORD. Did Mrs. Oswald, Marina, ever indicate to you her feeling toward guns; did she ever indicate any apprehension about having one in the house?

Mr. MARTIN. No.

Representative FORD. Related to rifles, pistols?

Mr. MARTIN. I have a 22 rifle in the house, for instance. Of course, she may never have seen it. But I don't believe the question ever came up at all.

Representative FORD. She never indicated to you that she had told Lee Harvey Oswald that she was apprehensive about his use of a gun or his having a gun in the household?

Mr. MARTIN. No.

Mr. REDLICH. Mr. Martin, I would like to ask you whether Mrs. Oswald ever discussed with you any aspects of the life of Marina Oswald and Lee Harvey Oswald while they were in Russia.

Mr. MARTIN. Let's see now—she mentioned one time to both my wife and I that Lee had gone to Moscow, I believe, and an old boy friend called her up and she went out with him while Lee was gone.

Mr. REDLICH. Did she indicate to you at that time the purpose of Lee's trip to Moscow?

Mr. MARTIN. No.

Mr. REDLICH. Did she indicate to you whether she had told Lee about her going out with this old boy friend?

Mr. MARTIN. She said she did tell him.

Mr. REDLICH. By the way, would you recall when Lee made this trip to Moscow?

Mr. MARTIN. No, I don't think she mentioned the date at all. She may have but I don't recall.

Mr. REDLICH. Did she indicate in connection with this trip of Lee Oswald to Moscow that she herself subsequently went to Moscow while he was there?

Mr. MARTIN. No. I think she said he was gone one day or one night and came back the next day.

Mr. REDLICH. So that on the basis of your recollection, if there was a trip in which Lee Oswald went to Moscow and she joined him there this was a different trip from the one you are talking about?

Mr. MARTIN. Yes.

Mr. REDLICH. Is that right?

Mr. MARTIN. Yes.

Mr. REDLICH. Just to make sure of this you say to the best of your recollection she said he went there for one day and returned?

Mr. MARTIN. Yes.

Mr. REDLICH. Can you think of any other aspects of their life in the Soviet Union that Marina discussed with you.

Mr. MARTIN. He used to like her aunt. Now, which aunt I don't know. Yes, I do. It is the aunt that is working as a secretary and her husband is on a pension. She has an aunt and an uncle by blood.

Now, the aunt's husband is on a pension, and the uncle's—The uncle is a lieutenant colonel in the Soviet Army.

Mr. REDLICH. Now, the aunt and uncle that you say she liked very much, is this the aunt and uncle with whom she was living at the time she met Lee Oswald or is this a different aunt and uncle?

Mr. MARTIN. That was all very—always confusing to me because she wouldn't call the spouse of the aunt, for instance, her uncle, and I couldn't tell all the time which party she was talking about.

Mr. DULLES. These were both relatives to Marina, therefore, they were not married.

Mr. MARTIN. Well, no; they were not married to each other.

Mr. DULLES. That is what I mean, yes.

Mr. MARTIN. There were two couples, and the aunt in one couple and the uncle in the other couple. But she didn't refer to the opposite spouse as an aunt and uncle.

Mr. REDLICH. Does the name Berlov refresh your recollection any?

Mr. MARTIN. Berlov?

Representative FORD. Did Marina ever indicate to you anything about her education, what school she attended?

Mr. MARTIN. No, just the school of pharmacy, and she compared her grade school or our grade school, which is, I guess similar to our grade school in high school or junior high, anyway.

Representative FORD. She only referred to the pharmacy training?

Mr. MARTIN. Yes.

Representative FORD. As any special training she received?

Mr. MARTIN. Yes.

Representative FORD. But she did discuss that with you?

Mr. MARTIN. Not at length. Just stated the fact that she had finished pharmacy school.

Representative FORD. But she didn't discuss any other training or schooling of a special nature.

Mr. MARTIN. No.

Representative FORD. Did she ever discuss any special training that Lee might have had while he was in Russia?

Mr. MARTIN. No.

Representative FORD. Did she ever discuss Lee's employment while he was in Russia?

Mr. MARTIN. Only that he was unhappy where he was working.

Representative FORD. Did she tell you where he worked, the kind of work he was doing?

Mr. MARTIN. I don't know, I have an idea it was in a factory of some kind, whether she told me that or whether it was an assumption, I don't know.

Mr. REDLICH. Did she ever discuss their apartment, their living quarters in Minsk?

Mr. MARTIN. Yes, she said she had a one-room apartment, and had a balcony on it, and that as soon as the baby was born they were going to move to a larger one. I questioned her about that because I understand it is quite difficult to get more than a one-room apartment in Russia and she said, well, Lee was an American and he could get things the Russians couldn't get.

Mr. REDLICH. Did Mrs. Oswald give you the impression that in general she and Lee Oswald had better treatment than other Russians?

Mr. MARTIN. Yes, and actually her past life even before she met Lee seemed a little bit strange to me, going to the opera, taking vacations and holidays as she says. I understand it is quite expensive to go to the opera, and she was making, what did she say, 45 rubles a month, and she would take a girl friend with her when she went to the opera.

Now, how much that cost, I don't know.

Mr. REDLICH. Did you ever question her about her financial situation in Russia?

Mr. MARTIN. I asked her how she could afford it and she said she got by. She was living at home or with her aunt and uncle. So I imagine their expenses there weren't high.

Mr. REDLICH. Did she mention any extra income which Lee Harvey Oswald may have had apart from his job?

Mr. MARTIN. No; I asked her about that specifically because I had heard an account that he was supposed to be getting Western Union money orders, and asked her about that. She didn't know what a Western Union money order was, for one thing, so I reworded the question and asked if he was getting money from anyone else other than where he was working, and she said no.

Mr. REDLICH. This was true of this life in the Soviet Union?

Mr. MARTIN. Yes, apparently.

Mr. REDLICH. Did Marina ever discuss with you the uncle with whom she lived who was apparently a lieutenant colonel in the Soviet army?

Mr. MARTIN. No; except she didn't like him.

Mr. REDLICH. Did she say why?

Mr. MARTIN. No. She preferred her aunt, who has the husband on the pension.

Mr. REDLICH. Can you search your memory at this point and tell this Commission anything that you have not yet told us about Marina's conversations with you concerning her life in the Soviet Union?

Mr. MARTIN. Her aunt used to bring food and liquor home after parties had at the government building where she was working. Other than talking about—she pulled one tooth out before she came to the United States. A tooth was either crooked or broken and she pulled the tooth out. That caused the other one to twist. I don't know what that was.

Representative FORD. Did Marina ever indicate to you while she was in the Soviet Union that she drank beer, wine, liquor?

Mr. MARTIN. Vodka.

Representative FORD. When she came to the United States, you could observe it, did she drink beer, wine, liquor of any kind?

Mr. MARTIN. She drank, I guess she drank a bottle of beer every day, and occasionally she would drink some vodka.

Representative FORD. But not a heavy drinker?

Mr. MARTIN. No.

(Discussion off the record.)

Mr. REDLICH. Mr. Martin, have you ever been curious about how Mrs. Oswald was ever able to leave the Soviet Union?

Mr. MARTIN. Well, I wasn't, until Don Levine brought up the subject. Of course, I have no idea what it entails to get into Russia or out of it as far as that is concerned.

But according to Mr. Levine, it is extremely difficult for people to get out of Russia, especially when they have had the training that Marina has had.

Mr. REDLICH. By training you mean what?

Mr. MARTIN. Pharmacy. He said they spent quite a bit of money on her training, and he doesn't understand how she got out of Russia on such short notice.

Mr. REDLICH. Did you ever ask this question of Marina Oswald?

Mr. MARTIN. She said that Lee arranged it, and that is all she would say.

Mr. REDLICH. She never discussed any other aspect of her departure from the Soviet Union?

Mr. MARTIN. No. Let's see, they were in Moscow, she waited a couple of days while he was, how did she put it, collecting money or getting money together to come over to the States. I have forgotten the name of the hotel they stayed in. She even remarked they had pancakes every morning and she didn't like pancakes.

Mr. REDLICH. In terms of her official negotiations to leave the Soviet Union, you asked her nothing other than the question that I have already discussed with you?

Mr. MARTIN. No, she said that Lee arranged everything.

Mr. REDLICH. I would like to ask you a few questions now about some of the individuals that Marina and Lee Harvey Oswald knew in Fort Worth and Dallas, and ask you in each case whether Marina Oswald discussed any of these individuals with you.

The first is George Bouhe.

Mr. MARTIN. I know the name but I don't think Marina has ever mentioned him; Katya Ford has though.

Mr. REDLICH. Are you personally acquainted with George Bouhe?

Mr. MARTIN. No.

Mr. REDLICH. Could you tell us what Katya Ford has told you about Mr. Bouhe?

Mr. MARTIN. It was relating to Marina—I think Katya Ford and Boube are friends, and they had been discussing Marina all the time she was in seclusion, and wondering what had happened to her, where she was. Now this was after the news was out where she was.

Mr. REDLICH. Are you acquainted with——

Mr. DULLES. Excuse me, by "in seclusion", you mean at the time she was with you in your house?

Mr. MARTIN. Yes, and the press didn't know where she was.

Mr. DULLES. I see.

Mr. REDLICH. Are you acquainted with George De Mohrenschildt or his wife Jean De Mohrenschildt?

Mr. MARTIN. No.

Mr. REDLICH. Have you ever discussed either George or Jean De Mohrenschildt with Marina Oswald?

Mr. MARTIN. No.

Mr. REDLICH. Have you ever discussed George and Jean De Mohrenschildt with anyone else?

Mr. MARTIN. No.

Mr. DULLES. Did you ever hear the name mentioned before?

Mr. MARTIN. No. I think I would remember that name.

Mr. REDLICH. Are you personally acquainted with Peter Gregory?

Mr. MARTIN. I met him once, maybe twice, at the Inn. He was interpreting for Marina, for the Secret Service, I believe, before Lee Gopadze got there.

Mr. REDLICH. Do you know who he is?

Mr. MARTIN. I understand he is a geologist, and he also teaches Russian.

Mr. REDLICH. Did Marina ever discuss either Peter Gregory or Paul Gregory with you?

Mr. MARTIN. She mentioned—I don't know which one.

Mr. REDLICH. One is the father and one is a son.

Mr. MARTIN. I think it is the older gentleman that I met. She mentioned that she liked him.

Mr. REDLICH. The older gentleman?

Mr. MARTIN. Yes. And I think she corresponded with him. I know she corresponded with him.

Mr. REDLICH. Do you have any knowledge of Mr. Gregory's son?

Mr. MARTIN. No.

Mr. REDLICH. Have you ever met him?

Mr. MARTIN. Not to my knowledge.

Mr. REDLICH. You have had no conversations with anyone else about him?

Mr. Martin. No. We were—I think John Thorne and I were talking about at sometime we may need an interpreter, and I mentioned his name in that instance.

Mr. Redlich. That would be the elder Mr. Gregory?

Mr. Martin. Yes. But nothing on Paul Gregory.

Mr. Redlich. Nothing on Paul Gregory?

Mr. Martin. No.

Mr. Redlich. Are you aware of the fact that Paul Gregory is a student at the University of Oklahoma?

Mr. Martin. No.

Mr. Redlich. Did Marina ever discuss with you the fact that she had helped tutor the son of Peter Gregory?

Mr. Martin. No.

Mr. Redlich. Are you familiar with—strike that.

Do you have any personal acquaintanceship with Gary Taylor?

Mr. Martin. No.

Mr. Redlich. Have you ever heard the name of Gary Taylor?

Mr. Martin. No.

Mr. Redlich. Marina Oswald has never discussed that name with you?

Mr. Martin. No.

Mr. Redlich. Do you know Mrs. Elena Hall?

Mr. Martin. Elena Hall? No.

Mr. Redlich. Has Marina ever discussed her with you?

Mr. Martin. No.

Mr. Redlich. The name John R. Hall, who is the husband of Mrs. Elena Hall?

Mr. Martin. No, it sounded a little familiar but I can't place anything on it.

Mr. Redlich. Do you know Mrs. Katherine Ford?

Mr. Martin. Yes.

Mr. Redlich. Could you tell us how you came to know her?

Mr. Martin. Let's see, she had contacted Marina a couple of times by letter, and——

Representative Ford. While she was staying at your home?

Mr. Martin. Yes—well, she sent the letter to Grand Prairie, the letters, Christmas cards, and I think two letters after that. So I called her and Marina wanted to, expressed a desire to, talk to her. So I called her and Marina talked to her on the phone. I think every time she talked to her she talked nearly an hour.

Representative Ford. In Russian or in English?

Mr. Martin. In Russian.

Mr. Dulles. Was it on the telephone?

Mr. Martin. Yes.

Mr. Redlich. Did Marina ever tell you the gist of these conversations?

Mr. Martin. No.

Mr. Redlich. Did Marina ever relate to you whether she had ever lived in Mrs. Ford's home?

Mr. Martin. I believe she had for a very short time.

Mr. Redlich. You mean Marina related this to you?

Mr. Martin. I think Mrs. Ford told me that.

Mr. Redlich. How did you get this knowledge, from Marina or from Mrs. Ford? Did you ever discuss this with Marina?

Mr. Martin. No. I know Marina likes her home, I mean likes the house that they live in.

Mr. Redlich. Did you ever ask Marina how it came about that she was separated from her husband and living at the home of Mrs. Ford?

Mr. Martin. No.

Mr. Redlich. Did any of Marina's other Russian-speaking friends in the Dallas-Fort Worth area write letters to her while she was at your home?

Mr. Martin. Mrs. Paine wrote at least once a week and——

Mr. Dulles. Once a week?

Mr. Martin. Yes. Marina did not answer, didn't answer any of the letters and didn't call her.

Mr. Redlich. Did Mrs. Paine attempt to reach Marina by phone?

Mr. MARTIN. Yes, until I had my telephone number changed and then she couldn't find the phone number so she came over to the house.

Mr. REDLICH. What happened when she came to the house?

Mr. MARTIN. Nothing, I let her in the house and Marina and the children were back in the den and the Secret Service men went back into the den, and I don't believe she knew that she was there.

Mr. DULLES. Was the change in number, did it have anything to do with Marina as objecting to receiving the calls?

Mr. MARTIN. No. That was strictly because the press pressure.

Mr. DULLES. The presence of the press?

Mr. REDLICH. I would like to go back to this incident when Mrs. Paine came to see Marina. You say Marina did not know that Mrs. Paine was there?

Mr. MARTIN. Yes, she knew it.

Mr. REDLICH. She knew that Mrs. Paine was there?

Mr. MARTIN. Mrs. Paine didn't know that Marina was there.

Mr. REDLICH. But Marina knew that Mrs. Paine was there?

Mr. MARTIN. Yes

Mr. REDLICH. Did Marina see Mrs. Paine at that time?

Mr. MARTIN. No.

Mr. REDLICH. Did you talk to Marina at that time?

Mr. MARTIN. Well, before and after.

Mr. REDLICH. At the time Mrs. Paine was there did you personally tell Marina that Mrs. Paine wanted to see her?

Mr. MARTIN. I told her before Mrs. Paine came in the door that Mrs. Paine was here, and she said she didn't want to see her. She stayed in the den, and Mrs. Paine was in the living room.

Mr. REDLICH. Then did you convey this message to Mrs. Paine yourself?

Mr. MARTIN. No.

Mr. REDLICH. Who did?

Mr. MARTIN. Well, she came with the intention or for the purpose of bringing a package to Marina that she had received in the mail, and I don't believe she knew that Marina was living there. I told her at that time that because of security that Marina wasn't seeing anyone but I don't believe she knew that Marina was at that address until later.

Mr. REDLICH. When Mrs. Paine called your home prior to the change of phone, did you speak to Mrs. Paine?

Mr. MARTIN. No, my wife did.

Mr. REDLICH. Do you recall the nature of the conversations between your wife and Mrs. Paine as reported to you?

Mr. MARTIN. Well, let's see, she called and asked for Marina or asked to get in touch with Marina. My wife gave me the number and I guess I called her back.

Mr. REDLICH. You called Mrs. Paine back?

Mr. MARTIN. A day or two later, yes.

Mr. REDLICH. What did you say to her?

Mr. MARTIN. I told her that under the present circumstances she just didn't want to see anybody, and also the security on her didn't permit her to go out too far. That we could possibly arrange a meeting at some middle point later on.

Mr. REDLICH. Was Marina free to see anyone she wanted to see?

Mr. MARTIN. Yes.

Mr. REDLICH. And the reason she didn't see Mrs. Paine was because she didn't want to see Mrs. Paine?

Mr. MARTIN. Yes. I asked her several times to call her, at least call Mrs. Paine and tell her she didn't want to see her, and she just shrugged her shoulders and said she didn't want to talk to her.

Mr. REDLICH. Did Marina ever tell you why she didn't want to talk to her?

Mr. MARTIN. She said something about Mrs. Paine talking too much, and she didn't like Mrs. Paine's children.

Mr. REDLICH. Were you aware at the time that Marina had lived with Mrs. Paine?

Mr. MARTIN. Yes.

Mr. REDLICH. Were you aware at the time that Mrs. Paine had taken the Oswald family to New Orleans and had——

Mr. MARTIN. Yes.

Mr. REDLICH. Gone to New Orleans and brought them back to Irving, Tex.?

Mr. MARTIN. Yes, that is why I felt she owed Mrs. Paine something.

Mr. REDLICH. What was Marina's attitude toward your comments?

Mr. MARTIN. She just didn't want to talk to her.

Mr. REDLICH. Did you yourself ever meet Mrs. Paine?

Mr. MARTIN. Yes.

Mr. REDLICH. Would you describe that meeting?

Mr. MARTIN. Well, the first time I met her was we went over to the Paine's house to pick up some of Marina's belongings.

Mr. REDLICH. Who is "we"?

Mr. MARTIN. John Thorne and I.

Mr. REDLICH. Do you recall about when this was?

Mr. MARTIN. I guess it was about a week after she had moved in, maybe shorter, maybe sooner than that. There was not much said at all at that meeting. Then when she came out to the house she talked at length, but it was——

Mr. REDLICH. There is another occasion when you say she came?

Mr. MARTIN. When she came to my house.

Mr. REDLICH. That was the same occasion that you referred to earlier when she came to pick up a package?

Mr. MARTIN. To deliver a package.

Mr. REDLICH. To deliver a package, I am sorry. Could you relate what happened at that time?

Mr. MARTIN. I was quite distracted by the children. It was rather a stiff meeting or conversation.

Representative FORD. This was the meeting at Mrs. Paine's house?

Mr. MARTIN. No, my house.

Representative FORD. Your house?

Mr. MARTIN. Mrs. Paine brought, I think, a package and some food, cookies, things like that, for Marina, and——

Mr. DULLES. Those are from Mrs. Paine to Marina, but the package was a third——

Mr. MARTIN. The package came through the mail.

Mr. DULLES. That you understand, but the cookies came from Mrs. Paine.

Mr. MARTIN. Yes.

I believe she brought some toys for the children. What the toys were, I don't recall. Her children were running back and forth through the living room making quite a bit of noise.

Mr. DULLES. Mrs. Paine's children?

Mr. MARTIN. Yes. And I wasn't really paying too much attention to what she was saying. I was wanting her to leave. I didn't ask her to leave but I wasn't saying much to foster the conversation. Then she left in, I guess, 15 minutes.

Mr. REDLICH. What did Mrs. Paine say to you?

Mr. MARTIN. Oh, boy——

Mr. DULLES. Was she disturbed, I mean was she annoyed, visibly annoyed, that Marina wouldn't see her. She didn't know Marina was in the house, I realize that.

Mr. MARTIN. She didn't know Marina was in the house. I am certain she didn't.

Mr. REDLICH. You mean her children were running around the house though, weren't they?

Mr. MARTIN. Her children were running in the living room and dining room.

Mr. DULLES. But not into the den?

Mr. MARTIN. But not into the den and kitchen.

Representative FORD. Do you have a door on the den so you can close the den off?

Mr. MARTIN. Yes. She talked mostly about generalities and she would like to see Marina to make sure she is well taken care of, and so on. She was concerned about her. And she came back after that time, she came back once more. I wasn't there. My wife answered the door and didn't invite her in.

Mr. DULLES. How long a trip is it from your house to Mrs. Paine's, roughly, a few miles?

Mr. MARTIN. No, a good 20 miles.

Mr. DULLES. A good 20 miles?

Mr. MARTIN. Because it is 30 miles out to the Inn, and she lives about 8 or 10 miles toward me from the Inn, so it is about 20 miles.

Mr. REDLICH. Your wife did not invite Mrs. Paine into the house at that time?

Mr. MARTIN. No.

Mr. REDLICH. Was this at Marina's urging?

Mr. MARTIN. Yes. Mrs. Paine was quite upset at that—that is what Wanda said, she looked upset at that time.

Representative FORD. On this occasion, did Mrs. Paine know Marina was in the house?

Mr. MARTIN. No, I don't believe so.

Mr. DULLES. Did she ask where she was, specifically?

Mr. MARTIN. No.

Mr. DULLES. She didn't ask?

Mr. REDLICH. What was the purpose of her visit?

Mr. MARTIN. I don't believe—let's see, she may have brought something that day, too. I don't recall whether she did or not. I know right after that, the Civil Liberties Union got into it. Well, Mark Lane, was first.

Mr. REDLICH. You say right after that Mark Lane got into it?

Mr. MARTIN. Yes.

Mr. REDLICH. Would you elaborate on that?

Mr. MARTIN. Mark Lane came to Dallas, and contacted John Thorne and I. We met him at the Statler and talked to him at lunch, and he expressed a desire to talk to Marina Oswald so that he could represent her husband, defend her husband in a hearing, and we told him that we would relay that information to her.

So we did, and she said that she didn't want to have any representation. She didn't want any more——

Mr. REDLICH. You mean she didn't want any representation for Lee Oswald?

Mr. MARTIN. Yes, she didn't want any more to do about it.

Representative FORD. Can you recall the date of this visit by Mr. Lane?

Mr. MARTIN. No.

Representative FORD. Was it in December or January?

Mr. MARTIN. It was in January, I believe.

Mr. REDLICH. And you transmitted Mr. Lane's message to Marina?

Mr. MARTIN. Yes, and she said that she didn't want any representation for Lee.

Mr. REDLICH. Did you tell her this in English?

Mr. MARTIN. Yes, and explained it to her, and at that time she could understand.

Mr. DULLES. To your knowledge, did Marina ever meet Mr. Lane?

Mr. MARTIN. Not to my knowledge, no.

Mr. REDLICH. And you also related the Ruth Paine, second Ruth Paine, visit to your home to something which you referred to as the American Civil Liberties Union business.

Mr. MARTIN. It was right after—these incidents happened rather closely. The letter from the Civil Liberties Union—well, first we received a telephone call from the Civil Liberties Union wanting to see Marina Oswald.

Representative FORD. Telephone call from Dallas or New York, or what?

Mr. MARTIN. From Richardson, the same person who wrote the letter which you have there. Do you have that?

Mr. REDLICH. We do have. We are inventorying many of these documents of which the American Civil Liberties letter is one and we will introduce it at an appropriate time.

Mr. MARTIN. Richardson is a suburb of Dallas.

This gentleman called, what was his name?

Mr. LEECH. I can't remember it.

Mr. REDLICH. Would it refresh your recollection if I mentioned the name Olds?

Mr. MARTIN. Yes, Greg Olds. He called on the phone and wanted to see Marina Oswald, wanted to make sure she was being properly represented, that she knew her rights, and so on and so forth.

John Thorne talked to him, and told him that he represented Marina Oswald, and that he was definitely sure that all her rights were being observed.

Then I think there was another phone call from them still wanting to see Marina Oswald, and I talked to Marina and she said well, she would talk to him. So they arranged a meeting with a third party, I can't remember his name, who was a minister of some kind, and then Marina changed her mind and said no, she didn't want to go at all, she didn't want to talk to any of them. So then they wrote the letter. They wrote a letter to her in Russian and sent one to me in English, one to John Thorne in English, and I believe one to the Secret Service and one to the FBI.

Mr. LEECH. Do you want to mention about their press releases at this time?

Mr. MARTIN. There were a number of press releases at that time also that she was being held incognito and not able to——

Mr. REDLICH. You mean incognito or incommunicado?

Mr. MARTIN. Incommunicado.

Representative FORD. Press releases by whom?

Mr. MARTIN. The Civil Liberties Union, and so they sent this letter to her and she answered it with a two-page letter in Russian.

Representative FORD. In Russian?

Mr. MARTIN. Yes.

Mr. REDLICH. Do you have a copy of that two-page letter?

Mr. MARTIN. No. She wrote it, put it in an envelope, put a stamp on it and I mailed it. I didn't open it or look in it in any way. And that seemed to be the end of it, but they still persisted they wanted to see her.

Mr. REDLICH. And the reason Marina did not see them was entirely her own volition?

Mr. MARTIN. Her own.

Mr. DULLES. She never talked to you about what was in the letter?

Mr. MARTIN. No, she said she just told them she didn't want to see them.

Mr. DULLES. In two pages?

Mr. MARTIN. Yes, sir; This was quoted, a portion of the letter was quoted, in the Worker.

Representative FORD. I suggest, Mr. Chairman, that we get, if possible, a copy of the original of that letter.

Mr. MARTIN. You probably can get it from Greg Olds.

Mr. DULLES. Would you make a note of that. I think we should do that.

That was dated sometime in the middle of January?

Mr. MARTIN. I believe so. The letter you have—she wadded the letter up that was written to her in Russian and threw it away, and I got it back out, and asked her to go ahead and write them a letter so it would quiet them. So she said she would and she wrote a letter, I think, that night, so it would be within a couple of days of the date of that letter, the English copy of which you have.

Mr. REDLICH. Mr. Chairman, if you would like, we could take a 3- or 4-minute recess and I could get the American Civil Liberties Union letter to Marina Oswald and introduce it at this time for the sake of clarity in the record.

Mr. DULLES. Good. It is a good time for a breather.

(Short recess.)

The CHAIRMAN. All right, gentlemen, the Commission will be in order.

You are familiar with, Mr. Dulles, you are familiar with, the hearing up to date. You go right ahead and preside, if you will.

Mr. DULLES. Mr. Redlich will you go right ahead with your questions?

Mr. REDLICH. I believe Congressman Ford, you said you wanted to ask your questions prior to your leaving.

Representative FORD. Do you wish to have that letter entered as an exhibit at this point before I ask several questions?

Mr. REDLICH. The witness has produced before this Commission a letter which I now mark Commission Exhibit No. 331 on the Dallas Civil Liberties Union stationery, addressed to Mr. John Thorne, James Martin, Mr. Sorrels, Secret Service, Mrs. Lee H. Oswald, and the Federal Bureau of Investigation.

I ask that it be introduced in evidence.

Mr. DULLES. Any objection?

Mr. LEECH. No.

Mr. DULLES. It will be introduced.

(The letter referred to was marked for identification as Commission Exhibit No. 331 and received in evidence.)

The CHAIRMAN. Have you seen it?

Mr. MARTIN. Yes.

Mr. REDLICH. Mr. Chief Justice, we have introduced that because just prior to the recess we were discussing it and Congressman Ford indicated he had to leave I believe and I wanted to ask some questions.

The CHAIRMAN. Go ahead.

Mr. DULLES. Could I ask one question on this letter for clarification? It is my understanding it is your belief that Mrs. Oswald received a copy of this letter in Russian?

Mr. MARTIN. Well, she received a letter on this letterhead written in Russian. Now whether it was an exact copy, I don't know.

Mr. DULLES. About the length of this letter as far as you could tell?

Mr. MARTIN. Yes.

Mr. DULLES. At about the same time?

Mr. MARTIN. Yes, it was the same day.

Mr. DULLES. That was the letter she crumpled up and put in the wastepaper basket?

Mr. MARTIN. Yes.

Mr. DULLES. But you retrieved it from the wastepaper basket, did you not say?

Mr. MARTIN. Yes, sir, and asked her to answer it.

Mr. DULLES Where is that copy that you retrieved from the wastepaper basket?

Mr. MARTIN. I don't know.

Mr. DULLES. Maybe reassigned to the wastepaper basket?

Mr. MARTIN. It may have been, yes.

Representative FORD. I believe that was the letter that Mr. Redlich indicated he would get a copy from the Dallas Chapter of the American Civil Liberties Union.

Mr. MARTIN. Her answer is what he wanted to get.

Mr. REDLICH. I think Congressman Ford is right. We might be able to get both a copy of the letter and their answer.

Mr. DULLES. Their statement in this letter is the English of the Russian translation which they sent to her. I think it would be adequate, wouldn't it?

Mr. REDLICH. Yes.

Mr. DULLES. It seems to me it would be adequate for our purposes.

Mr. REDLICH. We will contact the Dallas Division on that.

Representative FORD. Marina testified here, and she has said elsewhere, that based on the facts as she now knows them, she believes that Lee was guilty of the assassination of President Kennedy.

Mr. MARTIN. Yes.

Representative FORD. Was that her attitude when you first met her?

Mr. MARTIN. Well, when I first met her, we didn't converse very well at all. There was lack of communication because of the language barrier, and I didn't discuss it with her probably until the latter part of December, although she was speaking fairly good English by the 15th of December.

Representative FORD. When you first discussed it with her, what was her attitude?

Mr. MARTIN. Well, she said she thought he was crazy.

Representative FORD. But did she indicate when you first discussed the question of guilt or not being guilty, what was her attitude?

Mr. MARTIN. She thought he was guilty.

Representative FORD. The first time you discussed the matter?

Mr. MARTIN. Yes.

Representative FORD. Did she indicate why?

Mr. MARTIN. No. I asked her why, and she said it was just a feeling.

Representative FORD. At that point had she——

Mr. MARTIN. A woman's feeling.

Representative FORD. At that point had she been given or shown the evidence that had been accumulated by various agencies of the Federal Government?

Mr. MARTIN. I don't know. I assume she had through the FBI. The FBI were showing her pictures and numerous things. I was not in on any of the questioning at all.

Mr. DULLES. Had she read the papers or had them read to her as far as you know at that period?

Mr. MARTIN. Some of them, yes.

Mr. DULLES. Newspapers, I mean.

Mr. MARTIN. Yes.

Representative FORD. From that first conversation you had with her about this matter, the guilt of Lee Harvey Oswald, she has never changed her mind?

Mr. MARTIN. No, and I have never heard her say anything other than he was guilty.

Representative FORD. Did you ever discuss with Marina the conversation she had with Lee Harvey Oswald at the Dallas police station the day he was apprehended or the day following. Or at any time prior to his death?

Mr. MARTIN. The only time she said anything about it was that he told her not to worry and to make sure and get the—get June a pair of shoes.

Representative FORD. She told you that is what he said to her?

Mr. MARTIN. That is what he said, yes.

Representative FORD. There was nothing extraordinary that she told you about the conversation?

Mr. MARTIN. No, sir.

Representative FORD. Other than what you have indicated?

Mr. MARTIN. Yes. He said not to worry. Everything would be all right.

Representative FORD. Did you ever ask her about this conversation that she had with Lee Harvey Oswald while he was at the Dallas police station?

Mr. MARTIN. No.

Representative FORD. As her manager, as the manager of Marina, did you have anything to do with the change of her appearance? Many people have said to me the first picture they saw of her and the subsequent pictures they saw of her she was wearing different kind of clothes. She had a different hair-do, and so forth. Did you have anything to do with that?

Mr. MARTIN. Yes.

Representative FORD. What was the purpose of that?

Mr. MARTIN. Just to change her general appearance so she wouldn't be recognized when she went out.

Representative FORD. Did she agree to this, was she willing to do it?

Mr. MARTIN. Yes. She didn't like her haircut particularly.

Representative FORD. She liked the previous way it was?

Mr. MARTIN. Yes.

Representative FORD. How about the change in clothes, the type that she wore?

Mr. MARTIN. Well, of course, that was for the better.

Representative FORD. Did she like it?

Mr. MARTIN. She liked the clothes, yes.

Representative FORD. That is all.

Mr. MARTIN. She tried makeup but that didn't work, because she couldn't stand makeup.

Mr. REDLICH. We previously asked you, Mr. Martin, about various people that Marina Oswald knew in the Dallas-Fort Worth area and you have indicated the extent to which you knew them personally and the extent to which they had contacted Marina Oswald during the time she was in your home.

Are there any other friends of Marina Oswald's rather than those I have asked you about that you—who attempted to contact her while she was living at your home?

Mr. MARTIN. Ilya, I believe it is Mamatav or Mamantov—he is of the Dallas Police Department and he has asked of her how she is.

Mr. REDLICH. Has he ever seen her, to the best of your knowledge other than in an official capacity?

(At this point, Congressman Ford left the hearing room.)

Mr. MARTIN. Well, one time when we went to Sears, Sears Roebuck in Dallas, and walked into the store he was walking and practically ran into her, and they said hello and passed the time of day and he left.

Mr. REDLICH. There were no other friends of hers that you know about who attempted to see her or call her while she was living at your home?

Other than those we have already discussed on the record? If I mentioned the name of Mr. or Mrs. Teofil Meller—the first name is Teofil, the last name is Meller.

Mr. MARTIN. Well, there was someone that called the office one day and had a rather odd name, was that Meller, and said that Marina wanted to talk to her, and we took it just for a crank call. She wouldn't leave the number or anything like that. I am not sure whether that was Meller.

(Discussion off the record.)

(At this point, Senator Cooper entered the hearing room.)

Mr. MARTIN. There was no telephone number involved.

Mr. REDLICH. You have discussed at length the attempt of Ruth Paine to see Mrs. Oswald. Did Mike Paine ever attempt to see Mrs. Oswald while she was living at your home?

Mr. MARTIN. No.

Mr. REDLICH. Have you ever talked to Michael Paine?

Mr. MARTIN. No. When we went over to get the clothes, for instance, he stood back—I don't believe he said anything at all. It was a very odd situation. He was helping us move things but he didn't say anything.

Mr. REDLICH. Did Marina ever discuss Michael Paine with you?

Mr. MARTIN. No.

Mr. REDLICH. Only Ruth Paine but not Michael Paine?

Mr. MARTIN. Yes. She said they were separated.

Mr. REDLICH. Mr. Martin, did Marina ever discuss with you her husband's desire to go to Cuba?

Mr. MARTIN. She said that he had wanted to go to Cuba because he wanted—because he wasn't happy in Russia and he wasn't happy in the United States and then she said he wouldn't be happy in Cuba either.

Mr. REDLICH. Did she ever discuss with you a plan to hi-jack a plane?

Mr. MARTIN. No.

Mr. REDLICH. Did she ever indicate what steps he was taking to get to Cuba?

Mr. MARTIN. No. Not at all.

Mr. REDLICH. Do you have any knowledge at all of any plans he was making to get to and live in Cuba?

Mr. MARTIN. No.

Mr. REDLICH. Mr. Ford has asked you about the conversations which Marina had with Lee Oswald at the Dallas Police Station on November 23 and you have replied. I would like to ask you about any—your knowledge about any conversation which Robert Oswald had with Lee Oswald while he was in the custody of the Dallas Police prior to his death?

Mr. MARTIN. I have no knowledge at all of that.

Mr. REDLICH. You have never had any conversations with Robert Oswald concerning his conversations with Lee Oswald.

Mr. MARTIN. No.

Mr. REDLICH. Have you ever talked to Mrs. Marguerite Oswald concerning any conversations which she had with her son while he was in the custody of the Dallas police?

Mr. MARTIN. No.

Mr. REDLICH. Have you had any conversations at all with Mrs. Marguerite Oswald concerning the facts surrounding the assassination of President Kennedy?

Mr. MARTIN. No, I don't think any direct conversation, I mean between she and I. I was present at times out there at the Inn when she was talking to this person or that person. But I don't believe I have had any direct conversation with her at all.

Mr. REDLICH. Did Mrs. Marguerite Oswald ever discuss with you an incident concerning a photograph which was supposed to have been shown to her by agents of the FBI on November 23, 1963.

Mr. MARTIN. No, I have heard that through news media but that is the only place I heard it.

Mr. REDLICH. You have no direct knowledge of that incident yourself. Did Marina Oswald ever discuss that incident with you?

Mr. MARTIN. No.

Mr. REDLICH. Did Marina Oswald ever discuss with you her mother-in-law's allegations that Lee Oswald was acting as an agent of the United States Government?

Mr. MARTIN. No. She mentioned only one incident where the FBI came to their house when they were in Oak Cliff, and they took him down to the car, I believe he was about ready to sit down to dinner when they arrived, and they took him down to the car and talked to him, and Marina was upset because dinner was spoiling, and I think that is the only reference she has made to anything like that.

Mr. REDLICH. She has never discussed with you the specific claims of Marguerite Oswald in that respect?

Mr. MARTIN. No.

Mr. REDLICH. In the course of your conversations with Marina Oswald or in the course of the preparation of any stories or releases on Mrs. Oswald's behalf have you ever discussed with Mrs. Oswald the events of November 21 and the morning of November 22?

Mr. MARTIN. Yes.

Mr. REDLICH. Could you relate those conversations to us?

Mr. MARTIN. He came home Thursday night, which was unusual.

Mr. REDLICH. Just so the record is clear, I hope you are relating to us now what Marina Oswald has related to you and not what you have read in any publication.

Mr. MARTIN. Yes.

Mr. REDLICH. All right.

Mr. MARTIN. And, let's see, this was sometime in December that she was telling me this—no, I remember when it was, when she was moving from the Inn to my home.

Mr. REDLICH. By the Inn you mean——

Mr. MARTIN. The Inn of the Six Flags. She was in the back seat and Leon Gopadze was in the front seat talking with her, and she told him that he had come home Thursday night and that——

Mr. DULLES. In Russian?

Mr. MARTIN. Yes.

Mr. DULLES. This was a conversation in Russian?

Mr. MARTIN. Yes. Lee translated it for me, Gopadze translated it.

Mr. DULLES. Afterwards or as it took place.

Mr. MARTIN. As it took place, well, it was immediately afterwards, and she made a comment that he had left his wedding band on the dresser, I think, and she got up the next morning she found his wedding band on the dresser, which was strange.

Now, that is the only thing that relates to that period that I have heard her say. Now, I didn't actually hear her say that.

Mr. REDLICH. You have had no other conversations with her with regard to the period of November 21 and the morning of November 22?

Mr. MARTIN. No.

Mr. REDLICH. Do you have any knowledge of the story which Marina Oswald prepared in Russian and which she has sent to this Commission?

Mr. MARTIN. Yes.

Mr. REDLICH. Could you state the extent of your knowledge?

Mr. MARTIN. I knew it was written, and written by her, and that is about the extent of it.

Mr. REDLICH. Was it ever translated for you?

Mr. MARTIN. Well, we have part of it translated, a portion of it.

Mr. REDLICH. Are there any parts of that story which you now believe to be inaccurate?

Mr. MARTIN. No, I don't have the whole thing translated, but I think everything that is translated, I have no reason to doubt.

Mr. REDLICH. Did you assist Marina Oswald in the preparation for her television appearance in January on CBS television?

Mr. MARTIN. Yes.

Mr. REDLICH. Are there any portions of that interview which you now believe to be inaccurate in any respect?

Mr. MARTIN. No. We set a format for CBS to use, specific questions, and Marina was not prompted as to the answers to give. Those were impromptu. But we went over the ones with her off the camera, and asked her the questions so that she would understand them, and then she answered them, and the second time she did it on camera.

Mr. REDLICH. To the best of your knowledge and recollection those answers were accurate?

Mr. MARTIN. Yes. I can't remember them. But none of them struck me as being——

Mr. REDLICH. Apart from the newspaper clippings which we went through this morning and afternoon, are you familiar with any other narrative prepared by or for Marina Oswald?

Mr. MARTIN. Prepared by or for?

Mr. REDLICH. Yes.

Mr. MARTIN. You mean other than newspaper articles?

Mr. REDLICH. Other than the newspaper articles which we discussed this morning and this afternoon.

Mr. MARTIN. Life magazine.

Mr. REDLICH. Did you have anything to do with the recent story in Life magazine?

Mr. MARTIN. No, we had nothing on that other than the picture. Time magazine, she was interviewed for Time magazine.

Mr. REDLICH. When was that?

Mr. MARTIN. Saturday—Friday—she was here in Washington.

Mr. REDLICH. If I may refresh your recollection, she completed her testimony before this Commission at approximately 5:30 on Thursday, February 6.

Mr. MARTIN. Well, I believe it was Friday. We held a press conference on Friday afternoon, and I think it was Friday night then.

Mr. REDLICH. It would be sometime after the completion of her testimony is that correct?

Mr. MARTIN. Yes.

Mr. REDLICH. Were you with her during the course of that interview?

Mr. MARTIN. It must have been Thursday night. It was Thursday night because Secret Service was still with her.

Mr. REDLICH. You believe this interview took place on Thursday night?

Mr. MARTIN. Yes.

Mr. REDLICH. That would be February 6?

Mr. MARTIN. Yes.

Mr. REDLICH. Were you with her during the course of this interview?

Mr. MARTIN. Part of the time. I left John Thorne and Marina and the Time reporter at the table. June was restless, and I was walking her around the restaurant.

Mr. REDLICH. Have you read the interview?

Mr. MARTIN. Yes.

Mr. REDLICH. Are there any portions of it which you now believe to be inaccurate, to the best of your recollection?

Mr. MARTIN. I don't think so. I would have to re-read it to make it definite, make a definite statement on it.

Mr. REDLICH. On the basis of conversations which you had during the course of the testimony of Marina Oswald before this Commission and on the basis of conversations which you have had subsequent to that time, do you have any opinion concerning the truthfulness of the testimony which she presented before this Commission?

Mr. MARTIN. No. I think primarily she is truthful, and I think that under oath she would tell the truth.

Mr. REDLICH. Are you still Mrs. Oswald's business representative?

Mr. MARTIN. According to the contract, yes. According to my contract with her.

Mr. REDLICH. Have you received any communication from her which raises questions as to whether you are still her business representative?

Mr. MARTIN. Yes.

The CHAIRMAN. Are we really concerned with that?

Mr. REDLICH. Mr. Chairman, I intend to ask the witness why he was discharged in terms of whether it had anything to do with any business negotiations or anything to do with the testimony of Mrs. Oswald before this Commission.

The CHAIRMAN. You can ask him if it has anything to do with her testimony. We are not interested in her business affairs.

Mr. REDLICH. I merely wanted to establish the fact of——

The CHAIRMAN. This thing can go on interminably with all this minutia and things that don't bear on what we are here to find out, whatever his business relations are with Mrs. Oswald, it seems to me is his business and not ours.

Mr. REDLICH. Did Mrs. Oswald's attempt to terminate the relationship with you relate in any way to her testimony before this Commission?

Mr. MARTIN. No. There was no reason given.

Mr. REDLICH. Did it relate in any way, in your opinion, to any information which you may have given to anyone else with regard to your knowledge of the facts concerning the assassination of President Kennedy.

Mr. MARTIN. No.

Mr. REDLICH. Do you know Jack Ruby?

Mr. MARTIN. Yes.

Mr. REDLICH. Would you tell us about your association with him?

Mr. MARTIN. Well, it is a very minor association. I had been working in the Statler Hotel in Dallas as assistant manager for maybe six months before I met him, and met him through some of the other people in the hotel.

Mr. DULLES. What year was this?

Mr. MARTIN. About 1955.

Mr. DULLES. I just want to get the general area.

Mr. MARTIN. 1955 or 1956. And as a club manager, I was club manager in Dallas also, and didn't associate with him at all, even on a bilateral communication through the clubs. But it was just a nodding acquaintance, you might say. I knew him by his first name. He knew me by my first name and we spoke when we saw each other and I think I have been in his place twice.

Mr. REDLICH. Do you recall the approximate dates of those visits?

Mr. MARTIN. Let's see, once in 1962. I had some gentlemen from New Orleans with me. They were visiting Dallas on business at the Inn of the Six Flags, and they wanted to see the Carousel.

Mr. DULLES. That is what you mean by his place?

Mr. MARTIN. Yes. So I called Jack Ruby and asked if it would be all right if I brought them down. We stayed approximately an hour and a half.

The other time was during the daytime, let's see, as it was then, I had—I was walking in that area and just stopped in to say hello. The club was closed at that time, not closed for business but it was before opening hours.

Mr. REDLICH. Those are the only times you have been in Jack Ruby's business establishment?

Mr. MARTIN. Yes.

Mr. REDLICH. Do you consider yourself a friend of his?

Mr. MARTIN. No. An acquaintance.

Mr. REDLICH. Have you gone out socially?

Mr. MARTIN. No. He came out to the Inn one time with some little gimmick. It is called a Detwist Board. It is quite a piece of plywood about like this with a round plate on the bottom of it, seated in ball bearings and you are supposed to stand on this thing to twist, and came out to ask me to see who to ask at the park to merchandise it, the Six Flags over Texas Amusement Park, and I told him. Now, whether he went over there or not, I don't know.

Mr. REDLICH. I understand that you have had a conversation with an aid of General Walker concerning the General Walker incident.

Would you tell the Commission about that?

Mr. MARTIN. They contacted us——

Mr. REDLICH. Who is "they"?

Mr. MARTIN. General Walker's aide, Mr. Moore or Morse, a tall thin gentleman, about 55 or 60, and wanted actually an interview with Marina which we didn't think was necessary.

They came out to John Thorne's office and we sat and talked. They were of the opinion—what they were trying to do was find out who else was involved—this was right after the announcement was made in the paper about Lee Oswald shooting at Walker. They were trying to find out who else was involved because General Walker is still in fear of his life.

Mr. DULLES. This was some time before the 22d.

Mr. MARTIN. No, it was after.

Mr. DULLES. After November 22?

Mr. MARTIN. Yes, sir. This was after the announcement was made in the paper that——

Mr. DULLES. Oh, yes.

Mr. MARTIN. That Lee Oswald had attacked him.

Mr. DULLES. The actual attack was in April. This was after the newspaper announcement.

Mr. MARTIN. Yes.

The CHAIRMAN. After the newspaper announcements that Lee had tried to kill him which was after the assassination?

Mr. MARTIN. That is correct.

Mr. DULLES. Yes.

Mr. MARTIN. And they just wanted verification actually that or to try to get verification as to how many people were involved, and we told them that there was just one person involved.

Mr. REDLICH. At the time did you ask Marina about this?

Mr. MARTIN. Yes.

Mr. REDLICH. And this is what she told you?

Mr. MARTIN. Yes.

Mr. DULLES. The persons involved in the Walker incident?

Mr. MARTIN. Yes. She said that Lee did it alone without any help. There was no one with him.

Mr. REDLICH. Mr. Martin, I have at this time no further questions other than those which may be suggested by a perusal of the records which you have forwarded to this Commission.

As we indicated in the brief recess earlier, Mr. Dulles is able to be here at 9 o'clock this evening, and I would envisage then a very brief session at which time your testimony would be completed.

Mr. MARTIN. All right.

Mr. REDLICH. Are there any questions that anyone would like to ask of Mr. Martin at this time?

The CHAIRMAN. Would you like to ask your client any questions?

Mr. LEECH. No. I am not going to make that mistake.

(Laughter.)

The CHAIRMAN. All right.

Mr. DULLES. I have no questions. I will reserve them for tonight. I don't think I have any further questions.

The CHAIRMAN. Mr. Rhyne, do you have any questions you would like to ask.

Mr. Rankin, are you through for the day?

Mr. RANKIN. Until 9 o'clock.

The CHAIRMAN. Well then, gentlemen, we will adjourn until 9 o'clock.

(Whereupon, at 5:15 p.m., the President's Commission recessed.)

Evening Session

TESTIMONY OF JAMES HERBERT MARTIN RESUMED

The President's Commission reconvened at 9:20 p.m.

Mr. DULLES. The Committee will come to order.

Will you continue with the testimony?

Mr. REDLICH. Thank you, Mr. Dulles.

Mr. Martin, at our last session I asked you whether you knew Jack Ruby, and you replied that you did. You indicated the brief contact that you have had with him and the two times, I believe, that you have been to his business establishment?

Mr. MARTIN. Yes.

Mr. REDLICH. Apart from your own personal contact with Jack Ruby, do you have any other information about him and his activities which you would like to present before this Commission?

Mr. MARTIN. No, nothing that I definitely know about him. It is just he is a city character. He is very friendly to everyone.

Mr. REDLICH. Please understand I am not asking you for rumors or that type of thing.

Mr. MARTIN. No, I know. Well, just what I know of him, he seems very friendly to everyone, and he is always around. You are liable to see him anywhere.

Mr. REDLICH. Has he ever been to the motel that you have?

Mr. MARTIN. Yes, I mentioned that.

Mr. REDLICH. Oh, yes.

Mr. MARTIN. He brought that twist board out there one time.

Mr. REDLICH. Never been there as a guest?

Mr. MARTIN. No.

Mr. REDLICH. I hand you a copy of an invoice for a Revere recorder and a 1,200-foot reel of recording tape, and ask you if you have ever seen this?

Mr. MARTIN. Yes. That is a tape recorder that I rented and recorded the——

Mr. REDLICH. I will ask you about it shortly. I would just like to know if you are familiar with it.

Mr. MARTIN. Yes.

Mr. REDLICH. Mr. Chairman, I am marking this as Commission Exhibit No. 332, and ask that it be admitted in evidence.

Mr. DULLES. Any objection?

Mr. LEECH. No, sir.

Mr. DULLES. It may be admitted.

(The tape recorder and tape invoice referred to were marked Commission's Exhibit No. 332 for identification and received in evidence.)

Mr. REDLICH. Mr. Martin, I hand you Commission Exhibit No. 332, and ask you to tell the Commission the conditions under which this invoice arose?

Mr. MARTIN. We had Marina's manuscript interpreted by Ilya Mamantov, and this was part of it. He was only able to interpret about half of it.

Mr. REDLICH. He interpreted it and put it on tape?

Mr. MARTIN. And we recorded that on tape as he interpreted it.

Mr. DULLES. How do you mean interpreted?

Mr. MARTIN. He read it in English?

Mr. DULLES. Oh, I see, translated it.

Mr. MARTIN. Yes.

Mr. DULLES. From Russian into English?

Mr. MARTIN. Yes.

Mr. REDLICH. When I asked you this afternoon about your knowledge as to the accuracy of that story, I take it your reply was based upon this translation?

Mr. MARTIN. Yes.

Mr. REDLICH. And this only encompasses about half of the entire story, is that right?

Mr. MARTIN. It is more than half, it is about 15 pages, I guess.

Mr. REDLICH. Did she consult with you at all in the preparation of that story?

Mr. MARTIN. No.

Mr. REDLICH. And there is nothing on this tape other than the English translation of that Russian story?

Mr. MARTIN. That is true.

Mr. DULLES. Do we have that translation as well as the copy of the original?

Mr. REDLICH. Yes, Mr. Chairman, we have the original in Russian and then it was translated by Mr. Gopadze, of the Secret Service.

Mr. MARTIN. Actually our translation is very poor. He was not able to translate properly into English a lot of the phrases.

Mr. DULLES Who is "he," Illa? Isn't that Ilya, by the way?

Mr. MARTIN. I am not sure.

Mr. DULLES. That is generally the Russian, I don't know.

Mr. RANKIN. That is right.

Mr. MARTIN. It might be.

Mr. DULLES. Yes.

Mr. MARTIN. But he is professor at SMU. He has a list of titles that long. He is very well thought of. I think he works for Sun Oil Company, and is a well-respected individual. His wife and his mother, I believe, teach Russian also. I think his mother taught Mrs. Paine a good deal of her Russian.

Mr. REDLICH. Mr. Martin, I would like to show you Commission Exhibit No. 325 which was introduced earlier today. Mr. Leech, I believe you have a photostat of this. If you could hand it to me during the course of this questioning. I would appreciate it.

Mr. LEECH. Yes.

Mr. REDLICH. Thank you.

Could you tell the Commission what this document purports to state, and then I will ask you about individual items.

Mr. MARTIN. These are contracts that we have made both in writing and verbally for Marina Oswald's right, her story rights.

Mr. REDLICH. And the first item appearing on Commission Exhibit No. 325 is a contract with Texitalia Films.

Mr. MARTIN. Yes.

Mr. REDLICH. Would you describe the terms and conditions of that contract?

Mr. MARTIN. Texitalia Films is planning a 60-minute technicolor documentary to start. They will pay $75,000 for World-Wide movie and the TV rights.

Mr. DULLES. Excuse me, is this a documentary of Marina's life?

Mr. MARTIN. Yes. Any movie or television appearances Marina would be paid $7,500 plus expenses for each appearance. Then for each personal appearance, for instance, the film opens in St. Louis on such and such a date and they would like for her to be there to make a personal appearance for the showing, the opening of the film, she would receive $1,500 plus expenses for each public appearance of that nature.

Mr. REDLICH. And this contract according to this exhibit was signed on February 11, 1964?

Mr. MARTIN. Yes.

Mr. LEECH. By her?

Mr. MARTIN. No, by me acting for her.

Mr. REDLICH. By you acting on behalf of Mrs. Oswald?

Mr. MARTIN. Yes, in accordance with my contract with her.

Mr. REDLICH. The second item appearing here is a contract with Life magazine. Would you tell the Commission about that?

Mr. MARTIN. Life magazine purchased the rights, North American rights on a photograph of Lee Harvey Oswald with a rifle and pistol, primarily for their use on a cover issue.

Mr. Dulles. That is what appeared on the recent cover issue, I guess, it was 2 weeks ago.

Mr. Martin. Yes, sir.

Now, that $5,000 has been paid. We have the $5,000 in an escrow account.

Mr. Redlich. Did you actually have in your possession the photograph, a copy of which appeared on the cover of Life magazine?

Mr. Martin. No.

Mr. Redlich. Could you tell us how this contract was consummated, in view of the fact that Life magazine apparently printed on its cover a photograph which you never possessed?

Mr. Martin. They knew the photographs belonged to Marina. They have a common law copyright, and the only way they could legally use the film is to purchase the rights from Marina.

Mr. Redlich. Did Life magazine indicate to you where they obtained the photograph?

Mr. Martin. No.

Mr. Redlich. Have you had conversations with other publications concerning that photograph?

Mr. Martin. Yes. I made the contact with the London Daily Mirror for the purchase of the British Commonwealth rights on that same photograph, and they guaranteed $2,200 plus 50–50 split on what they sold in the Commonwealth. It was restricted to the Commonwealth only.

However, the London Daily Mail came out with the photograph prior to the Mirror, and I was informed by Mr. Weggand of the London Daily Express that the Detroit Free Press had sold this photograph to the London Daily Mail for $500.

Mr. Redlich. Do you have any idea how the Detroit Free Press obtained this photograph?

Mr. Martin. No. I talked to Ken Murray, who I was informed was the attorney for the Detroit Free Press.

Mr. Redlich. Where did you talk to him?

Mr. Martin. At his home in Detroit.

Mr. Redlich. By phone?

Mr. Martin. By telephone. And he stated that the photograph was public property, and not covered under common law copyright. I asked him where he got the photo, and he said he got it at the same place as Life did, through a leak in the Commission. I talked to Life magazine attorney—I can't remember his name. It is a very odd name. It begins with an "S". Now, Murray said that Life had informed him that they had gotten it from a leak through the Commission, and I contacted Life and he denied saying anything of the sort to Murray.

However, Murray insisted that that is where he got that and he figured it was public domain.

Mr. Redlich. At the start of today's testimony when you mentioned the possibility of a leak with regard to this photograph, something that you said prior to the actual start of hearings, Mr. Rankin and I commented on that assertion.

Would you tell the Commission what we said?

Mr. Martin. That there was definitely not a leak in the Commission, and that you would certainly find out what Murray was talking about.

Mr. Redlich. Did you talk to an editor of the Detroit Free Press with regard to this photograph?

Mr. Martin. I called at night. It was at night, and I asked for the news editor. He was not in, so I talked to a reporter, and he couldn't say anything about it. He referred me to Ken Murray and gave me his home telephone number.

Mr. Redlich. The next item on Commission Exhibit No. 325 has reference to Stern Magazine.

Would you tell the Commission about that, please?

Mr. Martin. Stern Magazine we have been working with since the middle of December. They have been quite patient actually. For $12,500 they wanted Marina's memoirs and photographs, available photographs for use in Germany and Italy only. They wanted exclusive use in those two countries. Then they would endeavor to sell these same memoirs and pictures to other European countries, limiting it only to European countries, and take a 30 percent commission on any sales that they made, the remaining 70 percent going to Marina.

Mr. REDLICH. Has this contract been signed?

Mr. MARTIN. Yes.

Mr. REDLICH. Do you know when it was signed? Can you approximate the date?

Mr. MARTIN. I confirmed it by wire to them. It is in the exhibits.

Mr. REDLICH. We have not introduced——

Mr. MARTIN. You haven't come to that yet.

Mr. REDLICH. We do not intend to introduce the specific documents into the record, just this summary.

Mr. LEECH. Give him an approximate date.

Mr. REDLICH. You say it was confirmed by telegram.

Mr. MARTIN. Yes, it was confirmed by telegram to Spiegelberg.

Mr. LEECH. When?

Mr. MARTIN. In New York. December 16 at 2:45 p.m.

Mr. REDLICH. The next item on Commission Exhibit No. 325 also refers to Stern Magazine, an item of $2,650.

Could you comment on that?

Mr. MARTIN. This was a recent development wherein since they could not send an author in to talk to Marina, they purchased seven photographs for a total of $2,650, to take the memoirs later.

However, they will not hold off the memoirs forever.

Mr. REDLICH. These seven photographs are photographs of what?

Mr. MARTIN. Of Marina and Lee Harvey Oswald together and separate.

Mr. REDLICH. These were photographs which were not turned over to the Dallas police?

Mr. MARTIN. No. They were photographs that we were given prints of by the FBI. The FBI sent prints of these photographs to us.

Mr. REDLICH. Am I correct in assuming that all of the photographs which were in the possession of Marina Oswald and Lee Harvey Oswald, either in his apartment or in the Paine's apartment, were turned over to the Dallas police?

Is that right?

Mr. MARTIN. As far as I know.

Mr. REDLICH. To the best of your knowledge?

Mr. MARTIN. Yes.

Mr. REDLICH. And that any photographs which you have and which have been the basis of any contract are copies which were made available to you by some law enforcement authority?

Mr. MARTIN. Yes. Now, there was a check, there was a $250 cash down payment made on this $2,650. Then a check for $2,400; the check was stopped, payment on the check was stopped because of a letter written by William McKenzie saying that I had no authority to sign any contracts whatsoever for Marina, and that if they did use anything that I had sold them, litigation would follow immediately. So consequently they stopped payment on the check. I still have the check. It is still attached to the letter that was sent with it.

Mr. DULLES. Could I ask who is that check made out to?

Mr. MARTIN. Made out to me.

Mr. DULLES. To you as agent?

Mr. MARTIN. Yes.

Mr. DULLES. Or to you just in your name?

Mr. MARTIN. I think it is just made out to me.

Mr. DULLES. I don't know if it is important.

Mr. LEECH. You go ahead and I'll find it.

Mr. MARTIN. Under the contract all checks were supposed to be made payable to me. Then I would deduct my fee and forward the balance to Marina.

Mr. REDLICH. The next item on Commission Exhibit No. 325 refers to Meredith Press.

25

Mr. MARTIN. The Meredith Press is a book publisher with their main office in Des Moines, Iowa. I had talked with Mr. Ted Purdy at great length and on numerous occasions by phone. We had negotiated world book rights for Marina Oswald's story. For this Meredith Press would pay a $25,000 advance to her. Then on the first printing would be a 10 percent commission of the retail price of the book.

On the second printing would be 12½ percent commission, and on the third and succeeding printings it would be 15 percent commission.

Now, of course, the commissions were to be deducted from the advance.

Mr. REDLICH. And this was to be her life story?

Mr. MARTIN. Yes.

Mr. REDLICH. Had you discussed with Marina at all the contents of this book? Had you started making any preparations for writing?

Mr. MARTIN. No. I am not a writer, and wouldn't know the first thing to do about a book. But we had negotiated with one writer, Isaac Don Levine, who Meredith Press felt would be the best writer available for this type of book because of the Russian attachment.

Mr. REDLICH. When you told us this morning of your initial concern over the Nixon shooting incident, did it relate to these various agreements that you have been working on concerning the sale of Marina Oswald's story?

Mr. MARTIN. Did it relate to them?

Mr. REDLICH. Yes.

Mr. MARTIN. How do you mean?

Mr. REDLICH. Were you concerned about the publicity, the effect of the publicity of the Nixon incident on these various agreements which you were negotiating at the time?

Mr. MARTIN. No. As a matter of fact, it would enhance the price of it.

For instance, the Post magazine, the Saturday Evening Post, said that they would like to buy American serial rights if there was something in Marina's story that the Commission did not know.

Mr. REDLICH. When did they tell you this?

Mr. MARTIN. Around the first of the year I guess.

Mr. REDLICH. Around the first of the year. Did Marina know about this?

Mr. MARTIN. No.

Mr. REDLICH. This is the Saturday Evening Post you are talking about?

Mr. MARTIN. Yes. I talked to a Mr. Black.

Mr. REDLICH. And the Saturday Evening Post said to you that they would buy the serial rights provided there was some information which would not be known to the Commission?

Mr. MARTIN. Yes. I told them there was no realm that would apply, and we closed negotiations.

Mr. REDLICH. And you say you didn't relate this fact at all to Marina Oswald?

Mr. MARTIN. No.

Mr. REDLICH. These negotiations with the Post.

Mr. MARTIN. No.

Mr. REDLICH. Was there in fact to the best of your knowledge material which she did not in fact relate to this Commission?

Mr. MARTIN. Not to my knowledge other than the Nixon affair.

Mr. REDLICH. And were you aware at the time she completed her testimony here that she had not related this information to the Commission?

Mr. MARTIN. Yes.

Mr. REDLICH. Was there any connection between her failure to tell the Commission of the Nixon incident and the negotiations, the temporary negotiations that you had had with the Saturday Evening Post?

Mr. MARTIN. No, none whatsoever. That was closed off at least 30 days before she testified.

Mr. REDLICH. Was there any attempt on your part or anyone acting on Marina Oswald's part that you know of to negotiate the sale of the information concerning the Nixon shooting incident?

Mr. MARTIN. No, not to my knowledge.

Mr. REDLICH. When Marina—did Marina ever give you an explanation for why she did not tell the Commission about the Nixon incident?

Mr. MARTIN. No. I have never talked to her about that other than the first time that she told me about it. I asked John Thorne if she had mentioned it. I didn't discuss it with her.

Mr. REDLICH. And since Marina Oswald's return from Washington after having testified here, you say you have never discussed the Nixon incident with Marina Oswald in any way?

Mr. MARTIN. No. I probably would have had there been sufficient time. Of course, she left my home the following day after she got back from Washington.

Mr. REDLICH. When you say you probably would have, in what way?

Mr. MARTIN. Well, since she didn't mention it to the Commission, I feel the Commission should know about it.

Mr. DULLES. Did you know at this time she had not mentioned it to the Commission?

Mr. MARTIN. I asked John Thorne.

Mr. DULLES. Oh, you asked John Thorne?

Mr. MARTIN. Yes.

Mr. REDLICH. What did John Thorne say?

Mr. MARTIN. Said she had not mentioned it.

Mr. REDLICH. Did you ask John Thorne why she had not mentioned it?

Mr. MARTIN. No.

Mr. REDLICH. Did John Thorne offer any information as to why she had not mentioned it?

Mr. MARTIN. No.

Mr. REDLICH. Do you know whether John Thorne had urged her to mention it?

Mr. MARTIN. No.

Mr. REDLICH. John Thorne was aware of the Nixon incident prior to Marina Oswald's appearance before this Commission, was he not?

Mr. MARTIN. Yes.

Mr. REDLICH. Because you had apparently told him about that shortly after you learned about it in January.

Mr. MARTIN. Yes.

Mr. REDLICH. Did you discuss the Nixon incident with Robert Oswald after Marina Oswald's appearance before this Commission in February?

Mr. MARTIN. No.

Mr. REDLICH. You had not?

Mr. MARTIN. I don't know if I discussed it with him prior to the Commission's testimony or not. I may or I may not have. I don't know. I don't know whether I mentioned it to him or not.

Mr. REDLICH. Coming back to Commission Exhibit No. 325, the next item under London Daily Mirror, am I correct in assuming that this is, that this item refers to the rifle photo which you discussed earlier in your testimony tonight?

Mr. MARTIN. Yes, that is right.

Mr. REDLICH. Do you have anything to add with regard to that rifle photo that you have not already told us?

Mr. MARTIN. No.

Mr. REDLICH. Did you discuss with Marina Oswald at any time this rifle photo and the circumstances under which it was taken.

Mr. MARTIN. I asked her at one time why he wanted a photograph taken of that type, and she said she didn't know. He just wanted pictures taken that way.

Mr. REDLICH. Did she tell you when this photograph was taken in relationship to any other incidents such as the General Walker incident or the Richard Nixon incident?

Mr. MARTIN. No.

Mr. REDLICH. Did you know where the photograph was taken?

Mr. MARTIN. I don't know. I don't even know if it was in Oak Cliff or not. I have an idea that it was in Oak Cliff but I don't know whether I know that or whether I have read it.

Mr. REPLICH. When you say Oak Cliff, some of us don't live in Dallas.

Mr. MARTIN. It is a suburb of Dallas, a section of Dallas.

Mr. REDLICH. Are you referring to the area where the Neely Street house was located?

To refresh your recollection, Mr. Martin, the Oswalds lived in two places in Dallas. One was on Elsbeth Street and the other on Neely. Are they both in Oak Cliff?

Mr. MARTIN. Yes. Elsbeth Street is right around the corner from Neely Street, I believe they lived in an apartment on Elsbeth.

It was a group of apartments in one building, and on Neely Street, I think, that was similar to a duplex.

Mr. REDLICH. And you are not certain as to where this photograph which was the subject of these negotiations was taken?

Mr. MARTIN. No, except that the Elsbeth address, I believe, was a brick residence, I mean a brick apartment, it is a dark building, and the Neely Street address is a white building.

I believe the photo shows a white building.

Mr. REDLICH. On the basis of that you would conclude the photograph was taken at which address?

Mr. MARTIN. At the Neely Street address.

Mr. REDLICH. At the Neely Street address. When you were negotiating with various publications for this photograph, didn't anyone ask you when and where it was taken?

Mr. MARTIN. Yes, I told them that it was while they were living in Oak Cliff. I didn't say where or when.

Mr. REDLICH. No one asked you.

Mr. MARTIN. And they apparently weren't concerned with the where or when.

Mr. REDLICH. Did they ask you anything about the publication which Lee Oswald had in his hand?

Mr. MARTIN. Yes, and I told them that it was either the Militant or the Worker. I was not sure which one. I am not even sure whether either one.

Mr. REDLICH. Your copy of the photograph did not indicate clearly which one it was?

Mr. MARTIN. Correct.

Mr. REDLICH. Do you now know which one it was?

Mr. MARTIN. No.

Mr. DULLES. Are you sure it is one of the two?

Mr. MARTIN. No, I am not. I assume that it would be one of the two.

Mr. REDLICH. For the record it is the Militant.

Mr. DULLES. It is?

Mr. REDLICH. Is there anything about the circumstances of this photograph, including the rifle, the pistol, the time, the place, anything concerning this photograph that you have not told this Commission about which you have knowledge?

Mr. MARTIN. No.

Mr. REDLICH. The last item on Commission Exhibit No. 325 is This Week magazine, $1,000. Could you tell us about that. At the conclusion of this list I will ask if there is anything else. We are now at This Week magazine.

Mr. MARTIN. When Marina was here in Washington, she had the press conference, and at the end of the press conference she mentioned, she made a statement "Now I go to church." On the way to the CBS studios we passed a Russian Orthodox Church, and she remarked about it, that she would like to come back and go inside, see what it looked like. Someone in This Week magazine caught that statement, and wanted to write a short article on Marina going to church, and that is what that is.

Mr. REDLICH. What happened? Could you tell us how this article got written?

Mr. MARTIN. It hasn't been written.

Mr. REDLICH. Did the reporter accompany Mrs. Oswald to church?

Mr. MARTIN. Oh, no. Actually when the television interview was over, we came back and went to the church, but the church was locked and we didn't get in at all. Now this contact was made after we left Washington. This Week magazine contacted us after, not while we were still here.

Mr. REDLICH. And what was the subject matter of this article specifically supposed to be?

Mr. MARTIN. The title of it was supposed to be "I go to church," and it would be an article written on Marina going to church.

Mr. REDLICH. Mr. Martin, the total figure on the bottom of Commission Exhibit No. 325 is $132,350. This presumably does not include any future royalties, is that correct?

Mr. MARTIN. That is correct.

Mr. REDLICH. Have you made an estimate as to the total earnings which would accrue as a result of these contractual arrangements?

Mr. MARTIN. It should be approximately $300,000 at a maximum, depending on what American serial rights and British Commonwealth serial rights, Asiatic serial rights would bring.

Mr. REDLICH. You say the maximum of $300,000?

Mr. MARTIN. I think so.

Mr. LEECH. Of those contracts?

Mr. REDLICH. That is what I am asking about are these.

Mr. MARTIN. Of these contracts, yes.

Mr. REDLICH. Could you tell us about any other contractual arrangements that you have made or are negotiating on behalf of Marina Oswald?

Mr. MARTIN. There are no others. I will have to refer to things. We had an offer from Australia and also from New Zealand as far as this photograph is concerned. However, it was thrown to the wind by the Detroit Free Press, so they got it from Detroit Free Press, we have been offered—we have not received an offer. The Australian newspaper——

Mr. DULLES. Do you need these details do you think?

Mr. REDLICH. I want to get the total figure, Mr. Chairman.

Mr. MARTIN. Associated Newspapers Limited of Australia would like to have Australian rights to a book that Marina would write, and also the London Evening Standard would like to have the British rights, of course, to the picture of Lee Harvey Oswald.

Mr. REDLICH. Mr. Martin, Mr. Thorne has indicated to this Commission that he estimated that Marina's earnings would approach approximately $500,000. Would you comment on that estimate?

Mr. MARTIN. I think it might be a little high. Of course, if you take into consideration she has $68,000, close to $70,000 in contributions alone, then the advances on this Exhibit No. 325, that is $200,000 right there. I think $500,000 might be just a little bit high.

Mr. REDLICH. The final document I would like to show you is a photostat of a letter which you presented to the Commission today, purporting to be a letter written in Russian together with an English translation. It starts, the English translation starts with the words "As the widow of Lee Oswald." I show you Commission Exhibit No. 333 and ask you if this is a photostat of the letter which you submitted to the Commission this morning.

Mr. MARTIN. Yes, apparently so.

Mr. DULLES. Who is that letter to?

Mr. REDLICH. We don't know yet.

Mr. DULLES. You don't know yet?

Mr. REDLICH. I will develop that in the questioning. I mark this Commission Exhibit No. 333, being a Russian letter and what purports to be its English translation and ask that it be admitted in evidence.

Mr. DULLES. Can you identify that any further than just a Russian letter?

Mr. REDLICH. On the top appears a date, and the day of the month is the 20th. I am unable to tell what month it is.

Mr. MARTIN. But the year is 1964, and the words "Dallas, Texas" then appear under the date.

Mr. DULLES. That helps identify it.

Mr. REDLICH. I ask that it be admitted in evidence.

Mr. DULLES. Any objection?

Mr. LEECH. No objection.

Mr. DULLES. It is admitted.

(The photostats of a Russian letter with an English translation were marked Commission Exhibit No. 333 for identification and received in evidence.)

Mr. REDLICH. Mr. Martin, with your permission I would just summarize the contents of this letter, and if I have summarized it inaccurately, just say so. This letter requests that the death penalty not be applied to Jack Ruby, the person who has been charged with the murder of Lee Harvey Oswald. Is that inaccurate?

Mr. MARTIN. No; that is correct.

Mr. REDLICH. That is a correct summary of the contents of the letter?

Mr. MARTIN. Yes.

Mr. REDLICH. Do you recall to whom that letter was written?

Mr. MARTIN. She originally wrote the letter to Melvin Belli.

Mr. REDLICH. By "she" you mean Marina Oswald?

Mr. MARTIN. Marina. I advised her against——

Mr. REDLICH. Melvin Belli?

Mr. MARTIN. Is the attorney for Jack Ruby. I advised her against such an action, because of the possibility of the letter itself in translating from Russian to English being misinterpreted and used in a manner that might be derogatory to Marina Oswald. I suggested that she send this letter to Henry Wade who would be the prosecutor in the case. Now whether she changed the salutation on the letter I don't know. I can't read Russian. And the salutation was not translated in the translation. The translation was made by Katya Ford.

Mr. REDLICH. To the best of your knowledge has this letter ever been sent to anyone?

Mr. MARTIN. No sir, it hasn't.

Mr. DULLES. You say it has not been?

Mr. MARTIN. It has not been.

Mr. DULLES. That is your belief or you have knowledge that it has not been?

Mr. MARTIN. I have the original. Now if a letter has been sent, it would be a different letter.

Mr. REDLICH. On the basis of your knowledge of Marina Oswald's handwriting, would you tell the Commission whether you believe that this letter is in her handwriting?

Mr. MARTIN. Yes, it is. I also observed her writing the letter.

Mr. REDLICH. Are you aware of the fact that Marina Oswald discussed this letter when she appeared before this Commission?

Mr. MARTIN. I believe you mentioned it sometime today.

Mr. REDLICH. Were you aware of it prior to your coming here?

Mr. MARTIN. No.

Mr. REDLICH. Do you know why it has not been sent?

Mr. MARTIN. She decided that it was best not to be sent unless she actually thought that Ruby was going to get the death penalty. Actually a letter like that should go to the Governor of the State.

Mr. REDLICH. Mr. Martin, do you have any additional information concerning the assassination of President Kennedy, Marina Oswald, or the assassination of her husband Lee Harvey Oswald which you would like to present before this Commission at this time?

Mr. MARTIN. No, I don't think so. Nothing.

Mr. REDLICH. If it would be helpful for the work of this Commission for you to return to Washington and appear again before this Commission, would you be willing to do so?

Mr. MARTIN. Yes, sir.

Mr. REDLICH. Mr. Chairman, I have no further questions of this witness, unless Mr. Rankin does or you do.

Mr. DULLES. I would just like to ask a question about this letter I am just glancing over. Where did this letter paper come from? Is that some personal paper with a tree on it?

Mr. MARTIN. Yes. I bought that.

Mr. DULLES. You bought it for her?

Mr. MARTIN. At a drug store, yes, sir, at a drug store in Arlington.

Mr. DULLES. Is this another draft or is this just a copy?

Mr. MARTIN. This is the original of the copy.

Mr. REDLICH. We have photographed what is now Commission Exhibit No. 333 and we are keeping the photostat. Mr. Martin, you will recall that at the start of today's proceedings Chief Justice Warren read into the record a copy of the letter which you received requesting certain notes, records, documents in connection with today's hearing. Have you made available to the Commission all of the material which was requested in that letter?

Mr. MARTIN. Yes, sir; I went through everything I had at home, and could find nothing else.

Mr. REDLICH. If you should find anything else which you inadvertently failed to bring before this Commission, will you mail it to us for examination and we will return it to you.

Mr. MARTIN. Yes, sir; there is a Worker that I have.

Mr. REDLICH. You mean by Worker the Daily Worker?

Mr. MARTIN. Yes. I think they dropped the "Daily."

Mr. DULLES. They are no longer daily.

Mr. MARTIN. It is called the Worker now. It has quite a lengthy article about Marina in it, and I will send that to you.

Mr. REDLICH. And you will send anything that you may come across which you may have inadvertently failed to produce before this Commission?

Mr. MARTIN. Yes, sir.

Mr. REDLICH. I have no further questions, Mr. Chairman.

Mr. DULLES. There were some questions that Senator Cooper had suggested. I don't know, have you looked those over? Have they been covered?

Mr. RANKIN. Yes.

Mr. REDLICH. Those have been covered.

Mr. DULLES. All been covered?

Mr. REDLICH. Yes.

Mr. DULLES. Did Marina ever express to you her opinion as to the guilt or innocence of her husband in connection with the assassination of the President?

Mr. MARTIN. Yes.

Mr. DULLES. What did she say?

Mr. MARTIN. She believes he was guilty. She believes he did it, and the first time she said it I questioned her as to why she thought he did it, and she said she just felt it. It was a woman's intuition. She didn't know the word intuition at that time. I had to look it up in the Russian-English Dictionary.

Mr. DULLES. Did she indicate any view as to whether he did it alone or had an accomplice or accomplices?

Mr. MARTIN. She remarked about the Walker incident, that that was definitely done alone, and that he always was alone. He never did anything with anyone else. I don't recall that she mentioned that specifically in the case of the assassination of the President. But she had made that remark before or during the interim about Walker.

Mr. DULLES. Did she ever at any time express to you any interest in returning to the Soviet Union or her desire to stay in the United States?

Mr. MARTIN. Well, she has always said that she wanted to stay in the United States. One time she said that she thought she would go back to Russia, and I asked her why and she said, well, she was just joking.

Mr. DULLES. Did she ever refer to you any letters she wrote to the Soviet Embassy with regard to a desire to return?

Mr. MARTIN. No. There was only one incident that she told me about was a letter to a friend in Russia.

Mr. DULLES. You mentioned that I think.

Mr. MARTIN. Yes.

Mr. DULLES. The one that she didn't put enough stamps on, enough postage on.

Mr. MARTIN. Yes, it came back "insufficient postage."

Mr. DULLES. Did she ever mention to you any names of any friends or associates of her husband that had not been discussed here at one time or another in this testimony, including the list of names that was read out to you?

Mr. MARTIN. No.

Mr. DULLES. Do you know any other friends that Marina has other than those that have been discussed in this testimony?

Mr. MARTIN. No. I was trying to think a while ago about that, and I can't think of anyone else.

Mr. DULLES. That is all I have.

Mr. REDLICH. Mr. Leech, would you like to ask Mr. Martin any questions at this time?

Mr. LEECH. Not a word.

Mr. DULLES. Mr. Rhyne? Mr. Rankin, have you any further questions?

Mr. RANKIN. Mr. Chairman, I merely wish to thank him for appearing voluntarily.

Mr. DULLES. I do thank you for coming and responding so fully to our questions.

Mr. MARTIN. Anything I can do.

Mr. DULLES. And if anything occurs to you or to your counsel as sometimes happens later, we will be very glad if you or your counsel will bring it to our attention.

Mr. MARTIN. Yes, sir; I certainly will.

Mr. REDLICH. May I before we adjourn ask another question?

Mr. DULLES. Certainly.

Mr. REDLICH. Have you ever discussed with Mrs. Marguerite Oswald the question of the guilt or innocence of Lee Harvey Oswald?

Mr. MARTIN. No. The only time I was in contact with Marguerite Oswald was at the Inn of the Six Flags in Arlington, Tex., and I don't believe I really discussed anything with her. I was more on the sidelines and didn't enter into any discussions with her at all.

Mr. REDLICH. And have you discussed with Robert Oswald the question of the guilt or innocence of Lee Harvey Oswald?

Mr. MARTIN. Yes. Let's see, on one occasion the article by Mark Lane, I think it was in the National Observer, was printed in the National Observer, and I called Robert's attention to that. I believe he cited 15 points where he believed that Lee Oswald was innocent, and I remarked to Robert that in nearly 100 percent of those points they were just completely out of line. The brief I believe was taken from newspaper accounts, from various newspaper accounts of the assassination, and a number of them contradicted each other.

Mr. REDLICH. Did Robert Oswald comment on this?

Mr. MARTIN. No.

Mr. REDLICH. For the record I believe the publication you are referring to is the National Guardian.

Mr. MARTIN. The National Guardian, yes.

Mr. REDLICH. Is that your recollection now?

Mr. MARTIN. Yes, National Guardian.

Mr. REDLICH. And Robert Oswald had no comment on this?

Mr. MARTIN. No.

Mr. REDLICH. We have no further questions.

Mr. DULLES. The Commission will stand adjourned, subject to call.

(Whereupon, at 10:20 p.m., the President's Commission recessed.)

Wednesday, March 4, 1964

TESTIMONY OF MARK LANE

The President's Commission met at 2:30 p.m., on March 4, 1964, at 200 Maryland Avenue NE., Washington, D.C.

Present were Chief Justice Earl Warren, Chairman; Senator John Sherman Cooper and Representative Gerald R. Ford, members.

Also present were J. Lee Rankin, general counsel; Norman Redlich, assistant counsel; Charles Murray and Charles Rhyne, assistants to Walter E. Craig.

The CHAIRMAN. The Commission will be in order.

The Commission has been informed that Mr. Lane has collected numerous materials relevant to the Commission's work.

The Commission proposes to question Mr. Lane on all matters of which he has knowledge concerning the assassination of President Kennedy and the subsequent killing of Lee Harvey Oswald, and to request of Mr. Lane that he make available to the Commission any documentary material in his possession which can assist the Commission in its work.

In accordance with the rules of this Commission, Mr. Lane has been furnished with a copy of this statement.

Mr. Lane, would please rise and be sworn? Do you solemnly swear to tell the truth, the whole truth, and nothing but the truth, so help you God?

Mr. LANE. I do.

The CHAIRMAN. Will you be seated, please.

Mr. Rankin, would you proceed with the examination, please?

Mr. RANKIN. Mr. Lane, will you state your name?

Mr. LANE. My name is Mark Lane.

Mr. RANKIN. Where do you live?

Mr. LANE. 164 West 79th Street, New York City, New York State.

Mr. RANKIN. Are you a practicing lawyer?

Mr. LANE. Yes; I am.

Mr. RANKIN. Will you state your age, please?

Mr. LANE. I am 37 years old.

Mr. RANKIN. How long have you been practicing law?

Mr. LANE. Thirteen years.

Mr. RANKIN. You have qualified in the State of New York?

Mr. LANE. Yes.

Mr. RANKIN. Are you qualified in any other jurisdiction?

Mr. LANE. Just in the Federal court.

Mr. RANKIN. Do you have some information concerning the matters being investigated by the Commission that you would like to present to the Commission?

Mr. LANE. Yes; I do.

Mr. RANKIN. Will you proceed to do so?

Mr. LANE. Yes.

I wonder if I might ask at the outset if I will be able to secure a copy of the transcript of my testimony tomorrow, or is that going to be rushing things?

The CHAIRMAN. You will be able to obtain it. I don't know whether we can promise it to you tomorrow morning or not. But we will do it just as quickly as it can be transcribed by the reporter.

Mr. LANE. Thank you, sir.

At the outset, I would like to request that this portion of the hearing, in any event, be opened to the public. I think that there are matters here of grave concern to all the people of our country, and that it would, therefore, be fruitful and constructive for the sessions to be conducted in a public fashion, open to the public and to the press.

Accordingly, I request that this session at least involving my testimony be so opened to the public.

The CHAIRMAN. You would have a right, as any witness would have, to request that, Mr. Lane. We will conduct this in an open hearing. We will adjourn at this time to the auditorium downstairs, and we will conduct the hearing there. It will be open to the public. I saw a good many members of the press around, so it will really be a public affair.

(Whereupon, at 2:45 p.m., the Commission recessed and then reconvened in the auditorium in open session.)

TESTIMONY OF MARK LANE RESUMED IN OPEN SESSION

The CHAIRMAN. The Commission will be in order.

The Commission convened in our committee room on the fourth floor.

A reporter has been appointed.

Mr. Lane has been sworn.

Mr. Lane has stated that he would like to give his testimony at a public hearing. I explained to him that that was thoroughly agreeable to the Commission. The Commission does not operate in a secret way. Any witness who desires to have his—give his testimony in public may do so.

We have done it in the quiet of our rooms for the convenience of witnesses, and in order to accelerate the program. But any witness who desires to have his testimony recorded at a public hearing may do so.

The purpose of this Commission is, of course, eventually to make known to the President, and to the American public everything that has transpired before this Commission. All of it will be made available at the appropriate time. The records of the work of the Commission will be preserved for the public. So, Mr. Lane, we will be happy to accommodate you, and to proceed with our hearing.

Now, Mr. Rankin will conduct the examination.

(Having been previously duly sworn.)

Mr. RANKIN. Mr. Lane, will you proceed to tell the Commission whatever you have that would bear upon this investigation? Start item by item, and give us whatever you have in support.

Mr. LANE. Yes, sir.

At the outset, I would like to call to the Commission's attention a matter which is somewhat peripheral, perhaps, and should the Commission determine it does not wish to hear my testimony in that regard, I will understand that. But I would like to call it to your attention, because although it is peripheral I think it is related to both the assassination and the investigation into the assassination of the President.

That is in relationship to a picture which has been widely publicized, probably in every single community of our country, allegedly showing Lee Harvey Oswald holding in his hand a rifle which has been described in at least one publication, Life magazine, as the weapon with which he assassinated President Kennedy.

I would like to indicate to the Commission at this time that the pictures which have been distributed throughout the country included doctored and forged photographs. I would like to present evidence to the Commission at this time in that regard.

I ask the Commission if it does conclude that the photographs have been doctored, whether it will consider determining whether or not a crime has been committed, or an effort has been made to submit evidence to the Commission members, though not directly through the press, from magazines, which evidence——

The CHAIRMAN. I didn't get that last sentence—something about the Commission?

Mr. LANE. I am asking the Commission if it does conclude that the pictures have been doctored, to consider investigating the method by which the doctoring took place, who was responsible, and whether or not an effort has been made to influence the members of the Commission, while not directly, through the publication of this picture, which certainly has been circulated very widely throughout our country.

The CHAIRMAN. You may be sure, Mr. Lane, that anything you present in that regard will be thoroughly considered by the Commission.

Mr. LANE. Thank you, sir.

I would like to offer the February 21, 1964 issue of Life magazine.

Mr. RANKIN. Will you mark that, Mr. Reporter, please, the next number.

Mr. LANE. A picture appears on the entire cover of Life magazine, and an identical picture appears in the interior pages, at page 80. The caption on the cover reads, "Lee Oswald with the weapons he used to kill President Kennedy and Officer Tippit."

I think it is quite plain from looking at both of the pictures that there appears on the rifle, what appears to be a rifle in the left hand of Lee Harvey Oswald, a telescopic sight.

Mr. RANKIN. Mr. Lane, we will mark that Exhibit No. 334.

(The document referred to was marked Commission Exhibit No. 334, for identification.)

Mr. LANE. Next I would like to offer a picture which is a glossy 8½-by-11 picture, of a photograph published in the New York Times, secured by the New York Times from the Associated Press.

Representative FORD. Is there any verification of the fact that that is as you have identified it?

Mr. LANE. That is what—a picture secured——

Representative FORD. From the New York Times, which in turn had acquired it from the Associated Press?

Mr. LANE. Well, that is a statement which I have made under oath, and it can be verified with the New York Times.

Mr. RANKIN. That is Exhibit 335 that you are just referring to, Mr. Lane.

(The document referred to was marked Commission Exhibit No. 335, for identification.)

Mr. LANE. I suggest that is the identical picture with the one published on the cover of Life magazine, Exhibit 334, in every respect, including the creases in the trousers, the background, with the exception of the rifle in the hands of Oswald, which appears to have no telescopic scope in Exhibit 335.

In addition, there clearly has been some other doctoring of the photograph around the head of Lee Harvey Oswald, and the trees and other background material over his left shoulder have been removed from the Associated Press picture, but are present in the Life magazine picture.

Shadows and fenceposts which can be observed between the legs of Lee Harvey Oswald in Exhibit 335 have been removed in the Life magazine picture. I would like to offer this picture as the next exhibit.

Mr. RANKIN. That will be marked Exhibit 336.

(The document referred to was marked Commission Exhibit No. 336 for identification.)

Mr. RANKIN. Will you tell us what that is, Mr. Lane?

Mr. LANE. Yes; 336 is an 8½-by-11 glossy photograph of a picture appearing in Newsweek magazine, March 2, 1964, credited by Newsweek magazine to the Detroit Free Press. I would suggest that that is an identical picture with the other two pictures in every respect, except that it has no telescopic sight on the rifle, and there is a great deal of metallic materials present on that rifle clearly not present in the other two pictures.

The CHAIRMAN. Did you say metallics?

Mr. LANE. Metallics.

Mr. RANKIN. Will you tell us what you mean by that, Mr. Lane?

Mr. LANE. Yes. Just below the hand, the left hand of Lee Harvey Oswald, there is clearly visible a series of pieces of metal, allegedly part of the rifle, which are in no way clear—which are in no way present in the other pictures.

The CHAIRMAN. I see.

Mr. LANE. To make that clearer, I would like to offer Exhibit 337, which is an enlargement of the picture 335, the New York Times picture.

(The document referred to was marked Commission Exhibit No. 337, for identification.)

Mr. LANE. This enlarges the area on the rifle just below what is allegedly Oswald's left hand. It clearly shows an absolute absence of all of the metallic material present in the Newsweek photo, 336.

This is a front page of the New York Journal American dated February 18, 1964, which is an identical picture with the one published in Life magazine, Exhibit 334, and the credit lines appearing on that publication indicate that the picture has been secured from the Associated Press through the Detroit Free Press.

(The document referred to was marked Commission Exhibit No. 338, for identification.)

Mr. LANE. That picture has a telescopic sight, and is not the picture in terms of the metal material on the rifle which Newsweek stated they secured through the Detroit Free Press, and is not the picture without the telescopic sight which the New York Times states that it secured through the Associated Press. In any event, I would like to submit a picture procured from Worldwide Photos.

Mr. RANKIN. 339.

(The document referred to was marked Commission Exhibit No. 339, for identification.)

Mr. LANE. This is allegedly a picture taken in the Dallas Police Station, showing the alleged murder weapon.

The CHAIRMAN. That is No. 339, Mr. Lane?

Mr. LANE. Yes, sir, and I would call the Commission's attention to the curved line of the stock present in Exhibit 339, and obviously absent from every other picture, indicating that in no event is the rifle allegedly in the hands of Lee Oswald, in Exhibits 334 through 338 comparable to the alleged murder weapon as shown in the Dallas police station.

And should the Commission decide to investigate the obviously doctored pictures that have been circulated so widely in our country, I would refer the Commission investigators to the Times Picayune of New Orleans, published on November 24, 1963, in which an Associated Press story indicated that the Dallas police chief, Jesse Curry, stated that he had in his possession photographs found in the home of Lee Harvey Oswald's Russian-born wife which linked Oswald with the rifle used in the assassination of President Kennedy. Curry said in the article attributed to Curry——

Mr. RANKIN. Do you wish to make that a part of the record?

Mr. LANE. Yes.

Mr. RANKIN. That will be Exhibit 340.

(The document referred to was marked Commission Exhibit No. 340 for identification.)

Mr. LANE. The article attributes a statement to Curry indicating that he, the Dallas Police Chief, found the pictures in the surburban Irving, Tex., home in which Marina Oswald lived, and stated that Mr. Curry had said that the pictures will be used in evidence in Oswald's murder trial. This was published, I assume, prior to the time that Oswald was himself killed on that day.

Representative FORD. Would the date of the paper be on the back side?

The CHAIRMAN. It is on the front. November 24th.

Mr. LANE. I would like to offer this as an exhibit.

Mr. RANKIN. This is marked Commission Exhibit 341.

(The document referred to was marked Commission Exhibit No. 341, for identification.)

Mr. LANE. Exhibit 341 is a page or portion of a page of the New York Times, on Sunday, December 8, with a picture of the alleged murder weapon, secured, according to the credit line under the picture, from the United Press International, indicating clearly that that rifle is not the rifle allegedly being held by Mr. Oswald in any of the pictures so widely circulated throughout our country.

Mr. RANKIN. On what do you base that last conclusion, Mr. Lane? Would you point out to the Commission the differences as you see them?

Mr. LANE. Yes: the reference of the stock. The stock has a clearly curved and bent line in this picture.

Mr. RANKIN. That is in Exhibit 341?

Mr. LANE. Yes, and it is present in none of the pictures of Oswald holding the rifle: 336, for example, in Newsweek magazine shows almost a straight stock. Some of them show even an absolutely straight stock.

Exhibit 335 from the New York Times shows a perfectly straight stock—which is not only a stock unlike this particular Italian 6.5 millimeter carbine, but is a stock I believe unlike any rifle stock produced during the 20th century, and possibly the 19th century, anywhere. Rifle experts seem to agree that every stock must have in it some break, so that it is possible to place your hand around the rifle while your finger holds the trigger. And there is no break in the doctored photographs, in the stock portrayed on the doctored photographs.

I have checked many rifle catalogs. This is not my field, and I don't qualify as an expert. But I have checked many rifle catalogs, and have only seen rifles with a break where the stock becomes narrow enough for one's hand to grasp it while pulling the trigger.

Mr. RANKIN. Is that the basis of your opinion that you have just given, that it doesn't have a break in it, and that other rifles for any period later than you have described do?

Mr. LANE. Well, several persons who have described themselves as rifle experts have made that statement to me.

Mr. RANKIN. Who are those?

Mr. LANE. I believe I have some of their names here. I don't have the names of those who have called, but I can secure that at our first break by a telephone call to my office.

Mr. RANKIN. Would you furnish that then?

Mr. LANE. Surely. In any event, whether there was another rifle or not, the rifle portrayed in the picture is clearly—in the picture in which Oswald is allegedly holding the rifle—clearly is not the rifle allegedly claimed to be the murder weapon. I wonder if I might ask the Commission if it might produce the rifle now, so that we might compare the actual rifle with the pictures.

The CHAIRMAN. We will do that in due course. But we don't have the rifle here now, Mr. Lane. We will make the proper comparisons, you may be sure, with experts.

Mr. LANE. Now, on another peripheral matter—unless there are any further questions in relation to this matter——

Mr. RANKIN. No, you may proceed. Do you have negatives of these pictures you have produced?

Mr. LANE. No. I am glad you asked that question, because I can now relate to you about a conversation that I had 2 or 3 days ago with a Mr. Dirksen, who is on the photo desk of the Associated Press. I called Mr. Dirksen and asked him for a glossy of the picture which the Associated Press sent out over the wire service.

Mr. RANKIN. Could you identify Mr. Dirksen a little more clearly?

Mr. LANE. He just told me he was employed. I called the Associated Press in New York City and asked for the photo desk, Mr. Dirksen answered and said he was employed there. I asked him what his specific position was there, and he declined to give me that information. He said he didn't think it was relevant.

In any event, I asked him if he could secure for me a glossy, a glossy copy of the picture sent by the Associated Press over the wires. And I described the picture as the one of Oswald allegedly holding the murder weapon in his left hand, and having on his right hip a pistol, allegedly the pistol with which he slew Officer Tippit.

Mr. Dirksen stated to me that he could not make a glossy of that picture available to me and I pointed out to him that in the past the Associated Press had been most cooperative when I asked for pictures, and he said, "Yes, we sent a whole batch up to you last week, didn't we?" I said, "Yes, you did, I appreciated that. I wonder why this picture is being treated differently from other pictures." He said, "This is not a normal picture and this is not the normal situation."

I asked him what he meant by that. He explained that there was a special contract—he did not have all the details, he said, because he is not one of the persons who was involved in drafting the contract—but there was a special contract between the Associated Press and the source of this picture, and they agreed, the Associated Press agreed in this contract that they would not make a glossy available to anyone, that they would send the pictures out only to their subscribers, and that no one else would be allowed to see the picture.

I said if that was the understanding, I certainly would not wish to have them breach their agreement, and asked if instead he would make the name of the source known to me, so that I might go directly to the source and see if I might secure the picture in that fashion. He stated he could not do that, because one of the other stipulations in the contract would be that they could not reveal the name of the source of the picture.

I discussed this with an employee of the New York Times thereafter, since I knew that the New York Times was a subscriber to the services made available by the Associated Press.

Mr. RANKIN. Could you identify that employee, please?

Mr. LANE. No, I am not going to be able to discuss sources, obviously, here, I am sorry.

But this employee indicated to me thereafter that an inquiry had been made by the New York Times to the Associated Press along the same lines as the inquiry which I had made, in terms of trying to determine the source of the

Associated Press picture. And I was informed by this employee of the New York Times that the Associated Press declined to name the source of the picture, even when the New York Times made a request. Therefore, I do not have the negative, and I do not know the source of the picture.

Mr. RANKIN. Is that true with regard to all of the pictures that you produced?

Mr. LANE. My office called Life magazine, and asked someone at Life magazine on the photo desk, the editorial department, if a picture could be made available and they stated that they would not make a glossy available—it was their policy in reference to all pictures in their possession.

Those are the only inquiries I made with reference to the source of the pictures.

Mr. RANKIN. Now you may proceed.

Mr. LANE. Yes. I would like to raise one other peripheral matter before going into the evidence, if I might. That is, I would like to call to the attention of the Commission this article, and ask that it be marked as an exhibit.

Mr. RANKIN. That has been marked Commission Exhibit 342.

(The document referred to was marked Commission Exhibit No. 342, for identification.)

Mr. LANE. Thank you.

This is an article appearing in the New York Journal American Sunday, February 23.

Mr. RANKIN. This consists of two separate pages, does it not?

Mr. LANE. It does—the first page being a masthead and front page, headline from the Journal American, dated Sunday, February 23, 1964, and the second page containing a portion of the front page of the Journal American on that date, and a portion of page 15, the continued story of the Journal American on the same date.

This is an article written by Bob Considine, who enjoys a reputation for being an excellent reporter. Mr. Considine states in his article that an eyewitness to the shooting of Officer Tippit by the name of Warren Reynolds was himself recently shot through the head by a man with a rifle.

Now, I don't believe that it is alleged that Reynolds actually saw the person pull the trigger which sent the bullets at Officer Tippit. As I understand it, Mr. Reynolds has stated that he, Reynolds, heard the shot, the shooting, left his office and saw a man running away, placing new shells into a pistol as he ran away. And Mr. Considine indicates that Reynolds thereafter identified Oswald as the person who was running from the scene.

This article indicated that during January, Mr. Reynolds was himself shot through the head with a rifle, and that he is in the hospital—I believe he was in the hospital at that time. I don't know what the state of his health is at the present time.

Mr. Considine indicates that a person was picked up in the Dallas area and charged with the shooting, but that someone who Mr. Considine refers to as "his girl"—I assume he is making reference to the gentleman who was charged with the attack upon Reynolds—testified in such a fashion, and took a lie detector test, so that the person charged with the crime was released.

This person, Betty Mooney MacDonald, who helped to free her friend, according to Mr. Considine, herself had worked as a stripper in the Carousel Club in Dallas, owned by Jack Ruby.

Two weeks before this article was written, Miss MacDonald was herself arrested for a fight with her roomate, and the week before the article was written, Mr. Considine states she hanged herself in her cell.

I would request the Commission to investigate into these series of most unusual coincidences, to see if they have any bearing upon the basic matter pending before the Commission.

The CHAIRMAN. It may be introduced as are all of these pictures, admitted.

(The documents heretofore marked for identification as Commission Exhibits Nos. 334 to 342, were received in evidence.)

Mr. LANE. In the course of my investigation, I have come across some material which would be relevant only if I was first able to examine the rifle, quite frankly. I wonder if that might be able to be accomplished sometime during the day?

The CHAIRMAN. During the day?

Mr. LANE. Today, if possible.

The CHAIRMAN. Well, I think not, because we don't have it. But we will make it available to you, though, at the very first opportunity, Mr. Lane.

Mr. LANE. Fine. Then I will reserve my comment in reference to the rifle for that occasion.

The CHAIRMAN. You may.

Mr. LANE. Thank you. I would like to, on behalf of Lee Harvey Oswald, make this information available to the Commission.

It, of course, has been alleged by the chief of police of Dallas, and by the district attorney of Dallas that Oswald was present on the sixth floor of the Texas Book Depository Building during the very early afternoon of November 22, 1963, and that from that area he fired an Italian carbine, 6.5 millimeters, three times, twice striking the President of the United States, wounding him fatally, and injuring the Governor of Texas by striking him with a bullet, on one occasion.

The physician who signed the death certificate of the President pronouncing him dead was Dr. Kemp Clark, whose name appeared on the official homicide report filed by the Dallas Police Department, and attested to by two police officers.

On the 27th of November, the New York Times reported, "Dr. Kemp Clark, who pronounced Mr. Kennedy dead, said one bullet struck him at about the necktie knot, 'It ranged downward in his chest and did not exit' the surgeon said."

On the same day the New York Herald Tribune stated, "On the basis of accumulated data, investigators have concluded that the first shot fired as the Presidential car was approaching, struck the President in the neck, just above the knot of his necktie, then ranged downward into his body."

According to Richard Dudman—Mr. Dudman is the Washington correspondent, as I am sure you all know better than I, for the St. Louis Post-Dispatch—according to him, the surgeons who attended the President while he was at the Parkland Memorial Hospital, described the wound—were in agreement in describing the wound in the throat as an entrance wound. The St. Louis Post-Dispatch on December 1 carried a rather long and involved story by Mr. Dudman, recounting his conversations with the physicians who were treating the President on the 22d at the Parkland Memorial Hospital.

Dr. Perry explained that he began to open an air passage in the President's throat in an effort to restore his breathing, and he explained that the incision had been made through the bullet wound in the President's throat—since that was in the correct place for the operation, in any event. Dr. Perry, according to Mr. Dudman, described to him the bullet hole as an entrance wound.

Dr. Robert N. McClelland, who was one of the three physicians who participated in that operation, later stated to Mr. Dudman, "It certainly did look like an entrance wound."

He went on to say that he saw bullet wounds every day in Dallas, sometimes several times a day, and that this did appear to be an entrance wound.

One doctor made reference to the frothing of blood in the neck wound. The doctor said, "He is bubbling air." Two of the doctors, Drs. Peters and Baxter, inserted a tube into the right upper part of the President's chest, just below the shoulder, to reexpand the lungs, and to keep them from collapsing.

Dr. Jones and Dr. Perry inserted a similar tube on the left portion of the President's chest.

The activity was necessitated because the bubbling air was the first clue that they had that the President's lung had been punctured.

The prosecuting authorities, confronted with what seemed then to be evidence that the President had been shot from the front, in the throat——

The CHAIRMAN. Are you reading now, Mr. Lane?

Mr. LANE. No, I am just making reference to this. That is not a quote.

The CHAIRMAN. It is not a quote. You are just paraphrasing what was in this article of Mr. Dudman's?

Mr. LANE. No, I am leaving Mr. Dudman now, and going on to statements made by the prosecuting authorities. I will submit quotations—I will try to remember to place quotation marks when I have a quotation.

The CHAIRMAN. Yes, all right.

Mr. LANE. The authorities who were confronted with what seemed to be irrefutable evidence that the President had been shot in the front of the throat, concluded that the Presidential limousine was approaching the Book Depository Building when the first shot was fired, because it seems at the very outset a theory was developed by the prosecuting authorities that Oswald was on the sixth floor of the Book Depository Building, that he was the assassin, and that he acted alone.

I think that the record and an examination of the activities of the Dallas police, and the Dallas district attorney's office, will show that the only area where they have been consistent from the outset was once this theory was enunciated, they stayed with the theory, and they were devoted to the theory, regardless of the discovery of new evidence and new facts.

For example, the New York Times stated on November 26, 1963, "The known facts about the bullets, and the position of the assassin, suggested that he started shooting as the President's car was coming toward him, swung his rifle in an arc of almost 180°, and fired at least twice more." At that time, the prosecution case had already been developed in terms of the theory that Oswald was the assassin and that Oswald acted alone.

There were newspaper pictures published in many portions of the country showing the Textbook Depository Building on Houston Street where the Presidential limousine approached the Book Depository Building, and Elm Street, where after the limousine made a sharp left turn it continued until it reached the underpass directly ahead.

And in these newspapers, there were superimposed dotted lines showing the trajectory of the three bullets, showing that the first bullet was fired while the Presidential car was still on Houston Street, still approaching the Book Depository Building.

However, it soon became essential for the prosecution to abandon that theory, because the eyewitnesses present, including Governor Connally, and Mrs. Connally, stated that the limousine had already made a left turn, had passed the Book Depository Building at the time that the first shot was fired.

In essence, then, the prosecution remained with the theory that Oswald, while acting alone, shot the President from the front from the back.

However, ——

Mr. RANKIN. I don't understand that.

Mr. LANE. I don't understand that either, but this was the theory of the prosecution—that the President had—it had been conceded at that time that the President had been shot in the front of the throat. However, the evidence then developed indicated that the Presidential limousine had already passed the Book Depository Building, and the President was not facing the Book Depository Building when the first shot was fired. At that time, Life magazine explains it all in a full page article entitled, "An End to Nagging Rumors, the 6 Crucial Seconds."

And Life conceded that the limousine was some 50 yards past Oswald when the first shot was fired, and that the shot entered the President's throat from the front, but explained that the President had turned completely around and was facing the Book Depository Building when the shot was fired.

But that theory, however, could not——

Mr. RANKIN. Do you have the date of that article?

Mr. LANE. That was December 6, Life magazine. The full page article was entitled "End to Nagging Rumors, the Six Critical Seconds."

The problem——

Senator COOPER. May I ask a question there—just to clarify? Did you say that in this article that Life said that the late President had turned around and was facing the Book Depository Building when the shot was fired?

Mr. LANE. Yes, Senator. The trouble with that theory, however, which was enunciated by Life, and from where they secured it I do not know, but they certainly were in Dallas very much in evidence on the scene—was that the week prior to then Life magazine itself printed the stills of the motion pictures, and in those stills, with Life's own captions, it was quite plain that the President was looking almost completely forward, just slightly to the right, but almost forward, and certainly not turned around when the first shot was fired. And so the stills printed in Life's own publication a week before they enunciated this theory proved that the Life theory was false.

In addition to this, persons present on the scene, such witnesses as Mrs. Connally and the Governor of Texas, indicated that the President was looking almost straight ahead. And I believe that Mrs. Connally stated that she had just made a statement to the President, tragically enough, something about, "You cannot say the people of Dallas have not given you a warm welcome today," and he was about to respond when the first bullet struck him.

In order for the prosecution to remain with the theory in the light of the new evidence that Oswald was the assassin and he acted alone, something would have to give, and it became plain that the third try would have to result in a new examination of the medical testimony.

Mr. Dudman stated that the doctors at Parkland Hospital, who had, of course, this vital evidence to offer, were never questioned about the vital evidence by the FBI or by the Secret Service, and that it was not until after an autopsy had been performed at Bethesda, that two Secret Service agents, armed with that report, journeyed down to the Parkland Hospital and talked to the doctors, for the purpose of explaining to them that the new medical testimony and evidence indicated they were all in error at the outset. And, eventually, that was the position agreed to by the physicians, that they all had been in error when they stated that it was an entrance wound in the throat.

Physicians seem to agree that a short period of time after death, as a result of the deterioration of tissue, it is much more difficult to examine wounds to determine if they are entrance wounds or exit wounds.

In addition to this, according to Mr. Dudman in the Post Dispatch there had been an operation performed on what the doctors thought then was an entrance wound; therefore, it would seem altering the wound in the throat so that it would probably be more difficult to determine if it were an entrance or an exit wound, after the operation had been completed.

However, I do not know, of course, what is in the autopsy report—very likely you have seen that report—but portions of it, whether accurately or inaccurately, have been leaked to the public through the press. And the portion which has been leaked to the press, to the public through the press, in reference to the wound in the President's throat, indicated that the bullet struck the back of the President's head, and either a fragment of the bullet or a fragment of bone from the President's head exited at the throat.

If this were so, while it could explain perhaps the wound in the throat, it would be difficult to understand why this was not apparent to the doctors in the Parkland Hospital, particularly in view of the fact that it would indicate that the path of the bullet ran from the top of the head down to the throat, not from the throat down to the back of the chest, a very different path entirely.

And since Dr. Perry indicated that he inserted a tube into the President's throat following the bullet wound, it would be difficult to understand how he was not aware of the path of the bullet, when it was absolutely in the opposite direction from the one he thought it was in when he inserted the tube.

Most remarkable of all, though, is that if the bullet entered the top of the head, and a portion of it or a portion of bone exited from the throat, the collapse of the lungs and the frothing of air at the throat are both indications of a punctured lung—it would be difficult to explain by that particular bullet's path.

I think that an openminded investigating and prosecuting agency would have found, at the outset, in view of the medical evidence available at the outset, that the President was shot from the front while facing slightly to the right, and after passing the book depository building—an openminded investigating body in Dallas, the district attorney's office or the police, or others who were associated in that investigation, might have considered abandoning their theory that Oswald was the assassin and that he acted alone, and

41

might have been led by the factual data to investigate in other areas as well—clearly something that they did not do.

I have been informed by reporters, for example, that—reporters from foreign countries covering the trial, that some of them were very concerned about the fact that they would now not be able to leave Dallas, that clearly the airports would be closed, there would be roadblocks placed on many of the streets, the trains would be stopped or searched, in order that the assassin or those who assisted him, or those who assisted the assassins, might be prevented from readily leaving the entire area.

I am informed by the reporters in the area that there were no such roadblocks, that planes continued to leave, trains continued to leave, and that the prosecution continued with its theory that Oswald was the assassin, that he acted alone, and they had secured his arrest, and there was nothing more to be done other than to prove as conclusively as possible, utilizing the press as we know, and the television, and the radio media for that purpose.

And while I am on this question, I wonder if I might ask the Commission to give consideration to—although I don't believe that it is present in any of the six panels which have been established by the Commission—but to give consideration nevertheless to the 48 hours in which Oswald was in custody, in reference to what happened to his rights as an American citizen, charged with a crime in this country.

The statement by the National Board of the American Civil Liberties Union, that had Oswald lived he could not have secured a fair trial anywhere in this country.

The CHAIRMAN. You may be sure, Mr. Lane, that that will be given most serious consideration by the Commission, and the Commission has already appointed as an act in that direction the President of the American Bar Association, with such help as he may wish to have, to make an investigation of that very thing. I assure you it will be done by the Commission.

Mr. LANE. Getting back to the evidence, Mr. Chief Justice, the spectator closest to President Kennedy, a Mrs. Hill, who was a substitute teacher in the Dallas public school system, stated to me that she was in her view the closest spectator to the President, and was standing alongside a Mary Moorman, who resides in Dallas.

Mr. RANKIN. Do you have the date of this interview, Mr. Lane?

Mr. LANE. It was within the last week. She stated to me that she was the closest spectator to the President, she and her friend, when the President was struck by a bullet. She said that she heard some four to six shots fired.

Now, she was standing on the grass across the—across Elm Street, across from the Texas Book Depository Building. She said that in her—it is her feeling that all of the shots, the four to six shots, came from the grassy knoll near the triple overpass which was at that time directly in front and slightly to the right of the Presidential limousine, and that in her view none of the shots were fired from the Book Depository Building which was directly across the street from her, and which was to the rear of the Presidential limousine.

She said further that after the last shot was fired, she saw a man run from behind the general area of a concrete facade on that grassy knoll, and that he ran on to the triple overpass.

She told me that standing alongside of her was Mary Moorman, who took a picture of the President just a brief moment before the first shot was fired, and that agents of the Federal Bureau of Investigation took the film from Miss Moorman, and gave her a receipt, which she still has in her possession, but that she has not been able to see the picture, and that it is possible that the picture included the entire Book Depository Building, taken just precisely a second or less before the shots were fired.

Tom Wicker, who is a member of the New York Times White House staff, who was the only New York Times reporter in Dallas when the President was shot, stated in an article which appeared in the Saturday Review, on January 11, 1964, "As we came out of the overpass, I saw a motorcycle policeman drive over the curb, cross an open area, a few feet up a railroad bank, dismount, and start scrambling up the bank." Ronnie Dugger, who is the editor of the Texas Observer, a statewide publication in Texas, stated in his publication on November 29, 1963, and later stated to me in two different interviews material of the same nature.

I am now quoting from the publication:

"On the other side of the overpass a motorcycle policeman was roughriding across some grass to the trestle for the railroad tracks, across the overpass. He brought his cycle to a halt and leapt from it and was running up the base of the trestle when I lost sight of him."

Mr. RANKIN. Can you give us the date of the paper that came from?

Mr. LANE. Yes. That was the Texas Observer, November 29, 1963. That statement has been confirmed by Mr. Dugger to me in two interviews in Dallas.

James Vachule, who is a reporter for the Fort Worth Star Telegram, said, "I heard the shots, several, at the triple overpass."

And Jerry Flemmons, reporting also for the Fort Worth Star Telegram, on November 22, 1963, stated, "Kennedy was gunned down by an assassin, apparently standing on the overpass above the freeway."

Now, I spoke to a Mary Woodward, who is an employee of the Dallas Morning News, and she stated that she was present with three coworkers, all employees of the Dallas Morning News, and they were standing near the—the base of the grassy knoll, perhaps 50 feet or so from the overpass, with the overpass to their right, and the book depository building to their left. And on November 23, 1963, the Dallas Morning News ran a story by Miss Woodward, and I have since that time spoken with Miss Woodward by telephone, and she has confirmed portions—the entire portion which I will quote from now—in her conversation with me.

That is, that as she and her three coworkers waited for the President to pass, on the grassy slope just east of the triple overpass, she explained that the President approached and acknowledged their cheers and the cheers of others, "he faced forward again, and suddenly there was an ear-shattering noise coming from behind us and a little to the right."

Here we have a statement, then, by an employee of the Dallas Morning News, evidently speaking—she indicated to me that she was speaking on behalf of all four employees, all of whom stated that the shots came from the direction of the overpass, which was to their right, and not at all from the Book Depository Building, which was to their left.

Miss Woodward continued, "Instead of speeding up the car, the car came to a halt. Things are a little bit hazy from this point, but I don't believe anyone was hit with the first bullet. The President and Mrs. Kennedy turned and looked around as if they, too, didn't believe the noise was really coming from a gun. Then after a moment's pause there was another shot, and I saw the President slumping in the car."

This would seem to be consistent with the statement by Miss Hill that more than three shots were fired.

In addition to these statements, James A. Chaney, who is a Dallas motorcycle policeman, was quoted in the Houston Chronicle on November 24, 1963, as stating that the first shot missed entirely. He said he was 6 feet to the right and front of the President's car, moving about 15 miles an hour, and when the first shot was fired, "I thought it was a backfire", he said.

Now, Miss Hill told me that when she was questioned—put that word unfortunately in quotation marks—by the U.S. Secret Service agents, that they indicated to her what her testimony should be, and that is that she only heard three shots. And she insisted that she heard from four to six shots. And she said that at least one agent of the Secret Service said to her, "There were three wounds and there were three shells, so we are only saying three shots." And they raised with her the possibility that instead of hearing more than three shots, that she might have heard firecrackers exploding, or that she might have heard echoes.

Despite this type of questioning by the Secret Service, Miss Hill continued to maintain, the last I spoke with her, about a week ago, that she heard from four to six shots.

Now, to the best of my knowledge, from my investigation, which has been very severely limited by lack of personnel and almost total lack of funds, and, there-

43

fore, is clearly not the kind of investigation which is required here—but from this limited investigation, it seems that only two persons immediately charged into the Texas Book Depository Building after the shots were fired. They were an officer of the Dallas Police Force, Seymour Weitzman, who submitted an affidavit to the Dallas police office, in which he stated that he discovered the rifle on the sixth floor of the Book Depository Building.

There was one other gentleman who ran into the building, and that was Roy S. Truly, who was and is, I believe, the director of the Book Depository Building.

However, Mr. Truly stated that he believed that the shots came from the direction of the overpass and from the grassy knoll. And although he was standing directly in front of the Book Depository Building, he did not believe that the shots came from that building.

Standing with him at the time of the assassination was O. V. Campbell, who was the vice president of the Book Depository Building.

In the Dallas Morning News on November 23, 1963, it was stated that "Campbell says he ran toward a grassy knoll to the west of the building where he thought the sniper had hidden."

So we have two persons that we know of standing in front of the Book Depository Building, and they both thought that the shots came from the grassy knoll near the overpass.

The police officer, Seymour Weitzman, submitted an affidavit to the Dallas district attorney's office, he and Mr. Truly, as I indicated a moment ago were the only two who charged into the Book Depository Building when the shots were fired.

Weitzman indicated in his affidavit—I assume you have the original of that affidavit—that he ran "in a northwest direction, scaled the fence toward where we thought the shots came from."

He indicated "then someone said they thought the shots came from the old Texas Building. I immediately ran to the Texas Building and started looking inside."

So even the two people who ran into the building indicated that they did not believe the shots came from the building.

Mr. Weitzman went into the building because someone whose name he did not give in his affidavit told him to go into the building, and then Truly explained that although he thought the shots came from the general direction of the grassy knoll or the overpass in front of the President's limousine, he saw this officer run into the building, of which he is a director, and he felt that since he knew the building and the officer did not, he should go in the building to assist the officer.

From published accounts, and from my investigation, I can only find one person who thought that the shots came from the building, and that was the Chief of Police in Dallas, Jesse Curry, who said as soon as the shots were fired, he knew they came from the building. From the Book Depository Building.

Now, of course, there were many persons present there whom I have not quoted, to whom I have no access.

Now, I spoke on several occasions with the reporter for the Fort Worth Star Telegram, whose name is Thayer Waldo. Mr. Waldo was standing with a police captain near the Dallas Trade Mart Building, which was the building, public building, where the President was going to have spoken that day. Mr. Waldo was awaiting his arrival, the President's arrival there, when a sergeant who was seated in a police cruiser called the captain over hurriedly to the police car. Mr. Waldo accompanied the captain to the police car. And Mr. Waldo stated to me that he heard the first bulletin which came over the Dallas police radio, and it was "Bulletin. The President has been shot. It is feared that others in his party have been wounded. The shots came from a triple overpass in front of the Presidential automobile."

So even the police, despite the Chief of Police's later assertion that he knew that the shots came from the Book Depository Building, behind the Presidential limousine, the first police radio broadcast indicated that it was the police position at that time that the shots came from the front, not from the rear.

Now, Patrolman Chaney, who I made reference to a little earlier, the motorcycle patrolman, stated that the Presidential car stopped momentarily after the first shot. That statement was consistent with Miss Woodward's statement in the Dallas Morning News, that the automobile came to almost a complete halt after the first shot, and the statement of many other witnesses as well.

Mr. RANKIN. When was that statement made?

Mr. LANE. That statement appeared in the newspaper I made reference to before, the Houston Chronicle, on November 24, 1963.

Mr. RANKIN. When you made an independent inquiry at any time, would you tell us, Mr. Lane?

Mr. LANE. Yes, I certainly shall do that.

Now, I think one has to conjecture as to why the Secret Service agent who was undoubtedly trained for this assignment, and particularly the agent who was driving the Presidential limousine in Dallas, where we were told that the greatest efforts ever to protect an American President were going to be made that day, because of the previous difficulties in Dallas, the attack upon our Ambassador to the United Nations and the attack upon the then Senator Johnson, when he spoke in Dallas in 1960—one would assume that the most qualified Secret Service driver that could be secured would be driving that automobile. It is difficult to understand why the automobile almost came to a complete stop after the first shot was fired, if the shots were coming from the rear. The natural inclination, it would seem, would be to step on the gas and accelerate as quickly as possible. However, if the driver were under the impression that the shots were from the front, one could understand his hesitation in not wanting to drive closer to the sniper or snipers.

In addition, however, Roy Kellerman, who was in the front right-hand seat of the automobile, who I am told was in charge of the Secret Service operation that day, the director of the Secret Service not being present in Dallas on that occasion—according to the pictures printed in Life magazine, Mr. Kellerman looked forward until the first shot was fired. Then he turned back, and looked at the President. He immediately looked forward again, and was looking in the direction of the overpass while the second shot was fired, and while the third shot was fired.

One would certainly expect that Mr. Kellerman was and is a trained observer, who would not panic in such a circumstance, for which he has received his training.

The pictures I make reference to are those in Life magazine which I referred to a little earlier in the afternoon.

Senator COOPER. May I ask a question there, Mr. Chief Justice?

The CHAIRMAN. Yes, go right ahead, Senator.

Senator COOPER. This last statement you made, about the Secret Service agent who turned, so that he was faced to the rear, toward the President, and then turned forward—I didn't quite understand what you deduced from that.

Mr. LANE. I assumed that he was looking toward the sound of the shots.

Senator COOPER. You mean when he turned to the rear, or turned ahead?

Mr. LANE. Well, when the President was shot, and was struck he then turned around, which I would imagine would be an ordinary response when somebody in an automobile with whom you are riding has been shot.

But immediately after that, before the second shot was fired, he turned completely to the front, and was looking at the overpass during the remainder of the time that the shots were fired. It would seem to indicate to me that it is possible that Mr. Kellerman felt that the shots were coming from the general direction in which he was looking.

Mr. RANKIN. What do you base your statement on that the car stopped, the President's limousine?

Mr. LANE. The statement made by various witnesses, including Mr. Chaney, a motorcycle policeman, Miss Woodward, who was one of the closest witnesses to the President at the time that he was shot, and others. I think that is the— I haven't documented that beyond that, because that seemed to be so generally conceded by almost everyone, that the automobile came to—almost came to a complete halt after the first shot—did not quite stop, but almost did. And, of course, you have the films, I assume, of the assassination and know more about that than I do, certainly.

Now, in reference to the rifle, there is on file—I assume that you have it or copies of it—in the Dallas district attorney's office or the police office in Dallas, an affidavit sworn to by Officer Weitzman, in which he indicates that he discovered the rifle on the sixth floor of the Book Depository Building at, I believe, 1:22 p.m., on November 22, 1963.

Now, in this affidavit, Officer Weitzman swore that the murder weapon— that the weapon which he found on the sixth floor was a 7.65 Mauser, which he then went on to describe in some detail, with reference to the color of the strap, et cetera.

Now, the prosecuting attorney, of course, took exactly the same position, and for hours insisted that the rifle discovered on the sixth floor was a German Mauser, adding the nationality. A German Mauser is nothing at all like an Italian carbine. I think almost any rifle expert will indicate that that is so.

I have been informed that almost every Mauser—and I am not able to document this, unfortunately, but I am sure that you have easy access to rifle experts— that almost every German Mauser has stamped upon it the caliber, as does almost every Italian carbine.

Mr. RANKIN. Do you know the difference between the two?

Mr. LANE. Do I know the difference?

Mr. RANKIN. Yes.

Mr. LANE. I know the difference between an Army M–1 and an American carbine—those are the only two weapons I fired—during the war. No, I don't know anything about rifles, other than those two rifles, which I used at one time.

I think it is most interesting to note that when Oswald was arrested we were informed immediately that he had an alias—his last name was Lee in that alias—as well as a great deal of material about his political background and activities on behalf of the Fair Play for Cuba Committee, and his defection to the Soviet Union, et cetera. But the alias was raised immediately.

The following day, on the 23d, when it was announced by the Federal Bureau of Investigation, that Oswald had purchased an Italian carbine, 6.5 millimeters, under the assumed name, A. Hidell, then for the first time the district attorney of Dallas indicated that the rifle in his possession, the alleged murder weapon, had changed both nationality and size, and had become from a German 7.65 Mauser, an Italian 6.5 carbine. And, further he indicated then for the first time that they knew of another alias maintained by Lee Oswald. In addition to the name Lee, which they discovered, they said, by going to the home where he lived—the house where he had lived in Dallas, where he rented a room, a rooming house, they discovered there he had secured the room under the name Lee. Mr. Wade stated that on Oswald's person, in his pocketbook, was an identification card made out to A. Hidell, and I have seen pictures of this reproduced in either Time magazine or Newsweek, or one of the weekly news magazines—I believe it was one or the other—with a picture of Oswald appearing on this card, plainly indicating that Oswald had the alias A. Hidell, to Mr. Wade.

I think it is interesting that the name Lee as an alias was released immediately, although some investigation was required to secure that alias. But the name A. Hidell, was not released as an alias, although that was present and obvious by mere search of Oswald's person when he was arrested.

Mr. RANKIN. Can you give us the time of the release of the information about the alias, A. Hidell?

Mr. LANE. That was on November 23.

Mr. RANKIN. And how about Lee?

Mr. LANE. November 22. The first release of the name A. Hidell came from the district attorney's office after the FBI had indicated that Oswald had purchased an Italian carbine under that name.

If I were permitted to cross-examine Mr. Wade, which evidently you have decided that I shall not be permitted to do, and Officer Weitzman, I would seek to find out how about the most important single element in probably this case or any other murder case, physical evidence, the murder weapon, in a case which I am sure is Mr. Wade's most important case—how he could be so completely in error about this.

Mr. Wade is a very distinguished prosecuting attorney, has been one for some 13 or 14 years, and I believe was an agent of the Federal Bureau of Investigation prior to that time.

I would like to know how he could have been so wrong about something so vital.

Now, assuming that the rifle found on the sixth floor was an Italian rifle, Italian carbine, one must wonder how it was possible for any number of things to happen for it to be fired there three times and strike the President in front of the throat, although he was past that building, and for the noise, according to the witnesses of the shooting, to have come from a different place entirely.

But in addition to that, one must wonder if that rifle is capable of the performance which the prosecuting authorities allege that it gave on that day. An Olympic rifle champion, Hubert Hammerer, said that he doubts that it could be done.

Mr. RANKIN. Could you give us his address?

Mr. LANE. He is not in the United States. The story appeared in the New York Times. I don't have the exact date.

Representative FORD. What nationality is he?

Mr. LANE. I don't know.

Representative FORD. Do you know when he was Olympic champion?

Mr. LANE. No, I don't know that. I do know it probably was some time after the Italian carbine was manufactured, since it is an extremely old weapon, manufactured back in 1938, as I recall. There seems to be an agreement that the period of time was between 5 and 6 seconds from the first shot to the last shot.

There is a serious question in the minds, I think, of persons who have fired that pistol—that rifle—first of all, as to its ability to be fired that quickly accurately with a telescopic sight, and secondly, in reference to the ammunition which is available. Various persons have tested various lots of ammunition. Someone from the National Rifle Association told me that he tested more than 30 rounds, a little over 30 rounds of the Italian 6.5——

Mr. RANKIN. When you refer to these people, will you tell us the names of any of them that you can? It might be of help to us.

Mr. LANE. I should remember this gentleman, because I just spoke with him. That is another name I am going to have to supply for you.

Mr. RANKIN. Thank you.

Mr. LANE. He is a member of the board of directors of the National Rifle Association. He purchased for one of the television networks some 30 rounds, a little over 30 rounds, and told me that 20 of them did not fire at all, and 6 of them were guilty of hanged fire, which is a phrase I don't know anything about, but he tells me that means it did not fire fully, and, therefore, could not be accurate. Therefore, a very small percentage of the ammunition was of any value.

Mr. Ed Wallace talked about making a similar test in the New York World Telegram and Sun, in a feature article, and I think he said that he went with an expert, and they got 20 rounds of this ammunition, and of those 17 did not fire—only 3 fired. It was very old ammunition.

Representative FORD. Who is Ed Wallace, and who is the individual that Ed Wallace referred to? Do you have that information?

Mr. LANE. I believe Mr. Wallace indicated that he was present when the test was made. But it was an article appearing in the New York World Telegram and Sun within a week after the assassination—from the 23d to the 30th of November. And I can secure and mail to you a copy of that article, if you prefer.

While there may be some question as to whether or not a rifle expert could secure such performance from a rifle, or whether or not one could secure enough good ammunition to get such performance, I think there is general agreement that only in the hands of a rifle expert could one attempt to come close to that kind of shooting that it is alleged Oswald did on November 22.

The Times reported on November 23, "As Marines go, Lee Harvey Oswald was not highly regarded as a rifleman." And you have in your files, of course, the scorecard indicating Oswald's marksmanship or lack of marksmanship while in the Marine Corps.

In addition to that, you have the documents given to you by Marguerite Oswald, Lee Oswald's mother, which contained a scorecard maintained by Oswald while in the Marine Corps, showing his score in fast and slow shooting at various different yardages, in reference to both an M-1, as I recall, and an American carbine. Now, of course, it has been alleged on occasion that Mr. Oswald practiced with his rifle, on occasion, on weekends, at rifle ranges.

Mrs. Paine, with whom Lee Oswald's wife lived for the 2 month period preceding the assassination, and where Lee Oswald himself spent weekends for that 2 months period preceding the assassination, told me that Oswald could not have ever gone to a rifle range on a weekend, since she can account for his whereabouts during that entire 2 month period just preceding the assassination.

Mr. RANKIN. Can you give us the day of that conversation with Mrs. Paine?

Mr. LANE. I have had about five conversations with her. The first one would be, oh, I believe, New Year's Day. I think that is the first time—this year—I believe that is the first time that she made the statement to me. She said she could account for Oswald's whereabouts during that 2 month period on weekends, from Friday late afternoon, when he left work in Dallas and arrived there in Irving, until early Monday morning.

She said the exception is during that time—she didn't watch him every moment, of course—there might be exceptions when she went shopping for half an hour, and he was left home to take care of the children, her two children, his children. But that unless he ran out quickly into the back yard with the rifle and shot and then quickly put the rifle away while caring for three children or four children, that it would be impossible for him to practice with the rifle on weekends.

Since it has been alleged that the rifle was in the garage during the entire period of time, of course—that was in Irving, Tex., and he was in Dallas, Tex.—it would have been impossible for him to practice during the week while he was in Dallas, with that particular rifle.

Of course one must zero in a rifle in order to be even fairly accurate with it. One must practice with the specific weapon which one is going to use, in order to have any accuracy, in any event.

Now, I spoke with Dial M. Ryder, who is a gunsmith in Irving, Tex., at the Irving Sport Shop, and he told me that he mounted a telescopic sight on a rifle for a man named Oswald during October 1963.

Now, unfortunately, he does not recall—that is around the deer season, he informed me, and a lot of people are getting rifles fixed or repaired or sights mounted on them during that time in the Dallas-Irving area. And he does not recall, therefore, what this gentleman named Oswald looks like.

But he does know that a rifle was brought to him by someone whose name now appears in this record as Oswald, and that he drilled three holes in the rifle for a mount, telescopic mount. He said he had only seen three rifles which required three holes for telescopic mount—a 303 British Enfield, a 303 American Springfield army surplus rifle, or an Eddystone, which is also an American rifle. He said, therefore, he did not attach a telescopic sight to the Italian carbine, because he would have only drilled two holes.

His employer, I think his name is Greener, he told me, checked with all the Oswalds they could find in the Irving area after this matter came to their attention, and could not find anyone in that area—and they called some people in Dallas also named Oswald—could not find anyone named Oswald who brought the rifle in to him.

I talked to Milton Klein, who is the owner of Klein's sporting goods store in Chicago—Klein's Sporting Goods is the name of the establishment, in Chicago.

Mr. RANKIN. When was this?

Mr. LANE. I spoke with him within the last 2 or 3 days. And he told me that—he runs the mail-order house which sent the carbine, Italian carbine, to Dallas, not to Oswald, but to A. Hidell, and that he sent that out with the holes already bored in the Italian carbine, and equipped with a telescopic sight which was already attached to the rifle.

48

Aguto Marcelli, who is a correspondent for an Italian publication which appears physically very much to be like Life magazine, called Leuropeo, stated to me that he had spoken with Mr. Klein, and Mr. Klein told him that the FBI—"The FBI warned me to keep my trap shut."

Mr. RANKIN. When was this?

Mr. LANE. He told me this about 2 weeks ago. When I spoke with Mr. Klein, about 3 days ago, 2 or 3 days ago, he indicated that he did not want to discuss any aspect of this matter with me. And I asked him if that was because he was told not to talk with anyone about this case, and he said yes.

And I said, "Who told you that?"

He said, "The FBI agents told me, ordered me not to discuss this case."

I pointed out to him that if he did not wish to discuss the case with me, I would not force him to. There was no way that he would be compelled to answer any of the questions that I asked him. But, however, in our democratic society, the FBI cannot order anyone not to discuss a case, and that such an order to him was not a valid order, if he wanted to discuss the case with me—he could.

So he did. And he told me what I informed you—that the FBI told him not to discuss the case, and that he mailed this rifle with the holes already bored and with the telescopic sight already mounted to someone named A. Hidell.

He also said that "No ammunition was purchased from me by Hidell at that time or since."

Senator COOPER. Mr. Chairman, may I ask a question?

The CHAIRMAN. Yes, sir.

Senator COOPER. Did he name any person with the FBI who told him not to discuss the case?

Mr. LANE. No; he did not.

Senator COOPER. Can you identify—did he identify him in any way?

Mr. LANE. He did not identify him. Earlier, perhaps before you arrived, Senator, I made reference to a statement made by Mrs. Hill, who was told by the Secret Service—I think perhaps you were here—that only three shots were fired. And I asked her specifically if she could identify that Secret Service agent, and she told me that she could not, there was such tremendous confusion at that time, there were so many agents of the FBI and Secret Service that she spoke to, that she did not think she could. But possibly if she saw him, she might be able to recognize him.

I didn't go any further into that question, however, with Mr. Klein. He seemed very reluctant to discuss that entire area—to discuss anything, but particularly that area.

I read in the Dallas Times Herald, on November 25, 1963, the statement made by Mr. Wade, when asked what they had tying Oswald to the "crime of the century" and his response was, according to the Dallas Times Herald, "If I had to single out any one thing, it would be the fingerprints on the rifle, and the book cartons which he used to prop the weapon on."

On the same day the World Telegram and Sun reported "Federal authorities have concluded that no readable print was found on the murder weapon when it was flown to Washington for laboratory studies."

There were certain leaks that a fingerprint or a palm print was discovered on the bolt of the rifle. If that is so, it would be remarkable if it were a print belonging to anyone other than Captain Fritz of the Homicide Squad in Dallas, because according to the affidavit signed by Officer Weitzman, who discovered the weapon, and I am quoting now from the affidavit on file—at that time on file with the district attorney's office, "The time the rifle was found was 1:22 p.m. Captain Fritz took charge of the rifle, and ejected one live round from the Chamber. I then went back to the office after this."

Now, you know if you have worked with that rifle that the—on most Italian carbines that bolt is not worked too easily. One really has to grab a hold of it and pull back. It would be unusual if a fingerprint belonging to someone other than the person who did that survived.

The first statement made by Mr. Wade in reference to the taxi driver who he alleged—he, Wade, alleged took Oswald generally from this scene, indicated that the driver's name was Daryl Click.

Now, that statement was not made in the first hours of the arrest. That statement was not made until after Chief Curry had announced to the press in Dallas, on that day, November 24th that the case was closed, there would be no further investigation—Oswald was the assassin, he had acted alone, he was then dead. And as a result of the change in policy, to reopen the case and have Mr. Wade assume a position in front of the radio and television microphones and cameras of the Nation, on that evening November 24, Mr. Wade then presented what he said was the evidence "for you piece by piece." And part of the evidence which he had secured was the proof that a taxi driver named Daryl Click drove Oswald roughly from the scene to his home, to Oswald's home.

When I was in Dallas—I suppose this was on January 2d, my first trip there in reference to this matter—I spoke with a Mr. Roseboro of the Teamsters Union—they have organized the taxi drivers in Dallas—and asked him if he knew—if he could give me any information about a Daryl Click. He said he did not have the name in his files, but Texas being a right-to-work law State, it is possible, he said, that Mr. Click was a driver but not a member of that union. He referred me to the personnel department of the City Transportation Co., which he told me was the one company monopoly running all the taxis in Dallas.

I spoke with the City Transportation Co. personnel office, Mr. Pott, as I recalled, who checked the records, and indicated to me that there was no Daryl Click who drove a taxi in Dallas.

Some time after Mr. Wade stated that Daryl Click was the taxi driver, he then stated that a person by the name of William Whaley was the taxi driver who took Oswald from the scene after he left the bus to his home.

It is therefore alleged by the prosecution that Oswald, after firing upon the Presidential limousine, walked the entire floor from the front of the Book Depository Building to the rear of the warehouse, almost to the extreme rear, where he hid the rifle, where it was found, and then took the stairs at the rear of the Book Depository Building and walked down four flights, until he arrived at the second floor, and then he walked to the Coca-Cola machine, which was at the front of the building, meaning he crossed the entire warehouse floor again, and he purchased a Coca-Cola, and was sipping it when a police officer arrived with a gun drawn, questioned him briefly. Mr. Truly explained to the officer that Oswald worked there. And eventually Oswald left the building, boarded a bus, then walked, after leaving the bus—walked two blocks and entered Mr. Whaley's taxi, at exactly 12:30, according to Mr. Whaley. The shots that killed the President were fired at 12:31.

Now, there is on file in the district attorney's office—I assume you have the original or copies of it—a report of a paraffin test taken of Oswald, of both his hands and his face. The test proved, according to Mr. Curry, and the statement that he made on Saturday, November 23, to the press that Oswald had fired the murder weapon. However, a reading of the test indicates that one could come to a very different conclusion.

The test in reference to the face proved negative, indicating that Oswald had not fired a rifle on November 22, 1963—although the test on the hands showed positive—indicating, according to the person who did the analysis, the kinds of patterns consistent with one having fired a revolver. That was the statement on the test taken and conducted by a Louis L. Anderson, on November 23, 1963, by the Dallas City County Crime Investigation Laboratory.

Now, it has, of course, been alleged that after Oswald shot the President and took a bus and a taxi, and went home and got a jacket, he then shot and killed Officer Tippit. The affidavit in the district attorney's office indicates that a person saw a stopped police car, walked up to the police car, leaned on it with his arms on the window, or what would be a windowsill or window ledge of the automobile, and then stepped back a step or two, the officer came out, and this person shot Officer Tippit to death.

The affidavit is peculiarly sparse in reference to the description of the assailant, the man who killed Tippit, by an eyewitness who said she was just 50 feet away.

Her description of this person is found in two different portions of the affidavit—he was young, white, male, and that is the entire description present in the affidavit at that time.

I spoke with the deponent, the eyewitness, Helen Louise Markham, and Mrs. Markham told me—Miss or Mrs., I didn't ask her if she was married—told me that she was a hundred feet away from the police car, not the 50 feet which appears in the affidavit. She gave to me a more detailed description of the man who she said shot Officer Tippit. She said he was short, a little on the heavy side, and his hair was somewhat bushy. I think it is fair to state that an accurate description of Oswald would be average height, quite slender, with thin and receding hair.

Helen Markham said to me that she was taken to the police station on that same day, that she was very upset, she of course had never seen anyone killed in front of her eyes before, and that in the police station she identified Oswald as the person who had shot Officer Tippit in the lineup, including three other persons. She said no one pointed Oswald out to her—she was just shown four people, and she picked Oswald.

She said—when I asked her how she could identify him—she indicated she was able to identify him because of his clothing, a gray jacket and dark trousers. And this was the basis for her identification—although Oswald physically does not meet the description which she indicated.

Representative FORD. When did you have this conversation with the deponent?

Mr. LANE. Within the last 5 days.

Representative FORD. Some time in late February 1964?

Mr. LANE. Or perhaps even early March, yes, sir.

Now, I inquired—I told her that I was coming here today, and that I was completing my investigation as Oswald's lawyer, and asked her if she would discuss the matter with me, and she said she would.

I asked her if anyone had asked her not to discuss this matter with me. At first she seemed reluctant, and she said she was reluctant because I called her at her place of employment, the Eat Well Cafe in Dallas. I tried her at home many times before then, but her phone was always busy. I believe it is a phone which is not her personal one, but is a common phone shared by others in the building where she resides.

I apologized for calling her at her place of employment. And she seemed reluctant to talk to me. I asked if anyone had asked her not to talk about this case with anyone. She said yes, she had been told by the FBI, by Secret Service agents, and by Dallas police, all three groups, not to discuss anything in relation to this case, and that by and large she had not.

I told her that somewhere it occurred to me that I had seen an article in a newspaper in which she described the assailant of Oswald as short, stocky, and with bushy hair—I'm sorry, the assailant of Tippit—as being short, stocky, with bushy hair. And she said she did talk to a reporter, she thinks, for one of the Dallas newspapers, the Dallas Times-Herald or the Dallas Morning News—but that is the only time she talked to anybody.

I would like to call to the Commission's attention the entire brief narrative of the entire case, as presented by the district attorney's office at this point, or at least on the 24th, because it seems to me to be so full of incredible happenings, that it would be very difficult to submit such a story to a jury by a prosecution generally.

If everything that the prosecution in this case says is true, one must conclude that Oswald behaved in a very, very unusual manner from the beginning to the end.

He decided on Thursday, November 21, that he was going to assassinate the President, and so he decided to go back to Irving, Tex., to secure a rifle there, in order to carry out that purpose. He had on his person some $13 when arrested, and almost $150 in cash in the top drawer of his dresser—so we can assume that on Thursday, the 21st, he had roughly that amount of money present.

One can purchase a rifle for less than $13 in many stores in Dallas. There is no question about that. By using a small portion of that $150, he could have purchased a rifle absolutely superior to the Italian carbine at home in Irving in many respects. And there are gun magazines which have had editorials dwelling on this question, saying that if Oswald did it with this weapon, and they do not move into the question of whether or not he did, it was an absolute miracle, because no one who knew anything about rifles would have chosen such a decrepit, worthless rifle, as this Italian carbine, manufactured in 1938, for which there is such pure ammunition. There are a series, I believe, of editorials in gun magazines proving that Oswald, I think, as a matter of pride, from a sportsman's viewpoint—that Oswald was in no way associated with weapons and did not belong in that category, because he could not have chosen such a weapon.

Representative FORD. Could you give us the citations of one of these magazines?

Mr. LANE. Yes. One is called Gun Magazine. I do not recall the names. But that is one of them. I am sure there was such an editorial in that one. I will get the other one and mail those to you also.

But I think there would have to be a more compelling reason for Oswald not to go home and get that particular inferior rifle if he decided on Thursday to kill the President. That was the only rifle in the whole world probably that could be traced to him. One can purchase a rifle in almost any community in this country, certainly in Dallas, without any notoriety attaching to it, without giving one's name or address, or having a serial number attached to a receipt kept by a store indicating who owns that particular rifle.

But here we have Oswald going home to get an inferior rifle, which rifle is the only rifle in the whole world which can be traced to him, which rifle he is going to leave behind as a calling card after the assassination is complete.

And so he goes home to Irving, Tex., and he gets this rifle, and he wraps it up in paper, we are told, and brings it in to the Book Depository Building.

Now, the rifle can be broken down, I believe, from examining other Italian carbines. But it would be not much shorter if it was broken down—perhaps 6 or 7 inches shorter. Evidently, though, he did not do that.

So he took this rifle into the book depository building, which I suggest, gentlemen, is a most remarkable thing. This was going to be the greatest series of precautions in the history of the United States to protect an American President. As we know now, and suspected then, with very good reason, because of the nature of what had gone before, with reference to public officials in Dallas—and here we have a man who has defected to the Soviet Union, who has married a Russian national, active on behalf of the Fair Play for Cuba Committee, we see a discharge less than honorable from the U.S. Marine Corps, who was working in the building exactly on the Presidential route. Not only is it on the Presidential route, but it is the building where the automobile is going to have to clearly slow down because of the sharp turn, sharp left turn, made right in front of the building.

And despite all of these precautions—and I have been informed that there were serious precautions taken in Dallas on that day by the Dallas police and by others, and that persons who did no more publicly, who did no more ever politically than to publicly speak in favor of school integration, were followed that day as potential assassins in Dallas.

Nevertheless, Oswald, with that background, is permitted to walk into the Book Depository Building, directly on the Presidential route, carrying with him in his hand a full rifle.

Mr. RANKIN. Can you tell us the information on which you base this, about anyone who merely spoke about school integration?

Mr. LANE. Yes. A reporter for the Dallas Morning News told me that, told me he was absolutely certain that was so. But before revealing his name, I am going to have to call him and indicate I am going to do that. I will be happy to do that. I am glad you are interested in that matter, because I think it is a most important one.

I suggest that the Federal Bureau of Investigation knew that Oswald worked at the Texas Book Depository Building, which was on the Presidential route. An FBI agent by the name of Hosty visited the home of the Paines in Irving, Tex., sometime during September and October. He visited that home on more than one occasion. Each of the at least two times that he was there, possibly three but I am not certain—but I was told he was there two times—I know I was told by Mrs. Paine in the presence of her husband, Michael Paine, that Agent Hosty was there at least on two occasions—each time he was there he asked where Oswald was. Mrs. Paine explained to Agent Hosty, she told me, that Oswald lived there only on weekends, and that during the week Agent Hosty could find him at his room in Dallas, where he stayed during the week, or during the daytime could find him at the Texas Book Depository Building, where he was an employee. Nevertheless—and that Oswald would not be found in Irving, Tex. at the Paine's home during the week. Nevertheless, Agent Hosty returned again at least one more time to the Paine home in Irving, during the week, during the day, I believe—certainly during the week—and again asked about Oswald, and again Mrs. Paine told him that he worked at the Book Depository Building, he would not be there, she said, "As we told you last time he won't be here during the week. During the daytime during the week you can find him at his job at the Book Depository Building, and during the nighttime during the week you can find him at his rooming house in Dallas."

Mr. RANKIN. Did she tell you whether she told him where the rooming house was?

Mr. LANE. I do not believe I asked her that question, and I don't believe she mentioned that.

Well, to go back to the prosecution narrative, or narrative according to the facts presented by the prosecution, Oswald was on the sixth floor, fired at the Presidential limousine, not as the automobile approached the building, when the automobile came extremely close to the building, so close that possibly even with that weapon one could have shot occupants of the automobile from that window—but it is alleged that Oswald never shot—it is now alleged that Oswald never shot when the automobile was right outside of the building, but fired when the automobile was some 75 yards beyond the building, when the first shot was fired.

Then Oswald walked the entire floor—or ran—the entire floor of the warehouse to the rear of the building, placing the rifle in between some boxes, but visible, so that one can see it when one arrives on the floor; went to the rear stairs, walked down the four flights to the second floor, then to the front of the building again, where he purchased a Coca-Cola—made no effort to leave the building at that time, evidently was going to wait until the building was surrounded by police before leaving.

He stayed at the top of the stairs near the Coke machine long enough so that a police officer could come up and place a pistol near him, and Roy Truly, the director, then intervened indicating that Mr. Oswald was employed at the building at that time, and the officer then went on to do other things in the building, including later on, I believe, to find the rifle, if it was the same officer.

Mr. Truly stated that Oswald was quite calm when the officer approached him on the stairs. He said although he did seem a little concerned about that pistol being stuck at him—but otherwise he seemed quite calm at that time.

Well——

Representative FORD. Where was this statement made, or testimony given?

Mr. LANE. By Truly?

Representative FORD. Yes.

Mr. LANE. This was reported very widely in probably dozens or scores of newspapers. The New York Times carried that, as did many other publications—direct quotations from Truly who was interviewed.

Then the next thing we heard from the prosecution in their opening or closing statement to the television cameras, after Oswald was killed was that—the next we hear of Oswald he was on a bus. Well, if Oswald boarded the bus where the busdriver claims he did, then Oswald walked a distance, in order to secure a bus which is going to take him directly back to the Book Depository Building, which one would think he was trying to flee after assassinating the President.

I would refer you to his story by Hugh Ainsworth in the Dallas Morning News published during the first week after the assassination. Hugh Ainsworth and Larry Grove published on November 28 in the Dallas Morning News—this is headed "Oswald Planned To Ride By Scene"—in which there are statements from the busdriver that—named C. J. McWatters, in which Mr. McWatters indicates that Oswald entered the bus at Elm and Griffin, and further indicates that the bus was going to go seven blocks further west and turn at Houston Street, exactly the scene of the assassination, or at least the scene of the Texas Book

Depository. So Oswald traveled somehow some seven blocks in order to secure a bus which is going to take him back to the place that he left.

Now, although I have talked to Mr. Ainsworth, and he tells me that the story is absolutely correct, and he questioned Mr. McWatters quite thoroughly, and he will so testify, I believe, if he is asked—Mr. Ainsworth will—and the affidavit which Mr. McWatters signed, or which the busdriver signed, he does not state that Oswald walked seven blocks and was going to get on a bus which was going to take him back. Indeed, he states that he picked him up about Elm and Houston Street, at the Book Depository Building. But the busdriver indicates that that story in his affidavit is not true. He indicated that after the affidavit was drawn and signed by him.

Mr. RANKIN. What did you say was not true, Mr. Lane—which part of it?

Mr. LANE. The affidavit. Mr. McWatters indicates that the affidavit in which—let me start that again.

There is an affidavit from the busdriver, which I am sure you have, which shows that according to his statement Oswald came into the bus at Elm and Houston Street. However, the busdriver since that time has indicated that Oswald came into the bus seven blocks from Elm and Houston Street, and had entered a bus which was going to take him to Elm and Houston Street. Elm and Houston Street of course is the location of the Book Depository Building.

Mr. RANKIN. Now, when you say since that time he has indicated that, you mean to you or to someone else?

Mr. LANE. To those two reporters for the Dallas Morning News with whom I discussed—one of them—I discussed this specifically. And he said that every word in that story is absolutely accurate, that he went to see the busdriver, and had a prolonged interview with him, and went over this in great detail with him. I think these two reporters will testify as to what the busdriver told them in their interview with him.

Mr. RANKIN. But they have not published this later story that you are telling about.

Mr. LANE. Yes, they have. That is the date that I gave you. The Dallas Morning News, on Thursday, November 28, under the headline "Oswald Planned To Ride By Scene".

Mr. RANKIN. Do you want to leave that with us?

Mr. LANE. I wonder if copies can be made of everything.

Mr. RANKIN. Yes.

Mr. LANE. Then I will be happy to leave it.

Mr. RANKIN. The story you were just referring to in the Dallas Morning News is Commission Exhibit 343.

(The document referred to was marked Commission Exhibit No. 343 for identification and received in evidence.)

Mr. LANE. That's correct.

Well, now, Oswald allegedly had shot the President and has walked some, talked to an officer, was calm, walked some seven blocks to find a bus which was going to take him back to where he left, and then got off and got—entered into a taxi after he had walked some two blocks from where he left the bus. And this taxi he entered of course a minute before the President was shot, if the taxi driver's log is accurate—after Oswald had done all these things, after allegedly shooting the President and the Governor.

Then the taxi driver drove him directly past his own home, according to the statement and—past Oswald's Dallas rooming house, until he arrived at a scene about a half a mile beyond Oswald's house, where Oswald then left the taxi, and then walked or ran home to secure a jacket—leaving behind, although one would assume he is now giving considering to escaping, the $150 in the dresser drawer, and taking just his jacket with him.

Mr. RANKIN. Which dresser drawer?

Mr. LANE. This is in Dallas.

Mr. RANKIN. Not at the Paine's?

Mr. LANE. Not at the Paine's. I do not know if there was money at the Paine's, but if he had money there, he left that behind the night before, knowing he was going to——

54

Mr. RANKIN. But the $150 you are speaking of was in his rooming house at Dallas.

Mr. LANE. Yes.

Mr. RANKIN. Do you have any affidavit or information in support of that statement about the $150?

Mr. LANE. I do not have an affidavit. I have the statement of a reporter who was told that—he was told this by a police officer who was present when the money was found in the Dallas rooming house. I have his statement. I can again ask for his permission to release that.

Mr. RANKIN. Would you do that, please.

Mr. LANE. Yes, sir.

Senator COOPER. Mr. Chairman—perhaps it has been done, but I think it would be proper in all cases in which he has referred to conversations that he has had with individuals who made statements to him about some aspect of this matter, and whose names he has not identified, that if he could give to the Commission in all of those cases the names of the individuals who gave him this information.

Mr. LANE. Yes, sir.

Senator COOPER. I mean at sometime—don't you think?

Mr. RANKIN. Yes, sir, it would be very helpful.

Mr. LANE. Yes, sir. I think there are only two occasions where I indicated I had to check the source, and one is the name of the rifle association board member whose name I will be happy to give to you, but I just do not recall it— my office has that.

Senator COOPER. I did not remember that you gave the name of this individual who told you that some policeman had told him that he had been present when the $150 was found.

Mr. LANE. Yes; that is one.

Senator COOPER. Did you give that name?

Mr. LANE. No; I did not give that name.

Mr. RANKIN. You said you were going to ask him his permission.

Mr. LANE. Yes; that's correct.

Then Oswald took a taxi, which took him approximately a half mile beyond his own house, his own room in Dallas, and he either walked or ran back to get his jacket—although it was a very warm day in Dallas. That day Mrs. Kennedy said later on that, reviewing the moment before the President was shot—she said she saw this overpass ahead and looked forward to being under it for a moment because there would be some brief shade to protect them from the powerful sun that day.

Well, Oswald ran home to get his jacket. He left the house, saw a police car parked, went up to the police car, according to the affidavit of Mrs. Markham, leaned on the car, and when the officer came out, he shot him to death, and then he went to the movies. And in the movies, and just before he went into the Texas Theatre, he was so extremely agitated that a gentleman on the outside of the theatre—I think his name is John Brewer—I am not certain—you have that affidavit, I am sure—indicated that Oswald was acting very agitated, the cashier made the same statement, and changing from seat to seat. The police were called and he was arrested.

Of course, one would wonder why Oswald, who might have thought that he had made his getaway while in the Texas Theatre unobserved, would become so extremely agitated, when just a moment after he allegedly shot the President and the Governor, with the policeman charging up the stairs, pointing a pistol at him, about to arrest him for these two terrible crimes, he was calm, according to Mr. Truly, but he became agitated only when he thought he had secured his getaway.

I think those of us who saw, as we all did, I guess, Oswald on television in his brief appearance would conclude that he seemed, even while in custody and charged with these two crimes, somewhat calm under the circumstances— calm when charged with the assassination, calm a moment after killing the President, when a policeman pointed a pistol at him, but agitated only in the theatre, and just before going to the theatre when he might have concluded that he was then in the clear.

I would just like to conclude on this note.

I hope the Commission will give consideration to my request, which the Commission has answered, but which again I would like at this time to renew. That is, that I be permitted, at the request of Mrs. Oswald, the mother of the accused defendant, really, before this Commission's hearing, to represent his interests here, to have access to the material which you have access to, and the right to present witnesses.

It is not usual for an attorney representing a party to be given an opportunity to testify, which is quite unusual—but rather to be given the opportunity to present witnesses and to cross-examine them. It has generally been my role in criminal cases. Never before have I testified in behalf of a client.

If it is the Commission's position that this is not a trial in any respect, and therefore Oswald is not entitled to counsel, that is the position with which I would like to respectfully offer a dissent.

The fact that Oswald is not going to have a real trial flows only from his death, and he is not responsible with that having taken place. Every right belonging to an American citizen charged with a crime was taken from him up to and including his life.

I think now that that episode is completed, hopefully never to reappear ever again in our history, or anything close to it—I think it would be proper to permit him to have counsel before the Commission, counsel who can function on his behalf in terms of cross-examining evidence and presenting witnesses. If it is the Commission's position now that he is entitled to counsel, and the Commission will appoint counsel, then I ask the Commission to consider that the Constitutional right to counsel involves the right to counsel of one's choice, or in the event of the death of a party, to counsel of the choice of the surviving members of the family.

If Marina Oswald, the widow, sought to have counsel represent her husband I would think—here—I would think that would cause a conflict and a problem, if the widow and also the mother made the same request. But as I understand it no request has been made by the widow, who has indicated to the press that she believes her husband is guilty, and through her former business agent, Mr. Martin, who I am told was secured for her by the Secret Service as a business agent, she indicated that even a trial which might prove he was innocent, she would still be sure he was guilty, and has indicated since that time no desire to my knowledge to secure counsel for her husband, her late husband, before the Commission.

I think, then, the mother would, in almost any jurisdiction, be the next person to make a decision in this area, and the mother has made a decision, as you know. She has retained me to represent the rights and interests of her son.

I think under those circumstances it would be proper for the Commission to permit me to participate.

This, of course, is not a jury trial. With all due respect to the integrity and background of each of the members of the Commission, I suggest that it is not the function of the trying body to appoint counsel, or the jury to appoint counsel, but in our society it is just the reverse; it is the function of defense counsel to participate in determining who the jury should be.

Many criminal lawyers, very noted counsel, would probably seek to excuse certain—and again no disrespect at all is meant to the background of members of this Commission—but defense counsel generally seeks to excuse as jurors those who are in any way associated with the Government in a criminal case. And here we have the Government appointing the jury, and then the jury picking counsel, who also is Government connected at this time. I in no way wish to raise the question of the integrity of any of the members of the Commission or counsel or anyone else, or their ability. But that truism about equality has some meaning in terms of impartiality—everyone is impartial to some people, and more impartial to other people. And counsel, in order to function, I believe, must be totally independent and totally committed to the responsibility of representing his client.

But above all, he must be secured by someone who has the ability to speak for the deceased, in this case his mother and his wife. And under those circumstances, I renew my request that I be permitted to, at the request of Lee Oswald's mother, who survives him—to function before this Commission as counsel on his behalf.

The CHAIRMAN. Mr. Lane, I must advise you that the Commission, as you already know, has considered your request and has denied it. It does not consider you as the attorney for Lee Oswald. Now, this is not for any discussion. We are not going to argue it. You have had your say, and I will just answer.

Lee Oswald left a widow. She is his legal representative. She is represented by counsel. This Commission is cooperating with her in any way she may request. If anyone else wants to present any evidence to this Commission, they may do so. But it is the view and the wish—the will of the Commission— that no one else shall be entitled to participate in the work and the deliberations of the Commission.

We asked you to come here today because we understood that you did have evidence. We are happy to receive it. We want every bit of evidence that you have. You may present anything that you wish to us. But you are not to be a participant in the work of the Commission. I assume you have some questions you would like to ask Mr. Lane, Mr. Rankin?

Mr. RANKIN. Yes, sir. Do you have any affidavits that you would like to submit to the Commission? I understood at one time you had some affidavits.

Mr. LANE. Well, I do have some affidavits. They are not originals—they are photostatic copies of affidavits taken by the Dallas police and on file in the Dallas district attorney's office. Now—including the paraffin test which I made reference to.

Now, if the Commission does not have copies of those, I would like to be so informed and I will see what I can do. I assume the Commission has copies of all those documents.

Mr. RANKIN. Yes. Do you have anything beyond that that you care to submit?

Mr. LANE. I have the various statements which I have made reference to from Mrs. Hill and Mrs. Markham, Mr. Klein, Mr. Ryder. But I have given you the essence of those statements. If you are interested in pursuing that, I think it might be best to call them.

Mr. RANKIN. I am interested if there was anything beyond what you have given us, Mr. Lane. And if you say you have given us the substance, then I take it that is complete as far as it could be of assistance to us, except our going directly to the witness. Is that what you have in mind?

Mr. LANE. Yes.

Mr. RANKIN. Now, do you have any witnesses that you would like to present for the Commission?

Mr. LANE. Well, I would like—I do not know that I would be able to do that, frankly.

Mr. RANKIN. Well, would you have any that you suggest that we should interview, bring before the Commission, that you have not presented up to this time in your testimony?

Mr. LANE. No; there is no one who I know of other than those names I have given, and two other persons whose permission I am going to have to secure in reference to other matters, and hopefully they will be willing to not only allow their names to be used, but to come forward and testify, if you wish to hear them.

Mr. RANKIN Now, is there any documentary evidence beyond which you have submitted that you would like to submit to the Commission?

Mr. LANE. Not beyond what I have submitted or made reference to.

Mr. RANKIN. In regard to the paraffin that you have referred to, do you have any particular materials or anything you want to refer the Commission to?

Mr. LANE. To that particular test taken by Mr. Anderson on November 23d?

Mr. RANKIN. Anything beyond that?

Mr. LANE. No; not at this time.

Mr. RANKIN. Now, I understand at one time you referred to some meeting in the Carousel Club a week or so before the assassination. Do you have any material on that or any information?

57

Mr. LANE. Yes.

Mr. RANKIN. Is there anything you would care to present to the Commission?

Mr. LANE. Yes. I have been informed—and this is the source I will have to check with again in order to secure his testimony——

Mr. RANKIN. You will advise us if you are permitted to.

Mr. LANE. Yes. But I can tell you the substance—that a meeting took place on November 14, 1963, in the Carousel Club between Officer Tippit and Bernard Weissman, Mr. Weissman being the gentleman who placed a full-page advertisement in the Dallas Morning News which was printed on November 22, asking a series of questions of President Kennedy. It was addressed "Welcome to Dallas, President Kennedy. Why have you traded the Monroe Doctrine for spirit of Moscow. Why has Gus Hall and the Communist Party endorsed your 1964 election" and such matter. I think these two give a rather clear indication of the kind of advertisement that it was. And I have been informed that Mr. Weissman and Officer Tippit and a third person were present there. I have been given the name of the third person. But for matters which I will make plain to the Commission, I will be pleased to give you the name of the third person as given to me, but not in the presence of the press. I would rather do that in executive session—that one piece of testimony.

The CHAIRMAN. That is satisfactory to do that, if you wish.

Mr. LANE. Thank you, sir.

Mr. RANKIN. Is there anything else about that incident that you know and want to tell the Commission at this time?

Mr. LANE. No.

The CHAIRMAN. That is the entire story, is it?

Mr. LANE. That they were there for more than 2 hours conferring—these three persons.

The CHAIRMAN. Your information does not—is not to the effect as to what they were conferring on.

Mr. LANE. No; they did not hear that.

Mr. RANKIN. I am not suggesting, Mr. Lane, that you have been selective about what you have told the Commission and what you have not told, but I do wish to make the inquiry as to whether there is any information you might have that the Commission should be informed of as to other people that you might have interviewed in regard to this matter.

Mr. LANE. I have given the Commission at this time everything that I know.

Mr. RANKIN. Is there anything about the palm prints that you can tell us in addition to what you have given us?

Mr. LANE. Not in addition to what I have said.

Mr. RANKIN. Well, I will ask you generally—is there anything in addition to what you have said that you would like to tell the Commission at this time that has any bearing upon this investigation?

Mr. LANE. All I can say in reference to that, Mr. Rankin, is that I am practically engaged in this project by myself, which means I am extremely limited. This is not my profession—investigator. I am an attorney. And there are many leads which I have followed, which have led me nowhere at all, obviously. Before finding Mrs. Markham or before finding Mrs. Hill, there were many other persons I talked to who were not even present, who I have heard were present. But there are still large numbers, probably at this point hundreds of leads which I have heard of, and which I have not yet been able to trace or to check through. I do not think it would be constructive just to tell you all of the things I have heard, because most of them are patently untrue, and they just require a great deal of work. But I will continue to do that, and should I come across any material which might in any way interest you, I will certainly either write to you for the purpose of presenting it to you through the mail in affidavit form, if you prefer, or indicate that I will be available to come and testify again if you prefer that.

The CHAIRMAN. Mr. Lane, your client, Mrs. Marguerite Oswald, when she was testifying before us, told us that she had sold some pictures to the press and she wanted the originals of all the pictures that she presented to us, because she said they were of great financial value to her. Do you know what sales she has made concerning pictures such as you have shown us?

Mr. LANE. In terms of the picture with the rifle, you mean, for example?

The CHAIRMAN. Well, we might start with that.

Mr. LANE. She has never seen such a picture, she has informed me, of Lee Harvey Oswald with the rifle—except after they had been published. She never had any knowledge of such pictures, and had never seen them.

I do not really represent Marguerite Oswald. She has retained me to represent the interests of her son. And so in her business dealings in terms of her sale of pictures and articles, I have not represented her. I believe she has a literary agent or perhaps even another lawyer—I don't know. But she has retained me to represent her son's interests, not to represent her at all.

The CHAIRMAN. I see.

Mr. LANE. Of course, we have conferred. But I do not have that information.

The CHAIRMAN. Yes.

Mr. RANKIN. Mr. Lane, I have a further question. Have you ever been prevented by any law enforcement officer from interviewing anyone concerning this matter when you wished to?

Mr. LANE. Well, I would say that I have been prevented by the statements made by the law enforcement persons or agents to the individual, that he should not talk to anyone about this case, that it is a secret matter. As I have indicated, Mr. Klein——

Mr. RANKIN. You have described those cases, have you?

Mr. LANE. I have also spoken to a reporter who is employed by a Dallas newspaper, who informed me that he sought to question more than 150 in the area, and that many of those persons informed him that they were ordered by the FBI not to talk to anyone about this case, and that almost none of the witnesses would talk with him about the case, and that some of them, when he asked the reason that they were not talking to him, it was "Was this because you have been told by the FBI?"—and he indicated they were not even allowed to answer that question. But many of them told him that the FBI or the Secret Service ordered them not to talk. In no other respect have I been interfered with to my knowledge.

Mr. RANKIN. Do you have the name of that reporter—can you reveal that to us?

Mr. LANE. I cannot reveal it at this time, but I am hopeful you will permit me to. He is one of the reporters I referred to earlier.

Mr. RANKIN. Thank you.

The CHAIRMAN. Senator, do you have any questions?

Senator COOPER. No; I have no questions.

The CHAIRMAN. Mr. Rhyne.

Mr. RHYNE. Mr. Chief Justice—I wanted to ask Mr. Lane, on his inquiry about what happened to Oswald during the 48 hours he was under detention—you suggested that the Commission make an inquiry into whether his civil rights were denied. Do you have any information on that subject?

Mr. LANE. Yes. I saw what happened—I read in the newspapers and heard on the radio.

Mr. RHYNE. It looked to me that most of the material presented here today was really in the newspapers. You are merely repeating what someone else has said.

Mr. LANE. I don't think that is an accurate characterization of my testimony at all, sir. For example, I told you before of conversations that I have had—I know you listened intently—I told you of conversations that I had with Mr. Klein. I told you of conversations I had with Miss Hill, who is probably the closest eyewitness to the assassination, with Miss Woodward, who is perhaps the second or third closest witness to the assassination, with Dial Ryder, with at least two or three other persons.

Mr. RHYNE. But on this one point, with respect to denial of any civil rights or protection of civil rights during this 48-hour period, you say that is all in the newspaper stories?

Mr. LANE. No. What I meant by that response was that the basic denial that I was discussing was the development of the case publicly against him, so that it would be impossible in securing a jury panel to secure 12 jurors probably anywhere in this country who had not reached a conclusion, first of all. And secondly, obviously the death of the accused, which I know is a matter for the Commission's inquiry already.

Mr. RHYNE. I notice that you said your investigation was incomplete. So I just wanted to be sure that I understood what you meant with respect to this 48-hour detention period.

Mr. LANE. No; I have no knowledge over and above that that I could give you in that area.

The CHAIRMAN. Mr. Murray, do you have any questions you would like to ask?

Mr. MURRAY. No: I have none, Mr. Chief Justice, at this time.

The CHAIRMAN. Well, Mr. Lane, if any evidence should come to your attention in the future, would you be willing to convey the information to the Commission?

Mr. LANE. Yes; I certainly would, sir.

The CHAIRMAN. We will appreciate it if you would. Thank you for your attendance.

We will adjourn at this time.

(Whereupon, at 5:35 p.m., the President's Commission adjourned, and reconvened in executive session.)

TESTIMONY OF MR. LANE RESUMED IN EXECUTIVE SESSION

The CHAIRMAN. The session will be in order.

Mr. RANKIN. Will you proceed, Mr. Lane, in executive session now, to describe the names?

Mr. LANE. The third name that I was informed—the person that I was informed was there, the third person, is named Jack Ruby. It was my feeling, of course, while his case was pending it would not be proper to comment on that in the presence of the press.

Mr. RANKIN. You mean the third person in the group apparently conferring?

Mr. LANE. Yes. Tippit, Weissman, and Ruby.

The CHAIRMAN. Have you made any public statement of this kind before on this subject—about this meeting?

Mr. LANE. Not about Ruby—about a meeting between Weissman and Tippit, yes.

The CHAIRMAN. But you never named Ruby publicly?

Mr. LANE. No; I have not. I shall not.

The CHAIRMAN. I see. Do you know any way by which we might corroborate that meeting—the fact that it was held?

Mr. LANE. I am going this evening to see, or tomorrow—I will try this evening first—to see if I can secure permission by my informant to reveal his name, and I hope he will be willing to come forward and testify as to what took place.

The CHAIRMAN. The Commission would like to know it, if you can do that.

Mr. LANE. Yes; I shall inform you as soon as I discover that. I would like very much for the Commission to have that information. Can I indicate to my informant that the matter can be so raised so that his name will not be known to anyone other than the Commission?

The CHAIRMAN. Yes, sir; you may.

Mr. LANE. That will be extremely helpful.

The CHAIRMAN. If you can think of any way that can be corroborated, it would be most helpful to us.

Mr. LANE. I understand.

The CHAIRMAN. Congressman, you just got in as we are about to adjourn. Mr. Lane was telling us of one piece of information that he had concerning a meeting that was held at the Carousel Nightclub, about a week, did you say——

Mr. LANE. Yes.

The CHAIRMAN. About a week before the assassination, at which the man who financed this full-page article in the paper, Dallas paper, this morning, concerning President Kennedy, and Officer Tippit, and he told us in private here—he didn't want to mention it before the press—Jack Ruby. And he tells us that he will try to find out from his informant more about that, and if he possibly can deliver the information to us.

Senator COOPER. May I ask one question?

I assume from what you have said you wouldn't be able to answer it, but was there any reason ascribed for the presence of Tippit?

Mr. LANE. My informant does not know the reason.

Senator COOPER. Or Ruby, with Weissman?

Mr. LANE. My informant does not know that information.

Representative FORD. May I ask a question, Mr. Chief Justice? When did this information come to your attention, Mr. Lane?

Mr. LANE. Some weeks ago.

Representative FORD. Do you consider the informant a reliable, responsible person?

Mr. LANE. Yes. I cannot vouch, of course, for the information personally, but I believe the informant is a reliable and a responsible person.

Representative FORD. Would your informant be willing, as far as you know—be willing to testify and give the Commission this information directly?

Mr. LANE. I am going to try to arrange that this evening. The Chief Justice has indicated that his name would not be known if he did that, and that I did not know that I could make that statement to him before now. I hope that will be decisive.

The CHAIRMAN. Is there anything further, gentlemen?

If not——

Representative FORD. May I ask, Mr. Chairman, are we going to have a schedule laid out, are we going to have a meeting of the Commission where maybe we will know what the schedule is in the next week or 10 days or 2 weeks?

Mr. RANKIN. We have a draft now.

The CHAIRMAN. We have a draft for you to see.

Mr. LANE. Perhaps I should withdraw at this time.

The CHAIRMAN. All right.

Mr. Lane, thank you very much, sir.

(Whereupon, at 5:45 p.m., the President's Commission recessed.)

Monday, March 9, 1964

TESTIMONY OF ROY H. KELLERMAN, WILLIAM ROBERT GREER, CLINTON J. HILL, AND RUFUS WAYNE YOUNGBLOOD

The President's Commission met at 9:10 a.m. on March 9, 1964, at 200 Maryland Avenue NE., Washington, D.C.

Present were Chief Justice Earl Warren, Chairman; Senator John Sherman Cooper, Representative Hale Boggs, and Representative Gerald R. Ford, members.

Also present were Norman Redlich, assistant counsel; Arlen Specter, assistant counsel; Walter Craig and Charles Murray, observers; and Fred Smith, Treasury Department.

TESTIMONY OF ROY H. KELLERMAN, SPECIAL AGENT, SECRET SERVICE

The CHAIRMAN. Gentlemen, the Commission will be in order. Will you be seated, please?

Would you state the names of the witnesses who are to be heard today, Mr. Specter?

Mr. SPECTER. Yes. Your Honor; the witnesses are to be Roy Kellerman of the Secret Service. William R. Greer of the Secret Service, Clinton Hill, also of the Secret Service, and Rufus Youngblood, representative of the Secret Service.

The CHAIRMAN. Very well, gentlemen; you know the purpose of the meeting, and we will call first, Mr. who?

Mr. SPECTER. Mr. Kellerman is our first witness.

The CHAIRMAN. Mr. Kellerman. Gentlemen, I want to announce that today it will be necessary for me to spend practically all of the morning with the Supreme Court, and in my absence Congressman Ford will conduct the hearing today because he can be here practically all the time. I will be here in and out throughout the day, however.

Congressman Ford, will you take over please?

Representative FORD. Thank you very much, Mr. Chairman.

The CHAIRMAN. Will you proceed? I believe the first thing is to swear the witness.

Mr. SPECTER. Very good, sir.

Representative FORD. Do you promise to tell the truth, the whole truth, so help you God?

Mr. KELLERMAN. I do, sir.

Mr. SPECTER. Will you state your full name for the record, please?

Mr. KELLERMAN. My name is Roy H. Kellerman.

Mr. SPECTER. By whom are you employed, Mr. Kellerman?

Mr. KELLERMAN. I am employed as a special agent for the Secret Service.

Mr. SPECTER. How old are you?

Mr. KELLERMAN. I am 48 years old.

Mr. SPECTER. Married?

Mr. KELLERMAN. Pardon?

Mr. SPECTER. Are you married?

Mr. KELLERMAN. Yes, sir; I am married and have two daughters; their ages are 20 and 17.

Mr. SPECTER. Where do you reside?

Mr. KELLERMAN. Bethesda, Md.

Mr. SPECTER. What is your current duty station with the Secret Service?

Mr. KELLERMAN. My current duty station is assistant special agent in charge of the White House detail.

Mr. SPECTER. How long have you been with the Secret Service?

Mr. KELLERMAN. This is my 23d year.

Mr. SPECTER. Will you sketch in a general outline what your duties have been with the Secret Service since the time you started with them, please?

Mr. KELLERMAN. I was appointed an agent with the Secret Service in Detroit, Mich., the 19th of December 1941. I was transferred to Washington, D.C., the field office, on February 9, 1942. Prior to that I had a 30-day assignment in the office of Cincinnati, Ohio, temporarily. I worked in the Washington field office from the 9th of February 1942 until the middle of March 1942, whereby I was temporarily transferred to the White House detail. This transfer became permanent, effective, I believe it was, the 17th of April or the latter part of April in 1942, still as a special agent.

At the White House detail we work on shifts around the clock, protecting the President and his family. I was a member of one of those three shifts. Presently, these shifts change on a two-weekly basis, from 8 to 4, 4 to midnight, and midnight to 8. I remained on the White House detail until February 7, 1951, when I was transferred to Indianapolis, Ind. Prior to that time I had received enough seniority whereby I grew up on this shift from the bottom to the top, and was in charge of one of the shifts prior to my departure to Indianapolis. This was fieldwork in Indiana.

On February 1, 1955, I was transferred back to the White House detail. On my return I was comparable to like, let's say, the No. 2 man of a shift. I was not in charge of it.

From 1955, I believe a couple of years later a vacancy occurred, a top man of that shift left and I received his position. That title was assistant to the special agent in charge. You at that time governed each man on your shift. You were in charge of him.

On October 1 of 1962 a vacancy was opened in the three top officials of the White House detail, which are comprised of, let me say, the special agent in charge, who has two assistants; one vacancy occurred. It was the oldest man on the White House detail; it was given to me and that is why today I have the title of assistant special agent in charge.

Mr. SPECTER. Now, since you brought us up to 1955, have your duties remained the same since that time?

Mr. KELLERMAN. I should bring you up to 1964. In 1955, I was transferred back to the White House detail, remained on that status on shift work until 1962, whereas I am now an assistant special agent in charge, which duties are the overseeing and the complete responsibility of the entire White House detail.

Mr. SPECTER. What is your educational background, Mr.——

Mr. KELLERMAN. I am a high school graduate only.

Mr. SPECTER. What year did you graduate from high school?

Mr. KELLERMAN. 1933.

Mr. SPECTER. What were your activities between graduation from high school and the time you joined the Secret Service, please?

Mr. KELLERMAN. In October of 1937 I completed the training with the Michigan State Police. I was sworn in as a trooper. I remained with the Michigan State Police until December 18, 1941, when I resigned and was appointed to the U.S. Secret Service.

Mr. SPECTER. How were you employed or occupied from the time of graduation from high school until the time you joined the Michigan State Police?

Mr. KELLERMAN. 1933 there wasn't too much work; 1935 was my first work with the Dodge Corp. of the Chrysler people in Detroit.

Mr. SPECTER. How long did you work there, sir?

Mr. KELLERMAN. Three years, off and on.

Mr. SPECTER. You described in a general way the organization of the Secret Service on the White House protective detail. Who is the special agent in charge?

Mr. KELLERMAN. Mr. Gerald A. Behn, sir.

Mr. SPECTER. Was he the special agent in charge back on November 22, 1963?

Mr. KELLERMAN. He was.

Mr. SPECTER. How many shifts are there?

Mr. KELLERMAN. Three shifts, sir.

Mr. SPECTER. And approximately how many men are assigned to each shift?

Mr. KELLERMAN. Ten men on each shift, sir.

Mr. SPECTER. What were your specific duties back on November 22 of 1963?

Mr. KELLERMAN. My specific duty, gentlemen, on the 22d of November of 1963, I was in charge of the detail for this trip of President Kennedy, for the trip to Texas in those 2 days.

Mr. SPECTER. How did you personally make the trip to Texas?

Mr. KELLERMAN. I rode on the President's plane on the entire tour.

Mr. SPECTER. Would you outline in a general way the times of departure and arrival on the trip to Texas up until the morning of November 22, please?

Mr. KELLERMAN. I just don't have the time we left Washington, D.C.

Mr. SPECTER. Without the precise times; just in a general way.

Mr. KELLERMAN. All right. We departed in the morning from Washington. Our first stop was in San Antonio, Tex.

Mr. SPECTER. Which morning was that, sir?

Mr. KELLERMAN. It was November 21; it was at San Antonio, Tex., that we picked up the then Vice President Johnson. The two people continued on this tour of the State in separate planes. During our stay in San Antonio, we then flew from San Antonio to Houston, Tex. There were ceremonies there, and the program there which had been set up. From Houston we flew into Fort Worth, Tex., where we remained overnight on November 21.

We arrived at the Texas Hotel, it was a little after 11 o'clock in the evening. There were no activities until the following morning, November 22.

Mr. SPECTER. What time did the activities start the following morning?

Mr. KELLERMAN. On November 22, the activities started at around 8:25 in the morning when the President, accompanied by the then Vice President Johnson, and a few congressional leaders walked out the front door, across this street which was a parking lot, and a few minutes' speech was made to the gathering there. It was a light drizzle at the time. From there we returned to the hotel and he attended a breakfast given by the chamber of commerce and, I believe it was, a citizens group of Fort Worth. On completion of the breakfast he returned to his suite. The weather was then changing. It had quit raining and it looked like it was going to break out and be a real beautiful day. In the neighborhood of 10 o'clock in the morning I received a call from Mr. Lawson, Special Agent Lawson, who had the advance from Dallas, Tex.

Mr. SPECTER. Mr. Lawson was with the Secret Service, was he?

Mr. KELLERMAN. Yes, sir; he is. He asked me to determine whether the bubbletop car that the President would ride in in Dallas that day should have the top down or remain up.

Mr. SPECTER. Let me interrupt you there for just a minute, Mr. Kellerman. I show you a photograph which has been marked as Commission Exhibit No. 344. Are you able to identify that picture and the automobile in that picture?

Mr. KELLERMAN. Yes, sir; this is the 1961 Lincoln Continental four-door convertible bubbletop. It is a special car.

Mr. SPECTER. For the purpose of the record, how many doors does that car have?

Mr. KELLERMAN. This vehicle has four doors.

Mr. SPECTER. And in the posture of the picture identified as Commission Exhibit 344, is the top up or down?

Mr. KELLERMAN. The top is down, sir.

Mr. SPECTER. And what top does that automobile have?

Mr. KELLERMAN. This top is a plastic top. From the rear of the passenger all the way to the windshield there are four sections of plastic glass. The one that comes over the top of the passengers in the back seat, two little sections that come over the two doors, and one over the driver and passenger in the front seat.

Mr. SPECTER. In what way is that attached, if any, to the car?

Mr. KELLERMAN. Securely bolted, screwed.

Mr. SPECTER. Mr. Chairman, may I ask that the Exhibit 344 be introduced formally in evidence, please?

Representative FORD. It will be so admitted.

(The photograph referred to was marked Commission Exhibit No. 344 for identification and received in evidence.)

Mr. SPECTER. I now hand you a photograph marked Commission Exhibit 345. Are you able to tell us what that depicts?

Mr. KELLERMAN. Yes, sir; this is the same vehicle as mentioned in 344. The difference being the top is up and there is a covering, a cloth covering that also fits over this plastic top.

Mr. SPECTER. And Exhibit No. 345 is taken from what angle, Mr. Kellerman?

Mr. KELLERMAN. From the rear, sir.

Mr. SPECTER. As contrasted with Exhibit No. 344, which is taken from what angle?

Mr. KELLERMAN. This is from the right side.

Mr. SPECTER. I ask that Exhibit 345 be introduced, if the Commission please.

Representative FORD. So admitted.

(The photograph referred to was marked Commission Exhibit No. 345 for identification and received in evidence.)

Mr. SPECTER. I now hand you a photograph marked Commission Exhibit 346, Mr. Kellerman, and ask you if you can tell us what that depicts.

Mr. KELLERMAN. This picture depicts the interior of this same automobile. It has a rear solid seat; there are two other jump seats that can be folded forward in the rear and the complete solid front seat for the driver and passenger. This is the same vehicle.

Mr. SPECTER. Will you describe what, if anything, is present between the front seat and the rear seat area?

Mr. KELLERMAN. Yes, sir. This metal partition that is erected in back of the driver, between the driver and the passengers in the rear seat, is a metal framework that goes over the car. It has four holes in it. These holes are utilized by the President for parades. As an example, say it was used in Washington where you had an official visitor, and in using one of the streets here as your parade route, he and his guest would stand in this car where the people could view them a little better than sitting in the rear seat.

Mr. SPECTER. Where is that metal bar positioned with respect to the front seat?

Mr. Kellerman. It is positioned over the front seat; the top of this bar would be 4 or 5 inches over my head.

Mr. SPECTER. Is it directly over the back portion of the front seat?

Mr. KELLERMAN. Yes, sir. Directly over the front seat.

Mr. SPECTER. And you describe it as 4 or 5 inches over your head. Can you give us an estimate of the distance above the top of the front seat?

Mr. KELLERMAN. Oh, I am guessing in the neighborhood of 15, 18 inches.

Mr. SPECTER. What is the width of that metal bar?

Mr. KELLERMAN. The bar, 4 to 6 inches, I would say.

Mr. SPECTER. Can you tell us approximately how wide the automobile itself is?

Mr. KELLERMAN. No; I can't.

Mr. SPECTER. With respect to the automobile, are there any running boards?

Mr. KELLERMAN. There are no running boards.

Mr. SPECTER. Is there any place on the car where someone can stand up and ride as it proceeds in motion?

Mr. KELLERMAN. Yes; on the rear of the vehicle, sir.

Mr. SPECTER. How many such positions are there?

Mr. KELLERMAN. There is a step on each side of the spare tire, one man on each one.

Mr. SPECTER. And is there any facility for holding on with a man riding in those positions?

Mr. KELLERMAN. Yes, sir; there is a metal arm erected on the trunk where a man can hold on while standing on the rear of the car.

Mr. SPECTER. All right.

May it please the Commission, I move that Exhibit 346 be introduced in evidence.

Representative FORD. It will be so admitted.

(The photograph referred to was marked Commission Exhibit No. 346 for identification and received in evidence.)

Mr. SPECTER. With reference to the bubble top which you have heretofore described, of what is that composed?

Mr. KELLERMAN. It is composed of plastic, clear plastic substance. Its use would be for a weather matter whereby the President or his occupants can see out. It is not an enclosed car.

Mr. SPECTER. Is it bulletproof?

Mr. KELLERMAN. It is not bulletproof.

Mr. SPECTER. Is it bullet resistant in any way?

Mr. KELLERMAN. It's not bullet resistant.

Mr. SPECTER. Could you describe in a general way at this point what efforts, if any, have been made to obtain a bulletproof clear top for the President's automobile?

Mr. KELLERMAN. Presently?

Mr. SPECTER. Presently or heretofore.

Mr. KELLERMAN. I am going to have to go in the present day.

Mr. SPECTER. Fine.

Mr. KELLERMAN. This same vehicle, I understand, is being completed with a bullet-resistant top and sides.

Representative FORD. Can you explain the difference between bullet resistant and the existing kind of the top?

Mr. KELLERMAN. I can't; I really can't. I have been behind on this thing and I am at a loss for a better answer.

Representative FORD. Could the present top deflect in any way, destroy the accuracy of a shot?

Mr. KELLERMAN. This would be a guess, Mr. Congressman. I would think that it would be deterred for, let's say, the velocity of a missile coming in at great speed, I think it would deter it; I don't think it would eliminate—it still would enter the top.

Representative Ford. The vehicle.

Mr. Kellerman. I am sure; yes, sir.

Representative Ford. But as far as you know the top that was available would not impede the projectile? Do you know whether or not it would deflect its accuracy?

Mr. Kellerman. Well, I have tried to study that, sir. The angle of the back as an example which is, what degree I don't recall, hoping that—of course, it was now known to be an upshot into the vehicle hoping that it would deter its force and so forth, but I really don't know. I kind of doubt it.

Mr. Specter. Mr. Kellerman, in describing the top as being not bulletproof and not bullet resistant, state whether you are describing the top which they are currently working on or the top which was present at the time of November 22, 1963?

Mr. Kellerman. That is the top that they are currently working on.

Mr. Specter. Well, as to the bubble top which accompanied this car on November 22, 1963, was that bulletproof or bullet resistant?

Mr. Kellerman. It was not; neither.

Mr. Specter. Do you know whether or not an effort is being made at the present time to develop a bullet-resistant or bulletproof top.

Mr. Kellerman. Yes, sir; it is.

Mr. Specter. Are you personally familiar with the progress of that effort?

Mr. Kellerman. I am not, sir.

Mr. Specter. Do you know how the President's automobile was transported from Washington, D.C., to Texas?

Mr. Kellerman. Yes, sir. The President's vehicle was transported to San Antonio by cargo aircraft. It was flown to San Antonio a day before the President arrived. It was then flown from San Antonio to Dallas, where it was used on November 22. This vehicle was not used in the other two stops at Houston and Fort Worth.

Representative Ford. When you say cargo aircraft——

Mr. Kellerman. Like a C-130, sir.

Representative Ford. A Government?

Mr. Kellerman. You are right, sir; that is right.

Mr. Specter. Mr. Kellerman, what were the President's activities, if you know immediately prior to the time he departed from Fort Worth?

Senator Cooper. Might I ask just one question?

Mr. Specter. Yes, sir.

Senator Cooper. Do you know whether or not prior to November 22 the President's car had ever been equipped with a top which had the capacity to stop or deflect a bullet?

Mr. Kellerman. Never had been, Senator.

Senator Cooper. There was none in existence?

Mr. Kellerman. No, sir.

Mr. Specter. Mr. Kellerman, what were the President's activities immediately before departing from Fort Worth on the morning of November 22?

Mr. Kellerman. First he walked from the hotel across the street, spoke to a group that were in a parking lot, with other congressional people there in Texas. From there he walked right into the hotel and entered the ballroom where a breakfast was held, given to him by the chamber of commerce and, I believe, the citizens group in Fort Worth.

From there he returned to his suite because there was time left before his departure for Dallas. It was up there in the neighborood of 10 o'clock in the morning that Special Agent Lawson called me from Dallas asking me to verify whether the top should be put on—should remain on the President's car or should be taken off due to the change of weather. It had been raining slightly in Dallas at that time. I said, "One moment and I will check with you one way or the other."

As I said earlier, the weather was clearing in Fort Worth; it was going to be a nice day. I asked Mr. Kenneth O'Donnell, who is President Kennedy's appointment secretary: "Mr. O'Donnell," I said, "the weather; it is slightly raining in Dallas, predictions of clearing up. Do you desire to have the bubbletop on the President's car or do you, or would you desire to have it removed for this parade over to the Trade Mart?"

His instructions to me were, "If the weather is clear and it is not raining, have that bubbletop off," and that is exactly what I relayed to Mr. Lawson.

Mr. SPECTER. Now, at about what time did President Kennedy depart from Fort Worth?

Mr. KELLERMAN. We were airborne from Fort Worth at 11:20 in the morning.

Mr. SPECTER. In what plane were you airborne?

Mr. KELLERMAN. In the President's special plane, sir.

Mr. SPECTER. What time did you arrive in that plane in Dallas?

Mr. KELLERMAN. We arrived in Dallas, Love Field, at 11:40 a.m.

Mr. SPECTER. Describe in a general way what President Kennedy's activities were at Love Field, please.

Mr. KELLERMAN. Very well. May I add this: Again I said there were two planes in this program. The then Vice President Johnson would be in a separate plane. He would land ahead of us by a minute or two, all right. He is in Dallas by the time we arrive at 11:40 a.m. As we are spotted on the apron at Love Field and when the ramp is pulled forward, the Vice President, then Vice President Johnson and Mrs. Johnson, together with a selected group of people would form a reception committee from the end of the ramp straight out to where the motorcade was in place.

At 11:40, as I said, the President and Mrs. Kennedy left that plane, met these people. As we finished greeting these folks here, there was an elderly lady wheeled up in a wheelchair; her name I do not know; the both of them met her. By this time the people are starting to get in their automobiles for this trip into town. The President then noticed that there was quite a gathering of people at this airport in back of a fenced area, and, with her, they both walked over to this crowded area and started shaking hands and greeting these people who had been there perhaps some time before we got in.

Mr. SPECTER. By "her", who do you mean, sir?

Mr. KELLERMAN. Mrs. Kennedy; I am sorry.

Mr. SPECTER. What would you estimate the crowd to be?

Mr. KELLERMAN. In the thousands; I would say there were two, three, four thousand people there.

Mr. SPECTER. Approximately how long did the greeting of the crowd at Love Field last, Mr. Kellerman?

Mr. KELLERMAN. Fifteen minutes. The motorcade left Love Field at 11:55.

Mr. SPECTER. Approximately how many cars were there in that motorcade?

Mr. KELLERMAN. At least 15.

Mr. SPECTER. What was the first car in line?

Mr. KELLERMAN. The first car in line, sir, was what we call the police pilot car. The duties of these police officers in that car—they would drive ahead.

Mr. SPECTER. Do you personaly know who was in that car?

Mr. KELLERMAN. No, sir.

Mr. SPECTER. How far ahead of the regular motorcade were they to be?

Mr. KELLERMAN. They could be several blocks ahead of us.

Mr. SPECTER. What is the general purpose of that pilot car?

Mr. KELLERMAN. The purpose of that pilot car is to clear the roadway and instruct the officers along the route that the President is in motion and coming in back of them. Next you will find a small group of motorcycles.

Mr. SPECTER. Do you know how many motorcycles there were in Dallas on that day?

Mr. KELLERMAN. No; I don't.

Mr. SPECTER. Will you tell us what the custom is with respect to motorcycles?

Mr. KELLERMAN. Yes, sir; those motorcycles that would be in back of that police car were to assist any officers along the way in any disturbance that they would run into before we got to that point, or secondly, in the event that we needed them back on our car they could be called, utilized.

Mr. SPECTER. What is the next car in line?

Mr. KELLERMAN. The next car is the lead car. That car on that day was driven by Chief Curry of the Dallas Police Department.

His occupants in that car was Special Agent Winston Lawson, who was carrying a portable radio with him. Also in this car was Special Agent in Charge Verne Sorrels, in charge of our Dallas office. The other occupant, I believe, was a deputy sheriff.

Mr. SPECTER. Was it Sheriff Decker, perhaps, of Dallas County?

Mr. KELLERMAN. The name doesn't reach me, sir; I am sorry.

Mr. SPECTER. You described a radio. Will you tell us a little more fully what radio transmission there was in the motorcade, please?

Mr. KELLERMAN. Yes, sir. This lead car which Mr. Lawson was in has a portable radio. The President's car is next. This is equipped with a permanent set radio on the same frequency as that gentleman up front. The next car is our Secret Service followup car which has a permanent installation. The Secret Service car, as I say, is equipped with a permanent installation which connects the President's car and the lead car. The next car in back of our Secret Service car was the then Vice President Johnson. The Secret Service agent in that car had a portable radio that he could read all three of us ahead. His car following was a small Secret Service followup car, and they, too, had a portable set, which could read all four.

So we had a net of five on our own frequency. In the police cars they had their own city police frequency radios.

Mr. SPECTER. How many frequencies were used by your own network?

Mr. KELLERMAN. One.

Representative FORD. Do you have an alternative frequency, emergency frequency?

Mr. KELLERMAN. Yes, sir; we do. We have two of them.

Mr. SPECTER. What automobile came behind the lead automobile?

Mr. KELLERMAN. The President's car.

Mr. SPECTER. Describe the occupants of that car, indicating their positions, if you can, please.

Mr. KELLERMAN. Yes. The President—President Kennedy sat on the right rear seat. Next to him on the left seat was Mrs. Kennedy. On the right jump seat in front of President Kennedy was Governor Connally. On the left jump seat in front of Mrs. Kennedy was Mrs. Connally. I sat on the right passenger seat of the driver's seat, and Special Agent William Greer drove the vehicle.

Mr. SPECTER. How far were you behind the lead car?

Mr. KELLERMAN. No more than two or three car lengths.

Senator COOPER. What is that? I didn't hear it.

Mr. KELLERMAN. No more than two or three car lengths, Senator Cooper.

Mr. SPECTER. What car immediately followed the President's car?

Mr. KELLERMAN. Our own Secret Service followup car.

Mr. SPECTER. What kind of a car was that?

Mr. KELLERMAN. This is a 1956 Cadillac, four-door touring car with the top down.

Mr. SPECTER. Was that also a special automobile flown in?

Mr. KELLERMAN. This is a special automobile, flown in with the President's car; yes, sir; that is correct.

Mr. SPECTER. And who were the occupants of that car, indicating their positions in the car?

Mr. KELLERMAN. All during this ride in from Love Field Special Agent Sam Kinney was the driver of this automobile. The assistant to the Special Agent in Charge Emory Roberts was sitting in the front seat, the passenger side. This car has running boards. Standing on the front of the left running board was Special Agent Clinton Hill. In back of him on the rear of that same running board on that side was Special Agent William McIntyre. On the right running board standing forward was Special Agent John Ready, and standing in back of him on the rear of the right running board was Special Agent Paul Landis.

Mr. SPECTER. Did that automobile have jump seats?

Mr. KELLERMAN. This automobile has jump seats.

Mr. Specter. And what people occupied the jump seats?

Mr. Kellerman. It was occupied by Mr. Kenneth O'Donnell, who was the appointment secretary of President Kennedy, and Mr. Dave Powers.

Mr. Specter. Do you know which sat on which side?

Mr. Kellerman. Mr. O'Donnell sat on the left; Mr. Powers sat on the right.

Mr. Specter. Who was in the back seat of that automobile?

Mr. Kellerman. The back seat of that automobile on the right side was Special Agent George Hickey, and on the left side Special Agent Glen Bennett.

Mr. Specter. How were the special agents in the followup car armed, if at all?

Mr. Kellerman. Each agent carries his own gun. This is a 4-inch revolver on their person.

Mr. Specter. Would that apply to you and Mr. Greer as well?

Mr. Kellerman. Absolutely.

Mr. Specter. Were there any other arms in the President's followup car?

Mr. Kellerman. Yes, sir; in this followup car we have what is now known as an AR-15. This is a rifle, and it is on all movements; this vehicle is out of the case; it won't be shown; it could be laying flat on the floor, but she is ready to go.

Mr. Specter. Now, how far behind the President's car did the Presidential followup car follow?

Mr. Kellerman. Not knowing how far it was behind, I would say, from the practice of that driver that he has, five feet would be a maximum.

Mr. Specter. What car was in the motorcade immediately behind the President's followup car?

Mr. Kellerman. That was Vice President Johnson's car then.

Mr. Specter. What kind of a car was that on that particular day?

Mr. Kellerman. This was a Lincoln four-door Continental convertible. This was a four-door car, with no top on it.

Mr. Specter. Is that a special car, also, or is that obtained on the market?

Mr. Kellerman. This is not a special car; it is a car that is on the market.

Mr. Specter. What car followed the Vice President's car?

Mr. Kellerman. The car following his car was a police car. It was driven by a member of the Dallas Police Force, or I just don't recall. I am sorry.

Mr. Specter. Do you have personal knowledge or detail of the occupants of the Vice President's car?

Mr. Kellerman. Yes; I do.

Mr. Specter. Who was present there?

Mr. Kellerman. Special Agent Rufus Youngblood sat in the front seat on the right side. In back of him on the right side and the rear was the then Vice President Johnson. Next to him was Mrs. Johnson, and next to Mrs. Johnson was Senator Yarborough.

Mr. Specter. Was Vice President Johnson seated on the right side or the left side of the rear seat?

Mr. Kellerman. On the right side, sir.

Mr. Specter. Were there jump seats in the Vice President's car?

Mr. Kellerman. No, sir.

Mr. Specter. Do you know the identity of the driver of the Vice President's car?

Mr. Kellerman. Yes, sir.

Mr. Specter. Who was that?

Mr. Kellerman. That was Mr. Hurchel Jacks. He is a Dallas police officer.

Mr. Specter. Might he be a Texas State police officer?

Mr. Kellerman. Yes, sir; you are right.

Mr. Specter. Do you know the identity of all of the individuals in the Vice President's followup car?

Mr. Kellerman. Not the driver. The agents, yes.

Mr. Specter. Who were they, sir?

Mr. Kellerman. Special Agent Thomas L. Johns, Special Agent Warren Taylor, and I believe that is all.

Mr. Specter. Are you able to indicate their precise positions?

Mr. Kellerman. No, no.

Mr. SPECTER. Now, what car, if you know, followed the Vice President's followup car?

Mr. KELLERMAN. That was car—as an example, car No. 1, which would be a congressional car; the occupants I do not know at the present time.

Mr. SPECTER. And behind that car, describe in a general way the balance of the motorcade, if you will, please.

Mr. KELLERMAN. All right. The balance of the motorcade, the back of that car No. 1 which would be the congressional people would be two press cars, one covering the wire people, and one would be the photographic group. Then you would have a series of guest cars, and then a press bus. And then a police car followup, bringing up the entire motorcade.

Mr. SPECTER. You described the motorcycles which followed the pilot car. Were there any other motorcycles in the motorcade?

Mr. KELLERMAN. Yes, sir; we had four other motorcycles opposite the back wheel of the President's vehicle, sir.

Mr. SPECTER. Were those on both sides or on each side?

Mr. KELLERMAN. On each side; two on each side.

Mr. SPECTER. Were there any other motorcycles in the balance of the motorcade?

Mr. KELLERMAN. Not that I recall.

Mr. SPECTER. At what speed did the motorcade proceed at the various times en route, say, from Love Field down to the downtown section of Dallas, Tex.?

Mr. KELLERMAN. As we left Love Field, the driveway from this apron on the field was sort of a winding thing, and there were many people that gathered on the roadside to view him as they passed. I don't think we traveled more than 12 to 15 miles until we left the airport apron proper.

Mr. SPECTER. Twelve to fifteen miles per hour?

Mr. KELLERMAN. Per hour.

Mr. SPECTER. Yes.

Mr. KELLERMAN. Then, as we were in the opening between there and the city limits of Dallas, we could have gone 25 to 30.

Mr. SPECTER. What was the size of the crowd at that specific point?

Mr. KELLERMAN. Nothing in between then until we hit the outskirts of the city. Of course, then you got into a residential, a school, area where all the people were out on the curb line.

Mr. SPECTER. What was the speed when you reached that area?

Mr. KELLERMAN. Then we would reduce the speed down to 15 miles an hour.

Mr. SPECTER. What is your best estimate of the minimum speed traveled until you reached the downtown area?

Mr. KELLERMAN. We could have been going 25 to 30 at several times, sir.

Mr. SPECTER. What were the crowds like in the downtown area itself?

Mr. KELLERMAN. A lot of people.

Mr. SPECTER. What was the speed of the motorcade when you came into the downtown area?

Mr. KELLERMAN. It would be reduced down to 10 to 15 miles an hour, sir.

Mr. SPECTER. Were there any unusual occurrences en route from Love Field until, say, you got to the downtown area of Dallas, Tex.?

Mr. KELLERMAN. As we were on the outskirts of this town and apparently reaching a crowded area there were a group of youngsters on the right side of the car curb-line-wise, that had a large sign, oh, perhaps the width of the two windows there, that said, "Please. Mr. President, stop and shake our hands," and he saw this and he called to the driver and said, "Stop," he said, "call these people over and I will shake their hands," which we did. The entire motorcade stopped. I got out of the car and stood alongside of it while these people were right up on me. The agents who were on the followup car, all around it. And then after a few seconds he said, "All right; let's travel on."

Mr. SPECTER. You say the agents in the followup car moved up at the stopping?

Mr. KELLERMAN. Always, sir.

Mr. SPECTER. Specifically, what did they do on that occasion?

Mr. KELLERMAN. They crowded right in between the President, the car, and the people.

Mr. SPECTER. Did the President actually leave the car?

Mr. KELLERMAN. No.

Mr. SPECTER. And how long did that stop last?

Mr. KELLERMAN. A matter of seconds.

Mr. SPECTER. Was there any other unusual occurrence en route to the downtown area itself?

Mr. KELLERMAN. No; I can recall, however, one small affair. I think we were in the heart of Dallas on this street when a young boy jumped off the curb and apparently he was thinking of running over to the President's car and shaking his hands when one of our people left the followup car and put him back on the curb, and that all happened in motion so there was nothing out of the way.

Mr. SPECTER. I show you a photograph marked Commission Exhibit No. 347 and ask you if you are at this time able to tell us what that photograph represents.

The CHAIRMAN. Congressman Ford, may I interrupt at this time to ask to be excused? I have a session in the Supreme Court, but I will be back later.

Representative FORD. Thank you very much, Mr. Chief Justice.

(Chief Justice Warren left the hearing room.)

Mr. KELLERMAN. This is an aerial photo of the downtown parade.

Mr. SPECTER. Are you able to identify the street on which you proceeded coming into the area depicted by that photograph?

Mr. KELLERMAN. Yes, sir. This is—this would be Main Street as we came into the heart of Dallas.

Mr. SPECTER. I think it might be helpful if we marked that as Main Street if we can get a pencil or pen that will mark on that.

Mr. CRAIG. May I suggest the witness mark it?

Mr. SPECTER. I think it is a good idea. Will you mark the street which you have identified as Main Street?

(Witness marking.)

Mr. SPECTER. Will you also mark——

Mr. KELLERMAN. We were traveling——

Mr. SPECTER. The street onto which you turned from Main Street?

Mr. KELLERMAN. As we were coming up from Main Street or down, either way.

Mr. SPECTER. In what general direction were you proceeding on Main Street?

Mr. KELLERMAN. This was a westerly direction.

Mr. SPECTER. Would you put an arrow indicating which way is north on the map? That is a general northerly direction on the map.

(Witness indicating.)

Mr. SPECTER. Will you mark an arrow on Main Street showing the direction on which you were proceeding on Main? And how far did you proceed on Main Street to what street?

Mr. KELLERMAN. Elm Street, sir. This is a very short block, maybe a couple of hundred feet at the most.

Mr. SPECTER. My question was to what street did you proceed on Main? You then drove to what street?

Mr. KELLERMAN. Houston Street.

Mr. SPECTER. Which way did you turn onto Houston Street?

Mr. KELLERMAN. Turned right, which would be north.

Mr. SPECTER. Will you mark the street that you have told us would be Houston Street?

(Witness indicating.)

Mr. SPECTER. How far did you proceed down Houston Street?

Mr. KELLERMAN. I am sure it wasn't more than 200 feet at the most. It was a real short block.

Mr. SPECTER. What street then did you turn onto as you turned off of Houston Street?

Mr. KELLERMAN. From Houston we turned onto Elm, which was a rather sharp turn with a downgrade, sir.

Mr. SPECTER. Was that a turn on the left or the right?

Mr. KELLERMAN. To the left, sir.

Mr. SPECTER. I ask that Exhibit 347 be admitted in evidence, may it please the Commission.

Representative FORD. It will be admitted.

Mr. SPECTER. I now show you a photograph marked Commission Exhibit No. 348, Mr. Kellerman, and I ask you if you are able at this time to identify what building is in that picture?

Mr. KELLERMAN. This building right straight ahead in the photo—I couldn't have told you on the day of the 22nd of November what it was, but as of now this is the Texas Depository Building.

Mr. SPECTER. Is that the building known as the Texas School Book Depository Building?

Mr. KELLERMAN. That is right, sir.

(The photograph marked Commission Exhibits Nos. 347 and 348 for identification and received in evidence.)

Mr. SPECTER. Will you mark on Exhibit 347—we have 348, we will get 348 back in a moment. I would like to have you mark in the aerial shot the precise location of that building with the initials "TS."

(Witness marks.)

Mr. SPECTER. For the written part of our record will you describe how many stories high the Texas School Book Depository building is?

Mr. KELLERMAN. This is a seven-story building. From here it appears to be a rather square-type constructed.

Mr. SPECTER. All right. As you were proceeding in a generally northerly direction on Houston Street, can you describe the layout of the street, indicating first the approximate width of that street?

Mr. KELLERMAN. Houston Street is a rather wide city street similar to anything we have here in Washington, really, and being in the heart of the business section, I would say that it was a six-lane street at the time.

Mr. SPECTER. What was on your right as you proceeded down Houston Street?

Mr. KELLERMAN. The buildings.

Mr. SPECTER. And how about on your left?

Mr. KELLERMAN. On my left it was open.

Mr. SPECTER. As you turned left onto Elm Street, will you describe what was on your right?

Mr. KELLERMAN. As we turned left onto Elm Street and left this building that we are speaking of here——

Mr. SPECTER. Is that the Texas School Book Depository Building?

Mr. KELLERMAN. Yes; then your area became clear.

Mr. SPECTER. On the right?

Mr. KELLERMAN. On the right, sir. This was an open field area with a hill. Now, there were, if I recall correctly, just at the brink of the hill, right beyond this building in question, there was a small white—how can I describe it?

Mr. SPECTER. A little park area?

Mr. KELLERMAN. A little park area; that is right. And beyond it it was all open.

Mr. SPECTER. What was on your left at about that time as you proceeded down Elm Street?

Mr. KELLERMAN. Right. As we turned left on Elm Street off Houston, this, too, was a little plaza area, and kind of a triangular thing where the street was on the opposite side; this is an apparently one-way street, and directly to our left as we turned you had to view, this looked like a little one-story plaza building or structure.

Mr. SPECTER. To complete the scene, as you looked ahead of you down Elm Street what, if anything, did you see immediately in front of you?

Mr. KELLERMAN. Yes. First thing that I saw was that the road was going to turn, and then a little further ahead we had a viaduct which we were going under.

Mr. SPECTER. Do you know what name the Dallas Texans give to that viaduct?

Mr. KELLERMAN. No; I really don't.

Mr. SPECTER. Have you heard it described since as the triple overpass?

Mr. KELLERMAN. No; I haven't.

Mr. SPECTER. What was the approximate width of Elm Street in lanes of travel, if you recall?

Mr. KELLERMAN. It is at least three lanes, sir.

Mr. SPECTER. And describe the terrain, whether it was smooth, level or in what way you went as you went down Elm Street.

Mr. KELLERMAN. As we went down Elm Street, there was a smooth road and the terrain on each side was a grassy plotted area, a very cleared-off area, visibility tremendous.

Mr. SPECTER. And describe the composure of the crowds at that time.

Mr. KELLERMAN. As we turned north on to Houston Street, this was primarily the end of the crowd in Dallas, Tex.; in the downtown section, there were still a few on the sidewalk until we got to Elm Street. As we turned in a northerly direction to Elm Street, which would be on our left, then the crowds just diminished. They were spotty, standing on the grassy plot. They were not on the side of the street. In fact, there were just a matter of a handful, that was all, and we were through it.

Mr. SPECTER. Do you know what time it was when you got to the intersection of Houston and Elm on November 22?

Mr. KELLERMAN. Not at Houston and Elm; no. No; I don't

Mr. SPECTER. What was the speed of the motorcade, Mr. Kellerman, as you were proceeding down Main Street at about the time you turned right onto Houston?

Mr. KELLERMAN. Ten, fifteen, no more: real parade speed.

Mr. SPECTER. How far ahead of you was the lead car at that time?

Mr. KELLERMAN. Again, it was four or five car lengths in front.

Mr. SPECTER. Do you know how far behind you the President's followup car was as you turned right onto Houston from Main Street?

Mr. KELLERMAN. No; I don't, but I am positive it was right on our rear wheels.

Mr. SPECTER. All right.

Now, as you turned left off Houston onto Elm, what is your best estimate of the speed of the President's automobile at that time?

Mr. KELLERMAN. As we turned onto Elm Street and the crowd, we were through the section of Dallas; we might have had—the driver picked it up because we were all through. Purely a guess, we could have been going at the most 25.

Mr. SPECTER. What would your estimate, your minimum estimate, of the speed be?

Mr. KELLERMAN. Fifteen.

Mr. SPECTER. As you turned left onto Elm Street, how far were you behind the lead car at that point?

Mr. KELLERMAN. I am going to say the same; three to five car lengths, but I can, to go a little further, I can see this car ahead of me. He is not running away from us.

Mr. SPECTER. How about the pilot car; was that car in sight?

Mr. KELLERMAN. No; that I didn't see; I didn't see it.

Mr. SPECTER. Do you know from your personal observation at the time you turned left onto Elm Street how far the President's followup car was behind you at that point?

Mr. KELLERMAN. Not from personal observation.

Mr. SPECTER. All right. Now, describe what occurred as you proceeded down Elm Street after turning off of Houston.

Mr. KELLERMAN. As we turned off Houston onto Elm and made the short little dip to the left going down grade, as I said, we were away from buildings, and were—there was a sign on the side of the road which I don't recall what it was or what it said, but we no more than passed that and you are out in the open, and there is a report like a firecracker, pop. And I turned my head to the right because whatever this noise was I was sure that it came from the right and perhaps into the rear, and as I turned my head to the right to view whatever it was or see whatever it was, I heard a voice from the back seat and I firmly believe it was the President's, "My God, I am hit," and I turned around and he has got his hands up here like this.

73

Mr. SPECTER. Indicating right hand up toward his neck?

Mr. KELLERMAN. That is right, sir. In fact, both hands were up in that direction.

Senator COOPER. Which side of his neck?

Mr. KELLERMAN. Beg pardon?

Senator COOPER. Which side of his neck?

Mr. KELLERMAN. Both hands were up, sir; this one is like this here and here we are with the hands——

Mr. SPECTER. Indicating the left hand is up above the head.

Mr. KELLERMAN. In the collar section.

Mr. SPECTER. As you are positioning yourself in the witness chair, your right hand is up with the finger at the ear level as if clutching from the right of the head; would that be an accurate description of the position you pictured there?

Mr. KELLERMAN. Yes. Good. There was enough for me to verify that the man was hit. So, in the same motion I come right back and grabbed the speaker and said to the driver, "Let's get out of here; we are hit," and grabbed the mike and I said, "Lawson, this is Kellerman,"—this is Lawson, who is in the front car. "We are hit; get us to the hospital immediately." Now, in the seconds that I talked just now, a flurry of shells come into the car. I then looked back and this time Mr. Hill, who was riding on the left front bumper of our followup car, was on the back trunk of that car; the President was sideways down into the back seat.

Mr. SPECTER. Indicating on his left side.

Mr. KELLERMAN. Right; just like I am here.

Mr. SPECTER. You mean, correct, left side?

Mr. KELLERMAN. Correct; yes, sir. Governor Connally by that time is lying flat backwards into her lap—Mrs. Connally—and she was lying flat over him.

Mr. SPECTER. Who was lying flat over him?

Mr. KELLERMAN. Mrs. Connally was lying flat over the Governor.

Mr. SPECTER. You say that you turned to your right immediately after you heard a shot?

Mr. KELLERMAN. Yes, sir.

Mr. SPECTER. What was the reason for your reacting to your right?

Mr. KELLERMAN. That was the direction that I heard this noise, pop.

Mr. SPECTER. Do you have a reaction as to the height from which the noise came?

Mr. KELLERMAN. No; honestly, I do not.

Representative FORD. Was there any reaction that you noticed on the part of Greer when the noise was noticed by you?

Mr. KELLERMAN. You are referring, Mr. Congressman, to the reaction to get this car out of there?

Representative FORD. Yes.

Mr. KELLERMAN. Mr. Congressman, I have driven that car many times, and I never cease to be amazed even to this day with the weight of the automobile plus the power that is under the hood; we just literally jumped out of the God-damn road.

Representative FORD. As soon as this noise was heard, or as soon as you transmitted this message to Lawson?

Mr. KELLERMAN. As soon as I transmitted to the driver first as I went to Lawson. I just leaned sideways to him and said, "Let's get out of here. We are hit."

Representative FORD. That comment was made to Greer; not to Lawson?

Mr. KELLERMMAN. Yes, sir; that is right.

Representative FORD. And the subsequent message was to Lawson?

Mr. KELLERMAN. Correct. That is right.

Mr. SPECTER. With relationship to that first noise that you have described, when did you hear the voice?

Mr. KELLERMAN. His voice?

Mr. SPECTER. We will start with his voice.

Mr. KELLERMAN. OK. From the noise of which I was in the process of turning to determine where it was or what it was, it carried on right then. Why I am so positive, gentlemen, that it was his voice—there is only one man in that back seat that was from Boston, and the accents carried very clearly.

Mr. Specter. Well, had you become familiar with the President's voice prior to that day?

Mr. Kellerman. Yes; very much so.

Mr. Specter. And what was the basis for your becoming familiar with his voice prior to that day?

Mr. Kellerman. I had been with him for 3 years.

Mr. Specter. And had you talked with him on a very frequent basis during the course of that association?

Mr. Kellerman. He was a very free man to talk to; yes. He knew most all the men, most everybody who worked in the White House as well as everywhere, and he would call you.

Mr. Specter. And from your experience would you say that you could recognize the voice?

Mr. Kellerman. Very much, sir; I would.

Mr. Specter. Now, I think you may have answered this, but I want to pinpoint just when you heard that statement which you have attributed to President Kennedy in relationship to the sound which you described as a firecracker.

Mr. Kellerman. This noise which I attribute as a firecracker, when this occurred and I am in the process of determining where it comes because I am sure it came off my right rear somewhere; the voice broke in right then.

Mr. Specter. At about the same time?

Mr. Kellerman. That is correct, sir. That is right.

Mr. Specter. Now, did President Kennedy say anything beside, "My God, I am hit."

Mr. Kellerman. That is the last words he said, sir.

Mr. Specter. Did Mrs. Kennedy say anything at that specific time?

Mr. Kellerman. Mr. Specter, there was an awful lot of confusion in that back seat. She did a lot of talking which I can't recall all the phrases.

Mr. Specter. Well, pinpoint——

Mr. Kellerman. But after the flurry of shots, I recall her saying, "What are they doing to you?" Now again, of course, my comparison of the voice of her speech—certainly, I have heard it many times, and in the car there was conversation she was carrying on through shock, I am sure.

Mr. Specter. Well, going back to the precise time that you heard the President say, "My God, I am hit," do you recollect whether she said anything at that time?

Mr. Kellerman. No.

Mr. Specter. Whether or not you can re-create what she said?

Mr. Kellerman. Not that I can recall right then, sir. This statement, or whatever she said, happened after all the shooting was over.

Mr. Specter. All right. Now, you have described hearing a noise which sounded like a firecracker and you have described turning to your right and described hearing the President's voice and, again, what was your next motion, if any, or movement, if any?

Mr. Kellerman. After I was sure that his statement was right that he was hit, turned from the back I come right down——

Mr. Specter. You just indicated that you had turned to the left. Had you turned to the left after hearing his voice?

Mr. Kellerman. Yes; certainly.

Mr. Specter. And what did you see? You have described what you saw in terms of position of his hands.

Mr. Kellerman. That was it.

Mr. Specter. What did you do next?

Mr. Kellerman. That is when I completely turned to my right and grabbed for the mike in the same motion, sideways telling the driver, "Let's get out of here; we are hit."

Mr. Specter. Will you give us the best estimate of the lapse of time from the instant you heard the sound which appeared to you to be a firecracker until you instructed Mr. Greer in the way you have described?

Mr. Kellerman. Seconds.

Mr. SPECTER. How many seconds?

Mr. KELLERMAN. Three or four.

Mr. SPECTER. Now, how long did it take you to relay the instructions which you have told us about to Special Agent Lawson; what your best estimate would be?

Mr. KELLERMAN. Instant, in seconds again. Again it is three to five.

Mr. SPECTER. Now, in your prior testimony you described a flurry of shells into the car. How many shots did you hear after the first noise which you described as sounding like a firecracker?

Mr. KELLERMAN. Mr. Specter, these shells came in all together.

Mr. SPECTER. Are you able to say how many you heard?

Mr. KELLERMAN. I am going to say two, and it was like a double bang—bang, bang.

Mr. SPECTER. You mean now two shots in addition to the first noise?

Mr. KELLERMAN. Yes, sir; yes, sir; at least.

Mr. SPECTER. What is your best estimate of the time, in seconds, from the first noise sounding like a firecracker until the second noise which you heard?

Mr. KELLERMAN. This was instantaneous.

Mr. SPECTER. No; let me repeat the question so I am sure you understand it. From the time you first heard the noise coming to your right rear, which you described as sounding like a firecracker, until you heard the flurry of shots?

Mr. KELLERMAN. This is about how long it took, sir. As I am viewing, trying to determine this noise, I turned to my right and I heard the voice and I came back and I verify it and speak to the driver, grab the mike, these shots come in.

Mr. SPECTER. Well, you have described it as 3 to 4 seconds from the time——

Mr. KELLERMAN. No more.

Mr. SPECTER. From the time of the first noise—wait a minute—until you gave the instruction to Mr. Greer and then as you made the statement to Special Agent Lawson over the microphone that was an instantaneous timespan as you have described it.

Mr. KELLERMAN. Yes, sir.

Mr. SPECTER. How soon thereafter did the flurry of shots come?

Mr. KELLERMAN. They came in, Mr. Specter, while I am delivering that radio message.

Mr. SPECTER. To Mr. Lawson. All right. Was there any timespan which you could discern between the first and second shots and what you have described as the flurry?

Mr. KELLERMAN. I will estimate 5 seconds, if that.

Representative FORD. But this flurry took place while you were occupied with these other activities; is that correct?

Mr. KELLERMAN. That is right, sir.

Representative FORD. You don't recall precisely a second shot and a third shot such as you did in the case of the first?

Mr. KELLERMAN. Let me give you an illustration, sir, before I can give you an answer. You have heard the sound barrier, of a plane breaking the sound barrier, bang, bang? That is it.

Representative FORD. This is for the second and the third, or the flurry as you described it?

Mr. KELLERMAN. That is right; that is right, sir.

Mr. SPECTER. On your 5-second estimate, was that in reference, Mr. Kellerman, to the total timespan from the first noise until the flurry ended?

Mr. KELLERMAN. That is right; that is right.

Mr. SPECTER. All right. Now, when the flurry occurred then, were you still facing forward talking into the microphone to Lawson?

Mr. KELLERMAN. That is right.

Mr. SPECTER. All right. Then precisely what was your next movement after completing the delivery of that message to Lawson?

Mr. KELLERMAN. When I completed the delivery of those instructions to Lawson, I just hung up the receiver and looked back.

Mr. SPECTER. To your right this time—to your left; pardon me.

Mr. KELLERMAN. To my left; that is right. This is when I first viewed Mr. Hill, who was on the back of the——

Mr. SPECTER. Precisely where was he in that instant?

Mr. KELLERMAN. Lying right across the trunk of the car with Mrs. Kennedy on the left rear, Mr. Hill's head was right up in back of her.

Mr. SPECTER. When you describe the left rear you mean as the car was facing?

Mr. KELLERMAN. As the car is traveling, sir; yes, sir. He was lying across the trunk of this car, feet on this side.

Mr. SPECTER. Was he flat across the trunk of the car?

Mr. KELLERMAN. Flat; that is right.

Mr. SPECTER. What was the position of Mrs. Kennedy's body at that time?

Mr. KELLERMAN. She was sitting up in the corner of this back seat, like this.

Mr. SPECTER. So that she was on the buttocks area of her body at that time?

Mr. KELLERMAN. Yes, sir.

Mr. SPECTER. And what movement, if any, did you observe Mrs. Kennedy make at that time?

Mr. KELLERMAN. I never did see Mrs. Kennedy leave that back seat, sir.

Mr. SPECTER. When you say the back seat, are you referring——

Mr. KELLERMAN. The seat she was sitting on.

Mr. SPECTER. Are you referring to the seat itself of the automobile?

Mr. KELLERMAN. Right.

Mr. SPECTER. Where did you look next; what did you observe following that?

Mr. KELLERMAN. Then I observed how the President was lying, which was—he was—flat in the seat in this direction.

Mr. SPECTER. On his left-hand side?

Mr. KELLERMAN. Yes, sir. Governor Connally was lying straight on his back with Mrs. Connally over him about halfway.

Mr. SPECTER. Did Governor Connally say anything up to this point?

Mr. KELLERMAN. No.

Mr. SPECTER. Did Mrs. Connally say anything up to that point?

Mr. KELLERMAN. No.

Mr. SPECTER. When was it that Mrs. Kennedy made the statement which you have described, "My God, what are they doing?"

Mr. KELLERMAN. This occurred after the flurry of shots.

Mr. SPECTER. At that time you looked back and saw Special Agent Hill across the trunk of the car, had your automobile accelerated by that time?

Mr. KELLERMAN. Tremendously so; yes.

Mr. SPECTER. Now, to the best of your ability to recollect, exactly when did your automobile first accelerate?

Mr. KELLERMAN. Our car accelerated immediately on the time—at the time—this flurry of shots came into it.

Mr. SPECTER. Would you say the acceleration——

Mr. KELLERMAN. Between the second and third shot.

Senator COOPER Might I ask a question there?

Mr. SPECTER. Yes.

Senator COOPER. A few minutes ago you said in response to a question that when you spoke to the driver the car leaped forward from an acceleration immediately. Did that acceleration occur before the second shot was fired?

Mr. KELLERMAN. Yes, sir. Just about the time that it came in.

Senator COOPER. About the time it came in?

Mr. KELLERMAN. Yes, sir.

Senator COOPER. Not before?

Mr. KELLERMAN. No.

Senator COOPER. One other question: You said the flurry of shots came in the car. You were leaning forward talking to the driver after the first shot. What made you aware of a flurry of shots?

Mr. KELLERMAN. Senator, between all the matter that was—between all the matter that was blown off from an injured person, this stuff all came over.

Senator COOPER. What was that?

Mr. KELLERMAN. Body matter; flesh.

Senator COOPER. When you were speaking of a flurry of shots, was there a longer interval between the first shot and the second shot as compared to the interval between the second shot and the third shot?

Mr. KELLERMAN. Yes, sir.

Mr. SPECTER. When did you first notice the substance which you have described as body matter?

Mr. KELLERMAN. When I got to the hospital, sir, it was all over my coat.

Mr. SPECTER. Did you notice it flying past you at any time prior to your arrival at the hospital?

Mr. KELLERMAN. Yes; I know there was something in the air.

Mr. SPECTER. When, in relation to the shots, Mr. Kellerman, did you notice the substance in the air?

Mr. KELLERMAN. Fine. When I have given the orders to Mr. Lawson, this is when it all came between the driver and myself.

Mr. SPECTER. Can you describe what it was in a little more detail as it appeared to you at that time?

Mr. KELLERMAN. This is a rather poor comparison, but let's say you take a little handful of matter—I am going to use sawdust for want of a better item—and just throw it.

Mr. SPECTER. Can you describe the sound of the flurry of shots by way of distinction with the way you have described the sound of the first shot?

Mr. KELLERMAN. Well, having heard all types of guns fired, most of them, rather, if I recall correctly these were two sharp reports, sir. Again, I am going to refer to it as like a plane going through a sound barrier; bang, bang.

Mr. SPECTER. Now, you are referring to the flurry?

Mr. KELLERMAN. That is right.

Mr. SPECTER. Did it sound differently from the first noise you have described as being a firecracker?

Mr. KELLERMAN. Yes; definitely; very much so.

Representative FORD. Was there any other noise going on at the time of the second and third shots different from the noise of the crowd or otherwise at the time of the first shot?

Mr. KELLERMAN. We had no crowd, sir. There was nothing there.

Representative FORD. So the external noise was identical as far as the——

Mr. KELLERMAN. Very much.

Representative FORD. First or second or the third shot?

Mr. KELLERMAN. Yes, sir. We are in an open-field area, so to speak, and everything was just clear.

Representative FORD. So there was no other sound that would have disturbed your hearing capability from the first through the third shot?

Mr. KELLERMAN. That is right; no other shot.

Representative FORD. Your only problem would be your personal activity after the first shot.

Mr. KELLERMAN. Correct.

Representative FORD. Your activity of speaking to Greer and talking to Lawson?

Mr. KELLERMAN. That is correct, sir; yes, sir.

Representative FORD. Was there any crowd reaction?

Mr. KELLERMAN. There was no crowd.

Representative FORD. There were a few stragglers?

Mr. KELLERMAN. A handful, and I didn't view any reaction, sir.

Representative FORD. All right.

Mr. SPECTER. Mr. Kellerman, you said earlier that there were at least two additional shots. Is there any area in your mind or possibility, as you recollect that situation, that there could have been more than two shots, or are you able to say with any certainty?

Mr. KELLERMAN. I am going to say that I have, from the firecracker report and the two other shots that I know, those were three shots. But, Mr. Specter, if President Kennedy had from all reports four wounds, Governor Connally three, there have got to be more than three shots, gentlemen.

Senator COOPER. What is that answer? What did he say?

Mr. SPECTER. Will you repeat that, Mr. Kellerman?

Mr. KELLERMAN. President Kennedy had four wounds, two in the head and shoulder and the neck. Governor Connally, from our reports, had three. There have got to be more than three shots.

Representative FORD. Is that why you have described——

Mr. Kellerman. The flurry.

Representative Ford. The noise as a flurry?

Mr. Kellerman. That is right, sir.

Mr. Specter. Excuse me, do you have any independent recollection, Mr. Kellerman, of the number of shots, aside from the inference that you make as to how many points of wounds there were?

Mr. Kellerman. Could you rephrase that, please?

Mr. Specter. Yes. You have drawn a conclusion, in effect, by saying that there were four wounds for the President and three wounds for the Governor; and from that, you say there must have been more than three shots in your opinion or your view. But my question is: Do you have any current recollection of having heard more than three shots?

Mr. Kellerman. No. I don't. I will have to say "No."

Senator Cooper. Has that been your recollection from the very time of the shooting?

Mr. Kellerman. No, sir; it has been my opinion.

Senator Cooper. Not your opinion, but from the time of the shooting you think then that you heard only three shots, or did you——

Mr. Kellerman. Yes.

Senator Cooper. Or did you ever think that you heard more than three?

Mr. Kellerman. No, sir; I can't say that, sir.

Mr. Specter. Now, you referred to four wounds, Mr. Kellerman, realizing, of course, your characterization is only lay opinion.

Mr. Kellerman. Very true.

Mr. Specter. Would you tell us which wounds you made reference to by that statement, please?

Mr. Kellerman. All right. Can I keep the train going from the time we got to the hospital?

Mr. Specter. Yes, sir; do it in your own way just as you please.

Mr. Kellerman. Fine. As we arrived at the hospital I immediately got out of the car. Our followup car is in back of us, as you will recall. I yelled to the agents, "Get in"—"Go get us two stretchers on wheels."

In the meantime in a matter of seconds—I don't know how they got out so fast—I turned right around to the back door and opened it. By this time Mrs. Connally had raised up, and the Governor is lying in her lap, face up. His eyes are open and he is looking at me, and I am fairly sure he is alive. By this time I noticed the two stretchers coming out of the emergency room, and I said to the Governor, I said, "Governor, don't worry; everything is going to be all right." And he nodded his head, which I was fairly convinced that that man was alive.

By this time the stretcher is there. I get inside on one side of him, and Special Agent Hill on the other. Somebody is holding his feet, and we remove the Governor and put him on the stretcher and they take him in.

We then get in and help Mrs. Connally out. Our next move is to get Mrs. Kennedy off from the seat, which was a little difficult, but she was removed. Then Mr. Hill removed his coat and laid it over the President's face and shoulder. He and I among two other people—I don't know—we lifted up the President and put him on a stretcher and followed him right into the emergency room.

Gentlemen, this emergency room is a, it looks like a, checkerboard; it has a walkway down the center and a crossway and there are rooms on each side. President Kennedy was put into the one on the right, Governor Connally across on the left. And as we pushed the wheelchair in—we pushed the stretcher inside, the medical people just seemed to form right in, right there, and I walked around him and I wanted to look at this man's face, they had him face up.

Senator Cooper. The President?

Mr. Kellerman. The President; I am sorry. I did not see any wounds in that man's face.

Mr. Specter. Indicating with your hand at that moment the front part of his face?

Mr. Kellerman. Right, sir.

Mr. SPECTER. May I interrupt you just to ask whether you had any view——

Mr. KELLERMAN. Surely.

Mr. SPECTER. Of the rear part of his head?

Mr. KELLERMAN. I did not, sir.

Mr. SPECTER. What was the rearmost or uppermost portion of President Kennedy's head which you could observe at that time?

Mr. KELLERMAN. It was the hairline to the ear, sir.

Mr. SPECTER. Proceed.

Mr. KELLERMAN. Having all the medical people in there, my business is left in their hands. So I left. Mrs. Kennedy, incidentally, was still in there.

Mr. SPECTER. In where, sir?

Mr. KELLERMAN. In the emergency room with him. Which after a few minutes they convinced her to leave, and she sat outside the room while they were working over the President. I walked into this center area of this emergency room—and I am looking for a telephone—which there is a little doctor's office and I walked inside, and I am alone at that time, except one medic who was in there. There are two phones and I said, "Can I use either one of these phones to get outside?" and he said, "Yes; just pick one up."

By this time Mr. Lawson enters and also Mr. Hill. I asked Mr. Lawson for the telephone number of the Dallas White House switchboard. He immediately has it and I said to Mr. Hill, "Will you dial it, please?" By that time a medic comes into the room from President Kennedy's section and he asks if anybody knows the blood type of the President—President Kennedy. We all carry it. I produce mine, and that is what I believe they used; I am not sure. By this time the connection is made with the White House operator in Dallas, and I took the phone, identified myself, and I said, "Give me Washington. Please don't pull this line; let's leave it open."

I got the Washington operator and I said, identified myself, and I said, "Give me Mr. Behn."

Mr. Behn was in the office at the time, and I said—his name is Gerald Behn—and I said, "Gerry, we have had an incident here in Dallas. The President, the Governor have been shot. We are in the emergency room of the Parkland Memorial Hospital." I said, "Mark down the time." Of course, since that time until now we have disagreed on about 3 minutes. I said it is 12:38, which would be 1:38 Dallas time. I am sorry—Washington time.

Mr. SPECTER. Was that at the time you were talking to Mr. Behn?

Mr. KELLERMAN. To Mr. Behn; yes, sir.

Mr. SPECTER. And your version is that it is 12:38 Dallas time?

Mr. KELLERMAN. 12:38. He said it was 12:41; he told me the next day.

Mr. SPECTER. May I interrupt you there for you to tell us how long after you arrived at the hospital did you make that telephone call to Mr. Behn, to the best of your recollection?

Mr. KELLERMAN. Three to five minutes.

Mr. SPECTER. All right. The topic we are on now, Mr. Kellerman, is your own way of relating the description of the wounds, starting with four wounds on President Kennedy.

Mr. KELLERMAN. Right; OK.

Mr. SPECTER. Proceed, then.

Mr. KELLERMAN. I can eclipse an awful lot here and get into the morgue here in Bethesda, because that is where I looked him over.

Mr. SPECTER. I will come back and pick up some of the other detail.

Mr. KELLERMAN. Fine.

Mr. SPECTER. But for the sequence at the moment, as it relates to your conclusions on the shots which you have already testified about——

Mr. KELLERMAN. OK.

Mr. SPECTER. I would like to develop your understanding and your observations of the four wounds on President Kennedy.

Mr. KELLERMAN. OK. This all transpired in the morgue of the Naval Hospital in Bethesda, sir. He had a large wound this size.

Mr. SPECTER. Indicating a circle with your finger of the diameter of 5 inches; would that be approximately correct?

Mr. KELLERMAN. Yes, circular; yes, on this part of the head.

Mr. Specter. Indicating the rear portion of the head.

Mr. Kellerman. Yes.

Mr. Specter. More to the right side of the head?

Mr. Kellerman. Right. This was removed.

Mr. Specter. When you say, "This was removed," what do you mean by this?

Mr. Kellerman. The skull part was removed.

Mr. Specter. All right.

Representative Ford. Above the ear and back?

Mr. Kellerman. To the left of the ear, sir, and a little high; yes. About right in here.

Mr. Specter. When you say "removed," by that do you mean that it was absent when you saw him, or taken off by the doctor?

Mr. Kellerman. It was absent when I saw him.

Mr. Specter. Fine. Proceed.

Mr. Kellerman. Entry into this man's head was right below that wound, right here.

Mr. Specter. Indicating the bottom of the hairline immediately to the right of the ear about the lower third of the ear?

Mr. Kellerman. Right. But it was in the hairline, sir.

Mr. Specter. In his hairline?

Mr. Kellerman. Yes, sir.

Mr. Specter. Near the end of his hairline?

Mr. Kellerman. Yes, sir.

Mr. Specter. What was the size of that aperture?

Mr. Kellerman. The little finger.

Mr. Specter. Indicating the diameter of the little finger.

Mr. Kellerman. Right.

Mr. Specter. Now, what was the position of that opening with respect to the portion of the skull which you have described as being removed or absent?

Mr. Kellerman. Well, I am going to have to describe it similar to this. Let's say part of your skull is removed here; this is below.

Mr. Specter. You have described a distance of approximately an inch and a half, 2 inches, below.

Mr. Kellerman. That is correct; about that, sir.

Mr. Specter. All right. What other wounds, if any, did you notice on the President?

Mr. Kellerman. The other wound that I noticed was on his shoulder.

Mr. Specter. Which shoulder.

Mr. Kellerman. Right shoulder.

Mr. Specter. And was it—what was its general position with respect to the breadth of the back?

Mr. Kellerman. Right straight.

Mr. Specter. No. Upper shoulder, lower shoulder; how far below the lower neckline would you say?

Mr. Kellerman. The upper neckline, sir, in that large muscle between the shoulder and the neck, just below it.

Mr. Specter. What was the size of that opening?

Mr. Kellerman. Again about the size of a little finger.

Mr. Specter. Now, have you described three wounds which you have observed?

Mr. Kellerman. That is three. The fourth one I will have to collaborate with—the medical people in Dallas said that he had entry in the throat or an exit.

Mr. Specter. Now, you are indicating a part on the throat right underneath your tie as you sit there, the knot of your tie.

Mr. Kellerman. Yes, sir.

Mr. Specter. Who told you that?

Mr. Kellerman. This comes from a report from Dr. Kemp Clark.

Mr. Specter. Did you talk to Dr. Clark personally?

Mr. Kellerman. I did not. This is a written report.

Mr. Specter. This is a written report which you have read?

Mr. Kellerman. Yes; that is right.

Mr. SPECTER. Do you have any knowledge of that wound on the front side aside from the written report of Dr. Kemp Clark?

Mr. KELLERMAN. Except that in the morgue it was very visible that they had incisioned him here to insert the tracheotomy that they performed on him.

Mr. SPECTER. So with the operative procedures to perform a tracheotomy, was there anything, in your view, left of the original entry?

Mr. KELLERMAN. No.

Mr. SPECTER. Entry or exit that you have described.

Mr. KELLERMAN. No, sir.

Mr. SPECTER. All you could see at that point was the operative procedure, the cutting of the surgeon's blade in Dallas?

Mr. KELLERMAN. That is right.

Senator COOPER. You are saying this, then, that you did not see, yourself, at any time the mark of any wound in his neck front?

Mr. KELLERMAN. When we took him into the hospital in Dallas; that is right.

Senator COOPER. What?

Mr. KELLERMAN. That is right; when we took him in the hospital in Dallas, I did not.

Senator COOPER. Did you ever see it?

Mr. KELLERMAN. Only after he was opened up in the morgue; yes, sir.

Senator COOPER. You saw some indication or some mark of a wound in the front of his neck?

Mr. KELLERMAN. Senator, from the report of the doctor who worked on him in Dallas, that he enlarged the incision here in his throat to perform that tracheotomy, and I believe in his own statement that that wound was there prior to this incision.

Senator COOPER. I know, but I am asking——

Mr. KELLERMAN. I didn't see it, sir.

Senator COOPER. What you saw yourself?

Mr. KELLERMAN. No; I didn't.

Representative FORD. Was that because Hill had thrown his coat over the President, or just didn't see the skin or the body at the time?

Mr. KELLERMAN. No, sir. When I—that coat was thrown over, sir, to eliminate any gruesome pictures.

Representative FORD. How far over that body? Did it go over the head only or down the chest?

Mr. KELLERMAN. No; the whole coat went all the way down to the waistline, sir.

Mr. SPECTER. You saw the President's face, though, at a later time as you have described?

Mr. KELLERMAN. Yes, thank you. This I had lost track of, to help you out, Mr. Congressman. While he lay on the stretcher in that emergency room his collar and everything is up and I saw nothing in his face to indicate an injury, whether the shot had come through or not. He was clear.

Representative FORD. But while he was on the stretcher in the emergency room you saw his face?

Mr. KELLERMAN. That is right.

Representative FORD. But he had his tie and his collar still——

Mr. KELLERMAN. Still on.

Representative FORD. Still on?

Mr. KELLERMAN. Yes, sir.

Representative FORD. You never saw his neck?

Mr. KELLERMAN. No, sir.

Representative FORD. At that time?

Mr. KELLERMAN. At that time, I did not observe him.

Representative FORD. The only time you saw him was later at the morgue?

Mr. KELLERMAN. Very much, sir.

Mr. SPECTER. Did you observe any blood on the portion of his body in the neck area or anyplace in the front of his body?

Mr. KELLERMAN. I don't recall any.

Mr. SPECTER. Did you observe any hole in the clothing of the President on the front part, in the shirt or tie area?

Mr. KELLERMAN. No, sir.

Mr. SPECTER. From your observation of the wound which you observed in the morgue which you have described as a tracheotomy, would that have been above or below the shirtline when the President was clothed?

Mr. KELLERMAN. It would have been below the shirtline, sir.

Mr. SPECTER. Now, have you described all of the wounds of the President to which you have referred?

Mr. KELLERMAN. Yes, sir.

Mr. SPECTER. Will you describe the three wounds which I believe you said Governor Connally sustained?

Mr. KELLERMAN. I am going to refer to the medical report on Governor Connally, wherein they said one wound was in his right back——

Mr. SPECTER. Indicating the upper shoulder area?

Mr. KELLERMAN. Yes, sir. One went through his wrist.

Mr. SPECTER. Indicating the right wrist.

Mr. KELLERMAN. I am using the numbers, and he was—a missile went into his thigh somewhere.

Mr. SPECTER. Do you know anything about Governor Connally's wounds aside from what you read in the medical report?

Mr. KELLERMAN. No; not personally.

Mr. SPECTOR. Do you have any independent knowledge of which wrist and which thigh, aside from what you read in the medical reports themselves?

Mr. KELLERMAN. Yes, sir; I do, I talked to the Governor several times later, and it is the right wrist, sir.

Mr. SPECTER. It is the right wrist?

Mr. KELLERMAN. Yes, sir.

Mr. SPECTER. And which thigh?

Mr. KELLERMAN. It would be the left one.

Representative FORD. Is this a good point for a recess?

Mr. SPECTER. This is fine.

Representative FORD. We will take a 5-minute break.

(Short recess.)

Representative FORD. The Commission will resume, and will you proceed, Mr. Specter, please?

Mr. SPECTER. Yes sir. One of your last answers was that the position of the wounds on Governor Connally was ascertained from a conversation between you and Governor Connally, as well as from the medical reports themselves. Is that correct?

Mr. KELLERMAN. No; it is really not.

Mr. SPECTER. Then tell us what your basis is for your testimony on Governor Connally's wounds.

Mr. KELLERMAN. I have never conversed with the Governor as to his other wounds outside of his wrist. Your medical report on Governor Connally which indicate the shoulder wound, wrist, and in the thigh.

Mr. SPECTER. When did you have occasion to talk to him about his wrist wound?

Mr. KELLERMAN. Over the holidays in Texas, sir.

Mr. SPECTER. The Christmas holidays?

Mr. KELLERMAN. Yes, sir.

Mr. SPECTER. Have you now told us everything you know, either from conversations or reports, about the wounds of Governor Connally?

Mr. KELLERMAN. That is right; yes, sir.

Mr. SPECTER. All right. Were you able to observe at the time of the shooting and immediately thereafter, as Governor Connally went into the hospital, any of his specific wounds?

Mr. KELLERMAN. Only the—I am presuming now of the hand because, when he was lying, he had it across his stomach here, and it was rather bloody.

Mr. SPECTER. And was it the hand that was bloody, the stomach, or both?

Mr. KELLERMAN. I would say so right now; yes.

Mr. SPECTER. Which?

Mr. KELLERMAN. The hand.

Mr. SPECTER. Was the stomach bloody at all?

Mr. KELLERMAN. Not that I remember.

Mr. SPECTER. Do you have anything to add, Mr. Kellerman, on the total number of wounds in relationship to your view that there were more than three shots?

Mr. KELLERMAN. Well, let's consider the vehicle.

Mr. SPECTER. Fine. What about the vehicle would you consider relevant in this regard?

Mr. KELLERMAN. The windshield itself, which I observed a day or two after the funeral here, had been hit by a piece of this missile or missiles, whatever it is, shell.

Mr. SPECTER. While you are referring to the windshield, permit me to hand you a photograph marked Commission Exhibit 349 and ask if you can tell us what that photograph depicts?

Mr. KELLERMAN. This photograph is the windshield of the Presidential special automobile that we used in Dallas on November 22. And it depicts a hit by some instrument on the metal railing that covers the windshield.

Mr. SPECTER. In what position is the hit on that metal railing?

Mr. KELLERMAN. Directly to the right of the mirror.

Mr. SPECTER. Is that on the top of the windshield?

Mr. KELLERMAN. That is on the top of the windshield. I am sorry; this is not the windshield itself; this is the top of the vehicle. This is the framework.

Mr. SPECTER. Would you draw a red arrow with the pen that you have to the mark which you have just described?

(Mr. Kellerman marked the photograph.)

Mr. SPECTER. Now, when did you first observe that indentation?

Mr. KELLERMAN. This was observed a day or two after the funeral, which funeral was the 25th of November; this would be upward of the 27th.

Mr. SPECTER. Where was the automobile at the time you observed that indentation?

Mr. KELLERMAN. At the White House garage, sir.

Mr. SPECTER. Was the windshield in the automobile at that time?

Mr. KELLERMAN. Yes, sir; it was in the automobile.

Mr. SPECTER. Did you observe or notice that indentation in the windshield when you were in Dallas after the shooting occurred?

Mr. KELLERMAN. No, sir.

Mr. SPECTER. Did you observe or notice that indentation before the shooting occurred?

Mr. KELLERMAN. No, sir.

Mr. SPECTER. Are you able to state positively whether or not that indentation was present before the shooting?

Mr. KELLERMAN. No, sir.

Mr. SPECTER. So that you observed it on the first occasion when you saw the car in the White House garage on or about November 27; is that correct?

Mr. KELLERMAN. That is correct, sir.

Mr. SPECTER. The indentation could conceivably have been present before the shooting?

Mr. KELLERMAN. It could have; yes.

Mr. SPECTER. But you didn't observe it before the shooting?

Mr. KELLERMAN. I did not.

Mr. SPECTER. And did you not observe it in Dallas after the shooting?

Mr. KELLERMAN. That is right; I did not.

Mr. SPECTER. Did you have any occasion to examine closely the windshield area after the assassination in Dallas?

Mr. KELLERMAN. No, sir.

Mr. SPECTER. Did you have any occasion to examine closely the windshield at any time after the assassination until you saw the car in the garage on or about November 27?

Mr. KELLERMAN. No, sir; I have not.

Mr. SPECTER. Would you describe for the record where that indentation occurs or is placed?

Mr. KELLERMAN. This indentation is placed on the metal-bar framework which is across the top of the windshield. The indentation is directly to the right of the mirror holder.

Mr. SPECTER. Is that on the inside or the outside of the car?

Mr. KELLERMAN. This is on the inside of the car.

Representative FORD. What prompted you to make that investigation on or about November 27?

Mr. KELLERMAN. First, Mr. Congressman, I wanted to look this car over for— let me go back a little bit. When this car was checked over that night for its return to Washington, I was informed the following day of the pieces of these missiles that were found in the front seat, and I believe aside from the skull, that was in the rear seat, I couldn't conceive even from elevation how this shot hit President Kennedy like it did. I wanted to view this vehicle, whether this was a slant blow off the car, whether it hit the car first and then hit him, or what other marks are on this vehicle, and that is what prompted me to go around and check it over myself.

Representative FORD. Had anybody told you of this indentation prior to your own personal investigation?

Mr. KELLERMAN. Not of the windshield; no, sir.

Representative FORD. You were the first one to find this indentation?

Mr. KELLERMAN. I believe I am the first one who noticed this thing up on the bar.

Representative FORD. That is what I meant.

Mr. KELLERMAN. Yes, sir.

Representative FORD. You are the first one to notice this particular indentation?

Mr. KELLERMAN. Yes; I believe I am, sir.

Representative FORD. All right.

Mr. SPECTER. Did you have occasion to examine the windshield or the framework closely before the assassination, either in Dallas or in Washington?

Mr. KELLERMAN. No; I honestly didn't.

Mr. SPECTER. Mr. Chairman, I move for the admission to evidence of Exhibit No. 349.

Representative FORD. It will be so admitted.

(The document referred to, heretofore marked Commission Exhibit No. 349 for identification, was received in evidence.)

Mr. SPECTER. Now I hand to Mr. Kellerman, through the Chairman, Commission Exhibit No. 350, and ask you to describe what this picture represents?

Mr. KELLERMAN. This picture represents the windshield of the President's special automobile as we are looking into it. This is an outside photo. My reason for this is that on inspection there is a—the windshield has been struck by an instrument and it has been cracked. This crack is opposite the mirror— facing the driver would be toward the right of the mirror, and——

Mr. SPECTER. The photograph, Exhibit 350, is from the outside of the car front looking toward the car; correct?

Mr. KELLERMAN. Yes, sir.

Mr. SPECTER. What mark, if any, appears in the photograph on the windshield itself?

Mr. KELLERMAN. There is the cracked windshield located to the right of the mirror as you look into the automobile.

Mr. SPECTER. That would be on the driver's side, as you previously stated?

Mr. KELLERMAN. Yes, sir; on the driver's side of the vehicle.

Mr. SPECTER. Now, is this picture an accurate representation of the appearance of the windshield at some time when you observed the windshield?

Mr. KELLERMAN. This windshield I observed on this same day.

Mr. SPECTER. On or about November 27, 1963?

Mr. KELLERMAN. That is correct.

Mr. SPECTER. Does that picture accurately represent what the windshield looked like on that day when you observed it?

Mr. KELLERMAN. Yes, sir; it is.

Mr. SPECTER. Did you observe any crack in the windshield as the President's automobile was being driven from the point of assassination to the hospital?

Mr. KELLERMAN. I did not.

Mr. SPECTER. Did you observe it at any time prior to the time you saw the automobile in the White House garage on or before November 27?

Mr. KELLERMAN. I did not, sir.

Mr. SPECTER. Did you have any occasion to examine closely the windshield after the time of the shooting up until the time you saw it in the White House garage?

Mr. KELLERMAN. No, sir.

Mr. SPECTER. Now, at the time of your examination of the windshield in the White House garage, did you feel the windshield?

Mr. KELLERMAN. On the day that I visited the White House garage and checked this car over for my own personal reasons, and this windshield crack was pointed out to me, I did——

Mr. SPECTER. When you say it was pointed out to you, by whom?

Mr. KELLERMAN. There were other people in the garage, Mr. Specter, like Mr. Kinney, I believe was there at the time, Special Agent Henry Rybka was the other person.

Mr. SPECTER. Was it sufficiently prominent without having to have it pointed out specially?

Mr. KELLERMAN. Oh, yes; very much. And I felt this windshield both inwardly and outwardly to determine first if there was something that was struck from the back of us or—and I was satisfied that it was.

Mr. SPECTER. When you say struck from in back of you, do you mean on the inside or outside of the windshield?

Mr. KELLERMAN. Inside, sir.

Mr. SPECTER. Inside of the car?

Mr. KELLERMAN. Right.

Mr. SPECTER. Did you have occasion to feel the outside of the windshield?

Mr. KELLERMAN. I did on that day; yes, sir.

Mr. SPECTER. What did you feel, if anything?

Mr. KELLERMAN. Not a thing; it was real smooth.

Mr. SPECTER. Did you have occasion to feel the inside of the windshield?

Mr. KELLERMAN. I did.

Mr. SPECTER. How did that feel to you?

Mr. KELLERMAN. My comparison was that the broken glass, broken windshield, there was enough little roughness in there from the cracks and split that I was positive, or it was my belief, that whatever hit it came into the inside of the car.

Mr. SPECTER. I move for the admission into evidence of Exhibit No. 350.

Representative FORD. It will be so admitted.

(The document referred to, heretofore marked Commission Exhibit No. 350 for identification, was received in evidence.)

Mr. SPECTER. I now call the attention of the Commission to Exhibit No. 351, which is the windshield itself which, as the Commission may observe, is present in the hearing room. Now, with reference to Exhibit No. 351, which is a marking placed over a glass object, Mr. Kellerman, can you describe for the Commission what that is?

Mr. KELLERMAN. Yes; this windshield, which has since been removed from the vehicle, at the time I first viewed it, this area marked in here was all that was cracked. These are later splints.

Mr. SPECTER. Before you proceed, Mr. Kellerman, do you have knowledge as to the general removal procedure during which this windshield was taken from the President's car?

Mr. KELLERMAN. I believe I do not. However, I believe Mr. Greer would be able to identify it better than I, on the removal side.

Mr. SPECTER. Would you describe the condition of the windshield in its present state as we are viewing it here this morning?

Mr. KELLERMAN. The windshield this morning has—has been hit by some object with sufficient force——

Mr. SPECTER. Perhaps we ought to start with the point of impact. Mr. Kellerman. First, are you able to positively identify this as the windshield from the President's automobile?

Mr. KELLERMAN. Yes, sir; I would say it was, sir.

Mr. SPECTER. Is this the same windshield as depicted in Exhibits 349 and 350?

Mr. KELLERMAN. Yes, sir.

Mr. SPECTER. All right. Now, starting with the principal point of impact, where does that exist on this windshield?

Mr. KELLERMAN. The principal point of impact is located to the left of the mirror, to the right above the driver's head, and to the right of his, I am going to say, view line.

Mr. SPECTER. As we view the windshield at this time, state whether or not there are spidering lines which have emanated from that point which you have described as the principal point of impact?

Mr. KELLERMAN. The spidering lines which extend in three different directions—you are speaking of the large ones or the others?

Mr. SPECTER. Well, I want to put on this record all of the spidering lines which exist here.

Mr. KELLERMAN. OK; the spidering lines which are in this encircled area reflect, in my opinion, that when the instrument hit this glass it shattered in half a dozen different ways.

Mr. SPECTER. Well now, with respect to the cracks themselves, is there a crack which goes in a generally upwardly direction slanting off in the general direction of the driver?

Mr. KELLERMAN. In the center of this, the impact of the center of this scratch, one goes directly to the top of the windshield.

Mr. SPECTER. On that line itself, is there a further splintering off of that line at another point?

Mr. KELLERMAN. It then continues on a small leg, a straight leg, about 3 inches from the original direction.

Mr. SPECTER. And is there a change of direction at that point, or a bifurcation, dividing it into two parts?

Mr. KELLERMAN. No.

Mr. SPECTER. Well, you have described in a generally upwardly direction of about 3 inches?

Mr. KELLERMAN. Yes.

Mr. SPECTER. And is there not a crack which then extends all the way to the top of the windshield moving, in the direction of the left side of the windshield from the driver facing it?

Mr. KELLERMAN. That is right. There is a complete crack from this so-called cutoff to the top right of the windshield right above the view line of the driver.

Mr. SPECTER. Taking that from a compass reading, would that be in a generally northeasterly direction?

Mr. KELLERMAN. Yes, sir; northeasterly.

Mr. SPECTER. All right. From a point 3 inches from the center crack, which we described as the principal point of impact, then, does there form a point of crack in a V-direction with the line you have already described?

Mr. KELLERMAN. Yes; there does. There is a small splint, about 2 inches, that heads directly north off from this splinter that goes in a northeasterly direction.

Mr. SPECTER. All right. Now, moving in a clockwise direction.

Mr. KELLERMAN. In a clockwise direction.

Mr. SPECTER. What crack do you observe, if any?

Mr. KELLERMAN. I next observe on the eastward side of this center crack a splint of about 3 inches long, which then makes a sharp veer to the southeast to the bottom of the windshield.

Mr. SPECTER. Now, moving further in a clockwise direction, what crack do you next observe emanating from the central point of impact?

Mr. KELLERMAN. The next crack from the central point of impact extends down about 3 inches, to the southeast, and then veers to a sharp southeast to the bottom of the windshield.

Mr. SPECTER. Now, moving further in a clockwise direction.

Mr. KELLERMAN. From this point——

Mr. SPECTER. Let's continue to move from the central point of impact to finish up what divergent cracks there are from the central point of impact. Is there one other?

Mr. KELLERMAN. There is one other point left. This is completely in a westerly direction about 3 inches from the center of impact, which then veers to the northwest to the top of the windshield.

Mr. SPECTER. Are there other cracks in the windshield?

Mr. KELLERMAN. There is one other splint, which is from the southeasterly leg——

Mr. SPECTER. That would be southwesterly leg.

Mr. KELLERMAN. Southwesterly leg—I am sorry—that drops to within an inch of the bottom of the windshield, whereby another splint travels in a northwesterly direction to about halfway of the windshield.

Mr. SPECTER. Now, have you described all of the visible cracks in the windshield?

Mr. KELLERMAN. That has completed it, sir.

Mr. SPECTER. As you have viewed this windshield, have you looked at it from the outside looking in or the inside looking out?

Mr. KELLERMAN. I have been looking from the outside looking in.

Mr. SPECTER. Where you would have been if you had been, say, on the front hood of the car when the windshield was in place on the automobile?

Mr. KELLERMAN. I would have been—pardon?

Mr. SPECTER. On the hood of the car?

Mr. KELLERMAN. On the hood of the car this would have been facing me as it is sitting here today.

Mr. SPECTER. Have there been any measures taken to protect the outer edges of this windshield in its position here in the hearing room?

Mr. KELLERMAN. Yes. A form of protective tape has been placed around the entire windshield to protect it, to keep it intact.

Mr. SPECTER. Are there any differences in the cracks on the windshield today as it sits in our hearing room from its condition when you observed it on or about November 27, 1963?

Mr. KELLERMAN. Yes, sir. From the point of impact the four cracks that looked in the four directions were the only ones on this windshield.

Mr. SPECTER. Is there any marking in color or otherwise on that piece of the windshield?

Mr. KELLERMAN. There has been a yellow crayon marking the circumference of these four cracks, apparently before the windshield was removed from the automobile.

Mr. SPECTER. Is that yellow or red?

Mr. KELLERMAN. It is red.

Mr. SPECTER. Were the cracks present within the circumference of that marking present at the time you observed the windshield on or about November 27?

Mr. KELLERMAN. Yes, sir.

Mr. SPECTER. Were any of the other marks present when you observed the windshield on or about November 27?

Mr. KELLERMAN. No, sir.

Mr. SPECTER. Would you at this time feel the outside of the windshield and describe what, if anything, you feel at the point of impact?

Mr. KELLERMAN. The outside markings from the point of impact, the extended lines——

Mr. SPECTER. Mr. Kellerman, I would like for you at this time to actually touch the outside and tell me, first of all, if it is the same or if it differs in any way from the sense of feel which you noted when you touched it on or about November 27?

Mr. KELLERMAN. As I touch the outside on the impact, it would be the same as I noticed on the 27th of November.

Mr. SPECTER. What do you notice, if anything?

Mr. KELLERMAN. It is a smooth surface without any——

Mr. SPECTER. Without any—finish your answer.

Mr. KELLERMAN. On the inside.

Mr. SPECTER. No; before. It is a smooth surface without any what?

Mr. KELLERMAN. Without any crack lines.

Mr. SPECTER. On the outside?

Mr. KELLERMAN. That can be felt.

Mr. SPECTER. On the outside?

Mr. KELLERMAN. That is right; on the outside of the windshield.

Mr. SPECTER. Feel the inside and tell us, first of all, whether it is the same or different from the way you touched it on November 27?

Mr. KELLERMAN. On November 27, when I felt the inside of this impact area, I was convinced that I could—that I felt an opening in one of these lines, which was indicative to me that the blow was struck from the inside of the car on this windshield.

Mr. SPECTER. Does it feel the same to you today as it did on or about November 27?

Mr. KELLERMAN. As a matter of fact, it feels rather smooth today.

Mr. SPECTER. It feels somewhat differently today than it felt before?

Mr. KELLERMAN. Yes; it does.

Representative FORD. Could we ask when the red circle was placed on the windshield, if you know?

Mr. KELLERMAN. I do not know.

Mr. SPECTER. With respect to the shattering which existed on or about November 27, which is within the red circle, could that condition have existed on November 22 after the assassination?

Mr. KELLERMAN. Absolutely not. I don't think so.

Mr. SPECTER. What is the reason for your expressing your thought that it could not have existed?

Mr. KELLERMAN. This automobile is never out of sight of any agent, or even a police officer, before it is used—used or afterward. Let me clarify that. The agent that accompanied these cars to Dallas was with the vehicles from the time they left Washington aboard this plane. One of his many duties outside of keeping it, having this car run perfectly, is that all the equipment is in perfect condition.

Mr. SPECTER. Mr. Kellerman, what you are saying, then, is there had been no crack in the windshield prior to the time of the shooting?

Mr. KELLERMAN. That is correct.

Mr. SPECTER. My next question is: Did you observe any crack in the windshield after the shooting on November 22?

Mr. KELLERMAN. No.

Mr. SPECTER. Did you have any occasion to look for or examine for any crack in the windshield after the shooting?

Mr. KELLERMAN. I had no occasion whatsoever.

Mr. SPECTOR. If the crack in the windshield had been as prominent as it was on or about November 27, 1963, would you have observed it after the shooting on November 22?

Mr. KELLERMAN. No, sir; I don't think I would have.

Senator COOPER. Is it correct then to say that you didn't find any occasion to examine the windshield after you heard the shots?

Mr. KELLERMAN. That is right, I did not have the opportunity.

Mr. SPECTER. And after the President was removed from the automobile, did you ever go back and examine the car, including the windshield?

Mr. KELLERMAN. Not in Dallas; no, sir.

Mr. SPECTER. To be absolutely certain our record is straight on this point, when you observed this windshield on or about November 27, 1963, was the windshield in or out of the car?

Mr. KELLERMAN. It was in the car. This was the same day they were going to remove it.

Mr. SPECTER. Did they remove it later that day, to your knowledge?

Mr. KELLERMAN. Yes; they did, and the mechanics were there.

Mr. SPECTER. Were you there at the time this was removed?

Mr. KELLERMAN. No, sir.

Mr. SPECTER. But the mechanics had arrived preparatory to removing it?

Mr. KELLERMAN. That is right.

Mr. SPECTER. Mr. Kellerman, we intended to describe the windshield in

89

detail prior to your mentioning it, but to go back to your train of thought, you had brought up the windshield in response to my question about whether you had told us everything that you had in mind when you expressed the view that there were more than three shots. Now, remaining on the subject of the windshield, what fact about the windshield was important in your mind when you expressed the view that there must have been more than three shots?

Mr. KELLERMAN. I may be a little—I am not ahead of myself in your investigation of this case, but I think with the evidence that you all have on the numbers, on the pieces of evidence that were found in the car, plus the fact that you have a missile that was received from Dallas, from one of the stretchers, plus the fact of the missile that, to my knowledge, hasn't been removed from Governor Connally—it may have, I don't know—count up to more than three to me, gentlemen.

Mr. SPECTER. All right; fine. But focusing just a moment on the windshield in and of itself, is there any physical factor or characteristic of the windshield other than those already described for the record which has any bearing on your conclusion about the number of shots?

Mr. KELLERMAN. No; it does not.

Mr. SPECTER. Now, moving on to the other pieces of evidence which you have just described, you referred to pieces of evidence in the car. What did you mean when you made that reference, sir?

Mr. KELLERMAN. I have—I was told, although this is a hearsay thing——

Mr. SPECTER. For these purposes, please tell us whatever you are referring to, whatever its source, hearsay or not.

Mr. KELLERMAN. Okay; fine. That when they examined that vehicle that night, when it was brought back to Washington, D.C., two pieces of a bullet or bullets were found on the passenger side on the floor of the front seat.

Mr. SPECTER. Did you observe those?

Mr. KELLERMAN. No, sir.

Mr. SPECTER. Who told you that, or what report?

Mr. KELLERMAN. Mr. Boring—Floyd Boring.

Mr. SPECTER. Who is Mr. Boring?

Mr. KELLERMAN. He is also an assistant special agent in charge.

Mr. SPECTER. Is he currently with the Secret Service?

Mr. KELLERMAN. He is currently with the Secret Service at the White House; yes.

Mr. SPECTER. Were those two pieces of bullet described with more particularity than you have mentioned?

Mr. KELLERMAN. No; they were not.

Mr. SPECTER. Were they described as fragments of bullets as distinguished from whole bullets?

Mr. KELLERMAN. Right, sir.

Mr. SPECTER. But do you have any information as to the size of the fragments?

Mr. KELLERMAN. No; I do not.

Mr. SPECTER. Are there any other pieces of evidence in the car that you were referring to there?

Mr. KELLERMAN. The only other piece of evidence in the car was President Kennedy's skull.

Mr. SPECTER. All right. Do you know what was done with those fragments that Mr. Boring told you about?

Mr. KELLERMAN. No; I don't.

Mr. SPECTER. Do you know whether or not those were turned over to the FBI?

Mr. KELLERMAN. I would say they were probably turned over to the FBI; yes, sir.

Mr. SPECTER. And why would you say they probably were?

Mr. KELLERMAN. Because they were assigned to going over the car.

Mr. SPECTER. Was it their procedure to turn over whatever they found to the FBI?

Mr. KELLERMAN. Oh, yes.

Mr. SPECTER. Now, is there anything special in the nature of the skull which you just mentioned which would have any bearing on the number of shots fired in this assassination?

Mr. KELLERMAN. No, but it would be one shell, one shot.

Mr. SPECTER. That would be your conclusion?

Mr. KELLERMAN. That would be my conclusion.

Mr. SPECTER. That it would take one shot to have separated that portion of skull?

Mr. KELLERMAN. Yes, sir.

Mr. SPECTER. You mentioned a missile found on a stretcher in Dallas. Will you elaborate on what you were referring to there?

Mr. KELLERMAN. This was given, I believe, in your statements there, to a Special Agent Johnsen. I haven't seen this missile.

Mr. SPECTER. Are you referring there to the missile which was found on the stretcher and to the sequence of events from which it was traced back to one of the two victims of this shooting?

Mr. KELLERMAN. Yes, sir.

Mr. SPECTER. Do you have any more knowledge about that other than that which you have already mentioned?

Mr. KELLERMAN. No; I do not.

Mr. SPECTER. You mentioned a missile which was not removed from Governor Connally. Specifically, what did you refer to there?

Mr. KELLERMAN. There was in the early—this was on the day in Parkland Memorial Hospital, and this information comes from Dr. George Burkley, the President's physician, when, I believe, I asked him the condition of Governor Connally, and have they removed the bullet from him.

Mr. SPECTER. What did Dr. Burkley say?

Mr. KELLERMAN. Dr. Burkley said that to his knowledge he still has the bullet in him.

Mr. SPECTER. And at what time on November 22 was that?

Mr. KELLERMAN. This was after we got into the hospital after the shooting, sir, between then and 2 o'clock.

Mr. SPECTER. So that the operation on Governor Connally had not been completed at that point?

Mr. KELLERMAN. That is correct, sir.

Mr. SPECTER. Do you have any additional knowledge about any bullet in Governor Connally?

Mr. KELLERMAN. I do not.

Mr. SPECTER. Have you now told us about all of the facts which you took into account in your conclusion that there were more than three shots?

Mr. KELLERMAN. Yes, sir.

Mr. SPECTER. Do you have anything to add, Mr. Kellerman, by way of explanation or elaboration, to tell us which might be helpful with respect to your conclusion based on all of these items which you have described to us that there were more than three shots?

Mr. KELLERMAN. Gentlemen, I think if you would view the films yourself you may come up with a little different answer.

Mr. SPECTER. Well, have you viewed the films, Mr. Kellerman?

Mr. KELLERMAN. I have; yes, sir.

Mr. SPECTER. Was there something special in your viewing of the films which led you to believe that there were more than three shots?

Mr. KELLERMAN. No; it doesn't point out more than three shots, sir.

Mr. SPECTER. Which films are you referring to?

Mr. KELLERMAN. These are the colored ones that were taken on the right side.

Mr. SPECTER. Taken by Mr. Abraham Zapruder?

Mr. KELLERMAN. I don't know.

Mr. SPECTER. You are not familiar with the photographer?

Mr. KELLERMAN. No; I am not.

Mr. SPECTER. Well, can you describe the view you say is from the right-hand side of the automobile?

Mr. KELLERMAN. That is right.

Mr. SPECTER. So that would be on the side of the road where the Texas School Book Depository Building was?

Mr. KELLERMAN. Yes, sir.

Mr. SPECTER. And approximately where did those pictures begin and end?

Mr. KELLERMAN. These pictures began as we turned off Houston Street onto Elm.

Mr. SPECTER. And where did they end?

Mr. KELLERMAN. As we are, just before we are, going into the viaduct.

Mr. SPECTER. Were those black and white or in color?

Mr. KELLERMAN. No; they were colored.

Mr. SPECTER. Have you seen any other films of the assassination?

Mr. KELLERMAN. Yes; I saw a black-and-white, but I didn't—I saw a black-and-white film. However, I didn't get enough out of it there to——

Mr. SPECTER. Before proceeding any further, I would like to move for the introduction in evidence of Exhibit 351.

Representative FORD. It is approved.

(The windshield referred to was marked Commission Exhibit No. 351 for identification and was received in evidence.)

Mr. SPECTER. Do you have anything at all to add which you think might be helpful, Mr. Kellerman, on the question of how many shots were fired, or have you told us everything you have in mind on that question?

Mr. KELLERMAN. I believe I have, Mr. Specter.

Senator COOPER. What was the name of the special agent driving the car—the President's car?

Mr. KELLERMAN. William Greer.

Senator COOPER. He was the one to whom you spoke when you heard the report?

Mr. KELLERMAN. Yes, sir.

Senator COOPER. Has he ever expressed any opinion to you as to the number of shots that were fired?

Mr. KELLERMAN. No, sir. I think we are all of the opinion, Senator, that we know of three.

Mr. SPECTER. Mr. Kellerman, referring to Commission Exhibit No. 347, will you pinpoint as precisely as you can on that aerial shot, aerial picture, where the President's car was at the time of the first shot? And mark that, if you would, please, with an "X" in red pencil.

Mr. KELLERMAN. My guess would be right in here, sir.

Mr. SPECTER. Now, would you mark as closely as you can where the President's car was at the time of the second shot and mark that with a "Y" in red.

(Mr. Kellerman marking the picture.)

Mr. SPECTER. Now, you have marked the cars being in approximately the middle of the road; is that accurate, as you recollect it?

Mr. KELLERMAN. That is the general procedure, Mr. Specter; they were traveling in the center of the road.

Mr. SPECTER. Now, with respect to the time of the third shot, would your marking be any different from the "Y" position?

Mr. KELLERMAN. No; it would not.

Mr. SPECTER. Now, from the time of the shooting until the time the automobile arrived at Parkland Hospital, did anyone in the President's car say anything that you have not already told us about?

Mr. KELLERMAN. No, sir.

Mr. SPECTER. Mr. Kellerman, there is a report from the Federal Bureau of Investigation designated "Bureau File No. 105"—I believe there is an "S", although it is somewhat illegible on my copy—"S2555, report of Special Agent Robert P. Gemberling," dated December 10, 1963, which refers to an interview of you by Special Agent Francis X. O'Neill, Jr., and James W. Sibert, in which the following is set forth:

"He"—and this obviously refers to you—"advised that he heard a shot and immediately turned around looking past Governor Connally who was seated directly in back of him, to the President. He observed the President slumped forward and heard him say 'get me to a hospital.' Mr. Kellerman then heard Mrs. Kennedy say, 'Oh, no,' as the President leaned toward her." That is the end of the quotation. My question is: Did you hear him; did you hear President Kennedy say, "Get me to a hospital"?

Mr. KELLERMAN. No, sir.

Mr. SPECTER. Did you hear Mrs. Kennedy say, "Oh, no"?

Mr. KELLERMAN. No, sir.

Mr. SPECTER. Do you have any knowledge or explanation as to why you would have been so quoted in the report of the FBI?

Mr. KELLERMAN. When these two gentlemen talked to me, I don't know where they got those quotes, because the only two things that I told them, they were interested in what I heard from the people in the back seat, and one said "my God, I have been hit," which was President Kennedy, and Mrs. Kennedy said, "What are they doing to you?"

Mr. SPECTER. You were interviewed, however, by Mr. O'Neill and Mr. Sibert on November 22, 1963?

Mr. KELLERMAN. November what?

Mr. SPECTER. November 22.

Mr. KELLERMAN. No. November 22 is when they were in the morgue with me. They interviewed me in the office that—it was around the 27th. This was after the funeral.

Mr. SPECTER. Did they have any conversation with you about these events in the morgue?

Mr. KELLERMAN. Not that I recall, sir.

Mr. SPECTER. Did you have a discussion with either of those gentlemen about anything while you were at the morgue on November 22?

Mr. KELLERMAN. The only thing I can recall discussionwise—I just forget which one it was, one of the two—this was before we even knew that a shell had been found from the hole in the President's shoulder. We couldn't determine what happened to it. They couldn't find it in the morgue; they couldn't find any leeway as to whatever happened to the shell when it hit the President's shoulder; where did it go. So our contention was that while he was on the stretcher in Dallas, and the neurosurgeon was working over him no doubt with pressure on the heart, this thing worked itself out.

Mr. SPECTER. When you say "our contention," what do you mean by that?

Mr. KELLERMAN. One of these agents—I forget which one it was; it could have been Sibert or O'Neill, but I am not sure.

Mr. SPECTER. Did what?

Mr. KELLERMAN. We—our discussion or my discussion.

Mr. SPECTER. You had a discussion and when you say "our contention" by that do you mean that was the conclusion you came to?

Mr. KELLERMAN. Conclusion—that is right, sir—as to where this bullet went into the shoulder and where did it go.

Mr. SPECTER. While you are on that subject, was there any conversation at the time of the autopsy on that matter itself?

Mr. KELLERMAN. Very much so.

Mr. SPECTER. Would you relate to the Commission the nature of that conversation and the parties to it?

Mr. KELLERMAN. There were three gentlemen who were performing this autopsy. A Colonel Finck—during the examination of the President, from the hole that was in his shoulder, and with a probe, and we were standing right alongside of him, he is probing inside the shoulder with his instrument and I said, "Colonel, where did it go?" He said, "There are no lanes for an outlet of this entry in this man's shoulder."

Mr. SPECTER. Did you say anything in response to that?

Mr. KELLERMAN. I said, "Colonel, would it have been possible that while he was on the stretcher in Dallas that it works itself out?" And he said, "Yes."

Mr. SPECTER. Was there any additional conversation between you and Colonel Finck at that time?

Mr. KELLERMAN. Not on that point; no, sir; not on that point.

Mr. SPECTER. Was there any conversation of any sort between you and Colonel Finck which would be helpful to us here?

Mr. KELLERMAN. Well, from Humes, who was the other gentleman out there, from the entry of the skull, from this hole here.

Mr. SPECTER. You are now referring to the hole which you describe being below the missing part of the skull?

Mr. KELLERMAN. Yes, sir; it was confirmed that the entry of the shell here went right through the top and removed that piece of the skull.

Mr. SPECTER. And who confirmed that?

Mr. KELLERMAN. One of the three gentlemen; I don't recall.

Mr. SPECTER. You don't recall which one, but it was one of the three doctors doing the autopsy?

Mr. KELLERMAN. That is right.

Mr. SPECTER. So you are saying it confirmed that the hole that was below the piece of skull that was removed, was the point of entry of the one bullet which then passed up through the head and took off the skull?

Mr. KELLERMAN. Right, sir. That is correct.

Mr. SPECTER. Then that was all done by one bullet, based on what you are telling us at this moment?

Mr. KELLERMAN. That is right.

Mr. SPECTER. From the confirmation that one of the three doctors made?

Mr. KELLERMAN. Yes, sir.

Mr. SPECTER. Now, was there any other conversation between you and Colonel Finck or Commander Humes——

Mr. KELLERMAN. No.

Mr. SPECTER. At that time, which was important on the subject we are discussing?

Mr. KELLERMAN. Actually, from all the X-rays that were taken, and we viewed them all together; when I say "we," I am saying the medical people who were in the morgue at the time, the two Bureau agents, myself, and also Mr. Greer, who was in there with me, naturally, they were looking for pieces of fragmentation of this bullet. There was none; only one piece to my knowledge. That was removed inside above the eye, the right eye.

Mr. SPECTER. You have now told us all about the conversations between you and Colonel Finck and Commander Humes and anyone else at the autopsy which are important on the positions of the hole and the wounds in the head?

Mr. KELLERMAN. Right, sir.

Mr. SPECTER. Did you have any other conversation with either Special Agent O'Neill or Special Agent Sibert of the FBI on November 22, 1963, other than your conversations about the wounds on President Kennedy?

Mr. KELLERMAN. No.

Mr. SPECTER. Mr. Kellerman, while we are discussing this in relationship to your conversations with Special Agents O'Neill and Sibert, were there any other comments made by anybody else present at the autopsy about the path of the bullet into Mr. Kennedy's back, relating to whether there was any point of exit or anything of that sort?

Mr. KELLERMAN. Colonel Finck did all the talking, sir. He was the only one.

Mr. SPECTER. Now, have you told us everything Colonel Finck said about that subject?

Mr. KELLERMAN. Very much so; yes, sir.

Mr. SPECTER. So that there is nothing that was said on that subject other than what you have already told us about?

Mr. KELLERMAN. No; that is right.

Mr. SPECTER. Mr. Kellerman, I have read to you a part of what Special Agents O'Neill and Sibert have attributed to you in an interview which they have written about on November 22, 1963. Referring to that in the portion which I have read to you and which I will reread, I want you to direct your attention to the issue about which way you turned. The report states, "He advised he heard a shot and immediately turned around looking past Governor Connally who was seated directly in back of him to the President."

Now, did that describe a turn to the right or to the left? This is a difficult question. Let me interject one thing. We are presupposing here, based on your testimony, that you did not discuss with Special Agents O'Neill or Sibert these specific events on November 22, to the best of your recollection as we sit here today.

Mr. KELLERMAN. That is right.

Mr. SPECTER. So that the question really goes to a situation where perhaps they have an inaccurate day or your recollection is inaccurate as to some of the things you might have told them. So, my prefatory question would be whether that is an accurate statement and is something you told them at some time.

Mr. KELLERMAN. I don't believe I did. I think I will stand on my original statement.

Representative FORD. The original statement you made here today?

Mr. KELLERMAN. Yes, sir; very much.

Mr. SPECTER. So that the statement I just read to you, so far as your best——

Mr. KELLERMAN. I can't——

Mr. SPECTER. So far as your best testimony is at this time, it was simply not made by you on November 22?

Mr. KELLERMAN. That is right, sir.

Mr. SPECTER. All right, now. Was that statement I just read to you, the short one about your turn, to the best of your recollection at this moment, did you ever make that statement to Special Agents O'Neill and/or Sibert?

Mr. KELLERMAN. Mr. Specter, everybody I have talked to I have always turned to the right when I first heard the noise. I turned to my left to view the people in my back seat because it is a more comfortable position. So I don't think the turning is correct, sir.

Mr. SPECTER. Would you say the report is incorrect?

Mr. KELLERMAN. That is right.

Representative FORD. May I ask—you have viewed these colored motion pictures which were taken during the assassination. Have you looked at those to see what your own actions were during this period of time?

Mr. KELLERMAN. Yes, sir.

Representative FORD. Do they coincide with what you have testified to here today?

Mr. KELLERMAN. They certainly do.

Mr. SPECTER. I now hand you a photograph marked Commission Exhibit No. 352, and ask you if you can tell us what that picture represents?

Mr. KELLERMAN. Yes, sir; this was the rear seat of the President's car, sir, after all the occupants were removed.

Mr. SPECTER. And when did the rear seat of the President's car look like the picture 352?

Mr. KELLERMAN. After all the occupants were removed on the 22d of November.

Mr. SPECTER. When the car was parked at Parkland Hospital?

Mr. KELLERMAN. I don't know where this picture was taken, sir. This could have been taken in the White House garage.

Mr. SPECTER. Yes; but aside from where the picture was taken, is that the way the car looked at the time it was at Parkland Hospital after President Kennedy and Governor Connally were removed from the car?

Mr. KELLERMAN. Yes, sir.

Mr. SPECTER. Will you describe for the written record very briefly what this picture shows?

Mr. KELLERMAN. The picture shows the complete rear seat of the Presidential limousine.

Mr. SPECTER. What, if anything, is on the rear seat?

Mr. KELLERMAN. On the seat part of this car is splattered with blood; there are a few petals of flowers, and the back seat cushion part is pretty well bloodied up.

Mr. SPECTER. I move for the introduction in evidence of Commission Exhibit No. 352.

Representative FORD. So admitted.

(The photograph referred to was marked Commission Exhibit No. 352 for identification, and received in evidence.)

Mr. SPECTER. I now hand you, through the Chairman, Commission Exhibit No. 353, move its admission into evidence, and ask you to tell us what this depicts.

Mr. KELLERMAN. This is the same Presidential vehicle after the occupants have been removed from the rear seat. It shows the—a goodly amount of blood that had remained on the cushion and back part of the seat and also little flower petals.

Mr. SPECTER. Is Exhibit No. 353 an accurate representation of the way the rear seat of the President's automobile looked after——

Mr. KELLERMAN. Yes, sir.

Mr. SPECTER. After President Kennedy and Governor Connally were removed to Parkland Hospital.

Mr. KELLERMAN. Yes, sir; it is.

Mr. SPECTER. You have described in answers to previous questions what occurred upon the arrival at Parkland of the President's automobile. What action, if any, did you take immediately after President Kennedy and Governor Connally were taken into the hospital?

Mr. KELLERMAN. I believe we had got to the point where I had made this phone call to Washington to alert these people back here of the incident.

Mr. SPECTER. And proceeding from that point?

Mr. KELLERMAN. From this point, the agents who were in this followup car had joined me in the emergency room. They took up security posts at entrance into the emergency room to keep it clear of all people except medical people. The only people allowed in there would be workers. After this was done, Special Agent Kinney came to me and asked permission to remove the President's car and our followup car to the airport, to load it aboard this aircraft for shipment to Washington, and I said, "Yes."

At that time the next move was Special Agent Warren Taylor, who was assigned to the then Vice President Johnson, came to me and he said, "Mr. Johnson wants to talk to you." So, I followed him into this room that they had the Johnson party in. He asked me the condition of President Kennedy, which I told him that President Kennedy is still in the emergency room, his condition is serious. He then said, "You let me know of any developments."

I then returned to the emergency room. By that time another shift of agents, who were at the Trade Mart on duty for prior to our arrival, reported into the emergency room. This is what is called as our afternoon shift, the 4 to 12. Mr. Roberts, whose group was on the followup car in the motorcade through Dallas, was the 8-to-4 shift. The 4-to-12 shift then was under the supervision of Mr. Stewart Stout. I then instructed Mr. Roberts to take his shift, which were the day people, and join Special Agent Rufus Youngblood and stay with Vice President Johnson.

Mr. SPECTER. How many agents were they to take with them?

Mr. KELLERMAN. They took the entire followup car, which would mean that they had Roberts, Ready, Bennett, McIntyre; those four.

Mr. SPECTER. Do you know where they went or what specifically they did by way of establishing security for Vice President Johnson?

Mr. KELLERMAN. No; I really don't.

Mr. SPECTER. What was your next activity?

Mr. KELLERMAN. My next move, then, my next part in this was—by this time it was after 1 o'clock—I am trying to pinpoint time—after 1, because Dr. Burkley said that the President had died; it was after 1 o'clock. By this time other people who were in with Mr. Kennedy, such as his staff—I am speaking of Mr. O'Donnell, Mr. Powers, I believe Larry O'Brien—through them, and I believe Mr. Hill, they had obtained a casket from one of the funeral people in town.

Mr. SPECTER. Where had Mrs. Kennedy been during this time?

Mr. KELLERMAN. Mrs. Kennedy was right outside the door to the emergency room.

Mr. SPECTER. How long, if at all, was she inside the emergency room with President Kennedy?

Mr. KELLERMAN. This I can't truly answer. However, I should say that, as for the casket being brought into the hospital, another gentleman came into this little doctor's room, his name I don't recall, but he represented himself to be from the Health Department or commission, some form. He said to me, he said, "There has been a homicide here, you won't be able to remove the body. We will have to take it down there to the mortuary and have an autopsy." I said, "No, we are not." And he said, "We have a law here whereby you have to comply with it."

With that Dr. Burkley walked in, and I said, "Doctor, this man is from some health unit in town. He tells me we can't remove this body." The Doctor be-

96

came a little enraged; he said, "We are removing it." He said, "This is the President of the United States and there should be some consideration in an event like this." And I told this gentleman, I said, "You are going to have to come up with something a little stronger than you to give me the law that this body can't be removed."

So, he frantically called everybody he could think of and he hasn't got an answer; nobody is home. Shortly he leaves this little room and it seems like a few minutes he is back and he has another gentleman with him, and he said. "This is"—the name escapes me—he said, "He is a judge here in Dallas," and he said, "He will tell you whether you can remove this body or not." I said, "It doesn't make any difference. We are going to move it," and I said, "Judge, do you know who I am?"

And he said, "Yes," and I said, "There must be something in your thinking here that we don't have to go through this agony; the family doesn't have to go through this. We will take care of the matter when we get back to Washington." The poor man looked at me and he said, "I know who you are," and he said, "I can't help you out." I said, "All right, sir." But then I happened to look to the right and I can see the casket coming on rollers, and I just left the room and let it out through the emergency entrance and we got to the ambulance and put it in, shut the door after Mrs. Kennedy and General McHugh and Clinton Hill in the rear part of this ambulance.

I am looking around for Mr. Greer and I don't spot him directly because I want to get out of here in a hurry, and I recognize Agent Berger and I said, "Berger, you get in the front seat and drive and, Mr. Stout, you get in the middle and I will get on this side," and as we are leaving—Mr. Lawson. I should say, was in a police car that led us away from Parkland Memorial Hospital. As we are leaving a gentleman taps on the driver's window and they roll it down and he says, "I will meet you at the mortuary." "Yes, sir." We went to the airport, gentlemen.

Mr. SPECTER. Who said, "Yes, sir"?

Mr. KELLERMAN. I did, sir. We went to the airport. In the meantime, Mr. Johnson had been taken to the airplane. They had secured the airport; nobody was there. They had removed seats off the rear part of the plane so we could put the body and the casket in it. As we got to the airport the ramp was there; we opened the door, and we moved the casket out and walked it right up to the plane.

Mr. SPECTER. Was there any further difficulty of any sort——

Mr. KELLERMAN. No.

Mr. SPECTER. Imposed by any Texas officials on the removal of the body?

Mr. KELLERMAN. No, sir. Whatever happened to the hearse, I don't know. I never left the plane.

Mr. SPECTER. Did you observe——

Mr. KELLERMAN. We left the hospital; we have a time on that; it is 4 minutes after 2. It is about a 10-minute ride to the airplane.

Mr. SPECTER. On the question of timing, pinning down these times as best we can, how long did it take you to get from the shooting incident to the time you arrived at Parkland, based on your best estimates?

Mr. KELLERMAN. Mr. Specter, it seemed like hours, but we flew there, I honestly don't know. I can't really tell you.

Mr. SPECTER. What is the best estimate of the speed of your vehicle en route from the shooting to the hospital?

Mr. KELLERMAN. I don't know.

Senator COOPER. Let the record show that Congressman Ford has to go to his official duties in the House and that I, Senator Cooper, am now acting as Chairman.

(At this point, Representative Ford left the hearing room.)

Senator COOPER. Go ahead.

Mr. SPECTER. Moving ahead, then, on to the sequences of time as best you can recollect them, Mr. Kellerman, at what time was it ascertained that the President had died and what was the basis of the pronouncement of death.

Mr. KELLERMAN. That was on the death certificate, sir.

Mr. SPECTER. Did you learn at or about 1 o'clock, while you were at Parkland Hospital, that he had died?

Mr. KELLERMAN. I would think so. However, at that time let me say that I wasn't watching any clock too closely and this time was given to me by Dr. Burkley.

Mr. SPECTER. Then you have no independent recollection of time at Parkland when the death was announced or pronounced?

Mr. KELLERMAN. No.

Mr. SPECTER. Now, then, you have specified the time of departure from Parkland Hospital and en route back to Love Field at what, sir?

Mr. KELLERMAN. We departed at 4 minutes after 2 from Parkland.

Mr. SPECTER. What time did you arrive at the President's plane?

Mr. KELLERMAN. 2:14.

Mr. SPECTER. What were your next activities?

Mr. KELLERMAN. Our next time, we had waited until Judge Sarah Hughes had arrived for the swearing-in ceremonies.

Mr. SPECTER. What time did the swearing-in ceremonies occur?

Mr. KELLERMAN. 2:37 p.m.

Mr. SPECTER. And what time did the plane depart from Dallas?

Mr. KELLERMAN. We left at 2:48.

Mr. SPECTER. Were you present during the swearing-in ceremonies?

Mr. KELLERMAN. Yes, sir.

Mr. SPECTER. In a general way, tell us who else was present there, recognizing that you don't know all the people there.

Mr. KELLERMAN. Yes. President Johnson, Mrs. Johnson, Mrs. Kennedy, Malcolm Kilduff. He was the press secretary for that trip. Congressman Thornberry, Congressman Thomas, Marie Fehmer, Mrs. Evelyn Lincoln, Jack Valenti, Bill Moyers, Special Agent Johns. There was another congressional man—I believe his name was Congressman Roberts—Brooks; I am sorry; Congressman Brooks. The picture was taken by Capt. Cecil Stoughton and myself.

Mr. SPECTER. What time did the President's plane arrive back at the Washington area?

Mr. KELLERMAN. May I look at my notes, sir?

Mr. SPECTER. Yes; you may. Identify for us, if you will, what notes you are referring to.

Mr. KELLERMAN. 5:58 p.m. This is my report.

Mr. SPECTER. Let the record show that Mr. Kellerman has just referred to a four-page report dated November 29, 1963, entitled "The Assassination of President John F. Kennedy on November 22, 1963, at Dallas, Tex.," which is a copy of a report he made, three of the sheets being carbon copies, and one being a photostatic reproduction. So that our record may be complete, let the record show that this is the same report which Mr. Kellerman submitted to the Secret Service which was, in turn, submitted by the Secret Service to the Commission, as one of the statements in Exhibit 12, statement 11, which was furnished by the Secret Service to the Commission as the report of the U.S. Secret Service on the assassination of President Kennedy, under the exhibits section. I will return that to you.

Mr. KELLERMAN. Fine; thank you.

Mr. SPECTER. What were your activities; specifically where did you land in the Washington area?

Mr. KELLERMAN. We landed at Andrews Air Force Base.

Mr. SPECTER. What were your activities then, immediately after landing at Andrews?

Mr. KELLERMAN. While en route from Dallas to Washington, D.C., I had several telephone communications with my special agent in charge, Gerald Behn, concerning this, transportation for the people aboard the plane, an ambulance for the body of President Kennedy, and my instructions. I was instructed to stay with the late President Kennedy. Aboard this plane were agents of the 4-to-12 shift which, as I mentioned earlier, was under the supervision of Mr. Stewart Stout; a conference was held with Mr. Rufus Youngblood, who was in charge of the Johnson detail at that time. He was informed that he would take all the agents under Mr. Stout's supervision and they would remain with them for the remainder of the day. That I would have Special Agents Hill, Landis, Greer, and O'Leary.

As we arrived at Andrews Air Force Base, arrangements were made prior to having a lift brought up to the rear end of the plane, whereby all the agents were requested by Mrs. Kennedy to carry this casket from the plane to the ambulance. It was put aboard this carrier; from there we took it from the carrier into the Navy ambulance. Mrs. Kennedy rode in the back seat, or in the rear part of the ambulance, with Mr. Robert Kennedy and General McHugh.

In the front seat the ambulance was driven by Special Agent Greer, of which Agents Landis and myself and Dr. Burkley rode in the front seat to the U.S. Naval Hospital in Bethesda. At that point Navy officials there instructed us where to take the ambulance, to what part of the building, and remove the casket into the morgue facilities.

As we landed in Andrews Air Force Base, I was met by our Chief, Mr. James Rowley, who informed me that Mr. Sibert and Mr. O'Neill of the FBI would join me at the Naval Hospital and to allow them in. I also informed him that the vehicles—that is, the President's car and our Secret Service followup car—are en route to Washington from Dallas, and that he should assign some members from our Washington field office to go over these cars for any evidence that might be left. In the morgue, I should say that Special Agent Greer and myself remained all night, Mr. O'Leary only briefly.

Mr. SPECTER. Where did the——

Mr. KELLERMAN. The family was placed——

Mr. SPECTER. Where did the family go?

Mr. KELLERMAN. They were placed in a room in the tower section of the Naval Hospital.

Mr. SPECTER. Did you actually accompany the body from the vehicle to the morgue room?

Mr. KELLERMAN. Yes, sir.

Mr. SPECTER. And were you present during the entire autopsy?

Mr. KELLERMAN. Yes, sir.

Mr. SPECTER. Tell us in a general way——

Mr. KELLERMAN. I only left on three different occasions.

Mr. SPECTER. For how long were you absent on those occasions?

Mr. KELLERMAN. A minute or two to make a phone call.

Mr. SPECTER. While the autopsy was in session, or when did you leave on those three occasions?

Mr. KELLERMAN. OK. First I was informed by a Navy personnel that I should call Mr. Rowley. There wasn't any phone—there was a phone in the room, but I wasn't aware of it at the time. So, I left and walked out into the corridor and called him. This was my first knowledge that they had found a projectile. The second call, I think I called home; that was my first call to home and that was it.

Mr. SPECTER. Now, the projectile that you just referred to was found where?

Mr. KELLERMAN. This was the projectile that was reportedly given to our Special Agent Richard Johnsen as we were leaving the hospital in Dallas.

Mr. SPECTER. How did you find out about that?

Mr. KELLERMAN. He says it was given to him by a security man or security officer in the hospital.

Mr. SPECTER. When did you first hear about it?

Mr. KELLERMAN. The phone call with Mr. Rowley that morning after we had got to the morgue.

Mr. SPECTER. What time was this?

Mr. KELLERMAN. I am only guessing; 9 o'clock in the evening.

Mr. SPECTER. Nine o'clock in the evening. You had said morning; you didn't mean morning; you meant 9 o'clock in the evening when you had a telephone call. From whom was the call again?

Mr. KELLERMAN. Mr. Rowley, Chief of Secret Service.

Mr. SPECTER. You got the phone call from Mr. Rowley?

Mr. KELLERMAN. Yes.

Mr. SPECTER. Who had called him, if you know?

Mr. KELLERMAN. This I don't know.

Mr. SPECTER. But at that time Chief Rowley advised of the detection of the bullet on the stretcher and brought you up to date with what information was known at that time?

Mr. KELLERMAN. Yes, sir.

Mr. SPECTER. Now, have you described all the times that you were absent from the room of the autopsy?

Mr. KELLERMAN. The only other time that I was absent was when the autopsy was about completed before the funeral directors were in, and it was my decision to get Mr. Hill down and view this man for all the damage that was done; so I went up to the floor where they were at and brought him down and he inspected the incisions.

Mr. SPECTER. What was your reason for that, Mr. Kellerman?

Mr. KELLERMAN. More witnesses, Mr. Specter; I think more to view the unfortunate happenings it would be a little better.

Mr. SPECTER. What time did that autopsy start, as you recollect it?

Mr. KELLERMAN. Immediately. Immediately after we brought him right in.

Mr. SPECTER. What time was that approximately, if you have a recollection?

Mr. KELLERMAN. I don't have a recollection.

Mr. SPECTER. What time did it end, if you recollect?

Mr. KELLERMAN. We left the hospital for the White House at 3:56 in the morning.

Mr. SPECTER. 3:56 a.m. on November 23?

Mr. KELLERMAN. Yes, sir.

Mr. SPECTER. Did the autopsy last all that time?

Mr. KELLERMAN. No. They were going to give these people a couple of hours that they worked on them.

Mr. SPECTER. Now, did you observe, during the course of the autopsy, bullet fragments which you might describe as little stars?

Mr. KELLERMAN. Yes, of the numerous X-rays that were taken mainly of the skull, the head. The reason for it was that through all the probing which these gentlemen were trying to pick up little pieces of evidence in the form of shell fragments, they were unable to locate any. From the X-rays, when you placed the X-ray up against the light the whole head looked like a little mass of stars, there must have been 30, 40 lights where these pieces were so minute that they couldn't be reached. However, all through this series of X-rays this was the one that they found, through X-ray that was above the right eye, and they removed that.

Mr. SPECTER. How big a piece was that above the right eye, would you say?

Mr. KELLERMAN. The tip of a matchhead, a little larger.

Senator COOPER. Let me ask a few questions. Mr. Kellerman, from what you have just said, I think it would be correct that from the time you began to assist in removing President Kennedy from his car to the time you left him in the emergency room that you never saw any bullet on a stretcher, either his stretcher or Governor Connally's stretcher?

Mr. KELLERMAN. I never saw any bullet, sir.

Senator COOPER. I believe you testified that, at the time you heard this first report, the President's car was approaching a viaduct?

Mr. KELLERMAN. Approaching, yes, but quite a little distance from it, sir.

Senator COOPER. Can you make any estimate as to how far away it was.

Mr. KELLERMAN. I don't know the footage, Senator Cooper.

Senator COOPER. Can you see it?

Mr. KELLERMAN. Yes; oh, yes, sir.

Senator COOPER. Can you see the viaduct plainly?

Mr. KELLERMAN. Oh, yes, sir.

Senator COOPER. Could you tell whether anybody was standing on top of the viaduct, or did you observe?

Mr. KELLERMAN. I didn't notice anybody up there at all, sir.

Senator COOPER. Did you observe whether anyone was in the immediate vicinity of the viaduct?

Mr. KELLERMAN. Not at this distance; no.

Senator COOPER. Do you have any—at the time of the shots, at the time that you were conscious of these shots being fired, do you have any judgment as to from what direction they came?

Mr. KELLERMAN. None whatsoever. Except I should say again that when this first one went off, which I indicated here that it sounded like a firecracker to my right and, say, rear, I looked to my right to see what it was.

Senator COOPER. Then it would be correct to say it was your judgment at the time, at the time of the report——

Mr. KELLERMAN. It was my judgment, sir.

Senator COOPER. That it was to the right and to the rear?

Mr. KELLERMAN. That would be correct. It was my judgment, sir.

Senator COOPER. Did you observe any persons standing to the right of the car?

Mr. KELLERMAN. Maybe a handful.

Senator COOPER. Did you see anything to indicate that any shot had been fired by those persons?

Mr. KELLERMAN. No, sir; not at the time.

Senator COOPER. When you heard the report and turned, could you see this building known as the Texas Book Depository?

Mr. KELLERMAN. Not by name. You could see the building because we passed right in front of it, sir.

Senator COOPER. You didn't know it as the Texas Depository Building?

Mr. KELLERMAN. Not then, no, sir.

Senator COOPER. Have you any idea how—what distance the President's car traveled from the time you heard the first report until the time you have described as hearing the flurry of shots?

Mr. KELLERMAN. No; I really don't know the distance. It wasn't too far.

Senator COOPER. What?

Mr. KELLERMAN. It wasn't too far.

Mr. SPECTER. For the record, I have some more questions when we reconvene.

Senator COOPER. We will recess then until 2 o'clock.

(Whereupon, at 12:35 p.m., the President's Commission recessed.)

Afternoon Session

TESTIMONY OF ROY H. KELLERMAN, SPECIAL AGENT, SECRET SERVICE, RESUMED

The President's Commission reconvened at 2 p.m.

Representative FORD. The Commission will come to order.

Will you proceed, Mr. Specter?

Mr. SPECTER. Yes, thank you. Mr. Kellerman, immediately before the luncheon recess, Senator Cooper had asked some questions relating to the presence of anyone on the triple overpass which was in front of the President's car. Did you have any occasion, immediately before or immediately after the shooting, to look for anyone on the triple overpass or in that vicinity?

Mr. KELLERMAN. No; I really didn't.

Mr. SPECTER. Are you in a position to state, then, whether there was or was not someone on the triple overpass?

Mr. KELLERMAN. No; I am in no position to state that.

Mr. SPECTER. At the time of the shooting, did you observe any bullets richochet off of the windshield or off of any other part of the automobile?

Mr. KELLERMAN. No. If any of the bullets richocheted off the windshield or front part of the car, this would have been matter that was blown over mine and the driver's head from, I would say, the explosion of President Kennedy's head.

Mr. SPECTER. But aside from the portions of President Kennedy's head which you have already testified about, you observed nothing detectable as being bullet fragments or bullets?

101

Mr. KELLERMAN. No, sir.

Mr. SPECTER. Richocheting off any part of the car?

Mr. KELLERMAN. No, sir.

Mr. SPECTER. And did you ever observe any bullet fragments in the car at rest after the shooting?

Mr. KELLERMAN. No, sir.

Mr. SPECTER. Did you observe a priest at Parkland Hospital?

Mr. KELLERMAN. Yes; there were two.

Mr. SPECTER. And approximately what time were they present at the hospital?

Mr. KELLERMAN. When we brought President Kennedy into the emergency room, the request for a priest was made immediately by one of the members of the staff. I do not recall who called for one. However, in the interim, a second call was sent out. Consequently, two showed; not at the same time, but one after the other.

Mr. SPECTER. How long were they at the hospital?

Mr. KELLERMAN. Just a matter of a couple of minutes of time.

Mr. SPECTER. And do you know where they went upon arrival at the hospital?

Mr. KELLERMAN. Yes, sir. They went right in the emergency room with the President.

Mr. SPECTER. Were you in the emergency room at the time they were there?

Mr. KELLERMAN. No, sir.

Mr. SPECTER. And do you know what services, if any, they performed while they were there?

Mr. KELLERMAN. No, sir.

Mr. SPECTER. Did you have any conversations with either of them while they were en route, either coming or going?

Mr. KELLERMAN. No, sir.

Mr. SPECTER. With respect to the state of readiness of Parkland Hospital at your arrival, how long after you got there were stretcher bearers at the front door?

Mr. KELLERMAN. To the best of my knowledge, there were no stretcher bearers at the car—none.

Mr. SPECTER. At your arrival?

Mr. KELLERMAN. Yes, sir.

Mr. SPECTER. Did some come shortly after you arrived?

Mr. KELLERMAN. No, sir.

Mr. SPECTER. Well, what sequence did follow with respect to the arrival of the stretchers?

Mr. KELLERMAN. When we arrived at the hospital, I had called to the agents to go inside and get two stretchers on wheels. Between those people and police officers who also entered the emergency room, they brought the stretchers out. I did not at any time see a man in a white uniform outside, indicating a medical person.

Mr. SPECTER. When did you first see the first indication of a doctor?

Mr. KELLERMAN. When we got in the emergency room itself proper.

Mr. SPECTER. And do you know which doctor that was?

Mr. KELLERMAN. Not by name or sight; no, sir.

Mr. SPECTER. How many doctors did you see at that time?

Mr. KELLERMAN. The room was full.

Mr. SPECTER. Who were the individuals who brought the stretchers on wheels if you know?

Mr. KELLERMAN. Agents who were in the followup car, police officers who were ahead of us on motorcycles.

Mr. SPECTER. Mr. Kellerman, did you state how long the autopsy lasted when you testified this morning?

Mr. KELLERMAN. No; I didn't. However, this is going to be an assumption on time; I think I can pin it pretty well.

Mr. SPECTER. Give us your best estimate on that, please.

Mr. KELLERMAN. Let's come back to the period of our arrival at Andrews Air Force Base, which was 5:58 p.m. at night. By the time it took us to take the body from the plane into the ambulance, and a couple of carloads of staff people who followed us, we may have spent 15 minutes there. And in driving from

Andrews to the U.S. Naval Hospital, I would judge, a good 45 minutes. So there is 7 o'clock. We went immediately over, without too much delay on the outside of the hospital, into the morgue. The Navy people had their staff in readiness right then. There wasn't anybody to call. They were all there. So at the latest, 7:30, they began to work on the autopsy. And, as I said, we left the hospital at 3:56 in the morning. Let's give the undertaker people 2 hours. So they were through at 2 o'clock in the morning. I would judge offhand that they worked on the autopsy angle 4½, 5 hours.

Mr. SPECTER. And were you present when the funeral director's personnel were preparing the body?

Mr. KELLERMAN. I was; yes, sir.

Mr. SPECTER. And about what time, then, did they complete their work?

Mr. KELLERMAN. They were all through at 3:30.

Mr. SPECTER. And what did you do immediately after they completed their work?

Mr. KELLERMAN. All right. Our communication between the Kennedy family and staff, who were on another floor in the hospital, was in this regard. We had telephone communication whereby we would tell them if the body is ready to be taken out of the morgue and into the ambulance. And they would hit the elevator and come right out the same way. So the 5 minutes it took to load the people in, we left the hospital morgue part at least at 3:50, and, as I say, we were off at 3:56, driving to the White House.

Mr. SPECTER. And did you go directly to the White House?

Mr. KELLERMAN. Yes, sir; we did.

Mr. SPECTER. Did that complete your tour of duty for that day?

Mr. KELLERMAN. Yes, sir; it did.

Mr. SPECTER. Now, with respect to the time you were present at the autopsy, was there any conversation of any sort concerning the possibility of a point of entry from the front of the President's body?

Mr. KELLERMAN. No.

Mr. SPECTER. You have testified about the impression you had as to the source of the first shot, which sounded to you like a firecracker. Did you have any impression as to the source of the other shots, which you described as being a flurry?

Mr. KELLERMAN. If you will excuse me just a minute. I was trying to elaborate on the last question.

Mr. SPECTER. Pardon me. Go ahead.

Mr. KELLERMAN. Just for the record, I wish to have this down. While the President is in the morgue, he is lying flat. And with the part of the skull removed, and the hole in the throat, nobody was aware until they lifted him up that there was a hole in his shoulder. That was the first concrete evidence that they knew that the man was hit in the back first.

Mr. SPECTER. When did they lift him up and first observe the hole in the shoulder?

Mr. KELLERMAN. They had been working on him for quite some time, Mr. Specter—through the photos and other things they do through an autopsy. And I believe it was this Colonel Finck who raised him and there was a clean hole.

Mr. SPECTER. What was said, if anything, by those present at the autopsy concerning the wound in the throat?

Mr. KELLERMAN. To go back just a little further, the reason for the hole in the throat, the tracheotomy; I am thinking they were of the opinion that when the—when he was shot in the head, and they had found this piece remaining above the eye underneath; I am sure there was some concern as to where the outlet was, and whether they considered—this is all an assumption now; whether they considered this—that there was a hole here in the throat prior to the tracheotomy. I don't know. But to complete the examination, they lifted him up by the shoulders, and there was this hole. Now, I think you asked me a question. Could you repeat it, please?

Mr. SPECTER. Well, let's be sure that we have your final answer on the question of any conversation at all about a point of entry in the front part of his body, in his throat, or any place else.

103

Mr. KELLERMAN. I don't believe, Mr. Specter, that it was ever concluded that there was an entry in the front.

Mr. SPECTER. Then that completes the conversations at the autopsy?

Mr. KELLERMAN. Yes, sir.

Mr. SPECTER. On any of the subjects I have asked you about?

Mr. KELLERMAN. Right.

Mr. SPECTER. The question which I had then started to ask you was whether you had any impression at the time of the second and third shots, which you described as a flurry of shots, as to the point of origin or source of those shots.

Mr. KELLERMAN. The only answer I can give to that is that they would have to come from the rear.

Mr. SPECTER. Well, is that the impression or reaction you had at the time of the flurry?

Mr. KELLERMAN. That is right, sir.

Mr. SPECTER. Have you ever, since the time of the assassination to this date, had any contrary impression, reaction, or view that the shots came from the front of the President?

Mr. KELLERMAN. No.

Mr. SPECTER. Now, Mr. Kellerman, with respect to the immediate reaction by you to the emergency situation, did you consider at any time leaving your seat, on the right front of the President's automobile, to go into the rear portion, where the President sat?

Mr. KELLERMAN. No, sir.

Mr. SPECTER. And what is the basis for—or what was the basis for your conclusion on that?

Mr. KELLERMAN. After I had heard President Kennedy's voice say, "My God, I am hit," I viewed him, which was enough for me that he was. My decision was to get this man to a hospital, because he needed medical treatment. And during the few seconds that I instructed the driver to get out of here, we are hit, my second instruction was to the man in the lead car ahead of us for the same, to lead us to a hospital, that we are hit. I then turn around, and I had two people injured. Not only was the President down in his seat; the Governor was down in his seat. My presence back there was gone. On top of that, I had Mr. Hill lying across that trunk.

Mr. SPECTER. What do you mean when you say, sir, that your presence back there was gone?

Mr. KELLERMAN. They were comfortable. if there is a comfort in this. Mr. Hill was taking care of Mrs. Kennedy. Mrs. Connally was over the Governor; there was no motion. The next thing was a doctor, sir.

Mr. SPECTER. Did you consider presenting a further shield for the President at that time?

Mr. KELLERMAN. No, sir.

Mr. SPECTER. Did the metallic handhold which you described early in your testimony as being about 15 inches off the top of the seat and going all the way across the width of the car, did that metal structure present any substantial impediment to your moving from the front seat to the rear seat of the automobile?

Mr. KELLERMAN. Mr. Specter, I think it would have been a small obstacle. However, let me say this: If I thought in my own mind that I was needed back there, there wouldn't have been an obstacle strong enough to hold me.

Mr. SPECTER. How about the presence of Governor Connally in the jump seat? Would the presence of Governor Connally or any passenger in the jump seat provide a substantial obstacle to your moving from your seat to shield the President's body?

Mr. KELLERMAN. Not at all. It wouldn't have made any difference, sir. Why? Because my job is to protect the President, sir, regardless of the obstacles.

Mr. SPECTER. Did Mr. Greer at any time use the radio in your car?

Mr. KELLERMAN. No, sir.

Mr. SPECTER. Mr. Kellerman, did the President's automobile at any time slow down after the first shot?

Mr. KELLERMAN. No; not that I recall.

Mr. SPECTER. Mr. Chairman, that completes our questions, sir.

Representative FORD. As you turned from Houston onto Elm, you were then facing the triple overpass?

Mr. KELLERMAN. Yes, sir.

Representative FORD. You were looking forward at the time?

Mr. KELLERMAN. Yes.

Representative FORD. You were not looking to the side particularly, or back at all?

Mr. KELLERMAN. Don't let me change your thought, Mr. Congressman. But as we turned left on Elm, there is also another curve before you get to this overpass.

Representative FORD. A rather slight curve to the right?

Mr. KELLERMAN. Very much. I still knew there was an overpass.

Representative FORD. But your concentration was ahead?

Mr. KELLERMAN. Ahead.

Representative FORD. Not to the side or to the rear?

Mr. KELLERMAN. No; not to the rear especially; that is true. Let me explain a little more. When you are riding in this automobile, which is with him, and on your right side, naturally you are observing more on the right. It is obvious. However, you still have time periodically to glance over to the left for viewing anything that might be of a danger—whether it is people or any other object.

Representative FORD. There is no way you would know from personal observation in what direction the President was looking at the time he was hit by the first shot?

Mr. KELLERMAN. That is right; I would not.

Representative FORD. Could you outline for us here the process by which you were put in charge of this particular operation?

Mr. KELLERMAN. Yes.

Representative FORD. Can you outline for us the procedure that is followed in such cases?

Mr. KELLERMAN. Yes, indeed. As I said earlier, we have three people, for a better word, in charge of the White House detail. Mr. Behn—Gerald Behn—is the special agent in charge. There are two assistants, Floyd Boring and myself. On all trips this was a divided matter. And this one was my trip. Not that I picked it or anything. It was my trip that Mr. Behn said, "You will make this one with the President." The other two people would have other duties to do. And this is how it fell on to me for that day, sir.

Representative FORD. Once this assignment is made by Mr. Behn, what happens after that?

Mr. KELLERMAN. In regard to who, sir?

Representative FORD. To your responsibilities.

Mr. KELLERMAN. The overall.

Representative FORD. In other words, from that assignment by Mr. Behn, you take charge; you execute; you make assignments and so forth?

Mr. KELLERMAN. Only one thing. I am not going to say that I don't make assignments. Mr. Congressman, these people all work in a team form. We have three shifts. They work together for a long time, and to say this, that they knew each other's footprints, is probably an overstatement. But they know each other's methods. Let me go back just one step further. I want to give it clear to you.

Let's say the four or five stops that we had in Texas on this visit—we had one overnight in Fort Worth. All right. Each time, each stop that we make, the individual that we had sent out ahead to set up and coordinate the program with the people in that area, whether it is security or otherwise, through communications for the days he is away, he keeps us abreast of what is going on, who to expect, and so forth.

And, again, I should say that in the morning of the 22d in Fort Worth, this lad called me—Mr. Lawson—asked about the top, whether it should remain on or off, which decision was reached from Mr. O'Donnell. I then asked him—I said, "Are we going to be all right in Dallas?" He said, "Oh, yes; it is a good program." Fine. If and when we ever arrived at that spot, I would ask this

105

man, is there anything unusual when we get here. That is a general question that I have given these people all the time.

Representative FORD. In other words, once the assignment has been made that you handle this trip, and in this case there was first a stop at El Paso, then at Houston——

Mr. KELLERMAN. San Antonio.

Representative FORD. San Antonio; then Houston, Fort Worth. You stayed overnight at Fort Worth?

Mr. KELLERMAN. Right.

Representative FORD. Then you proceeded to Dallas on the 22d?

Mr. KELLERMAN. Correct; yes, sir.

Representative FORD. As I understand it, when you arrived at San Antonio, the man that is in charge there, you immediately contacted.

Mr. KELLERMAN. Yes, indeed.

Representative FORD. When you go to Houston, the same process?

Mr. KELLERMAN. Yes, sir.

Representative FORD. Fort Worth, the same?

Mr. KELLERMAN. Fine.

Representative FORD. And when you got to Dallas, when you arrived there, whom did you see first?

Mr. KELLERMAN. Mr. Lawson.

Representative FORD. And what did he tell you?

Mr. KELLERMAN. He said, "Your program is all set. We have all the equipment and there should be no problem here." Fine.

Let me go back to Fort Worth again. On that night we had an overnight. The gentleman we had working that stop had an added thing thrown into him, which was the speech before breakfast. The President spoke to a crowd across the main street in front of the hotel. After the President retired that night, he and I went down to that parking lot. I said, show me where this man is going to be, where the platform is going to be, where are you going to have all these folks, and how close are they going to be; show me. He did.

You have got to keep abreast of these things, Mr. Congressman. Well, it is your job.

Representative FORD. Were all of these men that had charge of these various operations in San Antonio, Houston, Fort Worth, Dallas, men of experience?

Mr. KELLERMAN. Very much; very much so. I want to give you a little information on how these people are selected for doing your advance work out of Washington. In the first place, when they are brought in, you instruct them on everything you do securitywise around the White House. You instruct them in rangework, followup car work, every little phase entailed. Then say you have a little movement in town—the President has a press conference, as an example. He doesn't do that. Send him with an older fellow. Even if he just walks around, learn it. Take him another place, a departure from an airport, or a theater. Give him four or five. Then give him one, give him a little departure at an airport, or a hotel. But have somebody with him. Then there is no mistake made.

Representative FORD. Now, when these men are assigned to handle the responsibilities in a particular city, such as Lawson in Dallas, is Lawson on the staff here or is he a man from Dallas with the Secret Service?

Mr. KELLERMAN. These are all people we have in the White House detail, sir.

Representative FORD. In other words, Lawson was a White House detail man from Washington?

Mr. KELLERMAN. Right, sir. He is one of the men off those three shifts.

Representative FORD. Now, when was your assignment made as the man in charge of this particular operation?

Mr. KELLERMAN. Oh, I am going to say a week ahead, for lack of a better time—in fact, I knew that much of it.

Representative FORD. November——

Mr. KELLERMAN. Say the 17th, for a better day.

Representative FORD. On or before November 17th you got this assignment.

Mr. KELLERMAN. Surely. I knew that I was making a trip, and none of the other two gentlemen were.

Representative Ford. What did you do after you got this assignment—what steps did you take?

Mr. Kellerman. OK. The steps that I took—this entails work right here in Washington. First, to determine, to staff people in the White House, who is all going to make it, who are the passengers. This is a thing that those advance people out in the field do not know when they leave. You set up the time schedule—flight time—because the people on the other end want you there at 11:30 in the morning, you have to work back a flight time from Washington, or the helicopter time from the White House. All this is incorporated. Weatherwise—you will use an automobile. Allow a little more time. All right.

From the people that are out in the field on those 4 or 5 different spots, they are the ones that coordinate with the local folks what program they would like, which is forwarded back, conferred with staff people, whether it is approved, disapproved, added, or cut out. And about the day before you leave, then it is all gelled.

Representative Ford. But this is your principal responsibility, to pull everything together.

Mr. Kellerman. Right.

Representative Ford. Now, according to the various reports we have, when you know you are going to a particular city, or several cities, you have a method or a procedure to check to see if there are any individuals or organizations that present a serious threat to the President.

Mr. Kellerman. Yes, sir. We have what we call a Protective Research Section. This has been in existence for many years, through Roosevelt's days—I will go back that far. Through the combined efforts of various sources, through other agencies, they have a file on all the, let's say dangerous, for a better word, people that could be suspected in the city he arrives in. They will furnish the agents on those three shifts, if there are a number of them, or even one—it doesn't make any difference—all the data possible on that person— it will be given to each shift. It is a report form; can be read by all. And, if possible, there is a photograph included. That will be circulated around.

Representative Ford. Now, when you got your assignment on or about November 17, what did you do in this regard?

Mr. Kellerman. One little thing I should say. Well, I am sorry. One of the first things we do, when a trip is planned, is make a call on that PRS Section and tell them, "On November 21 we are going to be in San Antonio, Houston, and Fort Worth. On the 22d we will be in Dallas, Austin, and at the ranch." And they take it from there, sir.

Representative Ford. So, on or about November 22d, you made this inquiry.

Mr. Kellerman. This inquiry, sir, would be made a week ahead of time.

Representative Ford. A week ahead of the date that you were appointed?

Mr. Kellerman. That's right.

Representative Ford. Who would make that inquiry?

Mr. Kellerman. That would be made by any one of the three people—Mr. Behn, Mr. Boring, or myself, or one other person which I interrupted you a second ago. A departure is given to one man from one of the shifts who would set up a departure from the White House to Andrews. He, too, in turn notifies our Protective Research Section of this thing.

Representative Ford. Well, do you know who in this case for this trip made that inquiry of the Protective Research Section?

Mr. Kellerman. I don't have the name right now.

Representative Ford. Would there be a record of that made?

Mr. Kellerman. Yes, sir; yes, sir.

Representative Ford. I think we ought to have that for the record—the time it was made. You don't recall making it yourself, however.

Mr. Kellerman. No.

The Chairman. Do you know if it was actually done?

Mr. Kellerman. It is always done, sir.

The Chairman. I know. But do you know if it was done in this case?

Mr. Kellerman. Not for a fact; no.

Representative Ford. But you must assume it was done.

Mr. Kellerman. Very much so.

Representative FORD. Were you given the information from this inquiry, even though you didn't make it yourself?

Mr. KELLERMAN. What kind of information, sir?

Representative FORD. Well, about those people who are considered dangerous or a problem in any one of these four or five cities where the President was going on this trip.

Mr. KELLERMAN. I will have to check this, but there was no record.

Representative FORD. In other words——

Mr. KELLERMAN. No information.

Representative FORD. In other words, PRS never turned over to you any information about any dangerous individuals in any one of these communities on this trip.

Mr. KELLERMAN. That's right.

Representative FORD. Is this unusual?

Mr. KELLERMAN. Yes. But let me reserve the right to recheck that question again; may I?

Representative Ford. Absolutely. All we want in this case, as in any other, are whatever the facts are to the best of records that are available.

Mr. KELLERMAN. All right.

Representative FORD. In the report from the Secret Service it says, and I quote, "Because of the incidents on the occasion of the visit of Ambassador Stevenson to Dallas earlier in the fall, special attention was given to extremist groups known to be active in Dallas. Appendix A describes the action taken in Dallas in more detail." Were you familiar with that part of the Secret Service activity prior to your departure for Texas?

Mr. KELLERMAN. I have knowledge of that; yes, sir.

Representative FORD. How much knowledge?

Mr. KELLERMAN. But not enough to be written up, that I recall, sir.

Representative FORD. Well, could you describe for the Commission what knowledge you did have in this regard?

Mr. KELLERMAN. The only knowledge I can describe to you, sir, is the fact that we were aware of what this Ambassador went through down there. However, we had no information that such an incident would happen to President Kennedy on his trip into that State.

Representative FORD. But I gather from this report, which is the official report of the Treasury Department, that somebody knew of these previous incidents, and was thereby alerted to the possibility of—the potential of one, because the report says, "Special attention is given to extremist groups known to be in Dallas." Now, could you tell us what special attention was given?

Mr. KELLERMAN. No. Outside of the fact that everybody was alerted to this previous incident.

Representative FORD. PRS, Protective Research Section, didn't tell you, as the person in charge, of any individuals or of any groups that wanted special attention? I am using "special attention" as in the report.

Mr. KELLERMAN. Right as of this minute, the only knowledge that I have of any incident that could happen was in San Antonio, when I believe we had information of some pickets. Now, those pickets showed up outside of—he made a speech at that space hospital. Well, anyway, in view of that, I cannot reach the name right now—these pickets were out at, let's say, the main gate to the grounds, and just stayed right there with their placards.

Representative FORD. Also on the report it says, "In accordance with the usual practice, the local FBI office informed the local Secret Service office of any information which affected the President's visit."

Mr. KELLERMAN. They did. That is the normal practice.

Representative FORD. That was the normal procedure?

Mr. KELLERMAN. It is always the normal procedure; yes, sir.

Representative FORD. Now, whom would they have informed in this case in Dallas?

Mr. KELLERMAN. Their report would have come to Washington, and relayed to our Protective Research Section.

Representative FORD. And the FBI in this instance gave you what information, if any, that you should relay back to the people——

108

Mr. KELLERMAN. The only thing I can recall right now, sir, are those pickets in San Antonio.

Representative FORD. Well, may I say if on your return to your office you find any information on this particular point, I think it would be very helpful for the record, and it should be included in the record.

Mr. KELLERMAN. All right. I surely will.

Representative FORD. The report also says, "On October 30, 1963, the local FBI office gave the local Secret Service officer the name of a rightwing individual in the Dallas area. An investigation was made. On November 21 and 22 the local FBI office referred two pieces of information to the local Dallas office of the Secret Service." Were you familiar with that?

Mr. KELLERMAN. No.

Representative FORD. Who would, under your normal procedures, have been familiar with that?

Mr. KELLERMAN. It would be the same organization, Protective Research Section.

Representative FORD. But they did not give you any information of this.

Mr. KELLERMAN. No.

Representative FORD. Is this unusual or different?

Mr. KELLERMAN. If they evaluated this information, there would have to be a degree of seriousness.

Representative FORD. But, as far as you can best recollect at this point, you were never so informed.

Mr. KELLERMAN. No, indeed.

Representative FORD. The report does go on to say, and I quote, "One involved scurrilous literature already in the hands of the Secret Service, Exhibit 4. The second involved possible picket trouble which the local police were aware of." That is the picket trouble you were talking about?

Mr. KELLERMAN. Apparently so.

Representative FORD. The report also says on page 8, "Special Agent Lawson, SAIC Sorrel, and Special Agent Howlett met with Dallas law-enforcement officials. Special Agent Howlett also met with an informant. They followed up all leads and tips and checked scurrilous literature, Exhibit 4." Did you have any information personally about this activity by Lawson, Sorrel, and Howlett?

Mr. KELLERMAN. No, sir.

Representative FORD. Was it their responsibility to do it, to undertake that kind of an operation?

Mr. KELLERMAN. Everybody but Lawson. These other two gentlemen you are speaking of are field agents out of Dallas. Yes; they would investigate the seriousness of this thing, through the information furnished by the FBI. And, depending on the degree now, this would be furnished our Protective Research Section here in Washington.

Representative FORD. Now, did Lawson or anybody else communicate to you what was going on in this regard?

Mr. KELLERMAN. No, no. I do not think Mr. Lawson got in this investigative part at all. It would not be any part of his duties.

Representative FORD. I am only reading from the report.

Mr. KELLERMAN. Yes.

Representative FORD. And the report goes on to say, "Their investigations did not bring to light the name or the individual Lee H. Oswald, and he or his name was not known to them or any other Secret Service agent in Dallas or elsewhere prior to this shooting of the President." Would that be the same as far as you are concerned?

Mr. KELLERMAN. That is very true.

Representative FORD. You did not know of Lee H. Oswald?

Mr. KELLERMAN. None whatsoever.

Representative FORD. Was it surprising to you that when the President was going to a city as large as Dallas, that there were no names turned over to you, either by your Protective Research Section or by any other Federal agents—individuals or an individual dangerous to the President?

Mr. KELLERMAN. I recall, to give you an answer, Congressman, that it did seem strange that here we are hitting five cities in one State and—and from the apparent trouble Ambassador Stevenson had down there one evening, we certainly should have had some information on somebody.

Representative FORD. Hypothetically, if you go to other large metropolitan areas, do you normally get names from various agencies, including PRS, warning you of an individual or groups that might cause trouble?

Mr. KELLERMAN. Again I say that our PRS would recheck their files, from all the cities—from all the cases that they have in that city, and furnished us information, whether a report or photographwise. They in turn would—and I believe I am correct on this—they in turn notify the Bureau of this visit, or may have people check through their files. They can doublecheck this stuff. I don't recall any information whatsoever, except that picket thing.

Representative FORD. It is surprising to me, as well, and I gather it was certainly, on reflection, surprising to you——

Mr. KELLERMAN. Yes; it is.

Representative FORD. Was this in itself any warning to you that there might be some breakdown in the system?

Mr. KELLERMAN. Gee—no; I never cherished that thought, sir.

Representative FORD. You assumed that the proper liaison between various agencies was taking place, and your PRS was operating effectively?

Mr. KELLERMAN. Oh, yes; very much: yes indeed. Now, if I am wrong, when I check these two questions back here, I will let you know.

Mr. SPECTER. Congressman Ford, on this line, perhaps I should say that organizationally we are divided into phases where this is a separate phase in terms of protective devices. So, for the prepared part of what the staff has set up, we have by design omitted that portion here, with later witnesses to go into all these questions in some detail for the Commission.

Representative FORD. I was trying to get from Mr. Kellerman—from his testimony he was indicating that he was the person who from on or about November 17 had the responsibility. And I was trying to trace precisely how this responsibility was carried through, up to the point where you started out this morning. Do I understand, then, that at some later point in the Commission hearings with other witnesses we will go back into the process of how these decisions are made, as far as PRS is concerned?

Mr. SPECTER. Yes, sir. There will be detailed witnesses on the workings of PRS, and how they functioned with respect to this trip, and what information the FBI had or the State Department had about Lee Harvey Oswald, and whatever coordination, if any, was present. Our thought was that that would be handled separately, organizationally. Certainly, to some extent it is impossible to draw sharp lines of distinction here. But that is the way the staff has prepared the distinctions—with Mr. Kellerman going more specifically, as the other witnesses of today, on the sequence of events themselves at the assassination.

Representative FORD. But, as far as the procedures within PRS and the relationship between the Secret Service, the FBI, and other Federal agencies, that will come up later on in other witnesses who are more familiar with the precise workings.

Mr. SPECTER. Exactly; yes, sir.

Representative FORD. Who actually had the responsibility to check the route from the airport to the Trade Mart? I mean to check the route, lay out whatever security precautions should be taken from the outset until the day of the President's visit?

Mr. KELLERMAN. That was coordinated, Mr. Congressman, between Mr. Lawson and members of the Dallas Police Department, sir.

Representative FORD. You did not arrive in Dallas until the morning of the assassination?

Mr. KELLERMAN. Yes, sir; that is correct, sir.

Representative FORD. As you were in the car, in the right front seat, and the car turned from Main Street right into Houston, you had for a relatively short period of time an opportunity to look at the Texas School Depository Building. Did you look at it; did you notice anything about it? What was your reaction, if any, to that particular building?

Mr. KELLERMAN. Not knowing the name of the building—let me say this: When you are driving down this street, regardless of Houston or which, and you have buildings on either side of you, you are going to scan your eyes up and down this building.

Representative FORD. Did this building create, as you turned into Houston Street, any particular problem that would have alerted you one way or another?

Mr. KELLERMAN. None whatsoever. It did not produce a thing.

Representative FORD. Your eyes scanned the area. Did they scan sufficiently to identify anything, to be alerted by anything in any window, on the roof, or anyplace else?

Mr. KELLERMAN. No, sir.

Representative FORD. Did Mr. Lawson or anybody else indicate to you at any time that the Book Depository Building was a problem?

Mr. KELLERMAN. No, sir.

Representative FORD. I mean beforehand.

Mr. KELLERMAN. Never mentioned it.

Representative FORD. Did Mr. Lawson or anybody else discuss with you any particular danger involved in the overpass, the triple overpass?

Mr. KELLERMAN. No, sir.

Representative FORD. Did you have minute knowledge as to the route in Dallas, or was that left up to Lawson in his judgment?

Mr. KELLERMAN. Left up to Lawson and the people in Texas.

Representative FORD. But he did tell you when you arrived in Dallas; what, again?

Mr. KELLERMAN. And the people in Texas, the police department.

Representative FORD. What did he tell you? When you arrived in Dallas that morning, he told you something.

Mr. KELLERMAN. Yes, sir. He said, "This is your reception committee, which is at the bottom of the ramp leading out." I said, "Are we all right in Dallas here all the way for today?" And he said, "Yes; this will be fine." I said, "All right; let's get on with it."

Representative FORD. When were you first interviewed by anyone regarding the directions from which the shots came?

Mr. KELLERMAN. I don't recall ever being interviewed.

Representative FORD. Did you ever make a statement for submission to the Commission or to your supervisors?

Mr. KELLERMAN. Just this statement that I submitted here.

Representative FORD. Which is included in the Secret Service report.

Mr. KELLERMAN. Yes, sir.

Representative FORD. Did you have anything to do with setting up the method of trying to apprehend the alleged assassin? Was that outside or within your jurisdiction?

Mr. KELLERMAN. Outside, sir.

Representative FORD. You did nothing in that regard.

Mr. KELLERMAN. Nothing.

Representative FORD. I believe that is all. I have to go back to a very important committee meeting, Mr. Chairman. I may be able to get back later, Mr. Chief Justice.

The CHAIRMAN. I will be here the rest of the afternoon, so there will be no necessity of your coming back if you are tied up. Thank you very much for presiding all day.

Mr. Specter, have you some more questioning?

Mr. SPECTER. I have just one or two other questions.

Mr. Kellerman, you referred to a single statement which you said you had made. In the report of the U.S. Secret Service on the assassination of President Kennedy, on Exhibit 12, statement 11—we have the first statement which you made, which is four pages, and that is the one to which you referred, to refresh your recollection earlier today, and I show you what appears to be a second very brief report which you made 1 day later under date of November 30, 1963, with your name and initials, and ask you if you made this one, also.

Mr. KELLERMAN. That is right; yes, sir.

Mr. SPECTER. All right. You referred to you and Mr. Boring being the two assistant special agents in charge. Is that status the same at the present time, or are there now three assistant special agents in charge?

Mr. KELLERMAN. There are three. Mr. Rufus Youngblood is the third one.

Mr. SPECTER. Has that slight shift been made since the time of the assassination.

Mr. KELLERMAN. That is correct.

Mr. SPECTER. Mr. Chief Justice, those are my only additional questions, sir.

The CHAIRMAN. Mr. Craig, would you like to ask any questions, or do you think of any other avenue that we should explore here?

Mr. CRAIG. No, sir; thank you, Mr. Chief Justice. As the interrogation has progressed, I have been handing notes to counsel and he has been very kind in asking those questions.

The CHAIRMAN. Mr. Murray, can you think of anything?

Mr. MURRAY. No, thank you, Mr. Chief Justice.

Mr. SMITH. Off the record.

(Discussion off the record.)

Mr. CRAIG. Mr. Kellerman, is there any special agent in charge of the protection of the person next in line in succession, to your knowledge?

Mr. KELLERMAN. I think Mr. Rowley would like to man that. I think they have had a little difficulty to find a man.

Mr. CRAIG. There is no such person now?

Mr. KELLERMAN. No, they have made numerous attempts with the people, and so far they have got a negative reply.

The CHAIRMAN. Well, Mr. Kellerman, thank you very much, sir, for your attendance and for your testimony.

Mr. KELLERMAN. Thank you, sir.

(At this point, Representative Ford left the hearing room.)

The CHAIRMAN. Now, Mr. Specter.

Mr. SPECTER. We will call Mr. Greer.

The CHAIRMAN. Mr. Greer, how do you, sir.

Mr. Greer, will you raise your right hand and be sworn.

Do you solemnly swear to tell the truth, the whole truth, and nothing but the truth before this Commission, so help you God?

Mr. GREER. I do.

The CHAIRMAN. Would you be seated, please.

TESTIMONY OF WILLIAM ROBERT GREER, SPECIAL AGENT, SECRET SERVICE

Mr. SPECTER. Would you state your full name for the record, please.

Mr. GREER. William Robert Greer.

Mr. SPECTER. By whom are you employed, Mr. Greer?

Mr. GREER. The Treasury Department, Secret Service Division of the Treasury Department.

Mr. SPECTER. How old are you at the present time?

Mr. GREER. Fifty-four years old.

Mr. SPECTER. How long have you been with the Secret Service Department?

Mr. GREER. I have been with the Secret Service Department since October 1, 1945.

Mr. SPECTER. What is your educational background?

Mr. GREER. I have just education in public schools in Ireland, really.

Mr. SPECTER. And——

Mr. GREER. I took courses here in this country.

Mr. SPECTER. Are you a high school graduate, then?

Mr. GREER. Well, I have 2 years of high school.

Mr. SPECTER. And when did you complete this educational background?

Mr. GREER. I have to go back now.

Mr. SPECTER. Approximately.

Mr. GREER. About 1924 or 1925.

Mr. SPECTER. Would you outline in a general way what your activities have been since that time, up until your joining the Secret Service, please?

Mr. GREER. Yes, sir. I was born and raised on farmwork, a farmer. And

I done that until I came to this country in February 1930. I worked for a period of time—I lived in Boston for a little while. I worked one summer on the estate of Henry Cabot Lodge. I was a chauffeur for a family in Brookline, Mass., for about a year. And then I went to New York, Dobbs Ferry, N.Y. I lived there for 13 years as a chauffeur for a private family in Dobbs Ferry, N.Y. Then I went in the Navy in November 1942. I got discharged on September 18, 1945.

Mr. SPECTER. What were your principal duties while in the Navy?

Mr. GREER. I was seaman first class. I did almost 2 years at Bainbridge, Md., with the seaman guard there. And then I was assigned to the presidential yacht in May 1944, until I was discharged in September. But most of my duty was at the White House in that period, that year.

Mr. SPECTER. And how long after discharge from the Navy was it before you joined the U.S. Secret Service?

Mr. GREER. Well, I got out of the Navy September 18 and October 1 I went with the Secret Service—a matter of 14 or 15 days.

Mr. SPECTER. Describe your duties since joining the Secret Service, please.

Mr. GREER. Since joining the Secret Service I was assigned to the uniform force at first with the Secret Service at the Bureau of Engraving and Printing. For about 2 years I was with the physical education part of it. We had a gymnasium there. I was an instructor there part-time—part of the time. And then I was assigned for about 2 years to pick up the food of the President at the White House. I had that duty for about 2 years. And then I went back to the Treasury for a short period, a few months. And then I was reassigned to the White House as an agent in November—1950 I went there. I was made a full agent that following August 1951. I was there as a special officer from November to August 1951.

Mr. SPECTER. And have you been assigned to the White House staff since that time?

Mr. GREER. Yes, sir; I have been there ever since.

Mr. SPECTER. And while assigned at the White House staff, how much of your duty has involved driving the President's car?

Mr. GREER. Well, I drove the followup car for quite a long time—you know, off and on. And then I drove the President at intervals during President Truman's and President Eisenhower's terms. I was also assigned a great many times to Mrs. Eisenhower. When she left Washington, I was always assigned to her, to travel with her. And I have been assigned to the President, to drive the President, since election day, with President Kennedy. I was the senior agent assigned to him, to drive him.

Mr. SPECTER. How did you get to Dallas yourself back on November 22, 1963?

Mr. GREER. I flew—I was on a plane with the President all during the trip. And I flew from Fort Worth to Dallas that morning.

Mr. SPECTER. Mr. Greer, I hand you documents which have been marked Commission Exhibits 344, 345, and 346. I ask you if you can identify those, starting with 344, what that depicts.

Mr. GREER. Yes, sir; I can identify this automobile very well. That is the 1961 Lincoln, especially built for the President. And this is a rear view of that same automobile. This is the interior of that Lincoln Continental. Yes, sir, everything is very positive that I can identify.

Mr. SPECTER. How did that automobile—how was that automobile transported to Texas?

Mr. GREER. It was flown there in a C–130.

Mr. SPECTER. And do you know where it was flown to?

Mr. GREER. Well, it was flown—let's see, I forget the day before where our first stop was on that trip right now. I would have to go back into my papers. But we used I believe more than one stop. I am trying to think where we used it before we went to Dallas. It could have been at Houston. I am not too sure whether we used it at Houston the day before or not. I would have to go back in my records.

Mr. SPECTER. Is it possible the first time you used the automobile on that Texas trip was at Dallas?

Mr. GREER. Right now it is so long ago, I have almost forgotten whether we

113

did use it at Houston prior to that or not. I am not too sure where the first stop was. We sometimes use it more than one stop.

Mr. SPECTER. Is there any covering which can be put on the President's automobile?

Mr. GREER. There is—when we put the plastic—I put the plastic on it, we have a black canvass-type cover that buttons over the top of the plastic.

Mr. SPECTER. Will you please describe in a general way the plastic covering you just referred to.

Mr. GREER. The plastic covering is made in six pieces. Three of them—there are two corner pieces and a centerpiece on the back that we fasten together before we set it up onto the car. Then there is a front—one piece that goes across the front seat after that. Then the last pieces we put on are two that go in the center, and they meet together in the center—they come together in the center. That makes the six pieces that it comes down in. We have to break it down in the six pieces to store it in the trunk. It is kept in the trunk of the car whenever we are not using it.

Mr. SPECTER. Are the three pieces that you described as being joined together for the rear portion disassembled at all times?

Mr. GREER. We disassemble them to store them in the trunk, yes, sir. But we put them together on the floor, on the ground or something like that—we put the three pieces together, then we lift it up and set it in place, which covers the back seat of the car.

Mr. SPECTER. And after you put the three pieces together for the back portion of the car, how many additional pieces are there for the balance of the car?

Mr. GREER. Three; three more pieces.

Mr. SPECTER. And how are they secured to the automobile itself?

Mr. GREER. They are secured with—I don't know what you would call it— these fasteners, snaps, kind of snaps that snap on them. We have them made that way so that we can install them or take them apart very fast.

Mr. SPECTER. Now, is this cover transparent? Can it be seen through?

Mr. GREER. The plastic; yes. You can see through it.

Mr. SPECTER. And what is the plastic made of, if you know?

Mr. GREER. Well, it is a type of plastic. I just don't know who manufactures it. But it is clear plastic.

Mr. SPECTER. Is it bulletproof or bullet resistant?

Mr. GREER. No, sir. It is weather—the idea back of it was for inclement weather, that the President could be seen if the weather was too bad to have him outside. That is what we had in mind originally with it.

Mr. SPECTER. Do you have any personal knowledge of any efforts made to obtain a bulletproof or bullet-resistant transparent top?

Mr. GREER. Now, or before that?

Mr. SPECTER. Well, start beforehand.

Mr. GREER. No; I never had anything to do with that at all. I never had anything to do with anything being made for that.

Mr. SPECTER. Do you know what efforts have been made subsequent to the assassination of President Kennedy to obtain such a bulletproof transparent top?

Mr. GREER. Only just hearing conversation; nothing definite; no, sir.

Mr. SPECTER. Approximately what time, to the best of your recollection, did President Kennedy arrive in Dallas on November 22?

Mr. GREER. I would have to—I would not tell you right now. I would have to go back and look into my—you probably have it there. I have it also on my report.

Mr. SPECTER. If you don't recall the exact time, just give us your best estimate.

Mr. GREER. Approximately 11:35. I am guessing.

Mr. SPECTER. And what was his mode of transportation into Dallas?

Mr. GREER. He flew on an Air Force plane.

Mr. SPECTER. And where did he fly from?

Mr. GREER. From Fort Worth to Dallas.

Mr. SPECTER. Will you tell us in a general way what he did upon arrival in Dallas at Love Field?

Mr. GREER. Yes, sir. He got off the plane. He walked along the fence along there, and shook hands with a great many people. There was a large crowd there. He and Mrs. Kennedy both walked along and shook hands with many people.

Mr. SPECTER. Now, approximately how long after arrival at Love Field did he get into his automobile?

Mr. GREER. I would guess probably, say, approximately maybe 10 minutes.

Mr. SPECTER. What were the weather conditions like that day as he got into his automobile?

Mr. GREER. The weather was very nice that day. It was a beautiful day in Dallas, very fine day, warm, fairly warm, nice day.

Mr. SPECTER. Was the car open?

Mr. GREER. The car was open; no top.

Mr. SPECTER. Approximately how many automobiles were there in that motorcade?

Mr. GREER. I wouldn't have—couldn't tell you right now how many. There was quite a few cars.

Mr. SPECTER. Who were the occupants of the President's car?

Mr. GREER. On the back seat, on the right rear seat, the President. Mrs. Kennedy on the left rear seat, Governor Connally was on the right jump seat, and Mrs. Connally was on the left jump seat. Mr. Kellerman was riding on the right front, and I was driving.

Mr. SPECTER. At what speed did you travel as you proceeded at various points from Love Field, say, down into the downtown area of Dallas?

Mr. GREER. Well, we traveled at various speeds, according to the amount of people, the crowd. If it was—if we came to a large crowd, we would have to slow down, I would say, to probably 10 to 15 miles an hour. Then we would pick it up possibly 25 or somewhere around—25 maybe to 30, where there was few people.

Mr. SPECTER. What was the maximum speed at which you drove from the time you left Love Field until the time you got to downtown Dallas?

Mr. GREER. I wouldn't have the slightest idea now, after this length of time. I could not say how much it would be.

Mr. SPECTER. Can you give us your best estimate on the minimum speed from the time you left Love Field until the time you arrived at downtown Dallas?

Mr. GREER. The minimum speed traveling at all would probably be 10 to 15 miles an hour.

Mr. SPECTER. And what sort of crowds were along the way?

Mr. GREER. There was large crowds—at some places there was quite large crowds.

Mr. SPECTER. Did anything unusual occur en route from Love Field to the downtown area of Dallas?

Mr. GREER. Well, I think—it may have been—we may have stopped one time where he got out—didn't get out, but he stopped and spoke to some young people, I believe, en route. I think there may have been a group of people there.

Mr. SPECTER. I hand you a photograph which has already been marked Commission Exhibit No. 347 and ask you if at this time you are able to identify what that photograph depicts.

Mr. GREER. Yes, sir. That is the photograph of the route that we traveled in Dallas.

Mr. SPECTER. I show you a photograph marked Commission Exhibit No. 348 and ask you if you can identify what that picture represents.

Mr. GREER. With pictures that I have seen since then, I would recognize that as the Book Depository Building in Dallas—the street in front of it.

Mr. SPECTER. Are you familiar with the name of this street, which has since been marked by Mr. Kellerman, who identified this exhibit and marked the name of the street on it?

Mr. GREER. No, I wasn't at the time, but I know now that it is supposed to be Main Street.

Mr. SPECTER. And do you know in what general direction Main Street proceeds?

Mr. GREER. I am not too sure. No; I wouldn't really know. I didn't have enough time.

Mr. SPECTER. And are you familiar with the street which intersects with Main——

Mr. GREER. Houston Street.

Mr. SPECTER. And what street did you turn off of from Houston?

Mr. GREER. Houston to Elm Street.

Mr. SPECTER. Now, as you were proceeding down Main Street, which I will add is in a generally westerly direction, what is your best estimate of your speed as you turned the corner right onto Houston Street?

Mr. GREER. I would estimate the speed was somewhere between 12 to 15 miles per hour, coming through there.

Mr. SPECTER. And as you made that right-hand turn onto Houston Street, what was the composition of the crowds along the way, if any?

Mr. GREER. On Main Street there were very, very large crowds. They were almost close up against the automobile. Sometimes the motorcycles on the sides could not even get through. They were real close to us. And very large crowds. And when we got around on Houston Street, the crowds thinned out quite a lot. My recollection here is that there wasn't too many people on Elm Street—a few scattered people at that point.

Mr. SPECTER. And your finger indicated there the position near the Texas School Depository Building?

Mr. GREER. Yes, sir.

Mr. SPECTER. Now, you have described motorcycles. How many were present with the President's automobile, if any?

Mr. GREER. I could not tell the exact amount of motorcycles that were escorting us at that time. We usually do have them on the two front fenders and two rear fenders, and some probably preceding that, and some along the motorcade behind us. I could not tell you exactly how many there probably would be.

Mr. SPECTER. Do you recollect that there were some on this occasion, however?

Mr. GREER. Yes, sir; there were motorcycles.

Mr. SPECTER. Now, do you know how many cars back your car was in the motorcade?

Mr. GREER. No; I don't know how many police cars were ahead of us. I knew that the lead car was right directly ahead of me, with one of our agents, or maybe two, and the chief of police in that car. But how many police cars prior to that, I do not know how many there were at the time in front of us.

Mr. SPECTER. How far ahead of you was that police car as you turned off of Main Street onto Houston?

Mr. GREER. I usually allow 4 or 5 car lengths, if possible, between the car and myself, in case that there is any reason to speed up quick. I like to leave enough room that I can get out of there. I don't like to get too tight to the lead car when possible—unless the crowds are so big that I have to get in or they would close in on me—I have to get in closer.

Mr. SPECTER. Do you know how far behind you the first car immediately behind yours was?

Mr. GREER. The car behind me was only some few feet, because with our training and all, we stay very, very close to the President's car. Sometimes we are bumper to bumper. And the car never is much more than 10 to 12 feet away from the President's car, at slow speeds.

Mr. SPECTER. Did you endeavor to maintain a constant speed in the operation of the President's car so as to avoid contact with this close gap between the President's car and the President's follow-up automobile?

Mr. GREER. Yes, sir. We tried to drive at a very steady speed. We are used to driving with each other, and we almost can tell each other's thoughts what we do, because of the training we have had, and we work so long together. We drive at a steady pace of speed, so that we give each other enough ample time to stop or move in close.

Mr. SPECTER. After turning off Main onto Houston, did you have any opportunity to take a look at the building which you have since identified as the Texas School Book Depository Building?

116

Mr. GREER. No, sir. I had not any chance to look much at that building at all. When I made the turn into Elm Street, I was watching the overpass expressway—the overpass, or what was ahead of me. I always look at any—where I go underneath anything, I always watch above, so if there is anyone up there that I can move so that I won't go over the top of anyone, if they are unidentified to me, unless it is a policeman or something like that. We try to avoid going under them.

Mr. SPECTER. Now, when you turned off of Houston onto Elm, did you make a right-hand or a left-hand turn?

Mr. GREER. I made a right-hand turn off of Main onto Houston.

Mr. SPECTER. And when you turned from Houston onto Elm, was that a right-hand or a left-hand turn?

Mr. GREER. That was a left-hand turn.

Mr. SPECTER. And as you turned onto Elm Street, how far, to the best of your ability to estimate, was your automobile from the overpass which you have just described?

Mr. GREER. I wouldn't have a distance recollection at all on how far it was. It wasn't too far. I just could not give you the distance.

Mr. SPECTER. At that time, did you make a conscious effort to observe what was present, if anything, on that overpass?

Mr. GREER. Yes, sir. I was making sure that I could not see anyone that might be standing there, and I didn't see anything that I was afraid of on the overpass.

Mr. SPECTER. Did you see anything at all on the overpass?

Mr. GREER. Not that I can now remember.

Mr. SPECTER. What is your best recollection of the speed at which you were traveling as you turned left off of Houston onto Elm?

Mr. GREER. My best recollection would be between 12 and 15 miles per hour.

Mr. SPECTER. And how far were you at that time behind the police car which was in front of you?

Mr. GREER. Probably 50 feet maybe—approximately. I will say approximately 50 feet.

Mr. SPECTER. As you turned onto Elm, did you have any opportunity to observe how far behind you the President's follow-up car was?

Mr. GREER. No, sir. I was not looking in my mirror; I could not say how far it was behind me at the time.

Mr. SPECTER. And what was the nature of the crowd as you made the turn onto Elm Street, if you recall?

Mr. GREER. To the best of my memory, the crowd had thinned out a great deal, and there was not too many people in front of that building.

Mr. SPECTER. How many lanes of travel were there on Elm Street?

Mr. GREER. It was either three or four lanes wide. I have forgotten.

Mr. SPECTER. In what portion of the street were you traveling?

Mr. GREER. I was right in the center of the street.

Mr. SPECTER. Would you describe for us the contour of the street at that point—whether it was level, hilly, or what.

Mr. GREER. It was starting to go down—gradually going down toward this underpass. It was a down grade.

Mr. SPECTER. Now, would you tell us just what occurred as you were proceeding down Elm Street at that time?

Mr. GREER. Well, when we were going down Elm Street, I heard a noise that I thought was a backfire of one of the motorcycle policemen. And I didn't—it did not affect me like anything else. I just thought that it is what it was. We had had so many motorcycles around us. So I heard this noise. And I thought that is what it was. And then I heard it again. And I glanced over my shoulder. And I saw Governor Connally like he was starting to fall. Then I realized there was something wrong. I tramped on the accelerator, and at the same time Mr. Kellerman said to me, "Get out of here fast." And I cannot remember even the other shots or noises that was. I cannot quite remember any more. I did not see anything happen behind me any more, because I was occupied with getting away.

Mr. SPECTER. Now, how many shots, or how many noises have you just described that you heard?

117

Mr. GREER. I know there was three that I heard—three. But I cannot remember any more than probably three. I know there was three anyway that I heard.

Mr. SPECTER. Do you have an independent recollection at this moment of having heard three shots at that time?

Mr. GREER. I knew that after I heard the second one, that is when I looked over my shoulder, and I was conscious that there was something wrong, because that is when I saw Governor Connally. And when I turned around again, to the best of my recollection there was another one, right immediately after.

Mr. SPECTER. To the best of your ability to recollect and estimate, how much time elapsed from the first noise which you have described as being similar to the backfire of a motor vehicle until you heard the second noise?

Mr. GREER. It seems a matter of seconds, I really couldn't say. Three or four seconds.

Mr. SPECTER. How much time elapsed, to the best of your ability to estimate and recollect, between the time of the second noise and the time of the third noise?

Mr. GREER. The last two seemed to be just simultaneously, one behind the other, but I don't recollect just how much, how many seconds were between the two. I couldn't really say.

Mr. SPECTER. Describe as best you can the types of sound of the second report, as distinguished from the first noise which you said was similar to a motorcycle backfire?

Mr. GREER. The second one didn't sound any different much than the first one but I kind of got, by turning around, I don't know whether I got a little concussion of it, maybe when it hit something or not, I may have gotten a little concussion that made me think there was something different to it. But so far as the noise is concerned, I haven't got any memory of any difference in them at all.

Mr. SPECTER. Describe as best you can the sound of the third noise.

Mr. GREER. Just, to me it was similar, to the first two. They all sounded practically the same to me.

Mr. SPECTER. You testified that at the second noise you glanced over your shoulder.

Mr. GREER. Yes, sir.

Mr. SPECTER. Which shoulder did you glance over?

Mr. GREER. Right shoulder.

Mr. SPECTER. And describe or indicate how far you turned your head to the right at that time?

Mr. GREER. Just so that my eyes over, caught the Governor, I could see, I couldn't see the President. I just could see the Governor. I made a quick glance and back again.

Mr. SPECTER. Was the movement of your head just then approximately the same?

Mr. GREER. Yes, sir.

Mr. SPECTER. As the time?

Mr. GREER. Yes, sir.

Mr. SPECTER. You just indicated the turn of your head slightly to the right.

Mr. GREER. My eyes slightly more than my head. My eyes went more than my head around. I had vision real quick of it.

Mr. SPECTER. Exactly where was Governor Connally when you first caught him out of the corner of your eye?

Mr. GREER. He was—he seemed to be falling a little bit toward Mrs. Connally, to the left. He started to go over a little bit to the left.

Mr. SPECTER. And how far did you catch his movement during the time you were able to observe him?

Mr. GREER. Just a second. He probably hadn't gotten his shoulder, he hadn't fell down or anything. He probably was in a position such as I am now.

Mr. SPECTER. Did he fall to the rear or to the side or how?

Mr. GREER. In my opinion, he fell toward Mrs. Connally which would be to his left or to his side.

Mr. SPECTER. Did he fall then on his left shoulder and arm or in some other way?

Mr. GREER. He appeared to me to be falling on his left shoulder when I glanced. He had only started to move that way whenever he—when I saw him.

Mr. SPECTER. Were you able to see anything of President Kennedy as you glanced to the rear?

Mr. GREER. No, sir; I didn't see anything of the President. I didn't look, I wasn't far enough around to see the President.

Mr. SPECTER. When you started that glance, are you able to recollect whether you started to glance before, exactly simultaneously with or after that second shot?

Mr. GREER. It was almost simultaneously that he had—something had hit, you know, when I had seen him. It seemed like in the same second almost that something had hit, you know, whenever I turned around. I saw him start to fall.

Mr. SPECTER. Did you step on the accelerator before, simultaneously or after Mr. Kellerman instructed you to accelerate?

Mr. GREER. It was about simultaneously.

Mr. SPECTER. So that it was your reaction to accelerate prior to the time——

Mr. GREER. Yes, sir.

Mr. SPECTER. You had gotten that instruction?

Mr. GREER. Yes, sir; it was my reaction that caused me to accelerate.

Mr. SPECTER. Do you recollect whether you accelerated before or at the same time or after the third shot?

Mr. GREER. I couldn't really say. Just as soon as I turned my head back from the second shot, right away I accelerated right then. It was a matter of my reflexes to the accelerator.

Mr. SPECTER. Was it at about that time that you heard the third shot?

Mr. GREER. Yes, sir; just as soon as I turned my head.

Mr. SPECTER. What is your best estimate of the speed of the car at the time of the first, second, or third shots?

Mr. GREER. I would estimate my speed was between 12 and 15 miles per hour.

Mr. SPECTER. At the time all of the shots occurred?

Mr. GREER. At the time the shots occurred.

Mr. SPECTER. Now what, if anything, was Mr. Kellerman doing at the time of the first shot?

Mr. GREER. I couldn't really speak for where he was watching, what part of the street or the buildings or what he was watching at that time. I don't really know.

Mr. SPECTER. Do you know what Mr. Kellerman was doing at the time of the second shot?

Mr. GREER. He was sitting there in the front. No, sir; I don't know what his action was then. I was watching the overpass, I wasn't looking his way.

Mr. SPECTER. When you were watching the overpass at that time, did you observe anything on the overpass?

Mr. GREER. Not that I can remember now.

Mr. SPECTER. Did you observe that there was no one present on the overpass?

Mr. GREER. My recollection, there may have been a police officer up there. It is vague to me now everything that I had seen at that time.

Mr. SPECTER. Do you know what Mr. Kellerman was doing at the time of the third shot?

Mr. GREER. No, sir; I couldn't say what he was doing.

Mr. SPECTER. Was there any radio communication between your automobile and any of the other automobiles?

Mr. GREER. Yes, sir.

Mr. SPECTER. Who made that radio communication?

Mr. GREER. Kellerman.

Mr. SPECTER. Tell us as precisely as you can when he made that radio communication.

Mr. GREER. After he had said to me, "Get out of here fast." He got the radio and called to the lead car, "Get us to a hospital fast, nearest hospital fast."

Mr. SPECTER. Do you recall whether he said anything else at that time?

Mr. GREER. After he had said to me, he said, "12:30," and that is all I remember him saying to me was 12:30, and he had communications with the cars but I don't remember what he had said to them.

Mr. SPECTER. Did he say just "12:30," or was it 12:30 used in a sentence?

Mr. GREER. He said "12:30." He looked at his watch, he said "12:30," and we were in the underpass at the time.

Mr. SPECTER. Mr. Greer, would you on Commission's Exhibit 347, mark with an "A" as best you can indicate the position of the President's automobile at the time of the first shot?

Mr. GREER. Do you want me to mark it on this exhibit?

Mr. SPECTER. Right there, that is right, that red pencil with an "A," a small "A."

Mr. GREER. This is the center, I would say [indicating].

Mr. SPECTER. Will you mark your best estimate as to the position of the automobile at the time of the second shot with the letter "B"?

Mr. GREER. I would have to guess how far I had traveled at that time. I really wouldn't know. It was probably a little farther, only guessing how far I would go. I am guessing as to the distance between them. Maybe farther but I am only guessing to say at that. I wouldn't have any definite reason.

Mr. SPECTER. Would you make that "B" a little plainer, if you can?

Mr. GREER. Yes.

Mr. SPECTER. Could you give us the best estimate in feet as to the distance you traveled from the time of the first shot to the time of the second shot?

Mr. GREER. No, sir; I don't believe I could. Anything I would say would be guessing.

Mr. SPECTER. Would you be able to give us a meaningful mark on the overhead photograph as to the position of your car at the time of the third shot?

Mr. GREER. From this overhead. I probably was where this mark is here.

Mr. SPECTER. Would you mark it?

Mr. GREER. I will put it alongside.

Mr. SPECTER. Put a little "C."

Mr. GREER. This was for the third shot.

Mr. SPECTER. Yes, sir.

Mr. GREER. This is "C." This not having an idea really of how much footage is in there at all. I wouldn't——

The CHAIRMAN. I didn't understand.

Mr. GREER. I said I wouldn't probably know, Mr. Chief Justice, how many feet would be in that distance. I would be guessing how many feet.

The CHAIRMAN. Yes; I understand.

Mr. SPECTER. Did you have any opportunity to observe the overhead as you were driving along after the last shot occurred?

Mr. GREER. No, sir. I was fairly close to it, to the best of my memory, and I was trying to watch then where I was going. I had to look ahead to see, I was catching up on the lead car real fast, and I had to watch what was ahead of me.

Mr. SPECTER. How fast was it possible to accelerate your automobile at that time?

Mr. GREER. Well, it is a very heavy automobile, and it does not pick up too fast on account of the weight. I have never tested to see how many feet I could travel in a second. I have never had any reason to test it to see how much could travel. But it was in low gear at that time, and that helps you to accelerate a lot faster.

Mr. SPECTER. Would you characterize it as a very rapid or a rapid acceleration?

Mr. GREER. No.

Mr. SPECTER. Or how would you characterize it?

Mr. GREER. It is a very smooth car taking off anyway, and I would say I

120

wasn't rapid. It is fairly fast in low gear but not rapid like a light car will be.

Mr. SPECTER. Does that car have an automatic transmission?

Mr. GREER. Yes, sir.

Mr. SPECTER. And what are the varieties of forward speeds in the vehicle?

Mr. GREER. It has a low gear and then it has drive one and drive two. It has two top gears. One has, one probably has, free wheeling more than the other. The other is not a free wheeling gear.

Mr. SPECTER. How fast can the car be driven in the low gear?

Mr. GREER. I would say safely you can drive it up to 40 miles an hour in low gear. That is estimating it at 40.

Mr. SPECTER. From the time of the first shot until the time of the third shot, was your car moving in a straight line or in an arc or how would you describe it?

Mr. GREER. I was following the contour of the road, the center of the contour of the road as it goes.

Mr. SPECTER. What is the path of the contour of the road?

Mr. GREER. Well, at the time I didn't think much of it but it is a little, there is a little bend in the road going to the underpass.

Mr. SPECTER. Did you hear anyone in the car say anything from the time of the first shot until the time of the third shot?

Mr. GREER. Not to the best of my recollection, I don't remember.

(At this point, Representative Boggs entered the hearing room.)

(Discussion off the record.)

Mr. SPECTER. Mr. Greer, did you hear anyone say anything from the time of the third shot until the time of arrival at Parkland Hospital?

Mr. GREER. No, sir; I didn't. I didn't hear, I can't remember hearing anyone say anything at all. We were quite preoccupied to get to the hospital as fast as we can, as we could, and that was my mind was really occupied on what I was doing. I didn't hear anything.

Mr. SPECTER. Do you know what speed you were traveling at en route to the hospital?

Mr. GREER. No, sir; I couldn't say. I was just getting through the traffic and through the streets as fast as I could get through.

Mr. SPECTER. Would you have any estimate at all on speed?

Mr. GREER. I would estimate that I must have been doing 40 or 50, at least 50 miles an hour at times. We might have been going as fast as 50 miles an hour, I am sure.

Mr. SPECTER. When you accelerated your automobile, did you at any time come alongside of or pass the police car in front of you?

Mr. GREER. No, sir; I never passed it. I came up alongside one or two motorcycle men and I called to them "get to a hospital fast". You know, I called to them "hospital".

Mr. SPECTER. Were you led to the hospital?

Mr. GREER. Yes, sir; I was led to the hospital by the police car who was preceding me.

Mr. SPECTER. Did you have any independent knowledge of the route from where you were?

Mr. GREER. No, sir.

Mr. SPECTER. From the point of assassination to the hospital?

Mr. GREER. No, sir; I didn't.

Mr. SPECTER. Were you escorted by any other automobiles besides the police car in front of you?

Mr. GREER. We had motorcycles and I don't know if there were other police cars out in front of that or not. I am sure there may have been, but I couldn't say right now.

Mr. SPECTER. Was there any radio communication between your automobile and the hospital at any time prior to your arrival at the hospital?

Mr. GREER. No, sir; not between the hospital and our car.

Mr. SPECTER. Did Mr. Kellerman have any radio contact at all with anyone in addition to that which you have already described?

Mr. GREER. He may have had some more communications to the car, the lead car, but I can't remember what they were now.

121

Mr. SPECTER. Did you observe any bullets strike any portion of the car or ricochet in any way during the course of the shooting?

Mr. GREER. No, sir; I did not.

Mr. SPECTER. Did you observe any bullets or fragments of bullets at rest in the car after the shooting terminated?

Mr. GREER. No, sir; I didn't. I left the car at the hospital and I didn't see it any more until the next day.

Mr. SPECTER. I hand you Commission Exhibit No. 349, Mr. Greer, and ask if you are able to identify what that picture represents?

Mr. GREER. That represents the windshield of the car.

Mr. SPECTER. Of the President's car?

Mr. GREER. Yes, sir; it looks like the windshield of the President's car.

Mr. SPECTER. Now calling your attention to a small arrow——

Mr. GREER. Arrow.

Mr. SPECTER. Which points up on what appears to be an indentation, I ask you if you—when was the first time, if at all, that you observed that indentation?

Mr. GREER. I didn't observe that——

Mr. SPECTER. On the car?

Mr. GREER. Until after I got back to Washington, until the car came back to Washington, I saw it at the White House garage. It was the first time I had ever noticed that.

Mr. SPECTER. On what date did you observe that indentation on the car?

Mr. GREER. That was the day after, the 23, would be it. It would be the day after the shooting. We got back from Dallas.

Mr. SPECTER. And what time of the day did you observe the car at the White House garage on that date?

Mr. GREER. It was in the afternoon, I believe. I believe it was in the afternoon, I believe.

Mr. SPECTER. Did anyone call that indentation to your attention at that time?

Mr. GREER. Yes; I was asked if I knew about it.

Mr. SPECTER. Who was it who asked you?

Mr. GREER. I can't remember now who did say that, but I was shown that indentation at the same time I was the break in the glass. I was shown both and asked if I had known but I can't remember who might have asked me.

Mr. SPECTER. Had you ever observed that indentation before the assassination occurred?

Mr. GREER. No, sir. I had never noticed it before at any time. I had never seen it before.

Mr. SPECTER. Had you ever had any occasion to examine closely that metallic area to ascertain whether or not there was such an indentation prior to the assassination?

Mr. GREER. Well, it seems to me I would have prior to that had it been there because I do take care of the car sometimes, and it had never been—I had never noticed it at any previous time.

Mr. SPECTER. I hand you Commission Exhibit 350 and ask you if you are able to state what that depicts?

Mr. GREER. That depicts a break or a shatter in the windshield of it.

Mr. SPECTER. Does that picture accurately represent the status of the windshield on the President's car at sometime?

Mr. GREER. Yes, sir; that windshield looks real familiar to me on the way it——

Mr. SPECTER. At what time, based on your observation, did the windshield of the President's car look like that picture?

Mr. GREER. I had never seen that until the following day after it came back from Dallas.

Mr. SPECTER. But on November 23, did the President's car windshield look like that?

Mr. GREER. Yes, sir; it looked like there was a break that had a diamond, in the windshield whenever I was shown that at the garage, the White House garage.

Mr. SPECTER. Was the size and scope of the crack the same as that which is shown on that exhibit?

Mr. GREER. That I wouldn't remember whether it was quite that large or not. I don't believe it was that big. It might not have been but I wouldn't say for sure.

Mr. SPECTER. Did you observe any crack on the windshield after the time of the shooting on November 22?

Mr. GREER. No, sir; I didn't see it at all. I didn't know anything about it until I came back, until the car came back and I was shown that.

Mr. SPECTER. Did you have any occasion on November 22, after the shooting, to observe closely the windshield?

Mr. GREER. No, sir. The only time I was in the car was going to the hospital and I never—I didn't see the car any more. It was just from the shooting until we got to Parkland that I was with the car. I left the car there and never did see it until it was back at the White House garage.

Mr. SPECTER. Are you able to state with certainty there was no crack in that windshield prior to the shooting on November 22?

Mr. GREER. Yes, sir; I am sure there was nothing wrong with that windshield prior to that because I would have—it was almost in front of me and I examined the car, I looked it all over when I got there, I saw it was clean and everything, the windshield. I didn't see this ever at any time previous.

Mr. SPECTER. Mr. Greer, I now call your attention to a windshield which has been marked as Commission Exhibit No. 351, and I will ask you to take a look at it and identify it for us, if you can, calling your attention first of all to the windshield itself. Are you able to state——

Mr. GREER. Yes, sir; this is the windshield that came out of the Lincoln.

Mr. SPECTER. That you were operating on the day of the assassination?

Mr. GREER. Yes, sir.

Mr. SPECTER. Can you describe what cracks, if any, which you see now on that windshield were present?

Mr. GREER. When I looked——

Mr. SPECTER. When you observed the automobile windshield on November 23, the next day?

Mr. GREER. This little star, the star in here with the little star. These cracks were not there.

Mr. SPECTER. Now by these cracks you are indicating——

Mr. GREER. These.

Mr. SPECTER. The long cracks which radiate off from the center?

Mr. GREER. That is right. This was the only cracks that I could see was this star-type fragment.

Mr. SPECTER. There you are indicating what would be described as the principal point of contact which was present when you observed it on November 23?

Mr. GREER. Yes, sir.

Mr. SPECTER. Give me your best estimate on the diameter of the cracking of the windshield as it existed on November 23?

Mr. GREER. To the best of my estimate it would be these little stars that are here, the little shatters that are here.

Mr. SPECTER. Would it be fair to say that you are indicating a circle with a circumference or diameter of approximately an inch to an inch and a half?

Mr. GREER. I don't think it probably would be an inch. The whole diameter.

Mr. SPECTER. Approximately 1 inch as you estimate it?

Mr. GREER. Yes, sir.

Representative BOGGS. Excuse me, did you say you did not notice this crack from the time that you drove the car after the shooting to the hospital?

Mr. GREER. No, sir; I had flags on the car and you know they were waving at a high rate of speed and you have the Presidential flag and the American flag in front of you there; you know when you are going at a fast speed you get a lot of, well, I don't know how you would say it, it attracts you so much that I didn't have any recollection of what happened on the windshield.

Representative BOGGS. There was no glass or anything that spattered on you in any way?

Mr. GREER. No, sir; I didn't feel anything at all. I didn't feel a thing hit me.

I was kind of shocked at the time, I guess anything could have and I wouldn't have known what hit me. You are tense, I was pretty tense, and naturally my thoughts were the hospital, and how fast I could get there, and probably I could have been injured and not even known I was injured. I was in that position.

Mr. SPECTER. Mr. Greer, what is your best estimate and recollection of the time that the shooting occurred?

Mr. GREER. Well, Mr. Kellerman saying 12:30 to me makes me—that stays in my mind foremost, and that was when we had just left the scene of the shooting, a few seconds or a second or two from it. That is why that 12:30 stays in my mind, him saying 12:30 to me right after the shooting, he said. His watch may not have been correct but that is what he said to me at the time.

Mr. SPECTER. What is your best estimate of the distance between the point where the assassination occurred and Parkland Hospital?

Mr. GREER. No, sir; I haven't. It seemed like endless miles and probably wasn't very far, but it seemed like to me it was endless getting there. I was——

Mr. SPECTER. Are you able to give us an estimate with reasonable accuracy on the time it took?

Mr. GREER. No, sir.

Mr. SPECTER. From the time it took from the point of the shooting until you arrived at Parkland Hospital?

Mr. GREER. I didn't check anything but I thought that probably it would probably be 6 or 8 minutes, I am not too sure, somewhere in the vicinity of 5 and 10 minutes. I would have to guess at that.

Mr. SPECTER. How did you know which entrance of the hospital to go to?

Mr. GREER. I followed the car that was in front of me right to where he stopped and I was right at the entrance. The car stopped and I stopped alongside of him.

Mr. SPECTER. Which entrance was that?

Mr. GREER. It seems, I think it was the emergency entrance, I am almost sure. It was like a bay that you could pull in and out of. It looked like an ambulance entrance.

Mr. SPECTER. What did you observe with respect to President Kennedy's condition on arrival at the Parkland Hospital?

Mr. GREER. To the best of my knowledge he was laying, it seemed across Mrs. Kennedy, looked like laying across her lap or in front of her, I am not too sure which, I opened the doors—the doors were opened before I got to it, someone else had opened the doors and they were trying to get Connally out, and Mrs. Connally out of the seats so they could get to the President.

Mr. SPECTER. What did you observe about the President with respect to his wounds?

Mr. GREER. His head was all shot, this whole part was all a matter of blood like he had been hit.

Mr. SPECTER. Indicating the top and right rear side of the head?

Mr. GREER. Yes, sir; it looked like that was all blown off.

Mr. SPECTER. Yes.

Mr. GREER. I run around the front of the car and got hold of a stretcher or thing and I got hold of it to keep it steady while they lifted the President's body onto it and then I helped pull the front end of it into the emergency room.

Mr. SPECTER. Who was first removed from the automobile?

Mr. GREER. Governor Connally was first removed. He was on the jump seats.

Mr. SPECTER. And what, if anything, did you observe as to Governor Connally's condition on arrival at Parkland Hospital?

Mr. GREER. The best of my recollection he was lying across the seat toward Mrs. Connally when they picked him up and got him out of the car. And he was rushed in first into the hospital. That is when I got the stretcher to bring it, to hold it until they would get the President on it, on the right side of the car. They took him out on the side he was sitting on, that side of the car.

Mr. SPECTER. Were you able to make any personal observation about Governor Connally's specific wound?

Mr. GREER. No, sir. I didn't know how badly anyone really was injured. I had great thoughts the President was still living and that was the only thing I was thinking about was to get them in quick.

124

Mr. SPECTER. Did you observe anything specific which led you to the conclusion that the President was still living?

Mr. GREER. No, sir. When he was in the emergency room and I was there, I did see his chest expand and move, the movement of the chest a time or so.

Mr. SPECTER. Were you able to observe any wound on the front side of the President?

Mr. GREER. No, sir; I didn't, I never seen any on the front side of the President. The only thing I saw was on the head. I didn't know at the time of any other injuries on him.

Mr. SPECTER. As to the front side of the President's body, were you able to observe any hole or tear in either his shirt or tie?

Mr. GREER. No, sir; I didn't and I brought them back, those things, and I didn't see them at the time. I probably didn't inspect them very closely but they were handed to me in a paper bag to bring back.

Mr. SPECTER. When did you acquire custody and possession of those items of clothing?

Mr. GREER. After they had made the President's body ready for removal, I was in the emergency room, and a nurse got two shopping bags and I held them and she put the President's suit, his belongings into the two bags including his shoes and socks, and his pants and jacket which they had torn and the shirt they had torn, they had torn it to take it off him, and the nurse put these into the two bags and I got custody of them right then from the nurse at the emergency room.

Mr. SPECTER. Were there any other items of wearing apparel such as shorts or undershirt?

Mr. GREER. Yes, sir; his shorts and that brace he wore, whatever it was, and his sox and shoes, and shirt, and his trousers, and his suit coat.

Mr. SPECTER. Are you able to state with certainty that there was no undershirt?

Mr. GREER. Yes, sir; there was no undershirt. I am sure there was no undershirt. I would have to say it to the best of my recollection, there was no undershirt. I had been with him so many times and I knew he didn't normally wear an undershirt because I had heard him one time previously, I offered him a coat.

He said, "I have an undershirt on today," it was at some ballgame. He normally didn't wear an undershirt.

Mr. SPECTER. Can you describe with more particularity the brace you just said he was wearing?

Mr. GREER. It looked like a, I would say, a corset-type brace, maybe 6 inches wide, he wore it around his, down low around his, haunches, a little lower than the waist, probably, just probably below his belt he wore it there. It was something he normally wore, and I would guess, but I would say it was of a soft, maybe a kind of corset-type material, maybe elastic or something like that support.

Mr. SPECTER. Mr. Greer, when your automobile arrived at Parkland, was there any medical individual awaiting your arrival?

Mr. GREER. I can't remember—there were—who brought the stretchers out. There were some hospital people there, but who they were, I never got—I couldn't identify or knew who they were. There were some medical people there; yes.

Mr. SPECTER. Where were they when you first saw hospital personnel?

Mr. GREER. When I pulled into the ambulance entrance there were some people there on the right-hand side with these stretchers that they had rushed out. I don't know just who they were from the hospital staff. There was a great deal of confusion because everyone was trying to help, the agents were there.

Mr. SPECTER. Are you able to state whether there was a doctor in attendance at that time?

Mr. GREER. No, sir; I couldn't state that.

Mr. SPECTER. What did you do after your arrival at Parkland Hospital?

Mr. GREER. I helped pull it, take the stretcher into the emergency room that he was on. It is on wheels, and I helped to take that in, and I stayed inside the door of the emergency room most of the time while they were, the doctors were, working on the President's body.

Mr. SPECTER. How many doctors were working on him in the emergency room?

Mr. GREER. There were, between nurses and doctors, I would estimate there were, between 10 or 12 people, maybe not that many, 8 to 10 people in and out of that room. I don't know how many of them were doctors, attendants, nurses, and things like that with white jackets and they would come in and say, "I am doctor so-and-so."

Mr. SPECTER. How long were they working on him there in the emergency room?

Mr. GREER. I couldn't remember the time.

Mr. SPECTER. You say you were with him most of the time?

Mr. GREER. I was inside the door. I know, I kept the door closed most of the time, let doctors and nurses in and out while he was—while they were working on him. I stayed inside the emergency room door.

Mr. SPECTER. Was there any special reason for you to leave part of the time?

Mr. GREER. No, sir; I didn't go any farther away than outside the door.

Mr. SPECTER. Were there any other Secret Service agents inside the emergency room at that time?

Mr. GREER. Not at that time; I was inside the door.

Mr. SPECTER. Where was Mrs. Kennedy at this time?

Mr. GREER. Mrs. Kennedy was outside the door. They got her a chair out there for a little while and then she insisted on coming in and she got in the corner for a little while there and stayed there a little while and I don't quite remember the time she went over to his body but she did go over there, and I don't remember how far along the doctors had been on him when that happened.

Mr. SPECTER. Were you able to overhear any of the conversations among the doctors in the emergency room?

Mr. GREER. I don't understand anything that they were discussing at all.

Mr. SPECTER. Did a priest or more than one priest come upon the scene?

Mr. GREER. I believe there were two. To the best of my recollection there eventually was two.

Mr. SPECTER. How long after President Kennedy arrived at the emergency room did the priest arrive, if you recollect?

Mr. GREER. No, sir; I wouldn't have any idea, it seemed to me it was quite a little while in the matter, probably minutes.

Mr. SPECTER. Approximately how long did the priests stay?

Mr. GREER. I don't remember that, sir.

Mr. SPECTER. Did they say anything on leaving or in entering?

Mr. GREER. Not that I heard of personally. I was outside the room when the priest was in there. I wasn't in the emergency room while he was in.

Mr. SPECTER. When did you find that the President had died?

Mr. GREER. When the priest was in to give him the last rites then I knew that.

Mr. SPECTER. Do you have any reasonably close estimate on when the President did die?

Mr. GREER. No, sir; I haven't right off. I would have to look at some reports.

Mr. SPECTER. What did you do after the President was pronounced dead?

Mr. GREER. We stayed there until everything was settled up. I believe there was a judge came in there and I think, someone came in and made the decisions on removing the body and the casket was brought in, and the body was put in the casket. I had this, his clothing, I kept it in my hand at all times, all the time. Then I went, when they removed the casket from the emergency room, I was in front of it going out to make a path to get it to the ambulance.

So, I helped get it into the ambulance and then I drove a car with some agents and some people right behind the ambulance to Love Field back to the airport again and helped to get the casket aboard the airplane.

Mr. SPECTER. Were you present at the swearing in of President Johnson?

Mr. GREER. Yes, sir; I was—we were all asked to come back into the state room but I wasn't in too close. I was in the main part of the plane, as close as I could get to it, yes.

Mr. SPECTER. How did you personally return to Washington, D.C.?

Mr. GREER. I returned on Air Force 1 with the President's remains.

Mr. SPECTER. And at approximately what time did you leave Dallas to fly back?

Mr. GREER. I would have to look in my reports to say exactly. I would have to go back on the times. Two something but I don't remember.

Mr. SPECTER. Do you have any idea of the time you arrived in the Washington area?

Mr. GREER. I believe it was 6 or 6:15. As I say I have it in my reports but I haven't looked at the times recently.

Mr. SPECTER. Where did you arrive in the Washington area?

Mr. GREER. At Andrews Air Force Base.

Mr. SPECTER. What did you do next in connection with this matter?

Mr. GREER. I helped to get the casket out of the plane, and put it into a Navy ambulance and then I drove that Navy ambulance to Bethesda Naval Center.

Mr. SPECTER. What did you do upon arriving at the Bethesda Naval Center?

Mr. GREER. I stayed in, while the autopsy was being performed, I stayed in the autopsy room with Mr. Kellerman and the doctors and the people who were in there. I stayed in there and observed what was necessary that I could do.

Mr. SPECTER. Were any Secret Service Agents present besides you and Mr. Kellerman?

Mr. GREER. No, sir.

Mr. SPECTER. At the autopsy?

Mr. GREER. There may have been, Mr. Hill may have come in and out but he didn't stay there. Mr. Kellerman and I stayed permanently the whole time there. There may have been, Mr. Hill may have come in there and have gone back out but he didn't stay in there.

Mr. SPECTER. During the course of the autopsy did you hear any doctor say anything about the wound on the right side of Mr. Kennedy's back?

Mr. GREER. That was the first time that I had ever seen it, when the doctors were performing the autopsy, they saw this hole in the right shoulder or back of the head, and in the back, and that was the first I had known that he was ever shot there, and they brought it to our attention or discussed it there a little bit.

Mr. SPECTER. What conversation was there concerning the wound on the right back?

Mr. GREER. Well, the doctors and people who were performing the autopsy, when they turned the body apparently over they discovered that this wound was in the back, and they thought that they probably could get a bullet out of there, and it took a lot of—then they took more X-rays, they took a lot of X-rays, we looked at them and couldn't find the trace of any bullet anywhere in the X-rays at all, nothing showed on the X-rays where this bullet or lead could have gone.

Mr. SPECTER. Approximately where in the President's back was the bullet hole?

Mr. GREER. It was, to the best of my recollection it was, back here, just in the soft part of that shoulder.

Mr. SPECTER. Indicating the upper right shoulder area?

Mr. GREER. Upper right, yes.

Mr. SPECTER. Was there any effort made to probe that wound by any doctor?

Mr. GREER. I believe, yes, I believe the doctors probed to see if they could find that there was a bullet there.

Mr. SPECTER. Do you know which doctor that was?

Mr. GREER. No, sir; I don't, I don't have their names at this time.

Mr. SPECTER. Did any doctor make any statement about the results of his probing effort?

Mr. GREER. I questioned one of the doctors in there about that, and when we found out that they had found a bullet in Dallas, I questioned the doctor about it and he said if they were using pressure on the chest that it could very well have been, come back out, where it went in at, that is what they said at the time.

(At this point, Representative Ford entered the hearing room.)

Mr. SPECTER. Was anything said about any channel being present in the body for the bullet to have gone on through the back?

Mr. GREER. No, sir; I hadn't heard anything like that, any trace of it going on through.

Mr. SPECTER. Did you just mention, Mr. Greer, a hole in the President's head in addition to the large area of the skull which was shot away?

Mr. GREER. No. I had just seen that, you know, the head was damaged in all this part of it but I believe looking at the X-rays, I looked at the X-rays when they were taken in the autopsy room, and the person who does that type work showed us the trace of it because there would be little specks of lead where the bullet had come from here and it came to the—they showed where it didn't come on through. It came to a sinus cavity or something they said, over the eye.

Mr. SPECTER. Indicating the right eye.

Mr. GREER. I may be wrong.

Mr. SPECTER. You don't know which eye?

Mr. GREER. I don't know which eye, I may be wrong. But they showed us the trace of it coming through but there were very little small specks on the X-rays that these professionals knew what course that the bullet had taken, the lead.

Mr. SPECTER. Would you describe in very general terms what injury you observed as to the President's head during the course of the autopsy?

Mr. GREER. I would—to the best of my recollection it was in this part of the head right here.

Mr. SPECTER. Upper right?

Mr. GREER. Upper right side.

Mr. SPECTER. Upper right side, going toward the rear.

And what was the condition of the skull at that point?

Mr. GREER. The skull was completely—this part was completely gone.

Mr. SPECTER. Now, aside from that opening which you have described and you have indicated a circle with a diameter of approximately 5 inches, would you say that is about what you have indicated there?

Mr. GREER. Approximately I would say 5 inches; yes.

Mr. SPECTER. Did you observe any other opening or hole of any sort in the head itself?

Mr. GREER. No, sir; I didn't. No other one.

Mr. SPECTER. Specifically did you observe a hole which would be below the large area of skull which was absent?

Mr. GREER. No, sir; I didn't.

Mr. SPECTER. Did you have occasion to look in the back of the head immediately below where the skull was missing?

Mr. GREER. No; I can't remember even examining the head that close at that time.

Mr. SPECTER. When President Kennedy was being treated in the emergency room at Parkland Hospital, were any pictures or X-rays taken of him there?

Mr. GREER. No, sir; not that I know of. I didn't see any being taken.

Mr. SPECTER. Was he ever turned over that you observed while being treated at Parkland Hospital?

Mr. GREER. No, sir. I can't recollect him ever being turned over.

Mr. SPECTER. Do you have any recollection that he was in fact not turned over?

Mr. GREER. No, sir; I couldn't even say. I didn't see them turn him over in any way in my vision, although my back was to him quite often and because I was attending to the door and they could have done it.

Mr. SPECTER. Was he on a stretcher at the time he was being worked on at Parkland Hospital?

Mr. GREER. I can't remember whether they changed him from a stretcher to a table. I am not sure on that.

Mr. SPECTER. Mr. Greer, as to the return of the President's automobile to Washington, do you know how that was accomplished?

Mr. GREER. It was driven to Love Field, and put aboard the same C–130 it was taken out on and flown back to Andrews Air Force Base.

Mr. SPECTER. Do you know when it was returned from Dallas to the Washington area?

Mr. GREER. I believe it was returned shortly after, it left shortly after, the President's plane left, was flown back.

Mr. SPECTER. I hand you two photographs marked Commission Exhibit No. 352 and Commission Exhibit No. 353.

Do those photographs represent the condition of the back seat of the President's car at some time?

Mr. GREER. Yes, sir; they do.

Mr. SPECTER. And at what time do those pictures look just as the back seat of the President's car looked?

Mr. GREER. It looked like that when it came back from Dallas.

Mr. SPECTER. Did it look like that immediately after President Kennedy was removed from the back seat?

Mr. GREER. I wasn't there any more, sir. I was with the President after they lifted him out. I didn't see the car after he had been removed.

Mr. SPECTER. Did you observe the back seat of the car at any time from the time you arrived at Parkland Hospital until you observed the automobile in Washington?

Mr. GREER. No, sir.

Mr. SPECTER. On November 23?

Mr. GREER. No, sir; I didn't.

Mr. SPECTER. By the way, Mr. Greer, how much, approximately, does or did the President's automobile weigh?

Mr. GREER. It weighed between—well, for flight reason we said 8,000, but it wasn't that much. It probably was 7,500. We had extra weight on it.

Mr. SPECTER. Are you able to tell the Commission the dimensions of the automobile, indicating its length?

Mr. GREER. Yes, sir. It is 21 feet 8 inches long.

Mr. SPECTER. And how wide?

Mr. GREER. I would have to go back for the width on it. I have it all in black and white in the office, but I haven't got it with me in my head right now; I am sorry.

Mr. SPECTER. Could three people sit comfortably in the front seat of the automobile?

Mr. GREER. Yes, sir; it was wide enough for three. We many times had an aide in there; many times, an aide rode in the front.

Mr. SPECTER. Was it as wide or wider than, say, a Cadillac automobile?

Mr. GREER. No, sir; it would be probably the same width.

Representative BOGGS. Was that car specially made for the President?

Mr. GREER. Yes, sir; it was a specially built car.

Representative BOGGS. Was it a Lincoln Continental?

Mr. GREER. Yes, sir; a Lincoln Continental.

Representative BOGGS. How did it differ from the ordinary Lincoln?

Mr. GREER. Well, Lincoln doesn't make a seven-passenger car, and this was a seven-passenger car. The back seat on this car would raise 8 inches. It was electric, and you could lift, you could raise, the seat up 8 inches from the ground, from the floorboards. It had a little step that went with it. The President could raise it up and down himself. He had a button alongside that would cause it to go up and down when the top wasn't down. It wouldn't go up and down when the top was down. But when it was off he could raise it up or down, and it would be above the other seat.

Mr. SPECTER. Do you know whether the seat was actually raised at the time of the assassination?

Mr. GREER. No, sir; I couldn't say right off. I don't believe it was, but I wouldn't know.

Mr. SPECTER. Going back to the shots themselves, Mr. Greer, do you have any reaction as to the direction from which the shots came?

Mr. GREER. They sounded like they were behind me, to the right rear of me.

Mr. SPECTER. Would that be as to all three shots?

Mr. GREER. Yes, sir. They sounded, everything sounded, behind me, to me. That was my thought, train of thought, that they were behind me.

Mr. SPECTER. Have you ever had any reaction or thought at any time since the assassination that the shots came from the front of the car?

Mr. GREER. No, sir; I had never even the least thought that they could come. There was no thought in my mind other than that they were behind me.

Mr. SPECTER. Yes, sir.

The CHAIRMAN. Congressman Boggs, are there any questions you would like to ask the agent?

Representative BOGGS. I don't think so, Mr. Chairman.

The CHAIRMAN. Congressman Ford.

Representative FORD. Did you ever have any thought there were more than three shots?

Mr. GREER. No, sir; I never did.

Representative FORD. Did you positively identify the fact that there were one, two, three, or was there one, and then a delay, and then a flurry?

Mr. GREER. To the best of my recollection, Congressman, was that the last two were closer together than the first one. It seemed like the first one, and then there was, you know, bang, bang, just right behind it almost. The two seemed, the last two seemed, closer to me than the other.

Representative BOGGS. Did you speed up after you heard the first shot?

Mr. GREER. After I heard the second. The first one didn't sink into me, didn't give me the thought that it was a shot. I thought it was the backfire of a motorcycle. But when I heard the second one and glanced over my shoulder, I knew something was wrong then. I didn't know how bad anyone was injured or anything, but I knew there was something wrong, and right away after the second one I accelerated as fast as I could.

The CHAIRMAN. Mr. Craig, would you like to ask any questions?

Mr. CRAIG. Thank you, Mr. Chief Justice.

With respect to the position of the President's car that you were driving as it approached the underpass, you state now that you couldn't fix any specific distance. But would you say it was less than a mile that the President's car was from the overpass?

Mr. GREER. Oh, definitely. I couldn't say in feet or yards, but it was within— it was feet. I would say probably a hundred or 200 feet. It could be within that; it was definitely right up close to me, but I——

Mr. CRAIG. With respect to your vision, was it unobstructed down the roadway, looking at the overpass?

Mr. GREER. Yes, sir; there were no obstructions in the road that I could see.

Mr. CRAIG. As I recall your testimony, you were actually observing the overpass to see if there was any person there.

Mr. GREER. People up there at that time I would be doubtful of going underneath.

Mr. CRAIG. Yes, sir. And you say now you do not recollect that you saw anyone there?

Mr. GREER. Yes, sir.

Mr. CRAIG. You said also, I believe, that it was some time now since you made that observation. Did you make any report of any kind with respect to anyone being on the overpass immediately after this incident?

Mr. GREER. No, sir.

Mr. CRAIG. You made no written report to anybody as to whether or not there were people on the overpass or were not people?

Mr. GREER. No, sir; I haven't.

Mr. CRAIG. Do you believe if you had observed people on the overpass at that time you would now remember it?

Mr. GREER. Yes, sir; I believe I would; yes, sir.

Mr. CRAIG. If you had observed people on the overpass as you proceeded toward it, and they were other than a policeman or policemen or some other law-enforcement agent, what would you have done?

Mr. GREER. Well, I try never to go underneath a bridge if there are people up over it, if there are people who I don't know as law enforcement. I try not to go underneath them. I will probably veer to one side of them at any time. That is a matter of our training, that we try not to go underneath anyone with an open car where anyone could drop something.

Mr. CRAIG. Would you ever stop, if necessary, if you thought there were people up there that you couldn't veer around?

Mr. GREER. If there was any danger there I would have to either change my way of traveling. I have never had it happen, and never had any reason to, but we try, I try, not to go underneath a group of people standing on any overpass at any time. I try to move over, if the condition permits me to. Sometimes, when the road is too narrow, I couldn't. But that is part of our procedure, I think, to see that no one is on an overpass.

Mr. CRAIG. That is all.

The CHAIRMAN. If there are no further questions——

Mr. SPECTER. Mr. Chief Justice, may I ask one or two other questions?

The CHAIRMAN. Yes.

Mr. SPECTER. I have just noted that we have the report of the FBI which bears Bureau file No. 105–S, as it appears here somewhat indistinct, S–2555, "Report of Special Agent Robert P. Gemberling, dated December 10, 1963," and this refers, Mr. Greer, to an interview of you by Special Agents Francis X. O'Neill, Jr., and James W. Sibert. There is a report here of an interview of you and of Special Agent Kellerman, and the date here is listed as November 22, 1963, and there is this reference made in the report, and I will quote it verbatim:

"Greer stated that he first heard what he thought was possibly a motorcycle backfire, and glanced around and noticed that the President had evidently been hit. He thereafter got on the radio and communicated with the other vehicles stating that they desired to get the President to the hospital immediately."

Mr. GREER. I didn't go on the radio. It was Mr. Kellerman who done the radio talking. I didn't. It is a misquote if I done it. I didn't get on the radio. Mr. Kellerman did.

Mr. SPECTER. Did you ever make this statement, Mr. Greer, to Special Agent O'Neill or Sibert?

Mr. GREER. Those two agents were in during the autopsy; those two agents were in the autopsy room, with Mr. Kellerman and I, all night. Mr. Sibert and O'Neill were both in the autopsy room with us during that time, and the only time that any of us, either Mr. Kellerman or I, we never left the room, one or the other. We went and got some coffee and came right back, something like that, and the FBI did the same thing. One of them left; the other stayed.

Mr. SPECTER. Do you now recollect whether or not you ever said to them that you were the one who communicated on the radio with the other vehicles?

Mr. GREER. No, sir; I know I never remember saying that to them because I know I didn't do it. So that is how I know that I didn't say it, because I know I didn't do it. Mr. Kellerman did.

Mr. SPECTER. And the first part refers to your noticing that the President evidently had been hit. Did you ever——

Mr. GREER. I have no recollection of ever telling the agents that I said that; no, sir. If I said it, I don't remember saying it. The Governor was the person that I knew was—when we were first in trouble, when I see the Governor.

Mr. SPECTER. To the best of your current recollection, did you notice that the President had been hit?

Mr. GREER. No. sir; I didn't know how badly he was injured or anything other than that. I didn't know.

Mr. SPECTER. Did you know at all, from the glance which you have described that he had been hit or injured in any way?

Mr. GREER. I knew he was injured in some way, but I didn't know how bad or what.

Mr. SPECTER. How did you know that?

Mr. GREER. If I remember now, I just don't remember how I knew, but I knew we were in trouble. I knew that he was injured, but I can't remember, recollect, just how I knew there were injuries in there. I didn't know who all was hurt, even.

Mr. SPECTER. Are you able to recollect whether you saw the President after the shots as you were proceeding toward Parkland Hospital?

Mr. GREER. No; I don't remember ever seeing him any more until I got to the hospital, and he was lying across the seat, you know, and that is the first I had seen of him.

Mr. SPECTER. Your best recollection is, then, that you had the impression he was injured but you couldn't ascertain the source of that information?

Mr. GREER. Right. I couldn't ascertain the source.

Representative FORD. Did you hear the President say anything after the first shot?

Mr. GREER. No, sir; I never heard him say anything; never at any time did I ever hear him say anything.

Representative BOGGS. Did Mrs. Kennedy say anything to you while you were driving to the hospital?

Mr. GREER. No, sir; she didn't.

Representative BOGGS. Did Mrs. Connally say anything to you?

Mr. GREER. No. Mrs. Connally didn't say anything, either. There is quite a little distance between the front and the back seat of that car. As you know, it is 21 feet long, and you are quite a little bit away, and there was the sirens were all going. The following car had a siren wide—the big one on the fender was wide open. There wasn't much chance for me to hear anything, and I was really occupied with getting there just as fast as I could and not seeing that anything happened, avoid an accident or anything like that.

Mr. SPECTER. Did you have a siren on your car?

Mr. GREER. I didn't have mine going. There is a siren on that car, but I didn't even reach down to work it.

Representative BOGGS. There was another agent in the car with you?

Mr. GREER. Mr. Kellerman; yes, sir.

Representative BOGGS. And after the first shot, did he say to speed up or what?

Mr. GREER. I believe it was at the second that he and I both simultaneously— he said, "Get out of here fast," and I speeded up as fast as I could then and as fast as the car would go.

The CHAIRMAN. If there are no further questions, thank you very much, Mr. Greer.

Mr. GREER. Thank you, sir.

The CHAIRMAN. You may be excused.

Mr. GREER. Thank you, sir.

The CHAIRMAN. We will take a short recess.

(Short recess.)

The CHAIRMAN. Mr. Hill, come right in, sir. Would you raise your right hand, please, and be sworn? Do you solemnly swear that the testimony you give before this Commission will be the truth, the whole truth, and nothing but the truth, so help you God?

Mr. HILL. I do.

The CHAIRMAN. Would you be seated, please, Mr. Hill?

Mr. HILL. Thank you, sir.

The CHAIRMAN. Mr. Specter.

TESTIMONY OF CLINTON J. HILL, SPECIAL AGENT, SECRET SERVICE

Mr. SPECTER. Mr. Hill, would you state your full name for the record, please?

Mr. HILL. Clinton J. Hill.

Mr. SPECTER. How old are you, sir?

Mr. HILL. Thirty-two.

Mr. SPECTER. What is your educational background?

Mr. HILL. I went to secondary educational high school in Washburn, N. Dak., and then went on to Concordia College, Moorehead, Minn. I was a history and education major, with a minor in physical education.

Mr. SPECTER. What year were you graduated?

Mr. HILL. 1954.

Mr. SPECTER. What have you done since the time of graduation from college, Mr. Hill?

Mr. HILL. I went into the Army in 1954; remained in the Army until 1957. Then I couldn't determine what I wanted to do, whether to go to law school or not, and I took a couple of odd jobs. I worked for a finance company at one time. Then I went to work for the Chicago, Burlington & Quincy Railroad as a special agent in the spring of 1958, and entered the Secret Service in September 1958.

Mr. SPECTER. You have been with the Secret Service since September 1958 to the present time?

Mr. HILL. Yes; I have.

Mr. SPECTER. Will you outline for the Commission your duties with the Secret Service during your tenure there?

Mr. HILL. I entered the Secret Service in Denver, and during that period I did both investigative and protection work. I was assigned to Mrs. Doud, the mother-in-law of President Eisenhower. I attended the Treasury Law Enforcement School during my first year, and was sent to the White House for a 30-day temporary assignment at the White House in June 1959. In November of 1959, November 1, I was transferred to the White House on a permanent basis as a special agent assigned to the White House detail. I have been at the White House since that time.

Mr. SPECTER. Now, were you assigned to duties on the trip of President Kennedy to Texas in November 1963?

Mr. HILL. Yes, sir; I was.

Mr. SPECTER. Did you have any special duty assigned to you at that time?

Mr. HILL. Yes, sir.

Mr. SPECTER. In connection with the trip?

Mr. HILL. I was responsible for the protection of Mrs. Kennedy.

Mr. SPECTER. And, in a general way, what does that sort of an assignment involve?

Mr. HILL. I tried to remain as close to her at all times as possible, and in this particular trip that meant being with the President because all of their doings on this trip were together rather than separate. I would go over her schedule to make sure she knows what she is expected to do; discuss it with her; remain in her general area all the time; protect her from any danger.

Mr. SPECTER. Would you tell us, in a general way, what were the activities of the President and Mrs. Kennedy on the morning of Friday, November 22, before they arrived in Dallas?

Mr. HILL. I went to the fifth floor, I believe it was, where the President and Mrs. Kennedy were staying in the Texas Hotel in Fort Worth at 8:15 in the morning. President Kennedy was to go downstairs and across the street to make a speech to a gathering in a parking lot. I remained on the floor during the period the President was gone.

It was raining outside, I recall. About 9:25 I received word from Special Agent Duncan that the President requested Mrs. Kennedy to come to the mezzanine, where a breakfast was being held in his honor, and where he was about to speak. I went in and advised Mrs. Kennedy of this, and took her down to where the President was speaking; remained with her adjacent to the head table in this particular area during the speech; and accompanied she and the President back up to the, I believe it was, the fifth floor of the hotel, their residential area; remained on that floor until we left, went downstairs, got into the motorcade, and departed the hotel for the airport to leave Fort Worth for Dallas.

We were airborne approximately 11:20, I believe, in Air Force 1. I was in the aft compartment, which is part of the residential compartment, and we arrived in Dallas at 11:40.

Mr. SPECTER. Would you describe, in a general way, what the President and Mrs. Kennedy did upon arrival in Dallas?

Mr. HILL. They debarked the rear ramp of the aircraft first, followed by Governor and Mrs. Connally, various Congressmen and Senators. And Special Agent in Charge Kellerman and myself went down the ramp. There was a small reception committee at the foot of the ramp, and somebody gave Mrs. Kennedy some red roses, I recall. I walked immediately to the followup car and placed my topcoat, which is a raincoat, and small envelope containing some information concerning the Dallas stop in the followup car, returning to where the President and Mrs. Kennedy were at that time greeting a crippled lady in a wheelchair.

Mr. SPECTER. What do you estimate the size of the crowd to have been at Dallas that morning?

Mr. HILL. At the airport?

Mr. SPECTER. Yes, sir.

Mr. HILL. It is rather difficult to say. They were behind a chain-link fence, not on the airport ramp itself, and they were jammed up against the fence

133

holding placards, and many young people in the crowd. I would say there were probably 2,000 people there.

Mr. SPECTER. At approximately what time did the motorcade depart from Love Field to Dallas?

Mr. HILL. Approximately 11:55.

Mr. SPECTER. Do you know approximately how many automobiles there were in the motorcade?

Mr. HILL. No, sir; I do not.

Mr. SPECTER. In which car in the motorcade were you positioned?

Mr. HILL. I was working the followup car, which is the car immediately behind the Presidential car.

Mr. SPECTER. And how many cars are there ahead of the followup car, then, in the entire motorcade?

Mr. HILL. There was a lead car ahead of the President's car, the President's car, then this particular followup car.

Mr. SPECTER. Do you know whether there was any car in advance of the car termed the lead car?

Mr. HILL. There could have been a pilot car, but I am not sure.

Mr. SPECTER. Now, approximately how far in front of the President's car did the lead car stay during the course of the motorcade?

Mr. HILL. I would say a half block, maybe.

Mr. SPECTER. And how far was the President's car in front of the President's followup car during the course of the motorcade?

Mr. HILL. Approximately 5 feet.

Mr. SPECTER. Is there some well-established practice as to the spacing between the President's car and the President's followup car?

Mr. HILL. It would depend upon speed. We attempt to stay as close to the President's car as practical. At high rates of speed it is rather difficult to stay close because of the danger involved. Slow speeds, the followup car stays as close as possible so that the agents on the followup car can get to the Presidential car as quickly as possible.

Mr. SPECTER. What was the first car to the rear of the President's followup car?

Mr. HILL. The Vice-Presidential automobile.

Mr. SPECTER. What car was immediately behind the Vice President's automobile?

Mr. HILL. The Vice-Presidential followup car.

Mr. SPECTER. Do you know what cars in the Dallas motorcade followed the Vice President's followup car?

Mr. HILL. Well, I couldn't say which car any individual rode in after that particular automobile, but I could say they were occupied by members of the staff, both President Kennedy's and Vice President Johnson's; Congressmen and Senators who were on this particular trip; newspaper personnel who were on this trip.

Mr. SPECTER. Would you identify the occupants of the President's followup car and indicate where each was in the automobile.

Mr. HILL. The car itself was driven by Special Agent Sam Kinney, and Assistant to the Special Agent in Charge Emory Roberts was riding in the right front seat. I was assigned to work the left running board of the automobile, the forward portion of that running board. McIntyre was assigned to work the rear portion of the left running board. Special Agent John Ready was assigned the forward portion of the right running board; Special Agent Paul Landis was assigned the rear portion of the right running board. There were two jump seats, and they were occupied by two Presidential aides, Mr. O'Donnell and Mr. Powers. Mr. Powers was sitting on the right-hand side; Mr. O'Donnell on the left. The rear seat was occupied, left rear by Special Agent Hickey, right rear, Special Agent Bennett.

Mr. SPECTER. How were the agents armed at that time?

Mr. HILL. All the agents were armed with their hand weapons.

Mr. SPECTER. And is there any weapon in the automobile in addition to the hand weapons?

Mr. HILL. Yes. There is an AR–15, which is an automatic rifle, and a shotgun.

Mr. SPECTER. And where is the AR–15 kept?

Mr. HILL. Between the two agents in the rear seat.

Mr. SPECTER. How about the shotgun; where is that kept?

Mr. HILL. In a compartment immediately in front of the jump seats.

Mr. SPECTER. Is the President's followup car a specially constructed automobile.

Mr. HILL. Yes, sir; it is.

Mr. SPECTER. And what is the make and model and general description of that vehicle?

Mr. HILL. It is a 1955 Cadillac, nine-passenger touring sedan. It is a convertible type.

Mr. SPECTER. Was that automobile flown in specially from Washington for the occasion?

Mr. HILL. Yes; it was, sir.

Mr. SPECTER. Do you know how that automobile was transported to Dallas, Tex.?

Mr. HILL. Generally, it is flown in a C–130 by the Air Force. I am not sure how on this particular occasion.

Mr. SPECTER. Will you describe, in a general way, the composition of the crowds en route from Love Field down to the center of Dallas, please?

Mr. HILL. Well, when we left Love Field, we went away from the crowd to get to the exit point at Love Field, and there were no crowds at all, and then we, departing Love Field, found the crowds were sporadic. There were people here and there. Some places they had built up and other places they were thinned out. The speed of the motorcade was adjusted accordingly. Whenever there were large groups of people, the motorcade slowed down to give the people an opportunity to view the President. When there were not many people along the side of the street, we speeded up. We didn't really hit the crowds until we hit Main Street.

Mr. SPECTER. What is your best estimate of the maximum speed of the automobile from the time you left Love Field until the time you arrived at downtown Dallas?

Mr. HILL. I would say we never ran any faster than 25 to 30 miles per hour.

Mr. SPECTER. What is your best estimate of the minimum speed during this same interval?

Mr. HILL. Twelve to fifteen miles per hour. We did stop.

Mr. SPECTER. On what occasion did you stop?

Mr. HILL. Between Love Field and Main Street, downtown Dallas, on the right-hand side of the street there were a group of people with a long banner which said, "Please, Mr. President, stop and shake our hands." And the President requested the motorcade to stop, and he beckoned to the people and asked them to come and shake his hand, which they did.

Mr. SPECTER. Did the President disembark from his automobile at that time?

Mr. HILL. No; he remained in his seat.

Mr. SPECTER. At that time what action, if any, did you take?

Mr. HILL. I jumped from the followup car and ran up to the left rear portion of the automobile with my back toward Mrs. Kennedy viewing those persons on the left-hand side of the street.

Mr. SPECTER. What action was taken by any other Secret Service agent which you observed at that time?

Mr. HILL. Special Agent Ready, who was working the forward portion of the right running board, did the same thing, only on the President's side, placed his back toward the car, and viewed the people facing the President. Assistant in Charge Kellerman opened the door of the President's car and stepped out on the street.

Mr. SPECTER. What action was taken by Special Agent McIntyre, if you know?

Mr. HILL. I do not know.

Mr. SPECTER. How about Special Agent Landis?

Mr. HILL. I do not know.

Mr. SPECTER. What is your normal procedure for action in the event the President's car is stopped, as it did in that event?

Mr. HILL. Special Agent McIntyre would normally jump off the car and run to the forward portion of the left-hand side of the car; Special Agent Landis would move to the right-hand forward portion of the automobile.

Mr. SPECTER. Did anything else which was unusual occur en route from Love Field to the downtown area of Dallas?

Mr. HILL. Before we hit Main Street?

Mr. SPECTER. Yes, sir.

Mr. HILL. Not that I recall.

Mr. SPECTER. Did you have any occasion to leave the President's followup car at any time?

Mr. HILL. When we finally did reach Main Street, the crowds had built up to a point where they were surging into the street. We had motorcycles running adjacent to both the Presidential automobile and the followup car, as well as in front of the Presidential automobile, and because of the crowds in the street, the President's driver, Special Agent Greer, was running the car more to the left-hand side of the street more than he was to the right to keep the President as far away from the crowd as possible, and because of this the motorcycles on the left-hand side could not get past the crowd and alongside the car, and they were forced to drop back. I jumped from the followup car, ran up and got on top of the rear portion of the Presidential automobile to be close to Mrs. Kennedy in the event that someone attempted to grab her from the crowd or throw something in the car.

Mr. SPECTER. When you say the rear portion of the automobile, can you, by referring to Commission Exhibit No. 345, heretofore identified as the President's automobile, specify by penciled "X" where you stood?

Mr. HILL. Yes, sir [indicating].

Mr. SPECTER. Will you describe for the record just what area it is back there on which you stood?

Mr. HILL. That is a step built into the rear bumper of the automobile, and on top of the rear trunk there is a handguard which you grab for and hang onto when you are standing up.

Mr. SPECTER. Are identical objects of those descriptions existing on each side of the President's car?

Mr. HILL. Yes, sir; they do.

Mr. SPECTER. Did you have any other occasion en route from Love Field to downtown Dallas to leave the followup car and mount that portion of the President's car?

Mr. HILL. I did the same thing approximately four times.

Mr. SPECTER. What are the standard regulations and practices, if any, governing such an action on your part?

Mr. HILL. It is left to the agent's discretion more or less to move to that particular position when he feels that there is a danger to the President; to place himself as close to the President or the First Lady as my case was, as possible, which I did.

Mr. SPECTER. Are those practices specified in any written documents of the Secret Service?

Mr. HILL. No; they are not.

Mr. SPECTER. Now, had there been any instruction or comment about your performance of that type of a duty with respect to anything that President Kennedy himself had said in the period immediately preceding the trip to Texas?

Mr. HILL. Yes, sir; there was. The preceding Monday, the President was on a trip in Tampa, Fla., and he requested that the agents not ride on either of those two steps.

Mr. SPECTER. And to whom did the President make that request?

Mr. HILL. Assistant Special Agent in Charge Boring.

Mr. SPECTER. Was Assistant Special Agent in Charge Boring the individual in charge of that trip to Florida?

Mr. HILL. He was riding in the Presidential automobile on that trip in Florida, and I presume that he was. I was not along.

Mr. SPECTER. Well, on that occasion would he have been in a position comparable to that occupied by Special Agent Kellerman on this trip to Texas?

Mr. HILL. Yes, sir; the same position.

Mr. SPECTER. And Special Agent Boring informed you of that instruction by President Kennedy?

Mr. HILL. Yes, sir; he did.

Mr. SPECTER. Did he make it a point to inform other special agents of that same instruction?

Mr. HILL. I believe that he did, sir.

Mr. SPECTER. And, as a result of what President Kennedy said to him, did he instruct you to observe that Presidential admonition?

Mr. HILL. Yes, sir.

Mr. SPECTER. How, if at all, did that instruction of President Kennedy affect your action and—your action in safeguarding him on this trip to Dallas?

Mr. HILL. We did not ride on the rear portions of the automobile. I did on those four occasions because the motorcycles had to drop back and there was no protection on the left-hand side of the car.

Mr. SPECTER. When the President's automobile was proceeding in downtown Dallas, what was the ordinary speed of the automobile, based on your best estimate?

Mr. HILL. We were running approximately 12 to 15 miles per hour, I would say.

Mr. SPECTER. I show you a document which we have marked as Commission Exhibit No. 354, which is an aerial photograph identical with the photograph already marked as Commission Exhibit No. 347.

(The photograph referred to was marked Exhibit No. 354 for identification.)

Mr. SPECTER. I ask you if, referring only to Exhibit 354, you are able to identify what that scene is.

Mr. HILL. Yes, sir; I am.

Mr. SPECTER. Are you able to indicate the route which the President's motorcade followed through that area?

Mr. HILL. Yes, sir; I am.

Mr. SPECTER. And what does that scene depict—what city is it?

Mr. HILL. That is Dallas, Tex. It shows Main Street, Houston Street, and Elm Street.

Mr. SPECTER. Will you write on the picture itself where Main Street is? Would you now write, as best you can, which street is Houston Street?

Mr. HILL. Yes, sir.

Mr. SPECTER. And would you now write which street is Elm?

Mr. HILL. Yes, sir.

(At this point, Representative Ford entered the hearing room.)

Mr. SPECTER. Now, would you indicate, if you know, which is a generally northerly direction on that picture?

Mr. HILL. Yes, sir.

Mr. SPECTER. All right. What was the condition of the crowd as the motorcade made a right-hand turn off of Main Street onto Houston?

Mr. HILL. The crowd was very large on Main Street, and it was thinning down considerably when we reached the end of it, and turned right on Houston Street. Noticeably on my side of the car, which was the left-hand side of the street.

Mr. SPECTER. And what is your best estimate as to the speed of the President's car at the time it made the right-hand turn onto Houston Street?

Mr. HILL. In the curve?

Mr. SPECTER. The speed—in the curve itself; yes.

Mr. HILL. We were running generally 12 to 15 miles per hour. I would say that in the curve we perhaps slowed to maybe 10 miles per hour.

Mr. SPECTER. And how far behind the President's car was the Presidential followup car as the turn was made onto Houston Street?

Mr. HILL. Four to five feet, at the most.

137

Mr. SPECTER. I show you a photograph of a building which has already been marked as Commission Exhibit No. 348, and ask you if at this time you can identify what that building is.

Mr. HILL. I believe I can, sir; yes.

Mr. SPECTER. And what building is it?

Mr. HILL. It is the Texas School Book Depository.

Mr. SPECTER. Now, does that building appear on the Commission Exhibit No. 354?

Mr. HILL. Yes, sir; it does.

Mr. SPECTER. Did you have any occasion to notice the Texas School Book Depository Building as you proceeded in a generally northerly direction on Houston Street?

Mr. HILL. Yes, sir. It was immediately in front of us and to our left.

Mr. SPECTER. Did you notice anything unusual about it?

Mr. HILL. Nothing more unusual than any other building along the way.

Mr. SPECTER. What is your general practice, if any, in observing such buildings along the route of a Presidential motorcade?

Mr. HILL. We scan the buildings and look specifically for open windows, for people hanging out, and there had been, on almost every building along the way, people hanging out, windows open.

Mr. SPECTER. And did you observe, as you recollect at this moment, any open windows in the Texas School Depository Building?

Mr. HILL. Yes, sir; there were.

Mr. SPECTER. Are you able to recollect specifically which windows were open at this time?

Mr. HILL. No, sir; I cannot.

Mr. SPECTER. What was the condition of the crowd along the streets, if any, along Elm Street, in front of the Texas School Book Depository Building?

Mr. HILL. On the left-hand side of the street, which is the side I was on, the crowd was very thin. And it was a general park area. There were people scattered throughout the entire park.

Mr. SPECTER. Now, what is your best estimate of the speed of the President's automobile as it turned left off of Houston onto Elm Street?

Mr. HILL. We were running still 12 to 15 miles per hour, but in the curve I believe we slowed down maybe to 10, maybe to 9.

Mr. SPECTER. How far back of the President's automobile was the Presidential followup car when the President's followup car had just straightened out on Elm Street?

Mr. HILL. Approximately 5 feet.

Mr. SPECTER. Now, as the motorcade proceeded at that point, tell us what happened.

Mr. HILL. Well, as we came out of the curve, and began to straighten up, I was viewing the area which looked to be a park. There were people scattered throughout the entire park. And I heard a noise from my right rear, which to me seemed to be a firecracker. I immediately looked to my right, and, in so doing, my eyes had to cross the Presidential limousine and I saw President Kennedy grab at himself and lurch forward and to the left.

Mr. SPECTER. Why don't you just proceed, in narrative form, to tell us?

Representative BOGGS. This was the first shot?

Mr. HILL. This is the first sound that I heard; yes, sir. I jumped from the car, realizing that something was wrong, ran to the Presidential limousine. Just about as I reached it, there was another sound, which was different than the first sound. I think I described it in my statement as though someone was shooting a revolver into a hard object—it seemed to have some type of an echo. I put my right foot, I believe it was, on the left rear step of the automobile, and I had a hold of the handgrip with my hand, when the car lurched forward. I lost my footing and I had to run about three or four more steps before I could get back up in the car.

Between the time I originally grabbed the handhold and until I was up on the car, Mrs. Kennedy—the second noise that I heard had removed a portion of the President's head, and he had slumped noticeably to his left. Mrs. Kennedy had jumped up from the seat and was, it appeared to me, reaching for something coming off the right rear bumper of the car, the right rear tail, when she noticed that I was trying to climb on the car. She turned toward me and I grabbed her and put her back in the back seat, crawled up on top of the back seat and lay there.

Mr. SPECTER. Now, referring to Commission Exhibit No. 354, would you mark an "X", as best you can, at the spot where the President's automobile was at the time the first shot occurred?

Mr. HILL. Approximately there.

Mr. SPECTER. And would you mark a "Y" at the approximate position where the President's car was at the second shot you have described? What is your best estimate of the speed of the President's car at the precise time of the first shot, Mr. Hill?

Mr. HILL. We were running between 12 to 15 miles per hour, but no faster than 15 miles per hour.

Mr. SPECTER. How many shots have you described that you heard?

Mr. HILL. Two.

Mr. SPECTER Did you hear any more than two shots?

Mr. HILL. No, sir.

Mr. SPECTER. And what is your best estimate of the speed of the President's automobile at the time of the second shot?

Mr. HILL. Approximately the same speed as that of the first—although at the time that I jumped on the car, the car had surged forward. The President at that time had been shot in the head.

Mr. SPECTER. When, in relationship to the second shot, did the car accelerate—that is, the President's car?

Mr. HILL. Almost simultaneously.

Mr. SPECTER. You testified just a moment ago that the President grabbed at himself immediately after the first noise which you described as sounding like a firecracker.

Mr. HILL. Yes, sir.

Mr. SPECTER. Would you tell us with more particularity in what way he grabbed at himself?

Mr. HILL. He grabbed in this general area.

Mr. SPECTER. You are indicating that your right hand is coming up to your—to the throat?

Mr. HILL. Yes, sir.

Mr. SPECTER. And the left hand crosses right under the right hand.

Mr. HILL. To the chest area.

Mr. SPECTER. To the chest area. Was there any movement of the President's head or shoulders immediately after the first shot, that you recollect?

Mr. HILL. Yes, sir. Immediately when I saw him, he was like this, and going left and forward.

Mr. SPECTER. Indicating a little fall to the left front.

Mr. HILL. Yes, sir.

Representative BOGGS. This was after a head wound?

Mr. HILL. No, sir.

Representative BOGGS. Before the head wound?

Mr. HILL. Yes, sir; this was the first shot.

Mr. SPECTER. Now, what is your best estimate on the timespan between the first firecracker-type noise you heard and the second shot which you have described?

Mr. HILL. Approximately 5 seconds.

Mr. SPECTER. Now, did the impact on the President's head occur simultaneously, before, or after the second noise which you have described?

Mr. HILL. Almost simultaneously.

Representative FORD. Did you see the President put his hands to his throat and chest while you were still on the followup car, or after you had left it?

Mr. HILL. As I was leaving. And that is one of the reasons I jumped, because I saw him grab himself and pitch forward and to the left. I knew something was wrong.

Representative FORD. It was 5 seconds from the firecracker noise that you think you got to the automobile?

139

Mr. HILL. Until I reached the handhold, had placed my foot on the left rear step.

Mr. SPECTER. When, in relationship to the second shot, did Mrs. Kennedy move out of the rear seat?

Mr. HILL. Just after it.

Mr. SPECTER. You say that it appeared that she was reaching as if something was coming over to the rear portion of the car, back in the area where you were coming to?

Mr. HILL. Yes, sir.

Mr. SPECTER. Was there anything back there that you observed, that she might have been reaching for?

Mr. HILL. I thought I saw something come off the back, too, but I cannot say that there was. I do know that the next day we found the portion of the President's head.

Mr. SPECTER. Where did you find that portion of the President's head?

Mr. HILL. It was found in the street. It was turned in, I believe, by a medical student or somebody in Dallas.

Mr. SPECTER. Did you have any difficulty maintaining your balance on the back of the car after you had come up on the top of it?

Mr. HILL. Not until we turned off to enter the Parkland Hospital.

Mr. SPECTER. Now, what action did you take specifically with respect to placing Mrs. Kennedy back in the rear seat?

Mr. HILL. I simply just pushed and she moved—somewhat voluntarily—right back into the same seat she was in. The President—when she had attempted to get out onto the trunk of the car, his body apparently did not move too much, because when she got back into the car he was at that time, when I got on top of the car, face up in her lap.

Mr. SPECTER. And that was after she was back in the rear seat?

Mr. HILL. Yes, sir.

Mr. SPECTER. And where were the President's legs at that time?

Mr. HILL. Inside the car.

Mr. SPECTER. Now, what, if anything, did you observe as to the condition of Governor Connally at that time?

Mr. HILL. After going under this underpass, I looked forward to the jump seats, where Mrs. Connally and Governor Connally were sitting. Mrs. Connally had been leaning over her husband. And I had no idea that he had been shot. And when she leaned back at one time, I noticed that his coat was unbuttoned, and that the lower portion of his abdomen was completely covered with blood.

Mr. SPECTER. When was it that you first observed that?

Mr. HILL. Just after going under the underpass.

Mr. SPECTER. Were you able to observe anything which was occurring on the overpass as the President's motorcade moved toward the overpass?

Mr. HILL. From the time I got on the back of the Presidential limousine, I didn't really pay any attention to what was going on outside the automobile.

Mr. SPECTER. Had you noticed the overpass prior to the time you got on the Presidential automobile?

Mr. HILL. Yes; I had scanned it.

Mr. SPECTER. And do you recollect what, if anything, you observed on the overpass at that time?

Mr. HILL. There were some people there, but I also noticed there was a policeman there.

Mr. SPECTER. Approximately how many people would you say were there?

Mr. HILL. Very few, I would say—maybe five, six.

Mr. SPECTER. And how were you able to identify that there was a policeman there?

Mr. HILL. He was wearing the uniform—presumably a policeman.

Mr. SPECTER. What color uniform was it?

Mr. HILL. I think it was blue of some shade.

Mr. SPECTER. Did you identify it at that time as being of the identical color which other Dallas policemen were wearing whom you had observed in the area?

Mr. HILL. That's correct, sir.

Mr. SPECTER. Can you characterize the type of acceleration which the car made after it started to speed forward—that is, the Presidential car.

Mr. HILL. Well, the initial surge was quite violent, because it almost jerked me off the left rear step board. Then after that it was apparently gradual, because I did not notice it any more.

Mr. SPECTER. What is your best estimate of the distance from the time of the shooting to Parkland Hospital?

Mr. HILL. In time or——

Mr. SPECTER. Time and distance.

Mr. HILL. Distance, I have no idea.

Mr. SPECTER. How about time?

Mr. HILL. I would say roughly 4 minutes.

Mr. SPECTER. Did Mrs. Kennedy say anything as you were proceeding from the time of the shooting to Parkland Hospital?

Mr. HILL. At the time of the shooting, when I got into the rear of the car, she said, "My God, they have shot his head off." Between there and the hospital she just said, "Jack, Jack, what have they done to you," and sobbed.

Mr. SPECTER. Was there any conversation by anybody else in the President's automobile from the time of the shooting to the arrival at Parkland Hospital?

Mr. HILL. I heard Special Agent Kellerman say on the radio, "To the nearest hospital, quick."

Mr. SPECTER. Any other comment?

Mr. HILL. He said, "We have been hit."

Mr. SPECTER. Now, was there any other comment you heard Special Agent Kellerman make?

Mr. HILL. Not that I recall.

Mr. SPECTER. Did Special Agent Greer say anything?

Mr. HILL. No, sir.

Mr. SPECTER. Mrs. Connally say anything?

Mr. HILL. No, sir.

Representative BOGGS. Was Governor Connally conscious?

Mr. HILL. Yes, sir ; he was.

Mr. SPECTER. Did Governor Connally say anything?

Mr. HILL. No, sir.

Mr. SPECTER. Did President Kennedy say anything?

Mr. HILL. No, sir.

Mr. SPECTER. What is your best estimate on the speed at which the President's car traveled from the point of the shooting to Parkland Hospital?

Mr. HILL. It is a little bit hard for me to judge, since I was lying across the rear portion of the automobile. I had no trouble staying in that particular position—until we approached the hospital, I recall, I believe it was a left-hand turn and I started slipping off to the right-hand portion of the car. So I would say that we went 60, maybe 65 at the most.

Mr. SPECTER. Were you able to secure a handhold or a leghold or any sort of a hold on the automobile as you moved forward?

Mr. HILL. Yes, sir. I had my legs—I had my body above the rear seat. and my legs hooked down into the rear seat, one foot outside the car.

Mr. SPECTER. What is your best estimate of the time of the assassination itself?

Mr. HILL. Approximately 12 :30.

Mr. SPECTER. I am not sure whether I asked you about this—about how long did it take you to get from the shooting to the hospital?

Mr. HILL. Approximately 4 minutes.

Mr. SPECTER. What did you observe as to President Kennedy's condition on arrival at the hospital?

Mr. HILL. The right rear portion of his head was missing. It was lying in the rear seat of the car. His brain was exposed. There was blood and bits of brain all over the entire rear portion of the car. Mrs. Kennedy was completely covered with blood. There was so much blood you could not tell if there had been any other wound or not, except for the one large gaping wound in the right rear portion of the head.

Mr. SPECTER. Did you have any opportunity to observe the front part of his body, to see whether there was any tear or rip in the clothing on the front?

Mr. HILL. I saw him lying there in the back of the car, when I was immediately above him. I cannot recall noticing anything that was ripped in the forward portion of his body.

Mr. SPECTER. What action, if any, did you take to shield the President's body?

Mr. HILL. I kept myself above the President and Mrs. Kennedy on the trip to Parkland.

Mr. SPECTER. Did you do anything with your coat upon arrival at Parkland Hospital to shield the President?

Mr. HILL. Yes, sir. I removed it and covered the President's head and upper chest.

Mr. SPECTER. What, if anything, did you observe as to Governor Connally's condition on arrival at Parkland?

Mr. HILL. He was conscious. There was a large amount of blood in the lower abdominal area. He was helped from the automobile to the stretcher, and I do not recall him saying anything, but I know that he was conscious. He was wheeled immediately into, I think, emergency room No. 2.

Mr. SPECTER. And who was removed first from the automobile?

Mr. HILL. Governor Connally.

Mr. SPECTER. How long after the President's car arrived at Parkland Hospital did medical personnel come to the scene to remove the victims?

Mr. HILL. Seconds. They were there when we were there almost—almost simultaneously with the arrival.

Mr. SPECTER. Do you know where President Kennedy was taken in the hospital?

Mr. HILL. Yes, sir. I accompanied he, and Mrs. Kennedy to the emergency room.

Mr. SPECTER. Now, tell us what you did at the hospital from the time of arrival on, please.

Mr. HILL. I went into the emergency room with the President, but it was so small, and there were so many people in there that I decided I had better leave and let the doctors take care of the situation. So I walked outside; asked for the nearest telephone; walked to the nearest telephone. About that time Special Agent in Charge Kellerman came outside and said, "Get the White House."

I asked Special Agent Lawson for the local number in Dallas of the White House switchboard, which he gave to me. I called the switchboard in Dallas; asked for the line to be open to Washington, and remain open continuously. And then I asked for Special Agent in Charge Behn's office. Mr. Kellerman came out of the emergency room about that time, took the telephone and called Special Agent in Charge Behn that we had had a double tragedy; that both Governor Connally and President Kennedy had been shot. And that was about as much as he said. I then took the telephone and shortly thereafter Mr. Kellerman came out of the emergency room and said, "Clint, tell Jerry this is unofficial and not for release, but the man is dead." Which I did. During the two calls, I talked to the Attorney General, who attempted to reach me, and told him that his brother had been seriously wounded; that we would keep him advised as to his condition.

Mr. SPECTER. Where was Mrs. Kennedy all this time, if you know?

Mr. HILL. Immediately upon arrival, she went into the emergency room. And a few minutes afterward, she was convinced to wait outside, which she did, remained there the rest of the period of time that we were there.

Mr. SPECTER. And was there any pronouncement that the President had died?

Mr. HILL. Not that I know of. Apparently there was. I was requested by Mr. O'Donnell, one of the Presidential assistants, to obtain a casket, because they wanted to return to Washington immediately. I contacted the administrator of the hospital and asked him to take me where I could telephone the nearest mortuary, which I did, requested that their best available casket be brought to the emergency entrance in my name immediately.

Mr. SPECTER. And what action was taken as a result of that request by you?

Mr. HILL. The casket did arrive from the O'Neal Mortuary, Inc., in their own hearse, which we then wheeled into the emergency room. I left the emergency

Mr. YOUNGBLOOD. Forty.

Mr. SPECTER. And by whom are you employed?

Mr. YOUNGBLOOD. The U.S. Secret Service.

Mr. SPECTER. How long have you been so employed?

Mr. YOUNGBLOOD. Since March of 1951.

Mrs. SPECTER. What is your educational background, sir?

Mr. YOUNGBLOOD. I graduated from Georgia Institute of Technology, Bachelor of Industrial Engineering.

Mr. SPECTER. In what year?

Mr. YOUNGBLOOD. 1949.

Mr. SPECTER. How were you occupied from termination of your college work until starting with the Secret Service?

Mr. YOUNGBLOOD. I worked for Bradshaws, Inc., which was a refrigeration and air-conditioning concern in Waycross, Ga., and then worked for Alvin Lindstrom, who is a consulting mechanical engineer in Atlanta, Ga.

Mr. SPECTER. And would you outline in general terms what your duties have been with the Secret Service since the time you joined them?

Mr. YOUNGBLOOD. I began in the Secret Service as a special agent, criminal investigator, and started off at the Atlanta field office, and stayed there about a year and a half. This time was spent in investigation of Government forged check cases, bond cases, counterfeiting, and similar investigations.

(At this point, Chief Justice Warren withdrew from the hearing room.)

Mr. YOUNGBLOOD. I came to the Washington, D.C. area, and worked in the Washington field office, a continuation of the same type of work I had done in Atlanta, plus the beginning of the protective work, working on temporary assignment at the White House detail. And then in 1953 I was assigned to the White House detail and worked there during the Eisenhower Administration about 6 years, and returned to the Atlanta field office for 3 more years in that area, during which time President Eisenhower would come to Augusta and Albany, and on two occasions on foreign trips I was called in.

And after 3 years in that field office, I returned to Washington again, assigned to the White House detail. The last part of the Eisenhower Administration and the beginning of the Kennedy Administration.

And in March of 1961, I was assigned to the Vice-Presidential detail. This, at that time, was part of the Washington field office. And I have been on an assignment with the Vice-Presidential detail since March 1961, except for a 1-month period when I returned to the White House detail. And then back to the Vice-Presidential detail.

But during this time, the Vice-Presidential detail changed from a field office assignment to a small independent office, and then, later, in October of 1962, when legislation was passed, changing the laws relative to protection of the Vice President, it became a larger detail. And I have been on the Vice-Presidential detail in the occurrence at Dallas, and returned to the White House detail when Mr. Johnson became the President.

And during this period of time, I have been a special agent, assistant special agent in charge, and was scheduled to be the special agent in charge of the Vice-Presidential detail. But due to what occurred in Dallas, I went to the White House as an assistant special agent in charge.

Any other particulars?

Mr. SPECTER. Well, what was your rank at the time of the Dallas trip, specifically on November 22, 1963?

Mr. YOUNGBLOOD. I was the assistant special agent in charge of the Vice-Presidential detail.

(At this point, Chief Justice Warren entered the hearing room.)

Mr. SPECTER. And as such, were you responsible for the security of the Vice President on that trip?

Mr. YOUNGBLOOD. Yes, sir.

Mr. SPECTER. Now, what is your current rank?

Mr. YOUNGBLOOD. Assistant special agent in charge of the White House detail.

Mr. SPECTER. And, as such, do you hold one of the three positions of the assistant special agent in charge at the White House detail?

Mr. YOUNGBLOOD. Yes, sir.

Mr. Specter. And is that a rank comparable or exactly the same as that now held by Special Agent Kellerman?

Mr. Youngblood. Yes, sir; he is senior to me, but it is a comparable rank.

Mr. Specter. Now, would you outline briefly and in general terms the activities of Vice President Johnson during the few days immediately before Friday, November 22, 1963?

Mr. Youngblood. On Tuesday of that week we made a trip from the ranch to Dallas, and we went by commercial plane—actually, from the ranch to Austin in the Vice President's plane, and from Austin to Dallas on a commercial plane. And while in Dallas, he addressed the Bottlers Convention. And we returned to the plane, flew back to Austin, then flew back to the ranch later that night, and remained at the ranch the next day and through Thursday.

And on Thursday we went to San Antonio, to join the group coming down from Washington.

Mr. Specter. Now, when did Vice President Johnson then address the Bottlers Association in Dallas?

Mr. Youngblood. That was on Tuesday.

Mr. Specter. November 19?

Mr. Youngblood. I would have to look at a calendar.

Mr. Specter. The preceding Tuesday——

Mr. Youngblood. The preceding Tuesday before the 22d; yes, sir.

Mr. Specter. Now, outline in a general way Vice President Johnson's activities on the morning of November 22d, before he arrived in Dallas, if you would, please.

Mr. Youngblood. Well, our day began at the hotel in Fort Worth, where we had stayed overnight. And that morning we went down to a mezzanine floor where we met with President Kennedy and a group of White House people. We went across from this hotel to a parking lot across the street, and they had a speaker stand there, and they addressed an assembled gathering.

Then they returned to the hotel, and there was a breakfast meeting in the hotel. They attended that. And, after that, we formed a motorcade and went to the field nearby in Fort Worth and boarded Air Force 2, and flew into Dallas.

Mr. Specter. Approximately what time did the Vice Presidential plane arrive in Dallas?

Mr. Youngblood. About 11:35.

Mr. Specter. Now, will you tell the Commission in general terms what Vice President Johnson did upon arrival at the Love Field?

Mr. Youngblood. All right, sir.

This plane, Air Force 2, had on board the Vice President and Mrs. Johnson and other officials. And we disembarked from the plane and were met by a welcoming committee composed of local dignitaries. And then we moved from that area where we disembarked over to the area of the ramp, which would be pushed out when Air Force 1, the President's plane, arrived. And when his plane did arrive, which was just a few minutes after ours, roughly 10 minutes, we went out to the foot of the ramp and Vice President Johnson and Mrs. Johnson headed the reception committee to greet the people who came off of Air Force 1.

Mr. Specter. Approximately how long did the activities in greeting the crowd and the general reception last at Love Field on that morning?

Mr. Youngblood. Do you mean from the time we arrived on Air Force 2 until we left?

Mr. Specter. Yes.

Mr. Youngblood. I think it was about 15 minutes.

Mr. Specter. Now, in what position in the motorcade was Vice President Johnson's automobile?

Mr. Youngblood. We were following the Presidential followup car, and the motorcade up to our point—there was a lead car, the President's car, the Presidential followup car, and then our car.

Mr. Specter. Was there, to your knowledge, in advance of the lead car a car known as the pilot car?

Mr. YOUNGBLOOD. Yes, sir; in all probability. This is a normal police arrangement.

Mr. SPECTER. And would you identify the occupants of Vice President John-son's car, indicating the positions in the car of each individual?

Mr. YOUNGBLOOD. All right, sir. The driver of this car was Hurchel Jacks, and he is with the State Highway Patrol. And behind him was Senator Ralph Yarborough, from Texas. And in the middle back seat was Mrs. Johnson. And on the right-hand side of the back seat, behind me, was the Vice President. And I was in the front seat on the right-hand side.

Mr. SPECTER. And what kind of an automobile was it?

Mr. YOUNGBLOOD. This was a Lincoln convertible, a four-door convertible.

Mr. SPECTER. Is this a specially constructed automobile, or was it obtained locally for use during this trip?

Mr. YOUNGBLOOD. It was obtained locally for use during the trip.

Mr. SPECTER. And what car immediately followed the Vice President's automobile?

Mr. YOUNGBLOOD. The Vice Presidential detail had a followup car which followed our car.

Mr. SPECTER. What kind of an automobile was that?

Mr. YOUNGBLOOD. It was either a Lincoln or a Mercury, I don't know the exact make. It was a Ford product, and it was a four-door car. But it was closed.

Mr. SPECTER. Can you identify the occupants of that car, stating where each sat?

Mr. YOUNGBLOOD. The front seat, the driver, I think his name is Rich. He is always on the Texas Highway Patrol. In the front seat in the middle is Cliff Carter. He is an assistant to the Vice President's staff.

(At this point, Representative Boggs withdrew from the hearing room.)

Mr. YOUNGBLOOD. On the right-front side was Jerry Kivett. He is one of the agents on the Vice Presidential detail. And in the back seat, behind the driver, was Warren Taylor, and in the back seat on the other side was my agent, Lem Johns.

Mr. SPECTER. Do you know how many cars there were in the balance of the motorcade?

Mr. YOUNGBLOOD. No, sir; I don't.

Mr. SPECTER. What was the maximum speed at which the motorcade proceeded from Love Field down to the downtown area of Dallas?

Mr. YOUNGBLOOD. I doubt if the motorcade ever exceeded 20 miles or 25 miles an hour, and most of the time it was going slower than that.

Mr. SPECTER. What was the minimum speed, would you estimate, during that time?

Mr. YOUNGBLOOD. We actually came to stops during this time.

Mr. SPECTER. How many stops?

Mr. YOUNGBLOOD. More than one. Two or more.

Mr. SPECTER. What occurred during the course of those stops, or what prompted them?

Mr. YOUNGBLOOD. Well, these stops were made by the Presidential car to greet well-wishers, students on one particular occasion, and other groups of well-wishers, that were assembled along the streets.

Mr. SPECTER. Did Vice President Johnson greet anyone at those stops?

Mr. YOUNGBLOOD. He did greet them, but he didn't leave the car, I think. He remained in the car. I got out of the car and stood by the side of it on more than one occasion. He waved at people, and some did run over, and I think he did touch some. But he didn't leave the car.

Mr. SPECTER. How far behind the President's followup car did the Vice President's followup car drive?

Mr. YOUNGBLOOD. The Vice President's followup car?

Mr. SPECTER. Pardon me—the Vice President's automobile.

Mr. YOUNGBLOOD. We usually stayed on motorcades like this about two or three car lengths behind.

Mr. SPECTER. And did your distance on this occasion conform to your customary practice of being that distance behind?

147

Mr. YOUNGBLOOD. Yes, sir.

Mr. SPECTER. And what is the reason, if any, for staying that distance behind the President's followup car?

Mr. YOUNGBLOOD. Well, mainly so the crowd can see the Vice President, and he can see them. If you are too close behind the Presidential group, the crowd will be watching the President and will watch him as he goes by, and then they will miss the next man. So it gives the people a chance to recover and look back and see him, and they to see each other.

Mr. SPECTER. I show you a photograph which has been marked as Commission Exhibit No. 354, and ask you if you are able to identify what that is a picture of.

Mr. YOUNGBLOOD. Yes, sir.

Mr. SPECTER. And what does that depict?

Mr. YOUNGBLOOD. Well, it is a picture showing the main street, Houston Street and Elm Street, and the assassination occurred on Elm Street.

Mr. SPECTER. Are you familiar at this time with the identities of Main, Houston, and Elm?

Mr. YOUNGBLOOD. Yes, sir; when I have a map such as this ahead of me.

Mr. SPECTER. All right. How far behind the President's automobile was the Vice President's automobile in which you were riding when the Vice President's automobile turned right off of Main Street onto Houston?

Mr. YOUNGBLOOOD. You ask again how far were we behind the President's car? Did you mean, sir, how far were we behind the Presidential followup car?

Mr. SPECTER. No; I meant the President's car on that occasion.

Mr. YOUNGBLOOD. Well, we were a distance of about two car lengths behind the followup car, and they were probably one car length behind the Presidential car. But this would be a guess on my part.

Mr. SPECTER. What was the situation with respect to the crowd which was lined up on Houston and Elm as you approached that intersection?

Mr. YOUNGBLOOD. On Houston Street, on the side where the tall building is, the crowd was still somewhat continuous. On the side which is the park side, the crowd was smaller. They did have some people there, but it wasn't continuous in the same way it was on the building side.

Mr. SPECTER. What is your best estimate of the speed of the Vice President's car as you proceeded down Houston Street toward Elm Street?

Mr. YOUNGBLOOD. Well, our speed, of course, was governed by the vehicles in front of us, but I would say we had just made one turn, and it was only a block there before we would make another turn. It was approximately 10 miles an hour, between 10 and 15.

Mr. SPECTER. I show you a photograph which has been marked as Commission Exhibit No. 348, and I ask you if you are now able to identify what that building is?

Mr. YOUNGBLOOD. Yes, sir; I am now able to identify it.

Mr. SPECTER. What is that building, sir?

Mr. YOUNGBLOOD. That is the School Book Depository Building.

Mr. SPECTER. Where, as best you can recollect, was the Vice President's car at the time the first shots were heard? And would you take Commission Exhibit No. 354 and take the red pencil and mark as closely as you can the exact position on Commission Exhibit 354 of the Vice President's car with the capital letter "A" there?

Mr. YOUNGBLOOD. At the time of the first shot, did you say?

Mr. SPECTER. Yes, sir.

Mr. YOUNGBLOOD. It will be in this area here, I should think.

Mr. SPECTER. I want the Vice President's car at this time.

Mr. YOUNGBLOOD. Well, this is what I am attempting to locate. It would be in the vicinity of this "X" right here, I do believe.

Mr. SPECTER. All right. Now, will you describe——

Mr. YOUNGBLOOD. Excuse me. You said put an "A" here?

Mr. SPECTER. Yes, please. Will you describe just what occurred as the motorcade proceeded past the intersection of Houston and Elm Streets?

Mr. YOUNGBLOOD. Well, the crowd had begun to diminish, looking ahead and to the right the crowd became spotty. I mean it wasn't continuous at all, like it had been. As we were beginning to go down this incline, all of a sudden

148

there was an explosive noise. I quickly observed unnatural movement of crowds, like ducking or scattering, and quick movements in the Presidential followup car. So I turned around and hit the Vice President on the shoulder and hollered, get down, and then looked around again and saw more of this movement, and so I proceeded to go to the back seat and get on top of him.

I then heard two more shots. But I would like to say this. I would not be positive that I was back on that back seat before the second shot. But the Vice President himself said I was. But—then in hearing these two more shots, I again had seen more movement, and I think someone else hit a siren—I heard the noise of a siren.

I told the driver to close it up, and stick close to that car in front. And right away we started a hasty evacuation speed, and left this immediate area, and we were following close behind. And I had a radio which was on a Baker frequency, where I could communicate back with the agents in my followup car. And they had a Charlie frequency, which was on the same network of the Presidential motorcade. And I called back and said I am switching to Baker frequency—I said, "I am switching to Charlie." And as I switched, I heard some transmission over the Charlie sets saying for me to keep my man covered, and I heard Kivett reply to Emory Roberts that he was covered, and I saw agents in the followup car, the Presidential followup car signaling us to stay close. I asked the driver what his opinion was as to—I don't know for exact sure just where we were going, but I knew our best protection was to stay with that Presidential followup crew. And I asked the driver if he had passed the Trade Mart. He said he passed it and we were going on to the hospital. And I heard indications over the radio that we were going to the hospital. We had a very fast ride there.

I told the driver to go as fast as he could without having a wreck. There was some conversation between the Vice President and myself while we were going to the hospital. I told him that I didn't know how serious it was up in the front car, but when we arrived at the hospital, I would like to get out of the car and go into the building and not stop, and for him to stay close to myself and the other agents. He agreed to.

When we arrived at the hospital, we immediately went right in. As we stopped at the hospital, two of my agents from the Vice Presidential car, followup car, were coming up to meet us, and two from the Presidential followup were coming to meet us, and, with this group, we proceeded into the hospital and then went into a room. I posted one man at the door and said, not to let anyone in unless he knew him, was certain of his identity.

I told Jerry Kivett and Warren Taylor to pull all the shades and blinds, which they did. And they also busied themselves with evacuating a couple of people out of there. There was a nurse and a patient in there.

Mr. SPECTER. Before you go on, Mr. Youngblood, let me drop back and pick up a few of the details theretofore.

What would your best estimate be of the speed of the Vice President's car at the time you heard that first explosive noise?

Mr. YOUNGBLOOD. Oh, approximately 12 miles an hour.

Mr. SPECTER. And had you maintained the distance which you have described heretofore behind the President's followup car?

Mr. YOUNGBLOOD. Yes, generally. Sometimes as we went around corners, we tried to close up the gap a little bit. But as soon as we got on a straight stretch, we would drop back two or three car lengths.

Mr. SPECTER. Well, at this particular time, what is your best recollection of the distance between the Presidential followup car and the Vice President's car?

Mr. YOUNGBLOOD. We are on Elm Street now.

Mr. SPECTER. At the time the first shot occurred.

Mr. YOUNGBLOOD. We were two or three car lengths behind.

Mr. SPECTER. And how far behind the President's car was the Presidential followup car at the time of the first shot?

Mr. YOUNGBLOOD. I would think somewhat less than a car length.

Mr. SPECTER. What is your best estimate of the total timespan between the first and third shots which you have already described?

Mr. YOUNGBLOOD. From the beginning to the last?

Mr. SPECTER. Yes, sir.

Mr. YOUNGBLOOD. 1 would think 5 seconds.

Mr. SPECTER. And you have described the first shot as being an explosive noise. How would you describe each of the second and third shots?

Mr. YOUNGBLOOD. Well, there wasn't too much difference in the noise of the first shot and the last two. I am not really sure that there was a difference. But in my mind, I think I identified the last two positively as shots, whereas the first one I thought was just an explosive noise, and I didn't know whether it was a firecracker or a shot. It seems, as I try to think over it, there was more of a crack sound to the last two shots. That may have been distance, I don't know.

Mr. SPECTER. Now, as to time interval—was there longer or less time or the same between the first and second shots and the second and third shots?

Mr. YOUNGBLOOD. There seemed to be a longer span of time between the first and the second shot than there was between the second and third shot.

Mr. SPECTER. Now, did you have any reaction or impression as to the source or point of origin of the first shot?

Mr. YOUNGBLOOD. I didn't know where the source or the point of origin was, of course, but the sounds all came to my right and rear.

Mr. SPECTER. Now, how about as to the latter two shots, would the same apply, or would there be a different situation there?

Mr. YOUNGBLOOD. No; all of them seemed to sound that they were from the right.

Representative FORD. Did they sound on the surface or in the air or couldn't you discern?

Mr. YOUNGBLOOD. I couldn't say for certain. I don't know.

Mr. SPECTER. Now, did you then or have you ever had any contrary impression that the shots might have come from in front as opposed to the rear of the automobile?

Mr. YOUNGBLOOD. No, sir.

Mr. SPECTER. Now, you say that you hit the Vice President's shoulder, and at that time you were indicating your left hand, I believe.

Mr. YOUNGBLOOD. Yes, sir.

Mr. SPECTER. Which hand did you use in hitting the Vice President's shoulder?

Mr. YOUNGBLOOD. My left, sir.

Mr. SPECTER. And which shoulder of the Vice President did you hit?

Mr. YOUNGBLOOD. His right, because I turned this way. I turned to my left, with the hand out, and then came into his right shoulder.

Mr. SPECTER. And when you moved from the front to the rear seat, would you describe in as much detail as you can your relative position with respect to the position of President Johnson's body?

Mr. YOUNGBLOOD. Well, the Vice President says that I vaulted over. It was more of a stepping over. And then I sat on top of him, he being crouched down somewhat.

Mr. SPECTER. Indicating towards the left?

Mr. YOUNGBLOOD. He moved towards the center, or towards his left, yes, sir, and down. And then I sat on this portion of his arm here.

Mr. SPECTER. Indicating the right upper portion of the arm from elbow to the shoulder?

Mr. YOUNGBLOOD. Yes, sir; generally.

Mr. SPECTER. And what were the positions of the other occupants of the back seat at the time you sat on the Vice President?

Mr. YOUNGBLOOD. Mrs. Johnson more or less moved into a forward—just moved forward. And Senator Yarborough also moved forward, and possibly he moved over a little to the right. I am not sure. But we were all below the window level of the car. And those two generally were forward. But the Vice President was forward and a little to his left.

Mr. SPECTER. In what direction did you look when you were first sitting on the Vice President?

Mr. YOUNGBLOOD. In what direction did I look?

Mr. SPECTER. Yes.

Mr. YOUNGBLOOD. Almost all directions.

Mr. SPECTER. Did you have a reaction with respect to looking in the direction from which you thought the danger was emanating?

Mr. YOUNGBLOOD. I think I first looked to the right—but to the right, forward, up, as much as I could scan, and also the people in the Presidential followup car. Because I recall seeing at the time one of our agents, Hickey, who was in the Presidential followup car, in almost a standing position with an AR–15 looking back and up.

Mr. SPECTER. Are you able to fix the precise time of the assassination?

Mr. YOUNGBLOOD. I would say 12:30. I was to keep the times. The Vice President was asking me if we were running on time, and so forth. And so he asked me how much further, and I would call back to our followup car and ask them how many more miles and so forth.

So, for this reason, I was at that time keeping up with the time very closely. And when we turned the corner, I noticed an illuminated clock sign on this building, which I now know is the School Book Depository Building. And that clock indicated 12:30. And the reason it is significant is because this was the time we were supposed to arrive at the Trade Mart.

Representative FORD. As you looked at the school depository building, and noticed this clock, where is the clock? Can you identify it?

Mr. YOUNGBLOOD. This, right here.

Representative FORD. It is on top of the roof?

Mr. YOUNGBLOOD. Yes, sir; right up here.

Representative FORD. And this is after you turned from Main Street on to Houston Street?

Mr. YOUNGBLOOD. We were on Houston Street—just as soon as we got on Houston Street. And I looked up and I saw it there.

Representative FORD. Did you notice anything else on the building as you scanned it from the top down, or from the bottom up?

Mr. YOUNGBLOOD. I noticed open windows, and some people, I think. But I didn't notice this particular window.

Representative FORD. You saw nothing unusual in any of the open windows that you noticed?

Mr. YOUNGBLOOD. Well, sir, all through the day here we had been passing buildings with windows and people. And that I saw. But I saw nothing unusual.

Mr. SPECTER. Mr. Youngblood, what is your best estimate as to the time it took to get to Parkland Hospital after the shooting occurred?

Mr. YOUNGBLOOD. I believe it was between 5 and 8 minutes, something of that nature.

(At this point, Representative Ford withdrew from the hearing room.)

Mr. SPECTER. And at what speed did your automobile proceed, based on your best estimate, en route from the shooting to Parkland Hospital?

Mr. YOUNGBLOOD. I believe we were going around 60 or 70 miles an hour at times.

Mr. SPECTER. Now, did you observe President Kennedy or Governor Connally being removed from the President's automobile?

Mr. YOUNGBLOOD. No, sir; because I had—as I mentioned before—I had told the Vice President, or suggested to the Vice President that we did not want to linger, and get into the building as quickly as we could, and we would find out the condition of the other party after we got into a safe place.

Mr. SPECTER. Had they already been taken in by the time you arrived at the scene?

Mr. YOUNGBLOOD. No, sir; I don't hardly see how they could have been, because we arrived almost simultaneously with them. It was just a matter of opening the door and getting out of the car and hastily walking right on past. I think they were in the act of removing these people, but I don't think they would have had time to have removed them.

Mr. SPECTER. Did you enter the emergency entrance as well?

Mr. YOUNGBLOOD. Yes, sir.

Mr. SPECTER. Now, I interrupted you before when you were describing the security arrangements which you were making on the room to which you took the Vice President. Would you continue and describe for us what occurred thereafter?

Mr. YOUNGBLOOD. At what point?

Mr. SPECTER. I interrupted you. You were in the room, you had pulled the shades down, and were making security arrangements for the Vice President.

Mr. YOUNGBLOOD. Well, we were in a corner of this room, and there was the Vice President, Mrs. Johnson, and myself at first, with agents Kivett and Warren Taylor also in the big room, but not right over in the corner at the beginning. And shortly thereafter Emory Roberts came in. He was one of the White House detail agents. He told us that the situation—situation with President Kennedy looked very bad. The Vice President asked me what I thought—what we should do. And I said I think we should evacuate the hospital as soon as we can, and get on the plane, and return to Washington. And Emory Roberts concurred. And the Vice President agreed. But he wanted to get a better report on the condition and so forth.

Then we were joined by many others. Congressman Homer Thornberry came in, and Congressman Brooks, and Cliff Carter, and the Vice President had some conversations with these gentlemen. And at one time Cliff went out and got coffee. And then Mr. Ken O'Donnell and Roy Kellerman came down on one occasion, and Ken O'Donnell said for us to return to Washington, and to go ahead and take the President's plane.

The Vice President was worried about Mrs. Kennedy. So Mrs. Johnson thought that she would go see Mrs. Kennedy and Mrs. Connally. She did. Agents Kivett and Taylor went with her. Then later, after she came back, Ken O'Donnell and Roy Kellerman came down again and told us that the President had died.

Mr. SPECTER. About what time was that, sir?

Mr. YOUNGBLOOD. I don't know. I had told Lem Johns to try to keep up with all the times. I think it is a matter of record. I believe you have it in other documents.

Mr. SPECTER. Now, are you referring to a document which I will mark as Commission Exhibit 355?

(The document referred to was marked Commission Exhibit No. 355 for identification.)

Mr. YOUNGBLOOD. This is our shift report, and this is the times that Lem Johns was keeping that day. He shows 1 p.m., President Kennedy died at Parkland Hospital.

Mr. SPECTER. Was that daily shift report prepared under your supervision, Mr. Youngblood?

Mr. YOUNGBLOOD. Yes, sir.

Mr. SPECTER. Did you review it and approve it when it was completed, after the end of the workday on November 22?

Mr. YOUNGBLOOD. Well, not exactly at the end of the workday, sir. These agents would keep notes. And in this particular case you can see that this one, it says, "Date completed, December 2" down at the bottom. That is when he got around to typing it.

Mr. SPECTER. Well, does this document bear your initial in any place?

Mr. YOUNGBLOOD. Yes, sir; up at the top. The "RYW" is my initials.

Mr. SPECTER. And does that signify your approval shortly after completion of the document?

Mr. YOUNGBLOOD. Yes, sir.

Mr. SPECTER. All right. Would you go ahead and tell us what your activities were from the time you had learned that the President had died?

Mr. YOUNGBLOOD. Well, when Mr. O'Donnell and Roy Kellerman told us that he had died, the Vice President said, "Well, how about Mrs. Kennedy?"

O'Donnell told the Vice President that Mrs. Kennedy would not leave the hospital without the President's body. And O'Donnell suggested we go to the plane and that they just come on the other plane. And I might add that, as a word of explanation, there were two jet planes, one Air Force 1, in which the President flew, and the other Air Force 2, in which the Vice President and his party flew on. And O'Donnell told us to go ahead and take Air Force 1. I believe this is mainly because Air Force 1 has better communications equipment and so forth than the other planes.

President Johnson said that he didn't want to go off and leave Mrs. Kennedy in such a state. And so he agreed that we would go on to the airplane and board the plane and wait until Mrs. Kennedy and the body would come out. Shall I go on?

Mr. Specter. Yes. Proceed. Did you then depart from Parkland Hospital?

Mr. Youngblood. Yes, sir; previous to all of this, I had Johns, my agent, line up some unmarked police cars so that they would be ready when we did decide to evacuate the hospital.

So we left the room and proceeded out to these cars. The car that we went in was driven by Chief Curry, the Dallas Police Chief, and Congressman Thornberry was in the front seat, and the Vice President and I were in the back seat. And I had told the Vice President before we left the room that I would prefer that he stay below window level, and stay close with me as we went out, and that I would also prefer Mrs. Johnson to go in another car, but she would be accompanied by agents. And Mrs. Johnson did get in a second car. She was accompanied by Warren Taylor and Jerry Kivett and Congressman Brooks, and also Glen Bennett, another agent from the White House.

And as we started to leave the hospital area, that is drive away, just as we started away, Congressman Thomas saw us leaving—I imagine he saw Congressman Thornberry, and he said, "Wait for me." I don't think he saw the Vice President. And I told the driver to continue. I didn't want to stop there in front of the hospital. But by this time Congressman Thomas was right over at the side of the car, and the Vice President said, "Stop and let him get in."

So he got in in the front seat with Congressman Thornberry, having Congressman Thornberry move over closer to the driver. And then we started out again. This probably takes longer to tell about it than it actually took. It was about a 30-second stop.

We started out again, and the Vice President asked Congressman Thornberry to climb on over and get in the back seat, which he did, while the car was in motion. And then that put Congressman Thornberry behind the driver, and on the Vice President's left, and I was on his right.

And we continued on our way. We were momentarily stopped as we were leaving the hospital on this access road. There was a truck or delivery or something coming in there. We were stopped for one moment. But then the police got us on through, and we went on out to the main roads, and we were getting a motorcycle escort.

And they started using the sirens, and the Vice President and I both asked Chief Curry to discontinue the use of sirens, that we didn't want to attract attention. We were going on an unscheduled different route. We were not using any particular route. But in telling Lem Johns to get a car available, I told him to be sure and get a local driver who knew the area, a local policeman who could take us any route that we needed to go, and knew all the areas of evacuation and so forth.

So we went on to the airport. But we did have him stop using the sirens. And just before arriving at the airport, I called on the radio and told Air Force 1 to be ready to receive us, that we would be coming on board immediately. We arrived there and ran up the ramp onto the plane.

Mr. Specter. And how long after that did the swearing-in ceremonies occur? Approximately?

Mr. Youngblood. I would say in the neighborhood of about 40 or 45 minutes after that.

Mr. Specter. How long after the arrival of the Vice President on the plane did the party of the late President Kennedy and Mrs. Kennedy arrive at the plane?

Mr. Youngblood. Approximately—after we got on the plane, I would say it was approximately 30 or 35 minutes before Mrs. Kennedy and that party arrived.

Mr. Specter. And how long after the swearing-in ceremonies did the plane take off for the Washington area?

153

Mr. YOUNGBLOOD. After the swearing-in ceremonies, it took off immediately. It was just a matter of letting the people who had to get off the plane, such as Judge Hughes and Chief Curry disembark, and as soon as they had disembarked, we closed the door and started taxiing out.

Mr. SPECTER. Were there any conversations between Vice President Johnson and anyone else with respect to advice on the swearing-in ceremonies?

Mr. YOUNGBLOOD. Yes, sir. I think probably the first thing the Vice President did after he got on board the plane was to place a call to the Attorney General. In fact, he talked to the Attorney General, I believe, two times—at least two times.

Mr. SPECTER. Were you present when those conversations occurred?

Mr. YOUNGBLOOD. I was present when he placed the first call. I think he placed the first call from the bedroom there of the plane. Then someone from the Attorney General's office called back—not the Attorney General, but someone from the office—and gave the wording of the oath.

Mr. SPECTER. Were you informed as to what advice Vice President Johnson received from Mr. Kennedy with respect to the time of swearing in?

Mr. YOUNGBLOOD. I heard him discussing this—because after we got on board the plane I told them to pull down the shades, and then I told the Vice President, I am going to stick with you like glue while we are on the ground here. And so we were joined by Mrs. Johnson and then by Congressman Thornberry and Thomas, and Congressman Brooks. And I heard them discussing about taking the oath immediately, right there in Dallas. I heard the Vice President ask about anyone in particular that should administer the oath. And as I gathered from conversation, it was anyone who was authorized to administer a Federal oath. And then he put in calls to Judge Hughes, and he told me to expect Judge Hughes and to be sure she could get through the security lines.

Mr. SPECTER. Well, were you informed that Attorney General Kennedy advised Vice President Johnson that he should have himself sworn in as promptly as possible?

Mr. YOUNGBLOOD. Well, as I said, I was in the area, in their immediate vicinity, when they were talking about it. And this is what I gathered from hearing them talk—that the Attorney General had told him to go ahead and be sworn in there, as soon as possible.

Mr. SPECTER. And upon arrival back in Andrews Air Force Base, what activity, if any, were you engaged in then, along with President Johnson?

Mr. YOUNGBLOOD. Well, on the plane, on the flight up here, there had been numerous radio contacts in making arrangements and so forth. But when we actually arrived, Mrs. Kennedy and the body were removed first by the lift that was provided, and then when the ramp was in place, our party disembarked from the plane, and then President Johnson had a short statement that he was to make, and we went over to an area where the microphones were set up, and he made this brief statement. And then we proceeded from there to the awaiting helicopter, which was just a few yards away. We boarded the helicopter and flew in to the south grounds of the White House.

Mr. SPECTER. And did you then accompany President Johnson to his home?

Mr. YOUNGBLOOD. He didn't go to his home at that time; but the answer to your question is yes, when he did go later that night. You see, he went to his office in the EOB, the Executive Office Building, and conducted business there until in the vicinity of 9 o'clock. And then he went home, at which time I accompanied him, and many other agents.

Mr. SPECTER. Would you describe briefly what security arrangements if any were instituted on that day for the Vice President's daughters?

Mr. YOUNGBLOOD. Yes, sir.

While we were in the hospital, receiving these reports relative to President Kennedy's condition, I asked Mrs. Johnson—I knew generally where Luci and Lynda were, but I wanted to get the very latest from her, since sometimes these girls might visit a friend or a relative. And I knew that Lynda was going to the University of Texas, and that Luci was going to National Cathedral. So I confirmed the locations with Mrs. Johnson and then told Agent Kivett, who was in our presence at the time I was talking to her, to make the necessary calls to have Secret Service protection placed around Lynda and Luci. And Agent Kivett made these calls and then came back and reported to me that Lockwood, from Austin, who is in the San Antonio office, but he was in Austin at the time, had proceeded to the University of Texas to get Lynda, and that an agent from the Washington field office would go out and get Luci at the school.

Mr. SPECTER. Mr. Chief Justice, I move for the admission into evidence of Commission Exhibits No. 354, which is a reproduction of the overhead shot, and 355, which is a reproduction of the Vice Presidential detail schedules.

The CHAIRMAN. They may be admitted.

(The documents heretofore marked for identification as Commission Exhibits Nos. 354 and 355, were received in evidence.)

Mr. SPECTER. That concludes my questions, sir.

The CHAIRMAN. Mr. Craig, any questions?

Mr. CRAIG. No, sir.

Mr. MURRAY. I have no questions, Mr. Chief Justice.

The CHAIRMAN. Well, Agent Youngblood, thank you very much for coming and testifying. We appreciate it.

We will adjourn now. We will adjourn until 9 in the morning.

(Whereupon, at 6:20 p.m., the President's Commission recessed.)

Tuesday, March 10, 1964

TESTIMONY OF ROBERT HILL JACKSON, ARNOLD LOUIS ROWLAND, JAMES RICHARD WORRELL, JR., AND AMOS LEE EUINS

The President's Commission met at 9:15 a.m. on March 10, 1964 at 200 Maryland Avenue NE., Washington, D.C.

Present were Chief Justice Earl Warren, Chairman; Senator John Sherman Cooper and Representative Gerald R. Ford, members.

Also present were Joseph A. Ball, assistant counsel; David W. Belin, assistant counsel; Norman Redlich, assistant counsel; Arlen Specter, assistant counsel; and Edward L. Wright, Chairman, House of Delegates, American Bar Association.

TESTIMONY OF ROBERT HILL JACKSON

The CHAIRMAN. All right, gentlemen, are we ready? Would you raise your right hand and be sworn, Mr. Jackson? Do you solemnly swear to tell the truth, the whole truth and nothing but the truth, so help you God?

Mr. JACKSON. I do.

The CHAIRMAN. Will you be seated, please.

Mr. Specter will conduct the examination.

Mr. SPECTER. Will you state——

The CHAIRMAN. First, I will read a very small short statement for the record. The purpose of this day's hearing is to hear the testimony of Arnold Louis Rowland, Amos Lee Euins, James Richard Worrell, and Robert H. Jackson, who were in the vicinity of the assassination scene on November 22, 1963. The Commission proposes to ask these witnesses for facts concerning their knowledge of the assassination of President Kennedy.

You have seen a copy of this, have you, Mr. Jackson?

Mr. JACKSON. Yes, sir.

The CHAIRMAN. Very well, you may proceed, Mr. Specter.

Mr. SPECTER. Would you state your full name for the record, please?

Mr. JACKSON. Robert Hill Jackson.

Mr. SPECTER. And what is your address, Mr. Jackson?

Mr. JACKSON. 4030 Sperry.

Mr. Specter. What city is that located in?

Mr. Jackson. Dallas, Tex.

Mr. Specter. How long have you lived at that address, please?

Mr. Jackson. Since September of 1963.

Mr. Specter. And of what State are you a native?

Mr. Jackson. I am a native of Dallas, Tex.

Mr. Specter. Have you lived in Dallas all your life?

Mr. Jackson. Yes, sir.

Mr. Specter. What is your occupation at the present time?

Mr. Jackson. Staff photographer for the Dallas Times Herald.

Mr. Specter. How long have you been so employed?

Mr. Jackson. Since August of 1960.

Mr. Specter. Will you outline for us briefly——

The Chairman. 1950 or 1960?

Mr. Jackson. 1960.

Mr. Specter. Will you outline for us briefly your educational background, please?

Mr. Jackson. I attended Highland Park High School and then Southern Methodist University, where I studied for a business degree, and I did not finish. I lack about 8 hours of finishing, of getting a degree.

Mr. Specter. What year did you leave the university?

Mr. Jackson. 1957.

Mr. Specter. How were you occupied between the time you left the university and the time you started to work for the newspaper?

Mr. Jackson. I did some freelance photography work for a while, over a year, until I went into the service on the 6 month's plan through my National Guard unit, and I was a photographer there in the Army, on-the-job training, and then after I was released from the Army I did freelance work, I guess for about a year, until I got the job at the Herald.

Mr. Specter. How old are you at the present time?

Mr. Jackson. Twenty-nine.

Mr. Specter. What is your marital status?

Mr. Jackson. I am married.

Mr. Specter. Do you have children?

Mr. Jackson. One child. One girl 15 months today.

Mr. Specter. Going back to November 22, 1963, by whom were you employed at that time?

Mr. Jackson. Dallas Times Herald.

Mr. Specter. What was your assignment on that specific day?

Mr. Jackson. I was assigned to the motorcade to meet the President, Love Field, and go to the Trade Mart and that was the extent of it, cover the parade, I mean the motorcade and the speech.

Mr. Specter. Were you assigned to take pictures?

Mr. Jackson. To take pictures, yes, sir.

Mr. Specter. Did you meet the President at Love Field?

Mr. Jackson. Yes, sir.

Mr. Specter. And did you take photographs for your newspaper at Love Field?

Mr. Jackson. Yes, sir.

Mr. Specter. Describe briefly your activities at Love Field on the morning of November 22, please.

Mr. Jackson. Well, we got there, I guess, 30, 40 minutes early.

Mr. Specter. At about what time would that have been?

Mr. Jackson. I have to think to remember exactly what time, around 9, I guess, 9 to 9:15, I believe. And I took pictures there. There were other photographers from our paper there, our chief photographer. And we just took shots of the crowd, and waited for the President to arrive.

And then when he did arrive, our chief photographer left and went directly to the Trade Mart and I got into the motorcade to ride to town.

Mr. Specter. Do you know exactly which car you were in in the motorcade?

Mr. Jackson. We counted up, and it is either the seventh or eighth car. We said eighth car from the President, from the lead car.

Mr. Specter. When you say we counted up, whom do you mean?

Mr. Jackson. The photographers in the car. As we left Love Field, we were trying to figure how far back we were and we all decided it was the eighth car.

Mr. Specter. Can you reconstruct that count for us which provided the basis for your conclusion that you were in the seventh or eighth car. For example, how many cars ahead of you was the President's car or the Vice President's car, if you can recollect, please.

Mr. Jackson. Let me think a minute. I know there was a photographer's car directly in front of us which I believe had some of the local press. It was a convertible. Then in front were, I believe, two or three cars carrying the press, the White House press, and then President Johnson, I guess would be in the next car, and then the President in the lead car, or the next car, and I believe there was another car in the lead.

Mr. Specter. So as you recollect the scene there was the lead and immediately behind the lead car, whose car?

Mr. Jackson. The President's, I believe.

Mr. Specter. And then immediately behind the President's whose car?

Mr. Jackson. The Vice President's.

Mr. Specter. And immediately to the rear of the Vice President's car?

Mr. Jackson. Press vehicles and I was told it was the White House press, two or three cars.

Mr. Specter. And then there was one car filled with photographers?

Mr. Jackson. Directly in front of us.

Mr. Specter. Between your car and the cars which you believe to have been filled with White House newsmen?

Mr. Jackson. Yes, sir.

The Chairman. Wasn't there a Secret Service car directly behind the President's car?

Mr. Jackson. Yes, sir.

The Chairman. Between it and the Vice President's car?

Mr. Jackson. Yes, sir; that is right.

Mr. Specter. Wasn't there a Secret Service car immediately behind the Vice President's car, if you know?

Mr. Jackson. There must have been. That is what I can't recall is which was which in there. I knew the White House press was in there but I didn't know how many cars. I am sure there were Secret Service cars, yes, sir.

Mr. Specter. As you were proceeding along in the motorcade, were you within sight of the President's automobile?

Mr. Jackson. At times. When he was—when we could not get a clear view of it because of the photographers in the car ahead of us who were sitting up on the back of the seat just like we were, we did not have a clear view of the car at all times.

Mr. Specter. As you proceeded along approximately how far behind the President's car were you, expressed either in cars, block lengths or in any way that is convenient for you?

Mr. Jackson. Well, I would say approximately a block, average city block, maybe closer at times.

Mr. Specter. Mr. Jackson, I show you a photograph which has been marked heretofore as Commission Exhibit No. 347, and ask you to look at it for a moment, and see if you can identify what that photograph depicts.

Mr. Jackson. Yes, sir; this is the scene of the assassination, parade route, Main and Houston, left on Elm.

Mr. Specter. Now, which street did the Presidential motorcade take coming on to that scene which you have described as the assassination scene.

Mr. Jackson. They were on Houston.

Mr. Specter. And before Houston what street were they on?

Mr. Jackson. Main Street.

Mr. Specter. What direction were they proceeding on Main Street?

Mr. Jackson. West.

Mr. Specter. Now without reference to the photograph, will you tell us what happened as the motorcade proceeded west on Main Street?

Mr. JACKSON. Well, on Main, as we neared Houston Street everyone was more or less in a relaxed state in our car, because we were near the end of the route, I guess, nothing unusual happened on Main Street.

The final block on Main, before we turned on Houston I was in the process of unloading a camera and I was to toss it out of the car as we turned right on Houston Street to one of our reporters.

Mr. SPECTER. Had that been set up by prearrangement?

Mr. JACKSON. Yes, sir. And that I did as we turned the corner, and when— it was in an interval and as I threw it out the wind blew it, caught it and blew it out into the street and our reporter chased it out into the street and the photographers in our car, one of the photographers, was a TV cameraman whom I do not recall his name, and he was joking about the film being thrown out and he was shooting my picture of throwing the film out.

Mr. SPECTER. At this point could you tell us, to the best of your recollection, precisely who was with you in the car at that time?

Mr. JACKSON. Jim Underwood from KRLD–TV station, Tom Dillard, chief photographer for the Dallas Morning News, and me, and then two newsreel cameramen who I know by sight but I don't know their names.

One is with WFAA which is the Dallas Morning News station, and I believe the other was channel 11, I believe.

Mr. SPECTER. Can you position those people in the automobile for us with respect to where each was sitting?

(At this point Representative Ford entered the hearing room.)

Mr. JACKSON. Tom Dillard and Jim Underwood were in the front seat with the driver.

Mr. SPECTER. Can you identify who the driver was?

Mr. JACKSON. No, sir.

Mr. SPECTER. But he was a sixth individual separate and apart from the five heretofore described?

Mr. JACKSON. Yes, sir. And in the back seat were the two I know by sight but I can't remember the names.

And I was on the right side of the car.

Mr. SPECTER. On the right side of which seat?

Mr. JACKSON. Back seat, sitting up on the back of a seat.

Mr. SPECTER. What kind of a car was it, sir?

Mr. JACKSON. I believe it was a Chevrolet convertible.

Mr. SPECTER. Top down?

Mr. JACKSON. Yes, sir.

Mr. SPECTER. Were you carrying one camera or more than one camera?

Mr. JACKSON. Two cameras.

Mr. SPECTER. And was one camera loaded at the time you rounded the corner of Main and Houston?

Mr. JACKSON. Yes, sir; and one was empty.

Mr. SPECTER. Was it from the camera which was empty that you had taken the roll of film which you have just described?

Mr. JACKSON. Yes, sir.

Mr. SPECTER. All right. Will you now proceed to tell us what happened as you rounded the corner of Main and Houston, please?

Mr. JACKSON. Well, as our reporter chased the film out into the street, we all looked back at him and were laughing, and it was approximately that time that we heard the first shot, and we had already rounded the corner, of course, when we heard the first shot. We were approximately almost half a block on Houston Street.

Mr. SPECTER. Will you identify for me on Commission Exhibit 347, precisely as possible, where your automobile was at the time you heard the first shot?

Mr. JACKSON. Approximately right here, I would say the midpoint of this building. Approximately where we heard the first report.

Mr. SPECTER. Now, will you mark in a black "X" on 347 the spot where your car was at the time you heard the first shot?

Mr. JACKSON. Right here approximately. And as we heard the first shot, I believe it was Tom Dillard from Dallas News who made some remark as to that sounding like a firecracker, and it could have been somebody else who said that. But someone else did speak up and make that comment and before he actually finished the sentence we heard the other two shots. Then we realized or we thought that it was gunfire, and then we could not at that point see the President's car. We were still moving slowly, and after the third shot the second two shots seemed much closer together than the first shot, than they were to the first shot. Then after the last shot, I guess all of us were just looking all around and I just looked straight up ahead of me which would have been looking at the School Book Depository and I noticed two Negro men in a window straining to see directly above them, and my eyes followed right on up to the window above them and I saw the rifle or what looked like a rifle approximately half of the weapon, I guess I saw, and just as I looked at it, it was drawn fairly slowly back into the building, and I saw no one in the window with it.

I didn't even see a form in the window.

Mr. SPECTER. What did you do next?

Mr. JACKSON. I said "There is the gun," or it came from that window. I tried to point it out. But by the time the other people looked up, of course, it was gone, and about that time we were beginning to turn the corner.

Mr. SPECTER. Which corner were you beginning to turn?

Mr. JACKSON. Houston onto Elm.

Mr. SPECTER. I now show you a photograph marked as Commission Exhibit No. 348 and ask you if you can identify what that depicts?

Mr. JACKSON. This is the School Book Depository. This is the window the two colored men were looking out of. This is the window where the rifle was.

Mr. SPECTER. Will you mark the window where the rifle was with an "A" and would you please mark the window where you have identified the men below with a "B."

(Witness marking.)

Mr. SPECTER. Referring to your mark of "A," the photograph will show that you have marked the window on the sixth floor with the mark being placed on the window on the westerly half of the first double window.

Mr. JACKSON. I am sorry. This window here on the very end was the window where the weapon was. I am sorry, I just marked the double—actually this is the rifle window right here.

Mr. SPECTER. Will you take the black pencil again and draw an arrow—before you start to mark, hear the rest of the question—as precisely as you can to the exact spot where you saw what you have described as the rifle.

(Witness marking.)

Mr. SPECTER. Was the window you have just marked as being the spot from which the rifle protruded, open when you looked up?

Mr. JACKSON. Yes, sir.

Mr. SPECTER. What is your best recollection as to how far open it was at that time?

Mr. JACKSON. I would say that it was open like that window there, halfway.

Mr. SPECTER. Indicating a window on the sixth floor of the westernmost portion of the building open halfway as you have described it.

My last comment, as to the description of your last window, is only for the purpose of what you have said in identifying a window to show how far open the window was.

Mr. JACKSON. Yes.

Mr. SPECTER. Which you heretofore marked with an arrow, correct?

Mr. JACKSON. Yes, sir.

Also in that window I could see boxes, corrugated boxes on the left portion which would be my left, of the window, of the open window.

Mr. SPECTER. How many boxes could you see?

Mr. JACKSON. I couldn't tell. It just seemed like a stack of boxes.

Mr. SPECTER. How high were the boxes stacked?

Mr. JACKSON. Maybe two is all I saw. They were stacked, I believe they were as high as the window was open, halfway up the window.

Mr. SPECTER. What is your best recollection of the size of those boxes which you say you saw?

Mr. JACKSON. Maybe like that, that wide.

Mr. Specter. Indicating approximately 3 feet wide?

Mr. Jackson. Three feet or a little less maybe.

Mr. Specter. What was the height of those boxes?

Mr. Jackson. I would say high enough to hide a man. Let's say, between 5 and 6 feet high, I would say to the best of my recollection. From the angle I was looking at it, I would say they were 5 feet high at least.

Mr. Specter. That is each box would be 5 feet high?

Mr. Jackson. No; the stack, the stacked boxes.

Mr. Specter. Could you see how many boxes were stacked up to reach a total height of 5 to 6 feet?

Mr. Jackson. No, sir.

Mr. Specter. Now, were you able to see anyone in front of those boxes?

Mr. Jackson. No, sir.

Mr. Specter. Whether or not you could identify anyone, could you see even the form or outline of the man?

Mr. Jackson. No, sir. It looked to me like the man was over to the side of the window because the rifle was at quite an angle to me.

Mr. Specter. Which side of the window?

Mr. Jackson. Well, from the position of the rifle it would be the corner of the building, the east. It would be to the right of the window from my view.

Mr. Specter. Which direction was the rifle pointing?

Mr. Jackson. West. To my left.

Mr. Specter. Was it pointing in a straight westerly direction or was it pointing at an angle from the building.

Mr. Jackson. It was at an angle from the building. I am not—well, let's see—well, it wouldn't be directly west.

Mr. Specter. What was the general line of direction of the pointing of the rifle?

Mr. Jackson. Well, directly down the street.

Mr. Specter. And by down the street you are pointing out what street?

Mr. Jackson. Down Elm Street toward the triple, toward the underpass.

Mr. Specter. Was it pointed as you have indicated at the angle which Elm Street traverses heading toward the triple underpass?

Mr. Jackson. Yes, sir. And the rifle was pointing slightly down.

Mr. Specter. Did you at any time in this sequence observe the President's automobile?

Mr. Jackson. As we turned the corner—or we stopped where the intersection, actually we stopped before we began to turn left onto Elm Street, or rather I would say we hesitated and we were all looking down towards the President's car and I could see two cars going under the underpass. I barely saw the President's car. I would say just the rear end of it as it disappeared under the underpass.

Mr. Specter. Was that the only time you saw the President's car from the time you made a right-hand turn off of Main Street onto Houston Street?

Mr. Jackson. Yes, sir.

Mr. Specter. What is your best estimate as to the time span between the first shot you heard and the last shot you heard?

Mr. Jackson. I would say 5 to 8 seconds.

Mr. Specter. Can you give us a breakdown between the shots which you heard as to how many seconds elapsed between each one?

Mr. Jackson. I would say to me it seemed like 3 or 4 seconds between the first and the second, and between the second and third, well, I guess 2 seconds, they were very close together. It could have been more time between the first and second. I really can't be sure.

Mr. Specter. Are you sure you heard three shots?

Mr. Jackson. Yes, sir.

Mr. Specter. Now, will you mark on the overhead shot, which is Exhibit 347, with a "Y" as precisely as you can the position of your automobile at the time you heard the second shot?

Mr. Jackson. With a "Y"?

Mr. SPECTER. Yes, please.

(Witness marking.)

Mr. SPECTER. Would you now mark on the same exhibit the precise position of your car as closely as you can recollect it when you heard the third shot with a letter "Z"?

(Witness marking.)

Mr. SPECTER. When, in relation to the timing of the shots, which you have described, did you first look toward the Texas School Book Depository Building?

Mr. JACKSON. It couldn't have been more than 3 seconds before I looked at that window.

Mr. SPECTER. Three seconds from what point in time?

Mr. JACKSON. From the last shot.

Mr. SPECTER. Did you say from the last shot?

Mr. JACKSON. From the last shot, yes, sir.

Mr. SPECTER. What is your best recollection or estimate of the speed of your automobile as you were proceeding in a generally northerly direction on Houston Street at the time of the shooting?

Mr. JACKSON. I would say not over 15 miles an hour.

Mr. SPECTER. What would your best estimate be as to the minimum speed?

Mr. JACKSON. Ten, I would say.

Mr. SPECTER. Where, in the window were the two Negro men, whom you have described?

Mr. JACKSON. Well, there was one in each of those double windows.

Mr. SPECTER. On which floor was that?

Mr. JACKSON. The fifth floor.

Mr. SPECTER. And will you place an arrow where you saw each of those men, please?

Mr. JACKSON. Each one of them?

Mr. SPECTER. Yes.

(Witness marking.)

Mr. SPECTER. Did you observe any reaction from either or both of those two men when you saw them?

Mr. JACKSON. No, sir. Just looking up.

Mr. SPECTER. Could you see their faces reasonably clearly to observe that they were looking up.

Mr. JACKSON. I could tell they were looking up because they were leaning way out just like that. I couldn't see their faces very well at all.

Mr. SPECTER. The witness has leaned forward and turned his head to the right and looking upward as he sits in the witness chair, may the record show.

Representative FORD. Did they both turn the same way as you have indicated in answer to Mr. Specter's question?

Mr. JACKSON. To the best of my recollection one man looked up to his right and the other man looked up like this to his left, one in each window.

Representative FORD. Can you identify which to his right and which to his left?

Mr. JACKSON. I believe the one on the right window, my right, was looking to his right. The one on the west window, the one to my left was looking to his left. I believe I am right on that but I may not be because I just looked at them for a fraction of a second, I just followed them up.

Mr. SPECTER. What is your best estimate of the distance which separated you from those two men at the time you observed them?

Mr. JACKSON. I am not very good at distances. I was about the middle of the block, I guess. I would say around a hundred yards, I guess.

Mr. SPECTER. Did you see those two men before or after you observed the rifle?

Mr. JACKSON. Before.

Mr. SPECTER. What is your best estimate of how many inches of the rifle that you observed?

Mr. JACKSON. I saw the barrel and about half—well, I did not see a telescopic sight, but I did see part of the stock, so I guess maybe 8 or 10 inches of the stock maybe. I did see part of the stock, I did not see the sight.

Mr. SPECTER. Eight or ten inches of the stock, and how much of the barrel would you estimate?

Mr. JACKSON. I guess possibly a foot.

Mr. SPECTER. Did you see anyone's hands on the rifle?

Mr. JACKSON. No, sir.

Mr. SPECTER. Now, as best as you can recollect it, what exact words did you state at or about the time you made the observation of the rifle, if any?

Mr. JACKSON. I said, "There is the gun" and somebody said "Where?" And I said, "It came from that window" and I pointed to that window.

Mr. SPECTER. Do you recollect who it was who said "Where?"

Mr. JACKSON. Somebody in the car, I don't recall who.

Mr. SPECTER. Did anybody else in the car say anything else at that time?

Mr. JACKSON. Nothing that I could remember. I am sure they were all talking.

Mr. SPECTER. Did you say anything else at about that time?

Mr. JACKSON. If I did, I don't remember.

Mr. SPECTER. Did anyone in the automobile state that he, too, had seen the rifle from the window?

Mr. JACKSON. No, sir.

Mr. SPECTER. Did you have a conversation with all of the men in the car immediately after the incident?

Mr. JACKSON. No, sir; because as, I guess after the third shot, I do recall the driver speeding up, and we hesitated at the corner before turning left, and three of the occupants of the car got out, jumped out.

Mr. SPECTER. Who were those three?

Mr. JACKSON. That was Underwood, Jim Underwood, Tom Dillard and one of the TV cameramen. The WHAA channel 8 cameraman and I were left in the back seat. We couldn't make up our minds.

Mr. SPECTER. Was there an individual in the car by the name of Mr. Couch, to your knowledge?

Mr. JACKSON. Couch?

Mr. SPECTER. Yes, sir.

Mr. JACKSON. I don't know him.

Mr. SPECTER. Malcolm Couch?

Mr. JACKSON. The name is familiar. I might state what I did see as we did hesitate there at the corner, I don't recall whether this was before the other three fellows got out of the car or not, I believe we were still all in the car, as we observed these other things, but in a fleeting glance as I saw the cars go under the underpass, I did see people running. I saw a motorcycle policeman jump off his motorcycle, in fact, he just hit the curb and just let it fall, and he went down on his knees on the grass, on the lawn of that parkway.

I did see a family covering up their child, and I just saw a state of confusion, people running, and that is about all I saw at that point of the scene.

Mr. SPECTER. Mr. Jackson, at the time you heard the first shot, did you have any reaction or impression from the sound itself as to the source of the shot, point of origin?

Mr. JACKSON. No, sir; I didn't. It did sound like it came from ahead of us or from that general vicinity but I could not tell whether it was high up or on the ground.

Mr. SPECTER. When you say that general vicinity, what vicinity did you mean?

Mr. JACKSON. We were sure it came from ahead of us which would be in a northerly direction, northwesterly direction. It did sound as though it came from somewhere around the head of the motorcade.

Mr. SPECTER. From the second shot, did you have any reaction or impression as to the source of this shot?

Mr. JACKSON. No, sir. Through all three shots, I could just tell that it was ahead of me and not behind me, that is it.

Mr. SPECTER. And the same impression then prevailed through the third shot as well.

162

Mr. Jackson. Yes, sir. To me it never sounded like it was high or low.

Mr. Specter. Have you had occasion since this incident to relate the factual sequences, your observations and what you heard? Have you had occasion to tell anybody about what you saw and heard as you have described it to us?

Mr. Jackson. Yes, sir.

Mr. Specter. Has there been any variation in your recollection or impressions about your observations on these occasions?

Mr. Jackson. Not to my knowledge. The other times were not as thorough as this.

Mr. Specter. Mr. Chief Justice, those are all of the questions which I have, sir.

The Chairman. Congressman Ford, any questions you would like to ask Mr. Jackson?

Representative Ford. Mr. Jackson, when and by whom were you questioned or interrogated subsequent to the event? I was thinking of the FBI, the Secret Service, or any investigative organization.

Mr. Jackson. You say when, how soon afterwards?

Representative Ford. Right.

Mr. Jackson. I would say within 2 days afterwards, let's see, the next day was the first day.

Representative Ford. Saturday November 23?

Mr. Jackson. Yes, sir; I believe it was the first time.

Representative Ford. Who, by name, if you can, but if not by what organization?

Mr. Jackson. The FBI called me, I believe it was Friday evening, and I believe I did give some information on the phone Friday night.

Representative Ford. Was that followed up——

Mr. Jackson. And they came and saw me in the office, I believe on Saturday.

Representative Ford. How did they happen to contact you? Had you made a statement publicly before?

Mr. Jackson. Our newspaper ran an article by me or I got a byline on it stating this in general which I have stated today.

Representative Ford. Following this initial contact have you made subsequent statements to various organizations or any organization?

Mr. Jackson. I made statements to the Secret Service also. Other than that there was none other.

Representative Ford. How good are your eyes, do you wear glasses?

Mr. Jackson. No, sir.

Representative Ford. Have you had an eye examination recently or when was the last examination?

Mr. Jackson. I had a physical when I reenlisted in the National Guard, let's see, that was, I believe, about a year and a half ago, I had that physical and I had 20–20 vision.

Representative Ford. 20–20 vision?

Mr. Jackson. Yes, sir.

Representative Ford. You just indicated you were in the Texas National Guard?

Mr. Jackson. Yes, sir.

Representative Ford. How long have you been in the Texas National Guard?

Mr. Jackson. I joined in October 1958.

Representative Ford. And you have been in continuously since?

Mr. Jackson. Yes, sir.

Representative Ford. So you are familiar with guns in general?

Mr. Jackson. Yes, sir.

Representative Ford. So you would readily identify, if you saw it, a rifle?

Mr. Jackson. Yes, sir.

Representative Ford. Did any others in the automobile in which you were riding recollect as far as you know, hearing you say "There is the gun."

Mr. Jackson. I don't know whether they would remember it or not.

Representative Ford. Have you ever talked with any others in the car?

Mr. Jackson. I have never sat down and talked with them about the events, no, sir. I have seen them, of course, several times but I have never discussed it with them.

Representative FORD. You never discussed what you said or what they said?

Mr. JACKSON. No, sir. I guess the one man I have discussed it more with than anybody else was Tom Dillard, the chief photographer for the Dallas News, and we recalled to each other the scene but we really never went into any detail or as to what each one of us said either.

Representative FORD. At the time you were in the car, after it had turned from Main onto Houston, was there any noise from the crowd on either side of the street, Houston Street?

Mr. JACKSON. There was very little crowd on Houston, as I recall. On Houston itself. The crowd—I mean as compared to Main Street, to the other end of town and down through Main. The crowd thinned out as we got down near the intersection of Main and Houston, and there were a lot less people but I couldn't make an estimate of how many.

Representative FORD. There was no noise from the crowd at that point?

Mr. JACKSON. No, sir; no noise, I would say.

Representative FORD. At the time you heard the first shot, what was your position in the car? Were you standing or sitting?

Mr. JACKSON. I was sitting on the back of the seat, on the right-hand side of the back seat, sitting up.

Representative FORD. Did you have your camera in your hand?

Mr. JACKSON. Yes; I had one camera around my neck and the camera I had just emptied, it was in my lap. I had thrown my film out to this reporter over the side of the car as we rounded the corner and I still had the camera lying in my lap, and the other one was around my neck.

Representative FORD. Was this the position you were in at the time you heard the first shot?

Mr. JACKSON. Yes, sir.

Representative FORD. After the third shot and as the car hesitated, did you see any law enforcement officials move in any concentrated or concerted direction?

Mr. JACKSON. I saw at least one, there may have been more, run up the School Depository steps, toward the door. That is one of the things I saw in this confusion.

Representative FORD. This was separate from the policeman on the motorcycle?

Mr. JACKSON. Yes, sir. Yes. I should have said that a while ago. There was a policeman who moved toward the door of the Depository. But to my best knowledge there was no concentrated movement toward any one spot. It looked like general confusion to me, and of course, I stayed in the car. As we did turn the corner our driver speeded up and we went by the scene pretty fast and I do recall this Negro family covering up their child on the grass, and I, as we passed them, they were just getting up and he had the child in his arms and the child looked limp and I didn't know whether the child was shot or not. But then we were moving fast and went on under the underpass.

Representative FORD. That is all, Mr. Chairman.

The CHAIRMAN. Mr. Wright, do you have any questions?

Mr. WRIGHT. No, Mr. Chief Justice, I passed a question on.

Mr. SPECTER. I have just one additional question, and that is whether Mr. Jackson had any occasion to see anybody leave the scene of the Texas School Book Depository Building?

Mr. JACKSON. No, sir.

Mr. SPECTER. That is all, Your Honor.

The CHAIRMAN. Mr. Jackson, thank you very much for coming.

Mr. JACKSON. Thank you.

The CHAIRMAN. We appreciate it.

Who is next?

Mr. SPECTER. Mr. Rowland.

The CHAIRMAN. Would you raise your right hand and be sworn, please.

Do you solemnly swear the testimony given before this Commission will be the truth, the whole truth and nothing but the truth, so help you God?

Mr. Rowland. Yes, sir.

The Chairman. Mr. Specter will conduct the examination.

Mr. Specter. Will you state your full name for the record, please, but before you do, Mr. Chief Justice, is it your practice to read that statement to the witness?

The Chairman. Yes. I will read a short statement to you for the purpose of the hearing.

The purpose of today's hearing is to hear the testimony of Arnold Louis Rowland, Amos Lee Euins, James Richard Worrell, and Robert H. Jackson, who were in the vicinity of the assassination scene on November 22, 1963. The Commission proposes to ask these witnesses for facts concerning their knowledge of the assassination of President Kennedy.

A copy of that statement was furnished to you, was it not?

Mr. Rowland. No.

The Chairman. You didn't see it. You have one before you. Very well.

TESTIMONY OF ARNOLD LOUIS ROWLAND

Mr. Specter. Will you please state your full name for the record, Mr. Rowland?

Mr. Rowland. Arnold Louis Rowland.

Mr. Specter. What is your address?

Mr. Rowland. 1131 Aphinney.

Mr. Specter. And in what city do you reside?

Mr. Rowland. This is Dallas, Tex.

Mr. Specter. How long have you resided in Dallas, Tex.

Mr. Rowland. About 9 months at present.

Mr. Specter. Where did you live before coming to Dallas?

Mr. Rowland. In Salem, Oreg.

Mr. Specter. How long did you live in Salem, Oreg.

Mr. Rowland. About 3 months.

Mr. Specter. Where did you live before moving to Salem, Oreg.

Mr. Rowland. Dallas.

Mr. Specter. How long did you live in Dallas at that time?

Mr. Rowland. About 4 years.

Mr. Specter. Where were you born?

Mr. Rowland. Corpus Christi, Tex.

Mr. Specter. Have you lived in Texas most of your life?

Mr. Rowland. Most of my life.

Mr. Specter. What is your age at the present time, Mr. Rowland?

Mr. Rowland. Eighteen.

Mr. Specter. And what is your exact date of birth, please?

Mr. Rowland. April 29, 1945.

Mr. Specter. What is your marital status.

Mr. Rowland. Married.

Mr. Specter. Have you any children?

Mr. Rowland. No.

Mr. Specter. How long have you been married?

Mr. Rowland. Ten months.

Mr. Specter. What education have you had, sir?

Mr. Rowland. High school.

Mr. Specter. Are you attending high school at the present time?

Mr. Rowland. I have finished, and fixing to go to college.

Mr. Specter. When did you graduate from high school?

Mr. Rowland. June 1963.

Mr. Specter. How have you been occupied or employed since June of 1963?

Mr. Rowland. Worked in Oregon at three different jobs, Exchange Lumber Co. as a shipping clerk, Meier Frank Co. as a clothes salesman, and part time at West Foods. The business was mushroom processing. That was during the summer.

Upon my return to Dallas, I worked part time, while doing some postgraduate work, at the Pizza Inn. At present I am working with the P. F. Collier Co.

Mr. SPECTER. What sort of work are you doing with P. F. Collier?

Mr. ROWLAND. That is promotional advertising.

Mr. SPECTER. What college are you attending, if any, at the present time?

Mr. ROWLAND. None at the present.

Mr. SPECTER. What postgraduate work had you been doing that you just mentioned?

Mr. ROWLAND. Studies in math and science.

Mr. SPECTER. Where were you studying these courses?

Mr. ROWLAND. This was a high school in Dallas as advanced courses.

Mr. SPECTOR. Have you been accepted in any college?

Mr. ROWLAND. Yes; several. Texas A. & M., Rice, SMU, Arlington.

Mr. SPECTER. Do you have plans to attend one of those colleges?

Mr. ROWLAND. Yes.

Mr. SPECTER. Which one do you plan to enter?

Mr. ROWLAND. Preferably Rice.

Mr. SPECTER. Do you have an entry date set?

Mr. ROWLAND. No; I am trying for a scholarship for it.

Mr. SPECTER. Have you been in the military service?

Mr. ROWLAND. No; I haven't.

Mr. SPECTER. What is the general condition of your health.

Mr. ROWLAND. Good.

Mr. SPECTER. What is the condition of your eyesight?

Mr. ROWLAND. Very good.

Mr. SPECTER. Do you wear glasses at any time?

Mr. ROWLAND. No.

Mr. SPECTER. When, most recently, have you had an eye test, if at all?

Mr. ROWLAND. About 7 months ago.

Mr. SPECTER. And you know the results of that test?

Mr. ROWLAND. Very good vision.

Mr. SPECTER. Do you know what classification the doctor placed on it?

Mr. ROWLAND. No; I don't remember it.

Mr. SPECTER. Do you recollect if it was 20–20?

Mr. ROWLAND. He said it was much better than that.

Mr. SPECTER. And what doctor examined your eyes?

Mr. ROWLAND. This was the firm of doctors Finn and Finn.

Mr. SPECTER. F-i-n-n and F-i-n-n?

Mr. ROWLAND. Yes.

Mr. SPECTER. Where are they located?

Mr. ROWLAND. The Fidelity Union Life Building in Dallas.

Mr. SPECTER. Approximately how long ago was that examination?

Mr. ROWLAND. About 6 months.

Mr. SPECTER. Going to the day of November 22, 1963, how were you occupied at that time, Mr. Rowland?

Mr. ROWLAND. I was attending classes in school part of the day, working part time as a pizzamaker in Pizza Inn.

Mr. SPECTER. Had you regularly scheduled classes on the morning of November 22, 1963?

Mr. ROWLAND. Yes. I had classes up until 11. I just had two classes on Friday.

Mr. SPECTER. And what school were you attending at that time?

Mr. ROWLAND. W. H. Adamson High.

Mr. SPECTER. How far is that from the intersection of Houston and Elm Streets in Dallas, approximately?

Mr. ROWLAND. It must have been about a mile and a half.

Mr. SPECTER. Will you describe for the Commission what you did on that morning, in a general way, up until approximately noon time?

Mr. ROWLAND. I went to my classes. My wife got out of school early. We went to town. I had to go to work at 4, so we were going downtown to do some shopping. We went early so we could see the President's motorcade.

Mr. SPECTER. What time did you arrive in town?

166

Mr. ROWLAND. We rode a bus from the school. We got to town approximately a quarter to 12.

Mr. SPECTER. What school was your wife attending at that time?

Mr. ROWLAND. The same; Adamson.

Mr. SPECTER. What time did her classes end?

Mr. ROWLAND. She got out at 11 also.

Mr. SPECTER. And what did you do from the time you arrived in town at approximately a quarter of 12 for the next 15 minutes?

Mr. ROWLAND. Trying to find a good vantage point. We walked about five or six blocks.

Mr. SPECTER. From where did you walk?

Mr. ROWLAND. We got off at the junction, at the intersection of Main and Houston, walked up toward Ervay, about four blocks, I would say up to Akard. We walked from Houston to Akard on Main, and then we walked back down Commerce and then over to the sheriffs or the county courthouse, there was a lesser crowd there.

Mr. SPECTER. Is that the reason you selected the spot you ultimately picked to watch the parade?

Mr. ROWLAND. Yes, there was no one in front of us, no one around that area.

Mr. SPECTER. I am going to show you a photograph, Mr. Rowland. which has already been identified as Commission Exhibit No. 347 and first ask you if you can identify what scene this represents.

Mr. ROWLAND. Yes; I can.

Mr. SPECTER. What scene is that?

Mr. ROWLAND. This is the triple underpass, this is the scene where the President was assassinated.

Mr. SPECTER. What is this plaza called in Dallas?

Mr. ROWLAND. I don't know exactly. It is just known as the triple underpass.

Mr. SPECTER. Is it known as Dealey Plaza to your knowledge?

Mr. ROWLAND. I have never heard it called that.

Mr. SPECTER. Can you point with your finger for me at the spot where you were standing as best you can recollect it?

Mr. ROWLAND. We were about in this area on this sidewalk of this building. I say approximately two-thirds of the distance between here and here in this direction.

Mr. SPECTER. All right.

I have a substitute photograph for you to mark. I am now showing you an identical scene on a photograph which has been heretofore marked as Commision Exhibit No. 354. Will you mark with an arrow as closely as possible to the point where you were standing?

Mr. ROWLAND. There is an elevator shaft below this second window on that building that comes through a sidewalk. I was about 5 feet to the left of it, about the third window or right here in this area.

Mr. SPECTER. Will you mark that a little more heavily, please?

Mr. ROWLAND. Yes.

(Witness marking.)

Mr. SPECTER. What time were you so positioned?

Mr. ROWLAND. We got there about 5 after 12.

Mr. SPECTER. Did your position move at any time during the course of the next half hour?

Mr. ROWLAND. Yes. We did move to this corner, there were too many people on this corner.

Mr. SPECTER. You are indicating back to the corner of Houston and Main?

Mr. ROWLAND. Yes. Houston and Main there were too many crowds so we came back to this street here, Commerce is that right; no, Elm and Main. We came back to Elm and Main and figured it wouldn't be a very good vantage point because of the crowd there so we went back to where we were.

Mr. SPECTER. Where were you standing at the time the President's motorcade passed by you?

Mr. ROWLAND. At that position.

(Witness marking.)

Mr. SPECTER. The position you have marked with a "V," inverted "V."

Will you mark with the letter "A" the point to which you had moved when you described it as being at Commerce which you corrected to Elm and Houston.

Mr. ROWLAND. It was this corner.

(Witness marking.)

Mr. SPECTER. Approximately what time did you move to the position you have marked "A"?

Mr. ROWLAND. About 10 after 12.

Mr. SPECTER. How long did you stay at position "A"?

Mr. ROWLAND. Momentarily, just long enough to look, maybe a minute.

Mr. SPECTER. To look at what?

Mr. ROWLAND. To look at the position itself. There was too much of a crowd in that area. When the President would come by they would be pushing or rushing in that area and it would be too crowded for us.

Mr. SPECTER. At that point you did what?

Mr. ROWLAND. Then we went back to where we were.

Mr. SPECTER. To position "V"?

Mr. ROWLAND. Yes, and we stayed there for a minute or so, walked to the corner of Main and Houston.

Mr. SPECTER. Mark Main and Houston with the letter "B," if you would, where you moved next.

(Witness marking.)

Mr. ROWLAND. Stayed there momentarily, less than a minute. There was quite a crowd there and we went back to where we were, our original position.

Mr. SPECTER. To position "V"?

Mr. ROWLAND. Yes.

Mr. SPECTER. What time would you say you got back to your position "V"?

Mr. ROWLAND. We got back there 14 after, I noticed the time on my watch, and the Hertz time clock I noticed was about a minute later.

Mr. SPECTER. Where was the Hertz time clock located?

Mr. ROWLAND. That was on top of the school depository building.

Mr. SPECTER. Was your watch synchronized with the Hertz up on top.

Mr. ROWLAND. Yes; I always set it by the same clock whenever I pass it. I pass it coming into town and I set my watch at that time.

Mr. SPECTER. Now, did you observe at any time the building which is depicted in Commission Exhibit No. 348?

Mr. ROWLAND. Yes. We were looking around it, my wife and I, amongst the crowd, the different areas, making note of the policemen on top of the underpass itself, in that area, and the security precautions that were being taken.

Mr. SPECTER. Mr. Chairman, I would like to show the witness the same photograph, but a different picture on an exhibit marked Commission Exhibit No. 356.

Mr. Rowland, I show you a picture marked Commission Exhibit No. 356 and ask you if you can identify what that represents?

Mr. ROWLAND. That is Houston, Elm running in front of this building. This is the school book depository building.

Mr. SPECTER. Were you familiar with that building prior to November 22, 1963?

Mr. ROWLAND. Yes; I have been in there on occasion.

Mr. SPECTER. You have been in the building?

Mr. ROWLAND. Yes, to purchase books.

Mr. SPECTER. When were you in the building most recently prior to November 22, 1963?

Mr. ROWLAND. Within the first week of November. This was to buy a physics notebook.

Mr. SPECTER. What part of the building were you in at that time?

Mr. ROWLAND. Just inside the door of the main lobby.

Mr. SPECTER. On the first floor?

Mr. ROWLAND. Yes.

Mr. SPECTER. Had you ever had occasion at any time to be on any floor other than the first floor?

Mr. ROWLAND. No.

Mr. SPECTER. While you were standing on Houston Street in the various positions which you have described, did you have occasion at any time to observe the Texas School Book Depository Building?

Mr. ROWLAND. Yes. When we returned to position "V" we stayed there, we began looking around. My wife and I were discussing the security precautions that were taken in view of the event when Mr. Stevenson was there.

Mr. SPECTER. Before you go on, let me ask you at which time was this on your return to position "V"?

Mr. ROWLAND. This was 12:15.

Mr. SPECTER. All right; proceed to tell us what you saw and heard at about that time?

Mr. ROWLAND. We were discussing, as I stated, the different security precautions, I mean it was a very important person who was coming and we were aware of the policemen around everywhere, and especially in positions where they would be able to watch crowds. We talked momentarily of the incidents with Mr. Stevenson, and the one before that with Mr. Johnson, and this being in mind we were more or less security conscious. We looked and at that time I noticed on the sixth floor of the building that there was a man back from the window, not hanging out the window.

He was standing and holding a rifle. This appeared to me to be a fairly high-powered rifle because of the scope and the relative proportion of the scope to the rifle, you can tell about what type of rifle it is. You can tell it isn't a .22, you know, and we thought momentarily that maybe we should tell someone but then the thought came to us that it is a security agent.

We had seen in the movies before where they have security men up in windows and places like that with rifles to watch the crowds, and we brushed it aside as that, at that time, and thought nothing else about it until after the event happened.

Mr. SPECTER. Now, by referring to the photograph on this Commission Exhibit No. 356, will you point to the window where you observed this man?

Mr. ROWLAND. This was very odd. There were—this picture was not taken immediately after that, I don't think, because there were several windows, there are pairs of windows, and there were several pairs where both windows were open fully and in each pair there was one or more persons hanging out the window.

Yet this was on the west corner of the building, the sixth floor, the first floor—second floor down from the top, the first was the arched, the larger windows, not the arch, but the larger windows, and this was the only pair of windows where both windows were completely open and no one was hanging out the windows, or next to the window.

It was this pair of windows here at that time.

Mr. SPECTER. All right.

Will you mark that pair of windows with a circle?

(Witness marking.)

Mr. SPECTER. What is your best recollection as to how far each of those windows were open?

Mr. ROWLAND. To the fullest extent that they could be opened.

Mr. SPECTER. What extent would that be?

Mr. ROWLAND. Being as I looked half frame windows, that would be halfway of the entire length of the window.

Mr. SPECTER. Is that the approximate status of those windows depicted here in Exhibit 356?

Mr. ROWLAND. Yes.

Mr. SPECTER. In which of those double windows did you see the man and rifle?

Mr. ROWLAND. It was through the window to my right.

Mr. SPECTER. Draw an arrow right into that window with the same black pencil please.

(Witness marking.)

Mr. SPECTER. How much, if any, or all of that rifle could you see?

Mr. ROWLAND. All of it.

Mr. SPECTER. You could see from the base of the stock down to the tip of the end of the rifle?

Mr. ROWLAND. Yes.

169

Mr. Specter. The barrel of the rifle?

The Chairman. Congressman Ford, will you excuse me for just a few minutes to run across the street to my office. You conduct during my absence.

Representative Ford. Will you proceed, Mr. Specter?

Mr. Specter. What is your best estimate of the distance between where you were standing and the man holding the rifle whom you have just described?

(The Chief Justice left the hearing room.)

Mr. Rowland. 150 feet approximately, very possibly more. I don't know for sure.

Mr. Specter. Are you very good at judging distances of that sort?

Mr. Rowland. Fairly good.

Mr. Specter. Have you had any experience or practice at judging such distances?

Mr. Rowland. Yes. Even in using the method in physics or, you know, elementary physics of looking at a position in two different views, you can tell its distance. I did that quite frequently. And the best I can recollect it was within 150 to 175 feet.

Mr. Specter. Can you describe the rifle with any more particularity than you already have?

Mr. Rowland. No. In proportion to the scope it appeared to me to be a .30-odd size 6, a deer rifle with a fairly large or powerful scope.

Mr. Specter. When you say, .30-odd-6, exactly what did you mean by that?

Mr. Rowland. That is a rifle that is used quite frequently for deer hunting. It is an import.

Mr. Specter. Do you own any rifles?

Mr. Rowland. No; my stepfather does.

Mr. Specter. Have you ever gone hunting deer with such a rifle?

Mr. Rowland. Yes; I have.

Mr. Specter. And is that a .30-odd-6 rifle that you have hunted deer with?

Mr. Rowland. Yes.

Mr. Specter. Is that a popular size of rifle in the Dallas, Tex., area?

Mr. Rowland. I don't know about Dallas. I do know in Oregon it is one of the most popular for deer hunting.

Mr. Specter. Was the rifle which you observed similar to, or perhaps identical with, .30-odd rifles which you have seen before?

Mr. Rowland. The best I could tell it was of that size.

Mr. Specter. Have you seen such .30-odd rifles before at close range which had telescopic sights?

Mr. Rowland. Yes; one my stepfather has has a very powerful scope on it.

Mr. Specter. And did this rifle appear similar to the one your stepfather owned?

Mr. Rowland. From my distance, I would say very similar or of similar manufacture.

Mr. Specter. In what manner was the rifle being held by the man whom you observed?

Mr. Rowland. The way he was standing it would have been in a position such as port arms in military terms.

Mr. Specter. When you say port arms you have positioned your left hand with the left elbow of your hand being about level with your shoulder and your right hand——

Mr. Rowland. Not quite level with my shoulder, and the right hand being lower on the trigger of the stock.

Mr. Specter. So the waist of the imaginary rifle you would be holding would cross your body at about a 45-degree angle.

Mr. Rowland. That is correct.

Mr. Specter. How long was the rifle held in that position?

Mr. Rowland. During the entire time that I saw him there.

Mr. Specter. Did you see him hold it in any other position?

Mr. Rowland. No, I didn't.

Mr. Specter. For example, was he standing at any time in a parade-rest position?

Mr. Rowland. No; not to my knowledge.

Mr. SPECTER. Describe, as best you can, the appearance of the individual whom you saw?

Mr. ROWLAND. He was rather slender in proportion to his size. I couldn't tell for sure whether he was tall and maybe, you know heavy, say 200 pounds, but tall whether he would be and slender or whether he was medium and slender, but in proportion to his size his build was slender.

Mr. SPECTER. Could you give us an estimate on his height?

Mr. ROWLAND. No; I couldn't. That is why I said I can't state what height he would be. He was just slender in build in proportion with his width. This is something I find myself doing all the time, comparing things in perspective.

Mr. SPECTER. Was he a white man or a Negro or what?

Mr. ROWLAND. Seemed, well, I can't state definitely from my position because it was more or less not fully light or bright in the room. He appeared to be fair complexioned, not fair, but light complexioned, but dark hair.

Mr. SPECTER. What race was he then?

Mr. ROWLAND. I would say either a light Latin or a Caucasian.

Mr. SPECTER. And were you able to observe any characteristics of his hair?

Mr. ROWLAND. No; except that it was dark, probably black.

Mr. SPECTER. Were you able to observe whether he had a full head of hair or any characteristic as to quantity of hair?

Mr. ROWLAND. It didn't appear as if he had a receding hairline but I know he didn't have it hanging on his shoulders. Probably a close cut from—you know it appeared to me it was either well-combed or close cut.

Mr. SPECTER. What, if anything, did you observe as to the clothes he was wearing?

Mr. ROWLAND. He had on a light shirt, a very light-colored shirt, white or a light blue or a color such as that. This was open at the collar. I think it was unbuttoned about halfway, and then he had a regular T-shirt, a polo shirt under this, at least this is what it appeared to be. He had on dark slacks or blue jeans, I couldn't tell from that. I didn't see but a small portion.

Mr. SPECTER. You say you only saw a small portion of what?

Mr. ROWLAND. Of his pants from his waist down.

Mr. SPECTER. Which half of the window was open, the bottom half or the top half?

Mr. ROWLAND. It was the bottom half.

Mr. SPECTER. And how much, if any, of his body was obscured by the window frame from that point down to the floor?

Mr. ROWLAND. From where I was standing I could see from his head to about 6 inches below his waist, below his belt.

Mr. SPECTER. Could you see as far as his knees?

Mr. ROWLAND. No.

Mr. SPECTER. And what is your best recollection as to how close to the window he was standing?

Mr. ROWLAND. He wasn't next to the window, but he wasn't very far back. I would say 3 to 5 feet back from the window.

Mr. SPECTER. How much of the rifle was separated from your line of vision by the window?

Mr. ROWLAND. The entire rifle was in my view.

Mr. SPECTER. In the open part of the window?

Mr. ROWLAND. Yes.

Mr. SPECTER. And how much of his body, if any, was in the open view where there was no window between your eyes and the object of his body?

Mr. ROWLAND. Approximately two-thirds of his body just below his waist.

Mr. SPECTER. Up to what point?

Mr. ROWLAND. Mid point between the waist and the knees, this is again in my proportion to his height that I make that judgment.

Mr. SPECTER. So from the waist, some point between his knees and his waist, you started to see him clear in the window?

Mr. ROWLAND. Yes.

Mr. SPECTER. And from that point how far up his body were you able to see without any obstruction of a window between you and him?

Mr. Rowland. To the top of his head. There was some space on top of that where I could see the wall behind him.

Mr. Specter. What is your best estimate of the space between the top of his head and the open window at the perspective you were observing?

Mr. Rowland. Two and a half, three feet, something on that—that is something very hard to ascertain. That would just be an estimation on my part.

Mr. Specter. Is there anything else you observed about his appearance or his clothing or the rifle which you haven't already told us about?

Representative Ford. Was he facing toward you directly?

Mr. Rowland. Yes.

Representative Ford. In other words, did you get a full view of his face and his chest and the front of him?

Mr. Rowland. He appeared to me as though he were looking out the window and watching the crowd in particular.

Representative Ford. Excuse me, go ahead.

Mr. Rowland. That is all right.

Representative Ford. Was he looking toward the corner of Houston and Main?

Mr. Rowland. No; I would say he was looking in the area or the general vicinity of where I was.

Representative Ford. And you were on the sidewalk on Houston in front of the building that you have indicated?

Mr. Rowland. Yes. Now, I can't—here again I wasn't close enough to see his eyes but from the position of his head he was looking in that general area. It could have been that maybe he was—his eyes were a little bit off perspective and he was watching that corner, I don't know.

Representative Ford. In what position did you say his hands were on the rifle?

Mr. Rowland. One hand was at what is called the gun stock of the rifle, just above the trigger, it was around the rifle. The other was at the other end of the rifle about 4 inches below the end of the stock.

Representative Ford. Was the rifle held above his waist?

Mr. Rowland. The majority of it was, just a small portion of butt below his waist.

Representative Ford. The butt or the end of the rifle, the barrel end?

Mr. Rowland. The butt, the stock end, was below his waist. The barrel being pointed in the air toward the ceiling or the wall next to him.

Representative Ford. I see. The stock was down and the barrel was up.

Mr. Rowland. Yes.

Mr. Specter. Were you able to form any opinion as to the age of that man?

Mr. Rowland. This is again just my estimation. He was—I think I remember telling my wife that he appeared in his early thirties. This could be obscured because of the distance, I mean.

Mr. Specter. Were you able to form any opinion as to the weight of the man in addition to the line of proportion which you have already described?

Mr. Rowland. I would say about 140 to 150 pounds.

Representative Ford. When did you tell your wife you thought he was in his thirties?

Mr. Rowland. Right after I noticed the man, I brought him to my wife's attention, and she was looking at something else at that time, we looked at that, and when we both looked back she wanted to see also, and he was gone from our vision.

Representative Ford. So she never saw him?

Mr. Rowland. My wife never saw him.

Representative Ford. Did you say at that time how old he was or how old you thought he was?

Mr. Rowland. I think I remarked to my wife that he appeared in his thirties, early thirties.

Mr. Specter. When, after you first observed him did you have a conversation about him with your wife?

Mr. Rowland. Right afterwards. There was—just before I observed him there was a police motorcycle parked just on the street, not in front of us, just a little past us, and the radio was on it giving the details of the motorcade, where it was positioned, and right after the time I noticed him and when my wife was pointing this other thing to me. I don't remember what that was, the dispatcher came on and gave the position of the motorcade as being on Cedar Springs. This would be in the area of Turtle Creek, down in that area.

I can't remember the street's name but I know where it is at. And this was the position of the motorcade and it was about 15 or 16 after 12.

Mr. SPECTER. Well, did you tell your wife about the presence of this man immediately after you saw him?

Mr. ROWLAND. Yes.

Mr. SPECTER. And what was the quality or condition of her eyes?

Mr. ROWLAND. She has nearsightedness and has to wear glasses.

Mr. SPECTER. Was she wearing glasses at the time?

Mr. ROWLAND. No, she wasn't.

Mr. SPECTER. Based on your knowledge of her eyesight, would it have been possible for her to have seen him considering your relative positions?

Mr. ROWLAND. Had he still been there she would have been able to acknowledge the figure with no description.

Mr. SPECTER. How long did you see him there in total point of time?

Mr. ROWLAND. It was all relatively brief, short time, 15 seconds, maybe 20. I was looking at the building, looking at the people hanging out of the building, I noticed him, my eye contact was at that position for 15 to 20 seconds. This is all relatively very short length of time.

Mr. SPECTER. Now——

Mr. ROWLAND. But a lot can happen in that much time.

Mr. SPECTER. When you saw him, you told her about him, and then did she look in the direction of the man?

Mr. ROWLAND. After she pointed something else out to me she looked in that direction.

Mr. SPECTER. Did you then look back toward the direction of, to the window where you had seen him?

Mr. ROWLAND. Yes; I even pointed to it with my wife.

Mr. SPECTER. Did you look back at the same time she looked back?

Mr. ROWLAND. Yes.

Mr. SPECTER. And when you looked back what, if anything, did you observe in the window?

Mr. ROWLAND. There was nothing there then.

Mr. SPECTER. Following that did you and she have any additional conversation about this man in the window?

Mr. ROWLAND. We talked about it momentarily, just for a few seconds that it was of most likelihood a security man, had a very good vantage point where he could watch the crowds, talked about the rifle, it looked like a very high-powered rifle.

Mr. SPECTER. Did you mention that to your wife?

Mr. ROWLAND. Yes; I did.

Mr. SPECTER. Have you described as fully as you can everything you discussed with your wife at that juncture?

Mr. ROWLAND. I think so.

Representative FORD. Was there anybody else standing close to you as you had this conversation with your wife?

Mr. ROWLAND. There was a policeman about as far as me to the flag.

Representative FORD. That is about how many feet, would you say?

Mr. ROWLAND. Twelve, thirteen feet.

Representative FORD. There was no one between you and the policeman in that line of vision?

Mr. ROWLAND. No.

Then there were three or four colored men just behind the elevator, and a couple on the elevator that had come up through the sidewalk. This was a distance of—this was on the opposite side of us about 15 feet, just a little further than the officer.

Representative FORD. There was no one closer to you and your wife than 10 to 15 feet?

Mr. ROWLAND. That is correct. That is one of the main reasons we selected that spot.

Representative Ford. Did it ever enter your mind that you should go and tell the policeman of this sight or this vision that you had seen?

Mr. Rowland. Really it didn't.

Representative Ford. It never entered your mind?

Mr. Rowland. I never dreamed of anything such as that. I mean, I must honestly say my opinion was based on movies I have seen, on the attempted assassination of Theodore Roosevelt where they had Secret Service men up in the building such as that with rifles watching the crowds, and another one concerned with attempted assassination of the other one, Franklin Roosevelt, and both of these had Secret Service men up in windows or on top of buildings with rifles, and this is how my opinion was based and why it didn't alarm me.

Perhaps if I had been older and had more experience in life it might have made a difference. It very well could have.

Mr. Specter. Mr. Rowland, did the man with the rifle have any distinctive facial appearance such as a mustache or a prominent scar, anything of that sort which you could observe?

Mr. Rowland. There was nothing dark on his face. no mustache. There could have been a scar if it hadn't been a dark scar. If it was, you know, a blotch or such as this, there was nothing very dark about the color of his face.

Mr. Specter. Mr. Rowland, will you recount as precisely and as specifically as you can, the exact conversation between you and your wife from the time you first noticed this man until your conversation about the man concluded, indicating what you said and what she said in language as closely as you can recollect it?

Mr. Rowland. That is a whopper.

I am almost sure I told her or asked her, did she want to see a Secret Service agent. She said, "Where," and I said, "In the building there," and at that time she told me to look—I remember what she was looking at. Right directly across from us in this plaza in front of the pond there was a colored boy that had an epileptic fit or something of this type right then, and she pointed this out to me and there were a couple of officers there and a few moments later they called an ambulance, this is what she told me to look at then, and we looked at this for a short period of time, and then I told her to look in the building, the second floor from the top and on that end, the two open windows, is I think what I said, and I said, "He is not there now."

I think that is what I said. She said, "What did he look like," and I told her just that—I gave her more or less a brief description of what he looked like, open collared shirt, light-colored shirt, and he had a rifle, I described the rifle in as much detail as I have to you to her.

Mr. Specter. You described the rifle to her in as much detail as you have to us?

Mr. Rowland. Yes.

And then she said something about wishing she could have seen him but he was probably somewhere else in another part of the building watching people now. Then we were discussing again, just preceding that we were discussing the event with Mr. Stevenson, this was about 2 weeks beforehand, this was fresh on our mind, and right after that we started discussing that it was a security man.

We were looking around, we became very security conscious. We noted that policemen, I think there were maybe 2, maybe 3 on the viaduct itself; some 20 or 30, I would say 20 to 25 policemen being in that immediate area.

Representative Ford. About what time, as you can best recollect, did this conversation with your wife take place?

Mr. Rowland. About 5 minutes until about 22 after. I think I again looked at my watch.

Representative Ford. After you and your wife looked up and saw that there was no one in the window, did you ever again look at the window?

Mr. Rowland. Yes; I did, constantly.

Representative Ford. And as you looked at the window subsequently did you ever see anything else in the window?

Mr. Rowland. No; not in that window, and I looked back every few seconds, 30 seconds, maybe twice a minute, occasionally trying to find him so I could point him out to my wife.

Something I would like to note is that the window that I have been told the shots were actually fired from, I did not see that, there was someone hanging out that window at that time.

Representative FORD. At what time was that?

Mr. ROWLAND. At the time I saw the man in the other window, I saw this man hanging out the window first. It was a colored man, I think.

Representative FORD. Is this the same window where you saw the man standing with the rifle?

Mr. ROWLAND. No; this was the one on the east end of the building, the one that they said the shots were fired from.

Representative FORD. I am not clear on this now. The window that you saw the man that you describe was on what end of the building?

Mr. ROWLAND. The west, southwest corner.

Representative FORD. And the man you saw hanging out from the window was at what corner?

Mr. ROWLAND. The east, southeast corner.

Representative FORD. Southeast corner. On the same floor?

Mr. ROWLAND. On the same floor.

Representative FORD. When did you notice him?

Mr. ROWLAND. This was before I noticed the other man with the rifle.

Representative FORD. I see. This was before you saw the man in the window with the rifle?

Mr. ROWLAND. Yes. My wife and I were both looking and making remarks that the people were hanging out the windows. I think the majority of them were colored people, some of them were hanging out the windows to their waist, such as this. We made several remarks to this fact, and then she started watching the colored boy, and I continued to look, and then I saw the man with the rifle.

Representative FORD. After 12:22 or thereabouts you indicated you periodically looked back at the window in the southwest corner where you had seen the man with the rifle. What happened as the motorcade came along?

Mr. ROWLAND. As the motorcade came along, there was quite a bit of excitement. I didn't look back from then. I was very interested in trying to see the President myself. I had seen him twice before but I was interested in seeing him again.

Representative FORD. Did you notice a sedan come by with any officials in it at the outset of the motorcade?

Mr. ROWLAND. The first car in the motorcade was, I think it was, a white- or cream-colored Ford. This appeared to be full of detectives or such as this; rather husky men, large men.

I think there were four in this car.

Representative FORD. Was this an open or a closed car?

Mr. ROWLAND. This was a sedan, the doors were closed.

Representative FORD. What was the next car you noticed?

Mr. ROWLAND. The next car was the President's car.

Representative FORD. Did you notice again or did you look again during this period of time at the School Depository Building?

Mr. ROWLAND. No. From where we were standing the motorcade came down Main, and when it turned on Houston we watched the motorcade, my wife remarked at Jackie's clothing, Mrs. Kennedy, and we made a few remarks of her clothing and how she looked, her appearance in general, and we also discussed—we didn't immediately recognize Governor Connally and his wife being in the car, we were trying to figure out who that was.

Then the motorcade turned on Elm and was obscured from our vision by a crowd, and we were discussing the clothing of Mrs. Kennedy at that time. My wife likes clothes.

Representative FORD. You never again, after the motorcade once came into your view, looked back at the School Depository Building?

Mr. ROWLAND. I did after the shots were fired.

Mr. SPECTER. Had you finished telling us all about the conversation between you and your wife concerning this man?

Mr. ROWLAND. To the best of my recollection, yes.

Mr. SPECTER. All right.

You have described seeing someone in another window hanging out. Would you draw a circle and put an "A" beside the window where you say you saw someone hanging out. That is on Exhibit No. 356.

(Witness marking.)

Mr. Specter. At about what time was it that you observed someone hanging out of the window that you have marked as window "A"?

Mr. Rowland. Again about 12:15 just before I noticed the other man.

Mr. Specter. You have marked the double window there. Would you draw the arrow in the red pencil indicating specifically which window it was.

(Witness marking.)

Mr. Specter. Will you describe with as much particularity as you can what that man looked like?

Mr. Rowland. It seemed to me an elderly Negro, that is about all. I didn't pay very much attention to him.

Mr. Specter. At or about that time did you observe anyone else hanging out any window or observe any one through any window on the same floor where you have drawn the two circles on Exhibit 356?

Mr. Rowland. No; no one else on that floor.

Mr. Specter. You testified before that there were other windows where you had seen people hanging out, is that correct?

Mr. Rowland. Yes.

Mr. Specter. Would you tell us and indicate on the picture, Exhibit 356, to the best of your ability to recollect just which those windows were?

Mr. Rowland. There was either two or three people in this window.

Mr. Specter. Mark that with a "B" if you would, please.

(Witness marking.)

Mr. Rowland. Those pair of windows. I think this was all on that floor. Here on this floor.

Mr. Specter. Indicating the second floor?

Mr. Rowland. Yes.

Mr. Specter. Circle the windows and mark it with a "C" if you will.

Mr. Rowland. I think it was this pair immediately over the door, and this pair.

Mr. Specter. Mark one "C" and one "D," if you will.

(Witness marking.)

Mr. Rowland. Here I know there were two Negro women, I think.

Mr. Specter. Indicating window "C." You say two Negro women?

Mr. Rowland. Yes.

Mr. Specter. And were those women each in one window, both in one window or what?

Mr. Rowland. They were one in each window. Then at the window "D" there was one, one window open.

Mr. Specter. Which was that, indicate that by an arrow, if you please.

(Witness marking.)

Mr. Rowland. The one on the west side, and this appeared to have two heads just inside the window, no one hanging out the window as with the others.

Mr. Specter. Did you observe anyone else hanging out the window?

Mr. Rowland. There was someone on the third floor. I think it was—wait a minute—yes, the third floor had three adjoining sets of windows that were open. They were all open to the fullest extent they would open.

Mr. Specter. Would you mark those "E," "F" and "G," please.

(Witness marking.)

Mr. Specter. Did you observe any people in those windows marked "E," "F," and "G"?

Mr. Rowland. Yes, and this pair, "E," both windows were open, and there appeared to be one man in the eastern window.

Mr. Specter. Which you have now marked with an arrow.

Mr. Rowland. Yes.

Mr. Specter. How about as to window marked "F"?

Mr. Rowland. Both windows were completely up, and there appeared to be several people in that window, four or five, a number that I don't remember, you know I couldn't see all of them.

Mr. Specter. How about window "G"?

Mr. Rowland. This again, both windows were open all of the way and I think there was one person in each window.

Mr. Specter. Did you observe any other people either through any other window or hanging out of any other window in the building?

Mr. Rowland. There was no one in the fourth floor to my knowledge, to my recollection.

There were what appeared to be secretaries, several young white girls or ladies, standing on the steps of the building in this general area.

Mr. Specter. Indicating the door of the building.

Mr. Rowland. Yes.

Mr. Specter. Yes.

Mr. Rowland. And there was no one else in there, except I think there was a policeman in front of the door on the sidewalk.

Mr. Specter. Have you described everybody you have observed, with respect to everybody hanging out the windows?

Mr. Rowland. To the best of my recollection.

Mr. Specter. Or anybody you could see through the windows?

Mr. Rowland. Yes.

Mr. Specter. As to the window which you have marked "A", that double pair of windows, which, if either or both, was open?

Mr. Rowland. The one on the eastern side was open and not all of the way it would open.

Mr. Specter. Is that the one you have marked with an arrow?

Mr. Rowland. Yes.

Mr. Specter. How much of that window was open?

Mr. Rowland. It was open about that far.

Mr. Specter. Indicating 2½ feet?

Mr. Rowland. Two feet.

Mr. Specter. Two feet.

Mr. Rowland. Indicating 2 feet. It looked like the windows might open 3— two-thirds or three-fourths of the distance.

Mr. Specter. How about the other of the windows in the double-set marked "A," was that completely closed?

Mr. Rowland. Yes.

Mr. Specter. How about the windows in the group marked "B," was either of those windows open?

Mr. Rowland. They were both completely open.

Mr. Specter. Can you describe with any more particularity the people you saw in the window which you have marked "B"?

Mr. Rowland. There was a white man hanging out either "G" or "B," I do not remember which. He was the only white man, besides the man in these windows that I saw——

Mr. Specter. When you said "these windows" you mean the first window you marked with a black circle and a black arrow?

Mr. Rowland. Yes.

Mr. Specter. Is there anything else you can tell us about the people you saw in window "B"?

Mr. Rowland. I think to the best of my recollection there was either two or three people in window "B," and as I stated before, either "B" or "G" had a white man in the window. I do not remember which. I do remember it was one of the windows on the corner.

Mr. Specter. Do you recollect if the other people in window "B" were white or Negro?

Mr. Rowland. They were Negro.

Mr. Specter. Now, did you have any occasion to look back at window "A" from the time you saw the man whom you described as a Negro gentleman in that window until the President's procession passed by?

Mr. Rowland. Well, up until the time the procession was——

(Short recess.)

Representative Ford. I suggest, Mr. Specter, we resume the hearing.

Mr. Specter. Will you read the last question, Mr. Reporter, please.

(Question read.)

Mr. SPECTER. Would you like to start the question again or would you like the question repeated?

Mr. ROWLAND. I understand the question.

Let me see, the exact time I do not remember, but the man, the colored man, was in that window until the procession reached Commerce—I mean Main, and Ervay. I was looking back quite often, as I stated.

Mr. SPECTER. How do you fix the time that he was there until the procession reached the intersection of Commerce and Ervay?

Mr. ROWLAND. The police motorcycle was almost in front of me with the speaker on very loud, giving the relative position about every 15 or 20 seconds of the motorcade, and this is how I was able to note that.

Mr. SPECTER. Were you observing the window which you marked "A" at the time he departed?

Mr. ROWLAND. No, I didn't. I just know, I was looking at the crowd around, and then I glanced back up again, and neither did I see the man with the rifle nor did I see him. The colored man went away.

Mr. SPECTER. How long was that after you first noticed the colored man in the window "A"?

Mr. ROWLAND. Fifteen minutes.

Mr. SPECTER. Had you looked back at window "A" at any time during that 15 minute interval?

Mr. ROWLAND. Yes.

Mr. SPECTER. Had you seen anybody in window "A" during that time?

Mr. ROWLAND. The colored man was that——

Mr. SPECTER. So how many times did you notice him altogether?

Mr. ROWLAND. Several. I think I looked back about two, maybe three times a minute, an average. I was, you know, trying to find the man with the rifle to point him out to my wife. I noticed the colored man in that window. I looked at practically every window in the building but I didn't look at anything with the detail to see what I was looking for.

Mr. SPECTER. Over how long a time span did you observe the Negro man to be in the window marked "A"?

Mr. ROWLAND. He was there before I noticed the man with the rifle and approximately 12:30 or when the motorcade was at Main and Ervay he was gone when I looked back and I had looked up there about 30 seconds before or a minute before.

Mr. SPECTER. How long after you heard the motorcade was at Main and Ervay did the motorcade pass by where you were?

Mr. ROWLAND. Another 5 minutes.

Mr. SPECTER. So that you observed this colored man on the window you have marked "A" within 5 minutes prior to the time the motorcade passed in front of you?

Mr. ROWLAND. Approximately 5 minutes prior to the time the motorcade came, he wasn't there. About 30 seconds or a minute prior to that time he was there.

Mr. SPECTER. A few moments ago in your testimony you stated that in observing policemen in the area you had observed some officers on the overpass?

Mr. ROWLAND. Yes.

Mr. SPECTER. Approximately how far were you from the overpass at that time?

Mr. ROWLAND. 125 yards approximately.

Mr. SPECTER. Were you able to observe with clarity the individuals who were standing on the overpass?

Mr. ROWLAND. Not with detailed distinction. I do remember there were three women there, two or three men, a couple of boys, and two officers on the overpass itself.

Mr. SPECTER. How did you identify the officers as being policemen?

Mr. ROWLAND. They were uniformed officers.

Mr. SPECTER. What kind of uniforms were they wearing?

Mr. ROWLAND. Blue; I think trimmed in gold, uniforms.

Mr. SPECTER. Are those the regular uniforms worn by the Dallas police?

Mr. ROWLAND. Yes.

Mr. SPECTER. Where were you standing at the time you observed the people on the overpass whom you have just described?

Mr. ROWLAND. Position "B."

Mr. SPECTER. At about what time was it when you observed those individuals?

Mr. ROWLAND. This was between the time between 12:15 and 12:30. I think I looked more than once.

Mr. SPECTER. How many times did you look?

Mr. ROWLAND. I don't know really. I was more or less scanning the crowd.

Mr. SPECTER. Did the individuals present on the triple overpass change at the various times when you looked in that direction?

Mr. ROWLAND. I don't think so. I don't think anyone went off who was up there or anyone else went on.

Mr. SPECTER. Will you now relate what occurred as the Presidential motorcade passed by you?

Mr. ROWLAND. Well, the car turned the corner at Houston and Main. Everyone was rushing, pressing the cars, trying to get closer. There were quite a few people, you know, trying to run alongside of the car such as this; officers were trying to prevent this. The car turned—we had more or less a long period of time that they were within our sight considering some of the other people.

The car went down Houston, again turned on Elm, and it was proceeding down Elm when we heard the first of the reports. This I passed off as a backfire, so did practically everyone in the area because gobs of people, when I say gobs, I mean almost everyone in the vicinity, started laughing that couldn't see the motorcade. The motorcade was obscured from our vision by the crowd.

Mr. SPECTER. What would the occasion be for laughter on the sound of a backfire?

Mr. ROWLAND. I don't know. A lot of people laughed. I don't know. But a lot of people laughed, chuckled, such as this. Then approximately 5 seconds, 5 or 6 seconds, the second report was heard, 2 seconds the third report. After the second report, I knew what it was, and——

Mr. SPECTER. What was it?

Mr. ROWLAND. I knew that it was a gun firing.

Mr. SPECTER. How did you know that?

Mr. ROWLAND. I have been around guns quite a bit in my lifetime.

Mr. SPECTER. Was the sound of the fire different from the first and second sounds you described?

Mr. ROWLAND. No, that is just it. It did not sound as though there was any return fire in that sense.

Mr. SPECTER. What do you mean by return fire?

Mr. ROWLAND. That anyone fired back. You know, anyone in the procession such as our detectives or Secret Service men fired back at anything else. It gave the report of a rifle which most of the Secret Service men don't carry in a holster although I am sure they had some in the cars but the following two shots were the same report being of the same intensity, I state, because from a different position I know that the same rifle is not going to make the same sound in two different positions especially in a position such as it was, because of the ricocheting of sound and echo effects.

Mr. SPECTER. What is your basis for saying that, Mr. Rowland, that the rifle would not make the same sound in two different positions?

Mr. ROWLAND. This is due to a long study of sound and study of echo effects.

Mr. SPECTER. When had you conducted that study?

Mr. ROWLAND. In physics in the past 3 years.

Mr. SPECTER. Have you read any special books on that subject?

Mr. ROWLAND. Quite a few.

Mr. SPECTER. Do you recollect any of the titles and authors?

Mr. ROWLAND. No; I do not.

Mr. SPECTER. Did you take any special courses which would give you insight into that subject matter?

Mr. ROWLAND. This was more or less on my own initiative. The instructor gave me help and aided me when I requested this during my off periods of class.

Mr. SPECTER. What instructor was that?

Mr. ROWLAND. His name was Foster.

Mr. SPECTER. Do you recall his first name?

Mr. ROWLAND. Sam.

Mr. SPECTER. And at what school does he teach?

Mr. ROWLAND. He teaches at Crozier Tech, Downtown Technical High School.

Mr. SPECTER. Is he still there?

Mr. ROWLAND. To my knowledge.

Mr. SPECTER. How recently did you have a course with him?

Mr. ROWLAND. Last year, last school year.

Mr. SPECTER. Can you describe the second sound by comparison with the first sound which you have described as being similar to a backfire?

Mr. ROWLAND. The second to my recollection was identical or as closely as could be.

Mr. SPECTER. How about the third shot?

Mr. ROWLAND. The same.

Mr. SPECTER. Sounded the same to you?

Mr. ROWLAND. Yes.

Mr. SPECTER. Did you have any impression or reaction as to the point of origin when you heard the first noise?

Mr. ROWLAND. Well, I began looking, I didn't look at the building mainly, and as practically any of the police officers that were there then will tell you, the echo effect was such that it sounded like it came from the railroad yards. That is where I looked, that is where all the policemen, everyone, converged on the railroads.

Mr. SPECTER. When you say railroad yards, what area are you referring to? Identify it on Commission Exhibit No. 354, for example?

Mr. ROWLAND. In this area in here.

Now most of the officers converged on this area——

Mr. SPECTER. When you say "in here," I will get a black pencil here and see if we can draw a circle around the area where you have described the echo effect?

Mr. ROWLAND. The echo effect felt as though it came from this general vicinity.

Mr. SPECTER. Mark that with the letter "C" in the center of your circle.

(Witness marking.)

Mr. SPECTER. Now, as to the second shot, did you have any impression as to the point of origin or source?

Mr. ROWLAND. The same point or very close to it.

Mr. SPECTER. And how about the third shot?

Mr. ROWLAND. Very close to the same position.

Mr. SPECTER. Where did you look, if you recall, after you heard the first shot, in what direction?

Mr. ROWLAND. We were standing here at position "B." At the sound of the second report, I proceeded across the street. My wife was very anxious to find out what was going on. I proceeded to cross the street like this.

Mr. SPECTER. Indicating you were—she was pulling you ahead?

Mr. ROWLAND. Yes. She was very anxious to find out what was going on.

Mr. SPECTER. That was at the sound of the second report?

Mr. ROWLAND. Yes, it was.

Mr. SPECTER. And will you mark with this black pencil, with the letter "D," where you went to, as she pulled you across the street?

Mr. ROWLAND. We crossed the street in this area, proceeded down the sidewalk, around here, there was quite a bit of crowd, people were running.

Mr. SPECTER. Where were you at the time that you heard the second report?

Mr. ROWLAND. At the second report we were approximately at the curb, out from the curb, we were off the sidewalk.

Mr. SPECTER. At point "V"?

Mr. ROWLAND. Yes.

Mr. SPECTER. How about the third shot, where were you then?

Mr. ROWLAND. At the third shot I was in this vicinity halfway to where we crossed the street to the end of the block.

Mr. SPECTER. Would you indicate with the letter "D" where you were at the time of the third shot?

(Witness marking.)

Mr. SPECTER. Where did you look when you heard the third report?

Mr. ROWLAND. Well, we were trying to actually see the President's car, that is what my wife was trying to do, and then I decided I might as well give in to her.

Mr. SPECTER. After the shots occurred, did you ever look back at the Texas School Book Depository Building?

Mr. ROWLAND. No; I did not. In fact, I went over toward the scene of the railroad yards myself.

Mr. SPECTER. Why did you not look back at the Texas School Book Depository Building in view of the fact that you had seen a man with a rifle up there earlier in the day?

Mr. ROWLAND. I don't remember. It was mostly due to the confusion, and then the fact that it sounded like it came from this area "C," and that all the officers, enforcement officers, were converging on that area, and I just didn't pay any attention to it at that time.

Mr. SPECTER. How many officers were converging on that area, to the best of your ability to recollect and estimate?

Mr. ROWLAND. I think it would be a very good estimation of 50, maybe more.

Mr. SPECTER. Do you know how fast the President's automobile was driving as it proceeded in front of you when you were standing at position "B"?

Mr. ROWLAND. Very slow pace, 5, 10 miles an hour.

Mr. SPECTER. When, if at all, did you first report what you had observed in the Texas School Book Depositoiry Building about the man with the rifle to anyone in an official position?

Mr. ROWLAND. That was approximately 15 minutes after the third report that I went to an officer, he was a plainclothesman who was there combing the area, close to position "C," looking for footprints and such as this, some lady said someone jumped off one of the colonades and started running, there was an officer looking in this area for footprints and such as this.

Mr. SPECTER. Was that lady ever identified to you?

Mr. ROWLAND. No; I do not remember his name. He introduced himself and showed me his ID.

Mr. SPECTER. I mean the lady you talked about.

Mr. ROWLAND. No; I don't.

Mr. SPECTER. Now as to the officer to whom you made a report, was he a State, City or Federal official, if you know?

Mr. ROWLAND. It was a Dallas detective.

Mr. SPECTER. And did you give him a statement or what procedure did he follow?

Mr. ROWLAND. It happened such as this: He was looking in this area for footprints or any visible marks. I started looking around also. I found a fountain pen that someone had probably dropped during the confusion or fell out of their pocket when they fell on the ground or such. I picked it up and handed it to him. I had on gloves, I wasn't to mess up the fingerprints because it very possibly could have fallen out of the pocket of the man who supposedly had jumped down.

Mr. SPECTER. You were wearing gloves on that day?

Mr. ROWLAND. Yes.

Mr. SPECTER. Was it a chilly day?

Mr. ROWLAND. The sun was shining, it was a fair day but the wind was blowing and it was breezy.

Mr. SPECTER. Was it cold enough to have gloves?

Mr. ROWLAND. Yes; I had on my overcoat and my wife had a fairly heavy coat.

Mr. SPECTER. Proceed, and tell us what you did.

Mr. ROWLAND. I handed this pen to the officer and I started thinking and I went to him and told him again just before the motorcade came I saw a man in the building with a rifle, and he immediately took me to Sheriff Decker which, in turn, asked two other deputies to take me to his office. We went there to his office. There was quite a few reporters around, such as this.

They took my wife and I to a back room and shut us off completely from the reporters and everyone. There was no one in that room for 4 hours but this sheriff and a FBI agent, Agent Sorrels, and a stenographer, and I think another lady and a man that had seen another man carrying a rifle in a case on the other end of town earlier prior to this time.

Mr. SPECTER. Are you sure there was a court reporter present?

Mr. ROWLAND. It was one of the secretaries from the office of the sheriff, stenographer who was taking, using an electric typewriter every time.

Mr. SPECTER. Was she taking down in shorthand——

Mr. ROWLAND. Yes.

Mr. SPECTER. As you could observe——

Mr. ROWLAND. Yes.

Mr. SPECTER. Each word that you were saying?

Mr. ROWLAND. Yes.

Mr. SPECTER. Did she have any sort of a machine, such as a stenograph, as the gentleman who is serving as court reporter has?

Mr. ROWLAND. No; she took it down in shorthand and retyped it on an electric typewriter that she brought into the room.

Mr. SPECTER. Did she type up what you had said?

Mr. ROWLAND. Yes; typed up three or four copies and then I signed it at that time.

Mr. SPECTER. I now show you a photostatic copy of what purports to be an affidavit which you gave to the Sheriff's Department of the County of Dallas, Tex., on November 22, 1963, and has been marked as Commission Exhibit No. 357. Would you take a look at that, take your time, of course, and tell us whether or not that is the affidavit which you took on the occasion which you have just related?

Mr. ROWLAND. Yes. In fact, at this time I also noted that my wife dragged me across the street.

Mr. SPECTER. Just one detail on that statement: There is a reference here to the man holding the rifle being in a position which you describe as "a parade-rest sort of position." That appears——

Mr. ROWLAND. It does appear in there?

Mr. SPECTER. Eighteen lines down.

Mr. ROWLAND. Yes; I see it. It wasn't a parade-rest position. It was a port-arms position. I never noticed that in there before. There were—actually, I will say this, I said what I had to say. The FBI agent reworded it, and she took it down.

Now this happened; it wasn't my words verbatim, it was reworded.

Mr. SPECTER. Did you ever use the words "parade-rest" position?

Mr. ROWLAND. Not to my recollection.

Mr. SPECTER. So it is just an error in transcription which you did not notice when you signed it.

(At this point, Chief Justice Warren entered the hearing room.)

Is there any other aspect of the affidavit which you gave, which you have just observed, which is at variance with your current recollection of what you saw and heard on that date?

Mr. ROWLAND. Here it states we were at the west entrance of the sheriff's office, that is just a general approximation, we were 25 feet from there, in fact.

Mr. SPECTER. Are there any other portions of it which vary from your current recollection?

Mr. ROWLAND. I don't remember saying definitely that he was back about 15 feet. In fact, I think I said, as I said now, 3 to 5 feet, because from my point of view if he was back 15 feet I couldn't have even seen him.

Mr. SPECTER. Are there any other parts of the affidavit which vary from your current recollection?

Mr. ROWLAND. The actual time between the reports I would say now, after having had time to consider the 6 seconds between the first and second report and two between the second and third. It is very fast for a bolt-loading rifle.

Mr. SPECTER. Do you recall whether or not the statement is accurate in that you told the police officials at that time that there was a time span of 8 seconds between the first and second shots and a time span of 3 seconds between the second and third shots?

Mr. ROWLAND. I think I did tell them that, yes, sir.

Mr. SPECTER. And with respect to the facts which appear in the statement that you said the man was standing about 15 feet back from the windows, did you actually tell them that when you made the statement, or is that an error of transcription?

Mr. ROWLAND. I don't think I said that.

Mr. SPECTER. Now are there any other points where the affidavit is at variance from your current recollection?

Mr. ROWLAND. The time that it states here, we arrived in downtown Dallas at approximately 12:10. Actually we arrived before 12 but we took the position that we have, approximately 12:10, that position "V" on this other Exhibit 354.

Mr. SPECTER. Are there any other variances between your current recollection and this statement?

Mr. ROWLAND. I do not think so.

Mr. SPECTER. Did you tell the police officials at the time you made this statement that there was a Negro gentleman in the window on the southwest corner of the Texas School Book Depository Building which you have marked with a circle "A"—pardon me, southeast?

Mr. ROWLAND. At that time, no. However, the next day on Saturday there were a pair of FBI officers, agents out at my home, and they took another handwritten statement from me which I signed again, and this was basically the same. At that time I told them I did see the Negro man there and they told me it didn't have any bearing or such on the case right then. In fact, they just the same as told me to forget it now.

Mr. SPECTER. Mr. Reporter, will you please repeat that last answer for us? (Answer read.)

Mr. SPECTER. I am now handing you a document which I have marked as Commission Exhibit No. 358, which purports to be a reproduction of a statement which was purportedly given by you to the FBI, two agents of that Bureau.

Will you take a look at that and tell us if that is the statement which you gave to the FBI to which you just referred?

Mr. ROWLAND. Again, I have a variance of time and a variance of distance that he was from the window.

Mr. SPECTER. Before you direct your attention to those factors, Mr. Rowland, are you able to tell us whether or not this is the statement which you gave to the FBI?

Mr. ROWLAND. Yes. My wife was with me when I gave the statement.

Mr. SPECTER. And without looking at the statement which, may the record show, you are not now doing, do you recollect the names of the FBI, don't look there, just tell me if you can recollect without seeing their names on the statement?

Mr. ROWLAND. No, sir; I talked to seven different pairs of FBI agents and I don't remember their names.

Mr. SPECTER. Seven different pairs?

Mr. ROWLAND. Yes, sir; I had—this is only one of the statements. They came to my home or where I worked and took three more besides this one. There were four handwritten statements that I signed.

Mr. SPECTER. Before getting the details on those, tell me in what respect, if any, the statement which we have identified as Commission Exhibit No. 358 differs from what you told the FBI agents at that time?

Mr. ROWLAND. I do not think it differs.

Mr. SPECTER. Then that statement accurately reflects what you said at that time?

Mr. ROWLAND. Yes; I am sure it does.

Mr. SPECTER. Now, in what respects, if any, does that statement vary from your current recollection about the facts which are contained therein?

183

Mr. ROWLAND. The time factor, the time that we arrived in town. Here again it states 12:10. Now this is the time that we arrived at the position that we stayed at, not the time we arrived in town, and the distance the man was back from the window. Here it states 12 to 15 feet. I do not remember saying that although I very well could have. Everything was confusing.

Mr. SPECTER. But what is your current recollection on the distance that the man was back from the window?

Mr. ROWLAND. Three to four, five feet, somewhere in that neighborhood. He wasn't very far. Far enough for the sunlight to hit him and at the angle the sun was that wouldn't be very far.

Mr. SPECTER. Now noticing that the date on that statement is November 24, 1963, does that appear to you to be the date when that statement was taken, or was it taken on the 23d, the day after the assassination?

Mr. ROWLAND. It was Saturday morning, the 24th.

Mr. SPECTER. On what day was the assassination?

Mr. ROWLAND. It was Thursday, wasn't it?

Mr. SPECTER. No; the assassination occurred on Friday.

Mr. ROWLAND. I am sorry, that is right. It is so confused in this.

Mr. SPECTER. Well, was the statement taken the second day after the assassination or the morning of the first day after the assassination?

Mr. ROWLAND. No; it was taken on Saturday morning before I went to work because on Sunday there was another statement taken from me at my job where I was working. This occurred right after Oswald was shot himself.

Mr. SPECTER. Well, are you able to identify that statement which we have marked Exhibit 358, as the statement taken on Saturday, the 23d, as distinguished from the statement taken on Sunday, the 24th of November?

Mr. ROWLAND. Yes.

Mr. SPECTER. How can you be certain of that, Mr. Rowland?

Mr. ROWLAND. The one on Sunday, this particular one, I do remember the agent used a legal pad. He did have three pages of it handwritten. I made corrections on this in different parts of it. The one on Sunday was not a legal pad. It was a steno pad and it, in fact, covered a page and a half, I think, and it was concerned with mainly could I identify the man that I saw, his description.

Mr. SPECTER. Now, at the time you made the Saturday statement, which you say was transcribed and appears as Exhibit 358, did you at that time tell the interviewing FBI agents about the colored gentleman who you testified was in the window which you marked with an "A"?

Mr. ROWLAND. Yes; I did.

Mr. SPECTER. Did you ask them at that time to include the information in the statement which they took from you?

Mr. ROWLAND. No. I think I told them about it after the statement, as an afterthought, an afterthought came up, it came into my mind. I also told the agents that took a statement from me on Sunday. They didn't seem very interested, so I just forgot about it for a while.

Mr. SPECTER. Was that information included in the written portion of the statement which was taken from you on Sunday?

Mr. ROWLAND. No, it wasn't. It shouldn't but the agent deleted it though himself. I mean I included it in what I gave.

Mr. SPECTER. When you say deleted it, did he strike it out after putting it in, or did he omit it in the transcription?

Mr. ROWLAND. Omitted it.

Senator COOPER. I think you said a while ago that when you told the FBI agents on Saturday that you had seen this Negro man in the window, that they indicated to you that they weren't interested in it at all. What did they say which gave you that impression?

Mr. ROWLAND. I don't remember exactly what was said. The context was again the agents were trying to find out if I could positively identify the man that I saw. They were concerned mainly with this, and I brought up to them about the Negro man after I had signed the statement, and at that time he just told me that they were just trying to find out about or if anyone could identify the man who was up there. They just didn't seem interested at all. They didn't pursue the point. They didn't take it down in the notation as such.

Mr. Specter. It was more of the fact that they didn't pursue it, didn't include it?

Mr. Rowland. Yes.

Mr. Specter. Or that they said something which led you to believe they were not interested?

Mr. Rowland. It was just the fact they didn't pursue it. I mean, I just mentioned that I saw him in that window. They didn't ask me, you know, if was this at the same time or such. They just didn't seem very interested in that at all.

Mr. Wright. By man who was up there you mean man with the rifle?

Mr. Rowland. They were interested in the man with the rifle, and finding out if anyone could identify him. The other man was the colored man in the other window.

Representative Ford. A minute ago you indicated that you could see the man in the window with the rifle because of the light conditions, I think you referred to the sun shining in that direction toward the building. Was the sun bright, do you recall that at all?

Mr. Rowland. Yes; the sun was out, somewhat bright. I didn't have any sunglasses on at that time because I had broken them the week before, and I hadn't gotten any new ones. The sun was shining in from what I could tell he was standing where I seen him through the window on my right. This would be the east window of the pair. It appeared as though the sun were shining in through either a window on the other side of the building, on the west side of the building, or possibly the western pair, one of the pair. This sun was—that hit him about from the shoulders down as far as I could see, that is why I was able to tell the rifle was of the type or such that it was.

Representative Ford. As you faced the window, as you faced the building, the sun was shining over which shoulder, to your left or your right shoulder?

Mr. Rowland. As I faced the building the sun was shining—well, I would have been facing the building if the building were in this direction more or less this way and the sun would have been shining from this area.

Representative Ford. Over your left shoulder?

Mr. Rowland. Yes; forward.

Representative Ford. That is all.

Mr. Specter. Were you able to identify the man whom you saw in the window with the rifle for the FBI agents?

Mr. Rowland. No.

Mr. Specter. Did they have pictures with them at that time?

Mr. Rowland. I have seen three pictures of Lee Harvey Oswald, two of them in the paper. They had a morning newspaper was all they had. It wasn't a very good picture, and I couldn't tell. I didn't know, I wasn't going to say because I didn't, I mean. I just couldn't identify him. I wouldn't be—I had already resigned myself not to be given that task, because I couldn't definitely say any one man was that man.

Mr. Specter. And what was the basis of your concluding, as you put it, that you resigned yourself to that task?

Mr. Rowland. This was because I just didn't have a good enough look at his face.

Mr. Specter. Was that your conclusion at this moment that you are unable to identify, with precision and certainty, the man whom you saw holding the rifle in the window of the Texas School Book Depository Building?

Mr. Rowland. Yes; that is true.

Mr. Specter. Do you believe that you could identify the Negro gentleman in window "A" whom you testified you saw?

Mr. Rowland. I would have to say perhaps. I can't say for sure.

Mr. Specter. A moment ago you testified that you gave statements to seven different pairs of FBI agents. Have you already testified about three of those occasions, or, stated differently, start at the beginning and tell us, as best you

185

can recollect, what were those occasions, when they occurred, where you were when you had those meetings with the seven different pairs of agents.

Mr. Rowland. The first statement I gave was in the sheriff's office on that date.

Mr. Specter. Were there two FBI agents present?

Mr. Rowland. I think there were.

Mr. Specter. And do you recollect their names?

Mr. Rowland. No, I do not.

Mr. Specter. When was the second occasion?

Mr. Rowland. The Saturday morning.

Mr. Specter. Where was that statement given?

Mr. Rowland. That was in the agent's car in front of my mother-in-law's house.

Mr. Specter. Do you recollect the identities of those FBI agents?

Mr. Rowland. No, I do not.

Mr. Specter. That is the statement you have identified as being reproduced in Commission Exhibit 358?

Mr. Rowland. Yes.

Mr. Specter. Now, when was the third statement obtained?

Mr. Rowland. It was Sunday morning, the following day, November 25.

Mr. Specter. Where was that statement obtained?

Mr. Rowland. This was at my place of employment at the Pizza Inn.

Mr. Specter. Now, Sunday after the assassination would have been the 24th.

Mr. Rowland. Yes; that is right, I am sorry, sir.

Mr. Specter. Are you certain of the day of the week, however?

Mr. Rowland. Yes; I am certain of that because I went to work at noon on Sunday and they were there when I got to work, they were waiting on me.

Mr. Specter. That is the statement which you described as having been taken on a stenopad?

Mr. Rowland. Yes.

Mr. Specter. Did you sign that statement?

Mr. Rowland. Yes; I did. This was in the presence of my wife because she was there.

Mr. Specter. Do you recollect the identity of those FBI agents?

Mr. Rowland. No; I do not, sir.

Mr. Specter. When was the fourth statement taken?

Mr. Rowland. The fourth was Tuesday night of that week.

Mr. Specter. Of the following week?

Mr. Rowland. Yes.

Mr. Specter. Where was that statement taken?

Mr. Rowland. This was at my mother-in-law's house, and——

Mr. Specter. Was that reduced to writing?

Mr. Rowland. That was merely one paragraph. They were concerned with identification of the man that I saw.

Mr. Specter. What did you tell them essentially at that time?

Mr. Rowland. The description and that I could not positively identify him.

Mr. Specter. Did you sign a statement for them at that time?

Mr. Rowland. Yes; I did.

Mr. Specter. Do you know the identity of those FBI agents?

Mr. Rowland. No, sir; I don't.

Mr. Specter. Up to this point were any of the FBI agents the same who had interviewed you and taken statements from you?

Mr. Rowland. No, sir.

Mr. Specter. All different?

Mr. Rowland. Yes.

Mr. Specter. When did the fifth occasion take place when you were interviewed by the FBI?

Mr. Rowland. This was again where I worked. This was, it was not a formal written statement. They just took notes on what I said, had me recount that entire thing to the best of my knowledge.

Mr. Specter. When did this occur, the fifth one?

Mr. Rowland. It was on the following Friday.

Mr. Specter. About what time of the day or night was it?

Mr. ROWLAND. About 8:30 p.m.

Mr. SPECTER. At the Pizza Inn?

Mr. ROWLAND. Yes; Dallas time.

Mr. SPECTER. And do you recall the identities of those FBI agents?

Mr. ROWLAND. No; I don't.

Mr. SPECTER. Were they the same as any who had ever interviewed you before?

Mr. ROWLAND. No, sir; none of them are the same.

Mr. SPECTER. When was the sixth occasion when you were interviewed by the FBI?

Mr. ROWLAND. It was again on Sunday.

Mr. SPECTER. This would have been November—it would have been December 1st?

Mr. ROWLAND. I don't remember that date but it was——

Mr. SPECTER. The second Sunday after the assassination?

Mr. ROWLAND. Yes.

Mr. SPECTER. Where was the sixth interview conducted?

Mr. ROWLAND. This was at the Pizza Inn.

Mr. SPECTER. About what time of the day or night was that?

Mr. ROWLAND. About 1 o'clock. This was again right after I came to work.

Mr. SPECTER. Was the statement taken from you at that time reduced to writing?

Mr. ROWLAND. It was again informal, just taking notes on my statement, had me recount what I had told the other agents.

Mr. SPECTER. What were they interested in specifically at that time if you recall?

Mr. ROWLAND. They just wanted me to recount everything that I could recall.

Mr. SPECTER. Do you know the identity of those agents?

Mr. ROWLAND. No, sir; I don't.

Mr. SPECTER. Were they again different agents?

Mr. ROWLAND. Yes; they were.

Mr. SPECTER. From all those you had seen before?

Mr. ROWLAND. Yes.

Mr. SPECTER. When had you given the seventh statement to the FBI?

Mr. ROWLAND. The last statement I gave I think it was to one FBI agent and a Secret Service Agent.

Mr. SPECTER. When did that occur?

Mr. ROWLAND. That was either Tuesday or Wednesday of the week. I do not remember which.

Mr. SPECTER. On the week following the Sunday when you gave the sixth statement?

Mr. ROWLAND. Yes.

Mr. SPECTER. Do you recall the identities of those men?

Mr. ROWLAND. No, sir; I don't.

Mr. SPECTER. Had you ever seen either before?

Mr. ROWLAND. No, sir; I hadn't.

Mr. SPECTER. Did they reduce your statement to writing?

Mr. ROWLAND. No, sir; they just had me recount everything again.

Mr. SPECTER. In addition to the times you have already stated, have you ever been interviewed by the FBI on any other occasion?

Mr. ROWLAND. No, sir.

Mr. SPECTER. Have you ever been interviewed by the Secret Service on any other occasion?

Mr. ROWLAND. The afternoon of the 22d and the seventh time was the only two times of the Secret Service.

Mr. SPECTER. There was a Secret Service agent present in the sheriff's office?

Mr. ROWLAND. Yes; he was Agent Sorrels.

Mr. SPECTER. When you gave the affidavit which we have identified as Commission Exhibit 357?

Mr. ROWLAND. Yes.

Mr. SPECTER. In addition to the times you have mentioned, have you ever been interviewed by any agent or representative of the Federal Government?

Mr. Rowland. No, sir; I have not.

Mr. Specter. Have you been interviewed by any other agent or representative of the State Government of Texas?

Mr. Rowland. No, sir.

Mr. Specter. Now, on any of the other occasions, other than those you testified about, did you mention seeing the Negro gentleman in the window which we have circled with the "A"?

Mr. Rowland. No, sir.

Mr. Specter. Mr. Rowland, what was the quality of your grades in high school?

Mr. Rowland. Well, up until my senior year they were 4.0 straight A's, in my senior year I got a couple of B's.

Mr. Specter. Do you know what your IQ or intelligence quotient is?

Mr. Rowland. 147.

Mr. Specter. Do you know when you were tested for that?

Mr. Rowland. In 1963; in May.

Mr. Specter. Mr. Rowland, a couple of other questions.

Are you able to give us any other type of a description of the Negro gentleman whom you observed in the window we marked "A" with respect to height, weight, age?

Mr. Rowland. He was very thin, an elderly gentleman, bald or practically bald, very thin hair if he wasn't bald. Had on a plaid shirt. I think it was red and green, very bright color, that is why I remember it.

Mr. Specter. Can you give us an estimate as to age?

Mr. Rowland. Fifty; possibly 55 or 60.

Mr. Specter. Can you give us an estimate as to height?

Mr. Rowland. 5'8'', 5'10'', in that neighborhood. He was very slender, very thin.

Mr. Specter. Can you give us a more definite description as to complexion?

Mr. Rowland. Very dark or fairly dark, not real dark compared to some Negroes, but fairly dark. Seemed like his face was either—I can't recall detail but it was either very wrinkled or marked in some way.

Mr. Specter. Shortly after the assassination and before these interviews that you described were completed, Mr. Rowland, had you learned or heard that the shots were supposed to have come out of the window which we have marked with the "A"?

Mr. Rowland. No, sir. I did not know that, in fact until Saturday when I read the paper.

Mr. Specter. Which Saturday is that?

Mr. Rowland. The following Saturday.

Mr. Specter. Would that be the second day, the day after the assassination?

Mr. Rowland. Yes.

Mr. Specter. Well, knowing that, at that time, did you attach any particular significance to the presence of the Negro gentleman, whom you have described, that you saw in window "A"?

Mr. Rowland. Yes; that is why I brought it to the attention of the FBI agents who interviewed me that day. This was as an afterthought because I did not think of it firsthand. But I did bring it to their attention before they left, and they——

Mr. Specter. That was at the interview on the Saturday morning November 23?

Mr. Rowland. Yes.

Mr. Specter. Did you think it of sufficient significance to bring it to the attention of any of the other interviewing FBI agents on the balance of the interviews you have described?

Mr. Rowland. Yes: I did on the following Sunday to the agents who interviewed me where I worked.

Mr. Specter. How about the following Sunday?

Mr. Rowland. No; I did not.

Mr. Specter. Mr. Chief Justice, at this time I move for the admission into evidence of the three exhibits which we have shown this witness.

The Chairman. They may be admitted.

Mr. SPECTER. Exhibits Nos. 356, 357, and 358. That completes our questioning, Your Honor.

(The documents referred to were marked Commission's Exhibits Nos. 356, 357, and 358 for identification and admitted into evidence.)

The CHAIRMAN. Senator Cooper, have you any questions?

Senator COOPER. You said earlier that you had been much interested in and pursued studies in sounds, I believe?

Mr. ROWLAND. I have studied quite a bit of electronics, sound. Math and science is what I like.

Senator COOPER. You said you had read books on this subject. Did you ever conduct any experiments yourself?

Mr. ROWLAND. Yes; in the form of—there is a theory that sound is a basis of a transmitter and a receiver, that you have to have a receiver to have sound. There is a theory that if a tree falls down in the middle of a forest and there is nobody around where they can hear it, there is no sound.

Well, I have conducted experiments on this, and I—it is very interesting, very fascinating, but you can't prove it or you can't disprove it because if you have got a microphone there you have got a receiver.

Senator COOPER. Did you ever conduct any experiments with rifles, firing a rifle in relation to sound?

Mr. ROWLAND. Yes; in a firing range.

Senator Cooper. Beg pardon?

Mr. ROWLAND. Firing range.

Senator COOPER. Yes.

Mr. ROWLAND. I did conduct a few experiments. One of them was firing a bullet over water; you know, we were using a set of wood blocks to fire into, so we had a big vat of water that we were firing over, and we had several different articles and composition floating on the water, trying to measure the effect of the sound wave upon that. Such as this we did conduct.

Senator COOPER. I think you did say that when you heard the first report that you considered it to be a rifle shot?

Mr. ROWLAND. I did, but almost immediately everyone started laughing so I did not give it any further consideration until the second shot, second report.

Senator COOPER. At the time you saw a man standing near a window in the Texas School Book Depository with a rifle, can you state whether there were any, did you know whether or not any police officers were near you?

Mr. ROWLAND. There was an officer about 20 feet to my left.

Senator COOPER. Did you see any others?

Mr. ROWLAND. There were officers all over, that was the closest one. There were four or five on the block across the street from me, two of them being with the boy who had the epileptic fit.

There was also an officer in front of the doors to that building. There were several on the corners. I would say there were 20 uniformed officers right there in that 1½-block area.

Senator COOPER. Could any of the officers that you saw whose position you noted, have seen this window from the place where they were standing?

Mr. ROWLAND. They could have; yes, sir.

Senator COOPER. You don't remember whether any of them were looking up there?

Mr. ROWLAND. No; I don't remember whether they were. No; I don't.

Senator COOPER. Did it occur to you that you should speak to the officer about seeing a man in the window?

Mr. ROWLAND. It has. Do you ever have reoccurring dreams, sir?

Senator COOPER. What?

Mr. ROWLAND. Do you ever have reoccurring dreams?

Senator COOPER. Yes.

Mr. ROWLAND. This is a reoccurring dream of mine, sir, all the time, what if I had told someone about it. I knew about it enough in advance and perhaps it could have been prevented. I mean this is something which shakes me up at times.

Senator COOPER. I don't want to disturb you about that but my point was at the time did you—I think you said, though, you thought that he was a—he could have been a—Secret Service man, officer.

Mr. ROWLAND. Yes; that is right.

Senator COOPER. That is all.

The CHAIRMAN. Anything further, Congressman Ford?

Representative FORD. Mr. Rowland, have you ever had occasion to go back to the scene and reconstruct it? Have you ever gone back——

The CHAIRMAN. Supposing we take a few minutes recess.

Mr. ROWLAND. The answer to that question is yes; I do all the time. I pass that area very frequently.

The CHAIRMAN. Any other questions, gentlemen, Mr. Wright?

Mr. WRIGHT. No, Your Honor.

The CHAIRMAN. Very well, Mr. Rowland, I want to thank you for coming here and cooperating with the Commission. I know that this is a matter that recalls very sordid thoughts to your mind, and I can see how you would be somewhat distressed about it but you have been very frank and cooperative with us and I appreciate it.

We will take a short recess.

(Short recess.)

TESTIMONY OF JAMES RICHARD WORRELL, JR.

The CHAIRMAN. All right.

Will you raise your right hand and be sworn, please?

Do you solemnly swear that the testimony you give before this Commission will be the truth, the whole truth and nothing but the truth, so help you God?

Mr. WORRELL. Yes, sir.

The CHAIRMAN. Will you be seated, please.

Mr. Worrell, the purpose of today's hearing is to hear the testimony of Arnold Louis Rowland, Amos Lee Evins, yourself, and Robert Jackson, who were in the vicinity of the assassination scene on November 22, 1963. The Commission proposes to ask you and the other witnesses for facts concerning your knowledge of the assassination of the President.

Mr. WORRELL. Yes, sir.

The CHAIRMAN. Mr. Specter, will you proceed with the examination.

Mr. SPECTER. Will you state your full name for the record, please?

Mr. WORRELL. James Richard Worrell, Jr.

The CHAIRMAN. Senator, will you preside while I answer a phone call to another member of the Commission?

Mr. SPECTER. What is your address, Mr. Worrell?

Mr. WORRELL. 13510 Winterhaven Drive.

Mr. SPECTER. What city is that?

Mr. WORRELL. In Dallas, it is the Farmers Branch of the suburb of Dallas.

Mr. SPECTER. How long have you resided in Dallas, Tex.?

Mr. WORRELL. About 12 years.

Mr. SPECTER. And where did you live before that?

Mr. WORRELL. 3140 Storey Lane.

Mr. SPECTER. And in what city is Storey Lane located?

Mr. WORRELL. Dallas.

Mr. SPECTER. Where were you born?

Mr. WORRELL. Livermore, Calif.

Mr. SPECTER. And how old are you at the present time?

Mr. WORRELL. Twenty.

Mr. SPECTER. How long did you live in California?

Mr. WORRELL. I am not exactly sure. I was a little bitty old thing and I think it was 2 or 3 years.

Mr. SPECTER. Where did you move from California?

Mr. WORRELL. From California we moved to Abilene, I think.

Mr. SPECTER. Abilene, Tex.?

Mr. WORRELL. Yes.

Mr. SPECTER. And have you lived in Texas since that time?

Mr. WORRELL. Yes.

Mr. SPECTER. What is your marital status?

Mr. WORRELL. Sir?

Mr. SPECTER. Are you married or single?

Mr. WORRELL. Single, sir.

Mr. SPECTER. Do you live with your parents?

Mr. WORRELL. My mother and sister.

Mr. SPECTER. And how much schooling have you had?

Mr. WORRELL. Eleven years.

Mr. SPECTER. When did you end your schooling, if you have ended it?

Mr. WORRELL. I ended it October of this year, I quit.

Mr. SPECTER. What school were you going to at that time?

Mr. WORRELL. Thomas Jefferson.

Mr. SPECTER. High school?

Mr. WORRELL. High school; yes, sir.

Mr. SPECTER. Located in Dallas, Tex.?

Mr. WORRELL. Yes, sir.

Mr. SPECTER. And were you in the 11th grade or had you completed the 11th grade?

Mr. WORRELL. I was a senior.

Mr. SPECTER. How were your grades in school?

Mr. WORRELL. Average.

(The Chief Justice entered the hearing room at this point.)

Mr. SPECTER. How were you occupied or employed back on November 22, 1963?

Mr. WORRELL. I was in school then. I skipped school to go there.

Mr. SPECTER. You were attending Jefferson High School on that day or were enrolled at that time?

Mr. WORRELL. I was enrolled but I hadn't been going since October.

Mr. SPECTER. Was there any special reason for your not going since October?

Mr. WORRELL. No, sir.

Mr. SPECTER. Had you been employed anywhere from the time you stopped going to school?

Mr. WORRELL. Yes, sir. I was employed for El Capitan Oil Drilling out in Kermit, Tex.

Mr. SPECTER. What sort of work were you doing for them?

Mr. WORRELL. I was a floor man on a derrick.

Mr. SPECTER. Did you say floor man?

Mr. WORRELL. Yes.

Mr. SPECTER. On November 22, 1963, were you working on that day for your employer?

Mr. WORRELL. No. I didn't start this oil job until—it was the last of January.

Mr. SPECTER. Of 1964?

Mr. WORRELL. Yes.

Mr. SPECTER. And are you working for them at the present time?

Mr. WORRELL. No, sir.

Mr. SPECTER. Whom are you working for now?

Mr. WORRELL. I am not employed now.

Mr. SPECTER. Then going back to November 22, 1963, you had no job at that time?

Mr. WORRELL. Yes, sir.

Mr. SPECTER. And did you attend school that day at all?

Mr. WORRELL. No, sir.

Mr. SPECTER. Will you outline for us briefly what your activities were from the time you awakened until about noon time on November 22?

Mr. WORRELL. Well, I got up about, well, I got up at my usual time, about 6:30. I was going to go to school that day but I decided to go see the President and my mother left about 7:30, and my sister left about a quarter of 8. I left about 8, and hitchhiked down to Love Field and got there. It took me quite a while to get there, about 9, and just messed around there until the President come in, whatever time that was. And then I didn't get to see him good at all. So, I caught a bus and went over, went downtown and I just, I don't know, happened to pick that place at the Depository, and I stood at the corner of Elm and Houston.

Mr. SPECTER. Did you leave Love Field before the President did?

Mr. WORRELL. Oh, yes.

Mr. SPECTER. Why did you happen to leave Love Field before he left?

Mr. WORRELL. Well, so I could see him better.

Mr. SPECTER. Couldn't you get a good view of him at Love Field?

Mr. WORRELL. No, I just saw him off the plane and I figured that I wasn't going to see him good so I was going to get a better place to see him.

Mr. SPECTER. How did you travel from Love Field down to Elm and Houston?

Mr. WORRELL. Bus. No, no; I just traveled so far on the bus. I went down to Elm, and took a bus from there. I went down as far as, I don't know where that bus stops, anyway I got close to there and I walked the rest of the way.

Mr. SPECTER. What time, to the best of your recollection, did you arrive at the intersection of Elm and Houston?

Mr. WORRELL. Well, about 10, 10:30, 10:45, something around there. There weren't many people standing around there then.

Mr. SPECTER. Well, about how long before the Presidential motorcade came to Elm and Houston did you get there?

Mr. WORRELL. An hour; an hour and a half.

Mr. SPECTER. Are you sure you were at Love Field when the President arrived there?

Mr. WORRELL. Oh, yes.

Mr. SPECTER. All right. Now I am going to show you a photograph which I have marked as Commission Exhibit No. 359. Take a look at that, if you would, please, and tell us whether or not you can identify what scene that is?

Mr. WORRELL. Yes, this is Elm, Pacific, and Commerce. This is the Depository right here, and this is Stemmons, and this is the way the President come down.

Mr. SPECTER. So is that the assassination scene itself?

Mr. WORRELL. Yes, sir.

Mr. SPECTER. Now take a look at that picture and tell us where you were standing—and I will give you a pencil so you can mark it on that picture itself—at the time the Presidential motorcade came by. Mark it with an "X," if you would, just exactly where you were standing, as best as you can recollect it, at this moment, at the time the President went by.

Mr. WORRELL. Right underneath that window right there.

Mr. SPECTER. Now, how close were you standing to this building which I will ask you to identify; first of all, what building is that?

Mr. WORRELL. That is the Texas Depository.

Mr. SPECTER. All right.

Now how close to that building were you standing?

Mr. WORRELL. I was, I don't know, 4 or 5 feet out from it.

Mr. SPECTER. Were you standing with your face to the building, with your back to the building, or how?

Mr. WORRELL. My back was to the building.

Mr. SPECTER. I show you a photograph which has been identified as Commission Exhibit 360 and I will ask you if you can identify what that building is?

Mr. WORRELL. That is the Depository.

Mr. SPECTER. All right.

Now on this picture will you again, with an "X," mark where you were standing as closely as you can recollect it.

Mr. WORRELL. That car is in the way.

Mr. SPECTER. All right. Put the mark then right above where the car is, indicating where you were standing on the sidewalk near that building.

(Witness marking.)

Mr. SPECTER. Now, did you observe the President's motorcade come by?

Mr. WORRELL. Oh, yes.

Mr. SPECTER. Describe to us what you saw, heard, and observed at that time, as the motorcade came by.

Mr. WORRELL. Well, I saw him—I was standing looking—I don't know my directions very well; anyway, I was looking down towards Elm Street watching him come, and they filed by me——

Mr. SPECTER. On which street were you watching them come?

Mr. WORRELL. This way.

Mr. SPECTER. Look at Exhibit 359 and pick out which street they were on?

Mr. WORRELL. They were coming down this way, so on and so forth.

Mr. SPECTER. Well, now, were they coming down Elm Street or were they coming down Main Street with a righthand turn on to Houston Street with a curve on Houston down Elm, recollect it if you can?

Mr. WORRELL. That is right. They did turn around.

Mr. SPECTER. Did they come down——

Mr. WORRELL. I didn't see him up there.

Mr. SPECTER. Where was the President's motorcade at the time you first saw it?

Mr. WORRELL. Oh, about right in here.

Mr. SPECTER. Proceeding in this direction, indicating in a generally northerly direction on Houston Street, right?

Mr. WORRELL. Yes, north.

Mr. SPECTER. Then tell us what the President's motorcade did?

Mr. WORRELL. It turned and went down this way.

Mr. SPECTER. Made a left-hand or right-hand turn?

Mr. WORRELL. Left-hand turn.

Mr. SPECTER. Did it pass right by in front of where you were standing?

Mr. WORRELL. Within a hundred feet, I guess.

Mr. SPECTER. Were you able to get a pretty good view of the President's motorcade?

Mr. WORRELL. Yes, sir.

Mr. SPECTER. All right; go ahead and tell us.

Mr. WORRELL. Didn't get too good a view of the President either, I missed out on there too. But as they went by, they got, oh at least another 50, 75 feet on past me, and then I heard the shots.

Mr. SPECTER. How many shots did you hear?

Mr. WORRELL. Four.

Mr. SPECTER. Did you observe anything at about that time?

Mr. WORRELL. Yes, sir. I looked up and saw the rifle, but I would say about 6 inches of it.

Mr. SPECTER. And where did you see the rifle?

Mr. WORRELL. I am not going—I am not too sure but I told the FBI it was either in the fifth or the sixth floor on the far corner, on the east side.

Mr. SPECTER. Now looking at the picture which we have identified as Commission Exhibit No. 360, which is where you have drawn an "X," can you indicate the line of vision which you followed to the point where the rifle was to the best of your ability to recollect?

Mr. WORRELL. Well, when I heard the first shot it was too loud to be a firecracker, I knew that, because there was quite a big boom, and I don't know, just out of nowhere, I looked up like that, just straight up.

Mr. SPECTER. Indicating you looked straight over your head, raising your head to look over your body at the 90 degree angle?

Mr. WORRELL. Yes; and I saw it for the second time and I looked back to the motorcade.

Mr. SPECTER. What did you observe at that time?

Mr. WORRELL. I saw about 6 inches of the gun, the rifle. It had—well it had a regular long barrel but it had a long stock and you could only see maybe 4 inches of the barrell, and I could see——

Mr. SPECTER. Were you able to observe any of the stock?

Mr. WORRELL. Oh, yes.

Mr. SPECTER. How much of the stock were you able to observe?

Mr. WORRELL. Just very little, just about 2 inches.

Mr. SPECTER. How many inches of the barrel then could you observe protruding beyond the stock?

Mr. WORRELL. About 4 inches, I would say, not very much.

Mr. SPECTER. Now, at the time of the second shot were you able to observe anything at that precise instant?

Mr. WORRELL. You mean as to firing it.

Mr. Specter. As to anything at all. What did you see when the second shot went off?

Mr. Worrell. Well, I looked to see where he was aiming and after the second shot and I have seen the President slumping down in the seat, and——

Mr. Specter. Did you see the President slump in his seat after the second shot?

Mr. Worrell. Uh, huh. And about that——

Mr. Specter. Did you look up and see the rifle between the first and the second shots?

Mr. Worrell. Yes, sir. And saw the firing on the second and then before he could get a shot I was—I took in everything but especially the car, the President's car, and saw him slumping, and I looked up again and turned around and started running and saw it fire a third time, and then——

Mr. Specter. When did you see it fire a third time, when you looked up, the time you just described?

Mr. Worrell. When I was, I did it all in one motion, I looked up, turned around and ran, pivoted.

Mr. Specter. What did you hear, if anything, after that?

Mr. Worrell. Just a lot of commotion, everybody was screaming and saying "duck."

Mr. Specter. After the third shot, did you hear a fourth shot?

Mr. Worrell. Oh, yes. Just as I got to the corner of Exhibit 360, I heard the fourth shot.

Mr. Specter. Well, did these four shots come close together or how would you describe the timing in general on those?

Mr. Worrell. Succession.

Mr. Specter. Were they very fast?

Mr. Worrell. They were right in succession.

Mr. Specter. Now going back to the position of the rifle which you testified that you saw, you say it was either on the fifth or sixth floor?

Mr. Worrell. Yes, sir.

Mr. Specter. Is there any way you can tell us which floor it was on, or would the angle of your observation permit you to be sure it was the fifth or sixth floors?

Mr. Worrell. I am not going to say I am positive, but that one there.

Mr. Specter. All right, would you mark that one——

Mr. Worrell. Because that right there, I feel, would have obstructed my vision but I said it was either on the fifth or sixth floor.

Mr. Specter. Well, now, will you mark with a "Y" the window which you have just pointed to?

(At this point Chief Justice Warren departed the hearing room.)

Mr. Worrell. A "Y"?

Mr. Specter. A "Y."

(Witness marking.)

Mr. Specter. You have marked the "Y" over two windows. Was it the window—which window was it there as best you can recollect, as between those two?

Mr. Worrell. I didn't mean to bring it down that far but this one.

Mr. Specter. Would you put an arrow then at the window that you have just indicated, was the one where the rifle was protruding from?

(Witness marking.)

Mr. Specter. So, the sum of it is you are not sure whether it was the fifth or the sixth floor, but you believe it was on the floor where you have marked a "Y" which is the sixth floor and that was the line of vision as you looked straight up over your head?

Mr. Worrell. Yes, sir.

Mr. Specter. Where did you run, which is what you have just described that you did next?

Mr. Worrell. Well, a better view of it is here in 360. I ran down Houston Street alongside the building and then crossed over the street, I ran alongside the building and crossed over, and in 359, I was standing over here, and I saw this man come bustling out of this door.

194

Mr. SPECTER. Before you get to that, Mr. Worrell, let me show you a diagram which has been prepared here, which may be of some assistance to you in telling us your movements in running. I will mark this as Commission Exhibit 361 and ask Mr. David Belin, Staff Counsel, to make a statement as to the preparation of this exhibit for the record.

Mr. BELIN. The record will show that Exhibit 361 was prepared in the exhibit section of the Federal Bureau of Investigation by Inspector Leo. J. Gauthier and Eugene Paul Airy, exhibit specialist, with the assistance of Charles D. Musser, illustrator, with particular reference to showing the Texas School Book Depository Building, and the immediate area with relation to the parking lot that employees used.

Mr. SPECTER. Mr. Worrell, take a good look at this. Study it for just a moment in order to get your bearings on this particular map. This is the Texas School Book Depository Building designated as such. This is Houston Street and this is the direction I am indicating that the motorcade, as you have described from the other exhibit, came from, a generally northerly direction. This is generally north, and it made the left-hand turn which you have already described for the record, onto Elm Street Parkway going down the front there.

Now perhaps the best place to start on this is with this red pencil, to put a small "X" where you were standing on this map.

Mr. WORRELL. Where I was standing?

Mr. SPECTER. Where you were standing.

(Witness marking.)

Mr. SPECTER. Now will you describe your movement in running as you had started to a few moments ago, indicating with a line of the red pencil just exactly where you went and describe it as you go along.

Mr. WORRELL. Well, as I said on the third shot I was looking up and pivoting and turning to run at the same time. When I got here I heard the fourth shot.

Mr. SPECTER. Indicating that you were at that point right at the corner of the building on Houston?

Mr. WORRELL. Making a turn.

Mr. SPECTER. Having moved slightly to your left, and beginning to make a turn to go in a generally northerly direction on Houston Street?

Mr. WORRELL. I thought that was north.

Mr. SPECTER. No, this is north, there is a symbol showing which is north.

Mr. WORRELL. Okay. Then I turned the corner, went right down beside the building on the sidewalk and when I got to the corner——

Mr. SPECTER. Corner of what?

Mr. WORRELL. Of this building.

Mr. SPECTER. Of the Texas School Book Depository Building?

Mr. WORRELL. Yes.

Mr. SPECTER. And what did you do there?

Mr. WORRELL. Cut directly across, kind of at an angle.

Mr. SPECTER. Across Houston Street as you have drawn the red line there?

Mr. WORRELL. Yes, and I rested there, I was out of breath, I smoke too much, short winded.

Mr. SPECTER. Will you mark that "Y" where you stopped and rested and tell us how long you stopped there?

(Witness marking.)

Mr. WORRELL. How long?

Mr. SPECTER. Yes, sir.

Mr. WORRELL. I was there approximately 3 minutes before I saw this man come out the back door here.

Mr. SPECTER. All right.

Now will you put a "Z" where you first saw the man whom you have just described or mentioned?

Mr. WORRELL. It is here I am pretty sure, I am not positive.

(Witness marking.)

Mr. SPECTER. You are pretty sure—but you can't be positive—but you are pretty sure?

Mr. WORRELL. Yes.

Mr. SPECTER. Okay. Now, describe as best you can the man whom you have testified you saw at point "Z."

Mr. WORRELL. Describe his appearance?

Mr. SPECTER. Yes. Start by telling us how tall he was, to the best of your ability to recollect and estimate?

Mr. WORRELL. To the—it is going to be within 3 inches, 5-7 to 5-10.

Mr. SPECTER. What is your best estimate as to his weight?

Mr. WORRELL. 155 to 165.

Mr. SPECTER. What is your best estimate as to his height?

Mr. WORRELL. 5-7, 5-10.

Mr. SPECTER. Pardon me, your best estimate as to his age.

Mr. WORRELL. Well, the way he was running, I would say he was in his late twenties or middle—I mean early thirties. Because he was fast moving on.

Mr. SPECTER. Of what race was he?

Mr. WORRELL. White.

Mr. SPECTER. Can you describe the characteristics of his hair?

Mr. WORRELL. Black.

Mr. SPECTER. Did he have——

Mr. WORRELL. Well, I will say brunette.

Mr. SPECTER. Did he have a full head of hair, a partial head of hair, or what?

Mr. WORRELL. Well, see, I didn't see his face, I just saw the back of his head and it was full in the back. I don't know what the front looked like. But it was full in the back.

Mr. SPECTER. What clothes did the man have on?

Mr. WORRELL. Dark, like a jacket like that.

Mr. SPECTER. Indicating a dark gray jacket?

Mr. WORRELL. No, no. It was a jacket like that.

Mr. SPECTER. A suit jacket?

Mr. WORRELL. Yes.

Mr. SPECTER. Or was it a sports jacket?

Mr. WORRELL. Sports jacket.

Mr. SPECTER. Did not have on matching coat and trousers?

Mr. WORRELL. No.

Mr. SPECTER. Was it dark in color or light?

Mr. WORRELL. It was dark in color. I don't know whether it was blue, black, or brown, but it was dark, and he had light pants. And that is all I can say on his clothes, except his coat was open and kind of flapping back in the breeze when he was running.

Mr. SPECTER. Now, are there any other distinguishing characteristics that you can describe about him?

Mr. WORRELL. Not a thing.

Mr. SPECTER. What did he——

Mr. WORRELL. He wasn't holding nothing when he was running. He was just running.

Mr. SPECTER. What did you observe him do, if anything?

Mr. WORRELL. Well, when he ran out here, he ran along the side of the Depository Building and then when he got——

Mr. SPECTER. Make a dotted line as to where he went, or take this black pencil and make a line as to where he went.

(Witness marking.)

Mr. SPECTER. Where did you see him eventually go?

Mr. WORRELL. Well, he went on further.

Mr. SPECTER. Is that the last you saw him?

Mr. WORRELL. Yes, sir.

Mr. SPECTER. And did something come between you and him so that your vision was obstructed?

Mr. WORRELL. Yes, sir.

Mr. SPECTER. As of the point you have just dotted out there?

Mr. WORRELL. Yes, sir.

Mr. SPECTER. What obstructed your view of him at that juncture or at that point?

Mr. WORRELL. I can't really be sure, it was a building, but the type of building, I don't know.

Mr. SPECTER. During the course of your seeing him, did you ever get a view of his face?

Mr. WORRELL. Oh, no, no.

Mr. SPECTER. All right. What did you do next, Mr. Worrell?

Mr. WORRELL. Well, I went on down this way and headed up back to Elm Street.

Mr. SPECTER. Indicating you went on down to Pacific?

Mr. WORRELL. Yes.

Mr. SPECTER. And then proceeded——

Mr. WORRELL. No, no; that is wrong. I went on Pacific and——

Mr. SPECTER. Just a minute. You proceeded from point "Y" on in a generally northerly direction to Pacific and then in what direction did you go on Pacific, this would be in an easterly direction?

Mr. WORRELL. I went east.

Mr. SPECTER. You went in an easterly direction how many blocks down Pacific?

Mr. WORRELL. I went down to Market and from Market I went on Ross.

Mr. SPECTER. You went left on Market down to Ross, and then?

Mr. WORRELL. From Ross I went all the way to Ervay.

Mr. SPECTER. Where were you heading for at that time?

Mr. WORRELL. For the bus stop near my mother's office. And I rode the bus from there out to the school and hitchhiked the rest of the way to Farmers Branch.

Mr. SPECTER. All right. When did you first report to any official what you had seen and heard on this occasion?

Mr. WORRELL. Well, I turned the TV on early next morning to see what had happened, and Chief Curry was making a plea——

Senator COOPER. Is that going to become a part of the evidence at this point?

Mr. WORRELL. Chief Curry was making a plea for anyone who had seen the shooting, would they please come down and make a statement. So I called the Farmer Branch police, and told them, and they come and picked me up, and they called the Dallas police, and they come way out there and picked me up and took me downtown to make a statement and brought me back home.

Mr. SPECTER. Mr. Worrell, before we leave this Exhibit 361, are you able to testify as to the accuracy of the scale drawing here which represents the part of it that you have testified about, specifically the presence of the Texas School Book Depository Building on the northwest corner of Elm and Houston. Is that the accurate location of that building?

Mr. WORRELL. Yes, sir.

Mr. SPECTER. And is it an accurate reproduction of the intersection of Elm and Houston leading into the parkway on Elm Street?

Mr. WORRELL. As far as this?

Mr. SPECTER. Yes.

Mr. WORRELL. Yes.

Mr. SPECTER. As far as all the parts you have testified about Elm and Houston. Is it accurate that Pacific is one block in the northerly direction away from Elm Street?

Mr. WORRELL. Yes, sir.

Mr. SPECTER. And Ross is another block, generally, in a northerly direction away from Pacific?

Mr. WORRELL. No, Ross is over here. This is Record Street.

Mr. SPECTER. Well, first there is Elm, then there is Pacific, and then there is Ross. Is that much accurate as the map shows it to be, is that the way the streets are laid out?

Mr. WORRELL. I think so.

Mr. SPECTER. How about the general width of Houston Street in relation to the general width of the Texas School Depository Building, is that about right?

Mr. WORRELL. I don't know, sir.

Mr. SPECTER. All right, that is fine.

At the same time that we have marked Exhibit 361, Mr. Chairman, I would like to use the next number in sequence, No. 362 to mark the other half of this same exhibit which is designated Texas School Book Depository floor plan of the first floor, which we will not use at this time, but I would like to mark it in sequence.

And at this time I ask that Commission Exhibits Nos. 359, 360, 361, and 362 be admitted into evidence.

Senator COOPER. So ordered. Let those exhibits be admitted as part of the evidence.

(The documents referred to, heretofore marked Commission Exhibits Nos. 359, 360, 361, and 362 were admitted into evidence.)

Mr. SPECTER. Mr. Worrell, you had told us that you heard a plea by Chief of Police Curry for all witnesses to come forward.

Mr. WORRELL. Yes, sir.

Mr. SPECTER. And you heard that plea on the 23d of November?

Mr. WORRELL. It was on Saturday.

Mr. SPECTER. What action, if any, did you take in response to that request?

Mr. WORRELL. I called on the phone to the Farmers Branch police.

Mr. SPECTER. You called who?

Mr. WORRELL. The Farmers Branch police.

Mr. SPECTER. I see. And what did you do then?

Mr. WORRELL. Well, I told them what I had seen and they said, "Well, stay there and we will come and get you."

Mr. SPECTER. Did they come and get you?

Mr. WORRELL. Oh, yes, sir.

Mr. SPECTER. Did you then tell the police what you had seen and heard?

Mr. WORRELL. I told a Lt. Butler what I had seen, and I don't know if—they placed the call into the Dallas police and something like an hour later they came to pick me up there.

Mr. SPECTER. Did you make a statement or take an affidavit on what you had seen and heard?

Mr. WORRELL. To the Dallas police?

Mr. SPECTER. Yes.

Mr. WORRELL. Oh, yes, sir. I made a statement and signed five of them.

Mr. SPECTER. I will show you a paper which is marked Commission Exhibit 363 which purports to be an affidavit bearing your signature.

Mr. WORRELL. Yes, sir.

Mr. SPECTER. Let me ask you first of all if that is your signature?

Mr. WORRELL. Yes, sir.

Mr. SPECTER. And would you take just a minute, take your time and read that affidavit over, please.

Have you had a chance to read that over, Mr. Worrell?

Mr. WORRELL. Yes, sir.

Mr. SPECTER. Did you tell us that you signed five different statements or five copies of the same statement?

Mr. WORRELL. Five copies of the same statement.

Mr. SPECTER. Is this the statement which you signed in affidavit form at that time?

Mr. WORRELL. Yes, sir.

Mr. SPECTER. And——

Mr. WORRELL. Yes, sir.

Mr. SPECTER. As you have just—have you had time to read it over just now?

Mr. WORRELL. Oh, yes.

Mr. SPECTER. Is that statement accurate based on your current recollection of the event?

Mr. WORRELL. It is accurate down to, well, I changed my height to 5-8 from 5-7.

Mr. SPECTER. Aside from that minor variation, is it accurate in its entirety; that is, is it all accurate?

Mr. WORRELL. Well, I left out, when I was making my affidavit, I left out, while I was running I heard a gun fire two more times. Well, as I told you, I was turning the corner when I heard it and saw it fire the third time, and then the fourth.

Mr. SPECTER. Now, are there any other additions or modifications that you would like to make from the contents of your statement in accordance with your recollection at this moment?

Mr. WORRELL. I can't verify that—the time they got here because I am not too sure of that.

Mr. SPECTER. You are not sure of that now?

Mr. WORRELL. No.

Mr. SPECTER. All right.

Are there any other modifications that you would want to make in the contents of the statement?

Mr. WORRELL. Leave out firecracker. It sounded, it was too loud for a firecracker.

Mr. SPECTER. Your current recollection is that it was too loud for a firecracker?

Mr. WORRELL. Yes.

Mr. SPECTER. Is there any other respect in which your current recollection differs from this affidavit?

Mr. WORRELL. Instead of looking I ran, I looked up.

Mr. SPECTER. Is there any other respect in which your current recollection differs from the affidavit?

Mr. WORRELL. Well, I left out on the barrel of the rifle, I left out part of the stock. I didn't recollect that at that time.

Mr. SPECTER. Is there any other aspect in which your current recollection differs from the facts set forth in this affidavit?

Mr. WORRELL. Well, everything else is O.K.

Mr. SPECTER. What is your best estimate as to the length of time between the first shot and the last shot which you heard?

Mr. WORRELL. The best estimate 5, 6 seconds.

Mr. SPECTER. Have you talked to, been interviewed by or given a statement to any Federal agent?

Mr. WORRELL. The FBI down at Dallas.

Mr. SPECTER. How many times have you seen the FBI agents?

Mr. WORRELL. Once.

Mr. SPECTER. Do you recollect the names of the agents you saw?

Mr. WORRELL. No, sir.

Mr. SPECTER. Do you recollect when it was that you saw those agents?

Mr. WORRELL. It was on that Saturday, the 23d.

Mr. SPECTER. And where were you when you saw them?

Mr. WORRELL. In the Dallas Police Station.

Mr. SPECTER. How long did that interview last?

Mr. WORRELL. Thirty minutes.

Mr. SPECTER. Did you sign a statement for them?

Mr. WORRELL. I just signed it for the Dallas police. They didn't have me sign anything.

Mr. SPECTER. Have you been interviewed by any other Federal agent or representative?

Mr. WORRELL. Well, Mr. Sorrels interviewed me when he called me and asked me some questions when he called me up Wednesday night, I guess it was.

Mr. SPECTER. Was that in relationship to your coming here to this Commission hearing?

Mr. WORRELL. Yes.

Mr. SPECTER. What sort of questions did Mr. Sorrels ask you?

Mr. WORRELL. What I saw. And I told him.

Mr. SPECTER. Was that just on the telephone?

Mr. WORRELL. Yes.

Mr. SPECTER. How long did that conversation last?

Mr. WORRELL. Not very long. He talked to my mother first. He talked to her for 15 minutes, something like this.

Mr. SPECTER. Was he talking to her about what you saw or about travel arrangements to get you here?

Mr. WORRELL. I don't know. I was watching television, I didn't know even who she was talking to.

Mr. SPECTER. All right. Aside from that conversation with Mr. Sorrels and the interview you have had with the FBI, have you ever talked with any agent or representative of the Federal Government.

Mr. WORRELL. No, sir.

Mr. SPECTER. Have you talked to any police official of Dallas or the State of Texas after you gave this affidavit?

Mr. WORRELL. No, sir.

Mr. SPECTER. Based on seeing only the back of this man, were you ever able to make any identification of him?

Mr. WORRELL. No, sir.

Mr. SPECTER. Mr. Chairman, I move for the admission into evidence of the other exhibit which we have used with Mr. Worrell being Commission Exhibit No. 362.

Senator COOPER. The exhibit will be admitted to evidence.

(The document referred to was marked Commission Exhibit No. 362 for identification and received in evidence.)

Mr. SPECTER. That concludes our questions.

Senator COOPER. You stated that, I believe, you looked up after you had heard the first report?

Mr. WORRELL. Yes, sir.

Senator COOPER. You looked up and saw the barrel of a rifle, and then the rifle fired. What made you know that it fired?

Mr. WORRELL. Pardon?

Senator COOPER. How did you know it was fired when you were looking at it?

Mr. WORRELL. Well, I saw what you might call a little flame and smoke.

Senator COOPER. You saw something that came out of the barrel?

Mr. WORREL. Yes, sir.

Senator COOPER. Were you looking at it when you heard the third report?

Mr. WORRELL. Yes, sir, looking at it, turning around and started to run.

Senator COOPER. Did you see anything then?

Mr. WORRELL. Same thing, a little flash of fire and then smoke. I didn't see it on the fourth one.

Senator COOPER. Did you only look at the car in which the President was riding one time when you said you saw him slump?

Mr. WORRELL. Yes, sir.

Senator COOPER. Did you look back at the President's car then?

Mr. WORRELL. No, sir. I didn't do that because I mean I didn't know if there was one or more guns, because I wondered why if it was in such rapid succession being a bolt action, I found out later, and I didn't know what was coming off, so I was running to the back of the building because I figured that would be the safest place.

Senator COOPER. Did you see anyone in the windows, in the Texas Depository Building?

Mr. WORRELL. No, sir.

Senator COOPER. Did you notice where this man you have described later as running away from the building, did you see him come out of the building?

Mr. WORRELL. Yes, sir.

Senator COOPER. Where?

Mr. WORRELL. At the back entrance. Approximately where I put the mark "Z."

Senator COOPER. Was he running all the time you saw him?

Mr. WORRELL. Yes, sir, he sure was.

Senator COOPER. That is all.

Mr. WRIGHT. Prior to hearing the first shot, had you looked up at the School Book Depository Building?

Mr. WORRELL. No, sir; I sure didn't.

Mr. WRIGHT. That is all.

Mr. SPECTER. Were you able to observe the direction of the barrel which you have described?

Mr. WORRELL. Pointing right down at the motorcade.

Mr. SPECTER. Any special part of the motorcade?

Mr. WORRELL. I mean, I couldn't really say that because it was too high up and he could have been pointing at anyone of the cars. I mean I couldn't tell from where I was standing.

Mr. SPECTER. Was it on the part of the motorcade which had turned down Elm Street or on the part of the motorcade that was still on Houston or what?

Mr. WORRELL. It was the part that was turned down Elm Street.

Mr. SPECTER. Mr. Worrell, we have a report of the Federal Bureau of Investigation which contains a purported interview with you, designated as report of Robert P. Gemberling dated November 30, 1963, which has this statement:

"He"—referring to you—"stated that last night when he saw photographs of Lee Harvey Oswald on television he felt this was the person he had seen running away from the building. He stated this person did not look back but he was certain this was a white person since he had a profile view."

My question, first of all, to you: Did you have a profile view of the man who ran away from the building that you described?

Mr. WORRELL. No, sir.

Mr. SPECTER. The second question is, did you tell the FBI that you had a profile view?

Mr. WORRELL. No, sir, I sure didn't.

Mr. SPECTER. Did you tell the FBI agent who interviewed you, that you felt that this person was Lee Harvey Oswald?

Mr. WORRELL. I don't know if I did or not.

Mr. SPECTER. Did you see anyone else leave the building, that is the Texas School Book Depository Building, except the man you have already described to us?

Mr. WORRELL. No, sir.

Mr. SPECTER. I have no further questions, Mr. Chairman.

Senator COOPER. Are there any further questions? I believe we will stand in recess until 2 o'clock.

(Whereupon, at 1:10 p.m., the President's Commission recessed.)

Afternoon Session

TESTIMONY OF AMOS LEE EUINS

The President's Commission reconvened at 2:15 p.m.

The CHAIRMAN. The Commission will come to order.

Amos, will you stand up, please, and raise your right hand?

Do you solemnly swear the testimony you will give before this Commission will be the truth, the whole truth, and nothing but the truth, so help you God?

Mr. EUINS. Yes, sir.

The CHAIRMAN. You may be seated. How old are you?

Mr. EUINS. Sixteen.

The CHAIRMAN. All right.

Mr. SPECTER. Mr. Chief Justice, should we start by reading the purpose?

The CHAIRMAN. Yes. I think you received a copy of this statement. But I just want to say to you that the purpose of today's hearing is to hear the testimony of Arnold Louis Rowland, James Richard Worrell, Robert H. Jackson, and yourself who were in the vicinity of the assassination scene on November 22, 1963. The Commission proposes to ask you facts concerning your knowledge of the assassination of President Kennedy.

You understand that?

Mr. EUINS. Yes.

The CHAIRMAN. All right.

Mr. SPECTER. Would you tell us your full name for the record, please?

Mr. EUINS. Amos Lee Euins.

Mr. SPECTER. What is your exact date of birth, Amos?

Mr. EUINS. January 10, 1948.

Mr. SPECTER. January 10, 1948?

Mr. EUINS. Yes, sir.

Mr. SPECTER. And are you a school boy at the present time?

Mr. EUINS. Yes, sir.

Mr. SPECTER. What school do you go to?

Mr. EUINS. Franklin D. Roosevelt.

Mr. SPECTER. What grade are you in at that school?

Mr. EUINS. The ninth.

Mr. SPECTER. Do you live with your parents, Amos?

Mr. EUINS. Yes, sir.

Mr. SPECTER. How is your health generally?

Mr. EUINS. I guess it is all right.

Mr. SPECTER. How are your eyes?

Mr. EUINS. They are all right.

Mr. SPECTER. Can you see good at a distance?

Mr. EUINS. Yes, I can see good at a distance, but I can't see at real close range.

Mr. SPECTER. Are you able to read without glasses?

Mr. EUINS. Yes, sir.

Mr. SPECTER. You don't use glasses for any purposes, then?

Mr. EUINS. No, sir.

Mr. SPECTER. When you say you have trouble at close range, just what do you mean by that?

Mr. EUINS. You know, like I put something on real close.

Mr. SPECTER. Indicating about 4 or 5 inches from your eyes?

Mr. EUINS. Yes, sir. And then they kind of get dim. But on a long scene, I can see good.

Mr. SPECTER. How are your grades in school, Amos?

Mr. EUINS. They are all right.

Mr. SPECTER. Are they better than average, or what?

Mr. EUINS. They are about average.

Mr. SPECTER. All right.

Going back to November 22, 1963, that is last year, Amos, do you recall what you were doing early on that morning?

Mr. EUINS. Yes, sir. When I first got up, I went to school. Then about 11:30, well, the teachers called us and told us the ones that wanted to go downtown to see the President come down to the office and get an excuse and they could go. So I went down to the office, and I got an excuse, so I went downtown.

Mr. SPECTER. And what time did you leave school?

Mr. EUINS. 11:30.

Mr. SPECTER. And where did you go from your school?

Mr. EUINS. Downtown.

Mr. SPECTER. What part of downtown?

Mr. EUINS. Right over by the county jail.

Mr. SPECTER. Do you know the names of those streets, Amos?

Mr. EUINS. No, sir.

Mr. SPECTER. If I told you they were Elm and Houston, would that help your memory as to what the names of those streets were ?

Mr. EUINS. It was right by the freeway.

Mr. SPECTER. All right. Let me show you a photograph, Amos, which is on a document I have marked as Commission Exhibit No. 365.

(The document referred to was marked Commission Exhibit No. 365 for identification.)

Mr. SPECTER. Take just a minute and look at that, and see if you can recognize where that is.

Mr. EUINS. This is going across the railroad tracks, back up to here—right here at the corner is the Book Depository Building.

Mr. SPECTER. That is the Book Depository Building, you say?

Mr. EUINS. Yes, sir.

Mr. SPECTER. All right.

Why don't you just put an "X" with this pencil on the Book Depository Building, as you identify it there, Amos—on the building itself.

(Witness marking.)

Mr. SPECTER. Now, were you somewhere in that area when the President's motorcade went by?

Mr. EUINS. I was right here.

Mr. SPECTER. Why don't you take this black pencil and put an "A" right where you were, Amos.

(Witness marking.)

Mr. SPECTER. Now, what time did you get to the place where you have marked with an "A"?

Mr. EUINS. Oh, I would say around about 15 minutes or something like that to 12, because my mother brought me down there.

Mr. SPECTER. She drove you down, did she?

Mr. EUINS. Yes, sir.

Mr. SPECTER. Now, were you with anybody when you came to that spot, or did your mother leave you off there by yourself?

Mr. EUINS. She left me. She had to go on to work.

Mr. SPECTER. Now, about how long was it after you got there that the motorcade came by?

Mr. EUINS. Oh, I would say about—I had been there about 15, maybe 20 minutes. It come around the corner, come on around.

Mr. SPECTER. All right.

Amos, I want to show you another picture here that I have marked as Commission Exhibit No. 366.

(The document referred to was marked Commission Exhibit No. 366 for identification.)

Mr. SPECTER. I ask you if you can recognize what that building is.

Mr. EUINS. This here is the Book Depository Building.

Mr. SPECTER. All right.

Now, look back over here at 365. Can you tell us which direction the President's motorcade came from on this picture?

Mr. EUINS. It come from right in here.

Mr. SPECTER. First of all, do you know what the name of this street is? Would that be Main Street, in Dallas?

Mr. EUINS. Yes, sir; I think so.

Mr. SPECTER. Coming down Main Street, indicating in a general westerly direction. Turning which way?

Mr. EUINS. This way.

Mr. SPECTER. Turned right.

Do you know if that is Houston Street?

Mr. EUINS. No, sir; I don't.

Mr. SPECTER. Let the record show the witness is identifying a street heretofore identified as Houston.

Then which way did the motorcade go after proceeding in a general northerly direction on Houston?

Mr. EUINS. It come this way, turn.

Mr. SPECTER. Which way—right or left?

Mr. EUINS. It turned to the left, coming down, going on.

Mr. SPECTER. Do you know the name of the street it turned onto when it made the left turn?

Mr. EUINS. I was just trying to keep an eye on the President.

Mr. SPECTER. The witness has identified a street heretofore identified as Elm Street.

Tell us what you saw as the motorcade went by.

Mr. EUINS. I was standing here on the corner. And then the President come around the corner right here. And I was standing here. And I was waving, because there wasn't hardly no one on the corner right there but me. I was waving. He looked that way and he waved back at me. And then I had seen a pipe, you know, up there in the window, I thought it was a pipe, some kind of pipe.

Mr. SPECTER. When had you first seen that thing you just described as a pipe?

Mr. EUINS. Right as he turned the corner here.

Mr. SPECTER. Now, exactly where did you see that thing you have described as a pipe come from. And take a good look now before you tell us where it was.

Mr. EUINS. Right here.

Mr. SPECTER. Now, will you mark an "X" on Exhibit No. 366 where you saw the pipe? Mark the exact window, if you can, Amos.

(Witness marking.)

Mr. SPECTER. All right.

Proceed to tell us what happened, Amos.

Mr. EUINS. Then I was standing here, and as the motorcade turned the corner, I was facing, looking dead at the building. And so I seen this pipe thing sticking out the window. I wasn't paying too much attention to it. Then when the first shot was fired, I started looking around, thinking it was a backfire. Everybody else started looking around. Then I looked up at the window, and he shot again. So—you know this fountain bench here, right around here. Well, anyway, there is a little fountain right here. I got behind this little fountain, and then he shot again.

So after he shot again, he just started looking down this, you know.

Mr. SPECTER. Who started looking down that way?

Mr. EUINS. The man in the window. I could see his hand, and I could see his other hand on the trigger, and one hand was on the barrel thing.

Mr. SPECTER. All right.

Now, at the time the second shot was fired, where were you looking then?

Mr. EUINS. I was still looking at the building, you know, behind this—I was looking at the building.

Mr. SPECTER. Looking at anything special in the building?

Mr. EUINS. Yes, sir. I was looking where the barrel was sticking out.

Mr. SPECTER. How many shots did you hear altogether?

Mr. EUINS. I believe there was four, to be exact.

Mr. SPECTER. Now, where were you looking at the time of the third shot, if you remember?

Mr. EUINS. After he shot the first two times, I was just standing back here. And then after he shot again, he pulled the gun back in the window. And then all the police ran back over here in the track vicinity.

Mr. SPECTER. Slow down just a little bit in what you are telling us.

When the second shot occurred, were you still standing at the point where you marked with an "A" on 365?

Mr. EUINS. Yes, sir. But I was right behind this little——

Mr. SPECTER. Were you a little bit behind of where that "A" is?

Mr. EUINS. Yes, sir; right back here.

Mr. SPECTER. Let's mark that with a "B," where you were at the time the second shot occurred.

(Witness marking.)

Mr. SPECTER. All right.

Now, when the third shot occurred, Amos, let me ask you again, where were you looking then?

Mr. EUINS. I was still down here, looking up at the building.

Mr. SPECTER. What did you see in the building?

Mr. EUINS. I seen a bald spot on this man's head, trying to look out the window. He had a bald spot on his head. I was looking at the bald spot. I could see his hand, you know the rifle laying across in his hand. And I could see his hand sticking out on the trigger part. And after he got through, he just pulled it back in the window.

Mr. SPECTER. Did you see him pull it back in the window?

Mr. EUINS. Yes, sir.

Mr. SPECTER. And were you still standing at point B?

Mr. EUINS. Yes.

Mr. SPECTER. When he pulled it back in the window?

Mr. EUINS. I was still behind here, yes.

Mr. SPECTER. Where were you when you heard what you described as the fourth shot?

Mr. DUINS. The first shot I was standing here.

Mr. SPECTER. Now you are referring to 366. Put an "L" on 366 where you were standing at the first shot.

Mr. EUINS. Right here.

(Witness marking.)

Mr. EUINS. And then as I looked up there, you know, he fired another shot. you know, as I was looking. So I got behind this fountain thing right in there, at this point B.

Mr. SPECTER. At point B on 365?

Mr. EUINS. I got behind there. And then I watched, he did fire again. Then he started looking down towards my way, and then he fired again.

Mr. SPECTER. The question I have for you now is where were you when he fired on that fourth time.

Mr. EUINS. I was still behind point B.

Mr. SPECTER. You were still at point B when he fired the fourth time?

Mr. EUINS. Yes, sir. Then he pulled the gun back in the window.

Mr. SPECTER. Did you see him pull the gun back in the window after the fourth shot?

Mr. EUINS. Yes; he just come back like this.

Mr. SPECTER. Did you watch what he did after that?

Mr. EUINS. No, sir; because after he had pulled it back in the window, I ran this way, and went across the tracks.

Mr. SPECTER. All right.

You start on Exhibit 365, and put the black mark and show us the path of where you ran on 365.

Mr. EUINS. I was here at "B."

(At this point, Representative Ford entered the hearing room.)

(Witness marking.)

Mr. EUINS. I was coming down like this here, and there was a policeman, you know there is a little cut you can come through there. There was a policeman standing right around here.

Mr. SPECTER. Where was the policeman standing? Mark that with point "C," Amos.

Mr. EUINS. Right there.

(Witness marking.)

Mr. SPECTER. You ran past the policeman standing at point C?

Mr. EUINS. No, sir. You see, I come from point B, and ran here, and told the policeman I had seen the shot, because they were looking at the railroad tracks. So he put me on the cycle and he went to here.

Mr. SPECTER. He put you on the cycle and took you where?

Mr. EUINS. Up to the front of the building.

Mr. SPECTER. The Texas School Book Depository Building?

Mr. EUINS. Yes, sir; and then he called some more cars. They got all around the building. And then the policemen came from the tracks, and they got around the building.

Mr. SPECTER. Did you see the policemen come from the tracks to go around the building?

Mr. EUINS. Yes, sir.

Mr. SPECTER. About how many policemen were there, would you say, Amos?

Mr. EUINS. There was about 14 or something like that. They were coming from the tracks here.

Mr. SPECTER. Do you know what the name of that policeman was, who was in that position where you have marked C?

Mr. EUINS. No, sir. He was kind of an old policeman. I ran down and got him. And he ran up here.

Mr. SPECTER. You mean——

Mr. EUINS. The Book Depository Building.

Then he called some more cars. They got all the way around the building. And then after that, well, he seen another man. Another man told him he seen a man run out the back.

Mr. SPECTER. Do you know who that man was who said somebody ran out the back?

Mr. EUINS. No, sir. He was a construction man working back there.

Mr. SPECTER. Were you there when the man talked about somebody running out the back?

Mr. EUINS. Yes, sir. He said the man had—he said he had kind of bald spot on his head. And he said the man come back there.

Mr. SPECTER. Do you know what the name of the man was who told the police that someone had run out the back?

Mr. EUINS. No, sir.

Mr. SPECTER. What did you do next, Amos?

Mr. EUINS. So then they took me over to the county jail. And that is where I told them what happened. And then they was standing around the Book Depository Building, and I stayed over there to the jailhouse about 6 o'clock. And then they took me home.

Mr. SPECTER. And did they question you about what happened and what you observed on that occasion?

Mr. EUINS. At the jailhouse?

Mr. SPECTER. At the jailhouse.

Mr. EUINS. Yes, sir.

Mr. SPECTER. All right.

Amos, would you tell us everything that you can remember about what you saw about the gun itself?

Mr. EUINS. Well, when I first got here on the corner, the President was coming around the bend. That is when—I was looking at the building then.

Mr. SPECTER. What did you think it was when you first saw it?

Mr. EUINS. I thought it was a piece of pipe or something sticking out the window.

Mr. SPECTER. Did it look like it was a piece of metal to you?

Mr. EUINS. Yes, sir; just a little round piece of pipe.

Mr. SPECTER. About an inch in diameter, would you say?

Mr. EUINS. Yes, sir.

Mr. SPECTER. And how long was the piece of pipe that you saw?

Mr. EUINS. It was sticking out about that much.

Mr. SPECTER. About 14 or 15 inches?

Mr. EUINS. Yes, sir. And then after I seen it sticking out, after awhile, that is when I heard the shot, and everybody started looking around.

Mr. SPECTER. At that time, Amos, did you see anything besides the end of the pipe?

Mr. EUINS. No, sir.

Mr. SPECTER. For example, you didn't see anything about a stock or any other part of the rifle?

Mr. EUINS. No, sir—not with the first shot. You see, the President was still right along down in here somewhere on the first shot.

Mr. SPECTER. Now, when you saw it on the first occasion, did you think it was a rifle then? Or did that thought enter your mind?

Mr. EUINS. No, sir; I wasn't thinking about it then. But when I was looking at it, when he shot, it sounded like a high-powered rifle, after I listened to it awhile, because I had been in the NDCC for about a year.

Mr. SPECTER. What is NDCC?

Mr. EUINS. We call it a military army for the boys, at our school.

Mr. SPECTER. Is that ROTC?

Mr. EUINS. Yes, sir.

Mr. SPECTER. ROTC. And have you had any opportunity to fire a weapon in that ROTC class?

Mr. EUINS. No, sir; not outside of just .22's. We fire them on the firing range.

Mr. SPECTER. All right.

Now, when you looked up at the rifle later, you described seeing some of the trigger part.

Mr. EUINS. Yes, sir.

Mr. SPECTER. Now, describe as fully as you can for us what you saw then, Amos.

Mr. EUINS. Well, when he stuck it out, you know—after the President had come on down the street further, you know he kind of stuck it out more, you know.

Mr. SPECTER. How far was it sticking out of the window would you say then, Amos?

Mr. EUINS. I would say it was about something like that.

Mr. SPECTER. Indicating about 3 feet?

Mr. EUINS. You know—the trigger housing and stock and receiver group out the window.

Mr. SPECTER. I can't understand you, Amos.

Mr. EUINS. It was enough to get the stock and receiving house and the trigger housing to stick out the window.

Mr. SPECTER. The stock and receiving house?

Mr. EUINS. Yes.

Mr. SPECTER. Now, what direction was the rifle pointing?

Mr. EUINS. Down—what did you say—Elm?

Mr. SPECTER. Elm Street?

Mr. EUINS. Yes, sir; down Elm.

Mr. SPECTER. Was it pointing in the direction of the President?

Mr. EUINS. Yes, sir.

Mr. SPECTER. Now, could you see anything else on the gun?

Mr. EUINS. No, sir; I could not.

Mr. SPECTER. For example, could you see whether or not there was a telescopic lens on the gun?

Mr. EUINS. No, sir.

Mr. SPECTER. Now, is there anything else about the gun that you can describe to us that you have not already told us about?

Mr. EUINS. No, sir.

Mr. SPECTER. Now, what kind of a look, if any, did you have at the man who was there?

Mr. EUINS. All I got to see was the man with a spot in his head, because he had his head something like this.

Mr. SPECTER. Indicating his face down, looking down the rifle?

Mr. EUINS. Yes, sir: and I could see the spot on his head.

Mr. SPECTER. How would you describe that man for us?

Mr. EUINS. I wouldn't know how to describe him, because all I could see was the spot and his hand.

Mr. SPECTER. Was he slender or was he fat?

Mr. EUINS. I didn't get to see him.

Mr. SPECTER. Could you tell from where you looked whether he was tall or short?

Mr. EUINS. No.

Mr. SPECTER. Of what race was he, Amos?

Mr. EUINS. I couldn't tell, because these boxes were throwing a reflection, shaded.

Mr. SPECTER. Could you tell whether he was a Negro gentleman or a white man?

Mr. EUINS. No, sir.

Mr. SPECTER. Couldn't even tell that? But you have described that he had a bald——

Mr. EUINS. Spot in his head. Yes, sir; I could see the bald spot in his head.

Mr. SPECTER. Now, could you tell what color hair he had?

Mr. EUINS. No, sir.

Mr. SPECTER. Could you tell whether his hair was dark or light?

Mr. EUINS. No, sir.

Mr. SPECTER. How far back did the bald spot on his head go?

Mr. EUINS. I would say about right along in here.

Mr. SPECTER. Indicating about 2½ inches above where you hairline is. Is that about what you are saying?

Mr. EUINS. Yes, sir; right along in here.

Mr. SPECTER. Now, did you get a very good look at that man, Amos?

Mr. EUINS. No, sir; I did not.

Mr. SPECTER. Were you able to tell anything about the clothes he was wearing?

Mr. EUINS. No, sir.

Mr. SPECTER. Now, when you were at the sheriff's department in the police station that you have described, did they ask you to sign an affidavit or statement for them, Amos?

Mr. EUINS. Yes, sir.

Mr. SPECTER. I now show you a paper, Amos, which I have marked as Commission Exhibit No. 367.

(The document referred to was marked Commission Exhibit No. 367 for identification.)

Mr. SPECTER. This is supposed to be a statement which is signed. Let me first point out to you that it is a copy of it. I ask you if this is a copy of your signature?

Mr. EUINS. Yes, sir.

Mr. SPECTER. All right.

Now, will you take your time, Amos, and read that over, and then I want to ask you a couple of questions about it.

Did you have a chance to read it over?

Mr. EUINS. Yes, sir.

Mr. SPECTER. All right.

Let me ask you about a couple of specific things here, Amos.

In the statement you say here that he was a white man. By reading the statement, does that refresh your memory as to whether he was a white man or not?

Mr. EUINS. No, sir; I told the man that I could see a white spot on his head, but I didn't actually say it was a white man. I said I couldn't tell. But I saw a white spot in his head.

Mr. SPECTER. Your best recollection at this moment is you still don't know whether he was a white man or a Negro? All you can say is that you saw a white spot on his head?

Mr. EUINS. Yes, sir.

Mr. SPECTER. Then, did you tell the people at the police station that he was a white man, or did they make a mistake when they wrote that down here?

Mr. EUINS. They must have made a mistake, because I told them I could see a white spot on his head.

Mr. SPECTER. Now, is there anything else in this statement, Amos, which is different from the way you remember this event, as you are sitting here right now?

Amos, did you understand the last question?

Mr. EUINS. Yes, sir.

Mr. SPECTER. Did you answer it for us?

Mr. EUINS. No, sir; I don't think there is.

Mr. SPECTER. I don't understand you, Amos. The question I am trying to get at it, as you read that statement over now, you have testified or told us here today what you remember about this assassination?

Mr. EUINS. Yes, sir.

Mr. SPECTER. And I am asking you, when you read that statement over, is there anything on that statement which you think is wrong, based on what you remember right now?

For example, you told us that they were wrong when they wrote down that you identified him as a white man. Were they wrong about anything else that they wrote down?

Mr. EUINS. Not that I can see.

Mr. SPECTER. All right.

When you looked up and saw this man, Amos, did he have on a hat?

Mr. EUINS. No, sir.

Mr. SPECTER. Did you notice any boxes behind him at that time, Amos?

Mr. EUINS. Yes, sir; there were some boxes, you know, all the side of the window. Like this window—there were some boxes in these windows up here.

Mr. SPECTER. You saw some boxes in these windows?

Mr. EUINS. In these windows, and these windows, and there was boxes in half of this one.

Mr. SPECTER. All right.

Now, mark the windows where you saw those boxes, Amos. Start off with—mark the window "Y" where you saw boxes.

(Witness marking.)

Mr. SPECTER. You made a figure 9, as I read it, on the two places you saw boxes in the windows.

Mr. EUINS. Yes, sir; in this half.

Mr. SPECTER. Now, were there boxes in the window marked "X"?

Mr. EUINS. Yes, sir. There were about two or three of them right along here.

Mr. SPECTER. Indicating the middle dividing line there?

Mr. EUINS. Yes, sir.

Mr. SPECTER. Was that window marked "X" opened, Amos, or closed?

Mr. EUINS. It was open.

Mr. SPECTER. How far open was it?

Mr. EUINS. About that high.

Mr. SPECTER. Indicating about 19 inches?

Mr. EUINS. Yes, sir.

Mr. SPECTER. And was the window in the other double window immediately next to the window marked "X" open or closed?

Mr. EUINS. The top window, on the sixth floor?

Mr. SPECTER. I am referring to the window right next to it.

Mr. EUINS. No, sir; it was not open.

Mr. SPECTER. Amos, when you heard the first shot, did you have any reaction or impression as to where the noise was coming from at that exact time?

Mr. EUINS. No, sir; not at the exact time. You know, because everybody else started looking around. So I just started looking around, thinking it was a backfire, just like everyone else.

Mr. SPECTER. Did you look up towards that window before the second shot, or just when the second shot occurred?

Mr. EUINS. I think—just a little before, because as soon as I did, I looked at it—pow.

Mr. SPECTER. You heard a pow?

Mr. EUINS. Yes, sir.

Mr. SPECTER. Now, as you were watching and heard, did you have the impression that the noise you heard was coming from that rifle?

Mr. EUINS. No, sir; I didn't, because I wasn't thinking of the rifle at first—you know, because it looked like a pipe at first.

Mr. SPECTER. When you say the second—when you heard the second shot, when you say you were looking at the rifle, did you have the feeling that the noise came from the rifle when you heard the second shot, when you were looking at it?

Mr. EUINS. No, sir; I did not.

Mr. SPECTER. Well, did you have any impression at all about where the noise was coming from?

Mr. EUINS. No, sir; not on the first shot.

Mr. SPECTER. How about the second shot?

Mr. EUINS. Yes, sir.

Mr. SPECTER. Where did you think the noise was coming from on the second shot?

Mr. EUINS. I seen him shoot on the second shot.

Mr. SPECTER. So you thought the noise was coming from the rifle on the second shot?

Mr. EUINS. Yes, sir.

The CHAIRMAN. Did you say you thought, or saw?

Mr. EUINS. I saw him shoot the second shot.

Mr. SPECTER. How high were those boxes behind him, Amos?

Mr. EUINS. They was probably about 2 feet high stacked in the back of him.

Mr. SPECTER. Amos, were you questioned later by the FBI?

Mr. EUINS. Yes, sir; over in the office.

Mr. SPECTER. How many times were you questioned by the FBI?

Mr. EUINS. Oh, once.

Mr. SPECTER. Do you remember when that was?

Mr. EUINS. It was around about 2 or 3 o'clock.

Mr. SPECTER. Do you remember how many days after the assassination it was?

Mr. EUINS. About 4.

Mr. SPECTER. You think they might have talked to you more than once?

Mr. EUINS. No, sir.

Mr. SPECTER. Mr. Chief Justice, I move for the admission into evidence of the statement marked Commission Exhibit 367.

The CHAIRMAN. That may be admitted.

(The document heretofore marked for identification as Commission Exhibit No. 367 was received in evidence.)

Mr. SPECTER. That concludes the questioning I have, sir.

The CHAIRMAN. Mr. Wright?

Mr. WRIGHT. Nothing further, Mr. Chief Justice.

Mr. SPECTER. Mr. Chief Justice, I would like to move for the admission into evidence of all the exhibits here—365, 366, as well as 367.

The CHAIRMAN. Very well.

(The documents heretofore marked for identication as Commission Exhibits Nos. 365 and 366, were received in evidence.)

The CHAIRMAN. Amos, you may be excused, then. Thank you very much for coming and helping us out with your testimony.

We will recess until tomorrow morning at 9 o'clock.

Wednesday, March 11, 1964

TESTIMONY OF BUELL WESLEY FRAZIER, LINNIE MAE RANDLE, AND CORTLANDT CUNNINGHAM

The President's Commission met at 9:45 a.m. on March 11, 1964, at 200 Maryland Avenue NE., Washington, D.C.

Present were Chief Justice Earl Warren, Chairman; Senator John Sherman Cooper and Representative Gerald R. Ford, members.

Also present were J. Lee Rankin, general counsel; Joseph A. Ball, assistant counsel; David W. Belin, assistant counsel; Albert E. Jenner, Jr., assistant counsel; Wesley J. Liebeler, assistant counsel; Norman Redlich, assistant counsel; Charles Murray and Lewis E. Powell, Jr., observers.

TESTIMONY OF BUELL WESLEY FRAZIER

The CHAIRMAN. The Commission will be in order.

Mr. BALL. I would like to assign Commission Exhibit No. 364 to a paper sack which the FBI has identified as their C-109 Exhibit. That will be the Commission's Exhibit No. 364 for identification at this time.

The CHAIRMAN. All right.

(The paper sack referred to was marked Commission's Exhibit No. 364 for identification.)

Mr. BALL. Also for the record I would like to announce that prior to—this morning, Mr. Cortlandt Cunningham and Charles Killion of the Federal Bureau of Investigation laboratory, the Ballistics Division, Firearms Division, I guess it is, broke down, that is unscrewed Commission Exhibit No. 139, an Italian rifle, and that rifle has been placed in, after being disassembled, has been placed in Commission's No. 364 for identification, that paper sack.

The CHAIRMAN. All right.

Mr. BALL. We have also here before the Commission, Commission No. 142 which is a paper sack which is identified as the FBI's Exhibit No. 10. I think that has its number, exhibit number on it.

I have been informed that was 142. My notes show that the brown paper sack is 142.

I think we can call the witness now.

The CHAIRMAN. All right; would you call Mr. Frazier, please.

Raise your right hand to be sworn, please.

Do you solemnly swear the testimony you will give before this Commission will be the truth, the whole truth and nothing but the truth, so help you God?

Mr. FRAZIER. I do.

The CHAIRMAN. Will you be seated, please?

Mr. FRAZIER. Yes, sir.

The CHAIRMAN. Mr. Joseph Ball of our staff will examine you, Mr. Frazier, but I would like to read a very short statement concerning the purpose of the meeting.

The purpose of today's hearing is to hear the testimony of Buell Wesley Frazier, and Linnie Mae Randle. The Commission has been advised that these two witnesses have stated that they saw Lee Harvey Oswald on the morning of November 22, 1963. The Commission proposes to ask these witnesses questions concerning their knowledge of the assassination of President Kennedy.

You have a copy of this, have you not?

Mr. FRAZIER. Yes, sir.

The CHAIRMAN. All right, you may proceed, Mr. Ball.

Mr. BALL. You call yourself Buell or Wesley?

Mr. FRAZIER. I go by Wesley.

Mr. BALL. Well, Wesley, what is your age?

Mr. FRAZIER. Sir?

Mr. BALL. What is your age?

Mr. FRAZIER. Nineteen.

Mr. BALL. Where do you live?

Mr. FRAZIER. For the time being I am living in Irving now.

Mr. BALL. Irving, Tex.?

Mr. FRAZIER. Yes, sir.

Mr. BALL. What is the address where you live?

Mr. FRAZIER. 2439 West Fifth Street.

Mr. BALL. Did you live there in November 1963?

Mr. FRAZIER. Yes, sir; I did.

Mr. BALL. And who lives in that house with you?

Mr. FRAZIER. My sister and brother-in-law and their three children.

Mr. BALL. Will you state their names, your sister's name?

Mr. FRAZIER. Linnie Mae Randle and my brother-in-law. I believe his real name is William Edward Randle. We call him Bill. They have three little girls, Diana, Patricia and Caroline Sue.

Mr. BALL. Where does your mother live?

Mr. FRAZIER. She lives in Huntsville.

Mr. BALL. Where is that?

Mr. FRAZIER. That is about 200 miles south of Dallas there.

Mr. BALL. What is the name of the town?

Mr. FRAZIER. Town, you mean where my mother lives? Huntsville.

Mr. BALL. Huntsville?

Mr. FRAZIER. Yes, sir; that is about, it is about 70, 80 miles north of Houston.

Mr. BALL. What is your mother's name?

Mr. FRAZIER. Essie Mae Williams.

Mr. BALL. Was she visiting you and your sister sometime in November 1963?

Mr. FRAZIER. Yes, sir; she was.

Mr. BALL. How long was she there?

Mr. FRAZIER. She was there for, I believe, for a period of about 4 or 5 weeks because my stepfather was with her and he got sick and they had to put him in the hospital and he was in the hospital 3 or 4 weeks, somewheres, 4 or 5 weeks because they were there a week before he got sick.

Mr. BALL. Then on November 21 and 22, living with you in this residence at Irving, Tex., were your mother, Mrs. Williams, and your sister, Linnie Mae Randle?

Mr. FRAZIER. Right.

Mr. BELL. And her husband and their three children?

Mr. FRAZIER. That is right.

Mr. BALL. Where do you work?

Mr. FRAZIER. Work at Texas School Books.

Mr. BALL. How long have you worked there?

Mr. FRAZIER. I have been working there since September.

Mr. BALL. September of 1963?

Mr. FRAZIER. Correct.

Mr. BALL. What kind of work do you do there?

Mr. FRAZIER. I fill orders.

Mr. BALL. How did you happen to get that job?

Mr. FRAZIER. Well, I went to see, first I come up there and started looking for a job and couldn't find one myself so I went to one of these employment agencies and through that a lady called up one morning, I was fixing to go out and look for one, I was looking for myself in the meantime when they were, too, and so she called up and gave me a tip to it if I was interested in a job like that I could go over there and see about that and for the time being I wasn't working and needed some money and so I did and I went over there and saw Mr. Truly, and he gave me an interview, and then he hired me the same day I went over there.

Mr. BALL. You say you came up, you mean you came up from Huntsville?

Mr. FRAZIER. That is right; yes, sir.

Mr. BALL. That was in September 1963?

Mr. FRAZIER. Yes, sir; it was.

Mr. BALL. Looking for a job around Dallas?

Mr. FRAZIER. Yes, sir.

Mr. BALL. Did you go to live with your sister at that time?

Mr. FRAZIER. Yes, sir; I did.

Mr. BALL. What—where is the employment agency and what is its name when you first applied for a job?

Mr. FRAZIER. Well, I went to several but, see, this one got me this job the main one was Massey, the employment agency, and it is over there on Shady Grove Road.

Mr. BALL. In Dallas?

Mr. FRAZIER. No, sir; in Irving.

Mr. BALL. How do you spell that name, the name of the employment agency?

Mr. FRAZIER. Massey?

Mr. BALL. Yes.

Mr. FRAZIER. I believe it is M-a-s-s-e-y.

Mr. BALL. And it was a woman at the employment agency that called you and told you to go to see the Texas School Book Depository?

Mr. FRAZIER. Yes, right.

Mr. BALL. And you went to see Mr. Truly and after an interview he gave you a job?

Mr. FRAZIER. Correct.

Mr. BALL. Then you started work there about what date in September?

Mr. FRAZIER. It was the 13th. I say that was the same day I went for an interview. I went early enough that morning that he told me to come back after lunch.

Mr. BALL. And you are still working there?

Mr. FRAZIER. Yes, sir.

Mr. BALL. When Mr. Truly hired you did he tell you it would be a full-time job or just a temporary job?

Mr. FRAZIER. No, sir; he told me that he was looking for somebody full time and I told him, well, that is what I wanted, and so he said that would be just fine.

Mr. BALL. How much did he start to pay you?

Mr. FRAZIER. He started me off with a dollar and a quarter an hour.

Mr. BALL. That is for an eight-hour day?

Mr. FRAZIER. Right. Five days a week.

Mr. BALL. Did you commute back and forth from your sister's home in Irving?

Mr. FRAZIER. Over there to the Texas School Books?

Mr. BALL. To the Texas School Book Depository.

Mr. FRAZIER. Yes, sir.

Mr. BALL. From the first day?

Mr. FRAZIER. Yes, sir.

Mr. BALL. And you still do?

Mr. FRAZIER. Yes, sir.

Mr. BALL. Do you own a car?

Mr. FRAZIER. Yes, sir.

Mr. BALL. Your own car?

Mr. FRAZIER. Yes, sir.

Mr. BALL. You had it, did you, when you started to work?

Mr. FRAZIER. Yes, sir.

Mr. BALL. Still have it?

Mr. FRAZIER. Yes, sir.

Mr. BALL. And you have been since September driving that car from your sister's home in Irving over to the Texas School Book Depository?

Mr. FRAZIER. Correct.

Mr. BALL. Go there in the morning?

Mr. FRAZIER. Right.

Mr. BALL. What time do you get to work?

Mr. FRAZIER. I get there around 8 o'clock.

Mr. BALL. When do you quit?

Mr. FRAZIER. I quit at 4:45.

Mr. BALL. Then you drive home?

Mr. FRAZIER. Yes, sir.

Mr. BALL. How long for lunch?

Mr. FRAZIER. 45 minutes.

Mr. BALL. Do all the employees have the same lunch hour?

Mr. FRAZIER. Now, the ones who work down there filling book orders around where I work now, so we all work the same hours. Some people work up there in the offices, I hear that they come in a little bit later. Now, I don't know for sure but I see primarily the ones who does the same type of work I do, we all start the same time and work the same time

Mr. BALL. Those are the people who fill the orders?

Mr. FRAZIER. Right.

Mr. BALL. How far is it in miles from your sister's home to Texas School Book Depository?

Mr. FRAZIER. It is roughly around 15 miles.

Mr. BALL. And did you take the same route every day?

Mr. FRAZIER. You mean since I have been going over there; since the first day?

Mr. BALL. That is right.

Mr. FRAZIER. Up to now?

Mr. BALL. Yes, right.

Mr. FRAZIER. No, sir; I didn't.

You see, I found two ways, you can more judge by the traffic and you can go some days one way and the traffic will be easier than others, but most times I use just one route.

Mr. BALL. What route did you usually use?

Mr. FRAZIER. Used one like you go down from the house there.

Mr. BALL. Yes.

Mr. FRAZIER. Go down and right Storey Road, see Fifth Street is just one block off Storey Road, and just go down and hit Storey Road and stay on it until you come to Stemmons Freeway and you stay right on Stemmons until you come right on into Dallas there.

Mr. BALL. About what length of time does it take you to go from your sister's home to work in the morning?

Mr. FRAZIER. Usually, I usually leave not any later than 7:25. I usually try to leave about 7:20, and if you leave at 7:20, you usually get around there, by the time you get down to the parking lot now it is usually pretty close to 5 minutes to 8 and that gives you enough time to walk to the Book Depository, put up your lunch and take off your coat.

Mr. BALL. Did you have a place to park your car?

Mr. FRAZIER. Yes, sir.

Mr. BALL. Was it assigned to you by Mr. Truly?

Mr. FRAZIER. No, sir; he just said we had a parking lot there and showed me where it was and said you can park in the parking lot.

Mr. BALL. Was that the parking lot two or three blocks from the building.

Mr. FRAZIER. Yes, sir, it is down there; right across from the warehouse there.

Mr. BALL. Then you would walk from there from that parking lot——

Mr. FRAZIER. Up to the other Depository up there at the corner of Houston and Main.

Mr. BALL. We have here a map which has been marked as Commission's Exhibit No. 361.

Mr. FRAZIER. I see.

Mr. BALL. And north is to the bottom of the map.

Mr. FRAZIER. Yes.

Mr. BALL. Instead of the top, as usually the case.

Mr. FRAZIER. Right.

Mr. BALL. It has two pictures over here, one to the left and one to the right of the map.

Mr. FRAZIER. Right.

Mr. BALL. Let's take a look at the picture to the right of the map. Do you recognize that area?

Mr. FRAZIER. Yes, sir; I do.

Mr. BALL. What is it?

Mr. FRAZIER. I see that is right there where you say that is the street going up to the parking lot there.

Mr. BALL. Do you recognize this car?

Mr. FRAZIER. Yes, sir.

Mr. BALL. What car is that?

Mr. FRAZIER. That is my car.

Mr. BALL. Is that where you usually park every day?

Mr. FRAZIER. Well, I would say at the time being when I first started to work there I first started to park there but now I park on the other side of the fence there.

Mr. BALL. But that is a picture of the parking lot, is it?

Mr. FRAZIER. Right.

Mr. BALL. Where you park is in the parking lot?

Mr. FRAZIER. Yes, sir. I park inside the fence but what I am talking about—I park on the different side of the lot.

Mr. BALL. Different side of the same lot?

Mr. FRAZIER. Yes, sir; we just have one lot there.

Mr. BALL. Do you see the Texas School Book Depository Building?

Mr. FRAZIER. Yes, sir; right there.

Mr. BALL. And you walked from about the place where your car is parked?

Mr. FRAZIER. Yes, sir.

Mr. BALL. Usually up to the Depository Building?

Mr. FRAZIER. Right, correct.

Mr. BALL. Now, the map to the left, upper left-hand corner of the map, there is a picture.

Mr. FRAZIER. Yes, sir.

Mr. BALL. Do you see this area where I point my finger which is marked "parking lot No. 1."

Mr. FRAZIER. Yes, sir.

Mr. BALL. What is that?

Mr. FRAZIER. That is the same parking lot we were looking at right here.

Mr. BALL. What route do you walk, which way do you walk when you park in this parking lot No. 1, to the Texas School Book Depository Building?

Mr. FRAZIER. Do you want me to get up to where I can show it to you?

Mr. BALL. Yes; show it to us.

Mr. FRAZIER. I usually always come up, you know, you can come right, you see the building right down here, and you notice a series of railroad tracks, so usually early in the morning, now about 8 o'clock there is usually not any cars right here, but I say they are switching back and forth.

Mr. BALL. By "cars" you mean railroad cars?

Mr. FRAZIER. Yes, sir; they usually start switching around 8 o'clock. Usually, there are not any cars, it is usually a long train that moves up pretty soon but I usually move up in this direction here, especially when it is dry. When it is wet I walk on this because it is harder. But when it is raining, I usually walk around here, because in this area right here, when you get up closer to the railroad tracks it has more trenches, and it gets muddy and slimy and you can get bogged down.

So, when it is bad weather, I usually walk on this side. But I say nine times out of ten I come up right down here.

Mr. BALL. Let's look at the map. Here is the parking lot here, is that the parking lot where you usually park?

Mr. FRAZIER. Yes, sir; it is.

Mr. BALL. This is parking lot No. 1.

Mr. FRAZIER. That is parking lot No. 1, isn't it?

Mr. BALL. Right.

Mr. FRAZIER. Right.

Mr. BALL. We will show you this map later, but just to illustrate, how do you usually, what is the route you usually take, just show us on the board here, the route you usually take to the Texas School Book Depository Building in the morning?

Mr. FRAZIER. You mean when I am coming off of the freeway?

Mr. BALL. After you park here.

Mr. FRAZIER. You know right here, you say like the car, you notice that little house right there, I assume you have checked off. You know like I was telling you now, I usually park over in this corner. But at the time I parked right there. But anyway, there is a little cyclone fence and this was the series of railroad tracks, I was talking to you about.

Mr. BALL. That is right.

Mr. FRAZIER. I usually come down here.

Mr. BALL. Munger Street?

Mr. FRAZIER. That is right, and usually cross along the railroad tracks and come up here.

Mr. BALL. Houston Street?

Mr. FRAZIER. Houston runs into it, now they are doing some work across the tracks and you can't go any further than the tracks, right along here this line, cyclone, but that type of fence and I usually walk right up, you know.

Mr. BALL. To the buildings?

Mr. FRAZIER. Right.

Mr. BALL. And enter the rear of the building?

Mr. FRAZIER. Yes, sir.

Now, we call it a loading zone out there, dock area.

Mr. BALL. Fine.

Did anyone else ride with you in the morning, usually did anyone else ride with you in the morning from home to work?

Mr. FRAZIER. No, sir; they didn't.

Mr. BALL. Did anybody ride with you from work to home?

Mr. FRAZIER. No, sir; they didn't.

Mr. BALL. When did you first hear of Lee Harvey Oswald, first hear the name?

Mr. FRAZIER. I first heard, I never really did know his name, we just called him Lee around there. But the first time I ever saw him was the first day he come to work.

Mr. BALL. Had you heard he was coming to work before he came to work?

Mr. FRAZIER. I will say, you know, talking back and forth with the bossman all the time and from being around and getting along real fine and so he told me, I assume the day after he hired him that he was going to have him come in on Monday and he asked me had I ever seen him and I told him then no; I had never seen him.

(At this point, Representative Ford entered the hearing room.)

Mr. BALL. Had your sister told you that this fellow Lee was coming to work?

Mr. FRAZIER. Yes; she did. She said one afternoon when I went home she told me she found out from one of the neighbors there he came over for that interview with Mr. Truly and Mr. Truly had hired him.

Mr. BALL. You heard that from your sister?

Mr. FRAZIER. Yes.

Mr. BALL. Before you saw him?

Mr. FRAZIER. Right, before I saw him.

Mr. BALL. When you first saw him was it a Monday morning?

Mr. FRAZIER. Yes; it was.

Mr. BALL. Do you have any idea of the date itself, do you have any memory of the date when you first saw him?

Mr. FRAZIER. No, sir; I don't.

Mr. BALL. Was it sometime around the middle of October, do you think, would that be close to it?

Mr. FRAZIER. It could have been because it was sometime in October because I remember I went to work there on the 13th and I had been working there, 4 or 5 weeks and then he come there.

Mr. BALL. Where was he when you first saw him?

Mr. FRAZIER. I first saw him he was—we have a table not as large as this, but just about half as large as this, and we have just like you walk up to it where I am sitting over here and we have four or five boxes there and we have different names on it, you know, for different publishing companies, and he was there getting some orders, and I say, as well as I remember, I said, the foreman there was getting him out some real easy orders. Some of the orders we have are real easy to fill, easier than the others, you don't have to know so much about the textbooks to be able to fill them and he was getting some of them easy ones out to start on, when we have a great number of them, you see, the little pamphlet type books and all we do is count them out and read the invoice number.

Mr. BALL. What was the name of the foreman showing him?

Mr. FRAZIER. You mean the foreman, that was Mr. Shelly.

Mr. BALL. S-h-e-d?

Mr. FRAZIER. S-h-e-l-l-y.

Mr. BALL. Shelly.

What floor was this on?

Mr. FRAZIER. It was on the first floor there.

Mr. BALL. Did Shelly introduce you to him or did you go up and shake hands with him?

Mr. FRAZIER. No, sir; he didn't. I remember, I knew, you know that he was going to be coming to work so naturally I hadn't been there very long, you know, living in Dallas and so I wanted to make friends with everybody I could, because you know yourself friendship is something you can't buy with money and you always need friends, so I went up and introduced himself to myself, and he told me his name was Lee and I said "We are glad to have you."

We got talking back and forth and he come to find out I knew his wife was staying down there at the time with this other woman and so I thought he would go out there and I said, "Are you going to be going home this afternoon?"

And he told me then, he told me that he didn't have a car, you know, and so I told him, I said, "Well, I live out there in Irving,"—I found out he lived out there and so I said, "Any time you want to go just let me know."

So I thought he would go home every day like most men do but he told me no, that he wouldn't go home every day and then he asked me could he ride home say like Friday afternoon on weekends and come back on Monday morning and I told him that would be just fine with me.

I told him if he wanted a ride any other time just let me know before I go off and leave him because when it comes to quitting time some of these guys, you know, some of them mess around the bathroom and some of them quit early and some of them like that and some leave at different times than others.

But I said from talking to him then, I say, he just wanted to ride home on weekends with me and I said that was fine.

Mr. BALL. Did he say at that time he was living in Dallas, he had a room in Dallas?

Mr. FRAZIER. Yes, sir; he did. He had an apartment.

Mr. Ball. Did he say where?

Mr. Frazier. No, sir; he didn't. He just said he had an apartment over in Dallas.

Mr. Ball. Had you known his wife before that? Had you ever met his wife, Marina Oswald?

Mr. Frazier. No, sir; I never had.

Mr. Ball. Had you heard that a Russian girl was staying there in the neighborhood?

Mr. Frazier. Well, I say about this time I met him, you know, I knew that at the time then but I didn't think anything about it because, you know, the people travel from one country to the next all the time.

Mr. Ball. Did you know Mrs. Paine, Ruth Paine?

Mr. Frazier. No, sir; I didn't until all this had happened because I will be frank with you, people around there. I say, they just don't make friends very easy. I say you can have somebody living three doors from you and you can live a couple of years and you still might not know the name.

Mr. Ball. And you had never met Mrs. Ruth Paine before the day you met Lee Oswald?

Mr. Frazier. No.

Mr. Ball. What kind of work did Lee do, what kind of work was assigned to him?

Mr. Frazier. He filled orders like I do and several other men.

Mr. Ball. How many order fillers were there employed at that time?

Mr. Frazier. Oh, I would say roughly around five, six at that time. Because about the time we was real busy, the busy season. I come there, you know, and they was going pretty good when I went to work there and I say we were still going pretty good when he come to work there.

We had a lot of work to do and usually when we have a lot of work to do we have more order fillers.

Mr. Ball. Did he ride home with you in your car on weekends?

Mr. Frazier. Yes, sir; he did.

Mr. Ball. On Friday nights.

Mr. Frazier. Right.

Mr. Ball. From that time until November 22, did he ride home with you every weekend?

Mr. Frazier. No, sir; he did every weekend but one.

Mr. Ball. Do you remember that date?

Mr. Frazier. No, sir; I don't.

Mr. Ball. In the statement you made I believe you said it was the 16th and 17th of November. I am just reminding you of that.

Does it refresh your memory any?

Mr. Frazier. I remember one weekend, I say, right now I can't recall because just to be frank with you I couldn't tell you roughly; I say I might have at that time but I say it slipped my mind but the thing is I do know he rode home with me every weekend up to that but one.

Mr. Ball. And why did—did he tell you why he wasn't going to ride home that weekend?

Mr. Frazier. Yes, he did. He said he was working on his driving license and he was going to go take a driving test.

Mr. Ball. Did you ever ask him afterward if he had taken his driver's test?

Mr. Frazier. No, sir; I never did. I assumed that he had taken it and passed it what part of the test he was taking.

Most men do, I say, they usually work at it, study at it good enough so they don't flunk out.

Representative Ford. Do you have to get a learner's permit in Texas before you can get a driver's permit?

Mr. Frazier. No, sir; I say, you don't. Just two steps to it. I say, first no matter what age you are; say, when you have to be at least 14 is about the youngest you can get it in Texas and then you have to take a DE, Driver's Education, if you are going to school but otherwise, the age is 16 and you just go around to the driving license bureau there, they have an office in most any

217

town of any size in Texas, and you just go in and see the driving license man and just tell him that you plan to take your driving test and you would like to have the auto manual, and the manual covers any laws and so forth in the State of Texas, and you can either study for your operator's or your commercial and you pick out which one you want, and you study up for it and then he is there, he tells you what days he is in his office, and so he goes there a certain time and he gives you several sheets of paper, a quiz and you answer them questions, and if you—you have to make a grade of 70 on it to pass and if you make a grade of 70 or above, well, I say, in another week or two you go down there and you say like for instance if you are going to want a driver's license for a car——

Representative FORD. Did Lee ever ask you or did Lee ever tell you whether he had ever actually applied for a driver's license?

Mr. FRAZIER. No, sir; he never had, except I told you that weekend that he said he was going down to take his driving test, and so I knew from being in the State of Texas that you have to know something; you have to have the manuals and so forth to study up on it. Or there isn't any use going down there if you don't know the rules because you are not wasting any time but your own.

Mr. BALL. Do you remember whether or not one weekend that he didn't go down with you but he rode back with you, say, on the Armistice Day holiday? Do you remember?

Mr. FRAZIER. No, sir; I don't.

Mr. BALL. Your memory is that he went, he rode home with you every Friday and came back the following Monday?

Mr. FRAZIER. Yes.

Mr. BALL. Except this one weekend?

Mr. FRAZIER. Right, that is what I say. If he went home with me on Friday afternoon he always rode back with me on Monday morning. It wasn't no added job when he would come with me on the weekend. He would ride home with me on Friday and he would come back with me on Monday.

Mr. BALL. Did he ever tell you that he had or had not applied for a driver's license?

Mr. FRAZIER. No; he had not except he told me he was going down to take it.

Mr. BALL. He never told you that he had or had not?

Mr. FRAZIER. No.

Mr. BALL. And he never told you whether he had obtained a driver's license?

Mr. FRAZIER. No, sir; he didn't.

Mr. BALL. Did you ever talk to him on whether or not he could drive a car, knew how to drive a car?

Mr. FRAZIER. Well, I say, I believe the first afternoon, the first time we was going home and we were talking about that and he said he was working on his driving license then, and then naturally like I told you several weeks later, then he told me he was going to take his driving test and I assumed he could drive a car being as old as he was because most everybody in the State of Texas by the time you are my age if you can't drive a car something is wrong with you.

Mr. BALL. He did never say whether he could or couldn't?

Mr. FRAZIER. Right.

Mr. BALL. Did he ever ask you about the parts of a car?

Mr. FRAZIER. No, sir; I don't believe he did.

Mr. BALL. Do you remember any conversation when he asked you what the clutch was?

Mr. FRAZIER. Oh, yes. We got talking about that. He noticed, you know, most cars as old as mine, you know most of them are standard shift, and when I bought this old car it kind of fooled me it had automatic transmission on it so we got talking about it on the way home driving home and I told him that I really prefer a standard because you know, they are a lot easier to work on and you know, when an automatic goes dead it goes dead, there is no rolling

218

a couple of feet and jumping on the clutch and starting when the battery is down.

And I remember he said it was a little bit different to drive with a clutch. I said, if you are not used to it, but if you get used to it. You have to find a friction point on any car, even on Chevrolet or Ford, you know yourself the friction points on a clutch and the brakes are different adjusted on every car you drive.

And I told you there is nothing you do. You just have to get used to a car of the individual, you can drive one car to do it, and you can drive another one it may take you a couple of days to get used to it.

Mr. BALL. He is the one who mentioned the clutch, is he, that you didn't have a clutch?

Mr. FRAZIER. Right.

I guess he noticed that I didn't have a clutch.

Mr. BALL. I see.

Did he pay for any part of the trip, buy your gasoline?

Mr. FRAZIER. No, sir; he didn't. I never did ask him. Because like I said I drove over there anyway and it doesn't take any more to drive one guy than it does to drive a carload.

Mr. BALL. Did he offer to pay any time?

Mr. FRAZIER. No, sir; he never did.

Mr. BALL. At any time coming back after a weekend did you ever stop at a restaurant for breakfast?

Mr. FRAZIER. No, sir; we never did.

Mr. BALL. Did you ever stop on the way home on Friday night and buy anything?

Mr. FRAZIER. No, sir; stopped one time and bought some gas, I remember.

Mr. BALL. Did he pay for it?

Mr. FRAZIER. No, sir; he didn't.

Mr. BALL. Did he offer to?

Mr. FRAZIER. No, sir; he didn't.

Mr. BALL. Did you ever see him have any money in his possession, bills, change?

Mr. FRAZIER. No, sir; I never did see him out playing around with any money.

Mr. BALL. On the way back and forth did you talk very much to each other?

Mr. FRAZIER. No, sir; not very much. He is, probably in your line of business you have probably seen a lot of guys who talk a lot and some don't and he was one of these types that just didn't talk. And I have seen, you know, I am not very old but I have seen a lot of guys in my time, just going to school, different boys and girls, some talk a lot and some don't, so I didn't think anything strange about that.

About the only time you could get anything out of the talking was about babies, you know, he had one and he was expecting another, that was one way he had him get that job because his wife was pregnant and I would always get something out of it when I asked him about the babies because it seemed he was very fond of children because when I asked him he chuckled and told me about what he was doing about the babies over the weekend and sometimes we would talk about the weather, and sometimes he would go to work and it would be cloudy in the morning and it would come out that afternoon after work, sometimes during the day and it would turn to be just one of the prettiest days you would want anywhere, and he would say some comment about that, but not very much.

He would say a few words and then he would cut off.

Mr. BALL. Did he tell you he had been to Russia, say anything about that?

Mr. FRAZIER. Well, I say, we were talking about one time talking about the service, and so I asked him had he ever been overseas and he said he had, and I asked him had he ever been to Germany and he said he had been through there.

So, most times when boys are in the service in the United States they either go to Japan or, I say, they either go over there or you know, go to some of these, say, like Germany or France somewhere like that.

And so other than that he told me that he had been through there.

Mr. BALL. Did he say he had been to Russia?

Mr. FRAZIER. He said, you know, like I say, he said he had been over there and he said he had been there so I thought when he told me, yes; he had, so I thought maybe, you know, by being, I know he told me had been in service and I thought maybe that is how he got in.

Mr. BALL. In other words, your answer is yes; he did tell you he had been in Russia?

Mr. FRAZIER. Right.

Mr. BALL. Did he go into detail and tell you how he got there and what he did there?

Mr. FRAZIER. No, he didn't. I, to be frank with you I, was more interested about France and Germany and I asked him about them towns and he told me he liked France, I mean he said not that he didn't like France, he said people in France was more the kind to con the United States boys out of their money and he was in Germany there 2 or 3 days and he said he liked Germany better than France because that is one reason. Because he said if you didn't really know how to count that French money them French guys would really take you.

Mr. BALL. Did he say anything about being in the Marines?

Mr. FRAZIER. Yes; he told me he was a Marine.

Mr. BALL. That he had been to Japan?

Mr. FRAZIER. No, sir; he didn't say he had been to Japan.

Mr. BALL. Ever talk about politics?

Mr. FRAZIER. No, sir; he didn't.

Mr. BALL. Ever mention any subjects like, political parties, the Democrats, Republicans?

Mr. FRAZIER. No, sir; he didn't.

Mr. BALL. Ever mention anything about Communists, Marxists or any words like that did he use?

Mr. FRAZIER. No, sir.

Mr. BALL. Did he tell you where he met his wife?

Mr. FRAZIER. No, sir; he didn't.

Mr. BALL. Did he ever talk much about his wife?

Mr. FRAZIER. No, sir; he didn't. I say, like I said, he was just a guy who didn't talk very much at all.

Mr. BALL. At the Texas School Book Depository, you have lunch, 45-minute lunch hour, don't you?

Mr. FRAZIER. Right.

Mr. BALL. Did you pack your lunch from home?

Mr. FRAZIER. Yes, sir, I always took lunch.

Mr. BALL. Do you remember whether or not when Oswald came back with you on any Monday morning or any weekend did he pack his lunch?

Mr. FRAZIER. Yes, sir; he did.

Mr. BALL. He did?

Mr. FRAZIER. Yes, sir. When he rode with me, I say he always brought lunch except that one day on November 22 he didn't bring his lunch that day.

Mr. BALL. But every other day he brought a lunch?

Mr. FRAZIER. Right, when he rode with me.

Mr. BALL. Would he bring it in a paper sack or what kind of a container?

Mr. FRAZIER. Yes, sir; like a little paper sack you get out of a grocery store, you have seen these little old sacks that you could buy, sandwich bag, sack.

Mr. BALL. Did you carry your lunch in a paper sack?

Mr. FRAZIER. Yes, sir; I did.

Mr. BALL. There is a lunch room in the Texas School Book Depository?

Mr. FRAZIER. Yes, sir.

Mr. BALL. Is that on the first floor?

Mr. FRAZIER. No, sir; on the second floor.

Mr. BALL. There is some kind of a recreation room on the first floor?

Mr. FRAZIER. There is a little domino room there where some of the guys go in and play dominoes.

Mr. BALL. But the lunch room is on the second floor?

Mr. FRAZIER. Right.

Mr. BALL. Do they sell any food there?

Mr. FRAZIER. No, sir; they don't. About all they sell in the lunch room is different types of soft drinks and then near the window, the men who work in the offices there they have coffee there, you can drink coffee up there, I never did. Then you have an assortment of cookies and candies and peanuts and so forth on the machine there. That is about all they have.

Mr. BALL. Do you remember whether or not Oswald packed his lunch, brought his lunch on other days, the days that he didn't ride with you?

Mr. FRAZIER. To be frank with you, I don't know whether he brought his lunch because I will tell you one way, some guys bring their lunch there and some guys buy it there because we have a caterer service, you see, comes around about 10 o'clock the man comes around and several of the boys they go out there and buy their lunch from the catering service.

Mr. BALL. Then later on at 11:45?

Mr. FRAZIER. 12 o'clock is when we always eat lunch.

Mr. BALL. 12 to 12:45?

Mr. FRAZIER. Right.

Mr. BALL. When you get off your job, did you usually go to the lunch room on the second floor to eat your lunch?

Mr. FRAZIER. No, sir; most of the time I don't. Most of the time you see several of us guys sitting down at our own table and we just sit there. I say we usually go up there to get something to drink and I say I have ate up there several times but most of the times I eat with the guys I work with.

Usually we just sit down and eat, and we lay down on the big tables there and sometimes talk or go to sleep.

Mr. BALL. That is on the first floor?

Mr. FRAZIER. Right.

Mr. BALL. Did you notice where Oswald had his lunch usually?

Mr. FRAZIER. No, sir; I didn't.

Now, I say we have a refrigerator there, some of the boys put their lunches in there.

Mr. BALL. Did you ever eat lunch with Oswald?

Mr. FRAZIER. No, sir; I never have.

Mr. BALL. Did you ever see him eating lunch?

Mr. FRAZIER. No, sir; I never have seen him eat lunch. I have seen him go to the Doctor Pepper machine by the refrigerator and get a Doctor Pepper but I never have seen him, you might say, sit right down and eat his lunch.

Mr. BALL. In driving back and forth with Oswald did you ever hear him—did he ever talk about guns?

Mr. FRAZIER. No, sir; he never did.

Mr. BALL. Did he ever tell you he owned a gun?

Mr. FRAZIER. No, sir.

Mr. BALL. Did Oswald ever say anything to you about buying an automobile in any of these trips?

Mr. FRAZIER. One time we were talking about it, he said he thought he would just buy him an old car, you know, like mine. I say most models like that you can get them pretty cheap and as far as going back and forth for work that is about all they are good for.

I said, "You don't need a new car to be used for going back and forth. You don't need it unless you drive a good-sized distance."

But that is what he said in the long run he planned to buy one but so far as I know he never did.

Mr. BALL. Did he say that once or more than once?

Mr. FRAZIER. No, sir; just one time.

Mr. BALL. When he said he would get an old car?

Mr. FRAZIER. Yes.

Mr. BALL. Did he ever tell you he had gone to an old car dealer?

Mr. FRAZIER. No, sir.

Mr. BALL. Did he ever tell you that he had tried out a car?

Mr. FRAZIER. No, sir. So far as I—like I say, that one time, that is as far as I can ever recall that we even talked much about anything—about cars—except a while ago he asked me—we were talking about the clutch and automatic transmission and so forth.

Mr. BALL. There is a bus service between Dallas and Irving?

Mr. FRAZIER. Yes; there is.

Mr. BALL. Can you get the bus anywhere near the Texas School Book Depository?

Mr. FRAZIER. To be frank with you I will say I have never ridden the bus from Irving over there, but I assume you can get off there just like any other bus at any street corner you want to.

Mr. BALL. Do you know what the fare is?

Mr. FRAZIER. No, sir; I don't.

Mr. BALL. Is there a toll charge to call from Dallas to Irving?

Mr. FRAZIER. No, sir; it is not.

Mr. BALL. For 10 cents you can call there, can you?

Mr. FRAZIER. Well, I say just for your regular telephone bill, you just pick it up and call.

Mr. BALL. I see.

Now, there was the one date that Oswald came to you and asked you to drive him back to Irving, it was not a Friday, was it?

Mr. FRAZIER. No, sir; it wasn't.

Mr. BALL. It was on a Thursday.

Mr. FRAZIER. Right.

Mr. BALL. Was that the 21st of November?

Mr. FRAZIER. Yes, sir.

Mr. BALL. Well, tell us about that.

Mr. FRAZIER. Well, I say, we were standing like I said at the four-headed table about half as large as this, not, quite half as large, but anyway I was standing there getting the orders in and he said, "Could I ride home with you this afternoon?"

And I said, "Sure. You know, like I told you, you can go home with me any time you want to, like I say anytime you want to go see your wife that is all right with me."

So automatically I knew it wasn't Friday, I come to think it wasn't Friday and I said, "Why are you going home today?"

And he says, "I am going home to get some curtain rods." He said, "You know, put in an apartment."

He wanted to hang up some curtains and I said, "Very well." And I never thought more about it and I had some invoices in my hands for some orders and I walked on off and started filling the orders.

Mr. BALL. This was on what floor?

Mr. FRAZIER. This was on the first floor.

Mr. BALL. About what time in the morning?

Mr. FRAZIER. I would say sometime between eight and ten, because I go to work at eight and I would break at ten.

Mr. BALL. Was it at the break time or before?

Mr. FRAZIER. It was before the break.

Mr. BALL. It was before noon then?

Mr. FRAZIER. Yes, sir.

Mr. BALL. Did you see him at the noon hour?

Mr. FRAZIER. That day?

Mr. BALL. That day.

Mr. FRAZIER. I don't recall, to be frank with you. You know, I will just be frank with you, I say just like after a guy works there for a while and he comes by and he walks by you, you don't pay so much attention but say like somebody else comes in there strange, you automatically just look at them.

Mr. BALL. Did you talk to him again until quitting time?

Mr. FRAZIER. Well, to be frank with you, like I said, the only time—you know, like I say, he didn't talk very much and about the only time—other than like I told you about talking about them babies and about the weather sometimes he would ask me some questions about a book because down there, I say, if you have ever been acquainted with books a lot of times maybe just a little bit of difference in a title or something like that would make the difference in what type of book they want and sometimes maybe they will forget to put that on there and you look at the price.

If you can tell the price, some editions we have a paperback and some we have hard bound and the price can automatically tell you which one they want, and sometimes he would ask me something like that which book do they want and I would tell him and that was about the only conversation we had.

Mr. BALL. You didn't talk any more with him that day concerning the ride home?

Mr. FRAZIER. Right.

Mr. BALL. But you did go home with him?

Mr. FRAZIER. That is he rode home with me.

Mr. BALL. What time did you get off from work?

Mr. FRAZIER. 4:40.

Mr. BALL. What time did you get to Irving?

Mr. FRAZIER. Well, usually get there, if you make good time, get there maybe around 5:20 or 5:25. But if you catch the traffic and catch the train crossing the tracks, it is usually about 5:30 or 5:35, it is just according to how bad the traffic is.

If you get ahead of it before it starts coming out, you can make pretty good headway.

Mr. BALL. Did you make any stop in the car before you got home?

Mr. FRAZIER. No, sir; I don't believe we did.

Mr. BALL. Did the two of you walk together down to the parking lot?

Mr. FRAZIER. Yes, sir; we did.

Mr. BALL. And you dropped him off at the place where his wife was staying, did you?

Mr. FRAZIER. Yes, sir; I believe I did. I, to be frank with you I, say sometimes he rode home with me, sometimes—a little store not too far from the house, there and if I was going to the store I would just drop him off by the house, but if I wasn't going to the store he would usually go on to the corner near the house and walk the rest of the way to the house up to where his wife was staying just about a half a block from my house up to where he was, his wife was staying, so he would walk there just a little bit.

Mr. BALL. Do you remember if you talked to him any on the walk down two or three blocks down to the parking lot, anything said that you can remember?

Mr. FRAZIER. No, sir; I don't believe so.

Mr. BALL. When you got in the car and went home do you remember if you said anything, if you said anything to him, or if he said anything to you?

Mr. FRAZIER. No, sir; I don't believe he did. Like I said, he didn't talk very much. About the only time we would talk was about the weather and babies, something like that.

Mr. BALL. Do you remember this day whether or not you let him walk to the house where his wife was staying?

Mr. FRAZIER. To be frank with you, I can't remember positively whether I let him off at the house or whether he got out there where I lived, just to be frank with you.

Mr. BALL. You know where the house is, don't you?

Mr. FRAZIER. Yes, sir.

Mr. BALL. Where Mrs. Paine lives?

Mr. FRAZIER. Right.

Mr. BALL. How far is that from your house?

Mr. FRAZIER. Like I say, it is just about half a block up the street.

Mr. BALL. It is on the same street, is it?

Mr. FRAZIER. Well, I say, we lived at the corner of Westbrook and Fifth Street, and Fifth Street runs on up, you know, and I say they live on Fifth Street.

Mr. BALL. What direction does Fifth run, east, west, north or south?

Mr. FRAZIER. It runs east and west.

Mr. BALL. East and west. And you live on the corner of Westbrook and Fifth?

Mr. FRAZIER. Right.

Mr. BALL. And Paine's house is east or west of your house?

Mr. FRAZIER. It is west.

Mr. BALL. It is west of of your house?

Mr. FRAZIER. Right.

Mr. BALL. About a half block?

Mr. FRAZIER. Right.

Mr. BALL. On the same street, Fifth Street?

Mr. FRAZIER. Right.

Mr. BALL. What side of the street do you live on, the north side or south side of Fifth Street?

Mr. FRAZIER. North side.

Mr. BALL. What side of the street do the Paine's live on, the north or south side of Fifth Street?

Mr. FRAZIER. North.

Mr. BALL. You both live on the north side?

Mr. FRAZIER. Right.

Mr. BALL. So to walk from Paine's house to your house you walk east along the north side of Fifth Street across Westbrook, is that right?

Mr. FRAZIER. Now, from the corner of Westbrook and Fifth you walk west on the same side of the street on the north side.

Mr. BALL. On the north side?

Mr. FRAZIER. Right.

Mr. BALL. From your house to Paine's?

Mr. FRAZIER. Right, you walk west.

Mr. BALL. And from Paine's house to yours. OK.

Now, did you see Oswald any that night, the Thursday night——

Mr. FRAZIER. No, sir; I didn't.

Mr. BALL. You brought him home.

Next morning what time did you get up? What time did you get up the next morning?

Mr. FRAZIER. I believe I got up around 6:30, that is the time I usually get up, right around 6:30 there.

Mr. BALL. Always eat your breakfast before you go to work?

Mr. FRAZIER. Right.

Mr. BALL. Do you remember the night before, that is after you got home that night, that your sister asked you how it happened that Oswald came home with you?

Mr. FRAZIER. Yes; I believe she did or something. We got to talking about something and said, I told her that he had rode home with me and told her he said he was going to come home and pick up some curtain rods or something. I usually don't talk too much to my sister, sometimes she is not there when I am in because she is either at the store or something like that and I am either when she comes in as I say I am playing with the little nieces and we don't talk too much about work or something like that.

Mr. BALL. This night, this evening, do you remember you did talk to her about the fact that Oswald had come home with you?

Mr. FRAZIER. I believe I did.

Mr. BALL. Did you tell her what he had told you?

Mr. FRAZIER. Yes, sir. I believe she said why did he come home now and I said, well, he says he was going to get some curtain rods.

Mr. BALL. The next morning you had breakfast about what time?

Mr. FRAZIER. Between 7 and 7:15, that is the time I usually, I usually come to the breakfast table about 7.

Mr. BALL. Breakfast table in the kitchen?

Mr. FRAZIER. Yes, sir; it is in the den.

Mr. BALL. And the kitchen windows look out on what street, Westbrook or Fifth?

Mr. FRAZIER. Westbrook.

Mr. BALL. They look onto Westbrook?

Mr. FRAZIER. Right.

Mr. BALL. There is a back door, is there, to the kitchen?

Mr. FRAZIER. Yes; there is. I say when we come in there we have a double carport more or less type of garage.

Mr. BALL. Is that on Westbrook?

Mr. FRAZIER. Yes, sir; the entrance to the garage there, more or less carport; yes, the entrance is from Westbrook.

Mr. BALL. As you were having breakfast did your mother say anything to you about——

Mr. FRAZIER. Well, I say——

Mr. BALL. Oswald?

Mr. FRAZIER. I was sitting there eating my breakfast there, so sitting there, I usually talk to my little nieces, you know, they have them cartoons on for a while and we usually talk a little bit back and forth while eating breakfast and I was just finishing my coffee there and my sister, you know, was working over there around, you know the sink there, and she was fixing my lunch so she was somewhere around there over on the cabinets fixing the cabinets and mother just happened to glance up and saw this man, you know, who was Lee looking in the window for me and she said, "Who is that?"

And I said, "That is Lee," and naturally he just walked around and so I thought he just walked around there on the carport right there close to the door and so I told her I had to go, so I went in there and brushed my teeth right quick and come through there and I usually have my coat laying somewhere on the chair and picked it up and put it on and by that time my sister had my lunch, you know, in a sack and sitting over there on the washer where I picked it up right there by the door and I just walked on out and we got in the car.

Mr. BALL. Now, did your sister say anything as you were having breakfast?

Mr. FRAZIER. No; she didn't say anything to me at all.

Mr. BALL. She didn't say anything to you either about Oswald or did she?

Mr. FRAZIER. No, sir; say, she didn't say, you know, when I looked up and saw him I knew who it was.

Mr. BALL. You saw him?

Mr. FRAZIER. Right.

Mr. BALL. What was he doing?

Mr. FRAZIER. He just looked through the kitchen window. To see from there on the ground outside there. I say you don't have to be any height at all, you don't have to be too tall to be able to look in the kitchen window there.

I say, if you have the window open you can see in, if you have light on in there.

Mr. BALL. When your mother mentioned, "Who is that," you looked up and saw Lee Oswald in the kitchen window?

Mr. FRAZIER. I just saw him for a split second and when he saw I saw him, I guess he heard me say, "Well, it is time to go," and he walked down by the back door there.

Representative FORD. When he would go with you on Monday, on any Monday, was this the same procedure for getting to, getting in contact with you?

Mr. FRAZIER. You mean coming in there and looking through the window?

Representative FORD. Yes.

Mr. FRAZIER. No, sir; it wasn't. I say, that is the first time he had ever done that. I say, most times I would usually call him, you know, I was already out in the car fixing to go out the driveway there, and, you know, around to pick him up if he hadn't come down but most times, once in a while I picked him up at the house and another time he was already coming down the sidewalk to the house when I was fixing to pick him up and I usually picked him up around the corner there.

Representative FORD. Did this different method of him meeting you raise any questions in your mind?

Mr. FRAZIER. No, sir; it didn't. I just thought maybe, you know, he just left a little bit earlier but when I looked up and saw that the clock was, I knew I was the one who was running a little bit late because, as I say, I was talking, sitting there eating breakfast and talking to the little nieces, it was later than I thought it was.

Mr. BALL. When you went out the back door where was Oswald?

Mr. FRAZIER. He was standing just a few feet there outside the back door there.

Mr. BALL. He wasn't in the car?

Mr. FRAZIER. No, sir; he wasn't.

Mr. BALL. Was he near the car?

Mr. FRAZIER. No, sir; he wasn't.

You see, always I keep my car parked outside the carport there, on the other side.

Mr. BALL. He was just a few feet outside your back door when you came out?

Mr. FRAZIER. Right.

Mr. BALL. Did you walk together to the car?

Mr. FRAZIER. Yes; we did.

Mr. BALL. And you got in one side and he got in the other?

Mr. FRAZIER. Yes. Right in front there.

Mr. BALL. Did you say usually you had to go by and pick him up?

Mr. FRAZIER. Well, I said I had a couple of times. Most of the time, you know, he was usually walking down the sidewalk as I was driving out of the driveway so, therefore, I didn't have to go up to the house there to pick him up. I just usually picked him up around the corner because he was usually on the sidewalk and I just stopped and picked him up.

Mr. BALL. Were you later than usual that morning?

Mr. FRAZIER. No, sir; I don't believe we were, because we got to work on time. I say, when I looked at the clock, after I glanced he was there a split second and I just turned around and looked at the clock to see what time it was and it was right around 7:21 then and I went in and brushed my teeth real quick and running through the house put my coat on and we left.

Mr. BALL. You both got in the car about the same time?

Mr. FRAZIER. Right.

Mr. BALL. All right.

When you got in the car did you say anything to him or did he say anything to you?

Mr. FRAZIER. Let's see. when I got in the car I have a kind of habit of glancing over my shoulder and so at that time I noticed there was a package laying on the back seat, I didn't pay too much attention and I said, "What's the package, Lee?"

And he said, "Curtain rods." and I said, "Oh, yes, you told me you was going to bring some today."

That is the reason, the main reason he was going over there that Thursday afternoon when he was to bring back some curtain rods, so I didn't think any more about it when he told me that.

Mr. BALL. What did the package look like?

Mr. FRAZIER. Well, I will be frank with you, I would just, it is right as you get out of the grocery store, just more or less out of a package, you have seen some of these brown paper sacks you can obtain from any, most of the stores, some varieties, but it was a package just roughly about two feet long.

Mr. BALL. It was, what part of the back seat was it in?

Mr. FRAZIER. It was in his side over on his side in the far back.

Mr. BALL. How much of that back seat, how much space did it take up?

Mr. FRAZIER. I would say roughly around 2 feet of the seat.

Mr. BALL. From the side of the seat over to the center, is that the way you would measure it?

Mr. FRAZIER. If, if you were going to measure it that way from the end of the seat over toward the center, right. But I say like I said I just roughly estimate and that would be around two feet, give and take a few inches.

Mr. BALL. How wide was the package?

Mr. FRAZIER. Well, I would say the package was about that wide.

Mr. BALL. How wide would you say that would be?

Mr. FRAZIER. Oh, say, around 5 inches, something like that. 5, 6 inches or there. I don't——

Mr. BALL. The paper, was the color of the paper, that you would get in a grocery store, is that it, a bag in a grocery store?

Mr FRAZIER. Right. You have seen, not a real light color but you know normally, the normal color about the same color, you have seen these kinds of heavy duty bags you know like you obtain from the grocery store, something like that, about the same color of that, paper sack you get there.

Mr. BALL. Was there anything more said about the paper sack on the way into town?

Mr. FRAZIER. No, sir; there wasn't.

Mr. BALL. What route did you take into town that day?

Mr. FRAZIER. Went down—you know, I told you I had two routes; that day I went down, you know, Fifth Street runs into Sixth after you cross the Storey Road there, so I just went on down Sixth until I come to O'Connor, and then took a left on O'Connor and it takes you right on out to Stemmons and from there I went right on into Stemmons and come up Commerce, and you go up Commerce, there until you hit Record Street, that is one block over from Houston and then I went down until I hit McKinney and then it goes right down to the warehouse and then take a left and you go right around to the parking lot.

Mr. BALL. You didn't stop any place on your way in?

Mr. FRAZIER. No, sir.

Mr. BALL. Park in the parking lot?

Mr. FRAZIER. Right.

Mr. BALL. Where did you park in the parking lot this time?

Mr. FRAZIER. I parked in the same place the picture I showed you there.

Mr. BALL. As shown in the picture. That is Exhibit No. 361.

Anything else said about curtain rods?

Mr. FRAZIER. No, sir; there wasn't.

Mr. BALL. Anything else said about the package?

Mr. FRAZIER. No, sir; there wasn't.

Mr. BALL. Who got out of the car first?

Mr. FRAZIER. He did.

Mr. BALL. Do you remember any conversation on the way in about anything?

Mr. FRAZIER. Yes, sir; I asked him did he have fun playing with them babies and he chuckled and said he did. And so that morning I said just a few minutes after we started you know it was a cloudy day and it started misting and rain and by the time we got out on the Freeway I said, you know, how those trucks throw that grime on the windshield and finally it was getting pretty thick on there with spots of rain, and I turned on the windshield wiper and you know how grime spatters your windshield and I said, "I wish it would rain or just quit altogether, I wish it would do something to clear off the windshield," and the drops started getting larger so eventually it cleaned off the windshield and by the time I got down to Dallas there I just turned off the windshield.

Just a few clouds, and rained a little bit to get out of it. But other than that just saying the weather was messy, that is about all.

Mr. BALL. Was it foggy?

Mr. FRAZIER. No, sir; not in too particular. I say in other words, just old cloudy, dull looking day and like I say fine mist of rain and after we got a little bit further we got into larger drops.

Mr. BALL. Was there anything said about the President coming to Dallas that day?

Mr. FRAZIER. No, sir; it wasn't.

Mr. BALL. Did he say anything about that the day before?

Mr. FRAZIER. No, sir.

Mr. BALL. Did you ever have any conversation with him with reference to the President's visit to Texas?

Mr. FRAZIER. No, sir.

Mr. BALL. When you got to the parking lot who got out of the car first?

Mr. FRAZIER. He did.

Mr. BALL. You didn't get out immediately then?

Mr. FRAZIER. No, sir; I was sitting there, say, looked at my watch and somewhere around 7 or 8 minutes until and I saw we had a few minutes and I sat there, and as I say you can see the Freeway, Stemmons Freeway, from the warehouse and also the trains coming back and forth and I was sitting there.

What I was doing—glanced up and watching cars for a minute but I was letting my engine run and getting to charge up my battery, because when you stop and start you have to charge up your battery.

Mr. BALL. Did you have your lunch beside you?

Mr. FRAZIER. Yes, sir; I did.

Mr. BALL. Did you notice whether or not Lee had a package that looked like a lunch package that morning?

Mr. FRAZIER. You know like I told you earlier, I say, he didn't take his lunch because I remember right when I got in the car I asked him where was his lunch and he said he was going to buy his lunch that day.

Mr. BALL. He told you that that day, did he?

Mr. FRAZIER. Right. That is right. So, I assumed he was going to buy it, you know, from that catering service man like a lot of the boys do. They don't bring their lunch but they go out and buy their lunch there.

Mr. BALL. What did he do about the package in the back seat when he got out of the car?

Mr. FRAZIER. Like I say, I was watching the gages and watched the car for a few minutes before I cut it off.

Mr. BALL. Yes.

Mr. FRAZIER. He got out of the car and he was wearing the jacket that has the big sleeves in them and he put the package that he had, you know, that he told me was curtain rods up under his arm, you know, and so he walked down behind the car and standing over there at the end of the cyclone fence waiting for me to get out of the car, and so quick as I cut the engine off and started out of the car, shut the door just as I was starting out just like getting out of the car, he started walking off and so I followed him in.

So, eventually there he kept getting a little further ahead of me and I noticed we had plenty of time to get there because it is not too far from the Depository and usually I walk around and watch them switching the trains because you have to watch where you are going if you have to cross the tracks.

One day you go across one track and maybe there would be some cars sitting there and there would be another diesel coming there, so you have to watch when you cross the tracks, I just walked along and I just like to watch them switch the cars, so eventually he kept getting a little further ahead of me and by that time we got down there pretty close to the Depository Building there, I say, he would be as much as, I would say, roughly 50 feet in front of me but I didn't try to catch up with him because I knew I had plenty of time so I just took my time walking up there.

Mr. BALL. Did you usually walk up there together.

Mr. FRAZIER. Yes, sir; we did.

Mr. BALL. Is this the first time that he had ever walked ahead of you?

Mr. FRAZIER. Yes, sir; he did.

Mr. BALL. You say he had the package under his arm when you saw him?

Mr. FRAZIER. Yes, sir.

Mr. BALL. You mean one end of it under the armpit?

Mr. FRAZIER. Yes, sir; he had it up just like you stick it right under your arm like that.

Mr. BALL. And he had the lower part——

Mr. FRAZIER. The other part with his right hand.

Mr. BALL. Right hand?

Mr. FRAZIER. Right.

Mr. BALL. He carried it then parallel to his body?

Mr. FRAZIER. Right, straight up and down.

Representative FORD. Under his right arm?

Mr. FRAZIER. Yes, sir.

Mr. BALL. Did it look to you as if there was something heavy in the package?

Mr. FRAZIER. Well, I will be frank with you, I didn't pay much attention to the package because like I say before and after he told me that it was curtain rods and I didn't pay any attention to it, and he never had lied to me before so I never did have any reason to doubt his word.

Mr. BALL. Did it appear to you there was some, more than just paper he was carrying, some kind of a weight he was carrying?

Mr. FRAZIER. Well, yes, sir; I say, because one reason I know that because

I worked in a department store before and I had uncrated curtain rods when they come in, and I know if you have seen when they come straight from the factory you know how they can bundle them up and put them in there pretty compact, so he told me it was curtain rods so I didn't think any more about the package whatsoever.

Mr. BALL. Well, from the way he carried it, the way he walked, did it appear he was carrying something that had more than the weight of a paper?

Mr. FRAZIER. Well, I say, you know like I say, I didn't pay much attention to the package other than I knew he had it under his arm and I didn't pay too much attention the way he was walking because I was walking along there looking at the railroad cars and watching the men on the diesel switch them cars and I didn't pay too much attention on how he carried the package at all.

Mr. BALL. I will show you this picture again, this map, which is the Commission's Exhibit No. 361, and would you show us the way he walked, the course he walked from the place your car was parked up to the Texas School Book Depository. You come around here and here is a black pen. Show us the course that he walked.

Mr. FRAZIER. Like I say, I had that car parked.

Mr. BALL. Put an "X" there which will represent your car.

Mr. FRAZIER. All right (indicating).

Mr. BALL. That is where your car was parked?

Mr. FRAZIER. I would say roughly like in there, you know like the picture shows right in there.

Mr. BALL. Now, draw a line to show the way that he walked.

Mr. FRAZIER. O.K.

Mr. BALL. The direction he walked.

Mr. FRAZIER. All right.

Like I say, he was standing right about there when I got out of the car so naturally he started off walking so we just come on right on just like you would come across these tracks right here, and he was coming right on along the fence like that. Just coming right on, right here now is the School Book Depository, right, so he was coming right on down this fence there and he was coming across these tracks, and standing right in here somewhere at the door.

Mr. BALL. Door?

Mr. FRAZIER. Right.

Mr. BALL. At the end of that put a "XY", so "X" to "XY" will represent the course he walked. It shows "XY".

Mr. FRAZIER. Right.

Mr. BALL. Then "X" to "XY" is the course he took, is that right?

Mr. FRAZIER. Right.

Mr. BALL. Did you go in the same door?

Mr. FRAZIER. Yes, sir; I did.

Mr. BALL. You walked the same direction?

Mr. FRAZIER. Right.

Mr. BALL. Now when he went in the door you were about 50 feet behind him?

Mr. FRAZIER. Right. The last time I saw him I was right in this area coming across these railroad tracks and I just happened to glance up and see him going through the door there and shut the door.

Mr. BALL. Let's see, the last time you saw him he was at the door?

Mr. FRAZIER. Right.

Mr. BALL. Which is at "XY" and you were crossing the railroad tracks on Pacific Avenue?

Mr. FRAZIER. No, sir; I say this is Houston.

Mr. BALL. Pacific runs east and west?

Mr. FRAZIER. Right.

Mr. BALL. Put a mark there, put a "Z" there as to your location.

Mr. FRAZIER. Right in there.

Mr. BALL. That is about where you were, a "Z" when he entered the door at "XY"?

Mr. FRAZIER. Right.

Mr. BALL. Now, you went on in the Building, did you, afterwards?

Mr. FRAZIER. Right. I went on in.

Mr. BALL. Well, the first floor of the Texas School Book Depository is fairly clear, isn't it, it is clear of partitions?

Mr. FRAZIER. Pretty well. I will say we have bins after you get so far.

Mr. BALL. Toward the middle of the floor you have bins?

Mr. FRAZIER. Right.

Mr. BALL. Did you see Lee as you walked in the door?

Mr. FRAZIER. No, sir; I didn't.

Mr. BALL. Here is Commission 362 which we will show you. I will put it up high so everyone can see it. There is a picture in the lower left corner which is marked "Exterior View of Entrance Door from Houston Street Loading Dock."

Mr. FRAZIER. Right.

Mr. BALL. Is that the door?

Mr. FRAZIER. Right.

Mr. BALL. That is the door that Lee entered?

Mr. FRAZIER. That is right.

Mr. BALL. And that is also the door that you entered, is that correct?

Mr. FRAZIER. Yes, sir.

Mr. BALL. And over to the right here is the interior view of entrance door.

Mr. FRAZIER. Right.

Mr. BALL. That is the same door, isn't it?

Mr. FRAZIER. Now, this door, you see right there is that door right there.

Mr. BALL. In other words, the door in the lower left-hand corner is the outside door?

Mr. FRAZIER. Right.

Mr. BALL. And as you walk through—and this is the door, the outside door, is shown in the picture on the lower right-hand corner?

Mr. FRAZIER. That is right, right there, that is this same door you are looking at over here.

Mr. BALL. Then there is an interior door?

Mr. FRAZIER. Right.

Mr. BALL. Leading into the interior that is also shown there?

Mr. FRAZIER. Right.

Mr. BALL. That is sort of, what is it—a little corridor that you walk through?

Mr. FRAZIER. I say it is just about that distance from here over to that man over there.

Mr. BALL. Let's take a look there.

Mr. FRAZIER. It is called the loading zone there.

Mr. BALL. This map shows certain steps up, doesn't it?

Mr. FRAZIER. Right.

Mr. BALL. Where is the door that you entered or that he entered.

Mr. FRAZIER. Right here.

Mr. BALL. That is the door. Is that covered, is that area covered with a ceiling roof?

Mr. FRAZIER. Yes, sir; it it.

Mr. BALL. And this is also walled in, is it?

Mr. FRAZIER. Right. The railroad track runs along here.

Mr. BALL. After you get into this outside shed how did you get into the first floor of the Texas School Book Depository?

Mr. FRAZIER. Through that door.

Mr. BALL. Through the door there, into the interior door?

Mr. FRAZIER. Right.

Mr. BALL. How much of the first floor here is clear so that you can see anybody there?

Mr. FRAZIER. Roughly say, let's see, just a few feet back, you know here is the door right here.

Mr. BALL. Whose door?

Mr. FRAZIER. Mr. Shelley's.

Mr. BALL. Yes.

Mr. FRAZIER. Just a few feet back in here is where the bins start, they run this way.

Mr. BALL. Can you mark in this where the bins start, the place?

Mr. FRAZIER. Here.

Mr. BALL. Just draw a line across, you don't need to draw in the bins but just where the bins start and we we will know it is the area.

Mr. FRAZIER. Somewhere right in here.

Mr. BALL. Draw the line clear across.

We will mark the line "A" on one side and "B" on the other so that we can refer to it.

Now, the area between, all the area shown in here from entrance to line "AB", is clear, is it?

Mr. FRAZIER. Right.

Mr. BALL. Now, the line from "AB" to the Elm Street side there are bins, are they?

Mr. FRAZIER. Right.

Mr. BALL. And are those bins man high?

Mr. FRAZIER. Yes, sir.

Mr. BALL. 6, 7 feet?

Mr. FRAZIER. Yes, sir. Like I say these bins, we have two or three that run across this way, like I have this line drawn, and they have broken spaces, and you can see a man on the other side of these bins because they are not sealed up in the back.

In other words, you can put books in, say, from this side and go on the other side and have another. Anyway, we have more like these window here.

Mr. BALL. The windows on Elm Street?

Mr. FRAZIER. Right. We have some bins running this way, over here, several bins, two or three over here, and two or three over here.

Mr. BALL. Is this the only entrance to the first floor of the Building, the one you have shown us?

Mr. FRAZIER. No, sir, it is not.

Mr. BALL. What other entrance is there?

Mr. FRAZIER. Right here is the main entrance.

Mr. BALL. The main entrance?

Mr. FRAZIER. That is right, coming on through here.

Mr. BALL. There are two entrances. There is a main entrance in the front of the Building or the Elm Street entrance, and then there is the door through which you entered the first floor, is that right?

Mr. FRAZIER. Yes, then we have another.

Mr. BALL. Where?

Mr. FRAZIER. Out over here, let's see if I can find it, where the garage where we have the truck. Let's see.

Mr. BALL. There is an overhead door here.

Mr. FRAZIER. I see, right through here now, I see right through this door here we come out right here and we come out in this area right in here where we have another dock right out in this area right here, in that area there.

Mr. BALL. That would be——

Mr. FRAZIER. That would be one, two, three. From this loading, like I say, where we keep the truck.

Mr. BALL. Is this overhead door usually covered, usually down closed, rather?

Mr. FRAZIER. Yes, sir; I say we keep it closed, and we have it here back in cold weather and we kept it closed and like I say when you go out there and get into the truck like you are going to drive the truck.

Mr. BALL. Mark an arrow that you say is the entrance or exit, mark an arrow going out.

Mr. FRAZIER. Going out.

Mr. BALL. All right.

Now, this day did you see Lee Oswald the rest of the morning?

Mr. FRAZIER. Yes, sir; I saw him back and forth, you know, that morning walking around, filling books and so forth, filling orders, had invoices filling orders.

Mr. BALL. When you came in that morning to go to work where did you go first?

Mr. FRAZIER. I went like I did every morning, I went down in the basement there and hung up my coat and put up my lunch.

Mr. BALL. Did you see Oswald down there?

Mr. FRAZIER. No; I didn't.

Mr. BALL. Then you went to work?

Mr. FRAZIER. Right.

Mr. BALL. How did you get to the basement?

Mr. FRAZIER. Went down through the, now over there where they have—are you familiar with the Depository Building?

Mr. BALL. Only through the map.

Mr. FRAZIER. We have the——

Mr. BALL. There is the map of the first floor. Does it show the steps leading down to the basement?

Mr. FRAZIER. Yes, sir. You see the one there where you have the arrow that is one entrance to the basement and that is the entrance I used the biggest part of the time, that is the one I go down.

Mr. BALL. Did you see Oswald there?

Mr. FRAZIER. No, sir; I didn't.

Mr. BALL. During the morning you say you saw Oswald around filling orders?

Mr. FRAZIER. Yes, sir; I did.

Mr. BALL. Were you on the sixth floor any that morning?

Mr. FRAZIER. One time just a few seconds. I said to Mr. Shelley we had some book returns. They had sent back and he told me to count the books and make sure they were all there and put them in the space and so I took the elevator and loaded them on with a two-wheeler and so I know where they went, and I went to the shelf off the elevator and put them on the shelf and turned around and went right on down.

Mr. BALL. Were they doing some work there that day?

Mr. FRAZIER. Yes, sir; they were.

Representative FORD. What time was that?

Mr. FRAZIER. When I went to put up the stock?

Representative FORD. Yes. On the sixth floor.

Mr. FRAZIER. That was sometime between 8 and 10 o'clock. I say it was the early part of the morning.

Mr. BALL. What kind of work did you notice they were doing up there?

Mr. FRAZIER. As well as I remember they were moving stock, I believe putting up some stock, straightening up the stock.

Mr. BALL. Any work done on the floor?

Mr. FRAZIER. I don't remember if they were working on the floor or not. They may have because upon the fifth floor I know we have done the fifth floor.

Mr. BALL. Do you remember the names of any workmen you saw on the sixth floor that morning you were there?

Mr. FRAZIER. I believe Billy was up there, Billy Lovelady, but so far as I can say I went and put books on the shelf and turned around and walked back and glanced up when I was coming back, I didn't stay any length of time because when we are pretty busy, some fill out orders and some doing something else and if you have a lot of orders to fill you haven't got a lot of time to sit around and be talking.

Mr. BALL. Did you see Oswald on the sixth floor any time that morning?

Mr. FRAZIER. No, sir. I didn't because like I say that was the only time I went up there at all that day and I was just up there for a few seconds.

Mr. BALL. Did you talk to him any that morning?

Mr. FRAZIER. I don't believe I did much unless he asked me something about a book like I told you, and I was always willing to help anybody I can.

Mr. BALL. Now, you knew that the President was going to pass that building sometime that morning, didn't you?

Mr. FRAZIER. Well, I heard he would.

Mr. BALL. Did you talk to some of the men around there about it?

Mr. FRAZIER. No, sir; I didn't.

Mr. BALL. Did you ever talk to Oswald about that?

Mr. FRAZIER. No, sir; I didn't.

Mr. BALL. What time did you knock off for lunch?

Mr. FRAZIER. 12.

Mr. BALL. Did you eat your lunch?

Mr. FRAZIER. No, sir; not right then I didn't. I say, you know, he was supposed to come by during our lunch hour so you don't get very many chances to see the President of the United States and being an old Texas boy, and [he] never having been down to Texas very much I went out there to see him and just like everybody else was, I was standing on the steps there and watched for the parade to come by and so I did and I stood there until he come by.

Mr. BALL. You went out there after you quit work?

Mr. FRAZIER. Right, for lunch.

Mr. BALL. About 12 o'clock?

Mr. FRAZIER. Right.

Mr. BALL. And you hadn't eaten your lunch up to that time?

Mr. FRAZIER. No.

Mr. BALL. Did you go out there with somebody?

Mr. FRAZIER. Yes, sir; I did.

Mr. BALL. Who did you go out there with?

Mr. FRAZIER. I stayed around there pretty close to Mr. Shelley and this boy Billy Lovelady and just standing there, people talking and just talking about how pretty a day it turned out to be, because I told you earlier it was an old cloudy and misty day and then it didn't look like it was going to be a pretty day at all.

Mr. BALL. And it turned out to be a good day?

Mr. FRAZIER. Pretty sunshiny day.

Mr. BALL. Warm?

Mr. FRAZIER. Yes, sir; it was pretty warm.

Mr. BALL. Then let's see, there was Billy Lovelady and you were there.

Mr. FRAZIER. Right.

Mr. BALL. Anybody else you can remember?

Mr. FRAZIER. There was a lady there, a heavy-set lady who worked upstairs there whose name is Sarah something, I don't know her last name.

Mr. BALL. Were you near the steps?

Mr. FRAZIER. Yes, sir; I was, I was standing about, I believe, one step down from the top there.

Mr. BALL. One step down from the top of the steps?

Mr. FRAZIER. Yes, sir; standing there by the rail.

Mr. BALL. By steps we are talking about the steps of the entrance to the Building?

Mr. FRAZIER. Yes, sir.

Mr. BALL. Shown in this picture?

Mr. FRAZIER. Yes, sir.

Mr. BALL. Which is Commission's Exhibit No. 362. Can you come over here and show us about where you were standing?

Mr. FRAZIER. Yes, sir. Like I told you this was an entrance right here.

Mr. BALL. Yes, sir.

Mr. FRAZIER. We have a bar rail running about half way up here. This was the first step and I was standing right around there.

Mr. BALL. Put a mark there. Your name is Frazier, put an "F" there for Frazier.

Mr. FRAZIER. O.K.

Mr. BALL. In the picture that would show you about there, would it?

Mr. FRAZIER. Yes, sir; you can see, just see, the top, about the top rail there, I was standing right in there.

Mr. BALL. Right in there?

Mr. FRAZIER. To be frank with you, I say, shadow from the roof there knocked the sun from out our eyes, you wouldn't have any glare in the eyes standing there.

Mr. BALL. There was a roof over your head, was there?

Mr. FRAZIER. Right.

Mr. BALL. Did you stand there for 30 minutes or—tell us how long you stayed there?

233

Mr. FRAZIER. Well, I stood there until the parade come by.

Mr. BALL. Did you see the President go by?

Mr. FRAZIER. Yes, sir; I did.

Mr. BALL. Did you hear anything?

Mr. FRAZIER. Well, I say, just right after he went by he hadn't hardly got by, I heard a sound and if you have ever been around motorcycles you know how they backfire, and so I thought one of them motorcycles backfired because right before his car came down, now there were several of these motorcycle policemen, and they took off down toward the underpass down there, and so I thought, you know, that one of them motorcycles backfired, but it wasn't just a few seconds that, you know, I heard two more of the same type of, you know, sounds, and by that time people was running everywhere, and falling down and screaming, and naturally then I knew something was wrong, and so I come to the conclusion somebody else, somebody was shooting at somebody and I figured it was him.

Mr. BALL. You figured it was who?

Mr. FRAZIER. I figured it was somebody shooting at President Kennedy because people were running and hollering so I just stood still. I have always been taught when something like that happened or anywhere as far as that it is always best to stand still because if you run that makes you look guilty sure enough.

Mr. BALL. Now, then, did you have any impression at that time as to the direction from which the sound came?

Mr. FRAZIER. Well, to be frank with you I thought it come from down there, you know, where that underpass is. There is a series, quite a few number, of them railroad tracks running together and from where I was standing it sounded like it was coming from down the railroad tracks there.

Mr. BALL. Were you able to see the President, could you still see the President's car when you heard the first sound?

Mr. FRAZIER. No, sir; I couldn't. From there, you know, people were standing out there on the curb, you see, and you know it drops, you know the ground drops, off there as you go down toward that underpass and I couldn't see any of it because people were standing up there in my way, but however, when he did turn that corner there, there wasn't anybody standing there in the street and you could see good there, but after you got on past down there you couldn't see anything.

Mr. BALL. You didn't see the President's car at the time you heard the sound?

Mr. FRAZIER. No, sir; I didn't.

Mr. BALL. But you stood right there, did you?

Mr. FRAZIER. Right. Stood right where I was.

Mr. BALL. And Mr. Shelley was still standing there?

Mr. FRAZIER. Right.

Mr. BALL. And also Billy Lovelady?

Mr. FRAZIER. Yes, sir.

Mr. BALL. The three of you didn't go any place?

Mr. FRAZIER. I believe Billy and them walked down toward that direction but I didn't. I just stood where I was. I hadn't moved at all.

Mr. BALL. Did you see anybody after that come into the Building while you were there?

Mr. FRAZIER. You mean somebody other that didn't work there?

Mr. BALL. A police officer.

Mr. FRAZIER. No, sir; I stood there a few minutes, you know, and some people who worked there; you know normally started to go back into the Building because a lot of us didn't eat our lunch, and so we started back into the Building and it wasn't but just a few minutes that there were a lot of police officers and so forth all over the Building there.

Mr. BALL. Then you went back into the Building, did you?

Mr. FRAZIER. Right.

Mr. BALL. And before you went back into the Building no police officer came up the steps and into the building?

Mr. FRAZIER. Not that I know. They could walk by the way and I was standing there talking to somebody else and didn't see it.

Mr. BALL. Did anybody say anything about what had happened, did you hear anybody say anything about the President had been shot?

Mr. FRAZIER. Yes, sir; right before I went back, some girl who had walked down a little bit further where I was standing on the steps, and somebody come back and said somebody had shot President Kennedy.

Mr. BALL. Do you know who it was who told you that?

Mr. FRAZIER. Sir?

Mr. BALL. Do you know who the girl was who told you that?

Mr. FRAZIER. She didn't tell me right directly but she just came back and more or less in a low kind of hollering she just told several people.

Mr. BALL. Then you went back into the Building, did you?

Mr. FRAZIER. Right.

Mr. BALL. And police officers came in there?

Mr. FRAZIER. Yes, sir; I would say by the time, you know some of us went back in, and it wasn't just a few minutes, I say there were several.

Mr. BALL. Did you stay on the first floor?

Mr. FRAZIER. Well, stayed on the first floor there for a few minutes and I hadn't eaten my lunch so I had my lunch down there in the basement and I went down there to get my lunch and eat it and I walked back up on the first floor there.

Mr. BALL. When you came back into the Building, you came in the front door, didn't you?

Mr. FRAZIER. Right.

Mr. BALL. Did you go down to the basement immediately or did you stand around on the first floor?

Mr. FRAZIER. No, sir; I stood around for several minutes there, you know, and then, you know, eventually the ones who hadn't eaten their lunch, some of them had taken their lunch outside.

Mr. BALL. Did other people go downstairs with you?

Mr. FRAZIER. No, sir; they didn't.

Mr. BALL. You went down alone, did you?

Mr. FRAZIER. Yes, sir.

Mr. BALL. Did you go at any time in the back end of the Building back near the door to the loading dock?

Mr. FRAZIER. No, sir; I never did.

Mr. BALL. Perhaps I had better ask you to point out on the map here where you were. Come over here, please.

Mr. FRAZIER. O.K.

Mr. BALL. You came in back into the Building?

Mr. FRAZIER. Right.

Mr. BALL. Tell us where you went and what you did?

Mr. FRAZIER. Well, you know like I said I come back through here [indicating on Commission Exhibit No. 362, diagram of first floor].

Mr. BALL. By "coming back through here," you mean you came down the hallway and into the entrance into the first floor warehouse?

Mr. FRAZIER. Right, and you come by Mr. Shelley's office, that is his counter right here, after you get in, you get off here, that is his office, anyway, right out, I come out around here, you know where several of the people walked around here.

Mr. BALL. That is in the bin area?

Mr. FRAZIER. No, sir; the bins don't start automatically right up in here. I say, there is a little bit more or less, like more or less a hall through here, but anyway, you know, I say, you have two or three bins.

Mr. BALL. Through here you mean there is sort of a hall after you enter into the warehouse?

Mr. FRAZIER. Right.

Mr. BALL. Right.

Mr. FRAZIER. From it, after you come past this counter you have several rows of bins coming this way, but, I say, right after you get past, say, this last bin right here running that way, right out this general area right here you have a telephone and everything out in here.

Mr. BALL. Well, you indicated that everything that would be beyond this line, the bin lines, would be clear on the first floor.

Mr. FRAZIER. Right, beyond here.

Mr. BALL. Did you ever go into that area where it was clear before you went downstairs?

From the time you came back into the room, did you go down into this area which was clear before you went downstairs?

Mr. FRAZIER. No, sir; I didn't go in here. I was right over right close to Mr. Shelley's office right around here and sit around and talked with some guys around there.

Mr. BALL. You are indicating around Mr. Shelley's office?

Mr. FRAZIER. Yes, sir; pretty close right there, like I say more or less right out over in here we have a——

Mr. BALL. Put a mark there.

Mr. FRAZIER. Let's see——

Mr. BALL. Put a circle to show the general area where you and the rest of them stood around and talked.

Mr. FRAZIER. Right in there is right around near the telephone and we were just right around in there.

Mr. BALL. Where did you go?

Mr. FRAZIER. We left, you know, after we stood and talked with some guys there, some of them had eaten and some of them didn't, some of them had sandwiches in their hands, so naturally I felt like eating and I walked around the bin and walked down the steps there.

Mr. BALL. Got your lunch?

Mr. FRAZIER. Right.

Mr. BALL. Come back up?

Mr. FRAZIER. No, sir; I didn't come back up. I was sitting eating my lunch. I looked at my watch and didn't have but 10 minutes, so I naturally ate faster than normal, so I was eating a couple of sandwiches, and eat an apple or something and come right back up and the guys, the people who worked there, standing around on the first floor, some of them eating their lunches and others merely talking.

Mr. BALL. You never went back to work?

Mr. FRAZIER. No, sir; we didn't. I didn't work any more that day.

Mr. BALL. You stayed there on the job until you were told to go home?

Mr. FRAZIER. Yes, sir.

Mr. BALL. What time did they tell you to go home?

Mr. FRAZIER. It was between 1 and 2 there sometime, roughly, I don't know what time it was.

Mr. BALL. Had the police officers come in there and talked to you?

Mr. FRAZIER. Yes, sir; they come in and talked to all of us. They asked us to show our proper identification, and then they had us to write our name down and who to get in touch with if they wanted to see us.

Mr. BALL. Did they ask you where you had been at the time the President passed?

Mr. FRAZIER. Yes, sir; they had. I told them I was out on the steps there.

Mr. BALL. Asked you who you were with?

Mr. FRAZIER. Yes, sir; I told them and naturally Mr. Shelley and Billy vouched for me and so they didn't think anything about it.

Mr. BALL. Did you hear anybody around there asking for Lee Oswald?

Mr. FRAZIER. No, sir; I didn't.

Mr. BALL. At any time before you went home, did you hear anybody ask for Lee?

Mr. FRAZIER. No, sir; I don't believe they did, because they, you know, like one man showed us, we had to give proper identification and after we passed him he told us to walk on then to the next man, and we, you know, put down proper information where he could be found if they wanted to see you and talk to you any more, and then we went on up to a little bit more to the front entrance more toward Mr. Shelley's office there with another man and stood there for a little while and told us all that was there could go ahead and go home.

Mr. BALL. Then you went on home?

Mr. FRAZIER. Right.

Representative FORD. Did all this occur after you had finished your lunch?

Mr. FRAZIER. Yes, sir; it did.

Representative FORD. Did it ever occur to you at any time following the shooting there was something connecting the shooting with Lee Oswald and the package?

Mr. FRAZIER. Well, I say not particularly not at that time, I didn't think anything about it because, to be frank with you, some were over here, one or two would be over here talking and just strung out here, on the first floor and I didn't think anything about it. I see some of the guys, they go out for lunch and they come back 12:45 so I didn't know whether he had went out to lunch or not. Some of them do every week.

Representative FORD. Did any of the policemen interfere with your efforts to go into the Building and eventually down into the basement where you had your lunch?

Mr. FRAZIER. No, sir; they didn't.

Mr. BALL. Before you left, did you look for Oswald to see about taking him home?

Mr. FRAZIER. No; I didn't, sir.

Mr. BALL. Was there some reason why you didn't?

Mr. FRAZIER. Yes, sir; I did. Because like I told you, he was going home to get the curtain rods and I asked him at the time, the same time, it would be about that, would he be going home with me Friday afternoon like he had been doing, he said no. So naturally when they let us go I took on off because I thought maybe they had already dismissed him and he went on home.

Mr. BALL. When you talked to him on Thursday and he told you he wouldn't be going home on Friday, did he tell you what he was going to do, why he wasn't going to go home?

Mr. FRAZIER. No, sir; he didn't.

Mr. BALL. Did you talk to him again on Friday morning as to whether or not he had changed his mind? Did you ask him whether or not you could pick him up at the end of the day?

Mr. FRAZIER. To be frank with you, Mr. Ball, I am not sure.

Mr. BALL. Whether you did or not.

Did anybody tell you that Lee Oswald was missing before you went home?

Mr. FRAZIER. No, sir; they didn't.

Representative FORD. Could you describe for the Commission where you went on the sixth floor that morning in relationship to the overall picture of the sixth floor?

Mr. FRAZIER. Yes, sir; I could.

Representative FORD. Would you do so, please?

Mr. FRAZIER. Yes, sir.

Do you have a piece of paper I can draw? [Witness draws diagram on piece of paper.]

Let's see, right here is your two elevator shafts we have. That morning I used this one over here.

Representative FORD. Would you mark Houston, Elm and the other streets?

Mr. FRAZIER. This is Houston, this is Elm right out here. Anyway, like I said, I won't draw these buildings. I have these two elevator shafts here. Quickly you come off these elevator shafts right here, we have skids with books on them, and you see right on those skids you would have some shelves right about like this and so I merely walked over to the elevator with the two-wheeler we use on the dock and walked somewhere say maybe halfway, not quite halfway, there and put up some books, put them down on the floor there, on the floor level and so I just turned around and come back to the elevator and come on down, and went about my business. He had me putting up some books there on the shelves.

Representative FORD. From this point here could you see the windows or the area at the corner of Houston and Elm in the Building?

Mr. FRAZIER. Yes, sir; you could. I say you could look down and see this area back over here.

Representative FORD. Did you look over there?

Mr. FRAZIER. No, sir; I didn't.

Right on down there, I knew where the books went so normally I didn't have to look around. I say, I was going to get through, if you are not familiar with the books and so forth it would take you a little longer to find and put them up. But if you know where they go you can put them up very quickly.

So I knew this book went in the shelf because this book we don't handle very many of them and that is where I put books you don't handle very many, put them in the shelf.

So I put the books in the shelf and turned around and put them in the elevator and come on down.

Mr. BALL. Can I have this marked as Commission Exhibit 368, the diagram just drawn by the witness to illustrate his work on the sixth floor?

The CHAIRMAN. It may be marked.

(The document referred to was marked Commission Exhibit No. 368, for identification.)

Mr. BALL. I have here Commission's 163, a gray blue jacket. Do you recognize this jacket?

Mr. FRAZIER. No, sir; I don't.

Mr. BALL. Did you ever see Lee Oswald wear this jacket?

Mr. FRAZIER. No, sir; I don't believe I have.

Mr. BALL. Commission Exhibit No. 162, which can be described for the record as a gray jacket with zipper, have you seen Lee Oswald wear this jacket?

Mr. FRAZIER. No, sir; I haven't.

Mr. BALL. I have here Commission 150, which is described as sort of a rust brown shirt. Have you ever seen Lee Oswald wear this shirt? It has a hole in the sleeve near the elbow.

Mr. FRAZIER. No, sir; I don't believe I have because most time I noticed when Lee had it, I say he put off his shirt and just wear a T-shirt the biggest part of the time so really what shirt he wore that day I really didn't see it or didn't pay enough attention to it whether he did have a shirt on.

Mr. BALL. On that day you did notice one article of clothing, that is, he had a jacket?

Mr. FRAZIER. Yes, sir.

Mr. BALL. What color was the jacket?

Mr. FRAZIER. It was a gray, more or less flannel, wool-looking type of jacket that I had seen him wear and that is the type of jacket he had on that morning.

Mr. BALL. Did it have a zipper on it?

Mr. FRAZIER. Yes, sir; it was one of the zipper types.

Mr. BALL. It isn't one of these two zipper jackets we have shown?

Mr. FRAZIER. No, sir.

Mr. BALL. Do you know what kind of trousers he had on, what color?

Mr. FRAZIER. Not that day, I don't remember.

Mr. BALL. You wouldn't remember that day?

Mr. FRAZIER. I had seen him wear some gray ones before.

Mr. BALL. Here is Commission's Exhibit No. 157 which are gray trousers. Had you ever seen him wear these?

Mr. FRAZIER. Yes; to be frank with you. I had seen something more or less of that order, that type of material, but so far as that, being sure that, was his pants or some of his clothes, I couldn't be sure.

Mr. BALL. Here is Commission No. 156 which is a pair of gray trousers. Did you ever see him wear trousers of that type?

Mr. FRAZIER. Not that I know of.

Mr. BALL. You are not able to tell us then anything or are you able to tell us, describe any of the clothing he had on that day, except this gray jacket?

Mr. FRAZIER. Right.

Mr. BALL. That is the only thing you can remember?

Mr. FRAZIER. Right.

Mr. BALL. I have here a paper sack which is Commission's Exhibit 364. That gray jacket you mentioned, did it have any design in it?

Mr. FRAZIER. No, sir.

Mr. BALL. Was it light or dark gray?

Mr. FRAZIER. It was light gray.

Mr. BALL. You mentioned it was woolen.

Mr. FRAZIER. Yes, sir.

Mr. BALL. Long sleeves?

Mr. FRAZIER. Yes, sir.

Mr. BALL. Buttoned sleeves at the wrist. or do you remember?

Mr. FRAZIER. To be frank with you, I didn't notice that much about the jacket, but I had seen him wear that gray woolen jacket before.

Mr. BALL. You say it had a zipper on it?

Mr. FRAZIER. Yes, sir.

Mr. BALL. Now we have over here this exhibit for identification which is 364 which is a paper sack made out of tape, sort of a home made affair. Will you take a look at this. Does this appear to be anything like the color of the sack you saw on the back seat?

Mr. FRAZIER. Yes, sir; I would say it was, it was more a color like this.

Mr. BALL. It was more like this color, correct?

Mr. FRAZIER. Yes.

Mr. BALL. Did it have tape on it or did you notice it?

Mr. FRAZIER. Well, like I say, I didn't notice that much about it as I didn't see it very much.

Mr. BALL. Will you take a look at it as to the length. Does it appear to be about the same length?

Mr. FRAZIER. No, sir.

Mr. BALL. We will just use this. Was one end of the sack turned over, folded over? Do you remember that?

Mr. FRAZIER. Well, you know, like I was saying, when I glanced at it, but I say from what I saw I didn't see very much of it, I say the bag wasn't open or anything like it where you can see the contents. If you was going to say putting—to more or less a person putting in carefully he would throw it in carefully, you put it more toward the back. If he had anything folded up in it I didn't see that.

Mr. BALL. When you saw him get out of the car. when you first saw him when he was out of the car before he started to walk, you noticed he had the package under the arm?

Mr. FRAZIER. Yes, sir.

Mr. BALL. One end of it was under the armpit and the other he had to hold it in his right hand. Did the package extend beyond the right hand?

Mr. FRAZIER. No, sir. Like I say if you put it under your armpits and put it down normal to the side.

Mr. BALL. But the right hand on. was it on the end or the side of the package?

Mr. FRAZIER. No; he had it cupped in his hand.

Mr. BALL. Cupped in his hand?

Mr. FRAZIER. Right.

Mr. BALL. Take a look at this paper bag which is Commission Exhibit 364 for identification. with reference to the width.

Was the bag about that width or a different width?

Mr. FRAZIER. Well, I would say it appears to me it would be pretty close but it might be just a little bit too wide. I think it is, because you know yourself you would have to have a big hand with that size but like I say he had this cupped in his hand because I remember glancing at him when he was a walking up ahead of me.

Mr. BALL. This is another bag here which has been marked Commission's Exhibit 142. But I don't see the stamp on it. This is FBI No. 10. This was shown to you before, wasn't it, in Dallas?

Mr. FRAZIER. Yes, sir; it was.

Mr. BALL. You were asked if you had seen this before, weren't you?

Mr. FRAZIER. Yes, sir; I was.

Mr. BALL. When you first saw it, you felt that the bag you saw was of a different color, didn't you?

Mr. FRAZIER. Right, and I say they told me this one had been treated in the lab.

Mr. BALL. If you will note there is a part of this bag which has not been treated.

Mr. FRAZIER. Yes.

Mr. BALL. So I will show you this part of this exhibit that hasn't been treated, and tell me whether or not the paper, the color of the paper that has not been treated, is or is not similar to the color of the paper on the bag you saw on the back seat of your car that morning.

(At this point, Senator Cooper entered the hearing room.)

Mr. FRAZIER. To be frank with you, more like I say the color, the color I saw would be more like it but I imagine if this hadn't been run through that process that this color here that you unwrapped would be more closer to this. This seems to have a little bit different color to me.

Mr. BALL. I didn't get the answer because of the—let's refer to this bag, that is the colored bag.

Mr. FRAZIER. Okay, sir.

Mr. BALL. And the bag that is not colored, and the other is just a bag.

Mr. FRAZIER. Okay, sir.

Mr. BALL. We are talking about the colored bag, the one that has changed its color. There is a part of the colored bag that hasn't changed color, isn't it?

Mr. FRAZIER. Right.

Mr. BALL. That is the part I want to call your attention to.

Mr. FRAZIER. Right.

Mr. BALL. The color of this bag, the colored bag, has not been treated. Take a look at it. Is that similar to the color of the bag you saw in the back seat of your car that morning?

Mr. FRAZIER. It would be, surely it could have been, and it couldn't have been. Like I say, see, you know this color, either one of these colors, is very similar to the type of paper that you can get out of a store or anything like that, and so I say it could have been and then it couldn't have been.

Mr. BALL. Do you mean by that that it is similar to the color?

Mr. FRAZIER. Right.

Mr. BALL. And do you have a definite memory of the color of the bag you saw on the back seat of your car so that you can distinguish between one color and another?

Mr. FRAZIER. I believe it would be more on this basis here.

Mr. BALL. You say it would be more on the color of bag No. 364, is that right?

Mr. FRAZIER. Right.

Mr. BALL. You will notice that this bag which is the colored bag, FBI Exhibit No. 10, is folded over. Was it folded over when you saw it the first time, folded over to the end?

Mr. FRAZIER. I will say I am not sure about that, whether it was folded over or not, because, like I say, I didn't pay that much attention to it.

Mr. BALL. This is Commission Exhibit No. 142.

The CHAIRMAN. That is the dark bag?

Mr. BALL. The dark bag is Commission Exhibit No. 142.

When you were shown this bag, do you recall whether or not you told the officers who showed you the bag—did you tell them whether you thought it was or was not about the same length as the bag you saw on the back seat?

Mr. FRAZIER. I told them that as far as the length there, I told them that was entirely too long.

Mr. BALL. What about the width?

Mr. FRAZIER. Well, I say, like I say now, now I couldn't see much of the bag from him walking in front of me. Now he could have had some of it sticking out in front of his hands because I didn't see it from the front. The only time I did see it was from the back, just a little strip running down from your arm and so therefore, like that, I say, I know that the bag wouldn't be that long.

So far as being that wide like I say I couldn't be sure.

Mr. BALL. It could have been that wide?

Mr. FRAZIER. Right.

Mr. BALL. Now, you said that some of the bag might have been beyond his hands, did you say?

Mr. Frazier. Yes, sir; I said it could have, now I am not saying it was.

Mr. Ball. In other words, it could have been longer than his hands?

Mr. Frazier. Right.

Mr. Ball. It has been suggested that you take this bag, which is the colored bag, Commission Exhibit No. 142, and put it under your arm just as a sample, or just to show about how he carried the bag.

Mr. Frazier. Okay.

Mr. Ball. Put it under your armpit.

Mr. Frazier. Like that, normally your hand would come down like that and you would say, you would have an item, like you have seen people carry items like they would be walking along and your arm would come down like that, just like——

Mr. Ball. But are you sure that his hand was at the end of the package or at the side of the package?

Mr. Frazier. Like I said, I remember I didn't look at the package very much, paying much attention, but when I did look at it he did have his hands on the package like that.

Mr. Ball. But you said a moment ago you weren't sure whether the package was longer or shorter.

Mr. Frazier. And his hands because I couldn't see that about the package.

Mr. Ball. By that, do you mean that you don't know whether the package extended beyond his hands?

Mr. Frazier. This way?

Mr. Ball. No; lengthwise, toward his feet.

Mr. Frazier. No; now I don't mean that.

Mr. Ball. What do you mean?

Mr. Frazier. What I was talking about, I said I didn't know where it extended. It could have or couldn't have, out this way, widthwise not lengthwise.

Mr. Ball. In other words, you say it could have been wider than your original estimate?

Mr. Frazier. Right.

Mr. Ball. But you don't think it was longer than his hands?

Mr. Frazier. Right.

Mr. Ball. How tall are you?

Mr. Frazier. I am 6-foot, a little bit over 6-foot.

Mr. Ball. Do you know what your arm length is?

Mr. Frazier. No, sir; I don't.

Mr. Ball. We can probably measure it before you leave.

Did you ever see Lee taking home anything with him from the Texas Book Depository Building?

Mr. Frazier. No, sir; never did.

Mr. Ball. Did you ever see him taking a package home with him?

Mr. Frazier. No, sir.

Mr. Ball. When was the last time you can remember you saw Lee?

Mr. Frazier. You mean on the 22d?

Mr. Ball. On the 22d, that day.

Mr. Frazier. Somewhere between it was after 10 and somewhere before noon, because I remember I was walking down to the first floor that day, that was the only time I went up on the elevator was, like I say, for a few minutes and, I put that box of books up and put it down, and I was on the first floor putting up books all day and I seen him back and forth and he would be walking and getting books and put on the order.

Mr. Ball. That was the last time you saw him all day?

Mr. Frazier. Right.

Mr. Ball. You didn't talk to him again?

Mr. Frazier. No, sir; I didn't.

Mr. Ball. Did you wear a coat or jacket to work that morning?

Mr. Frazier. Yes, sir; I did.

Mr. Ball. It was chilly, was it?

Mr. Frazier. Yes, sir; it was.

Mr. BALL. When you stood out on the front looking at the parade, where was Shelley standing and where was Lovelady standing with reference to you?

Mr. FRAZIER. Well, see, I was standing, like I say, one step down from the top, and Mr. Shelley was standing, you know, back from the top step and over toward the side of the wall there. See, he was standing right over there, and then Billy was a couple of steps down from me over toward more the wall also.

Mr. BALL. Usually when Lee walked in the Building in the morning, when you came to work with him where did he go, do you know?

Mr. FRAZIER. No, sir. He just walked in, say, like inside the Building, and like I say I always went and put my lunch up and hang my jacket or coat up, whichever I wore, and he was usually around there on the first floor there after some of them put their lunch in the refrigerator, so far as that I never paid too much attention to what he usually did.

Mr. BALL. You usually walked in together?

Mr. FRAZIER. That is right, sir.

Mr. BALL. And you separated after you got in there?

Mr. FRAZIER. Yes; after we got into the interior I just went and put my lunch up.

Mr. BALL. Did you notice where Lee kept his lunch?

Mr. FRAZIER. No, sir; I didn't.

Mr. BALL. Did you ever see him come into the Building on other days than the days that he rode with you?

Mr. FRAZIER. You mean did I ever see him come in the Building when he rode with me?

Mr. BALL. Yes.

Mr. FRAZIER. Yes, sir; because when he rode with me we always walked together.

Mr. BALL. No; other than when he rode with you.

Mr. FRAZIER. Oh, other than when he rode with me. No, sir; I didn't.

The CHAIRMAN. Did he have any particular associates around there that you knew of?

Mr. FRAZIER. Not that I knew of. I say he didn't mingle with other guys like the rest of us. The rest of us usually joked back and forth with practically everybody who worked around there. But he usually kept to himself, that was the only time he talked to anybody was when he wanted to know something about a book or something like that.

Mr. BALL. We have got a picture taken the day of the parade and it shows the President's car going by.

Now, take a look at that picture. Can you see your picture any place there?

Mr. FRAZIER. No, sir; I don't, because I was back up in this more or less black area here.

Mr. BALL. I see.

Mr. FRAZIER. Because Billy, like I say, is two or three steps down in front of me.

Mr. BALL. Do you recognize this fellow?

Mr. FRAZER. That is Billy, that is Billy Lovelady.

Mr. BALL. Billy?

Mr. FRAZIER. Right.

Mr. BALL. Let's take a marker and make an arrow down that way. That mark is Billy Lovelady?

Mr. FRAZIER. Right.

Mr. BALL. That is where you told us you were standing a moment ago.

Mr. FRAZIER. Right.

Mr. BALL. In front of you to the right over to the wall?

Mr. FRAZIER. Yes.

Mr. BALL. Is this a Commission exhibit?

We will make this a Commission Exhibit No. 369.

(The document referred to was marked Commission Exhibit No. 369 for identification.)

Mr. BALL. That is written in. The arrow marks Billy Lovelady on Commission's Exhibit No. 369.

The CHAIRMAN. Do you have any lockers there in which you put your clothes, and so forth?

Mr. FRAZIER. No, sir; we don't.

(At this point, Representative Ford withdrew from the hearing room.)

Mr. FRAZIER. Some boys hang their jackets up in there in that little domino room where they were going to play dominoes. But here lately, I have been wondering, you know, most of us wear our jackets, what we have on, because if you are going out there on a dock in the cold air we usually keep them on.

The CHAIRMAN. I see.

Mr. BALL. On Thursday afternoon when you went home, drove on home, did he carry any package with him?

Mr. FRAZIER. No, sir; he didn't.

Mr. BALL. Did he have a jacket or coat on him?

Mr. FRAZIER. Yes, sir.

Mr. BALL. What kind of a jacket or coat did he have?

Mr. FRAZIER. That, you know, like I say gray jacket.

Mr. BALL. That same gray jacket?

Mr. FRAZIER. Yes, sir. Now, I can be frank with you. I had seen him wear that jacket several times, because it is cool type like when you keep a jacket on all day, if you are working on outside or something like that, you wouldn't go outside with just a plain shirt on.

Mr. BALL. I have no further questions.

The CHAIRMAN. Senator, have you any questions you would like to ask?

I think that is all.

Does anybody else have any questions to ask? Do you have any questions?

Mr. BALL. Mr. Frazier, we have here this Exhibit No. 364 which is a sack and in that we have put a dismantled gun. Don't pay any attention to that. Will you stand up here and put this under your arm and then take ahold of it at the side?

Now, is that anywhere near similar to the way that Oswald carried the package?

Mr. FRAZIER. Well, you know, like I said now, I said I didn't pay much attention——

Mr. BALL. Turn around.

Mr. FRAZIER. I didn't pay much attention, but when I did, I say, he had this part down here, like the bottom would be short he had cupped in his hand like that and, say, like walking from the back if you had a big arm jacket there you wouldn't tell much from a package back there, the physical features. If you could see it from the front like when you walk and meet somebody you could tell about the package, but walking from behind you couldn't tell much about the package whatsoever about the width. But he didn't carry it from the back. If this package were shorter he would have it cupped in his hands.

The CHAIRMAN. Could he have had the top of it behind his shoulder, or are you sure it was cupped under his shoulder there?

Mr. FRAZIER. Yes; because the way it looked, you know, like I say, he had it cupped in his hand.

The CHAIRMAN. I beg your pardon?

Mr. FRAZIER. I said from where I noticed he had it cupped in his hands. And I don't see how you could have it anywhere other than under your armpit because if you had it cupped in your hand it would stick over it.

Mr. BALL. Could he have carried it this way?

Mr. FRAZIER. No, sir. Never in front here. Like that. Now, that is what I was talking to you about. No, I say he couldn't because if he had you would have seen the package sticking up like that.

From what I seen walking behind he had it under his arm and you couldn't tell that he had a package from the back.

Mr. BALL. When you cupped the bottom of your package in the hands, will you stand up, again, please, and the upper part of the package is not under the armpit, the top of the package extends almost up to the level of your ear.

Mr. FRAZIER. Right.

Mr. BALL. Or your eye level, and when you put the package under your armpit, the upper part of the package, and take a hold of the side of it with your right hand, it extends on approximately about 8 inches, about the span of my hand, more than 8 inches, 8, 10 inches.

Mr. FRAZIER. If you were using a yardstick or one of these little——

Mr. BALL. I was using my hand.

Mr. FRAZIER. I know you were, but there are some different means to measure it. I will say it varies, if you use a yardstick. You can go and measure something with a tape measure, with a yardstick and come up with a different measurement altogether, maybe a quarter of an inch shorter or longer.

Mr. BALL. I was asked, there was some uncertainty in your testimony as to the direction from which you heard the shots fired. Let's see if we can illustrate it.

You heard the shots fired and you expressed an opinion that it came from a certain direction. I would like to clear that up, if I could, on this map.

Here is the Texas School Book Depository Building, and you were standing right here, you said, weren't you? Can you tell me?

Mr. FRAZIER. You know the entrance there is not quite at that corner.

Mr. BALL. That close.

Now, you say you heard these three sounds which you later thought were probably shots, you thought it came from a certain direction.

Can you tell us from what direction as illustrated on the map?

Mr. FRAZIER. Right. Now I say, you know where it is the straight curve that goes under the underpass.

Mr. BALL. That is the parkway?

Mr. FRAZIER. Right. I say it runs over this parkway, you don't have it on here—anyway, I say these railroad tracks there is a series of them that come up over this, up over this overpass there, and from where I was standing, I say, it is my true opinion, that is what I thought, it sounded like it came from over there, in the railroad tracks.

Mr. BALL. That would be east and south?

Mr. FRAZIER. No; that would be west and south.

Mr. BALL. West and south?

Mr. FRAZIER. No; it would be north.

Mr. BALL. No; it wouldn't be north.

Mr. FRAZIER. Yes; it wouldn't be south because that is in that direction.

Mr. BALL. This is north, and you say it, I believe, it came from north?

Mr. FRAZIER. It would be more or less west and north were these tracks from this overpass.

Mr. BALL. Your direction was west and north as the source of the sound.

Well, take a look at the map that does show the overpass and you will put a mark on that.

Did any other people who were standing there with you express any opinion as to where they thought the sounds came from?

Mr. FRAZIER. Well, I say, after we found out it was shots I see some of the other people around there said when they were staying there, said that is what it was, downward right back from us, like where we were standing. If we had been standing somewhere else you might have gotten a different opinion, but from where we were standing on the steps there it sounded like back down to the right.

Mr. BALL. Here is a Commission Exhibit, No. 347. It is an aerial photograph, and it shows the Texas School Book Depository Building.

Mr. FRAZIER. Here is the Depository Building here.

Mr. BALL. That is right, sir. Here is the parkway.

Mr. FRAZIER. Right.

Mr. BALL. Here are the overpasses here.

Can you show us on that map where you think—will that map—can you on that map indicate the general direction from which you thought the sounds came from?

Mr. FRAZIER. Yes, sir; because we were standing right here.

Mr. BALL. Don't mark it up right now.

Mr. FRAZIER. Right. But what I am trying to say is we were standing down there, and back over here, this over here is more or less a knoll, and you can look over there and see this. You see this furthest left line that curved around here is the ones we take to come out on Stemmons Expressway, and this is a high knoll up here which runs where the tracks are, from standing there it sounded like it came from this general area over here.

Mr. BALL. Just mark on that if you can, if you can mark a source.

Mr. FRAZIER. This is where is is.

Mr. BALL. Mark a circle.

Mr. FRAZIER. I would say just like over in here.

Mr. BALL. Let's make it a little heavier. In that general direction?

Mr. FRAZIER. Yes, sir. That was just part of the knoll.

Mr. BALL. The circle marked on No. 347, we will identify it with an "F," the circle marked "F" represents the direction, general direction, of a source of sound as you—as occurred to you as you stood on the front steps of the Texas Book Depository Building, is that right?

Mr. FRAZIER. Right.

Mr. BALL. I have no further questions.

The CHAIRMAN. Anything from you, Senator?

Well, that will be all. Thank you very much for coming and testifying before the Commission.

Mr. FRAZIER. Thank you, Mr. Warren.

The CHAIRMAN. All right, bring in the next witness.

The Commission will be in order.

Mrs. Randle, I will just read you a brief statement of the purpose of our meeting today.

The purpose of today's hearing is to hear the testimony of Buell Wesley Frazier and Linnie Mae Randle. The Commission has been advised that these two witnesses have stated that they saw Lee Harvey Oswald on the morning of November 22, 1963. The Commission proposes to ask these witnessees questions concerning their knowledge of the assassination of President Kennedy.

You have a copy of that, do you not?

Very well, Mr. Ball will conduct the examination.

Will you rise and be sworn, please?

Do you solemnly swear the testimony you give before this Commission will be the truth, the whole truth, and nothing but the truth, so help you God?

Mrs. RANDLE. Yes. sir.

The CHAIRMAN. Please be seated.

Mr. Ball?

TESTIMONY OF LINNIE MAE RANDLE

Mr. BALL. Mrs. Randle, where do you live?

Mrs. RANDLE. 2438 Westfield, Irving, Tex.

Mr. BALL. And you live there with your husband and three daughters, do you?

Mrs. RANDLE. Yes, sir.

Mr. BALL. And your brother?

Mrs. RANDLE. Yes.

Mr. BALL. Wesley?

Mrs. RANDLE. Yes, sir.

Mr. BALL. How long has Wesley been living there?

Mrs. RANDLE. Since September, somewhere around the first. I am not sure just the date.

Mr. BALL. Do you know Mrs. Ruth Paine?

Mrs. RANDLE. She is a neighbor that lives up the street from me.

Mr. BALL. When did you first meet Mrs. Paine?

Mrs. RANDLE. Well, for a period, I am not sure of this, it is quite 2 years, I lived across the street from her. I didn't visit with her, but I visited with her neighbor who lives next door.

Mr. BALL. What is her name?

Mrs. RANDLE. Mrs. Dorothy Roberts.

Mr. BALL. That is on Fifth Street in Irving, Tex.?

Mrs. RANDLE. That is right; yes.

Mr. BALL. That was before you moved down the street to the corner of Westfield and Fifth Street?

Mrs. Randle. Yes, sir.

Mr. Ball. You had never visited in Mrs. Paine's home?

Mrs. Randle. I was in her home on one occasion that I remember at a birthday party for one of her children and she invited mine.

Mr. Ball. How long ago?

Mrs. Randle. It has been about a year ago.

Mr. Ball. That is the only time you have visited Mrs. Paine?

Mrs. Randle. Yes, sir.

Mr. Ball. Did you ever meet Marina Oswald?

Mrs. Randle. Yes, sir; I did.

Mr. Ball. When did you meet her?

Mrs. Randle. The first time I met her was over at this Mrs. Roberts. I had gone up there to see Mrs. Roberts and her. Mrs. Oswald and Mrs. Paine was over there drinking coffee, that was the first time I met her.

Mr. Ball. When was that?

Mrs. Randle. Well, I believe it was the first week in October.

Mr. Ball. That is the first time you had ever met Mrs. Oswald?

Mrs. Randle. Officially met her. I had seen her out in the yard and through the neighbor I knew who she was. I hadn't met her until that time.

Mr. Ball. Did you ever see her again to talk to her, Marina Oswald?

Mrs. Randle. Well, she couldn't speak English. "How are you" and things like that was about all she could say and I did visit with Mrs. Roberts quite often and so she would be out in the yard and she would speak.

Mr. Ball. In whose yards, Mrs. Roberts' yard or Mrs. Paine's?

Mrs. Randle. Mrs. Paine's. She played with her children, and kept the yard and things like that.

Mr. Ball. But on this one occasion she was in the house, Mrs. Roberts' house?

Mrs. Randle. Mrs. Roberts.

Mr. Ball. With Mrs. Paine, Mrs. Roberts and yourself?

Mrs. Randle. That is right.

Mr. Ball. Was there some conversation at that time about her husband Lee Oswald?

Mrs. Randle. Well, they had—it was just general knowledge in the neighborhood that he didn't have a job and she was expecting a baby. Of course, I didn't know where he was or anything. And of course you know just being neighborly and everything, we felt sorry for Marina because her baby was due right away as we understood it, and he didn't have any work, so they said, so it was just——

Mr. Ball. Mrs. Paine told you that Lee didn't have any work?

Mrs. Randle. Well, I suppose. It was just in conversation.

Mr. Ball. Marina didn't take part in the conversation?

Mrs. Randle. No. She couldn't. So far as I know, she couldn't speak.

Mr. Ball. You and Mrs. Roberts and Mrs. Paine talked about it?

Mrs. Randle. Yes.

Mr. Ball. Was there anything said then about the Texas School Book Depository as a place he might get a job?

Mrs. Randle. Well, we didn't say that he might get a job, because I didn't know there was a job open. The reason that we were being helpful, Wesley had just looked for a job, and I had helped him to try to find one. We listed several places that he might go to look for work. When you live in a place you know some places that someone with, you know, not very much of an education can find work.

So, it was among one of the places that we mentioned. We mentioned several others, and Mrs. Paine said that well, he couldn't apply for any of the jobs that would require driving because he couldn't drive, and it was just in conversation that you might talk just any day and not think a thing on earth about it. In fact, I didn't even know that he had even tried any place that we mentioned.

Mr. Ball. What were some of the other places mentioned?

Mrs. Randle. Well, I remember two of them. Mrs. Roberts entered into the conversation and, of course, she is more familiar with the place than I am. It was Manor Bakeries which was a home delivery service.

Then there was this Texas Gypsum which makes sheet rock and things like that, and we mentioned because Wesley had tried those places that I mentioned those.

Mr. BALL. And then you also mentioned the Texas Book Depository?

Mrs. RANDLE. Well, I didn't know there was a job opening over there.

Mr. BALL. But did you mention it?

Mrs. RANDLE. But we said he might try over there. There might be work over there because it was the busy season but I didn't have any previous knowledge that there was any job opening.

Mr. BALL. Did you later learn that Lee had applied for a job?

Mrs. RANDLE. She told me, Mrs. Paine told me, later that he had applied for the job, and had gotten the job and she thanked us for naming the places and things like that.

Mr. BALL. Did you tell your brother that a fellow named Lee Oswald was going to work for them?

Mrs. RANDLE. No, sir; I didn't even know his name. She said Lee so I just assumed that was his last name and I just merely mentioned to Wesley that he had got the job or a job over there.

Mr. BALL. That Lee had the job?

Mrs. RANDLE. That Mrs. Paine said that, I had told Wesley that he might— that she said he was going to call over there.

In fact, Mrs. Paine asked me if I would call and see if there was a job available and I told her, no, that I didn't know anybody over there, and if she wanted to call over the place she would have to do it because I didn't know if there was any job openings over there.

Mr. BALL. You told Wesley, though, that you had—Mrs. Paine had told you that Lee had applied for a job and gotten a job there?

Mrs. RANDLE. Sir, I don't remember if I mentioned it to him or not.

Mr. BALL. When you said a moment ago that you had mentioned something to Wesley?

Mrs. RANDLE. I might have had. But I can't say for sure I did because at the time it was unimportant to me. It didn't really matter.

Mr. BALL. In other words, you are not sure whether you did or didn't?

Mrs. RANDLE. That is right. I might have, I don't know maybe for sure if I did.

Mr. BALL. Did Lee tell you at sometime that he had started to drive?

Mrs. RANDLE. I never talked to Lee.

Mr. BALL. Did Wesley tell you that he was driving Lee home weekends or driving him to Irving weekends?

Mrs. RANDLE. Wesley had told me that he asked to ride out on weekends.

Mr. BALL. Did you ever see him arrive with Lee?

Mrs. RANDLE. Yes, sir.

Mr. BALL. Do you recall on a Thursday night, November 21 that you saw Lee get out of Wesley's car?

Mrs. RANDLE. That is right.

Mr. BALL. About what time of night was it?

Mrs. RANDLE. About 5:20, I believe, 5:15 or 5:25 something like that.

Mr. BALL. Where were you when you saw him?

Mrs. RANDLE. I was on my way to the grocery store.

Mr. BALL. Did you talk to Wesley about the fact that he had brought Lee home on this night?

Mrs. RANDLE. No, sir.

Mr. BALL. Did you think it was unusual that he had come home that night?

Mrs. RANDLE. Well, I knew that he had—Friday is the only time he had ever ridden with him before which was a couple of times, I don't think he rode with him over three times, I am not sure but I never did know of him arriving, you know, except on Friday.

Mr. BALL. Well, did you mention to Wesley that night or did you ask Wesley that night how Lee happened to come home on Thursday?

Mrs. RANDLE. I might have asked him.

Mr. BALL. Do you remember anything about curtain rods?

Mrs. RANDLE. Yes.

247

Mr. BALL. What do you remember about that?

Mrs. RANDLE. He had told Wesley——

Mr. BALL. Tell me what Wesley told you.

Mrs. RANDLE. What Wesley told me. That Lee had rode home with him to get some curtain rods from Mrs. Paine to fix up his apartment.

Mr. BALL. When did Wesley tell you that?

Mrs. RANDLE. Well, that afternoon I suppose I would have had to ask him, he wouldn't have just told me.

Mr. BALL. You mean that night?

Mrs. RANDLE. Yes, sir.

Mr. BALL. After he came home?

Mrs. RANDLE. I was on my way to the store. So I probably asked him when I got back what he was doing riding home with him on Thursday afternoon.

Mr. BALL. You think that was the time that Wesley told you——

Mrs. RANDLE. Yes, sir; after I got back home.

Mr. BALL. That Lee had come home to get some curtain rods?

Mrs. RANDLE. Yes, I am sure he told me that.

Mr. BALL. The next morning did you get breakfast for Wesley, you, and your mother?

Mrs. RANDLE. Yes; mother and my children.

Mr. BALL. And you were packing his lunch, too, were you?

Mrs. RANDLE. Yes, sir.

Mr. BALL. Did you see Lee?

Mrs. RANDLE. Yes, I did.

Mr. BALL. Where did you see him?

Mrs. RANDLE. I saw him as he crossed the street and come across my driveway to where Wesley had his car parked by the carport.

Mr. BALL. What street did he cross to go over?

Mrs. RANDLE. He crossed Westbrook.

Mr. BALL. And you saw him walking along, did you?

Mrs. RANDLE. Yes, sir.

Mr. BALL. Was he carrying any package?

Mrs. RANDLE. Yes; he was.

Mr. BALL. What was he carrying?

Mrs. RANDLE. He was carrying a package in a sort of a heavy brown bag, heavier than a grocery bag it looked to me. It was about, if I might measure, about this long, I suppose, and he carried it in his right hand, had the top sort of folded down and had a grip like this, and the bottom, he carried it this way, you know, and it almost touched the ground as he carried it.

Mr. BALL. Let me see. He carried it in his right hand, did he?

Mrs. RANDLE. That is right.

Mr. BALL. And where was his hand gripping the middle of the package?

Mrs. RANDLE. No, sir; the top with just a little bit sticking up. You know just like you grab something like that.

Mr. BALL. And he was grabbing it with his right hand at the top of the package and the package almost touched the ground?

Mrs. RANDLE. Yes, sir.

Mr. BALL. He walked over to your house, did he?

Mrs. RANDLE. Well, I saw him as he started crossing the street. Where he come from then I couldn't say.

Mr. BALL. You don't know where he went from that?

Mrs. RANDLE. Where he went?

Mr. BALL. Did you see him go to the car?

Mrs. RANDLE. Yes.

Mr. BALL. What did he do?

Mrs. RANDLE. He opened the right back door and I just saw that he was laying the package down so I closed the door. I didn't recognize him as he walked across my carport and I at that moment I wondered who was fixing to come to my back door so I opened the door slightly and saw that it—I assumed he was getting in the car but he didn't, so he come back and stood on the driveway.

Mr. BALL. He put the package in the car.

Mrs. RANDLE. Yes, sir; I don't know if he put it on the seat or on the floor but I just know he put it in the back.

Mr. BALL. We have got a package here which is marked Commission Exhibit No. 364. You have seen this before. I guess, haven't you, I think the FBI showed it to you?

Mrs. RANDLE. Yes, sir.

Mr. BALL. Was the color of that package in any way similar to the color of this package which is 364?

Mrs. RANDLE. Yes, sir.

Mr. BALL. Similar kind of paper, wasn't it?

Mrs. RANDLE. Yes, sir.

Mr. BALL. Now, was the length of it any similar, anywhere near similar?

Mrs. RANDLE. Well, it wasn't that long, I mean it was folded down at the top as I told you. It definitely wasn't that long.

Mr. BALL. How about the width?

Mrs. RANDLE. The width is about right.

Mr. BALL. The width is about right.

Can you stand up here and show us how he was carrying it. Using this package as an example only?

Mrs. RANDLE. What he had in there, it looked too long.

Mr. BALL. This looks too long?

Mrs. RANDLE. Yes, sir.

Mr. BALL. About how long would you think the package would be, just measure it right on there.

Mrs. RANDLE. I would say about like this.

Mr. BALL. You mean from here to here?

Mrs. RANDLE. Yes, sir; with that folded down with this much for him to grip in his hand.

Mr. BALL. This package is about the span of my hand, say 8 inches, is that right? He would have about this much to grip?

Mrs. RANDLE. What I remember seeing is about this long, sir, as I told you it was folded down so it could have been this long.

Mr. BALL. I see. You figure about 2 feet long, is that right?

Mrs. RANDLE. A little bit more.

Mr. BALL. A little more than 2 feet.

There is another package here. You remember this was shown you. It is a discolored bag, which is Exhibit No. 142, and remember you were asked by the Federal Bureau of Investigation agents if this looked like the package; do you remember?

Mrs. RANDLE. Yes, sir.

Mr. BALL. Now, first of all with color, you told them the bag was not the color?

Mrs. RANDLE. Yes.

Mr. BALL. But they showed you a part of the bag that had not been discolored, didn't they?

Mrs. RANDLE. Yes, sir.

Mr. BALL. Looking at this part of the bag which has not been discolored does that appear similar to the color of the bag you saw Lee carrying that morning?

Mrs. RANDLE. Yes; it is a heavy type of wrapping paper.

Mr. BALL. Now, with reference to the width of this bag, does that look about the width of the bag that he was carrying?

Mrs. RANDLE. I would say so; yes, sir.

Mr. BALL. What about length?

Mrs. RANDLE. You mean the entire bag?

Mr. BALL. Yes.

Mrs. RANDLE. There again you have the problem of all this down here. It was folded down, of course, if you would take it from the bottom——

Mr. BALL. Fold it to about the size that you think it might be.

Mrs. RANDLE. This is the bottom here, right. This is the bottom, this part down here.

Mr. BALL. I believe so, but I am not sure. But let's say it is.

Mrs. RANDLE. And this goes this way, right? Do you want me to hold it?

Mr. BALL. Yes.

Mrs. RANDLE. About this.

Mr. BALL Is that about right? That is 28½ inches.

Mrs. RANDLE. I measured 27 last time.

Mr. BALL. You measured 27 once before?

Mrs. RANDLE. Yes, sir.

Mr. BALL. How was Lee dressed that morning?

Mrs. RANDLE. He had on a white T-shirt, I just saw him from the waist up, I didn't pay any attention to his pants or anything, when he was going with the package. I was more interested in that. But he had on a white T-shirt and I remember some sort of brown or tan shirt and he had a gray jacket, I believe.

Mr. BALL. A gray jacket. I will show you some clothing here. First, I will show you a gray jacket. Does this look anything like the jacket he had on?

Mrs. RANDLE. Yes, sir.

Mr. BALL. That morning?

Mrs. RANDLE. Similar to that. I didn't pay an awful lot of attention to it.

Mr. BALL. Was it similar in color?

Mrs. RANDLE. Yes, sir; I think so. It had big sleeves.

Mr. BALL. Take a look at these sleeves. Was it similar in color?

Mrs. RANDLE. I believe so.

Mr. BALL. What is the Commission Exhibit on this jacket?

Mrs. RANDLE. It was gray, I am not sure of the shade.

Mr. BALL. 163.

I will show you another shirt which is Commission No. 150.

Does this look anything like the shirt he had on?

Mrs. RANDLE. Well now, I don't remember it being that shade of brown. It could have been but I was looking through the screen and out the window but I don't remember it being exactly that. I thought it was a solid color.

Mr. BALL. Here is another jacket which is a gray jacket, does this look anything like the jacket he had on?

Mrs. RANDLE. No, sir; I remember its being gray.

Mr. BALL. Well, this one is gray but of these two the jacket I last showed you is Commission Exhibit No. 162, and this blue gray is 163, now if you had to choose between these two?

Mrs. RANDLE. I would choose the dark one.

Mr. BALL. You would choose the dark one?

Mrs. RANDLE. Yes, sir.

Mr. BALL. Which is 163, as being more similar to the jacket he had?

Mrs. RANDLE. Yes, sir; that I remember. But I, you know, didn't pay an awful lot of attention to his jacket. I remember his T-shirt and the shirt more so than I do the jacket.

Mr. BALL. The witness just stated that 163 which is the gray-blue is similar to the jacket he had on. 162, the light gray jacket was not.

Mrs. RANDLE. Yes.

Mr. BALL. I have no further questions.

The CHAIRMAN. Senator, have you any questions?

Senator COOPER. No questions.

The CHAIRMAN. Have you any questions, Mr. Powell?

Mr. POWELL. No, sir.

Senator COOPER. I think I do have one.

Prior to the assassination of President Kennedy, did any FBI agents or police officer ever visit your house?

Mrs. RANDLE. No, sir.

Senator COOPER. And said anything to you about Lee Oswald?

Mrs. RANDLE. No, sir.

Mr. JENNER. Could I ask, Mr. Chief Justice, along the line Senator Cooper touched on—whether there had been any conversation in the neighborhood prior to the assassination of any FBI agents or police officers having visited in the neighborhood?

Mrs. RANDLE. No, sir.

Mr. JENNER. You heard nothing along rumors of that kind?

Mrs. RANDLE. No. Later, after all this was over, I had heard that they had been to Mrs. Paine's residence.

Mr. JENNER. But there was no excitement in the neighborhood up to that point?

Mrs. RANDLE. No, sir.

Mr. BALL. I have one question, Mr. Chief Justice.

You used an expression there, that the bag appeared heavy.

Mrs. RANDLE. Yes, sir.

Mr. BALL. You meant that there was some weight appeared to be——

Mrs. RANDLE. To the bottom.

Mr. BALL. To the bottom?

Mrs. RANDLE. Yes. It tapered like this as he hugged it in his hand. It was more bulky toward the bottom than it was this way.

Mr. BELIN. Toward the top? More bulky toward the bottom than toward the top?

Mrs. RANDLE. That is right.

Mr. BALL. I have no further questions.

Senator COOPER. On that point—did you see Lee Oswald place the package in the automobile?

Mrs. RANDLE. In the automobile. I do not know if he put it on the seat or on the floor.

Senator COOPER. I mean did you see him throw open the door?

Mrs. RANDLE. Yes, sir.

Senator COOPER. When he placed the package in there do you remember whether he used one hand or two?

Mrs. RANDLE. No; because I only opened the door briefly and what made me establish the door on Wesley's car, it is an old car and that door, the window is broken and everything and it is hard to close, so that cinched in my mind which door it was, too. But it was only briefly that I looked.

Mr. JENNER. Mr. Chief Justice, could I ask—how far away were you? You were at the kitchen door and the automobile was in the driveway, what was the distance between yourself and Mr. Oswald?

Mrs. RANDLE. Sir, I don't know. The carport will take care of two cars, and then Wesley's car was on the other side of the carport so that would be three car lengths plus inbetween space.

Mr. JENNER. Car widths?

Mrs. RANDLE. Car widths, excuse me.

Mr. JENNER. Was it a light day?

Mrs. RANDLE. It was sort of cloudy, but there wasn't any—I mean it wasn't dark or anything like that.

Mr. JENNER. Would you be good enough as you can recall—can you recall what the fabric of the jacket was that Mr. Oswald had on this morning, was it twill or wool or gabardine? Cotton?

Mr. RANDLE. Probably cotton or gabardine, something like that that would repel water probably, and that is just my own opinion.

Mr. JENNER. That is your present recollection?

Mrs. RANDLE. Yes, sir.

Mr. JENNER. Thank you.

The CHAIRMAN. Mrs. Randle, thank you very much for coming, you may be excused.

TESTIMONY OF CORTLANDT CUNNINGHAM

Mr. BALL. Will you state your name for the record?

Mr. CUNNINGHAM. Cortlandt Cunningham.

The CHAIRMAN. Mr. Cunningham, will you raise your right hand and be sworn, please?

Do you solemnly swear the testimony given before this Commission will be the truth, the whole truth, and nothing but the truth, so help you God?

Mr. CUNNINGHAM. I do.

Mr. BALL. Mr. Cunningham, be seated there.

What is your business?

Mr. CUNNINGHAM. I am a special agent of the FBI.

Mr. BALL. What is your specialty with the FBI?

Mr. CUNNINGHAM. I am assigned to the FBI laboratory in the Firearms Identification Unit.

Mr. BALL. There is a rifle here that has been identified as Commission Exhibit No. 139, it has been in your custody, hasn't it?

Mr. CUNNINGHAM. It has.

Mr. BALL. You brought it over here this morning?

Mr. CUNNINGHAM. I did.

Mr. BALL. And I requested you disassemble it?

Mr. CUNNINGHAM. I did.

Mr. BALL. Let's take it out of the sack and put it before the Commission. Do you need any special tools to assemble this rifle?

Mr. CUNNINGHAM. No, sir.

Mr. BALL. I notice you have a screwdriver there. Can you assemble it without the use of a screwdriver?

Mr. CUNNINGHAM. Yes, sir.

Mr. BALL. What can you use?

Mr. CUNNINGHAM. Any object that would fit the slots on the five screws that retain the stock to the action.

Mr. BALL. Could you do it with a 10-cent piece?

Mr. CUNNINGHAM. Yes, sir.

Mr. BALL. Will you do that—about how long will it take you?

Mr. CUNNINGHAM. I know I can do it, but I have never been timed as far as using a dime. I have been timed using a screwdriver, which required a little over 2 minutes.

Mr. BALL. 2 minutes with a screwdriver.

Try it with the dime and let's see how long it takes.

Okay. Start now. Six minutes.

Mr. CUNNINGHAM. I think I can improve on that.

Mr. BALL. And the only tool you used was a 10-cent piece?

Mr. CUNNINGHAM. That is correct.

Mr. BALL. That is all.

Senator COOPER. Does the bolt work all right now?

Mr. CUNNINGHAM. Once in a while with regard to the top portion—namely the retaining screw and the top stock—you have trouble getting them engaged on this particular model.

The CHAIRMAN. Yes.

Mr. CUNNINGHAM. That is the case on this weapon. On that one over there, however, it slid right on when I put it together a little while ago; it was much faster.

The CHAIRMAN. Yes. This is a weapon identical to the one that has been identified as the assassination weapon?

Mr. CUNNINGHAM. This is the assassination weapon.

Mr. BALL. This is the weapon found on the sixth floor of the Texas Book Depository.

The CHAIRMAN. May I ask, have you fired it?

Mr. CUNNINGHAM. Many times.

The CHAIRMAN. That has been fired many times?

Mr. BELIN. You can disassemble it in a lesser amount of time, I assume.

Mr. CUNNINGHAM. Definitely, it comes apart much faster. I can do it for you.

The CHAIRMAN. I understand with a screwdriver you put the rifle together in 2 minutes.

Mr. CUNNINGHAM. Yes, sir; a few seconds over 2 minutes, somewhere around 2¼, 2½ minutes, readily.

The CHAIRMAN. Yes.

Mr. CUNNINGHAM. And I am sure I can assemble it faster the second time with a dime than I did the last time but I did have trouble with that one retaining screw.

The CHAIRMAN. Is there anything more you have on this?

Mr. BALL. No.

The CHAIRMAN. Anybody?

Well, Agent Cunningham, thank you very much, sir.

Mr. CUNNINGHAM. Thank you, sir.

The CHAIRMAN. Gentlemen, if there are no further witnesses today, we will adjourn for the day, and we will meet tomorrow morning at 9 o'clock for the purpose of taking further testimony.

(Whereupon, at 12:45 p.m., the President's Commission recessed.)

Thursday, March 12, 1964

TESTIMONY OF WILLIAM WAYNE WHALEY AND CECIL J. McWATTERS

The President's Commission met at 9:20 a.m. on March 12, 1964, 200 Maryland Avenue NE., Washington, D.C.

Present were Chief Justice Earl Warren, Chairman; Senator John Cooper and Representative Gerald R. Ford, members.

Also present were J. Lee Rankin, general counsel; Joseph A. Ball, assistant counsel; David W. Belin, assistant counsel; Melvin Aron Eisenberg, assistant counsel; Lewis F. Powell, Jr. and Charles Murray, observers.

TESTIMONY OF WILLIAM WAYNE WHALEY

The CHAIRMAN. Mr. Whaley, the purpose of our meeting today is to take some further testimony concerning the events surrounding the assassination of President Kennedy, and we understand you have some facts that will bear on it in a way and we would like to ask you questions concerning it.

Will you rise, please, raise your right hand to be sworn?

Do you solemnly swear to tell the truth, the whole truth and nothing but the truth, so help you God?

Mr. WHALEY. I do, sir.

The CHAIRMAN. Will you be seated, please? Mr. Ball will conduct the examination.

Mr. BALL. Mr. Whaley, what is your business?

Mr. WHALEY. I am a taxi driver, sir.

Mr. BALL. How long have you been a taxi driver?

Mr. WHALEY. 37 years.

Mr. BALL. You worked all that time in Dallas?

Mr. WHALEY. Yes, sir.

Mr. BALL. What is your residence?

Mr. WHALEY. 619 Pine Street, Route 2, Louisville, Tex., 26 miles north of Dallas.

Mr. BALL. But you drive a taxicab in Dallas?

Mr. WHALEY. Yes, sir.

Mr. BALL. Whom do you work for?

Mr. WHALEY. City Transportation Company.

Mr. BALL. You are an employee of theirs, are you?

Mr. WHALEY. Yes.

Mr. BALL. You don't own your own cab?

Mr. WHALEY. No, sir; they don't allow that in that city.

Mr. BALL. How long have you worked for that company?

Mr. WHALEY. 37 years. Not for that company, sir, but for the original owners, it started out. I have been in with that original company but all banded together in one cab company.

Mr. BALL. Were you on duty on the 22d of November 1963?

Mr. WHALEY. Yes, sir.

Mr. BALL. What were your hours that day at work?

Mr. WHALEY. Well, my hours run from 6 to 4, sir; 6 in the morning to 4 in the afternoon.

Mr. BALL. What kind of a cab were you driving on that day?

Mr. WHALEY. A 1961 Checker.

Mr. BALL. Was it equipped with radio equipment?

Mr. WHALEY. Yes, sir.

Mr. BALL. You can call in to your dispatcher?

Mr. WHALEY. Yes, sir; I can.

Mr. BALL. By a two-way radio?

Mr. WHALEY. Yes, sir.

Mr. BALL. Do you operate on cab stands or do you cruise?

Mr. WHALEY. No, sir; you just go out in the morning and wherever they send you you go to work and wherever you unload you check in they give you another call like that.

Mr. BALL. About 12:30 that day where were you?

Mr. WHALEY. Well, about 12:30 as you say, sir; I was at the Greyhound bus station. I have a copy of my trip sheet here.

Mr. BALL. Could I see that, please?

Mr. WHALEY. The FBI took the original and the pictures of the cab and everything.

Mr. BALL. That is what I have been waiting for.

Mr. WHALEY. I think it is supposed to be delivered to you, sir.

Mr. BALL. That is right. I am glad you have that copy.

Mr. WHALEY. I thought maybe you might need it. You look down there it says Greyhound, 500 North Beckley, I think it is marked 12:30 to 12:45. Now that could have been 10 minutes off in each direction because I didn't use a watch, I just guess, in other words, all my trips are marked about 15 minutes each.

Mr. BALL. I am going to let you use this manifest to refresh your memory, Mr. Whaley. I have seen it. I am going to ask you some questions and you refresh your memory if you will from the manifest.

First of all, describe the document you are using, what is that?

Mr. WHALEY. It is a trip sheet manifest. The company gets the amount of money you have run, your meter reading and all, and they have to keep it because of the city ordinance requirement that the taxis make this kind of manifest.

Mr. BALL. Tell me when you make the entries, you make the entries when?

Mr. WHALEY. Sometimes I make them right after I make the trips, sir, and sometimes I make three or four trips before I make the entries.

Mr. BALL. Are you required by your employer to describe the trip, where you went, how far it was?

Mr. WHALEY. Not by the employer, sir. All the employers are interested in are the meter reading and your tolls. The city of Dallas ordinance requires that you put down where you picked the passenger up, where you unload the passenger. They are not interested in the price, the number of passengers and the time.

Mr. BALL. Now, the manifest does contain that information, though, does it?

Mr. WHALEY. Yes, sir; it does.

Mr. BALL. Will you describe the different columns of the manifest, that information that is in each column generally?

Mr. WHALEY. Over on the left side, where you see call or pickup, if you get the call on your radio you mark with a "C" and if somebody hails you on the street that is marked "P" for pickup.

In the next column it has the trip numbers from one to fifty.

Mr. BALL. The number of the trips you make that day?

Mr. WHALEY. Yes, sir. In the third column it says "from." Like this first one, 4924 Belmont and then to the next column, to the airport.

The next column is the "meter reading," what the metter said, $1.75. The next column says "flat rate." If it had been an extra passenger or so and you had a flat rate you would put it in that column.

The third column is "charge," the people who have the charge accounts through the company in the car, you put the meter reading in there because you don't get cash and you put charge, the company takes it off.

The next column says the number of passengers and that first trip was four passengers, time out six o'clock, I got that trip out of the barn and it is marked "call."

6:20 is "time in." "Mileage in" was 44. Now, see I didn't put the mileage out on the first one, the mileage out is up here, 35 to 44. It would have been nine miles I made on the first trip.

Over here on the side here, it has the number of trips I made that day which is 21, on the meter registered 21 trips 45 cents a trip is $9.45. 157 units, a unit is a dime clicks every four-tenths of a mile. That would be 157 units at $15.70. Added total of $25.15. I used 5½ gallons of gas, had eight pickups in 13 calls and 29 passengers. That is it complete, sir.

Mr. BALL. I see.

Now, look at your manifest and tell me where you were at 12 o'clock the day of November 22, 1963.

Mr. WHALEY. 12 o'clock I got a call to the Travis Hotel. I have got it marked 16 which is the Continental bus station, stand No. 15. 55 cents. I unloaded that at 12:15.

Mr. BALL. Then where did you go at 12:15 according to you record?

Mr. WHALEY. According to my record I got a pickup at the Continental bus station which is stand 16 and went to the Greyhound which is 55 cents. I unloaded at the Greyhound. I have got it marked 12:30. See there is that 15 minutes you say I am off, I just mark it 15, I don't put the correct time on the sheet because they don't require it, sir, but anywhere approximate.

Mr. BALL. In other words, it took you about 15 minutes to go——

Mr. WHALEY. It actually took about nine minutes, sir.

Mr. BALL. And you put the trip ending Greyhound around 12:30?

Mr. WHALEY. Yes, sir.

Mr. BALL. You remember that trip, do you, you remember the fact that you took the trip to the Greyhound and parked your car at the Greyhound or your cab at the Greyhound, don't you?

Mr. WHALEY. Yes, sir; I remember it.

Mr. BALL. Were you standing at the Greyhound, at your cab stand at the Greyhound, long before you picked up another passenger?

Mr. WHALEY. No, sir, there was no one at the Greyhound stand and when I unloaded at the door I just pulled up about 30 feet to the stand and stopped and then I wanted a package of cigarettes, I was out so I started to get out and I saw this passenger coming so I waited for him.

Mr. BALL. He was coming down the street?

Mr. WHALEY. He was walking down the street.

Mr. BALL. What street was he walking down?

Mr. WHALEY. Lamar.

Mr. BALL. Would that mean he was walking south on Lamar?

Mr. WHALEY. He was walking south on Lamar from Commerce when I saw him.

Mr. BALL. That would be on which side of the street?

Mr. WHALEY. The west side of the street.

Mr. BALL. South on Lamar?

Mr. WHALEY. Yes, sir.

Mr. BALL. Did you notice how he was dressed?

Mr. WHALEY. Yes, sir. I didn't pay much attention to it right then. But it all came back when I really found out who I had. He was dressed in just ordinary work clothes. It wasn't khaki pants but they were khaki material, blue faded blue color, like a blue uniform made in khaki. Then he had on a brown shirt with a little silverlike stripe on it and he had on some kind of jacket, I didn't notice very close but I think it was a work jacket that almost matched the pants.

He, his shirt was open three buttons down here. He had on a T-shirt. You know, the shirt was open three buttons down there.

Mr. BALL. Now, what happened after that, will you tell us in your own words what he did?

Mr. WHALEY. Well, on this which was the 14th trip when I picked up at the Greyhound I marked it 12:30 to 12:45.

Mr. BALL. You say that can be off 15 minutes?

Mr. WHALEY. That can be off either direction.

Mr. BALL. Anything up to 15 minutes, you say?

Mr. WHALEY. Yes, sir; I wrote that trip up the same time I wrote the one up from the Continental bus station to the Greyhound, I marked this 12:15 to 12:30 and started 12:30 to 12:45. And the next one starts at 1:15 to 1:30 and it goes on all day long every 15 minutes the time keeps pretty approximate.

Mr. BALL. Let's take the 12:30 trip, tell me about that, what the passenger said.

Mr. WHALEY. He said, "May I have the cab?"

I said, "You sure can. Get in." And instead of opening the back door he opened the front door, which is allowable there, and got in.

Mr. BALL. Got in the front door?

Mr. WHALEY. Yes, sir. The front seat. And about that time an old lady, I think she was an old lady, I don't remember nothing but her sticking her head down past him in the door and said, "Driver, will you call me a cab down here?"

She had seen him get this cab and she wanted one, too, and he opened the door a little bit like he was going to get out and he said, "I will let you have this one," and she says, "No, the driver can call me one."

So, I didn't call one because I knew before I could call one one would come around the block and keep it pretty well covered.

Mr. BALL. Is that what you said?

Mr. WHALEY. No, sir; that is not what I said, but that is the reason I didn't call one at the time and I asked him where he wanted to go. And he said, "500 North Beckley."

Well, I started up, I started to that address, and the police cars, the sirens was going, running crisscrossing everywhere, just a big uproar in that end of town and I said, "What the hell. I wonder what the hell is the uproar?"

And he never said anything. So I figured he was one of these people that don't like to talk so I never said any more to him.

But when I got pretty close to 500 block at Neches and North Beckley which is the 500 block, he said, "This will do fine," and I pulled over to the curb right there. He gave me a dollar bill, the trip was 95 cents. He gave me a dollar bill and didn't say anything, just got out and closed the door and walked around the front of the cab over to the other side of the street. Of course, traffic was moving through there and I put it in gear and moved on, that is the last I saw of him.

Mr. BALL. When you parked your car you parked on what street?

Mr. WHALEY. I wasn't parked, I was pulled to the curb on Neches and North Beckley.

Mr. BALL. Neches, corner of Neches and North Beckley?

Mr. WHALEY. Which is the 500 block.

Mr. BALL. What direction was your car?

Mr. WHALEY. South.

Mr. BALL. The cab was headed?

Mr. WHALEY. South.

Mr. BALL. And it would be on the west side of the street?

Mr. WHALEY. Parked, stopped on the west side of the intersection, yes, sir.

Mr. BALL. When he got out of the cab did he go around in front of your cab?

Mr. WHALEY. He went around in front, yes, sir; crossed the street.

Mr. BALL. Across to the east side of the street?

Mr. WHALEY. Yes, sir.

Mr. BALL. Did you see whether he walked south?

Mr. WHALEY. I didn't see whether he walked north or south from there.

Mr. BALL. In other words, he walked east from your cab and that is the last time you saw him?

Mr. WHALEY. Yes, sir.

Mr. BALL. Was there anything in particular about him beside his clothing that you could identify such as jewelry, bracelets?

Mr. WHALEY. Yes, sir; he had on a bracelet of some type on his left arm. It looked like an identification bracelet. Just shiny, you know, how you see anything shiny, an unusual watchband or something shiny, you notice things like that.

Mr. BALL. I have a map of Dallas here, which I would like to have marked as the Commission's next exhibit which is Exhibit No. 371.

The CHAIRMAN. It will be so marked.

(The map referred to was marked Commission's Exhibit No. 371 for identification.)

Mr. BALL. I would like to offer into evidence Exhibits Nos. 368 and 369 that were marked yesterday.

The CHAIRMAN. They may be admitted.

(Commission Exhibits Nos. 368 and 369, heretofore marked for identification, were received in evidence.)

Mr. BALL. And 371 being a form map of Dallas can probably be offered in evidence at this time. It is going to be used to illustrate the witness' testimony.

The CHAIRMAN. That may be done.

(Commission Exhibit No. 371, heretofore marked for identification was received in evidence.)

Mr. BALL. There is a map here which is described as Dallas street map, Republic National Bank of Dallas, and in one corner of this map there is shown a small map of downtown Dallas.

Will you point on the map there to the Greyhound bus station?

Let's take the small map. It was on the corner of Jackson?

Mr. WHALEY. And Lamar.

Mr. BALL. And Lamar.

Mr. WHALEY. The northwest corner, Greyhound bus station.

Mr. BALL. You have seen this map before, have you not?

Mr. WHALEY. Yes, sir; I am very familiar with that map.

Mr. BALL. And let's take Lamar, here is Jackson.

Mr. WHALEY. Lamar is down here, sir.

Mr. BALL. This is Jackson, this is the Houston viaduct.

Mr. WHALEY. Yes, sir.

Mr. BALL. Here is Jackson, and Lamar is right there.

Mr. WHALEY. Well, the Greyhound bus station is on the northwest corner.

Mr. BALL. Suppose we make an "X" there at Jackson.

Mr. WHALEY. All right, sir.

Mr. BALL. And Lamar. That is where you picked your passenger up?

Mr. WHALEY. Yes, sir.

Mr. BALL. When you started out which direction did you go, and before you mark just take this blunt end and then we will mark it after you describe it on the map.

Now, the next street is Austin, just to the west of Lamar?

Mr. WHALEY. That is right.

Mr. BALL. All right.

Mr. WHALEY. I turned to the left.

Mr. BALL. All right.

Mr. WHALEY. I turned to the left off Lamar onto Jackson, went one block to Austin, then from Austin I turned to the left again and went one block over to Wood Street.

Now, the reason for that is if you catch this light right at Lamar and Jackson, this other light turns green as you make your turn here and the other one turns green as you make your turn at Wood. You just move through traffic. That was my reason for making the turn.

Then I turned left on Wood off Austin and went straight on down Wood to Houston which is the street which we call the old viaduct.

Mr. BALL. You call that the Houston Street viaduct?

Mr. WHALEY. Yes.

(At this point Representative Ford entered the hearing room.)

Mr. WHALEY. Went across the viaduct to Zangs, as soon as you get across the angle to the left, that is Zangs Boulevard.

Mr. BALL. Take the black pen and draw your course along this small map as far as you can go and we will go to the continuation of the map.

Now, can you tell us—did everybody see this course—now can you tell us

257

where you were when the sirens were blowing and you saw police cars all around?

Mr. WHALEY. I was still at the Greyhound, sir.

Mr. BALL. You were still there?

Mr. WHALEY. They were there when I loaded.

Mr. BALL. Now, in the course of your travel down to the Houston viaduct did you see any police cars?

Mr. WHALEY. Oh, yes, sir; lots of them, what we call triangle, three-wheeled motorcycle, they all seemed to be converging on one spot.

Mr. BALL. What spot?

Mr. WHALEY. Well, it seemed to be the courthouse, that is what it seemed to me at that time. I didn't know what had happened.

Mr. BALL. The courthouse is about a block from the Texas State Book Depository?

Mr. WHALEY. You could throw a baseball from one building to the other.

Mr. BALL. Now we will turn to the large map and we will still use the—get downtown. Here we are. Will you use—Lamar and Jackson again.

Mr. WHALEY. This will be kind of ticklish because that is very small.

Mr. BALL. That is right.

Mr. WHALEY. Main, Commerce, Jackson, Lamar.

Mr. BALL. Do the same thing.

Mr. WHALEY. To Austin, to Wood, to Houston, to the viaduct, across the viaduct, let's see, Colorado comes in off this, this is the Zangs Boulevard, the red line where it hits Marcel is here, that is Zangs Boulevard. Up past Colorado, still going Zangs here.

Mr. BALL. You are going along Zangs, will you go along——

Mr. WHALEY. I am trying to find Beckley, the green light changed from red to green on Beckley, right here is an intersection; Zangs Boulevard goes on up, and Beckley turns off.

Mr. BALL. Here is Neches right here.

Mr. WHALEY. Let me see where Neches is, is that right? Yes, that is it. This is the intersection right there.

Mr. BALL. We put an "X" there.

Mr. WHALEY. That is where he got off.

Mr. BALL. That is where you dropped your passenger, is that right?

Mr. WHALEY. That is—as far as I can see that is Neches.

Mr. BALL. That is Neches, that is Beckley.

Mr. WHALEY. Yes, sir; that is right, because that is the 500 block of North Beckley.

Mr. BALL. Now, we will mark the beginning of your trip on the large map as "Y", and where you dropped your passenger as an "X".

Mr. WHALEY. Yes, sir.

Mr. BALL. "Y" is the corner of Lamar and Jackson, and "X" is the corner of Neches and Beckley.

Mr. WHALEY. Yes, sir.

Mr. BALL. O.K.

Can you tell me what distance that was?

Mr. WHALEY. Well, it was 95 cents on the meter, the meter starts off at 45 cents, then it goes four-tenths of a mile and it clicks a dime which would be 55, then a dime every four-tenths of a mile after that and it was almost ready to click a $1.05 when it stopped, so I imagine that would be 55 cents, would be eight-tenths of a mile and then after the first 45 cents it runs 25 cents a mile, because it gets a dime every four-tenths.

Mr. BALL. So you had 95 cents?

Mr. WHALEY. 65 cents would be three, four-tenths, would be 1 mile and two-tenths. 75 would be one mile and six-tenths. 85 would be one—would be 2 miles. 95 would be 2 and four-tenths, almost ready to click.

Mr. BALL. What do you give them for 45 cents?

Mr. WHALEY. Four-tenths of a mile.

Mr. BALL. Four-tenths of a mile?

Mr. WHALEY. It goes four-tenths of a mile.

Mr. BALL. Five clicks after the first?

258

Mr. WHALEY. 45 cents.

Mr. BALL. Well, then, you ran about——

Mr. WHALEY. About 2½ miles, sir.

Mr. BALL. Two and one-half miles?

Mr. WHALEY. Approximately.

Mr. BALL. Two miles and four-tenths approximately.

Mr. WHALEY. Yes, sir.

Mr. BALL. Can you give me any estimate of the time it took you to go that 2½ miles?

Mr. WHALEY. Not actually, sir. I run it again with the policeman because the policeman was worried, he run the same trip and he couldn't come out the same time I did. But he was turning off of Jackson and Lamar when the light was wrong, and he was hitting a red light at Wood—I mean at Austin and Jackson and he hit a red light at Wood and Austin, then he hit a red light at Houston. Where I wait to make my turn until the light is right just after it has been green, almost ready for it to come red, turn right then, then the other lights turn green just as fast as you get to them, go on right through, you save about 2 minutes in traffic that way. That is where I got the 2 minutes on him he never could make up. So I had to go back with him to make that trip to to show him I was right.

Mr. BALL. How much time, in that experiment, when you hit the lights right, how long did it take you?

Mr. WHALEY. Nine minutes.

Mr. BALL. Nine minutes?

Mr. WHALEY. Nine minutes.

Representative FORD. Now on this particular trip with Oswald, do you recall the lights being with you?

Mr. WHALEY. They were with me, sir; for I timed them that way before I took off. Because I made that so much that I know the light system and how they are going to turn.

Representative FORD. So this was a typical trip?

Mr. WHALEY. Yes, sir.

The CHAIRMAN. The witness has been driving a taxicab in Dallas for 36 years.

Mr. WHALEY. Thirty-seven, sir.

The CHAIRMAN. Thirty-seven.

Mr. WHALEY. You name an intersection in the city of Dallas and I will tell you what is on all four corners.

Mr. BALL. Did you stop and let your passenger out on this run on the north or south side of the intersection?

Mr. WHALEY. On the north side, sir.

Mr. BALL. North side?

Mr. WHALEY. Yes.

Mr. BALL. That would be——

Mr. WHALEY. Northwest corner.

Mr. BALL. Northwest corner of Neches and Beckley?

Mr. WHALEY. Northwest corner of Neches and Beckley.

Mr. BALL. I have some clothing here. Commission Exhibit No. 150, does that look like the shirt?

Mr. WHALEY. That is the shirt, sir, it has my initials on it.

Mr. BALL. In other words, this is the shirt the man had on?

Mr. WHALEY. Yes, sir; that is the same one the FBI man had me identify.

Mr. BALL. This is the shirt the man had on who took your car at Lamar and Jackson?

Mr. WHALEY. As near as I can recollect as I told him. I said that is the shirt he had on because it had a kind of little stripe in it, light-colored stripe. I noticed that.

Mr. BALL. Here are two pair of pants, Commission Exhibit No. 157 and Commission Exhibit No. 156. Does it look anything like that?

Mr. WHALEY. I don't think I can identify the pants except they were the same color as that, sir.

Mr. BALL. Which color?

Mr. WHALEY. More like this lighter color, at least they were cleaner or something.

Mr. BALL. That is 157?

Mr. WHALEY. Yes, sir.

Mr. BALL. But you are not sure about that?

Mr. WHALEY. I am not sure about the pants. I wouldn't be sure of the shirt if it hadn't had that light stripe in it. I just noticed that.

Mr. BALL. Here is Commission No. 162 which is a gray jacket with zipper.

Mr. WHALEY. I think that is the jacket he had on when he rode with me in the cab.

Mr. BALL. Look something like it?

And here is Commission Exhibit No. 163, does this look like anything he had on?

Mr. WHALEY. He had this one on or the other one.

Mr. BALL. That is right.

Mr. WHALEY. That is what I told you I noticed. I told you about the shirt being open, he had on the two jackets with the open shirt.

Mr. BALL. Wait a minute, we have got the shirt which you have identified as the rust brown shirt with the gold stripe in it.

Mr. WHALEY. Yes, sir.

Mr. BALL. You said that a jacket——

Mr. WHALEY. That jacket now it might have been clean, but the jacket he had on looked more the color, you know like a uniform set, but he had this coat here on over that other jacket, I am sure, sir.

Mr. BALL. This is the blue-gray jacket, heavy blue-gray jacket.

Mr. WHALEY. Yes, sir.

Mr. BALL. Later that day did you—were you called down to the police department?

Mr. WHALEY. No, sir.

Mr. BALL. Were you the next day?

Mr. WHALEY. No, sir; they came and got me, sir, the next day after I told my superior when I saw in the paper his picture, I told my superiors that that had been my passenger that day at noon. They called up the police and they came up and got me.

Mr. BALL. When you saw in the newspaper the picture of the man?

Mr. WHALEY. Yes, sir.

Mr. BALL. You went to your superior and told him you thought he was your passenger?

Mr. WHALEY. Yes, sir.

Mr. BALL. Did the Dallas police come out to see you?

Mr. WHALEY. Yes, sir.

Mr. BALL. Or FBI agents?

Mr. WHALEY. The Dallas police came down and took me down and the FBI was waiting there.

Mr. BALL. Before they brought you down did they show you a picture?

Mr. WHALEY. No, sir.

Mr. BALL. They didn't?

Mr. WHALEY. No, sir.

Mr. BALL. They brought you down to the Dallas police station?

Mr. WHALEY. Yes, sir.

Mr. BALL. What did you do there?

Mr. WHALEY. Well, I tried to get by the reporters, stepping over television cables and you couldn't hardly get by, they would grab you and wanted to know what you were doing down here, even with the detectives one in front and one behind you. Then they took me in an office there and I think Bill Alexander, the Assistant District Attorney, two or three, I was introduced to two or three who were FBI men and they wanted my deposition of what happened.

So, I told them to the best of my ability. Then they took me down in their room where they have their show-ups, and all, and me and this other taxi driver who was with me, sir, we sat in the room awhile and directly they brought in six men, young teenagers, and they all were handcuffed together. Well, they wanted me to pick out my passenger.

260

At that time he had on a pair of black pants and white T-shirt, that is all he had on. But you could have picked him out without identifying him by just listening to him because he was bawling out the policeman, telling them it wasn't right to put him in line with these teen-agers and all of that and they asked me which one and I told them. It was him all right, the same man.

Mr. BALL. They had him in line with men much younger?

Mr. WHALEY. With five others.

Mr. BALL. Men much younger?

Mr. WHALEY. Not much younger, but just young kids they might have got them in jail.

Mr. BALL. Did he look older than those other boys?

Mr. WHALEY. Yes.

Mr. BALL. And he was talking, was he?

Mr. WHALEY. He showed no respect for the policemen, he told them what he thought about them. They knew what they were doing and they were trying to railroad him and he wanted his lawyer.

Mr. BALL. Did that aid you in the identification of the man?

Mr. WHALEY. No, sir; it wouldn't have at all, except that I said anybody who wasn't sure could have picked out the right one just for that. It didn't aid me because I knew he was the right one as soon as I saw him.

Mr. BALL. You don't think that that in any way influenced your identification?

Mr. WHALEY. No, sir; it did not. When you drive a taxi, sir, as long as I have, you can almost look at a man, in fact, you have to, to be able to tell whether you can trust or whether you can't trust him, what he is.

Now, like you got in my taxicab and I looked you over and you told me just wait for me here and went in the building, well, I will have to know whether I could just say, "OK, sir." Or say, "Will you leave me a $5 bill, sir?"

When you drive a taxi that long you learn to judge people and what I actually thought of the man when he got in was that he was a wino who had been off his bottle for about two days, that is the way he looked, sir, that was my opinion of him.

Mr. BALL. What was there about his appearance that gave you that impression? Hair mussed?

Mr. WHALEY. Just the slow way he walked up. He didn't talk. He wasn't in any hurry. He wasn't nervous or anything.

Mr. BALL. He didn't run?

Mr. WHALEY. No, sir.

Mr. BALL. Did he look dirty?

Mr. WHALEY. He looked like his clothes had been slept in, sir, but he wasn't actually dirty. The T-shirt was a little soiled around the collar but the bottom part of it was white. You have to know those winos, or they will get in and ride with you and there isn't nothing you can do but call the police, the city gets the fine and you get nothing.

Mr. BALL. Who was the other cab driver?

Mr. WHALEY. I don't know his name, sir. He worked for the same company but he works out of the Oak Cliff branch. They say he was the one who saw him kill the policeman, the one who used the policeman's microphone.

Mr. BALL. Is that Mr. Scoggins?

Mr. WHALEY. What is his name?

Mr. BALL. Scoggins.

Mr. WHALEY. It could have been, sir.

Mr. BALL. You don't know him?

Mr. WHALEY. I just know he drives taxi 213. He works out of Oak Cliff branch.

Mr. BALL. I would like to have a copy of the manifest temporarily marked 370.

Mr. WHALEY. You may have it, sir.

Mr. BALL. Commission 370, and offer it into evidence and ask leave to submit the original, if it is brought in, when it is brought here by the FBI.

The CHAIRMAN. Yes, it may be admitted.

(The manifest referred to was marked Commission Exhibit No. 370 for identification and received in evidence.)

Mr. BALL. This will be 370.

Could we excuse Mr. Whaley now? There are two pieces of evidence to be here and they are not here.

The CHAIRMAN. Excuse him and we will take the other witness.

Mr. BALL. We will excuse him and take the other witness.

Mr. CHAIRMAN. Mr. Whaley, will you wait outside until we get the other exhibits and we will finish with you very shortly.

Mr. McWatters, would you be seated please.

Mr. McWATTERS. Yes, sir.

The CHAIRMAN. The Commission is meeting today to take further testimony concerning the events surrounding the assassination of President Kennedy, and it is our understanding that you have some information that would bear on that subject, and that is the reason for our asking you to come here and testify.

Would you raise your right hand to be sworn please.

Do you solemnly swear the testimony you give before this Commission will be the truth, the whole truth and nothing but the truth, so help you God?

Mr. McWATTERS. I do.

TESTIMONY OF CECIL J. McWATTERS

The CHAIRMAN. Would you be seated please, and Mr. Ball will conduct the interrogation.

Mr. BALL. Mr. McWatters.

Mr. McWATTERS. Yes, sir.

Mr. BALL. What is your business?

Mr. McWATTERS. I am a bus driver.

Mr. BALL. How long have you been a bus driver?

Mr. McWATTERS. Let's see, this coming September will be 19 years.

Mr. BALL. Whom do you work for?

Mr. McWATTERS. The Dallas Transit Company.

Mr. BALL. How long have you worked for the Dallas Transit Company?

Mr. McWATTERS. It will be 19 years in September, I believe.

Mr. BALL. Where do you live?

Mr. McWATTERS. 2523 Blyth Drive, Dallas, Tex.

Mr. BALL. On November 22, 1963, were you on duty as a driver?

Mr. McWATTERS. Yes, sir.

Mr. BALL. What kind of a bus were you driving?

Mr. McWATTERS. Well, I was driving a 44-passenger, let's see, it is a 44-passenger city bus made by White, I believe is the maker of the bus.

Mr. BALL. What hours of work were you assigned that day?

Mr. McWATTERS. Well, I was assigned that day on the particular run from 11:52 until 2:27.

Mr. BALL. What was your run?

Mr. McWATTERS. Do you mean the name of the run?

Mr. BALL. What course did you take, what part of Dallas did you drive in.

Mr. McWATTERS. Well, I went from——

Mr. BALL. Describe it generally, you don't need to go into any detail.

Mr. McWATTERS. I would say from northeast Dallas in the Lakewood addition of Dallas to the Oak Cliff addition of Dallas, which is, would be southwest.

Mr. BALL. Would that be northeast to southwest?

Mr. McWATTERS. That is right.

Mr. BALL. There is a place near the downtown area of Dallas where you timed your run, wasn't it?

Mr. McWATTERS. Yes, sir; I have after I get into town, when I get into the downtown part of it, now St. Paul Street is my official time point going in, where they have a supervisor that stays at this checkpoint there, to check all incoming vehicles.

Mr. BALL. You would be coming in from northeast Dallas at that time?

Mr. McWATTERS. Yes, sir; I am coming in from the Lakewood addition of Dallas, which I came in on. The main thoroughfare is Gaston Avenue.

Mr. BALL. And you got to the intersection of what street and St. Paul when you were timed by your dispatcher?

Mr. McWATTERS. That is Elm, Elm Street.

Mr. BALL. Elm and St. Paul?

Mr. McWATTERS. Elm and St. Paul.

Mr. BALL. If you are ahead of time do you stop there until you are assigned a time to get in?

Mr. McWATTERS. Well, sir; no sir; you don't—a man he has his watch and schedule. If you are ahead of your schedule he will come out and stop you, in other words, and ask you if your watch is right or what is it, you know, the idea of you being there. There is no excuse, you know for a man being ahead of his schedule.

Mr. BALL. If you are ahead of your schedule does he stop you there until you leave?

Mr. McWATTERS. Yes, that is right.

Mr. BALL. What time are you due, according to your schedule, to leave the corner of St. Paul and Elm?

Mr. McWATTERS. 12:36.

Mr. BALL. What time did you leave there that day?

Mr. McWATTERS. Well, I left there that day on time because coming into town that day, I guess everybody done went to, down to, see the parade, I didn't have over four or five passengers coming into downtown.

Mr. BALL. Were you ahead of your schedule?

Mr. McWATTERS. Well, I stopped about a block before—now, just a block before we get to St. Paul, there is a big theater there, and it has all loading zones, no parking there and a lot of times if we are a minute or two ahead of our schedule when we pull in in front of this theater before we get there in time, in other words, we kill a minute.

Mr. BALL. What did you do this day?

Mr. McWATTERS. Well, I was a little ahead of my schedule and I killed about a minute, I guess, before I went to cross St. Paul Street.

Mr. BALL. After your dispatcher checked you in what time did you leave that corner of St. Paul and Elm?

Mr. McWATTERS. Well, the best I can remember I don't recall even picking up a passenger there. I think I discharged one lady passenger there on that, to the best I can recall, because I remember that I had, when I crossed Field Street, I think I had five passengers on my bus.

Mr. BALL. Well then, back to the question, what time did you leave that day, leave Elm and St. Paul?

Mr. McWATTERS. Well, I would have to say I left there around, in other words, 12:36 because I know I was on good time when I come in there.

Mr. BALL. And you think you left at the time you were supposed to leave?

Mr. McWATTERS. Well, I am almost positive I did, because, as I say, we generally come in on schedules on good time because from that street on is where we generally—for the next seven or eight blocks—is where we get all of our passengers going through the downtown area.

Mr. BALL. Had you heard any sirens before you got to St. Paul and Elm?

Mr. McWATTERS. No, sir.

Mr. BALL. Do you know if your dispatcher keeps a written record?

Mr. McWATTERS. The only way he keeps a written record is if you are ahead of your schedule. He has a little pad, and if a man is ahead of his schedule, in other words, he writes, of course, we all go by badge numbers, in other words, he would write your badge number, your bus number, and if you was ahead of schedule he would write how much ahead of schedule you were, and——

Mr. BALL. Do you think he did anything, did he write anything up on you on that day?

Mr. McWATTERS. No, sir; the guy that we have down there now, if you are ahead of schedule he will come out, in other words, because he stands on the corner all the time, and if you are a minute or two ahead of your schedule he will come out and if nothing else, converse with you for a minute or two to see that you leave it on time and very seldom, I mean, if ever—of course, a report goes in on you, it goes against your record.

Mr. BALL. In other words, if he did make a record it would be by way of a reprimand to you?

Mr. McWATTERS. Yes, sir.

Mr. BALL. As you went on down Elm you left your post at St. Paul and Elm, did you hear any sirens?

Mr. McWATTERS. No, sir.

Mr. BALL. Did you pick up any passengers?

Mr. McWATTERS. I picked up within a period of from the time I picked up two or three passengers, I can't recall just exactly which stop. I have after I leave St. Paul Street, I have Ervay Street and Akard Street, and Field Street which would be three stops where I can't recall that, exactly where I discharged or picked up passengers, because I had the few passengers that I had which I came into town with.

Mr. BALL. Well then, do you remember picking up a passenger at a place other than at a bus stop as you went down Elm?

Mr. McWATTERS. Yes, sir.

As I left Field Street, I pulled out into the, in other words, the first lane of traffic and traffic was beginning to back up then; in other words, it was blocked further down the street, and after I pulled out in it for a short distance there I come to a complete stop, and when I did, someone come up and beat on the door of the bus, and that is about even with Griffin Street.

In other words, it is a street that dead ends into Elm Street which there is no bus stop at this street, because I stopped across Field Street in the middle of the intersection and it is just a short distance onto Griffin Street, and that is when someone, a man, came up and knocked on the door of the bus, and I opened the door of the bus and he got on.

Mr. BALL. You were beyond Field and before you got to Griffin?

Mr. McWATTERS. That is right. It was along about even with Griffin Street before I was stopped in the traffic.

Mr. BALL. And that is about seven or, eight blocks from the Texas Book Depository Building, isn't it?

Mr. McWATTERS. Yes, sir. It would be seven, I would say that is seven, it would be about seven blocks.

Mr. BALL. From there?

Mr. McWATTERS. From there, yes, sir.

Mr. BALL. What did the man look like who knocked on your door and got on your bus?

Mr. McWATTERS. Well, I didn't pay any particular attention to him. He was to me just dressed in what I would call work clothes, just some type of little old jacket on, and I didn't pay any particular attention to the man when he got on.

Mr. BALL. Paid his fare, did he?

Mr. McWATTERS. Yes, sir; he just paid his fare and sat down on the second cross seat on the right.

Mr. BALL. Do you remember whether or not you gave him a transfer?

Mr. McWATTERS. Not when he got on; no, sir.

Mr. BALL. You didn't. Did you ever give him a transfer?

Mr. McWATTERS. Yes, sir; I gave him one about two blocks from where he got on.

Mr. BALL. Did he ask you for a transfer?

Mr. McWATTERS. Yes, sir.

Mr. BALL. Do you remember what he said to you when he asked you for the transfer?

Mr. McWATTERS. Well, the reason I recall the incident, I had—there was a lady that when I stopped in this traffic, there was a lady who had a suitcase and she said, "I have got to make a 1 o'clock train at Union Station," and she said, "I don't believe—from the looks of this traffic you are going to be held up."

She said, "Would you give me a transfer and I am going to walk on down," which is about from where I was at that time about 7 or 8 blocks to Union Station and she asked me if I would give her a transfer in case I did get through the traffic if I would pick her up on the way.

So, I said, "I sure will." So I gave her a transfer and opened the door and as she was going out the gentleman I had picked up about 2 blocks asked for a transfer and got off at the same place in the middle of the block where the lady did.

Mr. BALL. Where was that near, what intersection?

Mr. McWATTERS. It was the intersection near Lamar Street, it was near Poydras and Lamar Street. It is a short block, but the main intersection there is Lamar Street.

Mr. BALL. He had been on the bus about 2 blocks?

Mr. McWATTERS. About 2 blocks; yes, sir.

Mr. BALL. Up to that time had you heard any sirens?

Mr. McWATTERS. Not up until—now just about the time that, let's see, that is when I left Griffin, right about the time this gentleman got on the bus the traffic was starting and that was about the first that I can recall of hearing the sirens, but when, in other words, when they started it seemed to me like they was coming from all over town.

Mr. BALL. Did you have a radio in your bus?

Mr. McWATTERS. No, sir.

Mr. BALL. Did you hear a radio from nearby cars announcing anything about the President's assassination?

Mr. McWATTERS. Well, there was cars that were stopped alongside of the bus and I think someone raised the window but I couldn't hear. I never did hear anything outside of the——

Mr. BALL. Where were you when you first heard the President had been shot?

Mr. McWATTERS. Well, I was sitting in the bus, there was some gentleman in front of me in a car, and he came back and walked up to the bus and I opened the door and he said, "I have heard over my radio in my car that the President has been—" I believe he used the word—"has been shot."

Mr. BALL. Is that when you were stalled in traffic?

Mr. McWATTERS. That is right. That is when I was stalled right there.

Mr. BALL. Was that before or after the man got off the bus that asked for the transfer?

Mr. McWATTERS. That was before. In other words, at that time no one had gotten off the bus.

Mr. BALL. What was your location then, near what street?

Mr. McWATTERS. Between Poydras and Lamar, in other words, because I stayed stopped there for, I guess oh, 3 or 4 minutes anyway before I made any progress at that one stop right there and that is where the gentleman got off the bus. In fact, I was talking to the man, the man that come out of the car; in other words, he just stepped up in the door of the bus, and was telling me that what he had heard over his radio and that is when the lady who was standing there decided she would walk and when the other gentleman decided he would also get off at that point.

Mr. BALL. At that point.

What course did you take after that?

Mr. McWATTERS. Well, I still was going west, in other words, in the same direction, going west, in other words, towards Houston Street. In other words, I went there before I changed my course which was about, I would say, three or four blocks.

When I got to Houston Street, in other words, I turned to the left, which would be south——

Mr. BALL. You went by the Texas School Book Depository Building?

Mr. McWATTERS. Yes, sir; I turned at the corner of Elm Street and Houston which this book store is on the opposite corner from where I changed course there.

Mr. BALL. Was traffic still heavy along there?

Mr. McWATTERS. Yes, sir; the traffic was still tied up, but the police, they opened up a lane there, they had so many buses and everything that was tied up, they opened up, moved traffic around that they run quite a few of these buses through there.

In other words, from two blocks on this side of where the incident happened they had, in other words, they was turning all the traffic to the right and to the left, in other words, north and south.

Mr. BALL. You went on down to Houston viaduct then?

265

Mr. McWATTERS. Yes, I turned after they finally let—they weren't letting any cars through at that time but they just run a bunch of those buses through there.

Mr. BALL. Is there a bus stop in front of the Texas School Book Depository Building?

Mr. McWATTERS. No, sir.

Mr. BALL. Where do you stop for that intersection?

Mr. McWATTERS. Well, you stop, in other words, on this side of the street.

Mr. BALL. You stop on the south side of, the southeast corner of the intersection?

Mr. McWATTERS. Yes, sir.

In other words, like you would be going, direct south towards the Building, the bus stop is on this corner over here on this side.

Mr. BALL. You mean the corner of Houston and Elm?

Mr. McWATTERS. That is right.

Mr. BALL. Which corner, north, south, east, west?

Mr. McWATTERS. Well, it would be on the north.

Mr. BALL. North.

Mr. McWATTERS. On the north.

Mr. BALL. Here is a map and maybe you can show us where the bus stop is. This is Exhibit No. 371.

Mr. McWATTERS. In other words, this is south, in other words.

Mr. BALL. This is west. You are going west on Elm.

Mr. McWATTERS. In other words, I am going—right here is where the police had all traffic, they wasn't allowing anything to go any further than Market Street here.

In other words, all the traffic there they were moving was turning either to the right or left, on Market Street. But after they held us up there so long, of course, they run these buses in this right lane here and they did open up and let a bunch of these buses go right on down here to Houston, of course, a lot of them go straight on and a lot of them turn left to Houston Street, a lot of them go under the underpass here.

Mr. BALL. Wait a minute, you turned to the left?

Mr. McWATTERS. I turned to the left.

Mr. BALL. On Houston?

Mr. McWATTERS. In other words, my last stop, in other words at this corner right here on Record Street, all buses turning to the left have to stop at this corner right here.

Mr. BALL. At Record and Elm?

Mr. McWATTERS. At Record and Elm.

Mr. BALL. Do you have a bus stop at Houston and Elm?

Mr. McWATTERS. Yes, sir; there is a bus stop there for the buses that go on under the underpass.

Mr. BALL. Is there a bus stop for the buses that go south on Houston?

Mr. McWATTERS. No, sir; all the buses, we have to get in, this is a one-way street and you have to get over in this lane here.

Mr. BALL. By the lane you mean the extreme left lane?

Mr. McWATTERS. The extreme left lane to make——

Mr. BALL. To make the left turn south on Houston Street?

Mr. McWATTERS. Yes.

Mr. BALL. And your last bus stop, as you go west on Elm and before you turn is the northeast corner of Record and Elm?

Mr. McWATTERS. Yes, sir; that is correct.

Mr. BALL. You went on over to Houston Viaduct into the Oak Cliff section, didn't you?

Mr. McWATTERS. Yes, sir; to the Oak Cliff section.

Mr. BALL. And there was some conversation occurred on that bus that you told the FBI officers about?

Mr. McWATTERS. Yes, sir.

Mr. BALL. Tell us what that was?

Mr. McWATTERS. Well, there was a teenage boy, I would say 17 or 18 years of age, who was sitting to my right on the first cross seat and me and him had, we had conversationed a little while we was tied up in the traffic, you know, of the fact of we wondered where all, what all the excitement was due to the fact of the sirens and others, and after I turned on Houston Street I said to him and I made the remark, I wonder where the President was shot, and I believe he made the remark that it was probably in the head if he was in a convertible or something to that effect. I don't remember just exactly the way we worded it or what it was, but it was a conversation about the President, in other words, to where he was shot.

In other words, and he made the remark or something, he was probably shot in the head, if he was sitting in a convertible or to that effect. I really don't know just exactly at that time. Just like I say I never thought anything about it.

Mr. BALL. Didn't some lady say something?

Mr. McWATTERS. Well, yes, sir.

Now, as we got on out on Marsalis, along about it was either Edgemont or Vermont, I believe it was Vermont Street, there was a lady who was fixing to cross the intersection and I stopped and asked her if she was going to catch the bus into town from the opposite direction, and she said that she was and I told her that we was off schedule, that the other bus had done went into town, and I asked her did she care to just ride on to the end of the line and come back and she wouldn't have to stand there and wait, and she was getting on, and I asked her had she heard the news of the President being shot, at the time that was all I knew about it, and she said, "No, what are you—you are just kidding me."

I said, "No, I really am not kidding you." I said, "It is the truth from all the reliable sources that we have come in contact with," and this teenage boy sitting on the side, I said "Well, now, if you think I am kidding you," I said, "Ask this gentleman sitting over here," and he kind of, I don't know whether it was a grinning or smile or whatever expression it was, and she said, "I know you are kidding now, because he laughed or grinned or made some remark to that effect."

And I just told her no it wasn't no kidding matter, but that was part of the conversation that was said at that time.

Mr. BALL. Was this teenage boy—do you know where this teenage boy got on the bus?

Mr. McWATTERS. Yes, sir; he got on at between, he got on at the stop, in other words, I stopped in front of the Majestic theater which is a block before I get to St. Paul; in other words, it is a middle of the stop, block stop, in other words. We pull in and stop in the center of the block, and my next stop would be St. Paul; in other words, that is where the teenage boy got on.

Mr. BALL. He was on the bus when this man knocked on the door of your bus and got on?

Mr. McWATTERS. Yes, sir; he was.

Mr. BALL. He was on the bus when the man asked for the transfer and got off?

Mr. McWATTERS. Yes, sir. That is right.

Mr. BALL. Were you later called down to the—did the teenage boy ask for any transfer?

Mr. McWATTERS. No, sir.

Mr. BALL. Now, you were called down to the Dallas police department later, weren't you?

Mr. McWATTERS. Yes, sir.

Mr. BALL. What day was it?

Mr. McWATTERS. It was on the same day, the 22d.

Mr. BALL. 22d. Do you know how they happened to get in touch with you, did you notify them that you——

Mr. McWATTERS. No, sir; I didn't know anything to that effect.

Mr. BALL. Did they come out and get you?

Mr. McWATTERS. They come out and——

Mr. BALL. What did they ask you?

Mr. McWATTERS. Well, they stopped me; it was, I would say around 6:15 or somewhere around 6:15 or 6:20 that afternoon.

Mr. BALL. You were still on duty, were you?

Mr. McWATTERS. Yes, sir.

Mr. BALL. Still on your bus?

Mr. McWATTERS. I was on duty but I was on a different line and a different bus.

Mr. BALL. What did they ask you when they came out?

Mr. McWATTERS. Well, they stopped me right by the city hall there when I come by there and they wanted me to come in, they wanted to ask me some questions. And I don't know what it was about or anything until I got in there and they told me what happened.

Mr. BALL. What did they tell you?

Mr. McWATTERS. Well, they told me that they had a transfer that I had issued that was cut for Lamar Street at 1 o'clock, and they wanted to know if I knew anything about it. And I, after I looked at the transfer and my punch, I said yes, that is the transfer I issued because it had my punch mark on it.

Mr. BALL. Did your punch mark have a distinctive mark?

Mr. McWATTERS. It had a distinctive mark and it is registered, in other words, all the drivers, every driver has a different punch mark.

Mr. BALL. What makes it different?

Mr. McWATTERS. Well, it is, it would be, the symbol of it or angle, in other words, every one; it is different, in other words.

Mr. BALL. You have a punch there?

Mr. McWATTERS. Yes, sir; I have the punch right here.

Mr. BALL. Is that the punch that you used?

Mr. McWATTERS. That is the punch I used.

Mr. BALL. Will you punch a piece of paper and show us?

Mr. McWATTERS. In other words, that is the type of punch that this one makes right here, in other words.

Mr. BALL. That is a different type of punch than any other driver has?

Mr. McWATTERS. Any driver, in other words.

Mr. BALL. On any bus in Dallas?

Mr. McWATTERS. In other words, the superintendent has a list, in other words, it would be just like this and every man has a punch and he has his name, and everything. In other words, if anyone calls in about a transfer or anything, I mean brings one in he can look right down the list by the punch mark and tell whose punch it is, and who it is registered to.

Mr. BALL. Now, the sample of your punch there has been on a piece of paper and we would like to have it marked as 372 at this time.

(The paper referred to was marked Commission Exhibit No. 372 and received in evidence.)

Mr. BALL. If you punched, made a punch mark, on a transfer, did you designate the time of the punch or the place of the punch?

Mr. McWATTERS. Yes, sir; I designate the time of the—we have one general transfer point. In other words, Lamar Street is what we call our general transfer point in which all transfers are cut within the quarter of the hour in which you are supposed to be there.

In other words, if you was to arrive there at, say, 12:50 or in that vicinity, you always give the passenger the 15 minutes, in other words, within the hour of the transfer. In other words, is the way they have you to cut your transfers across your cutter.

In other words, it is just a little thing that you raise up and down and you can adjust them, and right here is a book of them in which you can see the time. It is one, in other words, 2:15, 3:30, and 4:45, and we set them in other words, if you wanted at 1:15, 1 o'clock would be across this direction. If you wanted it 1:15 you would cut across this direction or if you wanted it 1:45 you would cut it in this direction. In other words, 1:15, -:30 and -:45. In other words, the 15 minutes is always given at the time, at the general transfer point.

Representative FORD. It is 10:25 now. How would you cut it right now?

Mr. McWATTERS. At 10:25.

Representative FORD. Why don't you cut one?

Mr. McWATTERS. I have a regular cutter, you see; let's see if he can get something that would—in other words, 10:25, I will just cut it, in other words, cut across there, and cut it, in other words, at 10:30, in other words, it would show at 10:30.

(At this point, Senator Cooper entered the hearing room.)

Representative FORD. Where do you put your own identification?

Mr. McWATTERS. On here. Well, if it is in the morning or in the afternoon, here is your a.m., or your p.m. In other words, it is before 12:45, in other words, we consider up to 12:45 a.m., in other words, that is the way they are.

In other words, I would punch it in the a.m. side of it, and if it was in the afternoon, in other words, after that, it would be a p.m. transfer, and whatever line that you are working has the name on it right here.

In other words, at that time that transfer I had punched was punched a p.m. Lakewood, in other words, because I was coming from the Lakewood addition is the way that was punched on the transfer.

Mr. BALL. Well now, do you punch the transfer when the passenger asks for it?

Mr. McWATTERS. No. No, sir; in other words, when you leave this, you are inbound when you are going into town or when you are going, in other words, out of town, in other words.

I was coming in, in other words, when I got in Lakewood Addition I set my transfers for downtown.

Mr. BALL. For downtown and you set them for what time?

Mr. McWATTERS. I set them for 1 o'clock.

Mr. BALL. You set them for 1 o'clock?

Mr. McWATTERS. 1 o'clock.

Mr. BALL When you reached your end of the run in northeast Dallas then you set your transfers for 1 o'clock, did you?

Mr. McWATTERS. That is right, when I was coming back in.

Mr. BALL. And when you gave this transfer near Poydras and Elm——

Mr. McWATTERS. Yes, sir.

Mr. BALL. Did you pull out a transfer that had already been set for 1 o'clock time?

Mr. McWATTERS. Yes, sir. In other words, I just reached up on my cutter and just tore off one which is already punched.

Mr. BALL. Then did you punch it again or was it already punched?

Mr. McWATTERS It was already punched.

Mr. BALL. And you had punched it at the end of the line?

Mr. McWATTERS. Yes, sir.

Mr. BALL. So all you had to do is pull the transfer off of the pile of transfers and hand it to the man?

Mr. McWATTERS. That is correct.

Mr. BALL. And you had anticipated at the end of the line that when you got to about this point it would be a 1 o'clock transfer, is that correct?

Mr. McWATTERS. Well, that is right.

In other words, there is enough time on it, just like I say, within a quarter of an hour, but——

Mr. BALL. When you got to the police station that day did they show you a transfer?

Mr. McWATTERS. Yes, sir.

Mr. BALL. What did you tell them about the transfer?

Mr. McWATTERS. Well, I recognized the transfer as being the transfer that I had issued.

Mr. BALL. How did you recognize it?

Mr. McWATTERS. By my punch mark on it.

Mr. BALL. And what about the line?

Mr. McWATTERS. The line?

Mr. BALL. Lakewood.

Mr. McWATTERS The Lakewood punch on it, and where it was punched and Lakewood with my punch mark on it.

Mr. BALL. Were you able to identify it any further as a particular transfer you had given to any particular passenger?

Mr. McWATTERS. No, sir. Only——

Mr. BALL. Go ahead.

Mr. McWATTERS. I only gave two transfers going through town on that trip

269

and that was at the one stop of where I gave the lady and the gentleman that got off the bus, I issued two transfers. But that was the only two transfers that were issued.

Mr. BALL. Did you tell the police in Dallas that?

Mr. McWATTERS. I don't remember whether I did or not.

Mr. BALL. But you do remember it now?

Mr. McWATTERS. Yes.

(At this point Chief Justice Warren left the hearing room.)

Mr. BALL. All right. Now, what else did you do that day?

Mr. McWATTERS. Well, let's see—

Mr. BALL. Did they show you any prisoner?

Mr. McWATTERS. Yes, sir; when they stopped me over there and took me into the police department there, like I say, it was around 6:15 or 6:20, they took me down before the lineup there and asked me if I could identify anyone in that lineup as getting on my bus that day.

Mr. BALL. Did they take you down and show you a lineup?

Mr. McWATTERS. Yes, sir.

Mr. BALL. You sat there with police officers and they brought men in there?

Mr. McWATTERS. They brought four men out. In other words, four men under the lights; in other words, they was all——

Mr. BALL. All the same age?

McWATTERS. No, sir; they were different ages, different sizes and different heights. And they asked me if I could identify any man in particular there, and I told them that I couldn't identify any man in particular, but there was one man there that was about the size of the man. Now, I was referring back, after they done showed me this transfer at that time and I knew which trip, that I went through town on at that time, in other words, on the Lakewood trip and just like I recalled, I only put out two transfers and I told them that there was one man in the lineup was about the size and the height and complexion of a man that got on my bus, but as far as positively identifying the man I could not do it.

Mr. BALL. What was the size and the height and complexion of the man that knocked on the window of this bus?

Mr. McWATTERS. Well, I would say, just like I told the police, to me he was just a medium-sized man. To me he was, I would say, not, I wouldn't call him—just of average weight, and I would say a light-complected, to the best of my knowledge.

Mr. BALL. When you say "average weight" what do you mean?

Mr. McWATTERS. I figured just like I saw, the man, he looked like to me the best way I can describe him would be 135 or 140 pounds.

Mr. BALL. What about height?

Mr. McWATTERS. Well, just like I told them, it looked like to me he would probably be five-seven or five-eight, in that vicinity.

Mr. BALL. Anyway, you were not able to identify any man in the lineup as the passenger?

Mr. McWATTERS. No, sir.

Mr. BALL. As the passenger who had gotten on?

Mr. McWATTERS. No, sir.

Mr. BALL. You said there was one man who closely resembled in height, weight and color?

Mr. McWATTERS. That is right.

Mr. BALL. Do you know who that was?

Mr. McWATTERS. Just like I told them, I didn't know who was who or anything.

Mr. BALL. Did you ever learn who that person was?

Mr. McWATTERS. Well, I don't know whether that was really the man or not, I don't know.

Mr. BALL. I see.

Now, I have a map here.

(Discussion off the record.)

Representative FORD. All right, proceed.

Mr. BALL. You remember you told us about the man that knocked on the window of the door of your bus just before you got to Griffin, wasn't it?

Mr. McWatters. Yes, sir; along about the vicinity of Griffin Street, it comes to.

Mr. Ball. You let him on the bus, and he paid his fare, how much is that fare?

Mr. McWatters. It is 23 cents.

Mr. Ball. 23 cents, and you went about down almost to Poydras.

Mr. McWatters. Almost, between Poydras and Lamar.

Mr. Ball. Between Poydras and Lamar, closer to Lamar than to Poydras?

Mr. McWatters. Yes, sir.

Mr. Ball. And a man got on. Was it the same man?

Mr. McWatters. That was the same man who got on the bus that I picked up, in other words.

Mr. Ball. And the man you gave the transfer to?

Mr. McWatters. The man I gave the transfer to when the woman—in other words, when the man that got on Griffin Street there got off at the same place she did.

Mr. Ball. And he was only on the bus about 2 blocks?

Mr. McWatters. Two blocks was the only distance.

Mr. Ball. How long did it take you to go those 2 blocks?

Mr. McWatters. Now, he paid as far as from St. Paul Street. I made—there wasn't any traffic holding me up whatsoever, I come on right down to where I picked the man up there, in other words, about Field, and that is where the traffic was starting to back up to. So the best of my knowledge I would say it took me 3 or 4 minutes to get down there, so I will just have to say it was in the vicinity of around 12:40.

Mr. Ball. In other words, how long was the man on your bus, the man who got on, about Griffin and got off and you gave him the transfer, approximately?

Mr. McWatters. Well, he got on, and when he got on, I made that one block, and then the other, well, I would be safe in saying he wasn't on there 5 minutes.

Mr. Ball. And you think he got off or on around 12:40?

Mr. McWatters. 12:40 that is the best.

Mr. Ball. What time did you say he got on approximately?

Mr. McWatters. On the bus?

Mr. Ball. Yes.

Mr. McWatters. Well, I would say in the vicinity from where I left up there it would be probably it took me, I would say, 3 minutes to come, let's see, it would be Ervay, Akard and Field, that is about 3 blocks there where I left my time point which I would say just a rough estimation it would be with no traffic would be 2 or 3 minutes, I would say 3 minutes anyway.

So, it must have been somewheres 12:39 or—so.

Mr. Ball. When he got on the bus?

Mr. McWatters. 12:40.

Mr. Ball. And then he was on the bus about how many minutes?

Mr. McWatters. Well, just like I say he wasn't on the bus over 4 or 5 minutes, in other words, just made that 1 block there, and in other words, when the traffic stopped, well, that is when he got off the bus.

Representative Ford. During the time he was on the bus this man rapped at your door or was your door open, and spoke up and said that the President had been shot?

Mr. McWatters. He was on the bus, you mean was the door open?

Representative Ford. No. You previously testified that while you were stalled or jammed up in the traffic——

Mr. McWatters. Yes, sir.

Representative Ford. A man came to the door of the bus and indicated by word of mouth——

Mr. McWatters. Yes, sir.

Representative Ford. That the President had been shot.

Mr. McWatters. Yes, sir.

Representative Ford. Now, was the man to whom you issued the transfer on the bus at that time?

Mr. McWatters. Yes, sir.

Representative Ford. Now, the man who spoke up and said that the President had been shot, how loudly did he say that?

271

Mr. McWatters. Well, he said it loud enough that I guess everybody on the bus heard him when he stepped up in the bus.

Representative Ford. In other words, that would be your best impression or best recollection that whoever said this, that the President had been shot, said it loudly enough for not only you but the other bus passengers to hear it?

Mr. McWatters. Yes, sir. Because he stepped up in the bus and when he made the statement in other words, he said that the President had been shot, because I am pretty sure everybody—he said it to the fact. I think that everybody, there might have been some, if there was anybody in the extreme back of the bus, might not have heard it, but I think anyone who was near the front part of the bus could have.

Representative Ford. But at that time when this man made this statement, there was a teenager sitting in the first cross seat on the right-hand side of the bus?

Mr. McWatters. Yes, sir.

Representative Ford. And the man who had gotten on the bus to whom you later issued the transfer, was sitting in the second?

Mr. McWatters. In the second seat.

Representative Ford. What is the distance from the door of the bus where the man was standing who made this statement to the second cross seat?

Mr. McWatters. Well, I would say, let's see, it would be I would say 6 or 8 feet.

Representative Ford. Was he sitting alone in the second cross seat?

Mr. McWatters. He was sitting alone.

Representative Ford. Did you notice any reaction on the part of any of your passengers to this comment by this man who made this statement?

Mr. McWatters. Well, the only reaction that I knew is when he got up and said that, well, that is when the lady got off first, which she jumped up and got her suitcase and said, in other words, made a remark to something. "I am afraid you are going to be tied up here in this traffic and I want to get off."

Representative Ford. Where was this lady sitting who got up and asked for this transfer?

Mr. McWatters. Now, this lady was sitting behind me, in other words, I am the driver.

Representative Ford. On the left-hand side of the bus looking forward?

Mr. McWatters. Yes, sir; in other words, it is a cross seat. I mean a side seat, in other words, like the driver sitting here, the first seat is the one that runs parallel with the bus, in other words.

Representative Ford. Well now, the seat in which the lady was sitting would be parallel to the second cross seat on the other side of the bus?

Mr. McWatters. Yes, in other words——

Representative Ford. It would be on the same line?

Mr. McWatters. Yes, sir.

Representative Ford. The first seat would be ahead—the first seat on the right-hand side of the bus would be ahead of the seat where the lady was sitting?

Mr. McWatters. No, you mean the lady, I am referring to who got off first?

Representative Ford. Yes.

Mr. McWatters. No, the lady—I was sitting in the driver's seat, she was sitting right behind me, in other words, facing out his way.

Representative Ford. But she obviously heard what the man said about the President being shot?

Mr. McWatters. Yes, sir.

Representative Ford. There is no doubt in your mind she heard that?

Mr. McWatters. I wouldn't think so because when she got up and stated she wanted to get off——

Representative Ford. Was she any further from the man who made this statement about the President being shot than the man who was sitting in the second cross seat?

Mr. McWatters. She was closer to the man actually than the man that got off with her was.

Representative Ford. How many feet or how much difference?

Mr. McWatters. Well, the lady in other words, from the door here, it is just two cross seats, and two seats where you sit sideways and then the two seats in which he would be back here.

Representative FORD. Could you diagram that as best as you can?

Mr. BELIN. Congressman, we have a diagram. We have a picture of the side of the bus.

Mr. McWATTERS. Right here.

Representative FORD. Sit down.

Mr. McWATTERS. You can see it from this point right here, in other words. You see this cross seat, in other words, these first two right here, the driver's seat, you see the first two seats there, in other words.

Representative FORD. Could you sit down and mark it?

Mr. McWATTERS. This is the inside, let's see, this is the driver right here. Here is your cross seat right here. Here, about back here, is where the lady got off who was sitting on this seat.

Representative FORD. Will you mark that with an "L"?

Mr. McWATTERS. In other words, right here.

Representative FORD. Where was the man in the first cross seat sitting?

Mr. McWATTERS. Right here is the first. Right here is where the man that was sitting, got off, in this seat right here, I believe it is.

Representative FORD. Will you mark that "M" where the man who was sitting also got off who got the transfer?

Mr. BALL. Maybe we had better use a black pen that will show better on that glazed surface.

Representative FORD. This is where the man was sitting who you issued the transfer to at the same time the lady was issued the transfer?

Mr. McWATTERS. Yes, sir.

Representative FORD. And the teenager was sitting in what seat?

Mr. McWATTERS. Right here.

Representative FORD. Will you mark that "O"?

Mr. McWATTERS. Yes, sir.

Representative FORD. Where was the man standing who came to the bus and said the President had been shot?

Mr. McWATTERS. Right here.

Representative FORD. On the step?

Mr. McWATTERS. On the step. I guess, I presume this would be the second step there. To the best of my recollection he stepped up on the first step.

Representative FORD. Mark that "P."

Mr. McWATTERS. "P."

Representative FORD. Now, after the man who was standing at "P" said the President was shot, what did the lady do who was sitting in "L"?

Mr. McWATTERS. Well, the lady, she had a suitcase sitting right there beside me and she left. When the lady got up and said she would like to get off the bus, and that she was going to walk to the Union Station and asked me if I would give her a transfer in case that I caught up with her, and asked me if I would pick her up.

Representative FORD. You gave her a transfer?

Mr. McWATTERS. Yes, sir.

Representative FORD. What happened?

Mr. McWATTERS. She got off and by the time when she was talking to me that is when he got up, this gentleman here in the seat got up, at seat "M" got off. In other words, the door was never closed of the bus from the time the gentleman stepped up in the door of that there, in other words, when he said what he did, and got on back in his car, in other words, the lady got off, and the man got off, too, both at the same stop.

In other words, the bus hadn't moved at that stop.

Mr. BALL. I would like to mark this as the next exhibit, Commission's exhibit, which will be the diagram of the bus with the initials "M," "O," "L," "P," will be marked as Commission's Exhibit 373.

Representative FORD. It will be so admitted.

(The diagram referred to was marked Commission's Exhibit No. 373 for identification and received in evidence.)

Mr. BALL. And a photograph of the interior of the bus, I would like to have marked as 374.

And a diagram of the bus itself showing front and side as 375.

(The photograph and diagram referred to were marked Commission Exhibits Nos. 374 and 375, respectively, and received in evidence.)

Mr. BALL. I will hand you a photograph of the exterior of the bus.

Mr. McWATTERS. Yes, sir; in other words, that is the same bus number.

Mr. BALL. That is right.

Mr. McWATTERS. That is the bus it was.

Mr. BALL. That is the bus. Number ——

Mr. McWATTERS. 433.

Representative FORD. So admitted.

Mr. BALL. These are all admitted.

Now, we have this map which is Commission's Exhibit 371. Can you show me your starting point which is where you started your time on Elm and what street?

Mr. McWATTERS. That is Elm and St. Paul.

Mr. BALL. Will you mark an "X" there with your black pen, or let's take red pen this time for you, on this same map, here it is right there, that is where you commenced your time, is that right?

Mr. McWATTERS. Yes.

Mr. BALL. Put an "O" there.

Mr. McWATTERS. Put an "O" here.

Mr. BALL. Just circle that intersection.

Mr. McWATTERS. O.K.

Mr. BALL. Now, you went along Elm, westerly along Elm?

Mr. McWATTERS. That is right—

Mr. BALL. Put a "P" about the place where the man knocked on the window of your door of your bus and got on. Here is Griffin.

Mr. McWATTERS. This is Griffin right here, mark that with a "P".

Mr. BALL. And put an "R" at the place where the man got off the bus.

Mr. McWATTERS. Let's see.

Mr. BALL. Here is Lamar.

Mr. McWATTERS. Here is Lamar here. I want to find Poydras.

Mr. BALL. That is right in here.

Mr. McWATTERS. That would be, in other words, about the center here would be, in other words, a little bit closer to Lamar than——

Mr. BALL. Put an "R" there to indicate the approximate position where he got off.

"O" is where you started, so you had better raise those up to Elm. The place he got on and the place he got off.

Perhaps, if you would just draw a line up and put your "R" it would be easier.

Mr. McWATTERS. On Griffin here now that is where you want——

Mr. BALL. Where he got on, wherever it was.

Mr. McWATTERS. Is that where you want the "P"?

Mr. BALL. That is where he got on?

Mr. McWATTERS. Yes. O.K. right here.

Mr. BALL. And where he got off "R".

Mr. McWATTERS. That is a very short block right in between Poydras and Lamar here.

Mr. BALL. All right.

Now, let's use the map here. You made your start at St. Paul and Elm didn't you, and went west.

Mr. McWATTERS. Yes, sir.

Mr. BALL. Now, you picked up a man who knocked on the window of your bus at a place in the street that was not a bus stop, is that right?

Mr. McWATTERS. That is correct.

Mr. BALL. And its approximate location was where?

Mr. McWATTERS. At Griffin Street.

Mr. BALL. And you have marked that as "P"?

Mr. McWATTERS. Marked that as "P".

Mr. BALL. That same man stayed on your bus until you got to what location?

Representative Ford. How many hours a day do you work this route?

Mr. McWatters. Well, now, this one particular route right here, I work it only 2 hours and 35 minutes.

Representative Ford. Each day?

Mr. McWatters. Each day.

Representative Ford. How many days a week?

Mr. McWatters. 5 days, Monday through Friday. And after that, in other words, I work on another, a different bus line.

But this one particular one here is just 2 hours and 35 minutes each day.

Representative Ford. When you say a different bus line, you mean the same company but a different route?

Mr. McWatters. A different route.

Representative Ford. You would be familiar with the time schedules and all of the stops on this particular route from your 2 years' experience?

Mr. McWatters. Yes, sir.

Senator Cooper. May I ask a question?

Mr. McWatters. Yes, sir.

Senator Cooper. Have you testified that you saw this passenger whom you later recognized in the lineup, get on the bus in the vicinity of Murphy Street— is Murphy Street on your right?

Mr. McWatters. Murphy Street is the street that, in other words, that comes in.

Senator Cooper. Does it run into Elm Street?

Mr. McWatters. It runs into Elm Street, it dead ends, in other words, into Elm Street.

Here is Field Street, in other words, across this intersection and we stopped across the intersection of Field, and Murphy Street comes in to the intersection at about where the bus stops, in other words, where Field Street stops and I guess that Griffin is the next small street that comes in just, it is just a short distance below.

Senator Cooper. Well, did the passenger that you have testified about, and whom you stated that you later identified, did he get on in the vicinity of Murphy Street?

Mr. McWatters. Yes, sir.

Senator Cooper. Murphy Street—you proceeded from Murphy Street toward the Texas School Book Depository?

Mr. McWatters. Yes, sir.

Senator Cooper. Is that correct?

Mr. McWatters. That is correct.

Senator Cooper. Was the passenger that got on near Murphy Street the same passenger that you later have testified about who told you that the President had been shot in the temple?

Mr. McWatters. Well, they told me later that it was, but at the time they didn't tell me.

Senator Cooper. Who didn't tell you?

Mr. McWatters. The police didn't.

Senator Cooper. When you say this passenger got on near Murphy Street, was there anything about him that caused you to take notice of him particularly?

Mr. McWatters. Well, no, sir. I wouldn't say there was. He was, I would say, he didn't have on no suit or anything, he had on, I believe, some type of jacket, cloth jacket.

Senator Cooper. What caused you to remember him getting on?

Mr. McWatters. What caused me to remember?

Senator Cooper. Yes; at the time he got on.

Mr. McWatters. Because, the reason I remembered exactly because I didn't put out but two transfers, and that, in other words, from where he got on and everything, I didn't have but one, there wasn't but one man on the bus and that was the teenage boy, when he got on the bus, in other words, when he got off, he was the only man except the teenage boy who was on the bus at the time.

Senator Cooper. Now was this man that you saw got on the bus the same one who told you that the President had been shot in the temple?

Mr. McWatters. The man who got on the bus now?

Senator COOPER. Yes. The man to whom you have just referred as getting on the bus near Murphy Street.

Mr. McWATTERS. Yes.

Senator COOPER. Is he the same man who told you that the President had been shot in the temple?

Mr. McWATTERS. No, sir.

Senator COOPER. Who told you that?

Mr. McWATTERS. A man in an automobile in front of me, in other words, that was sitting in a car come back and told me.

Senator COOPER. Told you what?

Mr. McWATTERS. That the President had been shot, that he had heard over his radio in his car that the President had been shot.

Senator COOPER. I think you have testified that someone, some passenger on the bus, in response to a question that you had asked, "I wonder where they shot the President" said, "They shot him in the temple."

Mr. McWATTERS. Oh, that was now, that was after we had done, that is when I turned on Houston Street, the conversation with the teenage boy.

Senator COOPER. It was the teenage boy who told you that?

Mr. McWATTERS. Yes, sir; it was the teenage boy, sitting on his right side of the side seat there, the one that I conversationed with about the President being shot in the head or the temple, I don't remember, but the teenage boy was the one.

That was after the man that already got off that had boarded my bus up around Griffin there.

Senator COOPER. Then the one who told you the President had been shot in the temple was not the one you later identified in the police lineup?

Mr. McWATTERS. No, sir.

Senator COOPER. This probably has been testified to, but where did the man that you later identified in the police lineup get off the bus?

Mr. McWATTERS. Got off between Poydras and Lamar Street.

Senator COOPER. Was that after you crossed over the viaduct or before?

Mr. McWATTERS. No, sir; that was before I crossed over.

Senator COOPER. When did the teenage boy get off the bus?

Mr. McWATTERS. He got off at Oak Cliff, I believe. He got off at Marsalis and Brownley.

Senator COOPER. Was that after the bus had crossed the viaduct?

Mr. McWATTERS. That is after the bus had——

Senator COOPER. Past the Texas Depository?

Mr. McWATTERS. Yes, sir; that is about 3 or 4 miles out in the Oak Cliff section where the teenage boy got off of the bus.

Senator COOPER. From the time the man got on the bus, which you later identified in the police lineup until he got off, had you noticed him, had you looked at him again?

Mr. McWATTERS. Had I looked at him again?

Senator COOPER. Yes.

Mr. McWATTERS. Not until just like I say he was sitting—I was talking to this teenage boy and he was sitting right behind this boy, but I didn't pay him any particular attention, to the man.

Senator COOPER. You saw him get on the bus?

Mr. McWATTERS. Yes.

Senator COOPER. Did you see him get off?

Mr. McWATTERS. Yes; I gave him a transfer when he got off the bus, the same place that was, the same place I was stopped where the man come back and stepped up in the bus and told me what he had heard over his radio in his car, the same place that the lady got off, with a suitcase, is the place that the man got off.

Senator COOPER. The man you later identified in the police lineup?

Mr. McWATTERS. That is correct; yes, sir.

Senator COOPER. Did you pay any particular attention to him when he got off?

Mr. McWATTERS. Not no more than I did than, I think, when he got on.

Senator COOPER. Do you remember anything about his clothes or his general appearance in any way?

Mr. McWatters. Just like I say, I remember he had on, to me he had on just work clothes, he didn't have on a suit of clothes, and some type of jacket. I would say a cloth jacket.

Senator Cooper. I believe that is all.

Mr. Ball. You didn't—as I understand it, when you were at the police lineup, you told us that you didn't—weren't able to identify this man in the lineup as the man who got off, that you gave the transfer to.

Mr. McWatters. I told them to the best of my knowledge, I said the man that I picked out was the same height, about the same height, weight and description. But as far as actually saying that is the man I couldn't——

Mr. Ball. You couldn't do it?

Mr. McWatters. I wouldn't do it and I wouldn't do it now.

Mr. Ball. You signed an affidavit for the Dallas Police Department, do you remember that?

Mr. McWatters. Yes, sir.

Mr. Ball. I will show you a copy of it, we can get the original if you want, but there is a copy of it, a picture taken of it.

Will you read it, please?

(At this point, Representative Ford withdrew from the hearing room.)

Mr. Ball. This document, I would like to have marked as 377, at this time, Commission Exhibit, with the understanding that we may substitute the photostat for the original.

Senator Cooper. Very well; let it be substituted. It has been identified, and will be identified.

Mr. Ball. Yes, it will be; I will identify it for the record as a photostat of an affidavit of Cecil J. McWatters made before Patsy Collins, Notary Public of Dallas County, Tex., November 22, 1963.

(The document referred to was marked Commission Exhibit 377, and received in evidence.)

Mr. Ball, Now, having read that, first of all, does that look like your signature, Mr. McWatters?

Mr. McWatters. Yes, sir; it does.

Mr. Ball. Do you remember the circumstances under which you made that affidavit?

Mr. McWatters. Well, I just told them the best I could remember.

Mr. Ball. I am showing this to you for the purpose of refreshing your memory.

Mr. McWatters. Yes, I know.

Mr. Ball. I know it has been several months.

Mr. McWatters. Yes, I know what you mean.

Mr. Ball. And sometimes when you see something that you signed before it refreshes your memory.

Mr. McWatters. It sure does.

Yes, that is what you mean, I know what you mean, I said that looked like the man I saw.

Mr. Ball. In this affidavit, it says, it mentions the fact that when you went to Marsalis and picked up a woman.

Mr. McWatters. Yes.

Mr. Ball. You asked her if she knew the President had been shot, you told us about that a few moments ago.

Mr. McWatters. Yes.

Mr. Ball. She thought you were kidding, and you told her, "I told her if she didn't believe me to ask the man behind her, that he had told me the President was shot in the temple."

Mr. McWatters. Yes.

Mr. Ball. Was the man, was that the teenager?

Mr. McWatters. That is right, sir, that was the teenage boy. In other words, he was, I would say, around 17 or 18 years old.

Mr. Ball. You said here, "The man didn't say anything but he was grinning."

Mr. McWatters. Yes.

Mr. Ball. Do you think that happened?

Mr. McWatters. Well, when the lady asked him, he just kind of grinned, in other words, and she said, "This is not a grinning or laughing matter," or something to that effect I don't remember just exactly what she did say.

Mr. BALL. Now you told them at that time you didn't know where you let this man off.

Mr. McWATTERS. That is right, I didn't at that time, I didn't know where he got off.

Mr. BALL. You told us a few moments ago you thought he got off another place.

Mr. McWATTERS. That is right, sir.

Mr. BALL. What was that place?

Mr. McWATTERS. He got off at Brownley, because the man rode with me the next day.

Mr. BALL. You went out there the next day, did you?

Mr. McWATTERS. Yes, sir.

Mr. BALL. With an FBI man or a Dallas policeman?

Mr. McWATTERS. No, I mean——

Mr. BALL. The same teenager?

Mr. McWATTERS. The same teenager rode with me the next day.

Mr. BALL. And you noticed he got off there?

Mr. McWATTERS. Yes, and I noticed, and I asked him, like I told him, I said that I was—I thought that, you know, that he was, when he first got on down there, I says, "From all indications, we had you kind of pinpointed as the man who might have been mixed up in the assassination and everything." And—

Mr. BALL. Do I understand the day after you made the affidavit, this would be the 23d of November?

Mr. McWATTERS. Yes.

Mr. BALL. That this same teenager got on your bus again?

Mr. McWATTERS. Yes, he got on.

Mr. BALL. And you noticed where you let him off?

Mr. McWATTERS. I noticed where I let him off, yes, sir.

Mr. BALL. Is that the reason that today you remember he got off?

Mr. McWATTERS. That is it today I remember, just like I say, I remember I talked to him the next day, and he told me where he got on, and he told me where he got on, and where he got off and where he lived, and, you know that——

Mr. BALL. Has he been on your bus since?

Mr. McWATTERS. Yes.

Mr. BALL. He has?

Mr. McWATTERS. He has rode with me since.

Mr. BALL. Yes. I see.

Did you give him a transfer that day?

Mr. McWATTERS. No, because he gets on and he lives within about two blocks of the busline, in other words, where he gets off.

Mr. BALL. Do you know this boy's name?

Mr. McWATTERS. I believe his name is Milton Jones.

Mr. BALL. Milton Jones?

Mr. McWATTERS. Milton Jones. I don't believe I know where he lives, but I pass where he lives. But he told me his name was Milton Jones and he told me he was 17.

Mr. BALL. Did he ever tell you where he works?

Mr. McWATTERS. He told me that, I believe, he goes to school half a day, I believe he said and I believe he goes home and he has a part-time job, but he never did state where he works.

Mr. BALL. Did he tell you where he went to school?

Mr. McWATTERS. No, sir; he never did tell me where he went to school.

Mr. BALL. Or where he worked?

Mr. McWATTERS. Where he worked, either one.

Mr. BALL. You notice in the affidavit there it says, "This man"—referring to the man who was grinning——

Mr. McWATTERS. Yes.

Mr. BALL. "This man looks like the No. 1 man I saw in the lineup today."

Mr. McWATTERS. Yes.

Mr. BALL. Who was the No. 2 man you saw in the lineup on November 22, 1963?

Mr. McWATTERS. Well, just like I say, he was the shortest man in the lineup, in other words, when they brought these men out there, in other words, he was about the shortest, and the lightest weight one, I guess, was the reason I say that he looked like the man, because the rest of them were larger men than——

Mr. BALL. Well, now, at that time, when you saw the lineup——

Mr. McWATTERS. Yes.

Mr. BALL. Were you under the impression that this man that you saw in the lineup and whom you pointed out to the police, was the teenage boy who had been grinning?

Mr. McWATTERS. I was, yes, sir; I was under the impression——

Mr. BALL. That was the fellow?

Mr. McWATTERS. That was the fellow.

Mr. BALL. You were not under the impression then that night when you saw the lineup that the No. 2 man in the lineup was the man who got off the bus, to whom you had given a transfer?

Mr. McWATTERS. That is what I say. In other words, when I told them, I said, the only way is the man, that he is smaller, in other words, he kind of had a thin like face and he weighs less than any one of them. The only one I could identify at all would be the smaller man on account he was the only one who could come near fitting the description.

Mr. BALL. Let me ask you this, though. Did you tell them the man, the smaller man, you saw in the lineup, did you tell them that you thought he was the man who got off your bus and got the transfer or the man who was on the bus who was the teenager who was grinning?

Mr. McWATTERS. Well, I really thought he was the man who was on the bus.

Mr. BALL. That stayed on the bus?

Mr. McWATTERS. That stayed on the bus.

Mr. BALL. And you didn't think he was the man who got off the bus and to whom you gave a transfer?

Mr. McWATTERS. No, sir.

Mr. BALL. At that time you didn't?

Mr. McWATTERS. That is why I say I pinpointed that transfer on that boy as far as that is concerned. But at first, just like I say, I really thought from the height and weight of the two men, I mean was just like I say, was both of them were small. In the lineup they had, in other words, bigger men, in other words, he was the smallest man at the lineup.

Mr. BALL. We have got—we have this diagram that you have already drawn of the bus which has several initials on it. Could you tell me where on the bus this lady sat who told the teenager it was no grinning matter?

Mr. McWATTERS. Well, now, that is, in other words, I don't think at that time—now this teenager was still on the bus near, but I had a couple of more passengers on there, I believe I had two women on there, but I can't recall just, when I picked her up where she sat down on the bus.

Mr. BALL. Do you remember you said to the woman, "Look at that man behind you?"

Mr. McWATTERS. Yes, she was standing up here at the fare, paying fare.

Mr. BALL. And the teenager was where?

Mr. McWATTERS. He was sitting right here.

Mr. BALL. At the place "O", is that right?

Mr. McWATTERS. Yes, at the place "O".

Mr. BALL. I see.

Mr. McWATTERS. That is where the conversation was going on.

Mr. BALL. Mr. McWatters, that affidavit you have there, will you look at another item you have there?

Mr. McWATTERS. Yes, sir.

Mr. BALL. "Today, November 22, 1963, about 12:40 p.m., I was driving Marsalis Bus No. 1213."

Mr. McWATTERS. That is right.

281

Mr. BALL. First of all, you have referred to that as another bus, Munger Bus, is that the same bus?

Mr. McWATTERS. Yes, sir; in other words, that number there is my run number right here on my card.

Mr. BALL. I understand that, but do you call that run the Marsalis run as well as the Munger run?

Mr. McWATTERS. Yes, sir. Well, here you can—let me show you here on this schedule right here, Marsalis, Ramona, Elwood and Munger.

Mr. BALL. Can we take this and have a Xerox——

Mr. McWATTERS. You can just take the whole thing.

Mr. BALL. All right. We will have a Xerox of this and mark it 378, a Xerox copy.

Will you identify that document and tell me what it is?

(The document referred to was marked Commission Exhibit 378, for indentification.)

Mr. McWATTERS. This is a schedule, I will just say a bus schedule.

Mr. BALL. That is for the Marsalis-Ramona-Elwood-Munger run?

Mr. McWATTERS. That is correct.

Mr. BALL. Run 1213. Is this the run schedule that was in effect on November 22, 1963?

Mr. McWATTERS. Yes, sir; that is correct.

Mr. BALL. It shows here at St. Paul you were to leave at 12:36; is that correct?

Mr. McWATTERS. That is correct.

Mr. BALL. We will make a photostat of that and we will give you back the original.

Mr. McWATTERS. You can keep that if you want to. They made another copy of it.

Mr. BALL. All right, then, we will keep this as an original.

Can this be introduced into evidence, Senator?

Senator COOPER. Yes, let it be made a part of the evidence.

(The document heretofore marked for identification as Commission Exhibit No. 378, was received in evidence.)

Mr. BALL. I have a few more questions to ask you, a few more questions, Mr. McWatters.

Let's look again at this affidavit.

Mr. McWATTERS. Yes, sir.

Mr. BALL. "I picked up a man on the lower end of town on Elm around Houston," as I remember you didn't stop at Elm and Houston; you stopped at Record and Houston for a pickup.

Mr. McWATTERS. Yes.

Mr. BALL. Do you remember having picked up any man around the lower end of town at Elm around Houston?

Mr. McWATTERS. Elm and Houston?

Mr. BALL. Yes.

Mr. McWATTERS. No, no, sir; I didn't pick up. I made a statement here I picked up——

Mr. BALL. Take a look at it, "I picked up a man on the lower end of town on Elm around Houston."

Mr. McWATTERS. No, I didn't. I picked—"I picked a man up at the lower end of town at Elm," no, sir, I didn't pick up no man.

No, I was tied up in traffic there. Market Street is the—I must not have read that very good when I signed that, because I sure didn't. No, I didn't.

Mr. BALL. Did you pick up a man at Record and Houston?

Mr. McWATTERS. No, sir.

Mr. BALL. You didn't?

Mr. McWATTERS. No, sir; that is not even no stop.

Mr. BALL. In other words, this statement is not an accurate statement?

Mr. McWATTERS. That is right, sir, because in fact that day the police wouldn't let nobody, in other words they run them buses through but they wouldn't let nothing stop there, in other words.

Mr. BALL. Let's get back to that lineup.

Did you pick out one man or two men that night as people you had seen, as a person you had seen before?

Mr. McWATTERS. Well, I picked out, the only one that I told them it was the short man that I picked out up there.

Mr. BALL. And you thought he was the teenager whom you described?

Mr. McWATTERS. Yes, first that is what I thought he was.

Mr. BALL. Now you have named him Milton Jones.

Mr. McWATTERS. Yes, he was——

Mr. BALL. Now you realize you were mistaken in your identification that night?

Mr. McWATTERS. That is right.

Mr. BALL. As I understand it, neither then nor now are you able to identify or say that you have again seen the man that got off your bus to whom you gave a transfer?

Mr. McWATTERS. No, sir; I couldn't. I could not identify him.

Mr. BALL. This Beckley bus that we talked about, remember the one that has the starting point at St. Paul and Elm——

Mr. McWATTERS. Yes, sir.

Mr. BALL. The same as your bus, the Marsalis bus?

Mr. McWATTERS. Yes.

Mr. BALL. What is the difference in the time run, what time does the Beckley bus leave—let me withdraw the question.

Your bus leaves St. Paul and Elm at 12:36, scheduled to leave there as of November 22d?

Mr. McWATTERS. Yes, sir.

Mr. BALL. Using the same schedule, can you tell me at what time around 12:30 or so that the Beckley bus would leave Elm and St. Paul and proceed westerly on Elm?

Mr. McWATTERS. He is scheduled in there the same time as I am, 12:36.

Mr. BALL. 12:36. Was that bus in the line?

Mr. McWATTERS. No. In other words, that bus was behind me, in other words, because when I got there as a general rule, when we pull up there every day, in other words, I am coming in one direction and he is another, in other words, most every day, we will pull up at this intersection at the same time.

Now, whichever way the light changes is who gets, in other words, who gets in front of who. But at that day, I am sure that I was ahead of the Beckley bus.

Mr. BALL. You are sure you were ahead of it?

Mr. McWATTERS. Because there wasn't another bus in front of me. I was the first bus down there that was tied up in there in the traffic.

Mr. BALL. Did you see the Beckley bus?

Mr. McWATTERS. No, sir.

Mr. BALL. You don't remember whether he was behind you or not?

Mr. McWATTERS. I don't remember whether he was behind me or not.

Mr. BALL. Can you transfer from your bus to the Beckley bus?

Mr. McWATTERS. Yes, sir; sure can.

Mr. BALL. Any particular transfer point?

Mr. McWATTERS. Well, there are particular transfer points, but we don't question anybody within the downtown section with a transfer.

Mr. BALL. If you gave a transfer to your bus, then that transfer would be good on a Beckley bus any place along Elm, wouldn't it?

Mr. McWATTERS. That is right, it sure would.

Mr. BALL. Up to the place where you change courses?

Mr. McWATTERS. It would be accepted; yes, sir.

Mr. BALL. Your course is westerly on Elm, is identical with that of the Beckley bus between St. Paul and Houston, isn't it?

Mr. McWATTERS. That is correct.

Mr. BALL. And from that point you go south on Houston, and the Beckley bus continues west on Elm?

Mr. McWATTERS. That is correct.

Mr. BALL. So that would be a normal transfer point, wouldn't it?

Mr. McWATTERS. Yes, sir.

Mr. BALL. Houston and Elm?

Mr. McWATTERS. That would be a transfer. In other words, now, like I say, Lamar is the general transfer point of where all the buses cross.

Mr. BALL. Now, that night of the lineup, when you identified this one short man——

Mr. McWATTERS. Yes.

Mr. BALL. As being probably the teenager that had been on the bus——

Mr. McWATTERS. Yes.

Mr. BALL. Was there anything unusual in the conduct of anyone in the lineup?

Mr. McWATTERS. No.

Mr. BALL. Did any man in the lineup talk more than anyone else?

Mr. McWATTERS. No, I believe they had a guy that asked them their address, and they said, "address" and I don't know, he asked them, I believe he asked some of them where they lived or some of them where they worked, or I don't remember just what, in other words, he asked some enough, every one of them to say some few words.

Mr. BALL. You could hear them talk?

Mr. McWATTERS. Yes, sir; you could hear them talk.

Mr. BALL. Was any one man boisterous, mean, loud, anything of that sort?

Mr. McWATTERS. No, not that I could tell any difference. They all talked to me as, in other words, you just asked them their name and address. If they did, I didn't pay any attention to it.

(At this point, Representative Ford entered the hearing room.)

Mr. BALL. This is Exhibit No. 376 that I will show you again. You have indicated on the map the course of your bus south on Marsalis. Is there any other bus route that goes south on any street east of Marsalis?

Mr. McWATTERS. You mean that crosses it this way?

Mr. BALL. No, goes south.

Mr. McWATTERS. Well, let's see.

Mr. BALL. Is there a main highway called Denley? Is there a bus route on Ewing?

Mr. McWATTERS. Yes, sir. Bus route on Ewing.

Mr. BALL. That goes south on Ewing?

Mr. McWATTERS. Yes, sir.

Mr. BALL. Does that bus come anywhere near, does that bus run down Elm?

Mr. McWATTERS. Yes, sir.

Mr. BALL. Where does it turn to get to Ewing?

Mr. McWATTERS. In other words, it turns, it goes just like the Marsalis bus here goes, until he gets——

Mr. BALL. Let's start up at Elm here, Elm and Houston now. Does the bus that goes down Ewing come west on Elm?

Mr. McWATTERS. Yes, sir.

Mr. BALL. Does it go by St. Paul and Elm?

Mr. McWATTERS. Yes, sir.

Mr. BALL. Have a starting point there?

Mr. McWATTERS. Yes, sir; it is a final point for it right there.

Mr. BALL. And it goes west on Elm?

Mr. McWATTERS. Yes, sir.

Mr. BALL. Where does it turn off Elm?

Mr. McWATTERS. It turns the same place as I do, in other words.

Mr. BALL. South on Houston?

Mr. McWATTERS. South on Houston.

Mr. BALL. And then does it go across the Houston Street viaduct?

Mr. McWATTERS. Yes, sir.

Mr. BALL. Then it turns on, how does it get onto Ewing?

Mr. McWATTERS. It comes on out to Marsalis to, let's see, I have to find the zoo. That is where it turns right there at the Marsalis Park, and turns and goes over to Ewing, let's see, what is the name of that—this bus turns to the left off Marsalis there, it is a park—there is a big expressway there and it is the first street when it crosses over the expressway where it turns off of Marsalis on

284

Opera. The name of the bus is Ramona, it is the same, in other words, it is the same line as this other one.

Mr. BALL. As I understand it now the bus that goes down Ewing comes off the Houston Street viaduct as far as, comes down the Houston Street viaduct as far as Marsalis, does it?

Mr. McWATTERS. Yes, sir; and it goes south on Marsalis.

Mr. BALL. It goes south on Marsalis?

Mr. McWATTERS. That is right.

Mr. BALL. And it turns over to Ewing, that would be east on Ewing?

Mr. McWATTERS. Yes; that would be east.

Mr. BALL. At or about what point?

Mr. McWATTERS. Well, in other words, that is the Marsalis Zoo is where it is, after you cross the expressway there, it is the first street, Opera is the name of that and it goes right down to Ewing.

Mr. BALL. Then at the corner of 11th, at the intersection of 11th and Marsalis both buses travel the same route?

Mr. McWATTERS. Yes, sir; they sure do. Both buses travel the same route to Marsalis and the Ramona bus on that part travel the same route.

Mr. BALL. Probably on the same route.

Now, I show you this document which is the bus schedule of Marsalis-Ramona-Elwood-Munger, and it shows you leave St. Paul at 12:36 and you arrive at Lamar 12:40.

The bus transfers are punched you told me for 1 o'clock. We have a transfer here that you have seen or we will show you in a few minutes as soon as it gets here, which has a punch mark of 1 o'clock. You told Senator Cooper that you usually punched within 15 minutes of the time you reached the transfer points?

Mr. McWATTERS. Yes.

Mr. BALL. If that is the case, what——

Mr. McWATTERS. You mean why did I have it punched at 1 o'clock?

Mr. BALL. Yes.

Mr. McWATTERS. Because I punch it p.m. In other words, I have a punch, I am going to Lakewood, I mean I am going Marsalis and I am going back Lakewood, so I just take me two books of transfers. Instead of punching one of them a.m. and one p.m. I just punched them p.m.

Mr. BALL. Do you punch within 15 minutes of the time you reach the transfer points?

Mr. McWATTERS. That is the way that the transfers are supposed to be cut.

Mr. BALL. Well, if you reach Lamar, if you were to reach Lamar at 12:40, what time, according to the rules should you punch it?

Mr. McWATTERS. I should have punched it at 12:45.

Mr. BALL. At 12:45?

Mr. McWATTERS. But I would have to punch one book a.m. and another one p.m., so I just punched both of them p.m.

Mr. BALL. In other words, what you do is punch on the hour rather than the 45 and 15 minutes usually?

Mr. McWATTERS. Yes.

Mr. BALL. In other words, your usual practice is not to punch on the 15-minute interval, is that right, but to punch on the hour?

Mr. McWATTERS. Well, just like I say within the closest of the hour like that, in other words.

Mr. BALL. Suppose today you were wanting to punch some transfers at the end of the line and you knew you were going to get to Lamar at 12:40. Would you punch—what would you punch it?

Mr. McWATTERS. I work that run all the time, I punch at 1 o'clock every day. As I say I worked it 2 years and as I say in order to keep from punching one of them a.m. and one p.m., for the difference in the hour there, I just punch them p.m.

Mr. BALL. I don't quite understand that. Doesn't your p.m. start at after 12 o'clock?

Mr. McWATTERS. Well, the way the transfers are there, did you notice how they was, they run them until—see how 12:45 there, in other words, that is what they use that up to a.m. in other words.

Mr. BALL. It is 12:45 a.m., it runs up to a.m.

Mr. McWATTERS. That is what they run it to a.m. In other words, after 12:45 or in there, in other words, everything is punched p.m.

Mr. BALL. In other words, everything in the hour from 12 on is punched a.m., the day time, 12 to one is a.m., 12 to 12:45, for that hour, a transfer good in that hour is punched a.m., is that right?

Mr. McWATTERS. Yes, it can be punched a.m. up to, just like 12:45.

Mr. BALL. And the next punch is 1 o'clock and that is p.m?

Mr. McWATTERS. That is p.m.; yes, sir. That is the way they have them.

Representative FORD. The day that you punched this particular transfer, November 22?

Mr. McWATTERS. Yes, sir.

Representative FORD. You punched them the same that day as you did every other day?

Mr. McWATTERS. That is right. Every day, in other words, I just punch them p.m. I punch them p.m., and in other words, so it will be just a straight cut across it.

Representative FORD. Is that the usual practice for all bus drivers to use this practice?

Mr. McWATTERS. The practice they are supposed to cut them within the quarter of the hour, but in other words, I just have been working that run and I just, it is p.m., and I just make one trip one way and one back the other, and so I—all I carry are two books of transfers and so I just punch two books p.m., using one going one way at 1 o'clock and the other coming back at 2.

Representative FORD. This is the practice you have used for 2 years approximately?

Mr. McWATTERS. That is right, when I worked that run, in other words, when I am going one way at 1 o'clock, coming back from the other end of the line I set them at 2. I am back in there at, my next trip I am back in there at Lamar Street, I think it is 1:38 but I always just set them at 2 o'clock.

Mr. BALL. We have a couple of more pictures here. 378 and 379 which are pictures of the interior of the bus—Nos. 379 and 380. (Picture marked for identification as Commission Exhibit No. 374 is the same as Commission Exhibit No. 379.)

I will first show you 379. Is that a picture of the bus from front to rear of your bus?

Mr. McWATTERS. Yes, sir; that is the front and that is the rear.

Mr. BALL. Here is 380, is that a picture of the bus taken from the front taken looking towards the rear?

Mr. McWATTERS. Yes, sir.

Mr. BALL. I offer these in evidence, too.

Representative FORD. So admitted.

(The pictures referred to were marked Commission's Exhibits Nos. 379 and 380 and received in evidence.)

Mr. BALL. I have here an exhibit which I would like to have marked as 381 which can be identified as a transfer issued by Dallas Transit Company, Friday, November 22, 1963.

Do you identify it, can you tell me, if you have ever seen that transfer before?

Mr. McWATTERS. Yes, that is my punch mark right on that there; p.m.

(The transfer was marked Commission Exhibit No. 381 for identification.)

Mr. BALL. You issued it, did you?

Mr. McWATTERS. Yes.

Mr. BALL. Tell me when you issued it, on what run?

Mr. McWATTERS. I issued it on Marsalis and Munger line at I would say, around to the best of my knowledge it would be around 12:40 or somewheres in that vicinity on November 22.

Mr. BALL. And it has your punch mark, has it?

Mr. McWATTERS. Yes, sir; that is my punch mark.

Mr. BALL. Identify it punched in the p.m. section?

Mr. McWATTERS. Of the Lakewood column here on the transfer.

Mr. BALL. When did you punch it exactly? Where were you when you punched it?

Mr. McWATTERS. I punched it before I left the end of the line, in other words.

Mr. BALL. This is number 004459, is the transfer number. Entitled "The Shoppers Transfer." Every transfer has a separate number, has it?

Mr. McWATTERS. Yes, sir; everyone has a separate number.

Mr. BALL. What we would like to do is mark a photostat of the transfer as 381A and substitute the photostat and we can return the transfer to the custody of the FBI.

Representative FORD. The exhibit will be admitted.

(The photostat referred to was marked Commission Exhibit 381A and received in evidence.)

Representative FORD. How many of those transfers did you issue on this particular run?

Mr. McWATTERS. Well——

Representative FORD. Up to the time you passed the Texas School Depository.

Mr. McWATTERS. I really don't know because I didn't, see, I didn't know anything—I didn't put out any—most of the transfers that you put out at this time or that time of day are for elderly women which get the shopper's transfers, in other words. It has got a line there, and it entitles them to a free ride back to where they came from, in other words, and that time of the morning, because when I get downtown, in other words, you can catch a bus at Elm Street going to any place that I would go without having a transfer, in other words.

Representative FORD. Would you have any recollection of how many passengers you picked up from the beginning of the line to the time that this man got on at the middle of the block on Elm Street?

Mr. McWATTERS. Well, I don't—I recall that I didn't have very many passengers that day, because I figured that everybody had done gone to town to see the parade, to see the President, and it just wasn't what few passengers I recall was mostly elderly women that was going into town.

I don't recall just how many of them I did have on the bus.

Representative FORD. But you did have these two men, the teenager and this other young man?

Mr. McWATTERS. Yes, sir; that were on the bus.

Representative FORD. And you very specifically recall giving a transfer to this woman with the suitcase and the man who was in the second seat on the right-hand side?

Mr. McWATTERS. On the right side that got off. In other words, to the best of my knowledge that is the only two transfers that I put out going through town that I can recall at all, I mean, because I don't recall putting out any more transfers than those two that I put out when I was held up there in traffic.

Mr. BALL. Mr. McWatters, on this transfer is the name of Shopper's Transfer. Does that have any significance?

Mr. McWATTERS. Yes, sir; that is what I was telling him. In other words, if they want a Shoppers; well I put my punch mark in that Shoppers there, which they cannot use it for a transfer, in other words, any more than other than—all the stores, most of them in downtown Dallas, if you buy as much as a dollar's worth between the period of ten and four in the afternoon they give you a little white slip which entitled you to ride what is called the Shopper's Pass. It rides you back, but in other words you have to, a passenger has to, ask for it in other words.

When they say a Shopper, you take a punch and punch your punch mark where it says Shoppers, but they are not supposed to use the transfer then to transfer to another bus. They are supposed, in other words, where it is punched in the store, get it exchanged for their return fare.

Mr. BALL. In other words, all your transfers have on them printed the word "Shopper's Transfer"?

Mr. McWATTERS. Yes, sir; they do.

Mr. BALL. And in order to make it a Shopper's Transfer so that the transfer can be exchanged for a merchandise coupon to ride home, it has to have your punch in the Shopper's Transfer area, is that right?

Mr. McWATTERS. That is correct, yes, sir.

Mr. BALL. Did you know, did you remember, an elderly woman getting on your bus some place on Elm after you left St. Paul?

Mr. McWATTERS. Not that I recall.

Mr. BALL. Do you remember when this man, do you remember when this man knocked on your window, and you opened your bus and let him on, some place around Murphy or Griffin and Elm, that an elderly woman got up in the bus and moved?

Did you see that or anything like that?

Mr. McWATTERS. No, I don't recall.

Mr. BALL. Do you know whether or not you left an elderly woman off down around in the Oak Cliff area some place?

Mr. McWATTERS. The best I can recall I had two or three or four elderly women, the best I can remember on the bus when I left town, but I don't recall where any of them got off.

Mr. BALL. Do you know a woman named Mary Bledsoe?

Did you pick anybody up at St. Paul and Elm?

Mr. McWATTERS. I really don't—I really can't recall whether I did or not.

Mr. BALL. I have no further questions.

Senator COOPER. I would like to ask a few, if I may.

Am I correct in saying that the direction of your bus at the time of these events you have testified to it was going west on Elm Street?

Mr. McWATTERS. West on Elm. In other words, west, the streets of Dallas all run east and west.

Senator COOPER. But when you got to Houston Street, then you turned south?

Mr. McWATTERS. I turned south, that is correct.

Senator COOPER. Did your bus pass the Texas School Book Depository?

Mr. McWATTERS. Well——

Senator COOPER. I mean does it pass it directly?

Mr. McWATTERS. It doesn't pass it directly, no, sir. In other words, where I turn to the left on Houston Street, the book store is across on the opposite corner.

Senator COOPER. Now, as you reached Lamar Street, or did you reach Lamar Street on that date before you passed near the Texas School Book Depository?

Mr. McWATTERS. You mean—yes, I have to pass Lamar Street before I get down to there.

Senator COOPER. Now, this first affidavit you made on November 22——

Mr. McWATTERS. Yes, sir.

Senator COOPER. Which has been referred to in the testimony.

Mr. McWATTERS. Yes.

Senator COOPER. It stated in this affidavit that, "I picked up a man on the lower end of town on Elm around Houston."

Now, you picked up a man at that time it would have been after you passed Lamar Street?

Mr. McWATTERS. It would have been after I passed Lamar.

Senator COOPER. The remainder of the affidavit, which has been made a part of the testimony——

Mr. McWATTERS. Yes.

Senator COOPER. Refers to that you picked up a woman and you asked her if she knew the President had been shot, and then the man—you asked her then to speak to the man behind her.

Mr. McWATTERS. Yes.

Senator COOPER. "Who said the President was shot in the temple." Now, then, this incident that you testified to in this affidavit, was after you had passed Elm Street?

Mr. McWATTERS. Yes, sir; that is right.

Senator COOPER. Was the man that you were talking about in this affidavit the teenager?

Mr. McWATTERS. Yes, sir.

Senator COOPER. At the time this affidavit was made, were you asked about any other man who may have been on the run that day at that time?

Mr. McWATTERS. I don't remember whether I was or not.

Senator COOPER. What was it then that caused you at some time later to remember that another man had got on the bus near Murphy and had left the bus, as you have stated in 2 or 3 blocks in the vicinity of Elm Street?

Mr. McWATTERS. Well, just like I say, the best I can remember is the man, I believe in fact beside the boy. I believe he was the only man on board the bus. After I got to recall, in other words——

Senator COOPER. But what I am asking you is what it was that caused you to remember the teenager at the time you made this affidavit on the 22d, and what it was that, why it was that, you didn't at that time speak of the other man who had got on the bus?

Mr. McWATTERS. That is what I say, it just didn't—it just doesn't register, I don't know.

Senator COOPER. Were you asked whether or not any other man was on the bus?

Mr. McWATTERS. I don't remember whether I was or not.

Senator COOPER. When was it that you remembered about the second man being on the bus, the man that you now state got on around Murphy Street and got off at Elm?

Mr. McWATTERS. Well, I just studied and tried to remember everything that I could. In other words, I still, you know, just try to see if I could remember any incidents or anything that was said or done that I hadn't thought of and everything.

Senator COOPER. I think you stated you did not give the teenager any transfer?

Mr. McWATTERS. No, I don't—no.

Senator COOPER. Was the fact then that you were shown a transfer by the police that called your attention to that?

Mr. McWATTERS. I guess that would probably be——

Senator COOPER. Another man?

Mr. McWATTERS. That would probably be the reason.

I don't know of any other reason that it would be unless it was the transfer, that I can recall.

Senator COOPER. Are you absolutely certain that you did see another man on that bus?

Mr. McWATTERS. Do you mean the day?

Senator COOPER. A man other than the teenager?

Mr. McWATTERS. Yes, sir; I picked up a man.

Senator COOPER. Where?

Mr. McWATTERS. Along about Griffin Street that knocked on the door of the bus.

Senator COOPER. Is that near Murphy?

Mr. McWATTERS. That is near Murphy, in other words, Murphy is over here zig-zags, Griffin zig-zags across to Murphy.

Senator COOPER. Why was it then that when you made this affidavit, you wouldn't remember that a man knocked on the door to get in the bus?

Mr. McWATTERS. Just like I say, I guess it never did dawn on me until I just got to thinking about it and everything, and I had this boy, I mean was the one I was referring to in that affidavit right there.

In other words, he was just kind of a slight build, so far as him and Oswald, I guess they probably somewhere in the same size, I don't know. But I was mistaken in that. In other words, that was the boy right there—

Senator COOPER. Did the police ask you if any man other than the teenager was on the bus?

Mr. McWATTERS. I don't recall whether they did or not.

Senator COOPER. Did you tell the police at that time on the 22d or the Federal Bureau of Investigation on the 23d about a man knocking on the window and wanting to get into the bus?

Mr. McWATTERS. Yes, I believe I did.

Senator COOPER. What is it about this transfer that makes you know that it was a transfer which you issued?

Mr. McWATTERS. Well, you look at that old punch mark, I guess as many times as I have punched it——

Senator COOPER. Does each—does each driver have a different punch?

Mr. BALL. When you weren't here he showed us his punch and he punched it for us. He has got his punch.

Mr. McWATTERS. Each driver has a different punch. They all are registered. In other words, regardless of how many there are—that is my punch right there—there is some shape or form different, just like I say the superintendent has every man's name and a punch mark right on down, in other words, so when——

Senator COOPER. Do you know whether the punches are different in the shape that they make?

Mr. McWATTERS. No, sir; no, sir; I don't know anything about that. I know——

Senator COOPER. What you are saying is, then, you have punched so many of these transfer that you recognize your own punch?

Mr. McWATERS. I can recognize my own punchmark. I don't think there is supposed to be another——

Senator COOPER. Is there anything else on the transfer which indicates that it was one which would be issued on your bus?

Mr. McWATTERS. Well, except only where it is punched—in other words, I come off of Lakewood Boulevard there where that would be the only distinction right there, is the punchmark and the name of where I have it punched there.

Senator COOPER. Did anyone tell you, either the police or the FBI or any other officer or any other person, tell you at the time you made your first affidavit or later that there was another man reported to have been on your bus and got off?

Mr. McWATTERS. I don't recall.

Senator COOPER. Have you ever reported to the police the fact that you have carried as a passenger since November 22d the teenager whom you have now identified as having the name of Milton Jones?

Mr. McWATTERS. Did I ever report it to the police?

Senator COOPER. Yes.

Mr. McWATTERS. No, sir.

Senator COOPER. Have they ever been back to talk to you any more about this?

Mr. McWATTERS. No, sir.

Senator COOPER. About this matter?

Mr. McWATTERS. They have never been back to me. The only time they have talked to me——

Senator COOPER. Did you ever see——

Mr. McWATTERS. I beg pardon?

Senator COOPER. You saw—was any of the men in the police lineup ever identified to you as being Lee Oswald?

Mr. McWATTERS. Any men in the——

Senator COOPER. Yes, I think you saw the men in the lineup, didn't you?

Mr. McWATTERS. Yes.

Senator COOPER. Before you were asked to select a man in the lineup, did the police or any officer identify any one of them as bearing the name of Lee Oswald?

Mr. McWATTERS. No, sir; they never stated anything.

Senator COOPER. Later was he identified to you in any way?

Mr. McWATTERS. Was he identified to me?

Senator COOPER. As being Lee Oswald?

Mr. McWATTERS. No, they didn't tell me as far as saying, mentioning any name Lee Oswald, it was never, the name Lee Oswald, I don't believe was ever mentioned while we was back there.

Senator COOPER. Did you ever see this same man you call No. 2 in the lineup again—did you ever go back there after that time and see this same person again?

Mr. McWATTERS. No, sir.

Senator COOPER. Identified as No. 2?

Mr. McWATTERS. No, sir; I never did go back any more, that was the only time I was ever there was the one on November 22, about 6 something in the afternoon.

Senator COOPER. Have you seen photographs of a man who is named in those photographs as being Lee Oswald?

Mr. McWATTERS. Have I saw them?

290

Senator COOPER. Yes, sir.

Mr. McWATTERS. Yes, sir.

Senator COOPER. Well, now, you have seen this young man, Milton Jones, several times since then?

Mr. McWATTERS. Yes, sir.

Senator COOPER. Now after having seen him several times since then, and having seen these photographs of the man who is identified as Lee Oswald——

Mr. McWATTERS. Yes.

Senator COOPER. Does Milton Jones look like Lee Oswald?

Mr. McWATTERS. Well, they both, just like I say, about the same height, and same build, and everything, as far as identifying looking at a man in the face— of course, I know him now, distinctly.

Senator COOPER. But at this time would you identify him as Lee Oswald from the photographs you have seen of Lee Oswald?

Mr. McWATTERS. Right now?

Senator COOPER. Yes.

Mr. McWATTERS. No. At the time, I couldn't then, in other words, even from the recalling of what I seen him then, I mean just to say that the height and size of him, no, I wouldn't make the statement that I could now.

Senator COOPER. Are you certain that you did see some man who knocked on the window of your door of your bus and wanted to get in your bus at some point near Murphy?

Mr. McWATTERS. Yes, sir; I am positive about that. There was——

Senator COOPER. You saw that man get off later?

Mr. McWATTERS. Yes.

Senator COOPER. Before you got to——

Mr. McWATTERS. Before I got to Lamar Street, between Poydras and Lamar.

Senator COOPER. That is all.

Mr. McWATTERS. The best I can remember is that is where I issued two transfers. That is the best I can remember.

Mr. BALL. To clear this matter up with your punch, you have your punch there, have you?

Mr. McWATTERS. Yes.

Mr. BALL. That was issued to you by the Dallas Transit Company?

Mr. McWATTERS. Yes, sir.

Mr. BALL. Does that make a different mark in a transfer than any other punch issued to any other driver in the Dallas Transit Company?

Mr. McWATTERS. Yes, sir.

Mr. BALL. It is a distinctive mark?

Mr. McWATTERS. Yes, sir; it is supposed to be, there is not supposed to be any driver that has a punch that makes a punchmark like my punch.

Mr. BALL. So your supervisor could take this transfer and compare it with his list in his office?

Mr. McWATTERS. That is right.

Mr. BALL. And he could see McWatters issued this transfer?

Mr. McWATTERS. That is right; that is the way, if they have any complaint, any transfers brought in to him, he has a list. When he looked at the punchmark he knows the man's name, and his badge number.

Mr. BALL. And this document here which is 381, you have identified that punchmark as the one made by your punch?

Mr. McWATTERS. Yes, sir; that punchmark was made by that punch right there.

Mr. BALL. Now, there are on this transfer two punches, there is one in p.m., and there is marked punch Lakewood. Now, the p.m., refers to the time?

Mr. McWATTERS. Yes, sir.

Mr. BALL. But Lakewood refers to a certain location on your run, doesn't it?

Mr. McWATTERS. Yes, sir.

Mr. BALL. If this transfer was issued around the Lamar area or St. Paul— Elm area, is there any place that you could punch and show that particular location?

Mr. McWATTERS. No, sir.

Mr. BALL. You always punch at the end of your destination?

Mr. McWATTERS. Yes, that is the usual procedure on it.

Mr. BALL. Now, on one side of Lakewood is Beckley, where is that?

Mr. McWATTERS. Well, that is on the opposite of town from——

Mr. BALL. The other side is Capital. Where is that?

Mr. McWATTER. Capital, well, Capital is in north Dallas, I believe it is.

Mr. BALL. Are those Beckley lines listed on the transfer on your run?

Mr. McWATTERS. No, sir; I don't—you mean on the transfer?

Mr. BALL. Yes.

Mr. McWATTERS. Well, that is, in other words, we all—they have so many of the lines listed, in other words, I believe they have two divisions, I believe all the buses that work out of the east Dallas division have——

Mr. BALL. We can make this pretty simple. You have on this transfer certain names. When you are running Marsalis-Ramona-Elwood-Munger, how many possible punches would—location punches would you make?

Mr. McWATTERS. In other words, if I was—Marsalis when I left the end of Marsalis out there I would punch my transfer Marsalis, if I left the end of Ramona I would punch them Ramona. In other words, that is so they can't ride them, in other words, they can't ride the transfer.

Mr. BALL. Now, Lakewood is at one end of your run?

Mr. McWATTERS. That is right.

Mr. BALL. And Marsalis-Ramona-Elwood is the other, is that right?

Mr. McWATTERS. Yes, sir.

Mr. BALL. So you would punch one of those names?

Mr. McWATTERS. Going that way, while at Marsalis, I would punch the Lakewood when I would leave Marsalis coming toward Lakewood, I would have Lakewood on the front of my bus but I would punch the transfer Marsalis.

Mr. BALL. I have no further questions.

Representative FORD. Thank you very much, Mr. McWatters.

Mr. McWATTERS. Thank you, gentlemen.

TESTIMONY OF WILLIAM WAYNE WHALEY RESUMED

Mr. BALL. Mr. Whaley, I have here an exhibit which I will mark 370.

(The document was marked Commission Exhibit No. 370 for identification.)

Mr. BALL. 370 is a photostat of a manifest of yours, and it is dated November 22, 1963. I mark this 370. Do you recognize that?

Mr. WHALEY. That is the original trip sheet.

Mr. BALL. In your handwriting?

Mr. WHALEY. Yes, sir; in my handwriting.

Mr. BALL. I will offer this into evidence at this time, and the original trip sheet as Exhibit No. 382.

Representative FORD. So admitted.

(Commission Exhibits Nos. 370 and 382 were received in evidence.)

Mr. BALL. I have here a bracelet which is marked 383. Take a look at it and tell me if you have ever seen it before.

Mr. WHALEY. Yes, sir; as near as I can tell that is the bracelet he was wearing the day I carried him, the shiny bracelet I was talking about.

Mr. BALL. You mentioned the fact that the man who sat in the front seat of your cab, which you drove from the Greyhound Station on Lamar Street over to 500 North Beckley, had an identification bracelet on him.

Mr. WHALEY. Yes, it looked like an identification bracelet. It looks like this one, sir, it was shiny, I couldn't tell exactly whether that was the bracelet or not.

Mr. BALL. But it looks like one of them?

Mr. WHALEY. Yes, sir; it looks like it.

Mr. BALL. Offer this in evidence.

Representative FORD. So admitted.

(Commission Exhibit No. 383 was withdrawn and a photograph of the bracelet was received as Commission Exhibit No. 383-A.)

Representative FORD. What hand or what arm did he have it on?

Mr. WHALEY. He had it on the arm next to me, which was the left arm.

Representative FORD. Was it protruding below the sleeve or jacket?

Mr. WHALEY. His coatsleeve was like this when he stretches his arm out it was short, that is when I saw it.

Representative FORD. Where was his hand when you saw it, if you can recollect it?

Mr. WHALEY. Well, just moving. You know you catch any bright object, why you notice it, that is how I noticed it. He was just moving his hand around. When the old lady stuck her head in the door and asked me to call her a cab, why he reached over to the door to open it like he told her she could have that one but she decided that she would wait for the next one because he already had that one. And that is when I saw it, sir.

In the picture, I believe, I don't think he had it on in that picture in the paper the next morning.

Representative FORD. This is something you clearly noticed while he was riding in the car with you?

Mr. WHALEY. Yes, sir; I noticed it; yes, sir. I always notice watchbands, unusual watchbands, and identification bracelets like these, because I make them myself. I made this one.

Representative FORD. In other words, you have a particular interest in them?

Mr. WHALEY. Yes, I particularly notice things like that.

Representative FORD. Did you notice anything unusual about it?

Mr. WHALEY. No, sir, it was just a common stretchband identification bracelet. A lot of them are made of chain links and not stretchbands. Stretchbands are unusual because there is very few of them.

Representative FORD. In other words, this was an unusual band?

Mr. WHALEY. Yes, sir; this one was a stretchband like the one you showed me.

Representative FORD. It is sort of a hobby with you to make these kinds of wristbands?

Mr. WHALEY. Yes, sir; I make watchbands like that.

Mr. BALL. Do you recall when you told, talked to the Dallas police officers that you told them that you had seen a heavy identification bracelet on this passenger's wrist?

Mr. WHALEY. Yes, sir, I told them about the bracelet.

Mr. BALL. You told the FBI officers, also?

Mr. WHALEY. Yes, sir; but I don't remember saying it was heavy because I wouldn't have known how heavy it was without handling it.

Mr. BALL. You described the bracelet?

Mr. WHALEY. I just described the bracelet as a shiny bracelet.

Mr. BALL. A moment ago you told us about this man getting into your cab and an old lady coming up and asking for a cab.

Mr. WHALEY. Yes, sir.

Mr. BALL. Did the man sitting next to you open the door?

Mr. WHALEY. He just started to, sir, just reached for door handle and she said she wanted me to call one. She didn't want that.

Mr. BALL. Did the man who was sitting beside you in the cab say anything?

Mr. WHALEY. Only that she could have that one.

Mr. BALL. He said that?

Mr. WHALEY. Yes, sir.

Mr. BALL. I think that is all.

Any other questions of this witness?

Did you describe the shirt that this man had on to the police?

Mr. WHALEY. Yes, sir, I did.

Mr. BALL. What did you tell them?

Mr. WHALEY. To the best of my ability, I did, sir. I just told them it was a dark colored shirt with what looked like a silver lining.

Mr. BALL. Were you shown the shirt later?

Mr. WHALEY. About, it was at least a week later, sir, an FBI man brought the shirt over and showed it to me.

Mr. BALL. Is that the same shirt you saw here?

Mr. WHALEY. I think it is, sir. I am not positive but it had the same kind of silver streak in it.

Mr. BALL. What did you tell the FBI man who brought the shirt to you?

Mr. WHALEY. I told him to the best of my ability that was the shirt he had on.

Mr. BALL. Did the man riding with you say anything at all except tell you where he wanted to go?

Mr. WHALEY. That is all, sir, except he said when we got to where he wanted to go he said, "This will do fine," when I pulled over.

Mr. BALL. Now, in the police lineup now, and this man was talking to the police and telling them he wanted a lawyer, and that they were trying to, you say he said they were trying to, frame him or something of that sort——

Mr. WHALEY. Well, the way he talked that they were doing him an injustice by putting him out there dressed different than these other men he was out there with.

Mr. BALL. Now, did anyone, any policeman, who was there, say anything to him?

Mr. WHALEY. Yes, sir; Detective Sergeant Leavelle, I believe it was, told him that they had, would get him his lawyers on the phone, that they didn't think they were doing him wrong by putting him out there dressed up.

Representative FORD. Did the man you identified have any reaction when they brought the group out, did he have any reaction that you noticed at the time you identified him?

Mr. WHALEY. Only that he was the only one that had the bruise on his head, sir. The only one who acted surly. In other words, I told this Commission this morning you wouldn't have had to have known who it was to have picked him out by the way he acted. But he was the man that I carried in my taxicab. I told them when I identified him. I didn't identify him as the man who shot the President. I identified him as the man who rode from the Greyhound to 1500 North Beckley with me.

Representative FORD. Did you point him out with your hand?

Mr. WHALEY. No, sir; I did not. They asked me which number he was standing under and he was standing under No. 2.

Representative FORD. Could he hear you make this identification?

Mr. WHALEY. No, sir; he couldn't see me.

Representative FORD. He couldn't see you?

Mr. WHALEY. No, sir; they had the black silk screen that keeps the prisoners from seeing the people who show up.

Mr. BALL. I have no further questions.

Senator COOPER. I have no questions.

Mr. BALL. Do you know a taxi driver named Darrell Click?

Mr. WHALEY. I may know his face, sir, but not his name.

Mr. BALL. You don't know his name?

Mr. WHALEY. We go mostly by numbers.

Mr. BALL. Okay, no further questions.

The witness is excused.

Representative FORD. May we wait just a moment, please? Would you like to make a statement, Mr. Powell?

Mr. POWELL. Mr. Chairman, I think I might say just this: I am here representing Mr. Walter Craig, as I think the Commission understands. I have been here the last two days. In a conversation with Mr. Rankin yesterday morning we agreed that rather than my asking questions directly of witnesses, I would make suggestions to Mr. Ball or to one of his associates, and I have been following that practice yesterday and today, after consulting with Mr. Murray who is also here for Mr. Craig, and Mr. Ball and his associates have followed up these suggestions that we have made.

Representative FORD. The suggestions you have made have been transmitted to Mr. Ball or his associates and have been asked of the various witnesses?

Mr. POWELL. That is correct.

Representative FORD. Any other questions?

Thank you very much, Mr. Whaley.

Mr. WHALEY. Thank you, sir. I am glad to be able to be of service.

(Whereupon, at 12:30 p.m., the President's Commission recessed.)

TESTIMONY OF MRS. KATHERINE FORD, DECLAN P. FORD, AND PETER PAUL GREGORY

The President's Commission met at 9:10 a.m. on Friday, March 13, 1964, at 200 Maryland Avenue NE., Washington, D.C.

Present were Chief Justice Earl Warren, Chairman; Representative Gerald R. Ford, member.

Also present were Wesley J. Liebeler, assistant counsel; Norman Redlich, assistant counsel; and Charles Murray, observer.

TESTIMONY OF MRS. KATHERINE FORD

The CHAIRMAN. The Commission will be in order.

Mrs. Ford, I would just like to read to you a short statement concerning the purpose of the meeting.

I think you have had a copy of it but I will just read it for the record.

Mrs. FORD. Yes, sir.

The CHAIRMAN. The purpose of this hearing is to take the testimony of Mr. and Mrs. Declan P. Ford and Mr. Peter Paul Gregory. The Commission has been advised that Mr. and Mrs. Ford made the acquaintance of the Oswalds shortly after their arrival in the United States in June of 1962, and that Mrs. Marina Oswald lived in the Ford home on two different occasions in November 1962, and for a period following February 12, 1964.

The Commission has also been advised that Mr. Gregory was contacted by Mr. Lee Harvey Oswald shortly after Mr. Oswald's return from Russia as a result of which Mr. and Mrs. Oswald made the acquaintance of a large number of Russian-speaking people in the Dallas and Fort Worth area.

Since the Commission is inquiring fully into the background and possible motive of Lee Harvey Oswald, the alleged assassin, it intends to ask the above witnesses questions concerning Mr. Oswald, his associations and relations with others and any and all other matters relating to the assassination.

Would you please rise and be sworn, Mrs. Ford.

Do you solemnly swear the testimony you give before the Commission will be the truth, the whole truth and nothing but the truth, so help you God?

Mrs. FORD. I do.

The CHAIRMAN. You may be seated. Mr. Liebeler will conduct the examination.

Mr. LIEBELER. Would you state your full name for the record, please?

Mrs. FORD. My maiden name?

Mr. LIEBELER. Yes.

Mrs. FORD. Katrina Evstratova.

Mr. LIEBELER. Where were you born, Mrs. Ford?

Mrs. FORD. Nova Tchkarsk.

Mr. LIEBELER. Could you tell us just briefly how you came to come to the United States, Mrs. Ford?

Mrs. FORD. How I came to the United States; I was in Germany during the war. I was taken there by Germans, not in concentration camps, but in labor camp, and after we were liberated by Americans I got acquainted with an American soldier and was married to him, and that is how I came straight to Dallas.

Mr. LIEBELER. What was this soldier's name that you married?

Mrs. FORD. Skotnicki.

Mr. LIEBELER. And you were married to him in about 1946?

Mrs. FORD. That is correct.

Mr. LIEBELER. And you subsequently divorced him?

Mrs. FORD. Approximately 4 years ago, a little over 4 years.

Mr. LIEBELER. I want to ask you a few questions about Mr. Skotnicki and some of the people that he knew.

Do you still have any friends that were your friends when you were married to Mr. Skotnicki?

Mrs. FORD. Yes; I would think, some neighbors, I would say that we would be still—we don't see together, acquaintances together with those friends but I am sure they are still friendly. He is still friendly with the same people as I am. I would say Campbells down on 6468 Lane, the old house still stands there I would think he would still be friendly with them, and I know them very well.

Mr. LIEBELER. You don't continue to see Mr. Skotnicki in any way, do you?

Mrs. FORD. No, no; I have no reason for it.

Mr. LIEBELER. Do you know whether or not Mr. Skotnicki has a friend by the name of John M. Grizzaffi? That is spelled G-r-i-z-z-a-f-f-i.

Mrs. FORD. I think that he is friends, yes. It is a neighbor across the street. He was friendly with that man.

Mr. LIEBELER. Would you tell us just a little bit about Mr. Grizzaffi, if you know about him?

Mrs. FORD. I think he is in grocery business, that is what I know about him, and I believe, I wouldn't say he is busy in local politics but he is always talking about people he knows around town that are in politics, and that is about all I know. I was never very friendly with his wife and so I just know a little bit about him.

Mr. LIEBELER. Do you know whether Mr. Grizzaffi is a friend of Jack Ruby's?

Mrs. FORD. That I don't know. I was told by my son that Mr. Grizzaffi knew Ruby.

Mr. LIEBELER. Your son told you that?

Mrs. FORD. My young son.

Mr. LIEBELER. What is you son's name?

Mrs. FORD. My son's name is Gary.

Mr. LIEBELER. How old is he?

Mrs. FORD. Twelve.

Mr. LIEBELER. He is a son by Mr. Skotnicki?

Mrs. FORD. Yes.

Mr. LIEBELER. Is he living with you and Mr. Ford?

Mrs. FORD. He lives with me.

Mr. LIEBELER. Do you know whether Mr. Skotnicki knew the Oswalds?

Mrs. FORD. No; I don't think he did.

Mr. LIEBELER. Do you know whether he knew anything about the Oswalds?

Mrs. FORD. Unless something was told by my son or something, by children. I don't think he knew them personally.

Mr. LIEBELER. You yourself didn't have any conversations with Mr. Skotnicki about the Oswalds?

Mrs. FORD. No.

Mr. LIEBELER. I want to go through a list of names which I will go through fairly quickly and ask you if you recognize any of these names or if you know any of the people.

Do you know a gentleman by the name of George Senator?

Mrs. FORD. No; I don't.

Mr. LIEBELER. How about a man by the name of Ralph Paul?

Mrs. FORD. No.

Mr. LIEBELER. Andrew Armstrong?

Mrs. FORD. No.

Mr. LIEBELER. Do you know a lady by the name of Karen Bennett?

Mrs. FORD. No.

Mr. LIEBELER. Bruce Carlin?

Mrs. FORD. No.

Mr. LIEBELER. Do you know a man by the name of Roy William Pike?

Mrs. FORD. No.

Mr. LIEBELER. How about Larry Crafard?

Mrs. FORD. No.

Mr. LIEBELER. You yourself don't know Jack Ruby in any way?

Mrs. FORD. No.

Mr. LIEBELER. Does Mr. Ford know Mr. Ruby?

Mrs. FORD. No; I don't thing so; no.

Mr. LIEBELER. Do you know a lady by the name of Earlene Roberts?

Mrs. FORD. No.

Mr. LIEBELER. Mary Bledsoe?

Mrs. FORD. No.

Mr. LIEBELER. Bertha Cheek?

Mrs. FORD. No.

Mr. LIEBELER. John Carter.

Mrs. FORD. No.

Mr. LIEBELER. How about Mr. and Mrs. A. C. Johnson?

Mrs. FORD. A. C. Johnson, I don't think so.

Mr. LIEBELER. Do you know of any connection between Mr. Oswald, Lee Harvey Oswald and Jack Ruby?

Mrs. FORD. No; I don't know. I don't know that they knew each other.

Mr. LIEBELER. Would you tell the Commission, Mrs. Ford, how you first met the Oswalds?

Mrs. FORD. We were invited there after lunch, the Oswalds had a luncheon at Anna Meller's house, and we were invited after luncheon to meet them, and that was our first contact with them.

Mr. LIEBELER. Can you tell me when that was, approximately?

Mrs. FORD. I would say it was approximately at the end of August of 1962.

Mr. LIEBELER. Will you tell us who was at the luncheon?

Mrs. FORD. I believe there was Mr. and Mrs. Ted Meller and George Bouhe and the Oswalds and ourselves, I believe that is all I remember.

Mr. LIEBELER. Who first told you about the Oswalds? Did you hear of them the first time that you came to that luncheon or had you heard of them before?

Mrs. FORD. I had heard of them maybe a couple of weeks before from Mr. George Bouhe, I believe, who had told us that there was a young Russian girl came to Fort Worth and the man was out of a job, and that was the reason for us to try to help them. And she had a baby and so forth.

Mr. LIEBELER. Did Mr. Bouhe tell you anything else about the Oswalds?

Mrs. FORD. No; he was just telling that the man was having a very hard time finding a job because the last job he had was in Minsk or so.

Mr. LIEBELER. He told you that Mr. Oswald had been in Russia?

Mrs. FORD. Yes; he did. He told us about that he was in Russia and decided to come back and he brought a Russian wife with him who didn't speak English and had a tiny baby and both were having a very hard time at the moment.

Mr. LIEBELER. Did Mr. Bouhe tell you anything about the circumstances under which Mr. Oswald went to Russia?

Mrs. FORD. No; nothing like that was discussed.

Mr. LIEBELER. At the luncheon at which you and your husband, and Mr. and Mrs. Meller——

Mrs. FORD. Yes.

Mr. LIEBELER. And Mr. Bouhe were present——

Mrs. FORD. Yes.

Mr. LIEBELER. What was said at that time?

Mrs. FORD. At the time we were present, actually, I was only interested in economic conditions of Russia at the moment, for me to compare them with the time I was living there, and they were showing some pictures of Minsk and Leningrad and some of the pictures of some of the friends of Marina's friends, girl friends.

(At this point, Representative Ford entered the hearing room.)

Mr. LIEBELER. Did you have any conversations with the Oswalds at that time about the kind of apartment that they had when they lived in Minsk?

Mrs. FORD. I don't remember any particulars about that apartment, but they were talking about, I think, about the apartment, I don't know exactly what was said about it. I know it was, I think I remember they were saying they lived in one room and sharing a kitchen.

Mr. LIEBELER. Did they tell you how they came to meet each other in Russia and how they came to be married?

Mrs. FORD. It wasn't said at that particular time, but I remember Marina was telling me afterwards how they came to meet each other, and I believe it was at a dance some place at the Hall of Culture or some place they would have in Russia dances, and she met him there.

Mr. LIEBELER. Of the people that were at this luncheon, aside from yourself, how many of them were originally born in Russia?

297

Mrs. FORD. Mr. Bouhe and I believe and Mr. Meller would be—I believe Ted Meller was born in Poland.

Mr. LIEBELER. Did it appear to you at the time of that luncheon that Lee Harvey Oswald lived like other Russian people lived or did it appear that he might have received preferential treatment in some way.

Did you gather an impression about that during the course of your conversation?

Mrs. FORD. Yes; I believe he was still in something of a hardship in living in Russia, that was the reason for his leaving Russia. That it was rather difficult to make his ends meet as we say, because he was comparing it with his living standards of Marina's uncle who was a colonel or a major, I don't know, I wouldn't say because I don't know. He was saying that they had a very lovely apartment consisting of maybe four or five rooms and he was comparing it with his apartment, and such.

Mr. LIEBELER. Did he compare his apartment with the apartment of other workers who worked in Minsk?

Mrs. FORD. No; I don't think so. He was just comparing, I believe with her uncle.

Mr. LIEBELER. Did he tell you how much money he was paid at his job?

Mrs. FORD. I don't remember, he was saying or Marina was saying something, 80 rubles, I don't know which one gave me that.

Mr. LIEBELER. Did he indicate whether that was about the same that other people were paid or more?

Mrs. FORD. Yes; about the same as the workers were paid.

Mr. LIEBELER. Now, is there anything else you can remember about that luncheon, the conversation at that luncheon which you would like to tell the Commission about other than what we have already touched on?

Mrs. FORD. Well, I don't know what was important. I know he was saying— my husband made a sort of a joking statement that he had a child born in Russia, and he said, well, if it wasn't for the Americans she wouldn't be born over there because he had to wait so long to get a visa. I don't know what else he said.

Mr. LIEBELER. That was a visa for him to return?

Mrs. FORD. Yes; and the little girl, June, was born there because of that.

Mr. LIEBELER. And Lee Oswald blamed the Americans for causing the delay?

Mrs. FORD. Yes.

Mr. LIEBELER. Did he indicate what attitude the Russian authorities took when he told them he wanted to come back to the United States?

Mrs. FORD. No; I don't know. He didn't say anything. I don't remember discussing it.

Mr. LIEBELER. Did he say anything about the attitude they took toward letting Marina leave Russia and coming to the United States?

Mrs. FORD. I don't believe anything was said about that.

Mr. LIEBELER. Is there anything else you can remember about that luncheon now you think we ought to know about?

Mrs. FORD. Well, I am thinking, I really don't think I remember anything else.

Mr. LIEBELER. What was the next contact then that you had with the Oswalds?

Mrs. FORD. I think it must have been at—in late October or the first part of November when Mr. Bouhe called me and said that Marina made a call to Anna Meller and told her she is leaving her husband because of she can't stand the beating and treatment any longer from Lee Oswald, but none of us knew at the moment that he had mistreated her that way, but at the time at the party I remember seeing Marina with bruises on her face and she made excuses of running into a door or something at the night when attending the baby.

Mr. LIEBELER. This was the first time you saw her?

Mrs. FORD. That is right, the first time I saw her I did see bruises on her face. And George Bouhe was saying that Anna Meller, I don't know who picked her up, I believe George Bouhe because Anna Meller don't have a car, they went to Marina's apartment and picked up the baby things, playpen, and other things that she could take with her at the time, and she stayed there, I couldn't say how many days.

Mr. LIEBELER. Stayed with Mrs. Meller?

Mrs. FORD. With Mrs. Meller, I don't think it was longer than a week, and then my husband was supposed to go away for a week or so; I don't remember the time, I thought he was going—he said he had to go Austin and I told Mr. Bouhe that I could take her for a week, just take her in, if she didn't have a place to go, so I did, and she stayed with me.

Mr. LIEBELER. Why did she come to you as opposed to staying with Anna Meller?

Mrs. FORD. Anna Meller has a small two-room apartment and I have a bigger house. We have four bedrooms so I could make room for her and her children.

Mr. LIEBELER. When Mr. Bouhe called you and told you about this, did he tell you anything about why Marina was leaving Lee Oswald?

Mrs. FORD. Yes; he said because of mistreatment and she decided she is not going to return to him any longer, and Mr. Bouhe said, told her, if she made a promise to him she is not going to return to that man he will help her all he could to find a place to stay permanently such as maybe as help at home at somebody's house until she learns enough English to start going on her own whatever she could do.

· And I think he was trying to do, he was trying to find a place and that is the reason before that she needed a place to stay until she did find a place, and I kept her for a week until my husband returned and then another friend of mine, who also has a fairly large place where Marina could be comfortable, she told me she could keep her there for as long as Marina wished to stay.

Mr. LIEBELER. How did Marina actually get to your place? Did Mr. Bouhe bring her to your place?

Mrs. FORD. Yes; he did.

Mr. LIEBELER. Do you know how long Marina stayed with Anna Meller before she came to your place?

Mrs. FORD. It could be a week but I am not sure. But I don't think it is longer than a week.

Mr. LIEBELER. Did Lee Oswald come to see Marina while Marina was at your house?

Mrs. FORD. No; he did not but he did talk to her on the telephone, I think approximately after 3 days, after she stayed with me he called her up every night, I think he did call, every evening.

Mr. LIEBELER. Did Marina talk to him on the telephone?

Mrs. FORD. She was hesitating at first but he wouldn't leave the telephone until she came to telephone and she was talking to him. I didn't hear what he was saying but she was telling him not to call on her again and not to bother, she was not going to return to him.

Mr. LIEBELER. Did she tell you what the conversations were about?

Mrs. FORD. No. She did not say anything.

Representative FORD. When was this period that she stayed with you, October and November of 1963?

Mrs. FORD. I believe it must have been the first part of November.

Representative FORD. Of 1963?

Mrs. FORD. 1962.

Representative FORD. 1962.

Mrs. FORD. That is correct.

Mr. LIEBELER. Now, did Marina Oswald pay you anything for the privilege of staying at your home at that time?

Mrs. FORD. No; I did not expect it.

Mr. LIEBELER. Was there any arrangement she would work in the house?

Mrs. FORD. No; there was no arrangement; no.

Mr. LIEBELER. Tell us what Marina told you while she was staying there about her relations with Lee Oswald and particularly as to why she separated from him and what the difficulties were in their marriage?

Mrs. FORD. I think mostly it was a mistreatment by him that she couldn't stand any longer, she was saying.

Mr. LIEBELER. Mistreatment by him?

Mrs. FORD. Mistreatment by him; yes. That is what she was saying.

Mr. LIEBELER. Did she tell you any more specifically than that what the problem was?

Mrs. FORD. No; she didn't really. She did not elaborate. She did not go into explanations of their living together.

Mr. LIEBELER. Did she mention that Lee Oswald was jealous of the Russian friends that Marina had?

Mrs. FORD. Yes; she did. She told me that, that he was.

Mr. LIEBELER. Did they argue about that?

Mrs. FORD. Well, I didn't know if they were arguing about that. I know she said that he was very jealous of them helping Marina and jealous for the reason that he wasn't able to provide her at the time with any of the things that they were giving Marina, clothes, and baby clothes, and I think that he was—it was making him rather mad because he said he was unable to buy the things for her at the time, and I know that he was not accepting things people were giving him. He was telling her not to take them but she was taking them because she needed them. I suppose they were arguing about that but I don't remember the particulars.

Mr. LIEBELER. Did you form an impression at the time that Marina lived with you for that week as to what the cause of their difficulties might be?

Mrs. FORD. She mentioned one time that soon after marriage he told her he didn't love her any more in any way. So I don't know what is the difficulty, I don't know if that is what she mentioned. She did not explain and didn't go into explanations of this.

Mr. LIEBELER. Do you think, did you form an opinion as to whether this separation and the difficulties they were having was primarily the result of Oswald's behavior or did you think Marina might have been partially responsible for it, what did you think?

Mrs. FORD. My own opinion was that Marina was responsible for it. I think Marina was and I think now she is a rather immature girl.

The CHAIRMAN. She is what?

Mrs. FORD. I think she is rather immature in thinking.

The CHAIRMAN. Oh, yes.

Mrs. FORD. And a lot of times she agreed herself about provoking him in a way by arguing about his mother or things of some sort.

Mr. LIEBELER. What did she tell you about arguments concerning his mother?

Mrs. FORD. Well, I don't know really. She would say something that he was badly brought up or something like that.

Representative FORD. He was what?

Mrs. FORD. Badly brought up, some sort of thing, and he would get mad and slam her for that or something and then he was telling her not to let mother in, and when mother comes to the apartment she would let her in and then they would argue over that.

Representative FORD. He would tell her not to let the mother in?

Mrs. FORD. That is right, and she would because she said she just couldn't do that.

Mr. LIEBELER. Did Marina tell you at that time what her feelings toward Lee's mother were?

Mrs. FORD. I don't remember her saying anything one way or the other if she liked her or didn't.

Mr. LIEBELER. Do you remember whether Marina might have mentioned that Lee Oswald had spoken to a neighbor and told the neighbor that Marina was from Czechoslovakia?

Mrs. FORD. No; I don't know of anything like that.

Mr. LIEBELER. You didn't know at any time that Oswald didn't want people to know that his wife was from Russia? Marina didn't mention that?

Mrs. FORD. Not around us, we didn't because we knew it anyway.

Mr. LIEBELER. Marina didn't mention anything like that to you?

Mrs. FORD. No.

Mr. LIEBELER. When Marina lived with you during that time did she tell you anything about her background in Russia, did she tell you about her birthplace and youth in Russia?

Mrs. Ford. Yes; she was going into more of that in talking with me more than anything else, I think. Actually most of the time she was talking about her friends during, I think about when she was going to school, about her boy friends and things she was talking to me about her friends and she did go into talk about when she lived in, let's see, it is not Ukraine, I think it is Bessarabia, right now where would that place be, to live there, and she was very young, I believe, let's see she was born during the war, and they were sent somewhere, I don't know where they were sent, but then she lived there in Bessarabia for a few years, because there was a lot of food there and vegetables and they were sent there, to feed, like they sent the cattle to be fed up, I believe that is the expression she used after the war where the children could eat a lot of fruit and then she returned to Leningrad, I believe.

I don't know how long she lived in Bessarabia.

Mr. Liebeler. What did she tell you about her life in Leningrad, just briefly, if you will summarize it for us.

Mrs. Ford. Well, really, I don't know—the only thing I knew was about some of the things she was telling me about friends she had there, she had a friend that was a medical student and she told me she talked a lot on the telephone to him, and she was rather, I thought that is where I made the impression to me, it made an impression to me she was immature, she liked to talk to the man for a long time in the evening but she was afraid to be seen with him in the streets, he was ugly, so I thought it was rather strange, you know, and then——

Mr. Liebeler. Did she tell you who she was living with in Leningrad?

Mrs. Ford. Yes; she was living with her stepfather, that is what I remember, living with a stepfather she was telling me.

Mr. Liebeler. Did she tell you about her relations with her stepfather?

Mrs. Ford. Yes; she did. She didn't like him and I think he doesn't like her, either; they never did.

Mr. Liebeler. Did she tell you any reasons why she did not like him?

Mrs. Ford. She was telling me a lot of times, she was telling me about her mother, the mother didn't want to show affection to Marina or something like that because the father was jealous of that affection, and I think he did some sort of a cruel thing to her once that she doesn't—she still remembers as being very cruel, something of accusing her of taking some family silver and selling it while she knows that he had pawned the silver for buying liquor, because it showed up, she couldn't explain it to her aunt and it just made her feel very bad at that time.

I think she just could never forgive him for that.

Mr. Liebeler. Did Marina tell you about her move to Minsk?

Mrs. Ford. Well, she didn't tell me at that time. I just found it out not too long ago that was the reasons she wanted to get away from a friend that she found out later that he was married, she went with him for a short while she did not know he was married, but she did not go into particulars of explaining the whole thing to me.

Representative Ford. She was going with a man who was married?

Mrs. Ford. Yes. She met him somewhere, she had two tickets, she said, to a theater or to a movie, and she wanted to sell one ticket and he was the person who bought the ticket and they sat together in a movie house and later on, I believe, I don't know how they got to know each other later on, it was a few times they met, they have seen each other and at one time she went to his apartment, to the house that he lived, to call on him, and someone said that, "oh, that is the man who has that little boy," and she said she just turned around and went home. That is the time she found out he was married and was deceiving her.

But I don't know why she left, I mean why, exactly she left but I think this is the person that was her reason for leaving Leningrad.

Mr. Liebeler. Did she tell you that she had left in part at least to get away from this man?

Mrs. Ford. That is what I understood.

Mr. Liebeler. Now, did Marina tell you why she married Lee Oswald when she was in Russia, did she talk to you about that?

Mrs. Ford. Yes; she did.

I don't exactly know why she married him. But she said she met him at a dance, and soon after that, I don't know the reason why he was in the hospital but he was in a hospital, and she called on him, and I don't know how long he stayed there, either, and she liked the man, I think, and she bought him an Easter Egg, that was during Easter sometime and he was very surprised that such a thing could be done in Russia.

I think it rather pleased him very well. She said somehow she felt sorry for the man because none of her friends liked him, and mistrusted him, and she felt sort of like she was on the defensive, she wanted to, she felt sorry for him in a way.

Representative Ford. Did she tell you why her friends didn't trust him?

Mrs. Ford. Yes; she said they were thinking that he was an American spy or something like that, that is what they were trying to tell her. "Maybe he is a spy, and how can you trust a man like that?"

She told me the other day, she says no one trusted him, but she says, "I wasn't afraid of him," that is how she put it.

Representative Ford. Did Marina indicate to you whether she thought or had any reason to believe that Oswald was a spy?

Mrs. Ford. No; she didn't. She didn't think so. She never said that, I mean.

Representative Ford. Did Marina ever indicate to you or did you gather that one of the reasons that Marina married Lee Oswald was she had the possibility of leaving the Soviet Union in mind?

Mrs. Ford. Yes. She never did go out directly and say that but I think I got an impression that was her reason. She was telling me that way before she met Oswald she was dreaming of coming over here, and that is, I mean gathering by that later I thought that she wanted to come over, and he was, I suppose he was a reason.

Mr. Liebeler. In this connection, I wanted to ask you whether you ever had any contact with any newspaper reporters from the Dallas newspapers about this, did they ask you about this at any time?

Mrs. Ford. About this I don't remember if they asked me. I don't remember. But a couple of reporters came to my house soon after the assassination and talked to me.

Mr. Liebeler. I represent to you that there was a story in the November 27, 1963, issue of the Dallas Times Herald which told about some Russian-born woman in Dallas to whom Marina had supposedly confided some of the most intimate secrets of her stormy marriage, in the words of the newspaper article. Do you have any knowledge whether that would be you or somebody else?

Mrs. Ford. I think that would be me.

Mr. Liebeler. Did you tell the reporters that Marina had told you that Marina had felt sorry for Oswald because everybody hated him even in Russia?

Mrs. Ford. Yes; I might have said that.

Mr. Liebeler. Marina did say that to you?

Mrs. Ford. Yes; she did.

Mr. Liebeler. Did Marina tell you anything at this time about their trip back to the United States and the difficulties that they encountered, or how they did it, that sort of thing?

Mrs. Ford. No; I never talked with her about that.

Mr. Liebeler. Was there any conversation while Marina stayed with you during that week in November 1962, about the possibility of a divorce, of her divorcing Lee Oswald?

Mrs. Ford. The possibility—I know she didn't want to go back to him at the time she stayed with me.

Mr. Liebeler. But you don't remember any specific conversation?

Mrs. Ford. No; I don't remember any specific conversation.

Mr. Liebeler. About divorce?

Mrs. Ford. Frankly, there was talk about it, she didn't want to go back and I just told her, I felt that Marina wasn't really the domestic type she could stand very long being a help at home, not that I think she is not capable of taking care of her own house. I see now since she has got even her own place she keeps it very clean and her children are always neat. But she wasn't right for domestic help and I told her to stay with Lee, that is what I told her myself, and wait until she could be able to take care of herself other than working in a house.

Mr. LIEBELER. What did she say about that?

Mrs. FORD. She didn't say, she was really just listening, I think, and she didn't say anything.

Mr. LIEBELER. Did Marina say anything to you at this time about wanting to go back to Russia?

Mrs. FORD. No, no; she didn't want to.

In fact, she told me that Lee soon after he came to the United States, he was telling her that he would want to go back because he couldn't find a job here and he was, of course, seeing a lot of difficulties for himself, and Marina said, "If you want to go back, you can go but I am not going," that is what she told me.

Mr. LIEBELER. Marina told Lee if he wanted to go back he could but she wasn't going to go back to Russia.

Mrs. FORD. That is right.

Mr. LIEBELER. Is that all the conversation that you had with her about going back to Russia at that time?

Mrs. FORD. That is right. That is about all.

Mr. LIEBELER. Did you know where the Oswalds lived at this time when Marina came to the Meller's house and then to your house?

Mrs. FORD. No; I have never been at their apartment, and she couldn't tell me. I know she lived in Oak Cliff, the Dallas section about southwest, I believe.

Mr. LIEBELER. In Dallas?

Mrs. FORD. Yes.

Mr. LIEBELER. Did you know whether Marina had lived with a lady in Fort Worth before they came to Dallas?

Mrs. FORD. Yes; I know they stayed there but I didn't talk to her during the time and I didn't visit her. I know she stayed at Elena Hall's house and I think Elena had an accident just before that and she was—she stayed in bed most of the time. Marina was helping her out.

Mr. LIEBELER. Now, you had only seen Lee Oswald, up to this week that Marina came to live with you, one time, is that correct?

Mrs. FORD. That is correct.

Mr. LIEBELER. That was the Meller's luncheon party?

Mrs. FORD. That is correct.

Mr. LIEBELER. Were you surprised on the basis of any judgment you might have made of Lee Oswald to learn that he had beaten his wife?

Mrs. FORD. Just from seeing him once I would not have made—no; that he has beaten his wife; no, I didn't think at that time. I did, when she came in after I learned that he has beaten her, I was rather—I remember the bruises on her face and that rather made signs to me that he did.

Mr. LIEBELER. Did it surprise you that he would have done this?

Mrs. FORD. No; it did not surprise me. I just felt that young man as he was, if he was—decided to go to Russia after living in a country like the United States, I didn't feel he was very, what shall I say, how would you say, a person's mind won't work at this time——

The CHAIRMAN. Unstable?

Mrs. FORD. Unstable, that is how I felt. I felt a person like that, I felt frankly could do anything.

Representative FORD. Did she ever tell you that Lee Oswald was the cause of these bruises on her face?

Mrs. FORD. Well, she did tell me after she came to the house to stay with me.

Representative FORD. That is what I mean?

Mrs. FORD. That is right.

Representative FORD. The bruises you saw on her face at the house she told you Lee Oswald was the cause?

Mrs. FORD. Yes, that is right.

Mr. LIEBELER. Let's clarify that a little. Did Marina Oswald have any bruises at the time she came to live in your house in November 1962?

Mrs. Ford. No; that is right. But she stayed at Anna Meller's house for a week and when she came to Anna Meller's house I heard there were bruises at that time.

Mr. Liebeler. Did Anna Meller tell you that?

Mrs. Ford. Either Anna Meller or George Bouhe told me that. I don't remember.

Mr. Liebeler. And you yourself did see bruises on her face the first time?

Mrs. Ford. I did see the first time; yes.

Mr. Liebeler. Did she tell you that Lee Oswald had given her those bruises?

Mrs. Ford. That is right.

Mr. Liebeler. She told you that when she stayed with you?

Mrs. Ford. That is right.

Mr. Liebeler. Tell us the circumstances under which Marina left your home in November of 1962, where she went and what happened?

Mrs. Ford. Well, she stayed with me a week, and my husband came home on Saturday, and we discussed with another friend of mine for Marina to go to her house and stay there as long as she wanted, and I think Sunday morning this friend of mine, Anna Ray, came with a station wagon and picked all her things up, her playpen she had for baby, and diapers and things, and took her to her house and I believe my husband was with her, too, at that time and that is how she left.

Mr. Liebeler. Now, do you know how long she stayed with the Rays?

Mrs. Ford. With the Rays. I think she just stayed there, she had had dinner there, I believe she stayed one afternoon. I don't know how soon Lee came there but he came soon over to the house, but Marina said he cried and begged her to return, he would be nothing, if she didn't return, he would be finished, that is what he was telling her, and she said she just couldn't say, no to him.

Mr. Liebeler. So she returned to Oswald at that time?

Mrs. Ford. Yes; she returned to Oswald.

Mr. Liebeler. Did you ever talk with the Mellers about their experiences with Marina when she lived at their house for that time?

Mrs. Ford. No; I don't remember, she did not discuss it.

Mr. Liebeler. Did you remember or did you know where Lee Oswald was living prior to the time that Marina came to Dallas?

Mrs. Ford. No; I don't know where he lived at any time.

Mr. Liebeler. Did you know where he was working at that time or if he was working at all?

Mrs. Ford. During the time they lived in Dallas, I believe, I don't know exactly, though, either George Bouhe or Anna Meller's husband found him a job in a printing shop, I think, or I believe it is printing shop, somewhere in Oak Cliff, and that is why they had an apartment there. I remember that is the reason because George Bouhe was rather mad at Marina for taking an apartment in Oak Cliff because it was too far for him to drive and help her when she needed help and the baby, I think he was taking her to the dentist and taking the baby to a doctor to help her in ways that she couldn't do herself.

Representative Ford. Who was doing this driving?

Mrs. Ford. I believe George Bouhe did this. He has the car.

Mr. Liebeler. Where does Mr. Bouhe live?

Mrs. Ford. He lives, well, I don't know his address now. I know where he lives but I don't know the street number.

Mr. Liebeler. But it is not in the Oak Cliff Section of Dallas?

Mrs. Ford. No; it is not. I think it would be in the east part of Dallas.

Mr. Liebeler. During the time that Marina stayed with you, did she say anything to you about Lee Oswald's political beliefs or his attitudes concerning politics?

Mrs. Ford. No; she didn't talk to me about that and I didn't ask her.

Frankly, I didn't talk with Lee about that, I didn't feel the need of it myself to discuss politics with him.

Mr. Liebeler. Did you discuss that subject with any of your friends?

Mrs. Ford. Well, yes. They were telling me, those friends that went to his apartment, were telling me, that they have seen books like Karl Marx open in front of him, just lying there on the table, that he didn't even hide it when someone came in, and then someone else said there was a book laying there of How to Be a Spy, laying right open there.

Mr. LIEBELER. Do you remember who told you that?

Mrs. FORD. I believe it was Lydia Dymitruk.

Mr. LIEBELER. D-y-m-i-t-r-u-k.

Do you remember anything about that particular conversation?

Mrs. FORD. Well, she was telling me, she took, when the baby left my house, she had a cold, and it was getting worse, and I believe soon after she left Anna Ray, the baby began to have a fever, and Lydia, I believe, I don't know how she got to go to her apartment, really, I don't know the reason she went there; she went there and wanted to take the baby to the doctor and she told me of an incident that says even Marina was ashamed of Lee because when she took her to the hospital Lee was lying about that he didn't have a job at the time, which Lydia knew that he did have. He didn't want to pay for the services, and people at the hospital was asking him how does he pay for the apartment and he was telling them that, "My friends were helping me," and Marina just said something in Russian that Lydia remembers, "What a liar," you know, behind his back.

Mr. LIEBELER. Did she say that so he could hear it?

Mrs. FORD. I think so, because she said it aloud.

Mr. LIEBELER. And she said it in Russian?

Mrs. FORD. Yes; she did.

Mr. LIEBELER. In front of Lydia Dymitruk?

Mrs. FORD. Yes; that is right, and Lydia was rather mad about the whole thing and she said she is not going to help them any more if they are acting that way.

The baby wasn't helped at the hospital. I think the hospital didn't want to take the child because the father couldn't pay, that is what I got, the father couldn't pay for it.

Mr. LIEBELER. Did you ever see Marina say anything adverse to Oswald in his presence, did she run him down or make fun of him in public so far as you know?

Mrs. FORD. As far as I know, I don't, except the first time, the one time, I would think when she said, "What a liar," in front of him.

Mr. LIEBELER. You don't know of any other instance when she would have done that?

Mrs. FORD. I don't know of any other instance.

Mr. LIEBELER. Do you know whether she ever spoke of his political views before other people or make fun of him?

Mrs. FORD. No; I don't remember except lately I have been talking to her about that and she said she thought of him being young, and she thought she hoped it would pass with years, that he would mature, this is what she was telling me.

Mr. LIEBELER. Did she tell you whether or not she discussed politics with him herself? Did she argue with him about anything?

Mrs. FORD. She said she was arguing with him about that. Certainly, in fact, he called her, she was typical American girl, that she is not interested at all in politics, except in the material things that he wasn't interested in. She said she wanted a house and a family and he said, "All the American girls think that way" and he thought he married a different sort of a girl, a Russian girl.

Mr. LIEBELER. Now, think back on that week that Marina stayed with you. Is there anything else that happened or is there anything that Marina told you that you think we should know about and about which I haven't already asked you?

Mrs. FORD. I cannot think of it at the time.

Mr. LIEBELER. When was the next contact that you had with the Oswalds?

Mrs. FORD. It was right after Christmas before New Year's. I believe it was the 28th of December, a Friday. I gave, I had, a party for all the friends, and

I invited a family by the name of De Mohrenschildt, wife and husband, and Mrs. De Mohrenschildt called me up and asked me if she couldn't bring Marina and her husband over because she was saying it is a shame the way all their Russian friends have forsaken them during that time and they had no place to go and the De Mohrenschildts were the only ones helping them at the time, and I told her I didn't object to it. So she brought them over with them.

Mr. LIEBELER. Was Mr. Bouhe at the party?

Mrs. FORD. Yes; I think so.

Mr. LIEBELER. Mr. and Mrs. Frank Ray?

Mrs. FORD. Yes.

Mr. LIEBELER. Mr. and Mrs. Thomas Ray?

Mrs. FORD. Yes.

Mr. LIEBELER. Were Elena Hall and her husband there?

Mrs. FORD. I don't remember them being at that party. I don't think so.

Mr. LIEBELER. Were the Mellers there?

Mrs. FORD. Yes.

Mr. LIEBELER. You mentioned that De Mohrenschildt was there.

Mrs. FORD. Yes.

Mr. LIEBELER. And the Oswalds.

Mrs. FORD. That is right.

Mr. LIEBELER. Was there a gentleman by the name of Allen A. Jackson at the party?

Mrs. FORD. Yes.

Mr. LIEBELER. And his wife?

Mrs. FORD. And his wife.

Mr. LIEBELER. Do you remember any conversations or observe any conversations between Marina Oswald and Mr. Jackson?

Mrs. FORD. Marina Oswald, no; I don't think so. I don't think Marina spoke English at the time.

Mr. LIEBELER. Were Mr. and Mrs. Charles Edward Harris at the party?

Mrs. FORD. Yes.

Mr. LIEBELER. Did you talk to Mr. and Mrs. Harris about the party afterward?

Mrs. FORD. I might have.

Mr. LIEBELER. Did she mention translating a conversation between Mr. Jackson and Marina Oswald?

Mrs. FORD. No; she did not mention it to me.

Mr. LIEBELER. And you didn't see her doing that?

Mrs. FORD. No; I didn't see her doing that at the party.

Mr. LIEBELER. Did you have any conversation with Lee Oswald at the party that night?

Mrs. FORD. No.

Mr. LIEBELER. Did you notice anybody else talking to him?

Mrs. FORD. Yes; I did. I noticed a girl talking to him who was of Japanese descent but I don't remember her name.

Mr. LIEBELER. Was there anything striking about that?

Mrs. FORD. No; I think, the only thing it was that I think he talked to her most of the time and wasn't making any conversation with anyone else.

Mr. LIEBELER. Did Marina comment on that to you?

Mrs. FORD. No; she didn't. But I heard from somebody else that she did comment.

Mr. LIEBELER. Who told you that?

Mrs. FORD. I think George Bouhe again. He always spoke to everybody.

Mr. LIEBELER. What did Mr. Bouhe say about that?

Mrs. FORD. Well, he said something that I asked Marina afterward and she told me that it wasn't true. He said that Lee talked to that Japanese girl like a—it is an expression in Russia to take a bath and then beat themselves with the leaves from a tree, and the leaf would stick to the body, in the wintertime, and so the expression from that, like a leaf sticks to the hot body when you take a bath, you know. Then I suppose Lee struck her as just not saying anything—and I asked Marina and she said he did not do it.

Mr. LIEBELER. Was there any talk at the party about Oswald's experiences in Russia or his marriage to Marina?

Mrs. Ford. During the party?

Mr. Liebeler. Yes.

Mrs. Ford. No; I didn't talk to him at all.

Mr. Liebeler. And you didn't overhear anybody else talking about Oswald's experiences in Russia?

Mrs. Ford. No.

Mr. Liebeler. You mentioned that the Oswalds came with De Mohrenschildt. Did they go home with De Mohrenschildt?

Mrs. Ford. Yes; they did because Mrs. De Mohrenschildt stated that the lady who stayed with Oswald's child had to leave at 12 o'clock and they left before that.

Mr. Liebeler. After the Oswalds left the party, was there any discussion about the Oswalds that you can remember?

Mrs. Ford. No; really not. I don't think they made a big impression on that party on anybody.

Mr. Liebeler. Can you fix the date on which your party was held?

Mrs. Ford. The 28th of December.

Mr. Liebeler. What year?

Mrs. Ford. 1962.

Mr. Liebeler. Was there any other party the next day or the day after that?

Mrs. Ford. There were other parties. I don't think that Marina and her husband were present. I don't know if you would call it a party, there was a sort of a get-together at my house afterward because some people stayed over in town for a few days, I think that was the Rays, and the Harrises, and a friend of my husband from Louisiana, Sullivans, stayed there. But they hadn't met Oswald, they came much later after 12 o'clock. So we sort of had a get-together.

Mr. Liebeler. This would have been the next day?

Mrs. Ford. The next day.

Mr. Liebeler. On the 29th of December.

Was Mr. Bouhe——

Mrs. Ford. No; Mr. Bouhe wasn't present at that time.

Mr. Liebeler. Was there any conversation at that time about Oswald?

Mrs. Ford. I don't remember, I don't think so.

Mr. Liebeler. Do you remember that there was a party or open house at Mr. Bouhe's house on the 29th?

Mrs. Ford. If there was, I wasn't present, I didn't go.

Mr. Liebeler. Was there a party at Meller's house?

Mrs. Ford. There was a party or luncheon.

Mr. Liebeler. Did you go?

Mrs. Ford. No; I didn't go.

Mr. Liebeler. Did you hear any conversation during this period of 3 or 4 days about Oswald, anybody speculating about Oswald or discussing his experiences——

Mrs. Ford. No; I think——

Mr. Liebeler. In Russia?

Mrs. Ford. I think at that time everyone rather—George Bouhe said he was not going to help them any more, he was through, since Marina, he tried to help her very hard, and she did not hold her word about not going back to him. So he said since she went back, so now it is her problem.

Well, he is sort of that type of man, he is trying to help hard and if you are doing what he says otherwise he is not going to help, so that was it. So it was rather, sort of Marina and her husband were dropped at that time, nobody actually wanted to help, and I think what they heard about Lydia Dymitruk was saying that he couldn't help those people. I mean they were just sort of— he couldn't reach them. He was lying in hospital and things, we sort of gave it up.

Mr. Liebeler. Did Lydia make that remark at one of those parties or was that at a previous time?

Mrs. Ford. Oh, that was a previous time. As soon as she left to go back to her husband, George Bouhe even took the Russian dictionary back to him. He told her to give it back and he was just through with him.

Mr. Liebeler. So far as you know Mr. Bouhe had no more contact with the Oswalds after that?

Mrs. Ford. No; I don't think so.

Mr. Liebeler. Did you have any conversation with any of your friends in Dallas or Fort Worth on the question of Oswald's ability to leave Russia and come back to the United States and bring Marina with him?

Mrs. Ford. We didn't speculate on that until really later, until now, after the assassination that subject came up, and people asking why they left so soon. He was telling me it took them a year, so I don't know.

Mr. Liebeler. Was there any conversation prior to the assassination, during this period in 1962, any speculation as to whether Oswald might be an agent of any government?

Mrs. Ford. No. I frankly didn't think he was capable of it. That was my feeling on it.

Mr. Liebeler. Were there any conversations on that?

Mrs. Ford. No. There were not.

Mr. Liebeler. Do you remember that Mr. Bouhe suggested at one time that Oswald was a mental case?

Mrs. Ford. Mr. Bouhe, he might have; yes, I think we all thought that.

Mr. Liebeler. Do you remember that Mr. Bouhe said that?

Mrs. Ford. I don't remember particularly that he would say that.

The Chairman. Did you say, "We all thought that"?

Mrs. Ford. Yes; we thought that, that he was rather mentally—you just said the word before.

The Chairman. Unstable?

Mrs. Ford. Unstable.

Mr. Liebeler. Unstable.

Why did you think that, Mrs. Ford?

Mrs. Ford. In my own opinion, I just didn't think that a man as young as he was could come to the conclusions just by rather experiences or living a long time in America and I mean studying the whole economic structures of different governments, and things that he would come to the conclusion that is the best thing for him. I think he was just rather too young for that.

I thought he was just rather—something was rather wrong with the man.

Mr. Liebeler. You based this——

Representative Ford. In the conversation that Oswald had with this Japanese lady at your party, did you overhear any of that conversation?

Mrs. Ford. No; I did not. I did not have time, I was the hostess and I just didn't get to talk to anyone.

Representative Ford. Did you ever ask the Japanese lady what the gist of the conversation was or what the content of the conversation was?

Mrs. Ford. No; I never have. In fact, I have not seen her after that. That was the first time she came to my house. I mean I have seen her later on in the beauty shop but I have never talked to her about it.

Representative Ford. Did she speak English?

Mrs. Ford. Yes; she speaks English well.

Representative Ford. All right.

Mr. Liebeler. At this get-together that you mentioned at your house on, I think it was the 29th, after the party, the informal get-together, the Rays were there, and the Sullivans, and Mr. and Mrs. Harris.

Would it refresh your recollection if I suggested to you that some of the people that were there at that party said the possibility of Oswald being a Russian agent was discussed in detail at that party in that group?

Mrs. Ford. No.

Mr. Liebeler. You don't remember any of the discussion?

Mrs. Ford. I don't remember any of the discussion.

Mr. Liebeler. Is there anything other than what you told us that led you to believe that Oswald was unstable or a mental case?

Mrs. Ford. Nothing, except that I was thinking about him myself beating his wife. That would have been one reason. I don't think that any stable man would do that, especially she appeared to me very sick sort of a woman, not sick, but frail and fragile, I think any man who strikes a woman who is incapable of striking back, I would think would be unstable.

Mr. LIEBELER. This Russian group that we have been discussing, Mr. Bouhe and these other people, do they see each other regularly? Is there sort of a Russian community in Dallas, would you say?

Mrs. FORD. Yes; there are about, I think, maybe four families in Fort Worth and maybe half a dozen in Dallas or more than that, but that mainly we see each other, and there is one Eastern Orthodox Church in Russia where that is where we actually meet each other.

Mr. LIEBELER. In Dallas, you mean, or Fort Worth?

Mrs. FORD. Dallas, I am sorry. In Dallas, and we still observe our Eastern Orthodox religion during the holidays and sometimes like Christmas falls 13 days after the American Christmas so there is New Year's sometimes we celebrate those.

Mr. LIEBELER. How well do you know the De Mohrenschildts?

Mrs. FORD. Well, I know George De Mohrenschildt the same, approximately, I will say I was acquainted with him for approximately 14 years but I don't know him well.

Mr. LIEBELER. You mentioned before that De Mohrenschildt was the only member of the Russian community that kept on seeing the Oswalds and trying to help them.

Was there any discussion about that among your friends?

Mrs. FORD. Yes; George De Mohrenschildt is rather an odd ball, among Russians anyway, so it was nothing unusual about him doing that. He was always doing something unusual. He would even go to church with shorts on, you know, this is something, he would do something that nobody else would do.

Mr. LIEBELER. Shorts?

Mrs. FORD. Shorts.

Mr. LIEBELER. Short trousers?

Mrs. FORD. Yes.

Mr. LIEBELER. Do you remember any specific conversations about the reasons as to why De Mohrenschildt continued to associate with the Oswalds after the rest of you had given them up.

Mrs. FORD. Well, I remember his wife was telling me like she felt it was their duty now since everybody else dropped them and they needed help.

Mr. LIEBELER. Do you remember any conversation with the Oswalds among any of your friends as to whether or not Oswald went hunting in Russia and had access to weapons?

Mrs. FORD. Yes; I think that George Bouhe was telling me that. He was telling him that he was going hunting and he told him about killing ducks or something of that type.

Mr. LIEBELER. Can you remember that in any greater detail?

Mrs. FORD. No; I don't remember it. I only remember that because of the way he was saying, "ducks" in Russian, George was saying that he was using sort of a word when you call for it, it is a small duck rather than for ducks, he was saying that his Russian wasn't perfect.

I mean in that conversation he was using an example of he was saying, when he would go hunting for ducks, instead of "utki" for ducks he would say "utitschki" that would mean small ducks, and he was saying that his Russian was imperfect.

Mr. LIEBELER. That is Oswald's Russian?

Mrs. FORD. That is right.

Mr. LIEBELER. What about Marina's ability to speak English at that time, did she speak English at that time?

Mrs. FORD. I don't think she did. She could speak a few words but I don't think she did.

Mr. LIEBELER. Did any of you attempt to teach her English?

Mrs. FORD. Yes; George Bouhe was attempting to teach her to write and was giving her lessons.

Mr. LIEBELER. Can you tell us something about that?

Mrs. FORD. Well, he was telling me that he had gotten her a dictionary and he had—or some other book anyway and he was telling me that every time he saw her, made an attempt to see her I don't know how he did that but anyway he was giving her a lesson and she was supposed to have completed it by the next time in writing.

Mr. LIEBELER. Did Mr. Bouhe tell you anything about Marina's ability to speak English or write English? Did Marina learn as a result of that?

Mrs. FORD. He said she was doing very well. I don't know if she learned to speak but he said she was a good student.

Mr. LIEBELER. Did Lee Oswald ever object to this effort on Mr. Bouhe's part?

Mrs. FORD. Well, he was objecting to anyone of the Russians helping her.

Mr. LIEBELER. Helping her learn English?

Mrs. FORD. Not learning English, but I mean helping her about anything. I don't know whether he was objecting to that. But we talked with Lee about this, why he wasn't teaching her English and he wasn't speaking to her and he said that he didn't want to forget Russian and he really said, "If she wants," this is what Marina said the other day, that he didn't actually object, but he thought if she could learn Russian just by herself in any way she could, she could, but he is not going to help her. He just didn't want to help her by speaking English.

Mr. LIEBELER. You mean English.

Mrs. FORD. That is right. He is not going to talk English with her, he wanted Russian. He wanted for the little girl to learn Russian and for himself not to forget it.

Mr. LIEBELER. Did he indicate, in other words that he wanted Marina to speak Russian so that he could maintain his own ability in Russian?

Mrs. FORD. That is correct.

Mr. LIEBELER. And he also wanted his children to learn to speak Russian?

Mrs. FORD. That is right.

Mr. LIEBELER. After this party on the 28th of December, what was your next contact with either Lee or Marina Oswald?

Mrs. FORD. After the 28th? I think after the assassination, I only heard once about her, I just heard she went to New Orleans. Again a friend, Lydia Dymitruk, was in the bakery and she said she saw Marina coming in and she told her she thought Marina was pregnant and she told her Marina was going to New Orleans. That is the only time I have heard anything about them after that party. The next contact I had with her was, I don't know the date but it was soon after the assassination when I just felt sorry for Marina, I thought she was. I always felt she was innocent, I thought she was a naive girl in a lot of ways and that is why she got into a lot of problems and troubles.

I just felt if she didn't have anybody there except the FBI and nobody to speak in Russian, she didn't know how everybody felt, I would think she would feel very badly, so I called Mrs. Paine who, I found out after the assassination she was a friend of Marina's and I told her that if she would have a contact with Marina, tell her that we sympathize with her that she is in the position that she is, and to call me or to let me—that I would like to talk with her.

Mr. LIEBELER. Can you tell us approximately when it was that you talked to Mrs. Paine?

Mrs. FORD. I think that was either the first part of December, I think it must have been at least a week after the assassination.

Mr. LIEBELER. In early December?

Mrs. FORD. Yes.

Mr. LIEBELER. What happened after that?

Mrs. FORD. Right after that, I think the next day Marina called me, and she said the reason she called me was because Mrs. Paine told her that I called, and let her know.

Mr. LIEBELER. Do you remember specifically that Marina told you that she, Marina, had talked to Mrs. Paine?

Mrs. FORD. Well, this, I don't know. I think that is what she did. In fact, I think that Mrs. Paine told me she talked on the telephone with Marina but I couldn't be positive about it. I know she wrote letters, they wrote. I know Mrs. Paine wrote to Marina, and I couldn't exactly say she talked to her on the telephone or how it was, either Marina called Mrs. Paine or I don't know.

310

Mr. LIEBELER. You say you know Marina wrote Mrs. Paine a letter? Did Marina tell you that she wrote Mrs. Paine during that period?

Mrs. FORD. I don't remember. I know later Mrs. Paine kept calling me and asked if I heard from Marina, because she kept writing to Marina and Marina didn't answer, so she wanted to know if I talked to her, that she was the reason she was calling me.

Mr. LIEBELER. Did Mrs. Paine indicate to you after she called you trying to find out from Marina, did she indicate to you she had or had not heard from Marina since the assassination?

Mrs. FORD. I believe she told me she talked on the telephone with her right soon after, after I did.

Mr. LIEBELER. During this first telephone conversation with Marina, was there anything said about the events of the assassination in any way?

Mrs. FORD. No; not at all, except that Marina was very surprised the way people treated her. She was telling me that if it had happened in Russia, she just would—she just knew she wouldn't be talking to me or anybody else. She knew they would be sent to Siberia or shot right away is what she said.

Mr. LIEBELER. Is that what Marina said?

Mrs. FORD. That is what she said. I told her that was the big difference in Russian Government and the American Government. And then she asked me for advice. Someone contacted her at the time from a western paper and offered her $10,000 or something for the story and she asked me if it was the right thing to do because she felt she didn't want to make money on such a thing, a horrible thing as that, and I advised her to take the money because I thought she would need it for the children.

Mr. LIEBELER. Now, after that first—was there anything else you discussed in that telephone conversation?

Mrs. FORD. No; I think we talked mostly about that book deal, about the offer she had.

Mr. LIEBELER. After that first telephone conversation, what was the next contact you had with Marina?

Mrs. FORD. That was quite a long time after that when it was again Mrs. Paine contacted me, and wanted to know if I could go and translate for them for, we were saying about that yesterday, what is that union.

Mr. LIEBELER. I did talk to you yesterday afternoon.

Mrs. FORD. I have forgotten, I couldn't say because it is important.

Mr. LIEBELER. Was it the American Civil Liberties Union?

Mrs. FORD. That is right, it was the American Civil Liberties Union and I talked to my husband about that and he tried to find out; I told him to find out all he can if it had anything to do with a Communist front or something and if it was I didn't want to do anything about it, to be connected with it, and he couldn't find anything out, but at the same time I told him that I did not want to go with them but I didn't mind translating. So I did translate and they wanted to know if Marina was held incommunicado, and she answered. Mrs. Paine brought me that letter to translate from English to Russian, and the man in charge, I don't know his name, I have forgotten his name, you mentioned it yesterday, if you say it I will remember it.

Mr. LIEBELER. Let's come to that in a moment, let's develop the story first.

How did the question of the American Civil Liberties first come up, did Mrs. Paine bring it up?

Mrs. FORD. Yes; that is right, because she tried to write letters to Marina and she wouldn't answer and she thought she was held in sort of a protective custody and couldn't see anybody. That is what she felt, and she was rather imprisoned is what she thought.

Mr. LIEBELER. So Mrs. Paine came to you with a letter that was written in English, is that correct?

Mrs. FORD. That is right.

Mr. LIEBELER. And she asked you to translate into Russian?

Mrs. FORD. That is right.

Mr. LIEBELER. Was that a letter from Mrs. Paine to Marina or a letter from the Civil Liberties Union?

Mrs. FORD. No; from Civil Liberties Union.

Mr. LIEBELER. And so you translated that into Russian?

Mrs. FORD. That is right, I translated it into Russian.

Mr. LIEBELER. Up to that point was Mrs. Paine the only person who discussed that subject with you.

Mrs. FORD. That is right.

Mr. LIEBELER. Did you have any further discussions with Mrs. Paine or anybody else?

Mrs. FORD. We tried to find out about the Union and my husband called lawyers and friends of his who would know about it and called the Secret Service and FBI and nobody would tell us anything about it. They would send us somewhere else, refer it to someone else to find out, so we don't find out.

So, I just decided on my own not to go, just to translate.

Mr. LIEBELER. Well now, what is this about going with them, what did Mrs. Paine ask you?

Mrs. FORD. She thought that maybe since I knew Marina she would rather confide in me more than just anyone like reporters or someone just from the Union would go there.

Mr. LIEBELER. But you declined to go with them?

Mrs. FORD. Yes.

Mr. LIEBELER. Did there come a time when somebody else spoke to you about this subject?

Mrs. FORD. No, not at all. Just during that time I wanted to find out if she was in prison.

Mr. LIEBELER. Did Marina respond to the letter that you translated?

Mrs. FORD. Yes; they received an answer right the next day, and the man from Richardson, who I think is the head of that Union in Dallas, came to my house and asked me if I could translate it back into English.

Mr. LIEBELER. Do you remember that man's name?

Mrs. FORD. No; if you mention it I would know.

Mr. LIEBELER. Would it refresh your recollection if I mentioned the name of Gregg Olds?

Mrs. FORD. That is right; yes, that is his name.

Mr. LIEBELER. What did Mr. Olds say to you when he came to see you?

Mrs. FORD. He just brought the letter and he was rather standing and he wasn't talking very much. He was kind of a quiet person, I think. I took the letter—he thought I could just sit there and do it real fast in front of him, but I had to take it into a room and sort of concentrate in the living room and translated and giving it to him.

He said, "Thank you," and he left.

Mr. LIEBELER. Can you tell us approximately when this was?

Mrs. FORD. No; I cannot say. Let's see. I think it was sometime before Christmas, because after that I sent her a Christmas card.

No, wait a minute, I just can't say if it was before Christmas or afterward. I don't remember.

Mr. LIEBELER. Do you remember if it was before or after Marina testified before this Commission?

Mrs. FORD. That was before the Warren Commission.

Mr. LIEBELER. It was before the Warren Commission?

Mrs. FORD. That is right.

Mr. LIEBELER. Did you talk to Marina again on the telephone after this first time?

Mrs. FORD. Yes; I talked to her on the telephone because through my husband's brother who is a professor in one of the universities in California, he had a friend by the name of Isaac Levine who does write, who speaks Russian and writes rather—he wrote a book of on the mind of the assassin, Trotsky's story. He wanted to contact me and to find out if Marina had signed a contract on writing a book. So I told him that I would call the managers, since there was published in the newspaper at that time, and to find out if they did, and I did call. I called her lawyer and I asked if she signed for a book, and I called Levine long distance and told him she did not have a contract signed. Then he told me that he would like—he wanted to know if he could arrange to see

Marina, and I told him that I would ask the manager and he told me to contact, for Levine to contact, the attorney and the manager. I saw later on they have somehow gotten together. I think he wrote to them.

Mr. LIEBELER. Did there come a time when Marina came to your house to visit?

Mrs. FORD. Yes; she brought a letter she wanted me to translate. It was after this, after I had a contact about the writer Marina called me, this is the first time, the first time after the assassination that she called me on the telephone and we talked about that and I told her that the man had contacted me and he speaks Russian. I thought it would be a good opportunity for her to write if she wanted to since she could communicate easily with a writer that speaks Russian. I read his book that he sent me, and he makes real sense. I invited her to come out to dinner and, of course, I didn't expect that there would be a whole company with her.

Mr. LIEBELER. Did she come out?

Mrs. FORD. Yes; they did, they came out, the Secret Service and the manager were there and everybody so I cooked a Russian dinner.

Mr. LIEBELER. Can you tell us approximately when that was?

Mrs. FORD. It was shortly before the Commission, maybe about 2 weeks before the Commission.

Mr. LIEBELER. Late in January sometime?

Mrs. FORD. Yes.

Mr. LIEBELER. During that time that Marina was there did you have any discussion with her about the events of the assassination or anything relating to that?

Mrs. FORD. No.

Mr. LIEBELER. Did she discuss with you her possible testimony before this Commission?

Mrs. FORD. No, not during that time.

Mr. LIEBELER. Did Marina come back to your house again before she came to testify before the Commission?

Mrs. FORD. Yes, she was once more at my house. During the first time her manager brought a letter that she wanted to bring to the Governor about how she feels about Ruby's being executed. She told me she didn't want, she didn't feel, if she could help she didn't want to have the killing of a dead man on her conscience, on her mind. She wanted me to translate that letter and I did translate it.

And I left it at home and later on they came by, I told Mr. Martin that I would come by his house and bring the letter to her after I translated.

He said, "If you wanted to we can come back to your house like we did before." And they did and they picked up the letter.

Mr. LIEBELER. Do you have any copy of that letter?

Mrs. FORD. I think maybe I have a copy of it, of my translation. But I am not positive. I know I put it in a desk.

Representative FORD. This was a letter from whom to whom?

Mrs. FORD. From Marina to, I will say they did—I think it was advised to her to write it to the Governor, to Governor Connally.

Representative FORD. To Governor Connally?

Mrs. FORD. Yes.

Mr. LIEBELER. To the present Governor of Texas, that is the Governor of Texas?

Mrs. FORD. Yes.

Mr. LIEBELER. You said that Marina said to you she did not want to have another death on her conscience?

Mrs. FORD. That is right. She feels like, she told me she feels strongly about it, that people shouldn't kill one another, if there is no war.

Mr. LIEBELER. Did she use the words as you remember it, the words "on her conscience"?

Mrs. FORD. No; I don't remember that word really but I just feel this was, she would feel very badly if that would happen.

Mr. LIEBELER. Did she seem to feel that she had some responsibility for these things?

Mrs. FORD. What do you mean by that? I mean how, responsibility in what way?

Mr. LIEBELER. That she was in anyway a cause of any of these deaths herself?

Mrs. FORD. No; I wouldn't think she feels this way, no.

Mr. LIEBELER. Tell us about the conversations at the second meeting. Were there any conversations at that time about her testimony before the Commission or about the assassination?

Mrs. FORD. I believe she mentioned she was going to Washington at that time. She knew about going, I believe Martin said that.

Mr. LIEBELER. But she didn't talk about her testimony?

Mrs. FORD. No; she didn't, not at all she didn't.

Mr. LIEBELER. Did you talk to anybody else about her testimony before the Commisson?

Mrs. FORD. I don't know, I don't think so.

Mr. LIEBELER. Did Mr. Martin say anything about it?

Mrs. FORD. No; I don't remember, I don't know.

Mr. LIEBELER. When was the next time that you saw Marina?

Mrs. FORD. After she came back from Washington.

Mr. LIEBELER. Did she come to your house then?

Mrs. FORD. No; she did not. Her lawyer, in fact Mr. Martin, called me and told me she is staying at her brother-in-law's, and that he wanted to break the partnership with her, and he asked me if I could go with her attorney and translate for her the conditions of the break, the breaking of the contract, and I agreed to go with them.

Mr. LIEBELER. To Robert Oswald?

Mrs. FORD. To Robert Oswald's house; yes.

Mr. LIEBELER. Did there come a time after that when Marina came to live with you in your house?

Mrs. FORD. Yes; when I came there, Marina told me she couldn't stay another day, she thought, in Robert's house. It was such a small house and small children and she just didn't like to stay in there at all, and so I told her, "Well, you could come and stay at my place if you wanted to," and she said she would love to do that.

Mr. LIEBELER. After Marina moved in with you, did you talk to her about her testimony before the Commission, that she gave before the Commission?

Mrs. FORD. No; we never talked about what she did. She told me she had it, written something. She said something maybe that someone mentioned in the Commission that that was rather good for a novel but not for the testimony. She said, well, she had written the way she remembers her past, those are the words she made.

Mr. LIEBELER. She was referring to a statement she had written.

Mrs. FORD. She had written, yes.

Mr. LIEBELER. Did she show it to you?

Mrs. FORD. No; I have never seen it.

Mr. LIEBELER. During the time that Marina stayed with you or at any other time, did she say anything to you about this incident where Mr. Oswald was allegedly going to attack Mr. Nixon?

Mrs. FORD. No; I hadn't learned about that until later.

Mr. LIEBELER. Did you discuss it with Marina?

Mrs. FORD. Somehow she didn't feel, she didn't want to discuss it very much, she felt badly that it came out, I suppose or something. She didn't want it to.

Mr. LIEBELER. But she did talk to you about it?

Mrs. FORD. She talked to me because I had to translate it to her, the discussion with her lawyer, and he, I think, the FBI were at the lawyer's office while they went to talk to her about the subject, and I had to translate what she was telling the lawyer about it.

Mr. LIEBELER. Did you have any conversations with her about this Nixon affair at a time when the FBI was not present?

Mrs. FORD. I think going home, I just maybe, I don't know what I asked her. She said the same thing actually what she said in the office, that she held him in the bathroom and I asked her how was it finished, and she said, "I talked him out of it," and he said, "If you will keep me in the bathroom, just give me something to read." She didn't talk very much about it.

Mr. LIEBELER. Did you ask her how she could lock Lee in the bathroom?

Mrs. FORD. No; it never occurred to me to ask her and I did not ask her.

Mr. LIEBELER. Did you discuss this question with anybody else how she could lock anybody in the bathroom?

Mrs. FORD. Not until yesterday with my husband, how she could do it.

Mr. LIEBELER. Is there anything else that Marina told you about this Nixon affair that you can remember now?

Did she tell you when it happened?

Mrs. FORD. No; she told me only that, that she said she mixed up dates. She thought it was one month and it was, supposedly happened, another month and she said that a lot of times she doesn't remember exactly the month.

Mr. LIEBELER. Did she tell you anything about the General Walker affair?

Mrs. FORD. Yes; she told me something about that.

Mr. LIEBELER. What was that?

Mrs. FORD. She said in the first place, people are saying that maybe she knew ahead of time and she said she did not. Lee told her after it had happened, after he had shot, and he told her, "Well, I just tried to shoot Walker." She said she was rather angry and she told him if he ever does that again, she said, "Don't ever do that again," she was rather disgusted—that he shouldn't do such a thing.

Mr. LIEBELER. Did she tell you about any note that he had written in connection with the attack on General Walker?

Mrs. FORD. No; she didn't.

Mr. LIEBELER. Did she tell you whether the Walker incident occurred before or after the Nixon incident?

Mrs. FORD. I don't know. She never said it to me.

Mr. LIEBELER. Did she discuss with you during this period that she had been living in your house any of the details of the assassination?

Mrs. FORD. I, frankly, just didn't feel like asking her questions, I really felt like I just wanted to help her, that is all. She never brought the subject up herself.

Mr. LIEBELER. Did she say anything about what happened on Thursday night when Lee Oswald came back from Irving to Dallas?

Mrs. FORD. Yes; she said that was not long ago, and she somehow found out someone, I think Robert, told her there was some evidence that someone saw a boy running across—a boy saw someone running across the yard or something, and he thought maybe there was some other man involved. And she began to say, "Well, if Lee didn't kill the President why did he come home on Thursday and why did he leave his ring at home and why was the gun taken from the garage." I mean she was putting that together, she was making me believe that Lee was doing it.

Mr. LIEBELER. She was considering at that time the possibility that Lee Oswald was not?

Mrs. FORD. Yes.

Mr. LIEBELER. Guilty of this?

Mrs. FORD. Yes; Robert, I believe, was telling her that, that there was a possibility that somebody else did the crime and she was talking about that to me, and that is when she said about why would he come back on Thursday when he never did that before, and also that he would leave a ring that was to her it would mean something that he didn't want—he didn't feel like he would return or something.

Mr. LIEBELER. Did you discuss with Marina her feeling as to Lee Oswald's guilt or innocence in this matter?

Mrs. FORD. Well, she feels that—no, I don't remember her discussing it. I think she asked him after she saw him after the assassination he told her no, he did not kill anybody. He told her that. But I think her own conclusion is that he did.

Mr. LIEBELER. Did you have any discussions with her as to whether Lee Oswald was angry with President Kennedy for any reason?

Mrs. FORD. No; she told me that he actually never did say anything bad about Kennedy. He didn't like General Walker because he compared him rather with Hitler in some way. He said, he was telling her, she was asking him why would he kill a man like that, I mean that he should not kill anybody. He said, he told her, well, if somebody killed Hitler ahead of time that wouldn't have happened in Germany and he says he felt like it was his duty to get rid of men where he was a Fascist, speaking about General Walker.

Mr. LIEBELER. Did Marina say anything about Lee's attitude toward Governor Connally?

Mrs. FORD. No; she never discussed that.

Mr. LIEBELER. Did you talk to Marina about Marina's feelings toward Mrs. Paine?

Mrs. FORD. Lately, I have been talking to her about that, and Mrs. Paine, I know, tried to contact her and asked Marina why she did not want to write to her, because I know that she had written to her often. Somehow she doesn't like Mrs. Paine and then she said she feels that Martin told her that Mrs. Paine was making money on her articles about Marina, and she don't like that.

I got, even lately, Mrs. Paine called me up, and I believe it was only a pretense because she knew that I had a contact with Marina and she wanted to see Marina. She came to my house and told me she wanted for me to read in Russian very slowly that she could follow me for her students. She is teaching Russian to some students in private school and that she could record it and then listen to it, and she said she would pay me for the services, and at the time, the same time.

So, I had Marina that evening, I know she would want to see her, so I invited Marina to my house and at the time Mrs. Paine was coming.

Mr. LIEBELER. You told her Mrs. Paine was coming?

Mrs. FORD. Yes; I told her Mrs. Paine was coming and she only said she didn't want Mrs. Paine for her to know the telephone number or the house she lives in. She said she would come in all the time and she didn't exactly like her. She didn't want to see her at her house, not now anyway, she said.

Mr. LIEBELER. Did Marina and Mrs. Paine meet this evening at your house?

Mrs. FORD. Yes; they did, they talked.

Mr. LIEBELER. What did they say to each other?

Mrs. FORD. Well, frankly, I got an idea that Mrs. Paine came there to convince Marina to write a book with Mr. Levine who is rather persistent about it at the moment. He wants to start writing a book before Marina finishes with her lawyer and attorney—and her manager. She knows and she is advised by her attorney now not to do it before it is finished, and I think Mrs. Paine tried to talk her into it.

Mr. LIEBELER. They didn't discuss anything about the assassination or Mrs. Oswald's testimony before the Commission?

Mrs. FORD. No; I did not hear it.

Mr. LIEBELER. So far as you heard.

Did Marina ever tell you anything about the trip to Mexico that Lee Oswald took?

Mrs. FORD. Well, let's see. I think she was saying something about it that she did not mention to the FBI but she mentioned it to the Commission. She did say that. And that the FBI wanted to talk with her, that was the reason they wanted to come back again and talk with her. They came to my house quite often during the time she stayed at my house and talked with her, and she said that was the subject, and they asked her why she did not say it to start with, and she said well, she had begun to get tired of the FBI and she didn't like to talk with them.

Mr. LIEBELER. The FBI had been interviewing her while she stayed at your place?

Mrs. FORD. That is right.

Mr. LIEBELER. Have you been present at any of those interviews?

Mrs. FORD. No; unless they needed—no; I was not present.

Mr. LIEBELER. You were present at an FBI interview at Mr. McKenzie's office at one time?

Mrs. FORD. At Mr. McKenzie's office, that is right.

Mr. LIEBELER. Was there a translator present when the FBI interviewed Marina?

Mrs. FORD. Yes; there is at the moment.

Mr. LIEBELER. Do you know his name?

Mrs. FORD. Mr. Gopadze.

Mr. LIEBELER. Has Marina discussed with you the questions that the FBI has been asking her?

Mrs. FORD. No; except this particular Mexican trip.

Mr. LIEBELER. Did she tell you anything about the details of that trip?

Mrs. FORD. On that trip—she did not go into details of the trip; but certain things about—she asked Lee to bring her a bracelet and he didn't, things like that.

Mr. LIEBELER. Did she say anything about a desire that Lee Oswald had to go to Cuba?

Mrs. FORD. Well, this is something that she talked about but I don't remember how—she said he wanted to actually go to Cuba. He wanted to get a visa to go to Russia but he would go to Russia by the way of Cuba, and she thought that he would stay in Cuba and not go to Russia.

Mr. LIEBELER. Did Marina tell you what she was supposed to do when Oswald was in Cuba.

Mrs. FORD. Frankly, I don't know. I know that subject was discussed one time but I either had to go diaper the baby or something. I just cannot say— I know she tried to talk on this subject to Mr. Levine once and she explained it. It was a rather complicated sort of a thing and I cannot explain it.

Mr. LIEBELER. Did she express any fears that Oswald was going to leave her and go to Cuba and abandon her.

Mrs. FORD. There was a possibility—something she would stay here or something, and for a while, and we were asking her well, how did she intend to live while he was gone, and she thought, well, she said, well, Lee said, "You have a lot of Russian friends and they will help you," while he is not here, that was the conversation.

Mr. LIEBELER. Did Marina ever speak of any plans that Oswald had to hijack an airplane and go to Cuba?

Mrs. FORD. Yes; she said something like that.

Mr. LIEBELER. What did she say?

Mrs. FORD. Well, that was again, I believe she was discussing with Mr. Levine at the time about this Cuba and this airplane. It is again complicated, I don't think I can say it to make sense, somehow that he had to go, had to have enough gasoline or something to go there, not to make a stop anywhere. I could not say it to make any sense. I know she was talking about it.

Mr. LIEBELER. Did you ever talk to Robert Oswald about the assassination?

Mrs. FORD. No; we we never discussed it.

Mr. LIEBELER. Robert Oswald never expressed to you any thoughts that he had on Lee Oswald's guilt or innocence?

Mrs. FORD. I understand he didn't like the cover of Life magazine and I was rather surprised because it was in my mind like it seems there is no question. Nobody knows very sure but I feel like it was Lee that did it. And he was rather angry about the statement there that it was a gun with which the President was killed, and he was rather angry about that cover, and that is why I thought that maybe he didn't believe that Lee killed him.

Mr. LIEBELER. That is the only discussion you had with Robert Oswald?

Mrs. FORD. Yes; that is the only one, that is right.

Mr. LIEBELER. Have you talked to Marina about any rifle practice that Lee Oswald may have engaged in?

Mrs. FORD. I didn't discuss it with him but she said that she didn't think that he went to a rifle practice. She told me that about a lot of things that people would say that it was not true, she thought that she didn't think it was true about Lee being at practice.

Mr. LIEBELER. In Grand Prairie you are referring to?

Mrs. FORD. Yes; that is right.

Mr. LIEBELER. In Grand Prairie?

Mrs. FORD. That is right. She didn't think he was doing that.

Mr. LIEBELER. Did she say anything about him practicing with the rifle any place else?

Mrs. FORD. No; she didn't.

Mr. LIEBELER. Did she mention that he had practiced with the rifle at Love Field?

Mrs. Ford. She didn't say anything.

Mr. Liebeler. Did Marina ever say anything to you that indicated she wanted to go back to Russia?

You said before that she told Lee Oswald that if he wanted to go back to Russia he could go but she wasn't going to go.

But did she ever indicate to you at any time she wanted to go back to Russia?

Mrs. Ford. She did not. Again the first call after the assassination she asked me, she said. "You know I have a visa, a pending visa, to go to Russia and if they will send it to me, I may have to go." I sort of answered her, I am pretty sure they wouldn't send her a visa now so she doesn't have to worry about it.

Mr. Liebeler. Yesterday afternoon we discussed some of these things, did we not?

Mrs. Ford. Yes.

Mr. Liebeler. You mentioned the fact that Marina Oswald had told you that at one time she was thinking about committing suicide?

Mrs. Ford. Yes; she mentioned that.

Mr. Liebeler. Tell us about that.

Mrs. Ford. She said she didn't want to have it published anywhere, she is rather ashamed of it. But there was a time after all the—I think it was before she went to New Orleans and before she lived at Paine's house, that there was a time that she didn't have any friends, all the Russian friends left her, I believe De Mohrenschildts were gone during that time, and that Lee was treating her rather badly at the time and she just felt like she had no way out.

Mr. Liebeler. Did she tell you anything other than that? Did she tell you she actually tried to commit suicide or was it something she was thinking of?

Mrs. Ford. She didn't tell me the particulars but somehow Lee found out what was on her mind because he had beaten her again and told her only crazy people would consider doing a thing like that.

Mr. Liebeler. She said Lee had found out she had thought of committing suicide?

Mrs. Ford. Yes.

Mr. Liebeler. Did she ever tell you how he found out?

Mrs. Ford. No.

Mr. Liebeler. Did she indicate to you in any way that she had ever tried to do this?

Mrs. Ford. Well, she didn't tell me the particulars of it, I didn't want to, I mean I just didn't, ask her for all the details about it. But she was saying she was thinking about doing it at a certain time.

Mr. Liebeler. Well, I don't want to press you too hard about it but there is quite a difference between thinking about doing it and actually doing it.

The Chairman. She didn't hear it, she didn't hear it, did she?

Mr. Liebeler. That is right.

The Chairman. All right, that is enough.

Mr. Liebeler. Did you write to Marina at any time after the assassination?

Mrs. Ford. Did I write to her?

Mr. Liebeler. Yes.

Mrs. Ford. I sent her a Christmas card; yes.

Mr. Liebeler. Any other letters?

Mrs. Ford. No; no letters.

Mr. Liebeler. How many times have you been interviewed by the FBI, do you remember?

Mrs. Ford. FBI maybe twice. The first time, soon after the assassination; the same day that Lee Oswald was shot.

Actually we heard by radio, friends of ours had called us, anyone who knew Lee Oswald was supposed to come out and say it and call the FBI or the police. So we called the FBI and we said we did know and we came to the office ourselves and to talk about it.

Mr. Liebeler. Have you been interviewed by the Secret Service?

Mrs. Ford. No; I don't think so.

Mr. Liebeler. In our conversation yesterday we discussed your testimony and reviewed these matters. Is there anything you can remember that we discussed at that time that we have not talked about here now?

Mrs. FORD. I don't remember. I don't know.

Mr. LIEBELER. Is there any other information that you have that you think the Commission would like to know about that we don't have relating to the assassination?

Mrs. FORD. I don't think there is anything of importance that you don't know.

Mr. LIEBELER. Do you have any papers relating to these matters other than I think you mentioned a copy of the letter that you translated for the American Civil Liberties Union, other than that paper, do you have any papers that might relate to these questions I asked you?

Mrs. FORD. No; I might have a copy of the letter that Marina was writing for——

Mr. LIEBELER. To Governor Connally?

Mrs. FORD. To Governor Connally, and it is just rather a translation in my own handwriting.

Mr. LIEBELER. On this point about the rifle practice, did Marina tell you simply that he did not practice at the range at Grand Prairie or he did not practice at any place with the rifle?

Mrs. FORD. I think she was talking about the particular range.

Mr. LIEBELER. Particularly Grand Prairie?

Mrs. FORD. That is right.

Mr. LIEBELER. And she didn't say anything about any other practice?

Mrs. FORD. She was telling me that people were—supposedly saw him in San Antonio and she knew for sure he wasn't there, and then she was saying they saw him at Grand Prairie practicing and she thought that he wasn't there, and then again in Ruby's place and she knew sure that Lee would never go to a place like that, things like that.

Mr. LIEBELER. I have no further questions.

The CHAIRMAN. Congressman Ford, do you have some questions for Mrs. Ford?

Representative FORD. Mr. Chief Justice, I have one or two.

The CHAIRMAN. Proceed, please.

Representative FORD. Did Marina Oswald ever tell you about her schooling in Russia?

Mrs. FORD. Yes; she did. I think that would be a junior college here. She would finish 7 or 8 years, I don't know exactly, and then I think it is 4 years in a junior college which would make her in my opinion an assistant pharmacist.

Representative FORD. In other words, she went to the regular——

Mrs. FORD. School, yes.

Representative FORD. Primary school?

Mrs. FORD. That is right.

Representative FORD. Following that she went on to a secondary school.

Mrs. FORD. You don't have to finish primary school. Russian High School is 10 years, and if you want to specialize in some sort of assistant or technical work you would finish 7 or 8 years and then you would go 4 years after that, it is a finishing technical school, whether you would call it, where you would actually finish high school and at the same time you acquire some sort of a profession or technic, assistant to engineer or in this case assistant to a pharmacist.

Representative FORD. But those were the only schools that she has ever indicated to you that she attended?

Mrs. FORD. I think so, that is right.

Representative FORD. Did she ever indicate to you the participation that she had in the Komsomol.

Mrs. FORD. She said that she did join it and then she was kicked out or something.

Representative FORD. Did she ever give you any reason why she was kicked out?

Mrs. FORD. She told me that one time but I don't—I have forgotten the reason, I really don't remember.

Representative FORD. Was it an ordinary thing for a person to be kicked out of the Komsomol, so far as you know?

Mrs. FORD. Yes; I believe you have to be the sort, if you join it you have to perform your duty, you have to go the meetings and be sort of a leader in the community or in school or take on their work so if you don't do that, I think they just consider you not being a good young Komsomol. They wouldn't keep you there.

Representative FORD. Did Marina ever tell you that she did or didn't join the Communist Party in the Soviet Union?

Mrs. FORD. She couldn't join it.

Representative FORD. Why couldn't she join it?

Mrs. FORD. Well, not from my own experience but from what I know about it, I think you have to be over 20 years and you have to be 5 years, you have a 5-year waiting period until they check your background and see if you are good enough person to get by their standards to join the Party.

Representative FORD. Did Marina ever discuss with you any schools or training programs that Lee participated in while he was in the Soviet Union?

Mrs. FORD. No; she never has said anything of that sort. I think she said one time that they wanted to send him to a school which would give him a profession but it had nothing to do with military or anything like that but somehow he didn't go there. But I have forgotten what he had to be so he was just working regular labor in the factory.

Representative FORD. You don't recall anything, any details?·

Mrs. FORD. I don't recall any details of the school.

Representative FORD. You don't recall any of the details of the kind of school?

Mrs. FORD. Yes; but it was some sort of a civilian, it had nothing to do with military or espionage or anything like that that I remember.

Representative FORD. At the time that Marina and June stayed with you and your husband in October or November of 1962, did Lee Oswald visit her at your home?

Mrs. FORD. No. He did not.

Representative FORD. He called her?

Mrs. FORD. He called on the telephone.

Representative FORD. Did anyone else visit her while she was staying at your home on this occasion?

Mrs. FORD. On this occasion, I think the only person who visited was Anna Ray to whom she was to go later after she stayed with me.

Representative FORD. Excuse me, I didn't hear you.

Mrs. FORD. Anna Ray, that is another Russian-born person to whom Marina would go from my house, she came to visit her.

Representative FORD. The individual who kept Marina after she left you?

Mrs. FORD. That is right, that is correct.

Representative FORD. And his name was what?

Mrs. FORD. Her name.

Representative FORD. What is the name?

Mrs. FORD. Anna Ray.

Representative FORD. That is the only person who visited Marina during this period?

Mrs. FORD. At my house; yes.

Representative FORD. I would like to clarify the time and the circumstances of this discussion you had with Marina about the Nixon affair.

Mrs. FORD. Yes.

Representative FORD. You had gone to Mr. McKenzie's office with Marina?

Mrs. FORD. That is right. I had gone translating for her; yes.

Representative FORD. You were in Mr. McKenzie's office?

Mrs. FORD. Yes.

Representative FORD. With Marina. Who else was there?

Mrs. FORD. And at that time she had a date with the FBI, and we were doing, I was translating some legal work for her about dismissing her old attorney and manager and the FBI called me to come later after we finished with that, and they told Marina why they wanted to talk with her, and McKenzie took us in that other office and he asked Marina about that, and told her that that is what she had to talk about, and she was really angry. She said the thought Robert had said, I mean she did not tell anybody about it, and she didn't want to talk about it, and now she has to talk about it to the FBI since Robert mentioned it.

Representative Ford. In this meeting there was Mr. McKenzie?

Mrs. Ford. That is right. Mr. McKenzie, Marina and I.

Representative Ford. Just the three of you?

Mrs. Ford. Yes.

Representative Ford. In a room in Mr. McKenzie's office?

Mrs. Ford. Yes; in one of the rooms in his office.

Representative Ford. And Mr. McKenzie said what?

Mrs. Ford. Oh, I think that maybe—frankly, I don't know what he was telling her.

Representative Ford. Was this meeting only about the Nixon affair?

Mrs. Ford. I am very sorry, but I think that during that time when we were talking about that it was when he was talking about General Walker, that he was—it was not about Nixon that they talked about.

Representative Ford. This meeting with Mr. McKenzie, when Marina and you were discussing matters——

Mrs. Ford. That was about General Walker.

I think Mr. McKenzie didn't know what they would talk about but he advised her "They will ask you if there were two guns, you tell them there was one gun that was used," he told her.

Representative Ford. One gun used where?

Mrs. Ford. For Walker, I mean the same one they had at the house or something, frankly this is what I had——

Representative Ford. I think you just said at the outset of this meeting the prime purpose or the principal purpose was to discuss the Walker affair.

Mrs. Ford. Yes; that is right.

Representative Ford. How did the Nixon affair come up?

Mrs. Ford. I just can't recollect how.

Representative Ford. Did McKenzie raise the question or did Marina raise it?

Mrs. Ford. How it was raised, I didn't get to discuss it with her about the particulars about it, except one time in the car, I don't remember how it came up and I was asking well how did that happen, and she was rather hesitating to talk about it, but she said, "Well, I locked him in the bathroom, and he was screaming or something, he was wanting to get out", and she tried to talk him out of it and he said, "if you are going to keep me in here just let me have a book to read", and I told her how did he get out later, she said, "Well, he rather cooled off and I talked him out of it."

Representative Ford. You say this conversation took place in the car?

Mrs. Ford. Yes; this conversation right now took place in the car but I don't know how it got started, I have forgotten.

Representative Ford. When you say it took place in the car, was it in the car going from Mr. McKenzie's to your home?

Mrs. Ford. That is right, to my home. She was staying at my place at this time.

Representative Ford. Did she talk rather freely about this Nixon——

Mrs. Ford. She didn't talk about it freely, I thought she was rather hesitant about going into particulars.

Representative Ford. Did she ever indicate why she had not discussed this incident with anybody, including the Commission?

Mrs. Ford. Well, right during that time, just before that, in the office, Mr. McKenzie, and I told her before that, "if you know anything that I think that would help either the Commission or the FBI I thought it my duty to tell them," and I told her that if she doesn't want me to say to anybody just don't talk to me about it, that is what I told her.

But because and maybe that is why she was hesitating to talk to me, Mr. McKenzie told it to her and had a written statement to her, too, if he feels there is anything he will have to say he will say it in connection with the President.

So it was said right before that, and I feel maybe that is why she was hesitating to talk to me.

Representative Ford. That is all.

The Chairman. Mrs. Ford, you are an American citizen now, aren't you?

Mrs. FORD. Yes.

The CHAIRMAN. How did you acquire it, by marriage to your first soldier husband?

Mrs. FORD. No. I had to apply for it.

The CHAIRMAN. Where were you naturalized?

Mrs. FORD. In Dallas, Tex.

The CHAIRMAN. In the Federal court?

Mrs. FORD. That is correct.

The CHAIRMAN. When was that about?

Mrs. FORD. I have it on my bracelet, so I will give you the correct time, I got it in 1952.

The CHAIRMAN. In 1952?

Mrs. FORD. This I got on "This is Your Life". I was on "This is Your Life".

Representative FORD. Mr. Chairman, I have one or two more questions.

The CHAIRMAN. Go right ahead.

Representative FORD. I wish you could clarify, if you can, the comment you made about Marina mentioning two guns.

Mrs. FORD. She did not mention two guns ever to me or anything like that. But I don't know how or why he advised her to say that at all, I don't know, it was not clear to me.

Representative FORD. When you say he, was that Mr. McKenzie?

Mrs. FORD. That is right, because the only reason—the only thing I remember about Marina was saying that Lee had laughed about the attempt to kill General Walker, that he said that they were even too stupid to find out what gun was used to kill him because it was written up a different type of gun was used other than the one really used by Lee.

Representative FORD. Marina said that?

Mrs. FORD. That is right. Lee had commented on that they were not even smart enough to identify the gun by a bullet.

Representative FORD. When did Marina say Lee said that?

Mrs. FORD. Well, soon after he—maybe that evening or the next day but I mean after he had attempted to shoot the General.

Representative FORD. After he had attempted to shoot General Walker?

Mrs. FORD. That is right. And the bullet was found in the room and I suppose by the bullet they had tried to identify the gun or whatever he used to shoot him and it was identified wrong.

It was not, I don't know what kind of gun he used, frankly, I don't know, but he said, he just made a comment, they weren't even smart enough to identify the gun by the bullet.

Representative FORD. Lee said that to Marina?

Mrs. FORD. To Marina, that is right.

Representative FORD. Right after the incident?

Mrs. FORD. Right after the incident, that is correct.

Representative FORD. And Marina told Mr. McKenzie that?

Mrs. FORD. I don't know.

Representative FORD. You don't know?

Mrs. FORD. But I think right after that it was in the papers that a different type of gun was used, and to shoot the President was different again, there were supposedly two guns, you see, so maybe that is why he advised her, that he had only one gun. I really don't know how this came out.

The CHAIRMAN. That is all. Thank you very much for coming, you have been very helpful.

Mrs. FORD. I hope so. I frankly wish I had questioned her more but I didn't feel it was my duty, but I wanted to tell you what she said to me.

The CHAIRMAN. We will take a short recess.

(Short recess.)

TESTIMONY OF DECLAN P. FORD

The CHAIRMAN. Mr. Ford, you were given a copy of this statement were you? Mr. FORD. Yes, sir.

The CHAIRMAN. As to the purpose so you understand what we are doing here today?

Mr. FORD. Yes, sir.

The CHAIRMAN. Will you please rise. Do you solemnly swear the testimony you give before this Commission will be the truth, the whole truth and nothing but the truth, so help you God?

Mr. FORD. I do.

The CHAIRMAN. Be seated please and Mr. Liebeler will ask the questions.

Mr. LIEBELER. Will you state your name, sir?

Mr. FORD. Declan P. Ford.

Mr. LIEBELER. Where do you live?

Mr. FORD. Dallas, Tex.

Mr. LIEBELER. What is your employment?

Mr. FORD. I am a consulting geologist.

Mr. LIEBELER. Are you independently employed?

Mr. FORD. Yes; I am self-employed.

Mr. LIEBELER. Would you give us a brief statement of your educational background?

Mr. FORD. I was graduated from the University of California at Los Angeles in 1948, with a Bachelor of Arts degree in Geology, and was first employed by Tidewater Associated Oil Co. as a geologist, later with the Continental Oil Co. as a geologist, and then later with DeGollyer McNaughton, a consulting firm in Dallas, Tex., until 1962, October. I went into business for myself as a consulting geologist. All this time has been in exploration, development of oil and gas fields both in the United States and foreign countries.

Mr. LIEBELER. Have you been employed in and about the Fort Worth and Dallas area ever since you graduated from college?

Mr. FORD. No; I have only been in the Dallas area since January 1960.

Mr. LIEBELER. Your wife's name is Katherine Ford?

Mr. FORD. Yes.

Mr. LIEBELER. When were you married?

Mr. FORD. We were married July 1960. July 2.

Mr. LIEBELER. Were you married at any time prior to that?

Mr. FORD. No; I was not.

The CHAIRMAN. '62, did you say?

Mr. FORD. 1960.

Mr. LIEBELER. Are you acquainted with Jack Ruby?

Mr. FORD. No; I am not.

Mr. LIEBELER. Do you know of any connection between Lee Oswald and Jack Ruby?

Mr. FORD. No; I don't.

Mr. LIEBELER. Directly or indirectly?

Mr. FORD. No.

Mr. LIEBELER. Do you know Mr. John M. Grizzaffi?

Mr. FORD. Yes; I knew him.

Mr. LIEBELER. Do you know whether or not he is a friend or associate of Jack Ruby's?

Mr. FORD. I don't know. I have heard that he knows Jack Ruby. I don't know how well he knows him.

Mr. LIEBELER. Do you know whether Mr. Grizzaffi had any contact with the Oswalds or knew them?

Mr. FORD. None that I knew of.

Mr. LIEBELER. When did you first meet the Oswalds?

Mr. FORD. In 1962, and I think it was in August of 1962, I am not sure of the exact date.

Mr. LIEBELER. Would you tell us the circumstances of the meeting?

Mr. FORD. I was a guest at the house of some friends, the Mellers, and the Oswalds had been there for lunch, and we came over after lunch to have cocktails and to meet Lee and Marina Oswald.

Mr. LIEBELER. Who was there at that time?

Mr. FORD. Mr. Meller and his wife, Anna Meller, George Bouhe, my wife and myself, Marina and Lee Oswald, and I can't remember for sure if anybody else. It seems to me there was somebody else there but I can't remember who it was. Someone else may have come in later or something like that.

Mr. LIEBELER. Did you mention George Bouhe as being there?

Mr. FORD. Yes; George Bouhe was there.

Mr. LIEBELER. You mentioned him?

Mr. FORD. Yes.

Mr. LIEBELER. Who invited you to that luncheon?

Mr. FORD. Mrs. Meller.

Mr. LIEBELER. Had you heard of the Oswalds prior to that time?

Mr. FORD. Yes; I had.

Mr. LIEBELER. How?

Mr. FORD. I first heard of them, I think, from either George Bouhe or maybe from Max Clark who lives in Fort Worth but I think it was George Bouhe. He had mentioned the name of Lee Oswald and briefly described his history, his story of his going to Russia, attempting to give up his American citizenship, and later returning from Russia with a Russian wife and child, and living in Fort Worth, and we were, my wife is Russian and we were interested in meeting her. George Bouhe, I think, at the time was attempting to help Lee Oswald find employment.

Mr. LIEBELER. When you say "her" in that sentence you are referring to Mrs. Marina Oswald?

Mr. FORD. Yes; Marina Oswald.

Mr. LIEBELER. Is that the reason why basically you went to the lunch at the Mellers to meet Lee and Marina Oswald?

Mr. FORD. Yes.

Mr. LIEBELER. Was there any conversation with the Oswalds at that time?

Mr. FORD. There was, most of the conversation was in Russian which I don't understand. I had very little conversation with Lee himself because he spoke Russian most of the time that afternoon and Marina didn't speak any English at all.

Mr. LIEBELER. Did you have any conversations in English with Oswald about living conditions in Russia, about his expenses in Russia?

Mr. FORD. A little bit. He showed me pictures of people that he had worked with in Russia. I believe they were on a picnic together, a group of men, and various other pictures of places he had seen in Minsk, and he briefly described the living conditions in Russia, I guess the conditions under which he had lived in Russia, the small room they had to live in, and he said something about how much money he made there. I don't remember how much it was though.

Mr. LIEBELER. Did he tell you what kind of a job he had?

Mr. FORD. No, he didn't. I think George Bouhe told me he had been a sheet metal worker or something similar to that.

Mr. LIEBELER. In Minsk?

Mr. FORD. In Minsk, yes.

Mr. LIEBELER. Did Oswald compare to you the amount of money that he was paid with the amount of money that other workers in the plant were paid?

Mr. FORD. No; he said nothing about it.

Mr. LIEBELER. Did he indicate in any way any source of income other than from his job?

Mr. FORD. None.

Mr. LIEBELER. At any time did he do that?

Mr. FORD. No.

Mr. LIEBELER. Did you ever learn of anything like that?

Mr. FORD. No; I have heard people speak of it but I have never heard him or anybody that knew him say he had another source of income.

Mr. LIEBELER. You have heard people speak of it when, since the assassination?

Mr. FORD. Since the assassination.

Mr. LIEBELER. But you heard nothing of it prior to the assassination?

Mr. FORD. No.

Mr. LIEBELER. Did you get any impressions of Oswald at this first meeting?

Mr. FORD. I had an impression that he was not the type of person I could make friends with very easily. He didn't impress me as being friendly to me as a person. He was kind of closed up within himself. And it seemed to me he preferred to speak in Russian rather than in English. He wanted to practice speaking Russian with the Russian speaking people rather than talking to me.

Mr. LIEBELER. Did Mrs. Oswald have any bruises on her at that time?

Mr. FORD. Yes, she did. On her face.

Mr. LIEBELER. On her face. Was there any conversation about that?

Mr. FORD. Not directly with me. My wife told me that Mrs. Oswald told her it was due to some accident of running into a door at nighttime while she was getting up to see what—the baby crying, something like that.

Mr. LIEBELER. Did you accept that explanation?

Mr. FORD. I didn't—well, really, I didn't accept it. It just didn't make much sense but it didn't make an impression one way or the other to me. I frankly at the time thought of a standard cartoon joke of a kid explaining his black eye, by a kid explaining he ran into a doorknob.

Mr. LIEBELER. Was there anything that happened at this first luncheon that impressed you about Oswald or his attitude, in any way that you think the Commission should know about?

Mr. FORD. Very little. Except he seemed reserved, and I would call excessively polite, and the fact I don't think he made any effort to make friends with the other people.

Mr. LIEBELER. When was the next time that you had any contact with Oswald?

Mr. FORD. The next time I saw him was the night I drove Marina from our house to another friend's house, Mr. Frank Ray's house. She had been staying at our house for about a week and she had been separated from him.

I had been out of town and when I came home she was invited to stay over at Mr. Ray's house and I took her over there, I think it was on a Friday evening.

Lee Oswald called and wanted to talk to Marina and wanted then to come out and see her. Mr. Ray told him if he would get on the bus and come to the bus stop nearest their home that he would pick him up, and I went with Mr. Ray to pick up Lee Oswald at the bus stop.

We went back to Mr. Ray's home, and had a short conversation with Lee Oswald but he said he wanted to talk to Marina, and he and Marina went into another room. I don't know exactly how long it was but we sat down and had one or two drinks, and then Lee came back in and said he and his wife were going to have a reconciliation and she wanted to go home with him that evening. Mr. Ray offered to drive them back to their place in Oak Cliff, and then I went home.

Mr. LIEBELER. You were out of town throughout the entire time that Marina stayed with your wife?

Mr. FORD. Except for the last night. She stayed there one more night after I came home.

Mr. LIEBELER. Did you form any impression on Oswald that evening different from the one that you originally had of him?

Mr. FORD. Only it confirmed my original thought. I remember one instance. Frank asked him where he was working and he would never identify the place he was working. He would hedge, I forget his exact words, but he mentioned that he was working, I think in a printing shop, either printing or photographic developing shop, and Mr. Ray asked him the name of the place, I think, twice, and he avoided answering. He would just start talking about something completely different.

In other words, when he didn't want to answer a question he would either change the subject or just start talking to somebody else.

Mr. LIEBELER. You had no idependent knowldege of where he was working at that time?

Mr. FORD. I didn't know the name. I had heard he was employed in this shop that I think was a printing and photographic developing shop.

Mr. LIEBELER. You didn't have anything to do with his getting that job?

Mr. FORD. No, I didn't.

Mr. LIEBELER. Do you know whether your friend did?

Mr. FORD. I am not sure. I think either George Bouhe or maybe Theo

325

Meller may have introduced him to the owner of the shop but I am not sure about it.

Mr. LIEBELER. Did you have any conversations with either Mr. Meller or Mr. Bouhe about this?

Mr. FORD. I have had conversations with them, but it was prior to this night when Lee came to make a reconciliation with his wife.

Mr. LIEBELER. Did they tell you that they had anything to do with his getting this job?

Mr. FORD. I don't specifically remember that they said so. I either assumed this or something they said led me to believe it.

Mr. LIEBELER. Did you have any conversations with the Rays that evening while you were taking Marina over there about the difficulties that the Oswalds had in their marriage?

Let's expand the question. Think about that, and also think about any conversations that you may have had with your wife about that after you went back, and tell us the conversations that you had with anybody at that time about the incidents of the separation, what caused it and what was the trouble between the Oswalds?

Mr. FORD. I don't believe I had any discussion with either Mr. or Mrs. Ray about specifically the difficulties in their marriage between Marina and Lee Oswald.

The only thing I remember is frankly saying something to the effect, well, he is really a screwy nut, or something, he can't find ways to work, something to that effect.

I have not discussed their personal problems. But I have discussed it with my wife about it prior to that and after that and also after the assassination and it was my understanding when she left her husband it was because he had beat her up.

Mr. LIEBELER. Did anybody tell you any of the details about why he had done that or what the cause of the trouble was?

Mr. FORD. Not at the time. My wife didn't tell me anything about that. Again, after the assassination, she told me more about it, but I don't know if Marina had mentioned this prior to the assassination, the year before that when she stayed at our house, or whether she mentioned it after the assassination, I don't know the exact time that these details were brought out.

My wife did mention that perhaps Marina antagonized him by arguing with him, talking back to him, or something like that whereas if she just learned to be quiet when he said something he might not have hit her.

Mr. LIEBELER. But you don't recall whether that was developed during or at the time or later on?

Mr. FORD. I don't remember whether she told me that before the assassination or not. I know we have talked about it since the assassination.

Mr. LIEBELER. When was the next contact that you had with the Oswalds?

Mr. FORD. The next contact was after Christmas 1962. Between Christmas and New Year's we gave a cocktail party and some friends of ours, George De Mohrenschildt and his wife were invited and later called my wife and asked her if it would be all right to bring Lee and Marina to the party and my wife said sure, bring them along or might have asked me if it was all right to bring them along and I said sure. It was prior to December 28.

Mr. LIEBELER. Did Oswald come with De Mohrenschildt?

Mr. FORD. Yes, he came with De Mohrenschildt.

Mr. LIEBELER. Did you know anything about the relations between Oswald and the De Mohrenschildts?

Mr. FORD. I knew they were friends, no more than that. How often they saw each other or what they talked about or anything they talked about I don't know.

Mr. LIEBELER. How old are the De Mohrenschildts?

Mr. FORD. I guess George De Mohrenschildt is between 50 and 55 years old.

Mr. LIEBELER. Did it seem curious to you that a man that age would be close to Lee Oswald who was around 21 or 22 at that particular time?

Mr. FORD. Not in the particular case.

Mr. LIEBELER. Why do you say that?

Mr. Ford. Well, George De Mohrenschildt has a reputation for being a left-wing enthusiast or something, I don't mean a member of the Communist Party, but he is, I have heard other people say he has expounded the ideals of Marxism and since Lee Oswald was supposedly a Marxist or a Communist they would agree on their political views.

Again, I have never heard George De Mohrenschildt expound on any of these ideas. I have met him socially several times and he is very pleasant, a big, good looking man, but other than their agreement on what is the ideal political system, I can't think of anything else they would have in common.

Mr. Liebeler. Your knowledge of De Mohrenschildt's political views are hearsay?

Mr. Ford. All of it is hearsay.

Mr. Liebeler. How did you learn about Oswald's political views?

Mr. Ford. Also hearsay. from other people.

Mr. Liebeler. Can you tell us who told you about it?

Mr. Ford. I can't remember anybody, any specific statement from anybody, but I have discussed it with people like both my wife and George Bouhe and I don't remember if I discussed it with the Mellers or not but it seems I have heard this from several different people about just about everybody who knew them, the Oswalds, this was one of the things that people were leary about in dealing with him was his reputation for being a Communist.

Mr. Liebeler. Did he have that reputation in the community?

Mr. Ford. Yes, I think he had that reputation of either—not being a member, say, of the Communist Party, but his political ideas were either Marxist or Communist or something he had derived from reading Karl Marx, I suppose.

Mr. Liebeler. Do you know whether he expressed any extreme antagonism or antagonism of any sort toward the Government of the United States?

Mr. Ford. The only occasion I know of was the first time I met him. he did blame the U.S. Embassy for delaying his exit, the exit of he and his wife from Russia.

He did state if it had not been for their delaying the exit visa that his daughter would have been born in the United States rather than Russia.

Mr. Liebeler. Did he say anything more about that, do you remember any more in detail?

Mr. Ford. Not that I heard of or can remember.

Representative Ford. Did he think the birth of his daughter in Russia rather than in the United States was something important, did it appear that way?

Mr. Ford. I don't know how important he thought it was. It actually started as a joke. We also had a baby born shortly before that and I said, "Pretty little Russian girl" or something like that, and he made a statement, "She is just as much a Texan as your son," and then went on to explain that if the U.S. Embassy had acted more quickly that he and Marina could have left Russia and that June, the daughter, would have been born in the United States.

I don't know whether he placed any great importance on it or not.

Mr. Liebeler. Did Oswald ever appear to you to have any kind of a sense of humor?

Mr. Ford. None whatsoever.

Mr. Liebeler. Did he say anything about the attitude the Russian authorities took when he wanted to come back to the United States and bring his wife back with him?

Mr. Ford. He never said anything to me. I think he may have while he was talking Russian with these other people. He may have mentioned the fact that it was easier, they got their visa for he and his wife from the Russian authorities, the delay came from the American authorities, but I don't specifically know whether it did. He said these things, again it would be hearsay, again I would have heard it from my wife or somebody else who could speak Russian who had either discussed it with him or was present when he was discussing it with somebody else.

Mr. Liebeler. Did you ever hear Oswald or hear of Oswald making any remarks that would indicate a hostility toward President Kennedy?

Mr. Ford. No; never did.

Mr. Liebeler. What about Governor Connally?

Mr. Ford. Never heard that either, until after the assassination. I saw newspaper copies of a letter he wrote to Governor Connally when Governor Connally was Secretary of the Navy.

Mr. Liebeler. I would limit my question to before the assassination?

Mr. Ford. Before the assassination, no.

Mr. Liebeler. Did you hear anything about his military career prior to the assassination?

Mr. Ford. No; in fact I had assumed prior to the assassination that he had had an honorable discharge from the Marine Corps.

Mr. Liebeler. You never had any discussions with him about that or heard anybody discussing it?

Mr. Ford. He said something the first time I met him, I can't specifically remember what it was, but I got the impression that, at that time that he had been a Marine Corps guard at the U.S. Embassy in Russia and I can't remember whether he said this or somebody else mentioned it or whether I just assumed it on my own.

So I know my first idea was this was the way he had gotten to Russia. I later learned he had gone on his own.

Mr. Liebeler. But you don't remember any specific discussion with him about this question?

Mr. Ford. No.

Mr. Liebeler. Did you know where Oswald was living during this period that his wife was separated from him and living with you and Mrs. Meller?

Mr. Ford. I knew he had an apartment in this Oak Cliff section of Dallas. I don't remember the exact address. I don't know whether he stayed there while Marina was in our house or not.

Mr. Liebeler. You had no knowledge where he lived prior to the time that he took the apartment in Oak Cliff, did you?

Mr. Ford. Well, I think he lived in Fort Worth. I am not absolutely sure. I believe this apartment in Oak Cliff was the first place he lived in Dallas, but I am not absolutely sure about it.

Mr. Liebeler. You had never talked to him about it?

Mr. Ford. No; never.

Mr. Liebeler. Did you ever visit the apartment?

Mr. Ford. No.

Mr. Liebeler. Now, had we gotten to the Christmas party?

Mr. Ford. You asked me about it.

Mr. Liebeler. Tell us as best as you can recall the events of that period. I think you said there was a party at your house on the 28th of December.

Mr. Ford. Yes.

Mr. Liebeler. Tell me if there were parties or get-togethers at which you were present or of which you knew at other homes during that period.

Mr. Ford. Well, there were, but I don't remember the specific dates that they were. I think they were after the party at our house. There was a party at George Bouhe's home, an apartment, during that period. I think it was a few days after that, right in the period of New Year's Eve, and I went to several celebrations.

I would hate to try to recall exactly when each one of them was and who was there.

Mr. Liebeler. Do you remember going to George Bouhe's apartment?

Mr. Ford. Yes; I remember going there but I don't remember the exact date that it was.

Mr. Liebeler. Was Oswald at that meeting?

Mr. Ford. No; he was not.

Mr. Liebeler. Was there any discussion of Oswald at that time?

Mr. Ford. Not that I can remember.

Mr. Liebeler. Were there any other parties that you attended during that period?

Mr. Ford. I don't remember any formal parties. I stopped and had drinks with a lot of people.

Mr. Liebeler. Specifically, was there a get-together at your home the night after the party that you had on the 28th of December?

Mr. FORD. Not a formal party, just a group of people happened to show up and we started another party.

Mr. LIEBELER. Who was there?

Mr. FORD. Mr. and Mrs. Sullivan, friends of ours from New Orleans, and Mr. and Mrs. Harris who were from Georgetown, Tex., and another Mr. and Mrs. Ray, not the ones who live in Dallas, but these live in Paris, Tex.

Mr. LIEBELER. Would that be Mr. and Mrs. Thomas Ray?

Mr. FORD. Thomas Ray.

Mr. LIEBELER. Thomas Ray. And yourself and your wife?

Mr. FORD. Right.

Mr. LIEBELER. Anybody else?

Mr. FORD. Right now I can't remember anybody else who came in. It was not a formal gathering, just people happened to stop in and we started having a party.

Mr. LIEBELER. Do you have any recollection of any discussion of Oswald at that time?

Mr. FORD. No.

Mr. LIEBELER. Do you remember at any time having any discussion with any of your Russian friends on the question of whether or not Oswald was a Russian agent?

Mr. FORD. Prior to the assassination?

Mr. LIEBELER. Yes, sir.

Mr. FORD. No; I don't remember prior to the assassination. There may have been some but I don't remember any.

Mr. LIEBELER. At the party at your home on the 28th of December, did you have any conversation with Oswald?

Mr. FORD. Said "hello, how are you," to he and Marina, and after that, I can't remember Oswald talking to anybody there except one guest, a Japanese girl, Yaeko, I forget her last name; my wife will remember.

As nearly as I can remember she was the only person in the whole party that he ever bothered to talk to.

Mr. LIEBELER. Do you remember whether Oswald was drinking that evening?

Mr. FORD. I fixed one drink for him, in a little liqueur glass full of liqueur. As far as I remember he never touched it.

Mr. LIEBELER. Did you ever observe Oswald smoking?

Mr. FORD. No.

Mr. LIEBELER. And you don't remember any discussion about Oswald after he left that evening?

Mr. FORD. No; after he left that evening, I don't recall any discussion of him.

Mr. LIEBELER. Did you ever have any conversations with De Mohrenschildt about Oswald?

Mr. FORD. I don't remember any specific conversations with George De Mohrenschildt. I may have.

Mr. LIEBELER. What was your impression of Oswald at this time as far as his relations with the other members of the Russian community were concerned, and generally?

Mr. FORD. My impression was that he didn't want his wife to associate with them, and that he resented any aid or help people tried to give either he or his wife. I might say, I know, I have heard other Russian people there, for example, would take Marina to a grocery store and buy a load of groceries for her and take her back, and one girl that went by and found the baby had a fever and nobody was taking it to the hospital and she took Marina and the baby to the hospital for some medical treatment for it, and I had the impression that Lee Oswald resented this.

Mr. LIEBELER. You gained that impression from conversations that you had?

Mr. FORD. From conversations with other people, yes.

Mr. LIEBELER. Is there any——

Mr. FORD. I was also going to say——

Mr. LIEBELER. Pardon me.

Mr. FORD. I think during the period of 1962 that George Bouhe, for example, thought it would be helpful for Marina to learn English and he tried to encourage her to learn English and I had heard later that Lee Oswald resented this, he didn't want her to learn English.

Mr. LIEBELER. When did you hear that?

Mr. FORD. That was back in 1962. I can't remember the specific time, but——

Mr. LIEBELER. Did you have any conversation with Mr. and Mrs. Harris at the party at your place on the 28th of December?

Mr. FORD. Oh, yes; I had conversations with them.

Mr. LIEBELER. Did you hear of an incident where Mrs. Harris was trying to teach English to Marina at the party and certain American customs and Oswald objected to it?

Mr. FORD. I didn't observe it. She may have tried to teach her some American customs. I don't remember hearing Oswald say anything about it, Lee Oswald say anything about it.

Mr. LIEBELER. Did Mrs. Harris say anything about it to you?

Mr. FORD. Not that I can remember.

Mr. LIEBELER. So you have no knowledge of that incident if it occurred at all?

Mr. FORD. No. It seems to me I have heard somebody else mention this but I did not see it or hear anything myself.

Mr. LIEBELER. Now, after the party on the 28th of December that was held at your house, when was the next contact that you had with either one of the Oswalds?

Mr. FORD. Well, I heard a few times or my wife had heard something about Marina living in Irving, but never actually saw either one of them until after the assassination. Then the first contact we had with Marina was, I believe, my wife tried to get in touch with her, either invite her to come to my house or to tell her that once things had been cleared up, the investigation had been cleared up, to feel free to come by, and let her know she still had friends.

Mr. LIEBELER. Did anybody suggest to you shortly after the assassination that Marina should come and live with you?

Mr. FORD. No.

Mr. LIEBELER. Did you ever express any hesitancy to anyone in connection with any suggestion that Marina should come and live with you?

Mr. FORD. I don't remember ever expressing it. If somebody had mentioned it the afternoon or next day after the assassination I probably would have been a little bit hesitant about it. But I don't remember saying anything to anybody.

Mr. LIEBELER. Did there come a time when Marina moved into your home after the assassination?

Mr. FORD. Yes; but this was in February of this year.

Mr. LIEBELER. Did you express any hesitancy at that time?

Mr. FORD. No.

Mr. LIEBELER. And you don't recall expressing any immediately after the assassination or before?

Mr. FORD. No. I don't remember talking to anybody at all about it. I mean the first few days immediately after the assassination, I don't recall saying anything to anybody about it, where she was going to live at my house or anybody else's.

Mr. LIEBELER. Did you ever have any conversations with Mr. Jim Martin on that subject?

Mr. FORD. No.

Mr. LIEBELER. Now prior to the time that Marina came to live in your home, your wife has testified she talked to Marina on the telephone several times and that Marina came to visit on two or three occasions, two occasions, I believe, at your home.

Mr. FORD. Yes.

Mr. LIEBELER. Did you talk to your wife about what Marina had said during your wife's visits with Marina?

Mr. FORD. When she came to visit us in our home?

Mr. LIEBELER. Yes.

Mr. FORD. I talked to her about what she had talked to Marina, and I couldn't carry on much of a conversation with Marina myself because she didn't speak much English but I would ask my wife, and my wife would tell me what she had said.

Mr. LIEBELER. Do you remember whether there was any discussion about Marina's testimony before this Commission, either before she went to Washington or after she came back?

Mr. FORD. No; not—my wife never told me before she came to Washington to testify before the Commission. After she came back, I did overhear some conversation between Marina, my wife, and Mr. William M. McKenzie regarding the testimony given to the Commission.

Mr. LIEBELER. Can you tell us what that was to the best of your recollection? Let me ask you this: Where did this occur?

Mr. FORD. I think it was in Mr. McKenzie's office, it may have been either in his office or my home but I think it was in his office, and I believe the FBI had been questioning her this afternoon, I am not sure of the date, and I came back later to pick up my wife and Marina and in my presence Mr. McKenzie asked my wife to ask Marina in Russian if she had told the Commission this Nixon story. I don't know the details of the story, but something regarding the threat to Mr. Nixon.

And I think Marina, again through my wife, told Mr. McKenzie that she had not mentioned this to the Commission. But that she had mentioned it to the FBI, and she had mentioned it, I believe to the FBI prior to the Commission hearing.

Mr. LIEBELER. Who told you that?

Mr. FORD. Well, I was standing there while Mr. McKenzie was talking to Marina using my wife as a translator.

Representative FORD. Was this in your home, did you say?

Mr. FORD. I think it was in Mr. McKenzie's office; it might have been in my home. Several times I have overheard conversation either in Mr. McKenzie's office or at my home.

Representative FORD. It could have been in either?

Mr. FORD. It could have been either, but it seems to me it was at his office. I think as Marina said, she had not said anything to the Commission about this, and then I think Mr. McKenzie asked her why not, and she said well she hadn't thought of it or nobody asked her; something to that effect.

I think he was trying to establish whether or not she had purposely withheld information from the Commission and she said no.

Mr. LIEBELER. Did you ever hear Marina Oswald make any remark to the effect when she was before the Commission she just answered questions and did not volunteer anything?

Mr. FORD. I never heard her say that.

Mr. LIEBELER. Did anybody ever translate that, a remark like that, so that you heard it when it was translated?

Mr. FORD. No; I never heard anybody translate for Marina and say that; no. In my presence, I never heard her say that and have it translated by anybody.

Mr. LIEBELER. Did you ever hear from anybody else that she had said that?

Mr. FORD. Not until yesterday when I was talking about it with you, that I can remember anything.

Mr. LIEBELER. And yesterday when we talked about it, I asked you the question, had anybody said that, isn't that right?

Mr. FORD. Yes.

Mr. LIEBELER. Did you obtain any information concerning the Nixon, any detailed information concerning the Nixon affair as a result of detailed conversations with your wife after she had had conversations with Marina? I am assuming Marina would speak in Russian to your wife. Did your wife ever tell you what Marina had ever said to her about the Nixon affair?

Mr. FORD. A little bit, not all the details. But something to the effect that Lee Oswald was threatening, I don't know whether to shoot Nixon, and in some way she had locked him in a bathroom and kept him there, I think all day. He had calmed down or cooled off and wasn't going to do anything. Just how she managed to do this, I don't know.

Mr. LIEBELER. Did you discuss the question with your wife as to how?

Mr. FORD. No; not—again, I never discussed it until yesterday, last night. I was talking to her and wondered how the devil she managed to lock him in the bathroom.

Mr. LIEBELER. And you discussed that with your wife last night as a result of a similar question that I asked you yesterday afternoon when we were reviewing the testimony?

Mr. FORD. Right.

Mr. LIEBELER. Did you learn anything relating to the Walker affair as a result of conversations with your wife?

Mr. FORD. Well, I had read about it in the newspapers; I had read stories that Lee Oswald had told Marina that he had taken a shot at General Walker and my wife did tell me later on she asked Marina if this were true and I think Marina said this was true, that Lee Oswald had told Marina he was the one who had taken a shot at General Walker.

Mr. LIEBELER. Is that the extent of your conversations about the Walker incident?

Mr. FORD. No; she mentioned something else that my wife told me about. That after Lee had taken a shot at General Walker, he had hidden the gun somewhere and went back the next day or a few days later and recovered the gun. And that Lee was reading the reports in the newspaper and made some statement, "Well, how stupid can the police be," something to this effect. In other words, expressing the idea that the police were unable to find out what happened in the Walker incident. And then also Marina had said at one time, I believe the day after the shooting of Walker or attempted shooting of Walker, George De Mohrenschildt had come into the house and made some statement to them regarding it. I can't remember the exact words but it was referring to it, Walker, somebody shooting at General Walker, and asking Lee how he could miss and she was surprised that De Mohrenschildt knew about it and Marina thought Lee had told George De Mohrenschildt about it.

Mr. LIEBELER. Did you ever learn how George De Mohrenschildt had learned about it?

Mr. FORD. No; I imagine he was surprised that Lee had done the shooting and to him it would have been a good joke.

Mr. LIEBELER. Do you remember anything else about the Walker incident that you and your wife may have talked about?

Mr. FORD. Yes; we have discussed it some after, I believe, Marina came to stay with us, and I expressed the doubt that Lee Oswald was the one who took a shot at Walker.

Mr. LIEBELER. Did you have any basis for expressing that doubt?

Mr. FORD. The only basis for it was that there was a story in one of the newspapers that they could not identify the bullet taken out of the wood in Walker's home as having come from a gun that Lee Oswald owned, it was too badly destroyed and they couldn't be sure it was the gun, the same gun, that shot the bullets at President Kennedy and Governor Connally.

Mr. LIEBELER. So on the basis of that newspaper story you expressed doubts as to whether Oswald was actually involved in the Walker incident?

Mr. FORD. Well, I expressed the doubt. It was possible that he really wasn't the one who took a shot at General Walker but just claimed he did and this to me would not be surprising.

Mr. LIEBELER. Why do you say that?

Mr. FORD. Well, I think, my opinion of Lee Oswald is that he would do anything to gain attention for himself, draw attention to himself, make not necessarily a hero out of himself but just a well-known person. He wanted attention. He wanted to be a big shot.

Mr. LIEBELER. And you think in an attempt to do that he might claim he had been the one who shot at Walker where, in fact, he was not the one at all?

Mr. FORD. It is possible, I think it is possible.

Mr. LIEBELER. Did you have any conversations with your wife in which your wife told you anything that Marina said about the details of the assassination, about Lee's coming home to Irving and his leaving for Dallas the next morning?

Mr. FORD. Well, we talked about it; I don't recall all the details of what my wife told me, whether they were my wife's opinions or things she had heard directly from Marina.

Apparently Marina was surprised that he would come home in the middle of the week rather than on weekends or come to visit her, and I gathered that Marina had thought of these things after the assassination, as she tried to figure things out. Well this increased her belief that Lee Oswald was the man who assassinated the President, because he did so many strange things that week, I mean that day before, not the week, the day before the assassination.

Mr. LIEBELER. To your knowledge, has Marina expressed any feeling about Oswald's guilt while she lived with you or while you were acquainted with her after the assassination, other than the fact he was guilty?

Mr. FORD. No; so far as I know she just accepts the fact he was guilty. He was the man who shot the President. And she believes this is true.

Mr. LIEBELER. Did you ever discuss this question with Robert Oswald?

Mr. FORD. No, not specifically, I didn't. I never asked Robert Oswald if he believed that his brother shot the President.

Mr. LIEBELER. Did Oswald ever indicate to you that he did not believe that?

Mr. FORD. Not directly. The only thing that might have indicated it was when Life published a picture of Lee Oswald on the front cover and I read a newspaper article which stated that Mrs. Marguerite Oswald was intending to sue Life Magazine and I wondered why, was the picture faked, and Robert Oswald said no it was a true picture of Lee Oswald but the title of the picture, that is what he was upset about, and I think the title was Lee Oswald holding the gun he either used to shoot or used to kill the President, and I didn't pursue the subject further with him.

I don't know specifically what he was upset about, if he thought his brother did shoot the President. There was nothing wrong with the statement except he may not have liked it in print.

Mr. LIEBELER. That was the only statement Robert Oswald made to you about the subject.

Mr. FORD. But he never said he didn't believe his brother did it.

Mr. LIEBELER. Do you have any other reasons for thinking that Oswald is the kind of person who would claim to do something that he hadn't done just to get attention drawn to him?

Mr. FORD. Well, yes; I think he was erratic enough in his behavior throughout his whole life to indicate that. Of course, I have read a lot about his life since the assassination, so it is not all opinion I formed prior to the assassination.

It is hard for me to distinguish which things I thought before the assassination from those I have thought about since the assassination.

Mr. LIEBELER. In that respect let me ask you this question: Were you surprised when you heard that Oswald had been charged with the assassination?

Mr. FORD. Yes, I was.

Mr. LIEBELER. Did you think on the basis of your knowledge of him before the assassination that he would have been capable of such a thing?

Mr. FORD. No; I wouldn't have thought so prior to the assassination and when I first heard he was picked up, I first thought, well, as I said to my wife, "This nut has gone down and got himself mixed up just to get some publicity."

Representative FORD. You said that to your wife?

Mr. FORD. Yes; that was my first opinion. When I heard that Lee Oswald was the man arrested, and I said I think I said, "This idiot has got himself arrested and got himself mixed up to get some publicity".

Mr. LIEBELER. What made you say that?

Mr. FORD. Again, I considered him to be erratic and unpredictable, I don't know how to explain the things that he would do.

For example, he had gone to Russia and he didn't like it there, he had gone back to Fort Worth and he didn't like it there. He didn't seem to like any place that he was, he didn't seem to make lasting friendships with anybody. And he would hop from one job to another, and move from one town to another. He never seemed to be satisfied and I considered his whole behavior rather erratic, and I suppose the main reason was, I felt that he had no desire to support, and I felt this prior to the assassination, he had no desire to support his wife and child, and he wanted and would be quite willing to sponge off anybody to get their support, and this was my primary reason for not wanting to associate with him rather than any political feelings he had.

Mr. LIEBELER. How did these things lead you to think that he was not capable of doing the assassination or that he just went there to get involved?

Mr. FORD. Prior to the assassination I never even considered the possibility of his killing a man but if somebody had asked me prior to the assassination, I would have answered no. I don't think he would kill anybody. But I don't think I really even considered it.

Mr. LIEBELER. You would have——

Mr. FORD. When the President was assassinated.

Mr. LIEBELER. And you would have based that response on the things you mentioned already.

Is there anything else you would have based that reason on?

Mr. FORD. Well, it is difficult to say. My general opinion of the man was that he was strange and he did a lot of things I couldn't understand but I had no reason to think he would attack a person with the intent to kill him.

As far as I knew there was nothing he had ever done before that that would indicate he would ever kill anybody. I don't know how you tell ahead of time whether a man can commit murder. I was never worried about him going out and killing somebody; say I would have never said prior to the assassination that you have got to watch out for this guy, he is dangerous. He didn't impress me that way.

Mr. LIEBELER. You had information prior to the assassination that he had beaten his wife, did you not?

Mr. FORD. Right.

Mr. LIEBELER. And did you take that information, would you take that, into consideration in the judgment that you just expressed?

Mr. FORD. No; I don't think so. I think man and wife can fight over a lot of things and it isn't necessary that either one of them would intend to kill somebody. He might become violent toward his wife, who is a much smaller and weaker person but he never impressed me as the type of person who would violently attack another man, for example.

Mr. FORD. When did you first hear that Lee Oswald was held by the authorities?

Mr. FORD. It was the afternoon of the assassination, I heard on the radio.

Mr. LIEBELER. What was your reaction then?

Mr. FORD. Just what I said, my first reaction, "This idiot has gone down to get himself some attention and confuse the whole issue."

At that time I didn't know he was working in the School Book Depository Building.

Mr. LIEBELER. What did you do subsequent to hearing this radio broadcast?

Mr. FORD. Let's see; I heard it in a hardware store and I went and picked up my wife who was shopping at the grocery store, picked her up, and told her what I had heard and we went home. I didn't do anything specifically that I can think of. I did not mention it to anybody.

Mr. LIEBELER. Did you and your wife on the way home from this shopping trip discuss the apprehension of Lee Oswald and his implication in the affair?

Mr. FORD. Well, I told her the police had picked him up, and that he was apparently being held both for the assassination of the President and for shooting a police officer, and my wife was a little bit worried then, I think, about the people's reaction to the children, and she said, well, "Don't mention it in front of the children."

By the time we got home, I believe Linda, my stepdaughter, had already talked on the phone to Mrs. Anna Ray, who had also heard the radio broadcast and called up to ask if my wife had heard it, and, of course, by then it was too late, they knew who Lee Oswald was, they read who he was, that Marina stayed at our house.

Mr. LIEBELER. Then if I understand it you and your wife voluntarily went down to police headquarters?

Mr. FORD. Well, the next Sunday.

Mr. LIEBELER. Two days later?

Mr. FORD. Yes; the assassination was on a Friday afternoon. On Sunday morning, Mr. Frank Ray called me and said he heard on the radio that the FBI had requested anybody who knew Lee Oswald to please contact them, and he asked me what I was going to do, I said, "Well, I don't know, I will call an attorney and see what he suggests." I called Max Clark at Fort Worth and he was out, so I called my sister out in Los Angeles. She is an attorney and married to one, and I said, "Who are you supposed to contact if you know information about Lee Oswald," and she said she assumed it would be the FBI, so I then called the FBI office and made an appointment to talk to an agent and we made the appointment to talk in the FBI office in downtown Dallas. While we were driving downtown I stopped to get some gas and the attendant told me that somebody had just shot Lee Oswald and it was right about that time that I went down to talk with the FBI.

Mr. LIEBELER. In this interval between your first reaction and your going to the interview with the FBI, did you and your wife discuss any further the Oswald implications?

Mr. FORD. I am sure we discussed it, but I can't remember exactly what we said to each other about it.

I think she was worried at first that her children would suffer some prejudice from other people.

Mr. LIEBELER. Marina's children?

Mr. FORD. No; our children. And, of course, also that Marina was and her two children, my wife felt, would be sort of considered persona non grata in this country from then on, but I didn't consider this would happen as long as she was not implicated in a plot to kill the President.

I know we discussed it but I just can't remember specifically what we said.

Mr. LIEBELER. Mr. Ford, did you at any time learn of any desire on Oswald's part to return to Russia?

Mr. FORD. Yes; after the assassination I did.

Mr. LIEBELER. How did you learn that?

Mr. FORD. Well, partly from discussing it, I heard it through friends and then later when Marina talked to my wife, I don't remember if this was during the time she visited us during January or after she moved in, but she did tell the story to my wife of his desire, as expressing a desire, to return to Russia, and I am a little confused as to what the story was.

As nearly as I could make out he had told her he wanted to go back to Russia first and then later said, no, he was going—couldn't get a visa to Russia and he was going to try to get a visa and go through Cuba and then go to Russia, and then I think he changed his mind again and said he was going to ask for a visa to Cuba, using it as an excuse with the idea of going to Russia and then stay in Cuba, and somewhere in there I got the idea that Marina was not willing to go. He wanted Marina to return to Russia and I had the impression this was just a—but I couldn't even give you the details of her various statements which led me to the conclusions—as nearly as I could figure out, this was the story she had told my wife and she told me.

Mr. LIEBELER. Did you learn at any time through your wife or otherwise that Marina Oswald at one point had contemplated committing suicide?

Mr. FORD. Yes.

Mr. LIEBELER. Tell us about that?

Mr. FORD. Well, the first time I heard it was yesterday.

Mr. LIEBELER. During our conversations?

Mr. FORD. During our conversations, yesterday.

Mr. LIEBELER. And your wife explained to us in our conversations yesterday that she, Marina Oswald, had told her at onetime contemplated commiting suicide?

Mr. FORD. That is right.

Mr. LIEBELER. That was the extent of our conversations yesterday?

Mr. FORD. Yes, sir. That is right. I think my wife said Marina felt so desolate and downhearted that she felt that was the only way out at the time.

Mr. LIEBELER. Are you finished?

Mr. FORD. Yes.

Mr. LIEBELER. Do you have any other information or knowledge that you think the Commission should know about in connection with these matters that we haven't already asked you about?

Mr. FORD. There is nothing I can think of offhand.

Mr. LIEBELER. In our conversations yesterday you and your wife and I discussed your testimony today. Have we covered those matters here in the testimony and have there been any inconsistencies between what we discussed yesterday and what we have discussed today on the record that you can think of?

Mr. FORD. No; I can't think of any inconsistencies. I assume we have covered everything we discussed yesterday. I can't remember everything we discussed yesterday, so I am just assuming we covered it.

Mr. LIEBELER. I have no more questions then.

The CHAIRMAN. Have you anything further, Congressman Ford?

Representative FORD. Mr. Ford, you drove Marina Oswald from your home to the Ray home?

Mr. FORD. Yes.

Representative FORD. In October or November of 1962?

Mr. FORD. It was in November.

Representative FORD. It was November of 1962. How long a drive is that?

Mr. FORD. It is about 15 minutes. I guess it couldn't be over 7 or 8 miles, 6, 7, 8 miles, something like that.

Representative FORD. Did you have any conversation with her at that time?

Mr. FORD. No. She couldn't speak but about a half dozen words of English.

Representative FORD. So there was no real conversation between the two of you?

Mr. FORD. No.

Representative FORD. That is all.

Mr. MURRAY. Mr. Chief Justice, may I confer briefly with counsel?

The CHAIRMAN. Where were you born?

Mr. FORD. Los Angeles.

The CHAIRMAN. Did you go to the public schools there?

Mr. FORD. I attended both parochial and public schools in Los Angeles and Glendale.

The CHAIRMAN. Then you went to the University of California at Los Angeles?

Mr. FORD. Right.

The CHAIRMAN. Where did you go after that. You were in the service, did you say?

Mr. FORD. I was in the service. After I got out of the service I went back to UCLA and finished my education and then went to work in the oil industry first in Bakersfield and in Los Angeles, Ventura, and then went to work for DeGollyer and McNaughton overseas.

The CHAIRMAN. I see.

Representative FORD. How old are you, Mr. Ford?

Mr. FORD. Forty-one.

Mr. LIEBELER. Mr. Ford, were you at any time present in Mr. McKenzie's office, William McKenzie, when there was a discussion with Marina Oswald concerning guns and the gun that was used to or presumably used to attack Walker and the gun that was subsequently presumably used to attack the President?

Mr. FORD. I don't remember any discussion. I have been in his office several times when he was discussing things with Marina, but I don't remember him ever asking about this gun or discussing this gun.

Mr. LIEBELER. Did you hear McKenzie at anytime advise Marina if she were asked about these guns she should say there was only one gun?

Mr. FORD. I think I did hear him say that once or something to that effect but I don't remember specifically the words.

Mr. LIEBELER. Can you recall——

Mr. FORD. But I don't think it was any discussion about the gun used in shooting General Walker.

Mr. LIEBELER. Tell us about it.

Mr. FORD. As nearly as I can remember it, the whole discussion was, he was telling her, he had asked her if there was anything else but this one rifle and she said no, and he said "be sure you always say that there was just this one gun," but I thought he was referring to the gun used only in the case of the assassination.

Mr. LIEBELER. He asked her about this before he advised her?

Mr. FORD. Apparently this was after she had been interrogated by the FBI and I don't know—I just had the impression they were talking about the possibility that more than one gun was used in the assassination of President Kennedy.

Mr. LIEBELER. Is that the best you can recall about that conversation?

Mr. FORD. The best I can recall, yes.

Mr. LIEBELER. That is all.

The CHAIRMAN. Thank you very much, Mr. Ford. I appreciate your coming here with your wife. You have been very helpful.

The CHAIRMAN. Let's call Mr. Gregory.

TESTIMONY OF PETER PAUL GREGORY

Mr. Gregory, you were given a copy of a statement of the reason for our meeting today, were you not?

Mr. GREGORY. No, sir.

The CHAIRMAN. Then I will read it to you.   This is customary——

Mr. GREGORY. Yes, sir.

The CHAIRMAN. We read a statement to the witness.

The purpose of this hearing is to take the testimony of Mr. and Mrs. Declan P. Ford, and Mr. Peter Paul Gregory. The Commission has been advised that Mr. and Mrs. Ford made the acquaintance of the Oswalds shortly after their arrival in the United States in June of 1962, and that Mrs. Marina Oswald lived in the Ford home on two different occasions, in November 1962, and for a period following February 12, 1964.

The Commission has also been advised that Mr. Gregory was contacted by Mr. Lee Harvey Oswald shortly after Mr. Oswald's return from Russia as a result of which Mr. and Mrs. Oswald made the acquaintances of a large number of Russian speaking people in the Dallas and Fort Worth area.   Since the Commission is inquiring fully into the background and possible motive of Lee Harvey Oswald, the alleged assassin, it intends to ask the above witnesses questions concerning Mr. Oswald, his associations and relations with others, and any and all matters relating to the assassination.

Mr. GREGORY. Yes, sir.

The CHAIRMAN. Will you raise your right hand and be sworn, please, Mr. Gregory.

Do you solemnly swear that the testimony you give before this Commission will be the truth, the whole truth, and nothing but the truth, so help you God?

Mr. GREGORY. I do.

The CHAIRMAN. You may be seated.

Mr. Liebeler will ask the questions of you.

Mr. LIEBELER. Would you state your name for the record, please?

Mr. GREGORY. My name is Peter Paul Gregory.

Mr. LIEBELER. And will you tell us where you were born?

Mr. GREGORY. I was born in Chita, Siberia.

Mr. LIEBELER. Would you tell us briefly how you came to the United States?

Mr. GREGORY. Yes, sir.

I came to the United States on or about August 1, 1923. I landed in San Francisco; came from Japan where I lived for 2 years prior to that. And my purpose was, of course, to come as an immigrant and to attend the University of California.

Mr. LIEBELER. Did you attend the University of California?

Mr. GREGORY. Yes, sir; I enrolled at the University in 1923 and I stayed out of the University for a couple of years but I graduated in 1929 as a petroleum engineer at Berkeley.

Mr. LIEBELER. What educational background did you have in Russia or Japan before you came to the United States?

Mr. GREGORY. I started my primary education in Russia, in 1912, and my education was interrupted by civil war in 1919. I finished high school or the equivalent of high school in Tokyo, Japan, where I attended the American school in Japan.

Mr. LIEBELER. Where did you learn to speak English?

Mr. GREGORY. I learned it in Japan.

Mr. LIEBELER. Were you personally involved in the civil war in Russia?

Mr. GREGORY. Not personally, no. I was too young; I was only 16, 17 at the time.

Mr. LIEBELER. Were any of your relatives involved in that?

Mr. GREGORY. My older brother was an officer in the White Russian Army.

Mr. LIEBELER. Do you presently reside in Fort Worth?

Mr. GREGORY. Yes, sir. I have been residing in Fort Worth for the past 20 years, and prior to that in the oilfields in the western part of Texas for 15 years, and prior to that I resided in California from 1923 to 1929.

Mr. LIEBELER. You are presently self-employed in Fort Worth, is that correct?

Mr. GREGORY. I am presently chairman of the Yates Pool Engineering Committee which is a group of engineers supervising activities in the Yates oilfield in Pecos County, Tex., and I am also a consulting petroleum engineer.

Mr. LIEBELER. And you are fluent in the Russian language, are you?

Mr. GREGORY. I am, I think.

Mr. LIEBELER. In fact, you teach Russian at the Fort Worth Public Library, is that correct?

Mr. GREGORY. Yes, I do; as a civic enterprise. I teach Russian once a week from 10 to 20 weeks a year.

Mr. LIEBELER. Approximately how long have you been doing that, sir?

Mr. GREGORY. For about 3 or 4 years.

Mr. LIEBELER. Would you tell us about your first contact with Lee Harvey Oswald?

Mr. GREGORY. Yes, sir.

It was in the middle of June 1962. On that particular morning, I was in the office, my telephone rang, and the voice on the other end told me that my name was given to him by the Fort Worth Public Library. He knew I was teaching Russian at the library, that he was looking for a job as a translator or interpreter in the Russian and English languages, and that he would like for me to give him a letter testifying to that effect.

He spoke to me in English, so I suggested to him, not knowing who that was, that he might drop by my office and I would be glad to give him a test. He did. He came by the office, about 11 o'clock that morning, and I gave him a short test by simply opening a book at random and asking him to read a paragraph or two and then translate it.

He did it very well. So I gave him a letter addressed to whom it may concern that in my opinion he was capable of being an interpreter or a translator.

Mr. LIEBELER. What happened after you gave Mr. Oswald—this individual was Lee Harvey Oswald?

Mr. GREGORY. Yes, sir; that individual was Lee Harvey Oswald.

After that, I asked him—I noticed that he spoke with what I thought to be a Polish accent, so I asked him if he were of Polish origin, and he stated that he was not, that he was raised in Fort Worth, Tex., but that he learned Russian in the Soviet Union where he lived for 2½ or 3 years.

He also told me that he married a Russian girl, and that he brought his wife with him, and that they also had a baby. I told him that I knew of no openings at the time—I didn't know of any—for services of a translator or interpreter, but that if he would leave his address I would be glad to get in touch with him if and when I learned of any such openings.

He gave me his address. He lived with his brother at that time at the western edge of Fort Worth.

Mr. LIEBELER. Did you ever send him any work as a translator or interpreter?

Mr. GREGORY. No, sir.

Mr. LIEBELER. Did you and Mr. Oswald have lunch together that day.

Mr. GREGORY. Yes, sir. It was about noontime when I gave him that test, so I invited him to lunch, and during the lunch being naturally curious about the present day life in the Soviet Union, I was asking him questions, asked how people lived there, and so forth.

He told me that he was employed in a factory in Minsk as a sheetmetal worker. He told me a little bit about the working conditions and living conditions in that country.

Mr. LIEBELER. Did he tell you how he was paid as a worker?

Mr. GREGORY. Yes; I think I asked him what he was paid and my recollection is that he told me he was getting about 80 rubles a month. I may be wrong about that but that is my recollection.

Mr. LIEBELER. Did he compare his salary with the salary of other workers in Russia?

Mr. GREGORY. Other workers in the Soviet Union?

Mr. LIEBELER. Yes.

Mr. GREGORY. No, he did not. By way of comparison, I was curious as to what the purchasing power of his earnings would be, I asked him what 80 rubles would buy, and I think he mentioned, as I say, a pair of shoes cost around 15 rubles.

Mr. LIEBELER. Did he indicate to you that he had any source of income other than his job at the factory?

Mr. GREGORY. No, sir; he did not.

Mr. LIEBELER. Did he tell you anything about why he went to Russia?

Mr. GREGORY. The only statement he made that I remember, he said, "I went to the Soviet Union on my own," but I did not feel like prying into his affairs. I did not press the question.

Mr. LIEBELER. Did you notice anything about the way he was dressed or anything else about him that would seem strange to you?

Mr. GREGORY. Yes; it was a very hot morning. You know in Texas in the middle of June, it is generally hot. I remember that he wore a flannel, woolen coat, suit, and atrocious looking shoes that were made in Russia.

I know he was very uncomfortable because he was too warmly dressed for that time of the year.

Mr. LIEBELER. Did Mr. Oswald tell you anything else at that time about conditions in the Soviet Union or his attempt to come back to the United States or bringing his wife back that you can recall?

Mr. GREGORY. I don't recall of anything outstanding that he told me. But I think he did tell me that they, he and his wife, left Moscow by train, and they went through East Germany to Berlin, I believe, and that their destination was Amsterdam, I believe, where they took a ship to come to New York.

Mr. LIEBELER. Did he express anything about any difficulties that he might have had in returning to the United States?

Mr. GREGORY. No, sir; not to my recollection.

Mr. LIEBELER. Did it seem extraordinary to you that his wife was able to leave the Soviet Union with him or didn't you think about that?

Mr. GREGORY. I thought at the time it was more than extraordinary.

Mr. LIEBELER. Why do you say that?

Mr. GREGORY. Because simply from reading accounts of the difficulties experienced by so many Americans who married Russian girls in the Soviet Union, and all the difficulties they had to secure permits from the Soviet Government for an exit visa for their wives.

Mr. LIEBELER. Did you discuss that with Mr. Oswald?

Mr. GREGORY. I did not.

Mr. LIEBELER. When was the next time you saw him?

Mr. GREGORY. The next time was a few days later, and the occasion was this, to the best of my recollection. My youngest son Paul, who at the time was a junior at the University of Oklahoma, Paul majoring in economics and also studying the Russian and the German languages, Paul expressed a wish to meet Marina Oswald simply because she was fresh from the country, Russia; that presumably her language was pure Russian language as compared to mine which became, shall we say, affected by my 40 years living in the United States, is not pure Russian any more probably, in fact, he thought that maybe he could take lessons of the Russian language from Marina Oswald.

So, I arranged; I called Lee Oswald at his brother's residence, and asked if it would be, if they would be, at home, that my son and I would come out to visit them, and we did. I don't remember the date but it must have been within possibly within 10 days, the first 10 days after his initial contact with me at the office.

Mr. LIEBELER. Let us try to set the date of your initial contact. I have here a copy, not a confirmed copy, but just a typewritten copy of a letter entitled "To Whom it May Concern." I show it to you and ask you if that is the letter to the best of your recollection that you gave to Mr. Oswald?

Mr. GREGORY. I think that is a copy of the letter I gave. That was on June 19, 1962.

Mr. LIEBELER. I ask that it be admitted in evidence and marked as the next exhibit.

The CHAIRMAN. It may be marked.

It will be marked as Exhibit 384.

Very well, it is admitted as Exhibit 384.

(The letter referred to was marked Commission Exhibit No. 384 for identification and received in evidence.)

Mr. GREGORY. I would hazard a guess that the second contact with Lee Oswald that I just referred to was made, say, around the 25th, toward the end of June 1962.

Mr. LIEBELER. And you went to see him at his brother's house?

Mr. GREGORY. At his brother Robert's, Robert Oswald's house. Paul and I spent there perhaps an hour, speaking Russian with Marina, and mostly with Marina. They showed some pictures, snapshots of their friends, of themselves, taken in Minsk. We talked about the living conditions, just in a very general way.

Mr. LIEBELER. Did you discuss politics with Mr. Oswald?

Mr. GREGORY. No, sir; we did not.

Mr. LIEBELER. Did you discuss politics with him at any time?

Mr. GREGORY. Not with Lee Oswald, no.

Mr. LIEBELER. Did you get the impression from just talking to the Oswalds at this time that Oswald was treated pretty much as other Russians were in Russia or did you think he had a special situation there in any way?

Mr. GREGORY. My personal impression was that he was treated there as the rest of the Russians.

Mr. LIEBELER. Did your son subsequently have additional contacts with the Oswalds?

Mr. GREGORY. Yes. He and I made arrangements for Marina Oswald to give him lessons, conversational lessons, I believe it was twice a week, and Paul paid her for these lessons. I don't remember the exact amount, whether it came under the minimum or not, it was around a dollar and a half an hour. And he took those lessons after he made a visit to his aunt in San Francisco in July of 1962. So, I would say that he took lessons from Marina Oswald, say, from approximately August 1 to September 15 when he went back to the university of Oklahoma.

Mr. LIEBELER. Do you remember when the last contact was that your son had with the Oswalds?

Mr. GREGORY. To the best of my knowledge his last contact with them was the Thanksgiving Day of 1962.

Mr. LIEBELER. Did your son tell you whether he had discussions with Oswald concerning politics and economics and things like that?

Mr. GREGORY. He mentioned once, I believe, that there were political discussions.

Mr. LIEBELER. What did he tell you about that?

Mr. GREGORY. He told me that he thought Lee Oswald was pretty silly in his views.

The CHAIRMAN. Pretty silly?

Mr. GREGORY. Silly.

The CHAIRMAN. Silly.

Mr. LIEBELER. Did he express any other——

Mr. GREGORY. He also mentioned that he saw some book on Marxism, whether it was Das Kapital or some other book I don't recall now, but he saw a book on Marxism in Lee's residence when they lived on Mercedes Street in Fort Worth.

Mr. LIEBELER. Did he say in words or substance that he thought that Oswald was a half-baked Communist?

Mr. GREGORY. I think that is the expression he used, yes.

Mr. LIEBELER. Now, did there—did you ever go to Oswald's own apartment?

Mr. GREGORY. Yes, I went there once to take Paul to his lesson. I, in other words I visited in their so-called living room once, when they lived on Mercedes Street.

Mr. LIEBELER. In Fort Worth?

Mr. GREGORY. In Fort Worth, yes, sir.

Mr. LIEBELER. Would you tell us what the conditions in their home were like?

Mr. GREGORY. It was practically a bare room. There was no furniture to speak of. There was the bare necessities; there was no playpen or crib for the baby. The baby was playing in the middle of the floor in the living room, as I remember. It was an extremely primitively furnished room, and the rest of the house was the same way.

Mr. LIEBELER. Did you have any impression as to whether the Oswald baby was being adequately cared for?

Mr. GREGORY. No; that I don't know. I do know this, that Oswald showed outward signs of love toward the baby. He would pucker his lips and this and that.

Mr. LIEBELER. Indicating that he had affection for the child?

Mr. GREGORY. For the child.

Mr. LIEBELER. At that visit did you have any discussion with Oswald about living conditions or anything else in Russia?

Mr. GREGORY. No, sir; I simply took Paul in for that lesson, and I left before the lesson began.

Mr. LIEBELER. Now, did there come a time when you held a dinner party to which you invited Mr. Oswald?

Mr. GREGORY. Yes. Well, really, it was not a dinner party. It was a small dinner. I mentioned the fact that Marina Oswald went to school in Leningrad, formerly St. Petersburg prior to the revolution, and a friend of mine, George Bouhe of Dallas, who is an accountant, was born and raised in St. Petersburg. He indicated to me that he would like to meet Marina Oswald and his fellow townswoman and townsman, so I discussed it with my wife, and she thought she will invite Marina Oswald and Lee Oswald and Mr. Bouhe, and a friend of Mr. Bouhe, Mrs. Meller of Dallas, to their dinner. I am sure Paul was at home at that time, so there were six of us at the dinner and my wife and my son.

Mr. LIEBELER. Will you tell us when the dinner was held?

Mr. GREGORY. Yes; it was before Paul went back to school so I assume it was in the early party of September, maybe it was late in August.

Mr. LIEBELER. Mr. Bouhe is a native born Russian?

Mr. GREGORY. Yes; he was born in St. Petersburg.

Mr. LIEBELER. What about Mrs. Meller?

Mr. GREGORY. I assume Mrs. Meller was born in Ukrania.

Mr. LIEBELER. During this dinner party was there any discussion between Mrs. Meller and Mr. Bouhe with the Oswalds concerning their background, experiences in Russia?

Mr. GREGORY. The conversation, as I recall it, centered mostly on St. Petersburg. Bouhe brought with him his albums of St. Petersburg, and he was asking her and they were both looking at the pictures, and is such and such statue on the main street of St. Petersburg, and so on and so forth. I think that was the gist of the conversation.

They also discussed the present day life in the Soviet Union. I do recall, the conversation was mostly with Marina, and she did not speak any English at that time, so all of that conversation was in the Russian language, which my wife does not understand at all.

I remembered that Lee Oswald hazarded, he would interject into the conversation, and he was a little bit critical of the attitude of the Soviet Government toward its own people, and here is what I am trying to say; he said they make the best shoes in Minsk for export, and the people get the—and I think he indicated his own shoes, which he still wore at that time. Then just very, very slight criticism, not politically, but sort of in the sense of economics that the people were not getting the best products, they were all for export.

Mr. LIEBELER. Now, at that time was there any indication that Oswald was better treated than other people in the Soviet Union or did you maintain the impression throughout your acquaintance with Oswald that he was treated similarly to other Russians?

Mr. GREGORY. That was my impression, that he was treated the same as other Russians.

Mr. LIEBELER. Did you detect any friction between Marina Oswald and Lee Oswald at this dinner?

Mr. GREGORY. No, sir.

Mr. LIEBELER. Was there any indication at that time that Lee Oswald had beaten his wife in any way?

Mr. GREGORY. Not at that time; no, sir.

Mr. LIEBELER. Did you ever see any indication that Marina Oswald had been beaten?

Mr. GREGORY. No, sir; I haven't seen it personally. I have heard reports from my friends that he did mistreat her physically, and that he had blackened her eyes, and once even extinguished a cigarette on her shoulder, something like that.

Mr. LIEBELER. Who told you that?

Mr. GREGORY. To the best of my recollection it was either—I think it was Bouhe or it could have been Mrs. Meller, but I believe it was Bouhe.

Mr. LIEBELER. That was at a time subsequent to this dinner party?

Mr. GREGORY. Yes, sir; subsequent. It was after the assassination of the President.

Mr. LIEBELER. That Bouhe told you?

Mr. GREGORY. Yes.

Mr. LIEBELER. Did Oswald at all discuss the reason why he went to Russia?

Mr. GREGORY. No; he just told me, you know once, the very first time I met him that he went there on his own.

Mr. LIEBELER. Did he indicate any desire to return to Russia?

Mr. GREGORY. I learned subsequently that he did but he never indicated it to me.

Mr. LIEBELER. Do you know whether Oswald maintained contacts with people that he had associated with in Russia?

Mr. GREGORY. None to my knowledge.

Mr. LIEBELER. You don't know that he wrote them letters?

Mr. GREGORY. No, sir. Excuse me, sir, when you asked me about his relations with Marina Oswald, I don't know whether this is of any importance or not, but during my first visit at their apartment on Mercedes Street in Fort Worth, the second time I saw Marina, I suggested to him that he should insist that she learn English as quickly as possible because it would be so much easier for her to get along in this country, and he replied that he would prefer that she did not learn English at all or else he would lose his fluency in the Russian language.

So it showed to me that he didn't particularly care about her. He cared more about himself.

Mr. LIEBELER. Did you say anything to him in response to that?

Mr. GREGORY. No, sir; I was frankly very much disgusted with that sort of attitude.

Mr. LIEBELER. Did Oswald ever come to your office?

Mr. GREGORY. Yes, he came to my office once or twice more. Once I was in the office when he came, and at that time, apparently he was downtown, my office is downtown in Fort Worth, he brought with him some typewritten sheets which he told me he was writing his memoirs of his life in the Soviet Union.

I remember seeing, I did not read the manuscripts at all, but I saw some snapshots or photographs attached to some typewritten sheets.

Mr. LIEBELER. During this time that you—did you have any other contacts with Oswald?

Mr. GREGORY. Well, he came to the office once more but I was not in the office, my secretary told me that he came by.

Mr. LIEBELER. Do you remember what he came to your office for? Did he indicate any particular reason for coming there?

Mr. GREGORY. I don't recall. I don't know why he came back. Frankly, I don't remember. Here is something else that—one of the newspaper reporters came to the office and asked me if I would deliver a letter to Oswald, a reporter who tried several times to contact Oswald and get the story of his life or something like that, and they simply refused to see him. Why he choose me, I don't know. How he learned that Oswald came to my office, I don't know. But this man came and asked me to deliver this letter to Oswald the next time he came to the office, and I remember now that he did come once or twice more because I handed him that letter, and Oswald took it and put it in his pocket.

Representative FORD. When were these visits, the second and third visits to your office?

Mr. GREGORY. I would say that was probably during the month of July 1962.

Representative FORD. 1962.

Mr. LIEBELER. Did Oswald ever ask you to help him work on a book?

Mr. GREGORY. No, sir.

Mr. LIEBELER. That he was working on?

Mr. GREGORY. No, sir.

Mr. LIEBELER. Other than these contacts we have discussed, did you have any other contacts with Oswald ever?

Mr. GREGORY. Well, I was at home when my son Paul answered a telephone call from Lee Oswald and he asked if Paul would come to get them, I guess they were at his brother's, they were going to Dallas, they moved to Dallas by then, so it must have been in October or maybe it was——

Mr. LIEBELER. Was it Thanksgiving?

Mr. GREGORY. It could have been Thanksgiving. It was Thanksgiving. It was Thanksgiving Day. Paul went to Oswald. Robert Oswald, and brought Marina and Lee Oswald and the baby to the house. He fixed some sandwiches for them and he took them to the bus station and they went to Dallas where they had already established residence. That was the last time I saw Lee Oswald and Marina Oswald until after the assassination of the President.

Mr. LIEBELER. On the basis of your contacts with Lee Oswald during this period of time, did you form any judgment of him?

Mr. GREGORY. Yes, sir; I think I did. He impressed me as a man that, first, he carried some sort of a chip on his shoulder. I also had the impression that, probably unfounded on my part, I don't know, I just formed that impression, that he, Lee Oswald, felt that he did not get proper recognition from the people, say, in the United States, maybe even in the Soviet Union. I don't know. In other words, I felt like he thought that he was a better man than the other people thought he was.

Mr. LIEBELER. Did you have the feeling that he desired to achieve recognition?

Mr. GREGORY. That is my distinct impression of him.

Mr. LIEBELER. Did you have any opinion as to whether he was ever able to command this recognition and respect that he was seeking?

Mr. GREGORY. I don't think so.

Mr. LIEBELER. Did you think he was an intelligent person?

Mr. GREGORY. Fairly.

Mr. LIEBELER. Do you think he was capable of performing an act such as an assassination of a President?

Mr. GREGORY. Definitely.

Mr. LIEBELER. What do you base that opinion on?

Mr. GREGORY. Well, he was a Marine; he, as I said, he carried a chip on his shoulder. From the best—from what I have read and so forth, I personally am of the opinion that he assassinated the President.

Mr. LIEBELER. Well now, based on your knowledge of him prior to the assassination did you have any reason to believe that he might do such a thing?

Mr. GREGORY. Prior to that time, no, sir. I didn't.

Mr. LIEBELER. You didn't regard him as a dangerous individual or something of that sort, did you?

Mr. GREGORY. Well, I thought he was—I did not think he was an unbalanced person or crazy person or anything like that. I would say he was sort of, I would say I thought he was sort of a peculiar person but I never thought he would do an act like that.

Mr. LIEBELER. Did you ever make the acquaintance of the mother?

Mr. GREGORY. Yes.

Mr. LIEBELER. Would you tell us about that?

Mr. GREGORY. Yes. As I mentioned earlier, I teach Russian once a week at the library. We started a new series of lessons on November 12, 1963, and in my class there was a lady by the name of Marguerite Oswald. Frankly, I never connected her with Lee Oswald. Oswald was just a name to me, and I did not learn about it until the day of the assassination. Or the next day, the next day, that she was his mother.

Mr. LIEBELER. Did Mrs. Oswald call you on the telephone at any time after the assassination?

Mr. GREGORY. Yes. She called me——

Mr. LIEBELER. Tell us about it?

Mr. GREGORY. Sunday morning, November 24, about 7 o'clock in the morning, from Dallas.

Representative FORD. This is the mother called?

Mr. GREGORY. The mother. Sunday morning about 7 o'clock in the morning, and she said, I still remember, she said, "Mr. Gregory, I need your help. The reporters, the news media were badgering me." I think that is the word she used. She said, "I wonder if some of your friends or you could provide a place for me to hide from them." And it sounded like she was crying on the telephone, although I think that woman is not taken to crying.

So I told her—she did not want to identify herself when she called me first. I asked her, I said, "Who are you?" And she said, "I would rather not tell you who I am but I shall identify myself by saying I am one of the students in the Russian class in the library." Of course, I knew it was Mrs. Oswald. In fact, I guessed who she was before she even tried to identify herself. So I told her, I said, "Now, I will tell you what I will do, Mrs. Oswald, you stay where you are and I will promise to you that I will come to see you sometime today." Of course, I knew where she was because the Secret Service told me where they had her before.

Mr. LIEBELER. The Secret Service contacted you the day before?

Mr. GREGORY. Yes.

Mr. LIEBELER. On Saturday?

Mr. GREGORY. Yes.

Mr. LIEBELER. Isn't it a fact they had asked you to come and translate an interview with Marina Oswald?

Mr. GREGORY. That is correct.

Mr. LIEBELER. But you didn't do it because you didn't need to do it that day?

Mr. GREGORY. No, sir.

Mr. LIEBELER. Did you see Lee Oswald that day?

Mr. GREGORY. No, I did not see him.

Mr. LIEBELER. Did you later on Sunday go to see Mrs. Marguerite Oswald?

Mr. GREGORY. Yes. As soon as I hung up the phone, I was talking to Marguerite Oswald, I called the U.S. Secret Service and reported this call, of course, and an agent, I called Agent Howard, who lives just north of Fort Worth, and he said, "Well, that is fine, we will find a hiding place for her, for Marguerite and Marina Oswald and the babies," and he suggested he come by my house in a matter of 45 minutes or an hour and we will go to Dallas and then proceed from there. And that is what we did then. We went to Dallas.

Mr. LIEBELER. You went to the Executive Inn where Marina and Mrs. Oswald were staying at that time, is that right?

Mr. GREGORY. Yes, sir; we went to the Executive Inn, and on the way we stopped en route on the turnpike, where the agents arranged a rendezvous with Robert Oswald and other agents, and we went to the Executive Inn in Dallas by the airport, and Robert and I went in and we told the women to pack up, that we were going to take them to. Robert told them we were going to take them to, the farm of his wife's parents, north of Fort Worth.

Mr. LIEBELER. But Mrs. Oswald objected to that?

Mr. GREGORY. Yes, she objected, she said she didn't want to go there. But I told her that she bothered me to come, to call me at the house to provide a place for her and here I am, and if she doesn't like it then I am just through with her.

Mr. LIEBELER. You told her that?

Mr. GREGORY. So she packed up and we got with the agents in two or three cars, two cars, and we started toward that farm of Robert Oswald's parents. But en route we detoured because Marguerite Oswald mentioned the fact that the two little babies were all wet, and that there were no diaper change for them, that Marina and she had no change of dresses, and so forth, and she insisted that we go by Irving where Marina lived with Ruth Paine.

Mr. LIEBELER. Then you went and obtained some materials for the babies there?

Mr. GREGORY. Well, we didn't go to the house because we got the report that Lee Oswald was shot. You see, that all happened Sunday morning, it was 11 o'clock in the morning, we were driving from Dallas to Irving and we got this report that Lee was shot, and the police advised us not to go to the house because there was a mob, so we went to the Chief of Police of Irving, to his residence. Marina telephoned Ruth Paine from there to gather these things for the babies and a change of dress for her and some money and so forth.

Mr. LIEBELER. You went from there, then, to Parkland Hospital where some events occurred and then you came back to the Inn of the Six Flags?

Mr. GREGORY. That is correct.

Mr. LIEBELER. I want to ask you about something that might have happened or happened at the Inn of the Six Flags.

There has been a newspaper report, and Mrs. Marguerite Oswald has said that on Saturday night an FBI agent came to the Executive Inn and showed her a picture of a man who she claims to be Jack Ruby. Have you seen newspaper reports to that effect?

Mr. GREGORY. Yes, I have seen reports to that effect.

Mr. LIEBELER. Now, Mrs. Oswald says, also, that while at the Inn of the Six Flags she observed a newspaper that had Jack Ruby's picture in it and exclaimed in the presence of other people that that was the same picture as the FBI had showed her, that is what she says. Did you ever hear her say anything like that?

Mr. GREGORY. No, sir; not to my recollection.

Mr. LIEBELER. She never did anything like that in your presence?

Mr. GREGORY. No, sir.

Mr. LIEBELER. After you met Mrs. Oswald, Marguerite Oswald, and had a chance to observe her, did that further your judgment of Lee Harvey Oswald in any way?

Mr. GREGORY. Yes, sir. I felt that a lot of his, many of his, peculiarities, possibly were brought on by the influence of his mother.

To me, she impressed me as being not necessarily rational. She is quite clever, but she certainly is most peculiar. She demands public attention, she wants to be the center of attention. As, for example, standing there in the middle of the room at the motel of that Six Flags, standing in the middle of the room saying "I want to make a statement," and she made those statements throughout the frequent intervals and always she would precede the statement by saying, "I want to make a statement. I feel that my son can't be buried anywhere but at the Arlington National Cemetery."

Mr. LIEBELER. And you detected similarities between Mrs. Oswald and Lee?

Mr. GREGORY. Yes; I felt they both craved public recognition or to be craving attention or publicity or whatever you wish to call it.

Mr. LIEBELER. In our conversation last evening about your testimony, I asked you about Mrs Ruth Paine, and you told me that Mrs. Ruth Paine had come to visit you at a time subsequent to the assassination.

Mr. GREGORY. No, sir; she never did. Ruth Paine?

345

Mr. LIEBELER. Yes.

Mr. GREGORY. No. She called me on the phone once.

Mr. LIEBELER. Called on the telephone?

Mr. GREGORY. Yes. But I have never met her.

Mr. LIEBELER. What was the conversation between you and her?

Mr. GREGORY. She asked me if I would tutor her in writing letters in Russian. If I remember, she mentioned that she either was going to write to the Soviet Embassy or Soviet Union, something like that, but I told her I was just too busy, I have no time for that. In fact, I didn't want to have anything to do with that sort of—I didn't want to write letters to the Soviet Union or to the Embassy or anybody else.

Representative FORD. How long have you taught Russian, Mr. Gregory?

Mr. GREGORY. In the library?

Representative FORD. Yes.

Mr. GREGORY. For approximately 3 or 4 years from 10 to 20 weeks a year.

Representative FORD. Have you taught Russian in any other area or capacity?

Mr. GREGORY. Yes, sir; I taught Russian a couple of years ago, not more than 2 years ago, at Carswell Air Force Base at Fort Worth, where I had a class of officers and men in the Russian language. With the result that two out of my class passed the Russian examination, and the rest flunked.

Representative FORD. How long would you estimate it would normally take for a person of average intelligence to learn to speak and write Russian as fluently as Oswald did?

Mr. GREGORY. If he lived in this country or in that country? That would make a lot of difference.

Representative FORD. Well, let's take this country first.

Mr. GREGORY. This country. That would depend again on the effort put out by the particular individual. If he were in earnest I would think he could do it in about 4 years.

Representative FORD. That is an ordinary person living in the United States?

Mr. GREGORY. Living in the United States.

Representative FORD. Who made——

Mr. GREGORY. Going to study Russian, say at the university, normal load, maybe 4 hours a week, plus homework, it would take about 4 years.

If he lived in the country——

Representative FORD. In the Soviet Union?

Mr. GREGORY. In the Soviet Union, he probably could do it in 2 or 3 years.

Representative FORD. Did Oswald tell you when he first visited you that he had learned to speak Russian, where?

Mr. GREGORY. In the Soviet Union.

Representative FORD. He never gave you any indication he had learned or studied prior to going to the Soviet Union?

Mr. GREGORY. No, sir.

Mr. LIEBELER. I have about one or two more questions.

Did you discuss at any time with Marina Oswald the conversation that she had with Lee Oswald after the assassination?

Mr. GREGORY. Would you mind to state that again?

Mr. LIEBELER. Yes.

Marina Oswald spoke with Lee after the assassination, when he was in the jail.

Mr. GREGORY. Yes, sir.

Mr. LIEBELER. Did she tell you about that?

Mr. GREGORY. Well, I don't remember whether it was Marina or whether it was Marguerite Oswald, I don't remember now; they did go to see him in the jail in the city of Dallas, and it must have been Marguerite because she was bragging what a wonderful son he is because he looked at the little girl, June, she is 2 years old, and he said, "You have got to buy her a new pair of shoes," I remember that. It must have been Marguerite because she used that as an illustration of what a wonderful boy he was.

Mr. LIEBELER. Other than that, you have no information as to what transpired at that time, happened at that time?

Mr. GREGORY. No.

Mr. LIEBELER. Would it be fair to say, Mr. Gregory, that it was through Oswald's contact with you that he subsequently made the association with and contact with the other members of the Russian community in Dallas and Fort Worth?

Mr. GREGORY. I think that would be a fair statement, yes.

Mr. LIEBELER. I have no more questions.

The CHAIRMAN. Congressman?

Representative FORD. I have one more, Mr. Gregory.

I believe Marina has testified when she first met Lee Harvey Oswald it was approximately 17 months after he had arrived in the Soviet Union. She testified, also, that she could not tell whether he was a native born resident of the Soviet Union or a foreigner by the way he spoke.

Mr. GREGORY. Yes.

Representative FORD. Is that unusual?

Mr. GREGORY. Well, frankly, I don't know. You see, Congressman, the city of Minsk is what we call, they call it, not we call, they call it in the White Russia Republic. You know they called this the Union of Republics, you know, in the White Russian Republic, and Minsk, I guess, is the capital of it.

It is fairly close to Poland, and there are all sorts of people, Poles, Lithuanians, probably Latvians, that lived in that part of the country, and none of those people speak pure Russian.

Now, whether she had reference, whether that had anything to do with her statement——

Representative FORD. Her observations?

Mr. GREGORY. Right; I don't know.

Now, I thought that Lee Oswald spoke with a Polish accent, that is why I asked him if he was of Polish descent.

Representative FORD. But leaving——

Mr. GREGORY. But, otherwise, I would say it would be rather unusual, rather unusual for a person who lived in the Soviet Union for 17 months that he would speak so well that a native Russian would not be sure whether he was born in that country or not.

Representative FORD. That would be a very unusual kind of a person?

Mr. GREGORY. It would be, yes.

Representative FORD. Or a person who had unusual training?

Mr. GREGORY. Right, or unusual ability or training, yes, that is right.

Representative FORD. That is all, Mr. Chairman.

The CHAIRMAN. Thank you very much, Mr. Gregory. You have been very helpful.

(Whereupon, at 1 p.m., the President's Commission recessed.)

Monday, March 16, 1964

TESTIMONY OF COMDR. JAMES J. HUMES, COMDR. J. THORNTON BOSWELL, AND LT. COL. PIERRE A. FINCK

The President's Commission met at 2 p.m. on March 16, 1964, at 200 Maryland Avenue NE., Washington, D.C.

Present were Chief Justice Earl Warren, Chairman; Senator John Sherman Cooper, Representative Gerald R. Ford, John J. McCloy, and Allen W. Dulles, members.

Also present were J. Lee Rankin, general counsel; Francis W. H. Adams, assistant counsel; Norman Redlich, assistant counsel; Arlen Specter, assistant counsel; and Charles Murray, observer.

TESTIMONY OF COMDR. JAMES J. HUMES

The CHAIRMAN. The Commission will be in order.

Commander Humes, will you please step up. You know, Commander, what we have met for today to take your testimony concerning the autopsy and anything else you might know concerning the assassination of the President.

Would you raise your right hand, please?

Do you solemnly swear the testimony you give before this Commission will be the truth, the whole truth and nothing but the truth, so help you God?

Commander HUMES. I do.

The CHAIRMAN. Will you be seated?

You may proceed.

Mr. SPECTER. Dr. Humes, will you state your full name for the record, please?

Commander HUMES. James Joseph Humes.

Mr. SPECTER. And what is your profession or occupation, please?

Commander HUMES. I am a physician and employed by the Medical Department of the United States Navy.

Mr. SPECTER. What is your rank in the Navy?

Commander HUMES. Commander, Medical Corps, United States Navy.

Mr. SPECTER. Where did you receive your education, Commander Humes, please.

Commander HUMES. I had my undergraduate training at St. Joseph's College at Villanova University in Philadelphia. I received my medical degree in 1948 from the Jefferson Medical College of Philadelphia.

I received my internship and my postgraduate training in my special field of interest in Pathology in various Naval hospitals, and at the Armed Forces Institute of Pathology at Walter Reed in Washington, D.C.

Mr. SPECTER. What do your current duties involve?

Commander HUMES. My current title is Director of Laboratories of the Naval Medical School at Naval Medical Center at Bethesda. I am charged with the responsibility of the overall supervision of all of the laboratory operations in the Naval medical center, two broad areas, one in the field of anatomic pathology which comprises examining surgical specimens and postmortem examinations and then the rather large field of clinical pathology which takes in examination of the blood and various body fluids.

Mr. SPECTER. Have you been certified by the American Board of Pathology?

Commander HUMES. Yes, sir; both in anatomic pathology and in clinical pathology in 1955.

Mr. SPECTER. What specific experience have you had, if any, with respect to gunshot wounds?

Commander HUMES. My type of practice, which fortunately has been in peacetime endeavor to a great extent, has been more extensive in the field of natural disease than violence. However, on several occasions in various places where I have been employed, I have had to deal with violent death, accidents, suicides, and so forth. Also I have had training at the Armed Forces Institute of Pathology, I have completed a course in forensic pathology there as part of my training in the overall field of pathology.

Mr. SPECTER. Did you have occasion to participate in the autopsy of the late John F. Kennedy on November 22, 1963?

Commander HUMES. Yes, sir; I did.

Mr. SPECTER. What was your specific function in connection with that autopsy?

Commander HUMES. As the senior pathologist assigned to the Naval Medical Center, I was called to the Center by my superiors and informed that the President's body would be brought to our laboratories for an examination, and I was charged with the responsibility of conducting and supervising this examination; told to also call upon anyone whom I wished as an assistant in this matter, that I deemed necessary to be present.

Mr. SPECTER. Who did assist you, if anyone, in the course of the autopsy?

Commander HUMES. My first assistant was Commander J. Thornton Boswell, whose position is Chief of Pathology at the Naval Medical School, and my other assistant was Lt. Col. Pierre Finck, who is in the wound ballistics section of the Armed Forces Institute of Pathology.

When I ascertained the nature of the President's wounds, having had the facilities of the Armed Forces Institute of Pathology offered to me by General Blumberg, the commanding officer of that institution, I felt it advisable and would be of help to me to have the services of an expert in the field of wound ballistics and for that reason I requested Colonel Finck to appear.

Mr. SPECTER. Tell us who else in a general way was present at the time the autopsy was conducted in addition to you three doctors, please?

Commander HUMES. This, I must preface by saying it will be somewhat incomplete. My particular interest was on the examination of the President and not of the security measures of the other people who were present.

However, the Surgeon General of the Navy was present at one time or another, Admiral Galloway, the Commanding Officer of the National Naval Medical Center; my own commanding officer, Captain John H. Stover of the Naval Medical School, Dr. John Ebersole, one of the radiologists assigned to the Naval Hospital, Bethesda, who assisted with X-ray examinations which were made. These are the chief names, sir; that I can recall.

Mr. SPECTER. What time did the autopsy start approximately?

Commander HUMES. The president's body was received at 25 minutes before 8, and the autopsy began at approximately 8 p.m. on that evening. You must include the fact that certain X-rays and other examinations were made before the actual beginning of the routine type autopsy examination.

Mr. SPECTER. Precisely what X-rays or photographs were taken before the dissection started?

Commander HUMES. Some of these X-rays were taken before and some during the examination which also maintains for the photographs, which were made as the need became apparent to make such.

However, before the postmortem examination was begun, anterior, posterior and lateral X-rays of the head, and of the torso were made, and identification type photographs, I recall having been made of the full face of the late President. A photograph showing the massive head wound with the large defect that was associated with it. To my recollection all of these were made before the proceedings began.

Several others, approximately 15 to 20 in number, were made in total before we finished the proceedings.

Mr. SPECTER. Now were those X-rays or photographs or both when you referred to the total number?

Commander HUMES. By the number I would say they are in number 15 to 20. There probably was ten or 12 X-ray films exposed in addition.

Mr. SPECTER. What time did this autopsy end?

Commander HUMES. At approximately 11 p.m.

Mr. SPECTER. What wounds did you observe on the late President, if any?

Commander HUMES. The wounds which we observed on the President were— excuse me, at this point might I use the charts which I have prepared?

Would that be appropriate?

Mr. SPECTER. Yes; would you like to start with the neck wound?

Commander HUMES. All right, sir.

I might preface my remarks by stating that the President's body was received in our morgue in a closed casket. We opened the casket, Dr. Boswell and I, and the President's body was unclothed in the casket, was wrapped in a sheet labeled by the Parkland Hospital, but he was unclothed once the sheet was removed from his body so we do not have at that time any clothing.

Mr. SPECTER. Dr. Humes, before you identify what that represents let me place Commission Exhibit No. 385 on it so it may be identified.

(The drawing was marked Commission Exhibit No. 385 for identification.)

Commander HUMES. When appraised of the necessity for our appearance before this Commission, we did not know whether or not the photographs which we had made would be available to the Commission. So to assist in making our testimony more understandable to the Commission members, we decided to have made drawings, schematic drawings, of the situation as we saw it, as we recorded it and as we recall it. These drawings were made under my supervision and that of Dr. Boswell by Mr. Rydberg, whose initials are H. A.

He is a hospital corpsman, second class, and a medical illustrator in our command at Naval Medical School.

Mr. SPECTER. Did you provide him with the basic information from which these drawings were made?

Commander HUMES. Yes, sir.

Mr. SPECTER. Distances, that sort of thing?

Commander HUMES. Yes, sir. We had made certain physical measurements of the wounds, and of their position on the body of the late President, and we provided these and supervised directly Mr. Rydberg in making these drawings.

Mr. SPECTER. Have you checked the drawings subsequent to their preparation to verify their accuracy?

Commander HUMES. Yes, sir.

Mr. SPECTER. And proportion?

Commander HUMES. I must state these drawings are in part schematic. The artist had but a brief period of some 2 days to prepare these. He had no photographs from which to work, and had to work under our description, verbal description, of what we had observed.

Mr. SPECTER. Would it be helpful to the artist, in redefining the drawings if that should become necessary, to have available to him the photographs or X-rays of the President?

Commander HUMES. If it were necessary to have them absolutely true to scale. I think it would be virtually impossible for him to do this without the photographs.

Mr. SPECTER. And what is the reason for the necessity for having the photographs?

Commander HUMES. I think that it is most difficult to transmit into physical measurements the—by word the—exact situation as it was seen to the naked eye. The photographs were—there is no problem of scale there because the wounds, if they are changed in size or changed in size and proportion to the structures of the body and so forth, when we attempt to give a description of these findings, it is the bony prominences, I cannot, which we used as points of references, I cannot, transmit completely to the illustrator where they were situated.

Mr. SPECTER. Is the taking of photographs and X-rays routine or is this something out of the ordinary?

Commander HUMES. No, sir; this is quite routine in cases of this sort of violent death in our training. In the field of forensic pathology we have found that the photographs and X-rays are of most value, the X-rays particularly in finding missiles which have a way of going in different directions sometimes, and particularly as documentary evidence these are considered invaluable in the field of forensic pathology.

Mr. SPECTER. Will you now proceed to show us what Commission Exhibit 385 depicts, please?

Commander HUMES. Actually, I think, sir, at this time the view from the posterior aspect would also be of value to the Commission.

This is——

Mr. SPECTER. Doctor, I hand you the second exhibit which is marked Commission Exhibit No. 386.

(Commission Exhibit No. 386 was marked for identification.)

Commander HUMES. I believe at this point I would like to have, if you have my gross autopsy description because I will give the dimensions of these wounds at this time.

Mr. SPECTER. We will use the Commission Exhibit No. 387 and I will ask you first of all, for the record, to identify what this document is, Dr. Humes.

(The document referred to was marked Commission Exhibit No. 387 for identification.)

Commander HUMES. This document is a copy of the gross autopsy report which was prepared by myself, Dr. Boswell, and Dr. Finck, and completed within approximately 48 hours after the assassination of the President.

Mr. SPECTER. Does that report bear your signature at its end?

Commander HUMES. It bears my signature on the first or covering page as well as on my last page, sir.

Mr. SPECTER. Will you now proceed to tell us what you observed with respect to the wound which is marked as appearing in the upper back or lower neck?

Mr. McCLOY. Have you identified that?

Mr. SPECTER. The one on the side is 385 and the one of the rear view is 386. And that one is 387. For purposes of our record, if you will, put them in as 385 and 386 for our printed record. You might want to put them in chalk above them so you will see the one on the left is 385 and on the right is 386.

Commander HUMES. These exhibits again are schematic representations of what we observed at the time of examining the body of the late President.

Exhibit 385 shows in the low neck an oval wound which—excuse me, I wish to get the measurements correct. This wound was situated just above the upper border of the scapula, and measured 7 by 4 milimeters, with its long axis roughly parallel to the long axis of vertical column.

We saw—I would rather not discuss the situation of the anterior neck at this time or would you prefer it?

Mr. SPECTER. How would you prefer to do it, Dr. Humes?

Commander HUMES. I would prefer to discuss the wounds, two wounds, we saw posteriorly and the wound, other wound, of the skull before going to that.

Mr. SPECTER. That is fine. Dr. Humes, do it any way you find convenient. I will give you the other drawing and you can do them both together. Let the third drawing be marked as Commission Exhibit No. 388.

(The drawing referred to was marked Commission Exhibit No. 388 for identification.)

Commander HUMES. The wound in the low neck of which I had previously begun to speak is now posteriorly—is now depicted in 385, in 386 and in 388.

The second wound was found in the right posterior portion of the scalp. This wound was situated approximately 2.5 centimeters to the right, and slightly above the external occipital protuberance which is a bony prominence situated in the posterior portion of everyone's skull. This wound was then 2½ centimeters to the right and slightly above that point.

The third obvious wound at the time of the examination was a huge defect over the right side of the skull. This defect involved both the scalp and the underlying skull, and from the brain substance was protruding.

This wound measured approximately 13 centimeters in greatest diameter. It was difficult to measure accurately because radiating at various points from the large defect were multiple crisscrossing fractures of the skull which extended in several directions.

I have noted in my report that a detailed description of the lines of these fractures and of the types of fragments that were thus made were very difficult of verbal description, and it was precisely for this reason that the photographs were made so one might appreciate more clearly how much damage had been done to the skull.

Mr. SPECTER. Were the photographs made available then, Dr. Humes, when Exhibit 388 was prepared?

Commander HUMES. No, sir.

Mr. SPECTER. All right.

Commander HUMES. The photographs, to go back a moment, the photographs and the X-rays were exposed in the morgue of the Naval Medical Center on this night, and they were not developed, neither the X-rays or the photographs. They were submitted to me, and here, if I make a mistake I am not certain, to either the Federal Bureau of Investigation or to the Secret Service. I am not sure of those.

Mr. SPECTER. Did you submit those yourself immediately after they were taken, Dr. Humes?

Commander HUMES. Again, one of the senior people present, I believe my own Commanding Officer, Captain Stover, took care of turning this material over to these authorities, and receiving a receipt for this information, for this material. It was—I supervised the positioning of the body for various of these examinations but as far as beyond that, I did not consider that my responsibility.

These, then, were the three wounds which were quite obvious at the time of the examination.

I could expand further on the general appearances of these wounds or I could turn to the anterior portion of the body and describe various other wounds which were present.

Mr. SPECTER. You were focussing on 388 before I last asked a question, Dr. Humes. Why don't you describe in general terms the nature of the wound which was present at the top of the head of the late President?

Commander HUMES. With your permission, sir, and Mr. Chief Justice, I think I might describe those two wounds together, and describe the defects in the scalp and in the skull in each instance.

Mr. SPECTER. That would be fine.

Commander HUMES. Would that be appropriate?

Mr. SPECTER. Yes.

Commander HUMES. Turning now to Commission Exhibit 388, where we have depicted in the posterior right portion of the skull a wound which we have labeled "in" or a wound of entrance and a large roughly 13 cm. diameter defect in the right lateral vertex of the skull. I would go into some further detail in describing these wounds.

The scalp, I mentioned previously, there was a defect in the scalp and some scalp tissue was not available. However, the scalp was intact completely past this defect. In other words, this wound in the right posterior region was in a portion of scalp which had remained intact.

So, we could see that it was the measurement which I gave before, I believe 15 by 6 millimeters.

When one reflected the scalp away from the skull in this region, there was a corresponding defect through both tables of the skull in this area.

Mr. SPECTER. Will you describe what you mean by both tables, Dr. Humes?

Commander HUMES. Yes, sir.

The skull is composed of two layers of bone. We will put the scalp in in dotted lines.

The two solid lines will represent the two layers of the skull bone, and in between these two layers is loose somewhat irregular bone.

When we reflected the scalp, there was a through and through defect corresponding with the wound in the scalp.

This wound had to us the characteristics of a wound of entrance for the following reason : The defect in the outer table was oval in outline, quite similar to the defect in the skin.

Mr. SPECTER. You are referring there, Doctor, to the wound on the lower part of the neck?

Commander HUMES. No, sir ; I am speaking here of the wound in the occiput.

The wound on the inner table, however, was larger and had what in the field of wound ballistics is described as a shelving or a coning effect. To make an analogy to which the members of the Commission are probably most familiar, when a missile strikes a pane of glass, a typical example, a B–B fired by a child's air rifle, when this strikes a pane of glass there will be a small, usually round to oval defect on the side of the glass from whence the missile came and a belled-out or coned-out surface on the opposite side of the glass from whence the missile came.

(At this point, Mr. Dulles entered the hearing room.)

Commander HUMES. Experience has shown and my associates and Colonel Finck, in particular, whose special field of interest is wound ballistics can give additional testimony about this scientifically observed fact.

This wound then had the characteristics of wound of entrance from this direction through the two tables of the skull.

Mr. SPECTER. When you say "this direction," will you specify that direction in relationship to the skull?

Commander HUMES. At that point I mean only from without the skull to within.

Mr. SPECTER. Fine, proceed.

Commander HUMES. Having ascertained to our satisfaction and incidentally photographs illustrating this phenomenon from both the external surface of the skull and from the internal surface were prepared, we concluded that the large defect to the upper right side of the skull, in fact, would represent a wound of exit.

A careful examination of the margins of the large bone defect at that point, however, failed to disclose a portion of the skull bearing again a wound of—a point of impact on the skull of this fragment of the missile, remembering, of course, that this area was devoid of any scalp or skull at this present time. We did not have the bone.

In further evaluating this head wound, I will refer back to the X-rays which we had previously prepared. These had disclosed to us multiple minute fragments of radio opaque material traversing a line from the wound in the occiput to just above the right eye, with a rather sizable fragment visible by X-ray just above the right eye. These tiny fragments that were seen dispersed through the substance of the brain in between were, in fact, just that extremely minute, less than 1 mm. in size for the most part.

(At this point, Senator Cooper entered the hearing room.)

Mr. SPECTER. Dr. Humes, this would be a good juncture to produce two photographs.

May it please the Commission, Mr. Chief Justice Warren, I have identified as Commission Exhibits 389 and 390 which will at a later time be identified as being two frames from the motion picture camera operated by one Abraham Zapruder, being the amateur photographer who was on the scene, which I think would assist in evaluating the angle of the President's head corresponding to that exhibit designated as 388.

I will hand those to you, Dr. Humes, and ask you if you would state for the record the relative position of the President's head in 389 which is a frame about one-sixteenth of a second before the point of impact shown in Exhibit 390.

(The frames referred to were marked Commission Exhibits Nos. 389 and 390 for identification.)

Commander HUMES. It will be noted in Exhibit 389 that the President's head is bent considerably forward and perhaps somewhat to the left in this frame of the photograph 389.

Mr. SPECTER. Is that in approximately the same position as the angle of the head depicted in Commission Exhibit No. 388?

Commander HUMES. Yes, sir; it is.

Mr. SPECTER. Mr. Chief Justice, at this time I would like to move for admission in evidence of Exhibits 385 through 390.

The CHAIRMAN. They may be admitted under those numbers.

(Commission Exhibits Nos. 385, 386, 387, 388, 389, and 390, previously marked for identification, were received in evidence.)

Mr. SPECTER. Will you proceed now, Dr. Humes, to continue in your description of the head wound?

Commander HUMES. Head wound—a careful inspection of this large defect in the scalp and skull was made seeking for fragments of missile before any actual detection was begun. The brain was greatly lacerated and torn, and in this area of the large defect we did not encounter any of these minute particles.

I might say at this time that the X-ray pictures which were made would have a tendency to magnify these minute fragments somewhat in size and we were not too surprised in not being able to find the tiny fragments depicted in the X-ray.

Mr. SPECTER. Approximately how many fragments were observed, Dr. Humes, on the X-ray?

Commander HUMES. I would have to refer to them again, but I would say between 30 or 40 tiny dustlike particle fragments of radio opaque material, with the exception of this one I previously mentioned which was seen to be above and very slightly behind the right orbit.

Mr. DULLES. Were these all fragments that were injected into the skull by the bullet?

Commander HUMES. Our interpretation is, sir, that the missile struck the right occipital region, penetrated through the two tables of the skull, making the characteristic coning on the inner table which I have previously referred to. That one portion of the missile and judging by the size of the defect thus produced, the major portion of the missile, made its exit through this large defect.

A second portion of the missile or multiple second portions were deflected, and traversed a distance as enumerated by this interrupted line, with the major portion of that fragment coming to lodge in the position indicated.

Perhaps some of these minor fragments were dislodged from the major one as it traversed this course.

To better examine the situation with regard to the skull, at this time, Dr. Boswell and I extended the lacerations of the scalp which were at the margins of this wound, down in the direction of both of the President's ears. At that point, we had even a better appreciation of the extensive damage which had been done to the skull by this injury.

We had to do virtually no work with a saw to remove these portions of the skull, they came apart in our hands very easily, and we attempted to further examine the brain, and seek specifically this fragment which was the one we felt to be of a size which would permit us to recover it.

Mr. SPECTER. When you refer to this fragment, and you are pointing there, are you referring to the fragment depicted right above the President's right eye?

Commander HUMES. Yes, sir; above and somewhat behind the President's eye.

Mr. SPECTER. Will you proceed, then, to tell us what you did then?

Commander HUMES. Yes, sir. We dissected carefully in this region and in fact located this small fragment, which was in a defect in the brain tissue in just precisely this location.

Mr. SPECTER. How large was that fragment, Dr. Humes?

Commander HUMES. I refer to my notes for the measurements of that fragment.

I find in going back to my report, sir, that we found, in fact, two small fragments in this approximate location. The larger of these measured 7 by 2 mm., the smaller 3 by 1 mm.

To make my presentation of this wound of the skull more logical to the Commission, I would like to go forward in time that evening to at a later hour. I apologize—time and what happened exactly at what moment escapes me at this time.

I mentioned previously that there was a large bony defect. Some time later on that evening or very early the next morning while we were all still engaged in continuing our examination, I was presented with three portions of bone which had been brought to Washington from Dallas by the agents of the Federal Bureau of Investigation.

These were——

Mr. SPECTER. Might that have been by a Secret Service agent?

Commander HUMES. It could be, sir; these things——

Mr. SPECTER. At any rate, someone presented these three pieces of bone to you?

Commander HUMES. Someone presented these three pieces of bone to me, I do not recall specifically their statement as to where they had been recovered.

It seems to me they felt it had been recovered either in the street or in the automobile, I don't recall specifically.

We were most interested in these fragments of bone, and found that the three pieces could be roughly put together to account for a portion of this defect.

Mr. SPECTER. How much remained unaccounted for, Dr. Humes?

Commander HUMES. I would estimate that approximately one-quarter of that defect was unaccounted for by adding these three fragments together and seeing what was left.

This is somewhat difficult, because as back to when we were actually looking for the fragments of metal, as we moved the scalp about, fragments of various sizes would fall to the table, and so forth, so it was difficult to put that exact figure into words.

However, the thing which we considered of importance about these three fragments of bone was that at the margins of one of them which was roughly pyramidal in shape, there was a portion of the circumference of what we interpreted as a missile wound. We thus interpreted it this because there was, the size was, sufficiently large for us, for it to have the curve of the skull still evident. At the point of this defect, and I will draw both tables of the bone in this defect, at the area which we interpreted as the margin of a missile wound, there was a shelving of the margin.

This would, to us, mean that a missile had made this wound from within the skull to the exterior. To confirm that this was a missile wound, X-rays were made of that fragment of bone, which showed radio-opaque material consistent and similar in character to the particles seen within the skull to be deposited in the margins of this defect, in this portion of the bone.

Mr. SPECTER. Then what conclusion did you reach as to what caused that hole reconstructed from the three portions of the late President's scalp?

Commander HUMES. We reached the conclusion a missile entered the left— the right posterior inferior portion——

Mr. SPECTER. Doctor, perhaps it would be helpful if you would refer to that as letter "A" and the exit as letter "B", so that the record is clear on those two points and perhaps it will be helpful to your description as well.

And would you mark them as well, with a pencil?

Commander HUMES. That is not entry for the second.

Mr. SPECTER. Exit for the second?

Commander HUMES. I will label 388 with the letter "A" to indicate our opinion as to the wound of entrance into the skull.

I will label as Point "B" the area of exit of a portion of the missile that entered posteriorly. I say a portion because a small fragment was seen in the position previously noted which was recovered.

However, we concluded that a very significant portion, perhaps the largest portion, made its exit and accounted for this very large defect for the multiple fractures of the skull and for the loss of brain and scalp tissue at this point.

Mr. SPECTER. Will you describe at this juncture the damage which was inflicted upon the brain, please?

Commander HUMES. May I refer at this point to the gross description of the brain prepared separately?

Mr. SPECTER. Certainly, Dr. Humes, if you prefer to do it in that order.

Commander HUMES. I believe you have that. It is the second portion of the report.

Mr. SPECTER. Yes, sir. I can make that available to you here.

Commander HUMES. While that is being provided, when we reflected the scalp away from the badly damaged skull, and removed some of these loosened portions of skull bone, we were able to see this large defect in the right cerebral hemisphere. It corresponded roughly in size with the greatest diameter of the defect in the scalp measuring some 13 cm.

Mr. SPECTER. May the record now show I am handing to you, Dr. Humes, an exhibit marked Commission Exhibit 391, and will you identify what that is, please, Doctor?

Commander HUMES. Exhibit 391 is listed as a supplementary report on the autopsy of the late President Kennedy, and was prepared some days after the examination.

This delay necessitated by, primarily, our desire to have the brain better fixed with formaldehyde before we proceeded further with the examination of the brain which is a standard means of approach to study of the brain.

The brain in its fresh state does not lend itself well to examination.

From my notes of the examination, at the time of the post-mortem examination, we noted that clearly visible in the large skull defect and exuding from it was lacerated brain tissue which, on close inspection proved to represent the major portion of the right cerebral hemisphere.

We also noted at this point that the flocculus cerebri was extensively lacerated and that the superior sagittal sinus which is a venous blood containing channel in the top of the meninges was also lacerated.

To continue to answer your question with regard to the damage of the brain, following the formal infixation, Dr. Boswell, Dr. Finck and I convened to examine the brain in this state.

We also prepared photographs of the brain from several aspects to depict the extent of these injuries.

We found that the right cerebral hemisphere was markedly disrupted. There was a longitudinal laceration of the right hemisphere which was parasagittal in position. By the saggital plane, as you may know, is a plane in the midline which would divide the brain into right and left halves.

This laceration was parasagittal. It was situated approximately 2.5 cm. to the right of the midline, and extended from the tip of occipital lobe, which is the posterior portion of the brain, to the tip of the frontal lobe which is the most anterior portion of the brain, and it extended from the top down to the substance of the brain a distance of approximately 5 or 6 cm.

The base of the laceration was situated approximately 4.5 cm. below the vertex in the white matter. By the vertex we mean—the highest point on the skull is referred to as the vertex.

The area in which the greatest loss of brain substance was particularly in the parietal lobe, which is the major portion of the right cerebral hemisphere.

The margins of this laceration at all points were jagged and irregular, with additional lacerations extending in varying directions and for varying distances from the main laceration.

In addition, there was a laceration of the corpus callosum which is a body of fibers which connects the two hemispheres of the brain to each other, which extended from the posterior to the anterior portion of this structure, that is the corpus callosum. Exposed in this laceration were portions of the ventricular system in which the spinal fluid normally is disposed within the brain.

When viewed from above the left cerebral hemisphere was intact. There was engorgement of blood vessels in the meninges covering the brain. We note that the gyri and sulci, which are the convolutions of the brain over the left hemisphere were of normal size and distribution.

Those on the right were too fragmented and distorted for satisfactory description.

When the brain was turned over and viewed from its basular or inferior aspect, there was found a longitudinal laceration of the mid-brain through the floor of the third ventricle, just behind the optic chiasma and the mammillary bodies.

This laceration partially communicates with an oblique 1.5 cm. tear through the left cerebral peduncle. This is a portion of the brain which connects the higher centers of the brain with the spinal cord which is more concerned with reflex actions.

There were irregular superficial lacerations over the basular or inferior aspects of the left temporal and frontal lobes. We interpret that these later contusions were brought about when the disruptive force of the injury pushed that portion of the brain against the relative intact skull.

This has been described as contre-coup injury in that location.

This, then, I believe, Mr. Specter, are the major points with regard to the President's head wound.

Mr. SPECTER. Do you have an opinion, Dr. Humes, as to whether there were dumdum bullets used specifically on this wound which struck point "A" of the head, on 388?

Commander HUMES. I believe these were not dumdum bullets, Mr. Specter. A dumdum bullet is a term that has been used to describe various missiles which have a common characteristic of fragmenting extensively upon striking.

Mr. SPECTER. Would you characterize the resultant effect on this bullet as not extensive fragmenting?

Commander HUMES. Yes. Had this wound on point "A" on Exhibit 388 been inflicted by a dumdum bullet, I would anticipate that it would not have anything near the regular contour and outline which it had. I also would anticipate that the skull would have been much more extensively disrupted, and not have, as was evident in this case, a defect which quite closely corresponded to the overlying skin defect because that type of a missile would fragment on contact and be much more disruptive at this point.

Mr. SPECTER. At this point would you state for the record the size and approximate dimension of the major wound on the top of the head which you have marked wound "B"?

Commander HUMES. This was so large, that localization of it in a descriptive way is somewhat difficult.

However, we have mentioned that its major—its greatest dimension was approximately 13 cm. The reason it was difficult to measure is that various fracture lines extend out from it in a quite irregular fashion, but it was approximately 13 cm.

Mr. McCloy. This red that is marked on 388 on the base of the skull, is that seepage or what?

Commander Humes. No, sir; that is to depict the musculature at the base of the neck.

Mr. McCloy. I see.

Commander Humes. That is not taken to depict the blood, sir.

Mr. Specter. On the reconstruction of the three portions of the scalp which you described——

Commander Humes. Skull, sir.

Mr. Specter. Skull, which enabled you to reconstruct a point of exit of the bullet, will you state at this point of the record that size of opening or exit path of the bullet?

Commander Humes. As I mentioned previously, at one angle of this largest pyramidal shaped fragments of bone which came as a separate specimen, we had the portion of the perimeter of a roughly what we would judge to have been a roughly circular wound of exit. Judging from that portion of the perimeter which was available to us, we would have judged the diameter of that wound to be between 2.5 and 3 cm.

Mr. Specter. Doctor Humes, have you now described the major characteristics and features of the wounds to the late President's head?

Commander Humes. I believe that I have, sir.

Mr. Specter. All right. Will you now turn your attention, please to the wound which is noted on 385 and 386 being at the——

Mr. McCloy. Before we leave that, could I ask a question?

When you talk about dumdum bullets, do you include the ordinary type of soft nose sporting bullets, maybe this is something that Colonel Finck would be more expert on, but was that, was the bullet, could it possibly have been a sporting type of hunting bullet that has a soft nose but is still somewhat firm?

Commander Humes. From the characteristics of this wound, Mr. McCloy, I would believe that it must have had a very firm head rather than a soft head.

Mr. McCloy. Steel jacketed, would you say, copper jacketed bullet?

Commander Humes. I believe more likely a jacketed bullet because of the regular outline which was present.

Mr. McCloy. All right.

Mr. Dulles. Could I ask a question?

The Chairman. Mr. Dulles.

Mr. Dulles. Believing that we know the type of bullet that was usable in this gun, would this be the type of wound that might result from that kind of a bullet?

Commander Humes. I believe so, sir.

Mr. Dulles. If my question is clear——

Commander Humes. Yes, sir; it is.

Mr. Dulles. We think we know what the bullet is, we may be wrong but we think we know what it was, is this wound consistent with that type of bullet?

Commander Humes. Quite consistent, sir.

Mr. McCloy. There is no evidence of any keyholing of the bullet before it hit, before the point of impact?

Commander Humes. I don't exactly follow your question.

Mr. McCloy. Was the bullet moving in a direct line or had it begun to tumble?

Commander Humes. To tumble?

That is a difficult question to answer. I have the opinion, however, that it was more likely moving in a direct line. You will note that the wound in the posterior portion of the occiput on Exhibit 388 is somewhat longer than the other missile wound which we have not yet discussed in the low neck. We believe that rather than due to a tumbling effect, this is explainable on the fact that this missile struck the skin and skull at a more tangential angle than did the other missile, and, therefore, produced a more elongated defect, sir.

Senator Cooper. May I ask a question there? Perhaps you have done this.

but if not, how would you explain the difference of the courses of the fragments which you traced and described as, I think, being discovered behind the right eye?

Commander HUMES. Yes, sir.

Senator COOPER. And the course of the fragment which was believed caused the large defect?

Commander HUMES. Caused the large defect?

Senator COOPER. How do you explain——

Commander HUMES. The discrepancy?

Senator COOPER. The difference in the courses.

Commander HUMES. Yes, sir.

As this missile penetrated the scalp, it then came upon a very firm substance, the hard skull, and I believe that this track depicted by the dotted lines on Exhibit 388 was a portion of that missile which was dislodged as it made its defect in the skull. And that—that another portion, and, as I say, presumably, by the size of the defect, a more major portion made its exit through the right lateral side of the skull.

Mr. McCLOY. Is this piece of pyramidal bone that was brought in to you subsequently as I understand it——

Commander HUMES. Yes, sir.

Mr. McCLOY. Was that part of the outer table or the inner table?

Commander HUMES. It was both tables, sir.

Mr. McCLOY. Both tables?

Commander HUMES. Yes, sir; had it only been one it might have been difficult to ascertain whether it was.

Mr. McCLOY. Shelving or not?

Commander HUMES. Yes, sir; in or out, but it encompassed both tables, sir.

Mr. DULLES. Is the angle of declination that you—one sees there from in and out approximately the angle you think at which the bullet was traveling at the time of impact and exit?

Commander HUMES. That is our impression, sir.

Mr. DULLES. So then the shot would have been fired from some point above the head of the person hit?

Commander HUMES. Yes, sir.

Mr. SPECTER. Dr. Humes, would you elaborate a bit on the differences in the paths, specifically why the bullet went in one direction in part and in part in the second direction, terminating with the fragment right over the right eye?

Commander HUMES. Yes, sir.

I will make a drawing of the posterior portion of the skull showing again this beveling which we observed at the inner table of the skull.

Our impression is that as this projectile impinged upon the skull in this fashion, a small portion of it was dislodged due to the energy expended in that collision, if you will, and that it went off at an angle, and left the track which is labeled 388, which is labeled on Exhibit 388 from "A", point "A" to the point where the fragment was found behind the eye.

Why a fragment takes any particular direction like that is something which is difficult of scientific explanation. Those of us who have seen missiles strike bones, be it the skull or a bone in the extremity, have long since learned that portions of these missiles may go off in various directions and the precise physical laws governing them are not clearly understood.

Mr. SPECTER. Would the angle be accentuated in any way if you were to assume the President was in a moving automobile going in a slight downhill direction?

Commander HUMES. There are many variables under these circumstances. The most—the crucial point, I believe, to be the relative position of the President's head in relation to the flight of the missile.

Now, this would be influenced by how far his head was bent, by the situation with regard to the level of the seat in the vehicle, off of the horizontal, and so forth.

Mr. SPECTER. How about a decline in the path of the road itself?

Commander HUMES. I think that that would have a tendency to accentuate this angle, yes, sir.

Mr. Specter. Mr. Chief Justice, I would like to move for the admission in evidence now of Exhibit 391, which is the exhibit on the brain report.

The Chairman. It may be admitted.

(The document heretofore marked for identification as Commission Exhibit No. 391 was received in evidence.)

Mr. Specter. Dr. Humes, would you now move over to the wound which appears on the lower part of the neck and upper part of the back?

Mr. Dulles. Could I ask one more question before we get to that, I am sorry.

Mr. Specter. Certainly.

Mr. Dulles. Could one say as to what portion of the bullet was found in all these fragments, I mean arrive at an estimate, was it a tenth of the bullet, was it, how much was it, assuming the type of bullet that we believe was used in this particular rifle.

Commander Humes. Sir, I have not had the opportunity to personally examine the type of bullet which is believed to have been represented by this injury.

However, I would estimate—if I understand you correctly the total amount that was present in the President's skull and brain?

Mr. Dulles. Yes.

Commander Humes. Including the fragment?

Mr. Dulles. Including all the fragments.

Commander Humes. Including all these minute particles. I would say there was something less than one-tenth of the total volume of the missile.

Mr. Specter. Dr. Humes, do you make that calculation on the assumption that the bullets used here were 6.5 mm. Mannlicher-Carcano rifle bullet weighing 158.6 grams?

Commander Humes. Yes, I do; sir.

Mr. Specter. Had I brought that particular fact to your attention prior to the time you started testifying here today?

Commander Humes. Yes, sir. One point I intended to make clear these fragments which I recovered from this position were turned over to the Secret Service.

I presume that they have made physical measurements including the weight of them, and could give a much more intelligent estimate of the proportion than I. I would say, however, that we did not deliver these minute fragments because they were so small as to be essentially unrecoverable.

So, obviously they were of a very small portion of the major missile.

Mr. Dulles. These minute fragments were part of the bullet, emanations from the bullet?

Commander Humes. Yes, sir.

Mr. Dulles. They were not from the head?

Commander Humes. No, sir, they were small, dust, of the size of dust particles, however.

Mr. Dulles. Is the posture of the head of that figure there, the inclination of it, rovghly the inclination that you think the President's head had at the time from the other photographs?

Commander Humes. Yes, sir. From the photographs and based on the physical examination of this wound, yes, sir.

Mr. Dulles. That is all I have.

Mr. McCloy. Perhaps this was something that Colonel Finck could testify to exactly, but, he would be quite competent. Is there anything to indicate that this was, might have been a larger than a 6.5 or smaller than a 6.5?

Commander Humes. The size of the defect in the scalp, caused by a projectile could vary from missile to missile because of elastic recoil and so forth of the tissues.

However, the size of the defect in the underlying bone is certainly not likely to get smaller than that of the missile which perforated it, and in this case, the smallest diameter of this was approximately 6 to 7 mm., so I would feel that that would be the absolute upper limit of the size of this missile, sir.

Mr. McCloy. Seven would be the absolute upper limit?

Commander Humes. Yes, sir; and, of course, just a little tilt could make it a little larger, you see.

Mr. DULLES. I have one other question, if I may.

Is the incidence of clean entry as indicated there, and then great fragmentation on exit, is that a normal consequence of this type of wound?

Commander HUMES. Sir, we feel that there are two potential explanations for this.

One, having traversed the skull in entrance in the occiput as depicted on 388, the missile begins to tumble, and in that fashion it presents a greater proportion of its surface to the brain substance and to the skull as it makes its egress.

The other and somewhat more difficult to measure and perhaps Colonel Finck will be able to testify in greater detail on this, is that a high velocity missile has tremendous kinetic energy, and this energy is expanded against the structures which it strikes, and so that much of this defect could be of the nature of blast, as this kinetic energy is dissipated by traversing the skull.

Is that the sense of the question, sir?

Mr. DULLES. Yes.

Senator COOPER. I will ask a question, and perhaps this isn't in your field. But assuming that the shot which struck President Kennedy at point A was fired by a gun from the window of the Texas School Book Depository, and which has been testified to, and assuming that you could locate the position of the President at the time he was struck by a bullet, you could then, could you not, establish the degree of the missile?

Commander HUMES. The degree of angle?

Senator COOPER. The angle, yes, the degree of angle of the missile from the building.

Commander HUMES. Yes, sir; there is one difficulty, and that is the defect of exit was so broad that one has to rely more on the inclination of the entrance than they do connecting in this instance entrance and exit because so much of the skull was carried away in this fashion.

Senator COOPER. That was my second question.

My first question was would it be possible physically to establish the degree of angle of the trajectory of the bullet?

Commander HUMES. Within limited accuracy, sir.

Senator COOPER. Within limited accuracy.

That being true then my second question was whether the point of entry of the bullet, point A, and the, what you call the exit——

Commander HUMES. Exit.

Senator COOPER. Did you establish them so exactly that they could be related to the degree of angle of the trajectory of the bullet?

Commander HUMES. Yes, sir; to our satisfaction we did ascertain that fact.

Mr. DULLES. Just one other question.

Am I correct in assuming from what you have said that this wound is entirely inconsistent with a wound that might have been administered if the shot were fired from in front or the side of the President: it had to be fired from behind the President?

Commander HUMES. Scientifically, sir, it is impossible for it to have been fired from other than behind. Or to have exited from other than behind.

Mr. McCLOY. This is so obvious that I rather hesitate to ask it. There is no question in your mind that it was a lethal bullet?

Commander HUMES. The President, sir, could not possibly have survived the effect of that injury no matter what would have been done for him.

The CHAIRMAN. Mr. Specter.

Mr. SPECTER. What conclusions did you reach then as to the trajectory or point of origin of the bullet, Dr. Humes, based on 388?

Commander HUMES. We reached the conclusion that this missile was fired toward the President from a point above and behind him, sir.

Mr. SPECTER. Now, on one detail on your report, Dr. Humes, on page 4, on the third line down, you note that there is a lacerated wound measuring 15 by 6 mm. which on the smaller size is, of course, less than 6.5 mm.?

Commander HUMES. Yes, sir.

Mr. SPECTER. What would be the explanation for that variation?

Commander HUMES. This is in the scalp, sir, and I believe that this is explainable on the elastic recoil of the tissues of the skin, sir. It is not infrequent in missile wounds of this type that the measured wound is slightly smaller than the caliber of the missile that traversed it.

Mr. SPECTER. Would you proceed, now then to the other major wound of entry which you have already noted and described?

Commander HUMES. Yes, sir.

Mr. SPECTER. Its point of origin, where it hit the President.

Commander HUMES. I—our previously submitted report, which is Commission No. 387, identified a wound in the low posterior neck of the President.

The size of this wound was 4 by 7 mm., with the long axis being in accordance with the long axis of the body, 44 mm. wide, in other words, 7 mm. long.

We attempted to locate such wounds in soft tissue by making reference to bony structures which do not move and are, therefore, good reference points for this type of investigation.

We then ascertained, we chose the two bony points of reference—we chose to locate this wound, where the mastoid process, which is just behind the ear, the top of the mastoid process, and the acromion which is the tip of the shoulder joint. We ascertained physical measurement at the time of autopsy that this wound was 14 cm. from the tip of the mastoid process and 14 cm. from the acromion was its central point—

Mr. SPECTER. That is the right acromion?

Commander HUMES. The tip of the right acromion, yes, sir, and that is why we have depicted it in figure 385 in this location.

This wound appeared physically quite similar to the wound which we have described before in 388 "A," with the exception that its long axis was shorter than the long axis of the wound described above. When the tissues beneath this wound were inspected, there was a defect corresponding with the skin defect in the fascia overlying the musculature of the low neck and upper back.

I mentioned previously that X-rays were made of the entire body of the late President. Of course, and here I must say that as I describe something to you, I might have done it before or after in the description but for the sake of understanding, we examined carefully the bony structures in this vicinity as well as the X-rays, to see if there was any evidence of fracture or of deposition of metallic fragments in the depths of this wound, and we saw no such evidence, that is no fracture of the bones of the shoulder girdle, or of the vertical column, and no metallic fragments were detectable by X-ray examination.

Attempts to probe in the vicinity of this wound were unsuccessful without fear of making a false passage.

Mr. SPECTER. What do you mean by that, Doctor?

Commander HUMES. Well, the defect in the fascia was quite similar, which is the first firm tissue over the muscle beneath the skin, was quite similar to this. We were unable, however, to take probes and have them satisfactorily fall through any definite path at this point.

Now, to explain the situation in the President's neck, I think it will be necessary for me to refer back to Exhibit 385, I believe the number is correct.

Mr. SPECTER. Yes; please do, that is 385.

Commander HUMES. Now, as the President's body was viewed from anteriorly in the autopsy room, and saying nothing for the moment about the missile, there was a recent surgical defect in the low anterior neck, which measured some 7 or 8 cm. in length or let's say a recent wound was present in this area.

This wound was through the skin, through the subcutaneous tissues and into the larynx. Or rather into the trachea of the President.

Mr. SPECTER. To digress chronologically——

Commander HUMES. Yes.

Mr. SPECTER. Did you have occasion to discuss that wound on the front side of the President with Dr. Malcolm Perry of Parkland Hospital in Dallas?

Commander HUMES. Yes, sir; I did. I had the impression from seeing the wound that it represented a surgical tracheotomy wound, a wound frequently made by surgeons when people are in respiratory distress to give them a free airway.

To ascertain that point, I called on the telephone Dr. Malcolm Perry and discussed with him the situation of the President's neck when he first examined the President, and asked him had he in fact done a tracheotomy which was somewhat redundant because I was somewhat certain he had.

He said, yes; he had done a tracheotomy and that as the point to perform his tracheotomy he used a wound which he had interpreted as a missile wound in the low neck, as the point through which to make the tracheotomy incision.

Mr. SPECTER. When did you have that conversation with him, Dr. Humes?

Commander HUMES. I had that conversation early on Saturday morning, sir.

Mr. SPECTER. On Saturday morning, November 23d?

Commander HUMES. That is correct, sir.

Mr. SPECTER. And have you had occasion since to examine the report of Parkland Hospital which I made available to you?

Commander HUMES. Yes, sir; I have.

Mr. SPECTER. May it please the Commission, I would like to note this as Commission Exhibit No. 392, and subject to later technical proof, to have it admitted into evidence at this time for the purpose of having the doctor comment about it.

The CHAIRMAN. It may be so marked.

(The document referred to was marked Commission Exhibit No. 392, for identification.)

Mr. SPECTER. What did your examination of the Parkland Hospital records disclose with respect to this wound on the front side of the President's body?

Commander HUMES. The examination of this record from Parkland Hospital revealed that Doctor Perry had observed this wound as had other physicians in attendance upon the President, and actually before a tracheotomy was performed surgically, an endotracheal tube was placed through the President's mouth and down his larynx and into his trachea which is the first step in giving satisfactory airway to a person injured in such fashion and unconscious.

The President was unconscious and it is most difficult to pass such a tube when the person is unconscious.

The person who performed that procedure, that is instilled the endotrachea tube noted that there was a wound of the trachea below the larynx, which corresponded in essence with the wound of the skin which they had observed from the exterior.

Mr. SPECTER. How is that wound described, while you are mentioning the wound?

Commander HUMES. Yes, sir.

Mr. SPECTER. I think you will find that on the first page of the summary sheet, Dr. Humes.

Commander HUMES. Yes, sir. Thank you.

This report was written by doctor—or of the activities of Dr. James Carrico, Doctor Carrico in inserting the endotracheal tube noted a ragged wound of trachea immediately below the larynx.

The report, as I recall it, and I have not studied it in minute detail, would indicate to me that Doctor Perry realizing from Doctor Carrico's observation that there was a wound of the trachea would quite logically use the wound which he had observed as a point to enter the trachea since the trachea was almost damaged, that would be a logical place in which to put his incision.

In speaking of that wound in the neck, Doctor Perry told me that before he enlarged it to make the tracheotomy wound it was a "few millimeters in diameter."

Of course by the time we saw it, as my associates and as you have heard, it was considerably larger and no longer at all obvious as a missile wound.

The report states, and Doctor Perry told me in telephone conversation that there was bubbling of air and blood in the vicinity of this wound when he made the tracheotomy. This caused him to believe that perhaps there had been a violation of one of the—one or other of the pleural cavities by a missile. He, therefore, asked one of his associates, and the record is to me somewhat confused as to which of his associates, he asked one of his associates to put in a chest tube. This is a maneuver which is, was quite logical under the circumstances, and which would, if a tube that were placed through all layers of the wall of the chest, and the chest cavity had been violated one could remove air that had gotten in there and greatly assist respiration.

So when we examined the President in addition to the large wound which

362

we found in conversation with Doctor Perry was the tracheotomy wound, there were two smaller wounds on the upper anterior chest.

Mr. DULLES. These are apparently exit wounds?

Commander HUMES. Sir, these were knife wounds, these were incised wounds on either side of the chest, and I will give them in somewhat greater detail.

These wounds were bilateral, they were situated on the anterior chest wall in the nipple line, and each were 2 cm. long in the transverse axis. The one on the right was situated 11 cm. above the nipple—the one on the left was situated 11 cm. on the nipple, and the one on the right was 8 cm. above the nipple. Their intention was to incise through the President's chest to place tubes into his chest.

We examined those wounds very carefully, and found that they, however, did not enter the chest cavity. They only went through the skin.

I presume that as they were performing that procedure it was obvious that the President had died, and they didn't pursue this.

To complete the examination of the area of the neck and the chest, I will do that together, we made the customary incision which we use in a routine postmortem examination which is a Y-shaped incision from the shoulders over the lower portion of the breastbone and over to the opposite shoulder and reflected the skin and tissues from the anterior portion of the chest.

We examined in the region of this incised surgical wound which was the tracheotomy wound and we saw that there was some bruising of the muscles of the neck in the depths of this wound as well as laceration or defect in the trachea.

At this point, of course, I am unable to say how much of the defect in the trachea was made by the knife of the surgeon, and how much of the defect was made by the missile wound. That would have to be ascertained from the surgeon who actually did the tracheotomy.

There was, however, some ecchymosis or contusion, of the muscles of the right anterior neck inferiorly, without, however, any disruption of the muscles or any significant tearing of the muscles.

The muscles in this area of the body run roughly, as you see as he depicted them here. We have removed some of them for a point I will make in a moment, but it is our opinion that the missile traversed the neck and slid between these muscles and other vital structures with a course in the neck such as the carotid artery, the jugular vein and other structures because there was no massive hemmorhage or other massive injury in this portion of the neck.

In attempting to relate findings within the President's body to this wound which we had observed low in his neck, we then opened his chest cavity, and we very carefully examined the lining of his chest cavity and both of his lungs. We found that there was, in fact, no defect in the pleural lining of the President's chest.

It was completely intact.

However, over the apex of the right pleural cavity, and the pleura now has two layers. It has a parietal or a layer which lines the chest cavity and it has a visceral layer which is intimately in association with the lung.

As depicted in figure 385, in the apex of the right pleural cavity there was a bruise or contusion or ecchymosis of the parietal pleura as well as a bruise of the upper portion, the most apical portion of the right lung.

It, therefore, was our opinion that the missile while not penetrating physically the pleural cavity, as it passed that point bruised either the missile itself, or the force of its passage through the tissues, bruised both the parietal and the visceral pleura.

The area of discoloration on the apical portion of the right upper lung measured five centimeters in greatest diameter, and was wedge shaped in configuration, with its base toward the top of the chest and its apex down towards the substance of the lung.

Once again Kodachrome photographs were made of this area in the interior of the President's chest.

Mr. SPECTER. Would you mark the point on Exhibit 385, the one on the rear of the President as point "C" and the one on the front of the President as point "D" so we can discuss those, Dr. Humes?

Now, what conclusion did you reach, if any, as to whether point "C" was the point of entry or exit?

Commander HUMES. We reached the conclusion that point "C" was a point of entry.

Mr. SPECTER. What characteristics of that wound led you to that conclusion?

Commander HUMES. The characteristics here were basically similar to the characteristics above, lacking one very valuable clue or piece of evidence rather than clue, because it is more truly a piece of evidence in the skull. The skull as I mentioned before had the bone with the characteristic defect made as a missile traverses bone.

This missile, to the best of our ability to ascertain, struck no bone protuberances, no bony prominences, no bones as it traversed the President's body. But it was a sharply delineated wound. It was quite regular in its outline. It measured, as I mentioned, 7 by 4 mm. Its margins were similar in all respects when viewed with the naked eye to the wound in the skull, which we feel incontrovertibly was a wound of entrance.

The defect in the fascia which is that layer of connective tissue over the muscle just beneath the wound corresponded virtually exactly to the defect in the skin.

And for these reasons we felt that this was a wound of entrance.

Mr. SPECTER. Did you search the body to determine if there was any bullet inside the body?

Commander HUMES. Before the arrival of Colonel Finck we had made X-rays of the head, neck and torso of the President, and the upper portions of his major extremities, or both his upper and lower extremities. At Colonel Finck's suggestion, we then completed the X-ray examination by X-raying the President's body in toto, and those X-rays are available.

Mr. SPECTER. What did those X-rays disclose with respect to the possible presence of a missile in the President's body?

Commander HUMES. They showed no evidence of a missile in the President's body at any point. And these were examined by ourselves and by the radiologist, who assisted us in this endeavor.

Mr. SPECTER. What conclusion, if any, did you reach as to whether point "D" on 385 was the point of entrance or exit?

Commander HUMES. We concluded that this missile depicted in 385 "C" which entered the President's body traversed the President's body and made its exit through the wound observed by the physicians at Parkland Hospital and later extended as a tracheotomy wound.

Mr. SPECTER. Does the description "ragged wound" which is found in the Parkland report shed any light in and of itself as to whether point "D" is an exit or entry wound?

Commander HUMES. I believe, sir, that that statement goes on, ragged wound in the trachea. I don't believe that refers to the skin. And you might say that it is a ragged wound is more likely to be a wound of exit.

However, the trachea has little cartilaginous rings which have a tendency, which would be disrupted by this, and most wounds of the trachea unless very cleverly incised would perhaps appear slightly ragged.

Mr. SPECTER. Now, what was the angle, if any, that you observed on the path of the bullet, as you outlined it?

Commander HUMES. The angle which we observed in measuring, in comparing the point of entrance, our point of entrance labeled "C" on 385 and "D" point of exit is one that the point of exit is below the point of entrance compared with the vertical.

Mr. SPECTER. Have you had an opportunity to examine the clothing which has been identified for you as being that worn by the President on the day of the assassination?

Commander HUMES. Yes; yesterday, just shortly before the Commission hearing today was begun, Mr. Chief Justice, we had opportunity for the first time to examine the clothing worn by the late President.

In private conversation among ourselves before this opportunity, we predicted we would find defects in the clothing corresponding with the defects which were found, of course, on the body of the late President.

Mr. SPECTER. Mr. Chief Justice, may it please the Commission, I would like to have identified for the record three articles on which I have placed Commission Exhibits Nos. 393 being the coat worn by the President, 394 being the shirt, and 395 being the President's tie, and at this time move for their admission into evidence.

The CHAIRMAN. It may be admitted.

(The articles of clothing referred to were marked Commission Exhibits Nos. 393, 394 and 395 for identification, and received in evidence.)

Mr. SPECTER. Taking 393 at the start, Doctor Humes, will you describe for the record what hole, if any, is observable in the back of that garment which would be at or about the spot you have described as being the point of entry on the President's back or lower neck.

Commander HUMES. Yes, sir. This exhibit is a grey suit coat stated to have been worn by the President on the day of his death. Situated to the right of the midline high in the back portion of the coat is a defect, one margin of which is semicircular.

Situated above it just below the collar is an additional defect. It is our opinion that the lower of these defects corresponds essentially with the point of entrance of the missile at Point C on Exhibit 385.

Mr. SPECTER. Would it be accurate to state that the hole which you have identified as being the point of entry is approximately 6 inches below the top of the collar, and 2 inches to the right of the middle seam of the coat?

Commander HUMES. That is approximately correct, sir. This defect, I might say, continues on through the material.

Attached to this garment is the memorandum which states that one half of the area around the hole which was presented had been removed by experts, I believe, at the Federal Bureau of Investigation, and also that a control area was taken from under the collar, so it is my interpretation that this defect at the top of this garment is the control area taken by the Bureau, and that the reason the lower defect is not more circle or oval in outline is because a portion of that defect has been removed apparently for physical examinations.

Mr. SPECTER. Now, does the one which you have described as the entry of the bullet go all the way through?

Commander HUMES. Yes. sir; it goes through both layers.

Mr. SPECTER. How about the upper one of the collar you have described, does that go all the way through?

Commander HUMES. Yes, sir; it goes all the way through. It is not—wait a minute, excuse me—it is not so clearly a puncture wound as the one below.

Mr. SPECTER. Does the upper one go all the way through in the same course?

Commander HUMES. No.

Mr. SPECTER. Through the inner side as it went through the outer side?

Commander HUMES. No, in an irregular fashion.

Mr. SPECTER. Will you take Commission Exhibit 394 and describe what that is, first of all, please?

Commander HUMES. This is the shirt, blood-stained shirt, purportedly worn by the President on the day of his assassination. When viewed from behind at a point which corresponds essentially with the point of defect on the jacket, one sees an irregularly oval defect.

When viewed anteriorly, with the top button buttoned, two additional defects are seen. Of course, with the shirt buttoned, the fly front of the shirt causes two layers of cloth to be present in this location, and that there is a defect in the inner layer of cloth and a corresponding defect in the outer layer of the cloth.

Mr. SPECTER. Is there any observable indication from the fibers on the front side of the shirt to indicate in which direction a missile might have passed through those two tears?

Commander HUMES. From an examination of these defects at this point, it would appear that the missile traversed these two layers from within to the exterior.

Mr. SPECTER. Would it be accurate to state that the hole in the back of the shirt is approximately 6 inches below the top of the collar and 2 inches to the right of the middle seam of the shirt?

Commander HUMES. That is approximately correct, sir.

Mr. SPECTER. Now, how, if at all, do the holes in the shirt and coat conform to the wound of entrance which you described as point "C" on Commission Exhibit 385?

Commander HUMES. We believe that they conform quite well. When viewing—first of all, the wounds or the defects in 393 and 394 coincide virtually exactly with one another.

They give the appearance when viewed separately and not as part of the clothing of a clothed person as being perhaps, somewhat lower on the Exhibits 393 and 394 than we have depicted them in Exhibit No. 385. We believe there are two reasons for this.

385 is a schematic representation, and the photographs would be more accurate as to the precise location, but more particularly the way in which these defects would conform with such a defect on the torso would depend on the girth of the shoulders and configuration of the base of the neck of the individual, and the relative position of the shirt and coat to the tissues of the body at the time of the impact of the missile.

Mr. SPECTER. As to the muscular status of the President, what was it?

Commander HUMES. The President was extremely well-developed, an extremely well-developed, muscular young man with a very well-developed set of muscles in his thoraco and shoulder girdle.

Mr. SPECTER. What effect would that have on the positioning of the shirt and coat with respect to the position of the neck in and about the seam?

Commander HUMES. I believe this would have a tendency to push the portions of the coat which show the defects here somewhat higher on the back of the President than on a man of less muscular development.

Mr. SPECTER. Mr. Chief Justice, may it please the Commission, I would like to mark for identification Exhibit 396, which later proof will show is a picture of President Kennedy shortly before the first bullet struck him, and ask the doctor to take a look at that.

Will you describe, Doctor Humes, the position of President Kennedy's right hand in that picture?

Commander HUMES. Yes. This exhibit, Commission Exhibit No. 396, allegedly taken just prior to the wounding of the late President, shows him with his hand raised, his elbow bent, apparently in saluting the crowd. I believe that this action——

Mr. SPECTER. Which hand was that?

Commander HUMES. This was his right hand, sir. I believe that this action would further accentuate the elevation of the coat and the shirt with respect to the back of the Presideent.

Mr. SPECTER. Now, Doctor Humes, will you take Commission Exhibit No. 395——

Mr. McCLOY. Before you go, may I ask a question? In your examination of the shirt, I just want to get it in the record, from your examination of the shirt, there is no defect in the collar of the shirt which coincides with the defect in the back of the President's coat, am I correct?

Commander HUMES. You are correct, sir. There is no such defect.

Mr. SPECTER. As to Commission Exhibit 395, Dr. Humes, will you identify what that is, please?

Commander HUMES. We had an opportunity to examine this exhibit before the Commission met today, sir. This is Commission Exhibit No. 395, and is the neck tie purportedly worn, purportedly to have been worn, by the late President on the day of his assassination.

Mr. SPECTER. What defect, if any, is noted on the tie which would correspond with the path of a missile apparently passing through the folds of the shirt which you have already described?

Commander HUMES. This tie is one of those—this tie is still in its knotted state, as we examine it at this time. The portion of the tie around the neck has been severed apparently with scissors or other sharp instrument accounting for the loop about the neck.

The tie is tied in four-in-hand fashion but somewhat askew from the way a person would normally tie a four-in-hand knot.

Situated on the left anterior aspect of this knotted portion of the tie at a point approximately corresponding with the defects noted previously in the two layers of the shirt is a superficial tear of the outer layer only of the fabric of this tie which, I believe, could have been caused by a glancing blow to this portion of the tie by a missile.

Mr. SPECTER. Mr. Chief Justice, I move at this time for the admission into evidence of Exhibits 393 through Exhibit 396, the three articles of clothing and the photograph which we have just used.

The CHAIRMAN. They may be admitted.

(Exhibits Nos. 393 through 396 were received in evidence and may be found in the Commission files.)

Mr. McCLOY. Commander, did you say left or right?

Commander HUMES. No, sir. In fact, the way this bow is tied now it would appear to be on the left of this tie, but it is kind of twisted out of shape.

Mr. McCLOY. Yes. It is twisted. It is not too clear.

Commander HUMES. It is not too clear, it is not clear how that might have been in position with the shirt, sir.

Mr. SPECTER. Now, Doctor Humes, at one point in your examination of the President, did you make an effort to probe the point of entry with your finger?

Commander HUMES. Yes, sir; I did.

Mr. SPECTER. And at or about that time when you were trying to ascertain, as you previously testified, whether there was any missile in the body of the President, did someone from the Secret Service call your attention to the fact that a bullet had been found on a stretcher at Parkland Hospital?

Commander HUMES. Yes, sir; they did.

Mr. SPECTER. And in that posture of your examination, having just learned of the presence of a bullet on a stretcher, did that call to your mind any tentative explanatory theory of the point of entry or exit of the bullet which you have described as entering at Point "C" on Exhibit 385?

Commander HUMES. Yes, sir. We were able to ascertain with absolute certainty that the bullet had passed by the apical portion of the right lung producing the injury which we mentioned.

I did not at that point have the information from Doctor Perry about the wound in the anterior neck, and while that was a possible explanation for the point of exit, we also had to consider the possibility that the missile in some rather inexplicable fashion had been stopped in its path through the President's body and, in fact, then had fallen from the body onto the stretcher.

Mr. SPECTER. And what theory did you think possible, at that juncture, to explain the passing of the bullet back out the point of entry; or had you been provided with the fact that external heart massage had been performed on the President?

Commander HUMES. Yes, sir; we had, and we considered the possibility that some of the physical maneuvering performed by the doctors might have in some way caused this event to take place.

Mr. SPECTER. Now, have you since discounted that possibility, Doctor Humes?

Commander HUMES. Yes; in essence we have. When examining the wounds in the base of the President's neck anteriorly, the region of the tracheotomy performed at Parkland Hospital, we noted, and we noted in our record, some contusion and bruising of the muscles of the neck of the President. We noted that at the time of the postmortem examination.

Now, we also made note of the types of wounds which I mentioned to you before in this testimony on the chest which were going to be used by the doctors there to place chest tubes. They also made other wounds, one on the left arm, and a wound on the ankle of the President with the idea of administering intravenous blood and other fluids in hope of replacing the blood which the President had lost from his extensive wounds.

Those wounds showed no evidence of bruising or contusion or physical violence, which made us reach the conclusion that they were performed during the agonal moments of the late president, and when the circulation was, in essence, very seriously embarrassed, if not nonfunctional. So that these wounds, the wound of the chest and the wound of the arm and of the ankle were performed about the same time as the tracheotomy wound because only a very few moments of time elapsed when all this was going on.

So, therefore, we reached the conclusion that the damage to these muscles on the anterior neck just below this wound were received at approximately the same time that the wound here on the top of the pleural cavity was, while the President still lived and while his heart and lungs were operating in such a fashion to permit him to have a bruise in the vicinity, because that he did have in these strap muscles in the neck, but he didn't have in the areas of the other incisions that were made at Parkland Hospital. So we feel that, had this missile not made its path in that fashion, the wound made by Doctor Perry in the neck would not have been able to produce, wouldn't have been able to produce, these contusions of the musculature of the neck.

Mr. DULLES. Could I ask a question about the missile, the bullet, I am a little bit—the bullet, I am a little bit—confused. It was found on the stretcher. Did the President's body remain on the stretcher while it was in the hospital?

Commander HUMES. Of that point I have no knowledge. The only——

Mr. DULLES. Why would it—would this operating have anything to do with the bullet being on the stretcher unless the President's body remained on the stretcher after he was taken into the hospital; is that possible?

Commander HUMES. It is quite possible, sir.

Mr. DULLES. Otherwise it seems to me the bullet would have to have been ejected from the body before he was taken or put on the bed in the hospital.

Commander HUMES. Right, sir. I, of course, was not there. I don't know how he was handled in the hospital, in what conveyance. I do know he was on his back during the period of his stay in the hospital; Doctor Perry told me that.

Mr. DULLES. Yes; and wasn't turned over.

Commander HUMES. That is right.

Mr. DULLES. So he might have been on the stretcher the whole time, is that your view?

The CHAIRMAN. He said he had no view. He wasn't there, he doesn't know anything about it.

Mr. DULLES. Yes. I wonder if there is other evidence of this.

Mr. SPECTER. There has been other evidence, Mr. Dulles. If I may say at this point, we shall produce later, subject to sequential proof, evidence that the stretcher on which this bullet was found was the stretcher of Governor Connally. We have a sequence of events on the transmission of that stretcher which ties that down reasonably closely, so that on the night of the autopsy itself, as the information I have been developing indicates, the thought preliminarily was that was from President Kennedy's stretcher, and that is what led to the hypothesis which we have been exploring about, but which has since been rejected. But at any rate the evidence will show that it was from Governor Connally's stretcher that the bullet was found.

Mr. DULLES. So this bullet is still missing?

Mr. SPECTER. That is the subject of some theories I am about to get into. That is an elusive subject, but Dr. Humes has some views on it, and we might just as well go into those now.

Mr. MCCLOY. Before he gets into that, may I ask a question?

The CHAIRMAN. Surely, go right ahead.

Mr. MCCLOY. Quite apart from the President's clothing, now directing your attention to the flight of the bullet, quite apart from the evidence given by the President's clothing, you, I believe, indicated that the flight of the bullet was from the back, from above and behind. It took roughly the line which is shown on your Exhibit 385.

Commander HUMES. Yes, sir.

Mr. MCCLOY. I am not clear what induced you to come to that conclusion if you couldn't find the actual exit wound by reason of the tracheotomy.

Commander HUMES. The report which we have submitted, sir, represents our thinking within the 24–48 hours of the death of the President, all facts taken into account of the situation.

The wound in the anterior portion of the lower neck is physically lower than the point of entrance posteriorly, sir.

Mr. MCCLOY. That is what I wanted to bring out.

Commander HUMES. Yes, sir.

Mr. McCLOY. May I ask this: In spite of the incision made by the tracheotomy, was there any evidence left of the exit aperture?

Commander HUMES. Unfortunately not that we could ascertain, sir.

Mr. McCLOY. I see.

Mr. DULLES. There is no evidence in the coat or the shirt of an exit through the coat or shirt.

Commander HUMES. There is no exit through the coat, sir. But these two, in the shirt, of course—excuse me, sir—there is. The entrance by our calculations—

Mr. DULLES. The entrance I know.

Commander HUMES. Posteriorly.

Mr. DULLES. What about the exit?

Commander HUMES. The exit wounds are just below.

Mr. DULLES. But there was no coat to exit through.

Commander HUMES. No; anteriorly the coat was quite open.

Senator COOPER. May I ask a question?

Commander HUMES. Yes, sir, Senator.

Senator COOPER. Assuming that we draw a straight line from Point "C" which you have described as a possible point of entry of the missile, to Point "D" where you saw an incision of the tracheotomy——

Commander HUMES. Yes, sir.

Senator COOPER. What would be the relation of the bruise at the apex of the pleural sac to such a line?

Commander HUMES. It would be exactly in line with such a line, sir, exactly.

Senator COOPER. What was the character of the bruise that you saw there?

Commander HUMES. The bruise here, photographs are far superior to my humble verbal description, but if I let my hand in cup shaped fashion represent the apical parietal pleura, it was an area approximately 5 cm. in greatest diameter of purplish blue discoloration of the parietal pleura. Corresponding exactly with it, with the lung sitting below it, was a roughly pyramid-shaped bruise with its base toward the surface of the upper portion of the lung, and the apex down into the lung tissue, and the whole thing measured about 5 cm., which is a little—2 inches in extent, sir.

Senator COOPER. What would be the—can you describe the covering around the apex of the pleural sac, the nature of its protection. My point is to get your opinion as to whether some other factor, some factor other than the missile could have caused this bruise which you saw.

Commander HUMES. A couple of ways we might do this, sir. One with regard to temporal, it was quite fresh. When examined under the microscope, the lung in this area had recent hemorrhaging in it. The red blood cells were well-preserved, as they would be if it happened quite recently before death, as was the red blood cells where they had gotten out into the lung tissue near there.

The discoloration was essentially of the same character as the discoloration in the muscles adjacent thereto, which would roughly again place it temporally in approximately the same time since bruises change color as time goes by, and these appeared quite fresh.

This is with regard to time—I don't know whether that is the right parameter in which you wished to study it, Senator.

Senator COOPER. My question really went to this point: Considering the location of the bruise at the apex of the pleural sac——

Commander HUMES. Yes, sir.

Senator COOPER. And of the tissue or muscles around it, was there any other factor which you could think of that might have caused that bruise other than the passage of a missile?

Commander HUMES. It was so well localized that I truthfully, sir, can't think of any other way.

Senator COOPER. That is all.

Mr. McCLOY. May I ask you one question which, perhaps, the answer is quite obvious. If, contrary to the evidence that we have here, that anterior wound was the wound of entry, the shot must have come from below the President to have followed that path.

Commander HUMES. That course, that is correct, sir.

369

Mr. SPECTER. Dr. Humes, can you compare the angles of declination on 385, point "C" to "D", with 388 "A" to "B"?

Commander HUMES. You will note, and again I must apologize for the schematic nature of these diagrams drawn to a certain extent from memory and to a certain extent from the written record, it would appear that the angle of declination is somewhat sharper in the head wound, 388, than it is in 385.

The reason for this, we feel, by the pattern of the entrance wound at 388 "A" causes us to feel that the President's head was bent forward, and we feel this accounts for the difference in the angle, plus undoubtedly the wounds were not received absolutely simultaneously, so that the vehicle in which the President was traveling moved during this period of time, which would account for a difference in the line of flight, sir.

Mr. SPECTER. Aside from the slight differences which are notable by observing those two exhibits, are they roughly comparable to the angle of decline?

Commander HUMES. I believe them to be roughly comparable, sir.

Mr. SPECTER. Could you state for the record an approximation of the angle of decline?

Commander HUMES. Mathematics is not my forte. Approximately 45 degrees from the horizontal.

Mr. SPECTER. Would you elaborate somewhat, Doctor Humes, on why the angle would change by virtue of a tilting of the head of the President since the basis of the computation of angle is with respect to the ground?

Commander HUMES. I find the question a little difficult of answering right off, forgive me, sir.

Mr. SPECTER. I will try to rephrase it. Stated more simply, why would the tilting of the President's head affect the angle of the decline? You stated that was——

Commander HUMES. The angle that I am making an observation most about is the angle made that we envisioned having been made by the impingement of the bullet in its flight at the point of entry. This angle we see by the difference of the measurement of the two wounds.

Therefore, this is—we have several angles we are talking about here, unfortunately, this is—the angle of which we speak in this location, "A" to "B", and it is difficult.

I have to retract. Since we feel from their physical configurations, wounds 385 "C" and 388 "A" are entrance wounds, if there wasn't some significant change in the angulation of the President's head with respect to the line of flight from these missiles, the physical measurements of 385 "C" and this 388 "A" should be similar. They aren't, in fact, dissimilar in that there is a greater angulation in 388 "A". Therefore, there has to be either a change in the position of the vehicle in which the President is riding with respect to the horizontal or a change in the situation of the President's head. I believe that the exhibits submitted earlier, the photograph——

Mr. SPECTER. I believe the ones were given to you so far—excuse me, you are right, 389.

Commander HUMES. 389, in fact at this point shows the President's head in a slightly inclined forward position, and I am not enough aware of the geography of the ground over which the vehicle was traveling to know how much that would affect it.

Mr. SPECTER. If you were to be told that there was a distance traversed of approximately 150 feet from the time of Point "C" on 385 to Point "A" on 388, and you would assume the additional factor that there was a slight angle of decline on the street as well, would those factors, assuming them to be true, help in the explanation of the differences in the angles?

Commander HUMES. I think that they would make the figure as depicted in 388 quite understandably different from 385.

Mr. DULLES. Was it possible, in view of the condition of the brain to point with absolute accuracy to the point of exit there? I can see that the point of exit in 385 can be clearly determined. Is it equally possible to determine the point of exit in 388?

Commander HUMES. No, sir; it was not, other than through this large defect because when——

370

Mr. DULLES. Therefore, that angle might be somewhat different.

Commander HUMES. Might be somewhat different, sir. I think we made reference to that somewhat earlier. The fragments were so difficult to replace in their precise anatomic location——

Mr. DULLES. That is what I thought, but I wasn't sure.

Commander HUMES. That is correct.

Mr. McCLOY. I would like to ask a question in regard to 385 similar to that I asked as to 388. In your opinion, was the 385 wound lethal?

Commander HUMES. No, sir.

Mr. DULLES. With the wound in 385, would it have affected the President's power of speech?

Commander HUMES. It could have, sir. The wound caused a defect in his trachea which would most usually have caused at least some defect in the proper phonation, sir.

(Discussion off the record.)

The CHAIRMAN. On the record.

Mr. SPECTER. In response to Mr. Dulles' question a moment ago, Doctor Humes, you commented that they did not turn him over at Parkland. Will you state for the record what the source of your information is on that?

Commander HUMES. Yes. This is a result of a personal telephone conversation between myself and Dr. Malcolm Perry early in the morning of Saturday, November 23.

Mr. SPECTER. At that time did Doctor Perry tell you specifically, Doctor Humes, that the Parkland doctors had not observed the wound in the President's back?

Commander HUMES. He told me that the President was on his back from the time he was brought into the hospital until the time he left it, and that at no time was he turned from his back by the doctors.

Mr. SPECTER. And at the time of your conversation with Doctor Perry did you tell Doctor Perry anything of your observations or conclusions?

Commander HUMES. No, sir; I did not.

(A short recess was taken.)

The CHAIRMAN. Gentlemen, the Commission will be in order. We will continue with the examination.

Mr. SPECTER. Doctor Humes, as to points of entry on the body of the late President, how many were there in total?

Commander HUMES. Two, sir, as depicted in 385–C and 388–A.

Mr. SPECTER. And to points of exit, how many were there?

Commander HUMES. Two, sir, as depicted in 385–D and the vicinity of 388–B. I make the latter remark as was developed earlier, in that the size of the large defect in the skull was so great and the fragmentation was so complex that it was impossible to accurately pinpoint the exit of the missile in the head wound.

Mr. SPECTER. Now as to that last factor, would the X-rays be of material assistance to you in pinpointing the specific locale of the exit?

Commander HUMES. I do not believe so, sir. The only path that the X-rays show in any detail are of the minor fragments which passed from point A to point B.

Mr. SPECTER. Now that you have finished your major descriptions of the wounds, can you be any more specific in telling us in what way the availability of the x-rays would assist in further specifying the nature of the wounds?

Commander HUMES. I do not believe, sir, that the availability of the X-rays would materially assist the Commission.

Mr. SPECTER. How about the same question as to the pictures?

Commander HUMES. The pictures would show more accurately and in more detail the character of the wounds as depicted particularly in 385 and 386 and in 388–A. They would also perhaps give the Commissioners a better—better is not the best term, but a more graphic picture of the massive defect in 388.

Mr. SPECTER. Going back for a moment, Doctor Humes——

The CHAIRMAN. Before we get off that, may I ask you this, Commander: If we had the pictures here and you could look them over again and restate your opinion, would it cause you to change any of the testimony you have given here?

Commander HUMES. To the best of my recollection, Mr. Chief Justice, it would not.

The CHAIRMAN. Mr. McCloy.

Mr. McCLOY. May I ask this question?

The CHAIRMAN. Go right ahead.

Mr. McCLOY. Do you have any knowledge as to whether or not any photographs were taken in Dallas?

Commander HUMES. I have none, sir, no knowledge.

Mr. McCLOY. No knowledge that any were taken?

Representative FORD. May I ask what size are the pictures to which you refer?

Commander HUMES. We exposed both black and white and color negatives, Congressman. They were exposed in the morgue during the examination. They were not developed. The kodachrome negatives when developed would be 405. They were in film carriers or cassettes, as were the black and white. Of course they could be magnified.

Representative FORD. Have those been examined by personnel at Bethesda?

Commander HUMES. No, sir. We exposed these negatives; we turned them over. Here I must ask the counsel again for advice—to the Secret Service.

Mr. SPECTER. Yes; it was the Secret Service.

Commander HUMES. They were turned over to the Secret Service in their cassettes unexposed, and I have not seen any of them since. This is the photographs. The X-rays were developed in our X-ray department on the spot that evening, because we had to see those right then as part of our examination, but the photographs were made for the record and for other purposes.

Representative FORD. But they had never been actually developed for viewing.

Commander HUMES. I do not know, sir.

Mr. SPECTER. Doctor Humes, back to the angles for just a moment.

Commander HUMES. Yes, sir.

Mr. SPECTER. Hypothesize or assume, if you will, that other evidence will show that the wound inflicted on Commission Exhibit 385 at point C occurred while the President was riding in the rear seat of his automobile approximately 100 feet from a point of origin in a six-floor building nearby, and assume further that the wound inflicted in 388 at point A occurred when the President was approximately 250 feet away from the same point.

With those assumptions in mind, there would be somewhat different angles of declination going from C to D on 385 and from A to B on 388.

Commander HUMES. I would expect there would.

Mr. SPECTER. You have already testified earlier today that you were unable to pinpoint with precision angle A to B on 388 because of the reconstruction of the scalp.

Now my question to you, in that elongated fashion, is from what you know and what you have described, are the angles, as you have expressed them to be in your opinion, consistent with a situation where the two wounds were inflicted at the angles and at the distances just described to you?

Commander HUMES. I believe they are consistent. I would state that the path outlined on 388–A to B is to a certain extent conjectural for the reasons given before.

Mr. SPECTER. Now, Doctor Humes, I hand you a group of documents which have been marked as Commission Exhibit No. 397 and ask you if you can identify what they are?

Commander HUMES. Yes, sir; these are various notes in long-hand, or copies rather, of various notes in long-hand made by myself, in part, during the performance of the examination of the late President, and in part after the examination when I was preparing to have a typewritten report made.

Mr. SPECTER. Are there also included there some notes that you made while you talked to Doctor Perry on the telephone?

Commander HUMES. Yes, sir; there are.

Mr. SPECTER. Are there any notes which you made at any time which are not included in this group of notes?

Commander HUMES. Yes, sir; there are.

Mr. SPECTER. And what do those consist of?

Commander HUMES. In privacy of my own home, early in the morning of Sunday, November 24th, I made a draft of this report which I later revised, and of which this represents the revision. That draft I personally burned in the fireplace of my recreation room.

Mr. SPECTER. May the record show that the Exhibit No. 397 is the identical document which has been previously identified as Commission No. 371 for our internal purposes.

Is the first sheet then in that group the notes you made when you talked to Doctor Perry?

Commander HUMES. That is correct, sir.

Mr. SPECTER. And do the next 15 sheets represent the rough draft which was later copied into the autopsy report which has been heretofore identified with an exhibit number?

Commander HUMES. That is correct, sir.

Mr. SPECTER. And what do the next two sheets represent?

Commander HUMES. The next two sheets are the notes actually made in the room in which the examination was taking place. I notice now that the handwriting in some instances is not my own, and it is either that of Commander Boswell or Colonel Finck.

Mr. SPECTER. And was that writing made at the same time that the autopsy report was undertaken; that is, did you review all of the markings on those papers and note them to be present when you completed the autopsy report?

Commander HUMES. Yes, sir. From the time of the completion of this examination until the submission of the written report following its preparation, all of the papers pertinent to this case were in my personal custody.

Mr. SPECTER. Have you now described all of the documents which were present in that 397, Exhibit No. 397?

Commander HUMES. Yes, sir; with the exception of the certification to the fact that I, in fact, detailed them in my custody, and a certification that I had destroyed certain preliminary draft notes.

Mr. SPECTER. And these represent all the notes except those you have already described which you destroyed?

Commander HUMES. That is correct, sir.

Mr. SPECTER. Now, just one point on the notes themselves. Page 14 of your rough draft, Doctor Humes, as to the point of origin, the notes show that there was a revision between your first draft and your final report.

Commander HUMES. Yes, sir.

Mr. SPECTER. Will you first of all read into the record the final conclusion reflected in your final report.

Commander HUMES. I would rather read it from the final report. The final report reads:

"The projectiles were fired from a point behind and somewhat above the level of the deceased."

Mr. SPECTER. And what did the first draft of that sentence as shown on page 14 of your rough draft state?

Commander HUMES. It stated as follows:

"The projectiles were fired from a point behind and somewhat above a horizontal line to the vertical position of the body at the moment of impact."

Mr. SPECTER. Now would you state the reason for making that modification between draft and final report, please?

Commander HUMES. This examination, as I have indicated, was performed by myself with my two associates. The notes which we have just admitted as an exhibit are in my own hand and are my opinion, was my opinion at that time, as to the best way to present the facts which we had gleaned during this period.

Before submitting it to the typist, I went over this with great care with my two associates. One or the other of them raised the point that perhaps this sentence would state more than what was absolutely fact based upon our observations, pointing out that we did not know precisely at that time in what position the body of the President was when the missiles struck, and that therefore we should be somewhat less specific and somewhat more circumspect than the way we stated it. When I considered this suggestion, I agreed that it would be better to change it as noted, and accordingly, I did so.

Mr. SPECTER. Mr. Chief Justice, I move now for the admission into evidence of Exhibit No. 397.

The CHAIRMAN. It may be admitted.

(The documents, previously marked Exhibit No. 397 for identification, were received in evidence.)

Mr. McCLOY. May I ask one question about the notes? The notes that you made contemporaneously with your examination, you said you put those down and then you put some in later. How much later were the notes, within the best of your recollection of the final notes made, not the final report, but the final notes that you made in your own handwriting?

Commander HUMES. The examination was concluded approximately at 11 o'clock on the night of November 22. The final changes in the notes prior to the typing of the report were made, and I will have to give you the time because whatever time Mr. Oswald was shot, that is about when I finished. I was working in an office, and someone had a television on and came in and told me that Mr. Oswald had been shot, and that was around noon on Sunday, November 24th.

Mr. SPECTER. Mr. Chief Justice, I have now marked another photograph as the next exhibit number, Commission Exhibit 398. May I say to the Commission that this is a photograph which, subject to later proof, will show it to be taken immediately after the President was struck by the first bullet.

The CHAIRMAN. It may be marked.

(The photograph was marked Commission Exhibit No. 398 for identification.)

May I move for its admission into evidence at this time for this purpose?

The CHAIRMAN. It may be admitted.

(The photograph, previously marked Commission Exhibit No. 398 for identification, was received in evidence.)

Looking at Commission Exhibit 398, Doctor Humes, with that as a background, have you had an opportunity to review the medical reports on Governor Connally at Parkland Hospital in Commission Exhibit 392?

Commander HUMES. I have.

Mr. SPECTER. Have you noted the wounds which he sustained on his right wrist, that is, Governor Connally's right wrist?

Commander HUMES. Yes, sir; I have noted the report of it in these records.

Mr. SPECTER. What does the report show as to those wounds on the right wrist?

Commander HUMES. The report shows a wound of entrance on the dorsal aspect of the right wrist. Let's get the precise point here. The wound of entry is described as on the dorsal aspect of the right wrist above the junction of the distal fourth of the radius and the shaft. It was approximately two centimeters in length and rather oblique, with the loss of tissue, and some considerable contusions at the margins. There was a wound of exit along the volar surface of the wrist about two centimeters above the flexion crease of the wrist in the midline.

Mr. SPECTER. Doctor Humes, I show you a bullet which we have marked as Commission Exhibit No. 399, and may I say now that, subject to later proof, this is the missile which has been taken from the stretcher which the evidence now indicates was the stretcher occupied by Governor Connally.

I move for its admission into evidence at this time.

The CHAIRMAN. It may be admitted.

(The article, previously marked Commission Exhibit No. 399 for identification, was received in evidence.)

Mr. SPECTER. We have been asked by the FBI that the missile not be handled by anybody because it is undergoing further ballistic tests, and it now appears, may the record show, in a plastic case in a cotton background.

Now looking at that bullet, Exhibit 399, Doctor Humes, could that bullet have gone through or been any part of the fragment passing through President Kennedy's head in Exhibit No. 388?

Commander HUMES. I do not believe so, sir.

Mr. SPECTER. And could that missile have made the wound on Governor Connally's right wrist?

Commander HUMES. I think that that is most unlikely. May I expand on those two answers?

Mr. SPECTER. Yes, please do.

Commander HUMES. The X-rays made of the wound in the head of the late President showed fragmentations of the missile. Some fragments we recovered and turned over, as has been previously noted. Also we have X-rays of the fragment of skull which was in the region of our opinion exit wound showing metallic fragments.

Also going to Exhibit 392, the report from Parkland Hospital, the following sentence referring to the examination of the wound of the wrist is found:

"Small bits of metal were encountered at various levels throughout the wound, and these were, wherever they were identified and could be picked up, picked up and submitted to the pathology department for identification and examination."

The reason I believe it most unlikely that this missile could have inflicted either of these wounds is that this missile is basically intact; its jacket appears to me to be in tact, and I do not understand how it could possibly have left fragments in either of these locations.

Mr. SPECTER. What wounds did Governor Connally sustain in his chest area, based upon the records of Parkland Hospital, which you have examined, Doctor Humes?

Commander HUMES. Governor Connally received in his chest a wound of entrance just—this is again from 392—"just lateral to the right scapula close to the axilla which had passed through the lattisimus dorsi muscle, shattered approximately ten centimeters of a lateral and anterior portion of the right fifth rib, and emerged below the right nipple anterially."

These were the wounds of the chest of Governor Connally.

Mr. SPECTER. Now assuming that there were only three missiles fired, and bearing in mind the positions of President Kennedy and Governor Connally from the photograph marked Commission Exhibit 398, do you have an opinion as to the source of the missiles which inflicted the wound on President Kennedy marked 385–C to D, and the wound in Governor Connally's chest which you have just referred to?

Commander HUMES. Yes. I would preface this statement by the following: As I testified earlier in the afternoon, as much as we could ascertain from our X-rays and physical examinations, this missile struck no bony structures in traversing the body of the late President. Therefore, I believe it was moving at its exit from the President's body at only very slightly less than that velocity, so it was still traveling at great speed.

I believe in looking at Exhibit 398, which purports to be at approximately the time the President was struck, I see that Governor Connally is sitting directly in front of the late President, and suggest the possibility that this missile, having traversed the low neck of the late President, in fact traversed the chest of Governor Connally.

Mr. SPECTER. How much of the velocity, if any, or would there be an appreciable diminution of the velocity of the projectile on passing through the portions of President Kennedy's body which you have described?

Commander HUMES. I would have to defer to my associate, Colonel Finck, for an opinion about this.

Mr. SPECTER. Fine. As to any damage to the rib which you described Governor Connally sustained, would that impact or trauma be consistent with the markings which are shown on Exhibit 399?

Commander HUMES. I think it quite possible. Here I think if this point were to be explored further, a most valuable piece of evidence would be an X-ray of the chest of Governor Connally, because I believe that this missile could have struck the rib a glancing blow.

The rib is a rather rigid structure, and the missile would not have to strike it directly to cause the fracture that was described, and the fracture is not very clearly described to me, and if an X-ray, for instance, showed no metallic fragments in the chest of the Governor, I would think it quite likely that this was the missile that had traversed his chest, because I doubt if this missile would have left behind it any metallic fragments from its physical appearance at this time.

Mr. SPECTER. Could that missile have traversed Governor Connally's chest without having him know it immediately or instantaneously?

Commander HUMES. I believe so. I have heard reports, and have been told by my professional associates of any number of instances where people received penetrating wounds in various portions of the body and have only the sensation of a slight discomfort or slight slap or some other minor difficulty from such a missile wound. I am sure he would be aware that something happened to him, but that he was shot, I am not certain.

Representative FORD. Would that have been the potential reaction of the President when first hit, as shown in 385?

Commander HUMES. It could very easily be one of some type of an injury—I mean the awareness that he had been struck by a missile, I don't know, but people have been drilled through with a missile and didn't know it.

Mr. SPECTER. Dr. Humes, under your opinion which you have just given us, what effect, if any, would that have on whether this bullet, 399, could have been the one to lodge in Governor Connally's thigh?

Commander HUMES. I think that extremely unlikely. The reports, again Exhibit 392 from Parkland, tell of an entrance wound on the lower midthigh of the Governor, and X-rays taken there are described as showing metallic fragments in the bone, which apparently by this report were not removed and are still present in Governor Connally's thigh. I can't conceive of where they came from this missile.

Representative FORD. The missile identified as Exhibit 399.

Commander HUMES. 399, sir.

Mr. SPECTER. Doctor Humes, would you have an opinion as to whether the wounds on Governor Connally's wrist and thigh were caused by the same bullet?

Commander HUMES. In reading the description of the fragmentation that was found, fragments were found in the wrist, one fragment was found imbedded in his femur, I would feel it was definitely within the realm of possibility that the same missile could have produced both of those injuries.

Mr. SPECTER. Those are all my questions, Mr. Chief Justice.

The CHAIRMAN. Are there any other questions? If not, thank you very much, Commander. You have been very helpful to us, indeed.

Commander HUMES. Thank you very much, sir.

The CHAIRMAN. Thank you.

Mr. SPECTER. Commander Boswell.

Mr. McCLOY. May I ask one more question?

The CHAIRMAN. Of course you may.

Mr. McCLOY. Earlier in the afternoon we had taken out of cellophane bags here the clothing of the President.

Commander HUMES. Yes, sir.

Mr. McCLOY. And amongst them was the shirt.

Commander HUMES. Yes, sir.

Mr. McCLOY. From your examination of the wounds, of the defects, I guess you would call it in the shirt——

Commander HUMES. Yes, sir.

Mr. McCLOY. Would you from examining the tissues of that shirt have any conclusions as to how that wound, how that missile passed through the shirt? Was it from the rear to the front, or from the front to the rear?

Commander HUMES. As I examined that exhibit today, sir, the threads are fragmented and distorted in such a fashion which would indicate to me that the missile passed through the shirt from the rear to the front.

TESTIMONY OF COMDR. J. THORNTON BOSWELL, MEDICAL CORPS, U.S. NAVY

The CHAIRMAN. Commander Boswell, will you raise your right hand and be sworn, please?

Do you solemnly swear the testimony you give before this Commission will be the truth, the whole truth, and nothing but the truth, so help you God?

Commander Boswell. I do, sir.

The Chairman. Be seated, please.

Mr. Specter. Will you state your full name for the record, please?

Commander Boswell. J. Thornton Boswell, Commander, Medical Corps, U.S. Navy.

Mr. Specter. What is your profession?

Commander Boswell. Physician.

Mr. Specter. And where did you obtain your medical degree, please?

Commander Boswell. At the College of Medicine, Ohio State University.

Mr. Specter. And what experience have you had in your professional line subsequent to obtaining that degree?

Commander Boswell. I interned in the Navy and took my pathology training at St. Albans Naval Hospital in New York. I was certified by the American Board of Pathology in both clinical and pathological anatomy in 1957 and 1958.

Mr. Specter. And what is your duty assignment at the present time?

Commander Boswell. I am the Chief of Pathology at the National Naval Medical School.

Mr. Specter. Did you have occasion to participate in the autoposy of the late President Kennedy?

Commander Boswell. I did.

Mr. Specter. And did you assist Doctor Humes at that time?

Commander Boswell. Yes, sir.

Mr. Specter. Have you been present here today during the entire course of Doctor Humes' testimony?

Commander Boswell. I have, sir; yes.

Mr. Specter. Do you have anything that you would like to add by way of elaboration or modification to that which Doctor Humes has testified?

Commander Boswell. None, I believe. Doctor Humes has stated essentially what is the culmination of our examination and our subsequent conference, and everything is exactly as we had determined our conclusions.

Mr. Specter. And are you one of the three coauthors of the autopsy report which has been previously identified as a Commission Exhibit?

Commander Boswell. Yes; I am.

Mr. Specter. All the facts set forth therein are correct in accordance with your analysis and evaluation of the situation?

Commander Boswell. Yes.

Mr. Specter. And specifically, as to the points of entry and points of exit which have been testified to by Doctor Humes, do his views express yours as well?

Commander Boswell. They do, yes.

Mr. Specter. Doctor Boswell, would you state for the record what your conclusion was as to the cause of death of President Kennedy?

Commander Boswell. The brain injury was the cause of death.

Mr. Specter. And in the absence of brain injury, what, in your view, would have been the future status of President Kennedy's mortality, if he had only sustained the wound inflicted in 385?

Commander Boswell. I believe it would have been essentially an uneventful recovery. It could have been easily repaired, and I think it would have been of little consequence.

Mr. Specter. Those are my only questions, Mr. Chief Justice.

The Chairman. Does anyone have any questions of the Commander? If not, Commander, thank you very much, indeed. You have been very helpful to us.

Mr. Specter. Colonel Finck.

TESTIMONY OF LT. COL. PIERRE A. FINCK, PHYSICIAN, U. S. ARMY

The Chairman. Colonel Finck.

Colonel, will you raise your right hand and be sworn? Do you solemnly swear that the testimony you give before this Commission will be the truth, the whole truth, and nothing but the truth, so help you God?

Colonel FINCK. I do.

The CHAIRMAN. Will you be seated, please, Colonel?

Mr. SPECTER. Would you state your full name for the record, please?

Colonel FINCK. My first name is Pierre. My middle initial is "A". My last name is Finck.

Mr. SPECTER. What is your profession, sir?

Colonel FINCK. I am a physician.

Mr. SPECTER. And by whom are you employed?

Colonel FINCK. By the United States Army.

Mr. SPECTER. And what is your rank?

Colonel FINCK. I am a lieutenant colonel in the Medical Corps.

Mr. SPECTER. Where did you obtain your medical degree?

Colonel FINCK. At the University of Geneva Medical School in Switzerland.

Mr. SPECTER. And in what year did you obtain that degree?

Colonel FINCK. In 1948.

Mr. SPECTER. What has your experience been in the medical profession subsequent to obtaining that degree?

Colonel FINCK. I had 4 years of training in pathology after my internship, 2 years, including 2 years of pathology at the University Institute of Pathology in Geneva, Switzerland, and 2 years at the University of Tennessee Institute of Pathology in Memphis, Tenn.

Mr. SPECTER. And how long have you been in the United States Army?

Colonel FINCK. Since 1955.

Mr. SPECTER. And what have your duties consisted of in the Army?

Colonel FINCK. From 1955 to 1958 I performed approximately 200 autopsies, many of them pertaining to trauma including missile wounds, stationed at Frankfort, Germany as pathologist of the, United States Army Hospital in Frankfurt, Germany.

Mr. SPECTER. Have you had any additional, special training or experience in missile wounds?

Colonel FINCK. For the past 3 years I was Chief of the Wound Ballistics Pathology Branch of the Armed Forces Institute of Pathology and in that capacity I reviewed personally all the cases forwarded to us by the Armed Forces, and some civilian cases from the United States and our forces overseas. The number of these cases amounts to approximately 400 cases. I was called as a consultant in the field of missile wounds for this particular case, and also last year in February 1963, the Surgeon General of the Army sent me to Vietnam for a wound ballistics mission. I had to testify in a murder trial involving a 30/30 rifle in the first week of March this year, and I came back yesterday after one week in Panama where I had to testify. I was sent to Panama by the Secretary of the Army regarding the fatalities of the events of 9–10 in January of 1964.

Mr. SPECTER. Have you been certified by the American Board of Pathology, Doctor Finck?

Colonel FINCK. I was certified in pathology anatomy by the American Board of Pathology in 1956, and by the same American Board of Pathology in the field of forensic pathology in 1961.

Mr. SPECTER. Would you describe briefly for the Commission what forensic pathology involves?

Colonel FINCK. Forensic pathology is the study with the naked eye and with the microscope of injuries, including missile wounds, trauma in general. In summary, it is the part of pathology in relation to the law, violent death being homicide, be it suicide, accidental or undetermined. It also includes unexplained deaths, sudden deaths, and poisoning.

Mr. SPECTER. Did you have occasion to participate in the autopsy of the late President Kennedy?

Colonel FINCK. Yes; I did.

Mr. SPECTER. And are you one of the three coauthors of the autopsy report which has been previously marked and introduced into evidence here?

Colonel FINCK. Yes, I am.

Mr. SPECTER. Have you had occasion to conduct any experiments on the effect of missile penetration of the brain reflected in the chart which you have brought with you here today?

Colonel FINCK. No, sir.

Mr. SPECTER. Of the skull—let me phrase the question this way: What does the test which is depicted on the document before you relate to?

Colonel FINCK. It is based on my observations, not on experiments.

Mr. SPECTER. Would you pass that to me, sir, so that I may mark that as a Commission Exhibit, and then I will ask you to identify it, please?

Mr. Chief Justice, may I mark as Commission Exhibit No. 400 a document?

The CHAIRMAN. It may be marked.

(The document was marked Commission Exhibit No. 400 for identification.)

Mr. SPECTER. I will ask Doctor Finck to describe it for us, please.

Colonel FINCK. This is a scheme which I prepared before the 22d of November. It is a teaching scheme, but it applies to the case in discussion. It will be of help in understanding how I could identify the entrance and the exit by examination of bone. "A" represents the bony portion of the skull. "B" represents the cavity of the head, the cranial cavity. "C" represents the entrance and "D" represents the exit. The arrows indicate the missile path.

This scheme is based upon observation of through and through wounds of bone, and the same differences apply to a pane of glass. The surface struck first by the missile in relation to the surface struck next by the missile, this one, shows a smaller diameter, which means that if you look at the route of entrance in this case here, C, from the outside you will not see a crater. If you examine it from the inside, you will see a crater corresponding to the bevelling, coning, shelving, previously described by Commander Humes.

In the case we are discussing today, it was possible to have enough curvature and enough portion of the crater to identify positively the wound of entrance at the site of the bone.

Mr. SPECTER. Relating then your evaluation of the situation with respect to President Kennedy, and turning to Commission Exhibit No. 388, what is your opinion as to whether point A is a wound of entrance or exit?

Colonel FINCK. My opinion as regards Exhibit 388, letter A, is that this wound is the wound of entrance.

Mr. SPECTER. And what are the characteristics of that wound which lead you to that conclusion?

Colonel FINCK. The characteristics were that seen from the inside of the skull, I could see a beveling in the bone, a beveling that could not be seen when the wound was seen from outside the skull.

Mr. SPECTER. Are there any other individual characteristics that led you to conclude A was the wound of entrance?

Colonel FINCK. No.

Mr. SPECTER. Were you present when the three pieces of scalp were reconstructed to form the major portion of the absent part of President Kennedy's skull which Doctor Humes described?

Colonel FINCK. I was present when several portions of bone were brought.

Mr. SPECTER. And what did you observe, if anything, as to a reconstructed hole from those three portions of skull?

Colonel FINCK. May I refer to my scheme?

Mr. SPECTER. Please do.

Colonel FINCK. For the sake of demonstration.

Mr. SPECTER. Fine.

Colonel FINCK. At the level of the wound of exit, E, in my scheme, Commission Exhibit No. 400, when viewed from the inside of the skull, there was no crater, whereas when the wound is seen from the outside of the skull, there was beveling, cratering, or coning—this is possible to determine an exit even if only a portion of the bone is submitted, for the reason that if there was enough bone submitted, there is enough curvature to identify the inside and outside of the skull. Therefore the fragment, to give you an example, this portion at the level of the wound of exit can be oriented, and the outer surface of the skull and the inner surface of the skull may be identified due to the curvature.

And then you look at the direction of the beveling and you do see the beveling when looking from the outside and you can identify an exit wound. And that is what I did, and now I am referring to the actual case in discussion, Commission Exhibit 388.

Mr. SPECTER. That is B?

Colonel FINCK. Letter B. We will see portions of bone in this general area, the large wound in the bone on the right side of the skull of President Kennedy. I had enough curvature to identify outside of the skull, and inside of the skull, as the first step to orient the specimen, and then I could determine the location of the beveling, and I could therefore say that B, Commission Exhibit 388, is a wound of exit.

Mr. SPECTER. Based on your observations and conclusions, was President Kennedy shot from the front, rear, side or what?

Colonel FINCK. President Kennedy was, in my opinion, shot from the rear. The bullet entered in the back of the head and went out on the right side of his skull, producing a large wound, the greatest dimension of which was approximately 13 centimeters.

Mr. SPECTER. And as to angle, was he shot from below, from level, from above, or what, in your opinion?

Colonel FINCK. In my opinion, the angle can be determined only approximately due to the fact that the wound of entrance is fairly small and could give enough precision in the determination of the path, but the dimension of the wound of exit, letter B of Exhibit 388, is so large that we can only give an approximate angle. In my opinion, the angle was within 45 degrees from the horizontal plane.

Mr. SPECTER. Is that to say that there was a 45-degree angle of declination from the point of origin to the point of impact, from the point of origin of the bullet where the bullet came from a gun until the point where it struck President Kennedy?

The CHAIRMAN. In other words, you mean was he shot from above or below.

Mr. SPECTER. Yes.

Colonel FINCK. I think I can only state, sir, that he was shot from above and behind.

Mr. SPECTER. At this time I move for admission into evidence Exhibit 400, Mr. Chief Justice.

The CHAIRMAN. It may be admitted.

(The document was marked Commission Exhibit No. 400 for identification, and was received in evidence.)

Mr. SPECTER. As to Exhibit 385, Dr. Finck, was point C a point of entry or a point of exit, in your opinion?

Colonel FINCK. In my opinion point C of Commission's Exhibit 385 is a wound of entrance.

Mr. SPECTER. And what is the basis for that conclusion?

Colonel FINCK. The basis for that conclusion is that this wound was relatively small with clean edges. It was not a jagged wound, and that is what we see in wound of entrance at a long range.

Mr. SPECTER. Were you present here today and did you hear the entire testimony of Doctor Humes?

Colonel FINCK. Yes; I did.

Mr. SPECTER. And do you concur in Dr. Humes' statements and opinions regarding the point of entry C, point of exit D, and general angle on the flight of the missile?

Colonel FINCK. I certainly do.

Mr. SPECTER. Then from what direction was President Kennedy shot on entry point C?

Colonel FINCK. From behind and above.

Mr. SPECTER. Were the bullets used dumdum bullets, in your opinion, Dr. Finck?

Colonel FINCK. In what wound, sir?

Mr. SPECTER. Well, start with the head wound, or the back wound, either one.

Colonel FINCK. In all the wounds considered, on the basis of the aspect of the wound of entrance, dumdum bullets were not used.

Mr. Specter. And what characteristics of dumdum bullets were absent, in your opinion—in your evaluation of these wounds?

Colonel Finck. I would expect more jagged, more irregular and larger wounds of entrance than described in this case.

Representative Ford. With a dumdum bullet?

Colonel Finck. With a dumdum bullet.

Mr. Specter. With respect to the question of likelihood of Governor Connally having been wounded in the back and chest with the same bullet which passed through President Kennedy in 385, what reduction would there be, if any, in the velocity, considering the relative positions of the two men in the automobile as reflected in photograph, Exhibit 398?

Colonel Finck. Of course, to reach precise figures we would need experiments and similar circumstances with the same type ammunition at the same distance through two human cadavers, which I did not do.

On the basis that if we assume that this is one bullet going through President Kennedy's body and also through Governor Connally's body, the reduction of velocity would be of some extent after passing through President Kennedy's body, but not having hit bones, the reduction in velocity, after going through President Kennedy's body, would be minimal.

Mr. Specter. Would there be sufficient force then to inflict the wound which Dr. Humes described from the Parkland Hospital records as having been inflicted on Governor Connally's back and chest?

Colonel Finck. There would be enough energy to go through the body of the Governor.

Mr. Specter. In expressing your opinion on that subject, Doctor Finck, have you taken into account the assumptions on distance, that we are dealing here with a weapon that has a muzzle velocity in the neighborhood of slightly in excess of 2,000, and that the vehicle carrying these two individuals was approximately 150, about 150 feet away from the site of origin of the missile?

Colonel Finck. At this range, a bullet of this velocity loses very little velocity, and keeps upon impact a large amount of kinetic energy.

Mr. Specter. You heard the whole of Doctor Humes' testimony, did you not?

Colonel Finck. Yes; I did.

Mr. Specter. Do you have anything that you would like to add to what he said?

Colonel Finck. No.

Mr. Specter. Or would you like to modify his testimony in any way?

Colonel Finck. No.

Mr. Specter. Do you subscribe to the observations and procedures which he outlined during the course of his testimony?

Colonel Finck. I do.

Mr. Specter. As having been conducted on President Kennedy?

Colonel Finck. I do.

Mr. Specter. And do you share the opinions which he expressed in their entirety in the course of his testimony here today?

Colonel Finck. I do.

The Chairman. You might be seated, Colonel.

Mr. McCloy. Just as truthful seated as standing.

Representative Ford. How many cases did you investigate to develop this theory shown by Commission Exhibit 400?

Colonel Finck. Among the more than 400 cases I have reviewed, several of them—I cannot give you an exact figure, I do not tabulate them, but many of them had through and through wounds of the skull as well as of flat bones, as, for instance, the sternum, the bone we have in front of our chest, and this would apply also to a through and through wound of the sternum. I have cases like that.

There was a specific case in which I was able to identify the entrance at the level of the sternum on the same basis as the criteria I have given for the skull. Whenever a bullet goes through a flat bone, it will produce that beveling, that cratering, shelving, and that I have seen in numerous cases.

Representative Ford. Is this a generally accepted theory in the medical profession?

Colonel Finck. Yes, sir; it is. Am I allowed to quote a standard textbook?

The CHAIRMAN. You may; yes sir.

Colonel FINCK. The textbook of legal medicine, pathology and toxicology by Gonzalez, Vance, Halpern and Umberger does not give a scheme like I have shown to you today, but describes similar criteria.

As you know, one of the authors of the book I mentioned is still chief medical examiner of New York City, with 20,000 medical-examiner cases a year.

Mr. SPECTER. Doctor Finck, after the path C–D described in No. 385, would that be a straight line starting with the weapon itself, or was that line deviated in any way or altered when it passed through the body of President Kennedy?

Colonel FINCK. For practical purposes line C–D is a straight line with little or no deviation, the bullet not having hit bony structures.

Mr. SPECTER. Dr. Finck, have you had an opportunity to examine Commission's Exhibit 399?

Colonel FINCK. For the first time this afternoon, sir.

Mr. SPECTER. And based upon your examination of that bullet, do you have an opinion as to whether in its current condition it could have passed through President Kennedy at point C–D in 385 and then inflicted the wound in the back and chest of Governor Connally?

Colonel FINCK. Yes; I do. This is a bullet showing marks indicating the bullet was fired. The second point is that there was practically no loss of this bullet. It kept its original caliber and dimensions. There was no evidence that any major portion of the jacket was lost, and I consider this as one bullet which possibly could have gone through the wounds you described.

Mr. SPECTER. And could that bullet possibly have gone through President Kennedy in 388?

Colonel FINCK. Through President Kennedy's head? 388?

Mr. SPECTER. And remained intact in the way you see it now?

Colonel FINCK. Definitely not.

Mr. SPECTER. And could it have been the bullet which inflicted the wound on Governor Connally's right wrist?

Colonel FINCK. No; for the reason that there are too many fragments described in that wrist.

Mr. SPECTER. And is the condition of Exhibit 399 consistent with the type of a wound which Doctor Humes described on Governor Connally's rib?

Colonel FINCK. Yes.

Mr. McCLOY. I have a question.

The CHAIRMAN. Go right ahead.

Mr. McCLOY. From your examination of Exhibit 399, can you identify the caliber of that bullet?

Colonel FINCK. The caliber of this bullet, if I could measure it, but I cannot touch it.

The CHAIRMAN. We can.

Colonel FINCK. I would say it is consistent with a 6.5 mm.

Mr. McCLOY. Are you familiar with the Mannlicher 6.5 rifle?

Colonel FINCK. I am familiar with the caliber 6.5. I can draw the calibers for you on the blackboard.

Mr. McCLOY. What is the initial velocity of a 6.5 mm. bullet of that character?

Colonel FINCK. Of the order of 2,000 feet per second.

Mr. McCLOY. And you say there would not be a substantial diminution of that velocity either at the point of impact or at the point of exit?

Colonel FINCK. That is correct.

Mr. SPECTER. One more question, Mr. Chief Justice.

On 388, point A to B, what is your view, Dr. Finck, as to whether or not that is represented by a straight line going back to the point of origin of the weapon?

Colonel FINCK. The difficulty in interpreting the path in line A–B of Commission's Exhibit 388 is that, one, there is, as stated before, a large wound of exit, and, two, there is a secondary path as indicated by the fragments recovered. So we can have an assumption and state that the general direction, the general path, the general angle of this missile was from behind and above, and that the bullet, markedly fragmented, went out of the President's head on the right side, but that a portion of this bullet which badly fragmented was recovered within the skull.

Mr. SPECTER. In view of the impact on the skull at point A, it is unlikely to be a straight line to B all the way back to the muzzle of the weapon as it is, say, in 385 C–D, all the way back to the muzzle of the gun.

Colonel FINCK. In C–D, Commission's Exhibit 385, due to the fact that there was no fragmentation, I can say that it is a straight line from behind and above, whereas here, due to the fragmentation and to the dual path, I can't give a precise angle, but I can say that the injury is consistent with a wound produced by one bullet producing many fragments.

The CHAIRMAN. Senator, have you any questions you want to ask?

Mr. McCLOY. May I ask one?

The CHAIRMAN. Yes; go right ahead.

Mr. McCLOY. Did you examine any of the fragments which were removed from the President's skull?

Colonel FINCK. I only saw one fragment shown to me when I arrived at Bethesda, and it was an elongated black metallic fragment, and that is the only one I saw to my recollection. I was told that it had been removed from the brain of President Kennedy in the anterior portion of his head.

Mr. McCLOY. From that bullet, that fragment, could you determine, was it sufficiently large to determine from the ballistic evidence the caliber of the bullet?

Colonel FINCK. No, sir; for the reason that to determine the caliber you need the entire bullet, or at least an entire portion. You need a portion of the bullet showing the entire diameter, and I was not shown that. I was shown a fragment which represented a very small portion of the original bullet. Therefore, at that time I could not say anything on the possible original caliber.

Mr. McCLOY. You examined no fragment which did contain those characteristics?

Colonel FINCK. No, sir; I did not see any entire bullet or bullet showing the entire diameter.

The CHAIRMAN. Congressman Ford?

Representative FORD. I believe you testified, Colonel, that you concurred in the previous testimony by Commander Humes and Commander Boswell, and that you were one of the co-authors of the autopsy. At any time during this process where you were conducting the autopsy, was there any disagreement between any one of you three, any difference of opinion as to anything involved in the autopsy?

Colonel FINCK. No, sir.

Representative FORD. There has been complete unanimity on what you saw, what you did, and what you have reported?

Colonel FINCK. Yes, sir.

The CHAIRMAN. Senator Cooper?

Senator COOPER. Colonel, I would like for you to look at Exhibit 388 and at the possible trajectory of the bullet which entered President Kennedy's head at A and then mark it as a possible point of exit by "out". You remember there was testimony about a portion of the bullet from point A to the place on the diagram marked "fragment" where a fragment was found. I would like to ask if it is possible that the trajectory of the bullet, from the point of origin, could have been A to this point marked "fragment" as well as from A to the place marked "out"?

Colonel FINCK. I don't think so, sir.

Senator COOPER. Why? Would you explain that answer?

Colonel FINCK. I would think that I would consider the midportion of this exit would labeled B, Exhibit 388, as the wound produced by most of the fragments and the major portions of the fragmenting bullet. This is only a small portion of it which makes me say that this is a secondary path.

Senator COOPER. What was the size of the fragment relative to the size of the missile of the 6.5 Mannlicher, fired from the 6.5 Mannlicher rifle?

Colonel FINCK. Approximately one-tenth, or even less.

Representative FORD. From your numerous case studies, is it typical for a bullet, for a missile in this circumstance as shown in 388, to fragment to the degree that this one apparently did?

Colonel FINCK. Yes, it is quite common to find a wound of exit much larger than the wound of entrance for weapons commonly used.

Representative FORD. But is it typical for the missile to fragment to the degree that this one did as shown in Exhibit 388?

Colonel FINCK. Yes; it is.

Representative FORD. Is it typical to find only a limited number of fragments as you apparently did in this case?

Colonel FINCK. This depends to a great extent on the type of ammunition used. There are many types of bullets, jacketed, not-jacketed, pointed, hollow-nosed, hollow-points, flatnose, roundnose, all these different shapes will have a different influence on the pattern of the wound and the degree of fragmentation.

Representative FORD. That is all.

The CHAIRMAN. Thank you, Colonel, very much for your help.

Colonel FINCK. You are welcome, sir.

Representative FORD. May I ask just one question?

The CHAIRMAN. Yes; Colonel, we would like to ask just one more question.

Representative FORD. Do these two wounds represent the same or a different kind of bullet?

Colonel FINCK. You are referring to one wound and this other wound here?

Representative FORD. I am referring to the wound shown in Exhibit 388 identified as point of entry A, and wound in Exhibit 385 identified as C.

Colonel FINCK. Due to the difference in the nature of the tissue, difference in the nature of the target, it is perfectly possible that these two wounds came from the same type of bullet, that one hit bony structures and the other one did not, and that explains the differences between the patterns of these two wounds.

Representative FORD. Why one fragmented and one did not.

Colonel FINCK. Yes.

(Discussion off the record.)

The CHAIRMAN. Gentlemen, again thank you very much.

(Whereupon, at 3:45 p.m., the President's Commission recessed.)

Wednesday, March 18, 1964

TESTIMONY OF MICHAEL R. PAINE AND RUTH HYDE PAINE

The President's Commission met at 9 a.m. on March 18, 1964, at 200 Maryland Avenue NE., Washington, D.C.

Present were Chief Justice Earl Warren, Chairman; Senator John Sherman Cooper, Representative Gerald R. Ford, John J. McCloy, and Allen W. Dulles, members.

Also present were J. Lee Rankin, general counsel; Wesley J. Liebeler, assistant counsel, Albert E. Jenner, Jr., assistant counsel; Dr. Alfred Goldberg, historian; and Charles Murray, observer.

TESTIMONY OF MICHAEL R. PAINE

The CHAIRMAN. The Commission will be in order.

Mr. Paine, I will just read a brief statement concerning the purpose of the meeting today which is our practice.

The purpose of this hearing is to take the testimony of Mr. and Mrs. Michael R. Paine. The Commission has been advised that Mr. and Mrs. Paine made the acquaintance of the Oswalds during 1963, and that Mrs. Marina Oswald lived in the Paine home from late September 1963 up to the time of the assassination.

Since the Commission is inquiring fully into the background and possible motive of Lee Harvey Oswald, the alleged assassin, it intends to ask the above witnesses questions concerning Mr. Oswald, his associations and relations with others, as well as questions concerning any and all matters relating to the assassination.

You have been furnished a copy of this, have you not?

Mr. PAINE. I have seen something to that effect.

The CHAIRMAN. You have seen it.

Very well, will you rise and raise your right hand, please.

Do you solemnly swear the testimony you give before this Commission will be the truth, the whole truth and nothing but the truth, so help you God?

Mr. PAINE. I do.

The CHAIRMAN. You may be seated; Mr. Liebeler will propound the questions to you.

Mr. LIEBELER. Would you state your name, please?

Mr. PAINE. Michael R. Paine.

Mr. LIEBELER. And your address?

Mr. PAINE. 2515 West Fifth Street, Irving, Tex.

Mr. LIEBELER. When were you born, Mr. Paine?

Mr. PAINE. June 25, 1928.

Mr. LIEBELER. Where?

Mr. PAINE. New York City.

Mr. LIEBELER. Would you tell us briefly your educational background, where you attended schools?

Mr. PAINE. I went to school, high school in New York, went to 2 years of Harvard and a year of Swarthmore, I have not finished college.

Mr. DULLES. What class would you have been in Swarthmore?

Mr. PAINE. 1953.

Mr. DULLES. You would have been 1953 if you finished or did you finish?

Mr. PAINE. No; I did not.

Mr. DULLES. Excuse me.

Mr. LIEBELER. You are presently married, are you not?

Mr. PAINE. That is right.

Mr. LIEBELER. Your wife's name is?

Mr. PAINE. Ruth Hyde Paine.

Mr. LIEBELER. You have two children?

Mr. PAINE. Yes.

Mr. LIEBELER. Tell us who your parents are.

Mr. PAINE. Lyman Paine is my father and Ruth Forbes Paine Young, or Young is her present name. Mrs. Arthur Young now. She is my mother.

Mr. LIEBELER. Where is your father living at the present time?

Mr. PAINE. He is in Los Angeles.

Mr. LIEBELER. Your mother?

Mr. PAINE. Philadelphia.

Mr. LIEBELER. Do you have any brothers and sisters?

Mr. PAINE. I have a brother in Baltimore.

Mr. LIEBELER. What is his name?

Mr. PAINE. Cameron Paine.

Mr. LIEBELER. By whom are you presently employed?

Mr. PAINE. Bell Helicopter, Fort Worth.

Mr. LIEBELER. Do you have a security clearance in connection with your work at Bell Helicopter?

Mr. PAINE. I suppose it is. I don't happen to know what the classification is.

Mr. LIEBELER. Where did you work prior to working for Bell Helicopter?

Mr. PAINE. I worked in Pennsylvania for Arthur Young.

Mr. LIEBELER. What was the nature of your employment with Mr. Young?

Mr. PAINE. I had set up a shop in his barn and started work for myself and then he employed me making models, helicopter models for himself.

Mr. LIEBELER. Approximately at what time, what period of time did you work for Mr. Young?

Mr. PAINE. That is very difficult to say. I began more or less gradually first. I was doing other things. I am very vague about the dates.

Mr. LIEBELER. Do you know the year approximately?

Mr. PAINE. I suppose I went to work at Bell in 1958. I have been there 4½ years.

Mr. DULLES. Is this Mr. Young your stepfather?

Mr. PAINE. That is right.

Mr. LIEBELER. And you worked for him immediately prior to your going to Bell Helicopter?

Mr. PAINE. Yes, sir.

Mr. LIEBELER. Prior to working for Mr. Young, did you have any other employment?

Mr. PAINE. I think I came from the Army. Before that I worked at Bartol Research Foundation in Swarthmore.

Mr. LIEBELER. You were going to tell us what that was.

Mr. PAINE. That was mostly a job of setting up a laboratory to—was nuclear research laboratory, Van Der Graaf generators it had there.

Mr. LIBELER. What was the nature of your work with Bartol?

Mr. PAINE. Mostly all the work in making those machines, setting those machines so they would run; making counters, coincidence counters, instrumentation to operate the machine.

Mr. LIEBELER. How long did you work for Bartol?

Mr. PAINE. That was just about a year, I believe.

Mr. LIEBELER. Prior to that did you have any other employment?

Mr. PAINE. No, that was Swarthmore.

Mr. LIEBELER. Did you ever work for the Griswold Manufacturing Co.

Mr. PAINE. Oh, I did; yes. That was after—well, after the Army. I think it was only a few months, I don't remember when it fitted in.

Mr. LIEBELER. What was the nature of your work with that company?

Mr. PAINE. That was very boring. It was engraving precision scales.

Mr. LIEBELER. You worked in the actual engraving of the scales?

Mr. PAINE. That is correct.

Mr. LIEBELER. What is the nature of your work with Bell Helicopter at the present time?

Mr. PAINE. I am called a research engineer. I work in a lab and design and build and test models of new concepts of helicopter configurations.

Mr. LIEBELER. Have you been engaged in that type of work for Bell throughout the entire time you have been employed by them?

Mr. PAINE. I have been in the research laboratory research group that long. It has all been problems——

Mr. DULLES. Are you a helicopter pilot by any chance yourself?

Mr. PAINE. I am an airplane pilot.

Mr. LIEBELER. But your work basically for Bell has been in the research of design and operation of helicopters?

Mr. PAINE. Yes.

Mr. LIEBELER. Would you tell us the circumstances under which you met your wife and subsequently married her?

Mr. PAINE. I met her at a folk dance party, folk dance meeting, and I had known her for about 2 years before we married.

Mr. LIEBELER. When did you meet her approximately?

Mr. PAINE. We were married, I think, in 1958, it was the end of the year so maybe it was 1957. What was the question again?

Mr. LIEBELER. Approximately when you met her.

Mr. PAINE. Two years before that would be, 1957.

Mr. LIEBELER. 1956 or 1957.

Mr. PAINE. Yes.

(At this point, Representative Ford entered the hearing room.)

Mr. LIEBELER. We understand that you are a Quaker, Mr. Paine, is that correct?

Mr. PAINE. That is not quite correct.

When I was in Philadelphia, I sang in various churches, and Ruth being a Quaker, started going to Quaker meetings. Had I remained there I would have become a Quaker. Moving to Texas there was a very small Quaker community, and I joined the Unitarian Church after a while.

Mr. LIEBELER. When did you first become interested in the Quaker religion; was it about the time you met your wife or was it before that.

Mr. PAINE. No; I think she was instrumental in bringing me into that circle.

Mr. LIEBELER. Give us a brief description of the outside interests that you and your wife and that your wife had during the time subsequent to your meeting and until the time you left Philadelphia. Was she active in church activities?

Mr. PAINE. No; I wouldn't say so. She was active in the Young Friends Committee of North America which was making an effort to bring a group of Russians on tour of this country. It was in the first flush or enthusiasm of East-West contacts, and after a couple of years they did succeed in bringing those Russians on tour. That was the beginning of her interest in Russian, learning the Russian language. I think that was her only activity that I am aware of or remember right now.

Mr. LIEBELER. Do you know whether your wife engaged in a writing campaign or a pen pal campaign between people in the United States and people in the Soviet Union?

Mr. PAINE. That was another part of this East-West contacts committee's duties or tasks they took upon themselves and I think she was chairman, accepted the chairmanship of that committee.

For a while, it was almost moribund, very inactive.

Mr. DULLES. Which committee was that, the committee to stimulate letters between Russia and the United States?

Mr. PAINE. Yes; to find names and addresses on each side to connect people together.

Mr. LIEBELER. Did you yourself ever take part in any activity of that group?

Mr. PAINE. No; I didn't.

Mr. LIEBELER. You spoke of the East-West contacts committee as being active in trying to bring a group of Russians to the United States. Did they engage in any activities other than this attempt to bring Russians to the United States that you know of?

Mr. PAINE. That is the only one I know of, yes.

Mr. LIEBELER. Did they succeed in bringing some Russians to the United States?

Mr. PAINE. Yes; they did. They brought three Russians, and then the Russians reciprocated by taking a group of Quakers who knew Russian on a tour of Russia.

Mr. LIEBELER. Were you married to Ruth Hyde Paine at the time these Russian people came to the United States under the auspices of the East-West contacts committee?

Mr. PAINE. I might have been; I don't know.

Mr. LIEBELER. Do you know whether she actively participated in the program to bring the Russians to the United States?

Mr. PAINE. Well, she participated insofar as going to the meetings. I don't believe she did most of the writing to the State Department and what-not to try to arrange clearances and itineraries and things like that, but she was at the meetings at which those things were discussed.

Mr. LIEBELER. Did she ever discuss them with you in any detail?

Mr. PAINE. We, I would often—I went to several of those meetings myself.

Mr. LIEBELER. Do you know the names of any of the Russians who came to the United States in connection with this program?

Mr. PAINE. I might recognize them if I saw them again, but right now the names have escaped me.

Mr. LIEBELER. You say there were just three of them?

Mr. PAINE. I think there were three; yes.

Mr. LIEBELER. Are you a member of the American Civil Liberties Union?

Mr. PAINE. Yes.

Mr. LIEBELER. When did you become a member of that organization?

Mr. PAINE. I suppose you become a member as soon as you contribute money, and I may have contributed money a good many years back. I didn't start going to a meeting of the organization until I was—I have only been to about four perhaps, in Dallas, four meetings.

Mr. LIEBELER. Is Dallas the only place you have attended meetings of the ACLU?

Mr. PAINE. To my knowledge.

Mr. LIEBELER. Are you acquainted with an organization known as the Friends Peace Committee?

Mr. PAINE. It is a familiar name. I guess not, though. I don't think I have been to a meeting of theirs.

Mr. LIEBELER. Do you know if it is connected in any way with the Young Friends Committee of North America.

Mr. PAINE. I take it to be a Friend, you know, a Quaker committee but I believe it is connected.

Mr. LIEBELER. Do you know a gentleman by the name of Dennis Jamison, who I believe is active in the Friends Peace Committee?

Mr. PAINE. I don't think so.

Mr. LIEBELER. Or George Lakey?

Mr. PAINE. For practical purposes; no. The names seem a little familiar but I can't place them.

Mr. LIEBELER. Do you have any recollection of the connection in which it is familiar to you?

Mr. PAINE. No.

Mr. LIEBELER. Are you familiar with the Committee for Non-Violent Action?

Mr. PAINE. Many of these things sound familiar. I don't—I really am saying no.

Mr. LIEBELER. Are you a member or have you ever attended any meetings of the John Birch Society?

Mr. PAINE. I am not a member. I have been to one or, I guess chiefly one meeting of theirs.

Mr. LIEBELER. Where was that?

Mr. PAINE. That was in Dallas?

Mr. LIEBELER. When?

Mr. PAINE. That was the night Stevenson spoke in Dallas.

The CHAIRMAN. When?

Mr. PAINE. The night Stevenson spoke in Dallas, U.N. Day.

Representative FORD. Was that 1963?

Mr. PAINE. Yes.

Mr. LIEBELER. Would you tell us the circumstances of your attendance at that meeting and what happened?

Mr. PAINE. I had been seeking to go to a Birch meeting for some time, and then I was invited on this night so I went. It was an introductory meeting.

Mr. DULLES. On the 9th of November?

Mr. PAINE. It was November something, I don't know what, a Wednesday or Thursday night.

Mr. LIEBELER. For the record I think the record should indicate that Mr. Stevenson was in Dallas on or about October 24, 1963. Who invited you to this meeting?

Mr. PAINE. I had tried once before to go to a meeting which didn't occur. There happens to be a member of our choir, a paid soloist who is a John Birch advocate so I have been applying—so I have been telling her, that I wanted to go. I suppose, I don't remember for certain but I suppose she was the one who told me where and when.

Mr. LIEBELER. Did this meeting have anything to do with the activity that occurred at Mr. Stevenson's meeting in Dallas?

Mr. PAINE. No. You see they were taking place at the same time. It was rather sparsely attended, most of them were down spitting on Stevenson.

Mr. LIEBELER. The Birch meeting which you were down to was sparsely attended?

Mr. PAINE. Yes.

Representative FORD. Was this an evening meeting or afternoon?

Mr. PAINE. This is evening.

Representative FORD. Evening.

Mr. DULLES. May I ask, did you go out of curiosity rather than sympathy or rather how did you happen to go?

Mr. PAINE. I am not in sympathy.

Mr. DULLES. So I gathered.

Mr. PAINE. I have been to a number of rightist meetings and seminars in Texas. I was interested in seeing more communication between the right and the left; there isn't much liberal out there and so I wanted to be able to speak their language and know that their fears—and be familiar with their feelings and attitudes.

Mr. LIEBELER. Was there any discussion at this meeting as far as you can recall of Mr. Stevenson's appearance in Dallas?

Mr. PAINE. No; I don't believe there was any.

Mr. LIEBELER. Was there any discussion of the policy of the Kennedy administration?

Mr. PAINE. There was no discussion at that meeting. It was a 2- or 3-hour lecture on a movie by Welch, and then a young man gave a few more explanations about the organization. It was mostly an introductory meeting. I think for newcomers.

Mr. LIEBELER. Telling them about the John Birch Society itself?

Mr. PAINE. That is right.

Mr. LIEBELER. Mr. Welch was not there, was he?

Mr. PAINE. No; he was not.

Representative FORD. Was this a movie in which he participated?

Mr. PAINE. He was the speaker at a lectern in this movie.

Mr. LIEBELER. Do you have any knowledge of the political attitudes or activities of your father, George Lyman Paine?

Mr. PAINE. I have very little specific knowledge of what he does.

Mr. LIEBELER. Would you tell us what you do know about your father's political activities?

Mr. PAINE. I have seen my father rather rarely. Since I have been in Texas, I have seen him more frequently. I think I have been out there three times now in the last 5 years.

Mr. LIEBELER. When you say out there—you mean Los Angeles?

Mr. PAINE. Yes; I have seen him twice. He was out to Texas. I have been to Los Angeles twice, and he came at least once to Dallas.

Mr. LIEBELER. Please fix the time when you went to Los Angeles?

Mr. PAINE. Last summer, 2 weeks in August or something. I was there for 3 days, the first, the middle of August.

I would guess it was about 2 years before that that I had been there. I could be off by a year both ways. I can't even remember whether he came—I think he probably interspersed his visit between mine.

Mr. LIEBELER. Do you recall that he visited Irving on two different occasions, once in Christmas, 1962?

Mr. PAINE. One was a Christmas party, that is right.

Mr. LIEBELER. And once in the summer of 1961.

Mr. PAINE. I don't remember '61. I do remember pictures now, we have pictures showing us outside so that was balmy weather.

Mr. LIEBELER. So that in the period that you have been living in Texas you have gone to Los Angeles on two different occasions and visited your father there and he has been in Irving on two different occasions, is that correct?

Mr. PAINE. That seems, I think, to be right.

Mr. LIEBELER. Would you go on and tell us what you know about your father's political activities?

Mr. PAINE. Yes.

Well, we would have to go back to a little to when I lived in New York as a school student in school, grammar school and high school. There I would see him very infrequently considering our close proximity and the fact that I found him stimulating and I liked him.

He took me to a few, one or possibly two, Communist meetings at my considerable insistence. He didn't urge this upon me. I wanted to go, to get the feeling of the—I asked him what he did or something and I wanted to know all this, my mother said he was on the radical left.

So, I went to a few of those meetings, and didn't—was unfamiliar with the issues and questions they were debating. I got the feeling, I came away with the impression, that these people, there were three Communist groups apparently in New York at the time, and they were most up in arms with each other, or there——

Mr. DULLES. Excuse me, how old were you at this time approximately?

Mr. PAINE. This was somewhere from eighth grade to high school.

Mr. DULLES. Yes.

Representative FORD. What year about, what time span would that be?

Mr. PAINE. Well 1947, I think I got out of high school, so it is 1943 to 1947.

Then I didn't—I got the flavor of those meetings. I found sort of an intense people, people of high intensity. I didn't feel very much at home there, and I guess I didn't go to any more.

Mr. DULLES. Did they try to recruit you at all or to get you to be a member or attend or join meetings?

Mr. PAINE. No; they were glad to meet Lyman's son. That is he would introduce me to friends or people he knew there, and I liked—I had some favorable attitudes to the zeal of the group or the zeal of the assembled people.

They were fully committed to what they believed in. I had my own dreams of how I would like to see society at the time and it wasn't along the same line.

So, I felt happy to have them there and I would go my course and just—I didn't feel opposed to them; neither did I feel drawn to them, although I tried to read some of Das Kapital at that time and Communist manifesto.

Mr. LIEBELER. Did you ever join any of these organizations?

Mr. PAINE. Well, I didn't know of any organization as such.

I went to this meeting in downtown New York. I didn't know—so therefore I knew three groups. Maybe it was the Socialist group and the Stalinist group and I think the group that Lyman was in, I don't know, maybe he was a Socialist.

Mr. LIEBELER. Which was the second group, was it the Stalinist?

Mr. PAINE. I mentioned the Stalinist, Dubinsky, David Dubinsky, was the only name I remember aside from Stalin, was a name I remember there, and I can't now remember whose side who was on.

Mr. LIEBELER. Do you have any clear recollection of what particular group your father was associated with?

Mr. PAINE. No; I never had—never knew what the name of any group he might be associated with.

Now, I suppose it was Trotsky. Trotskyite was a different distinct group at that time. They probably wouldn't be mentioning their own group. They would be mentioning their opponent's group.

Mr. LIEBELER. Subsequent to your attendance at the meetings of these groups at the time you have spoken of did you ever attend any other meetings of similar groups either in New York or any other place?

Mr. PAINE. I can't remember anything of a similar nature.

Mr. LIEBELER. Did you know of your father ever using any aliases?

Mr. PAINE. No; I don't.

Mr. LIEBELER. You are not familiar with the name Thomas L. Brown or Lyman Pierce?

Mr. PAINE. No.

Mr. LIEBELER. When was the——

Mr. PAINE. I was aware that my father didn't talk readily about his affairs. When we met we would talk at great length and we always do talk. There is an amazing similarity in our natures. I have almost thought there was one person trying to live in two bodies.

But we have always been completely absorbed in subjects that were closer to my—without going into what he was doing day to day or what he was—I was aware that I didn't know, and I didn't pry or probe as to what he might be doing there.

Mr. LIEBELER. So far as you know, however, he was actively participating in the meetings and activities of this group?

Mr. PAINE. Oh, yes.

Mr. LIEBELER. Am I correct in understanding that your father and mother were divorced when you were about 4 years old?

Mr. PAINE. That is right.

Mr. LIEBELER. You were at that time living in New York City?

Mr. PAINE. Yes.

Mr. LIEBELER. Subsequently you and your mother.

Mr. PAINE. She got a divorce in Reno, Nev., she had a house in Virginia City.

The CHAIRMAN. In New York you were living with your father or mother?

Mr. PAINE. They lived together in New York. Then there was a year, a part of a year, we moved to Philadelphia. They may have separated and he tried to come back or something like that, and then we went to Reno, Nev.

Mr. LIEBELER. During the time you lived in Philadelphia, was your father living with the family?

Mr. PAINE. I think he was there part time. I don't remember that for sure. We had two houses there. One I think I remember him slightly and the other one I don't.

Mr. LIEBELER. Your father was not present during the time that you stayed in Nevada?

Mr. PAINE. No; he was not.

Mr. LIEBELER. You and your brother stayed in Nevada with your mother?

Mr. PAINE. And a housekeeper also.

Mr. LIEBELER. After you left Nevada where did you live?

Mr. PAINE. We went over to California, Santa Barbara.

Mr. LIEBELER. Who lived there at that time with you?

Mr. PAINE. A friend of hers, Kathleen, now she was originally Kathleen Schroeder, a sister of my uncle, now Kathleen Forbes, and a distant cousin of my mother's, and I think my grandfather, grandparents, would come out occasionally.

Mr. LIEBELER. Was your father present at that time?

Mr. PAINE. No; he was not.

Mr. LIEBELER. He wasn't there at any time during your stay in Santa Barbara?

Mr. PAINE. I don't remember that. I am not certain of it.

Mr. LIEBELER. How long did you live in Santa Barbara, Calif.?

Mr. PAINE. Each year my grandfather paid our way back across the country to Naushon Island in Massachusetts. We lived there 3 years.

Mr. LIEBELER. Where did you go after that?

Mr. PAINE. Cambridge, Mass.

Mr. LIEBELER. How long were you there?

Mr. PAINE. From the third to the sixth grade.

Mr. LIEBELER. With whom did you live?

Mr. PAINE. With my mother on Fairweather Street.

The CHAIRMAN. Is this of particular importance to the investigation, it is very lengthy, and I don't know particularly what it bears upon. If it is in relation with his father, let's get at that and get it over with, but I don't see what this man's history from the time he was born—I don't see how it bears on it. It just takes altogether too much time for an extraneous purpose, it seems to me. Let's get on with the thing.

Mr. LIEBELER. It bears on the point only on what connection he has with his father.

Mr. PAINE. Let me go to that. I have seen him on a few times, once a year would be a frequent—we felt great affinity in our bent, not in the actual application of the way we would like to do things but in a concern for the value of people. I know very little about what he does, and he has not tried to proselytize me, and he has not volunteered information about what he did.

I think a certain change has come over him since. For many years or years in college or something I thought he was still interested in his revolutionary groups and that was a pity because that wasn't going to happen, and it was to be a dead end, a blind, he would come to the end of his life and his cause had fizzled out.

When I went out to California more recently, the last time we were talking about the civil rights movement and, shall we say, the revolution occurring in this country spearheaded by the Negroes' demand for dignity, that was a subject that completely absorbed the weekend and there were various Negroes who came around the country, who happened to pass through at that time.

You probably might be interested in regard to Cuba. I was surprised sometime in the conversation someone there had spoken favorably of the revolution in Cuba. This was a surprise to me, I didn't realize that this was part of the—was the present thrill, shall we say. I don't know whether that applied to Lyman also or whether—I think he went along with that. We didn't get around to arguing on that point. I only mention that in passing. That was about the full extent of it.

She mentioned Cuba in this favorable way, and it was a subject I didn't——

Mr. DULLES. Who was this she?

Mr. PAINE. It was Grace somebody, I have forgotten.

Mr. DULLES. One of the people present in these conversations?

Mr. PAINE. Yes. So that was my only knowledge that he was, or the people around him were, interested in Cuba, and that is the only thing I can see has any bearing in your interest here.

Mr. LIEBELER. To what extent would you say that your father has influenced your own political views and attitudes?

Mr. PAINE. I would have guessed it was almost negligible. I was aware that sometime in the beginning of college or something I used the language of the masses or I used jargon which I recognized, came to perceive was of quite leftist nature, and I think that at the time I used to get The Nation, that was in high school. I probably picked it up more from the magazines and things of that sort than from him.

Mr. LIEBELER. Did you ever discuss your father with Lee Oswald?

Mr. PAINE. On a phone call shortly after the assassination he called and thought it was outrageous to be pinning Lee Oswald who was a scapegoat, an ideal person to hang the blame on.

Mr. LIEBELER. Your father called you?

Mr. PAINE. Yes; he called me, yes. He didn't suppose it was true, I told him I thought it probably was true. And I told him to keep his shirt on.

Mr. LIEBELER. Do you remember anything else about that conversation?

Mr. PAINE. No. It was chiefly both he and Freddy, his wife, had to be calmed down. They thought it was a steamrollered job of injustice or something. And I didn't think their admonitions were—I think not to say anything, not to join the hubbub or jump on the things I said or I took it to be things I said would be distorted and blown up and added to the hullabaloo to lynch Lee.

Representative FORD. Did they infer or imply that the allegations or accusations against Oswald bore the semblance of a lynching? And I use lynching in the broad sense.

Mr. PAINE. They did not use lynching at all. I added that. They thought he was——

Representative FORD. Being railroaded?

Mr. PAINE. No; he said that no one, no member of the Friends of Cuba would want to assassinate the President. That was a crazy idea.

Representative FORD. You said that was a crazy idea?

Mr. PAINE. No; he said that. Therefore, he concluded, and this was the same, similar to my feeling, that I first didn't think Oswald had done it because I didn't see how it fitted in, how it helped his favorite ideals.

And Lyman then said the same thing. Therefore, including himself, Lyman, that Lee couldn't have done it, and that this must be—Lee was the ideal person to hang it on.

Representative FORD. How soon was this phone call after the assassination?

Mr. PAINE. I think it was—he did not know, I think, that we had Marina staying with us, but he was one of the first to connect, guess that it was us. He called and asked us, "Is this you?"

Representative FORD. "Is this you?" What? I don't quite understand the context here.

Mr. PAINE. He heard it on the news and he heard Mrs. Paine, and Marina had been staying with a Mrs. Paine and he called to ask, "Are you the Paines?"

Mr. LIEBELER. Had you discussed Lee Oswald with your father prior to this time?

Mr. PAINE. No; I don't think I mentioned him.

Mr. LIEBELER. Do you know whether your father knew Lee Oswald?

Mr. PAINE. No; I do not know. Or I gather since he had such a funny idea of him over the phone.

Mr. LIEBELER. To the best of your judgment the only way your father heard of Lee Oswald, connected Lee Oswald to you, was through a news broadcast that he had heard connecting Oswald with somebody named Paine?

Mr. PAINE. Or Marina had stayed with the Paines.

Mr. LIEBELER. Did you ever discuss your father with Lee Oswald?

Mr. PAINE. No; I did not.

Mr. LIEBELER. And Oswald never asked you about your father in any way or did he indicate that he knew of your father?

Mr. PAINE. No; he did not. I think Ruth came closer to revealing that my father had—you will have to ask her about that question. I did not mention my father to Lee.

Mr. LIEBELER. When did you meet Lee Oswald?

Mr. PAINE. I met him sometime in the spring of 1963.

Mr. DULLES. This is Oswald?

Mr. LIEBELER. Yes; Lee Oswald.

Mr. PAINE. We were invited to a party, Ruth and I were invited to a party, given by Everett Glover. I had a cold and wasn't able to go. Ruth went at that time and subsequently went once or twice to see Marina. And she invited Marina and Lee to our house for dinner, and here the date that comes to mind is April 10.

Mr. DULLES. Where was Marina staying at this time?

Mr. PAYNE. Berry Street.

Mr. DULLES. Berry Street in Dallas.

Mr. LIEBELER. Berry Street or would it be Neely Street?

Mr. PAINE. Neely Street. So this was the first time I saw them. I had to go over, he didn't drive a car and I had to go over, and pick him up in my car and bring him back to the house. So I went over to Neely Street and saw them. Marina took about half an hour to pack all the things for Junie. Meanwhile I was talking to Lee at their house there.

Mr. LIEBELER. Would you tell us about that conversation?

Mr. PAINE. I asked him what he was doing, his job, and he showed me a picture on the wall, which was a piece of newspaper. I think—that is beside the point. I asked him about Russia, what he liked about——

Mr. DULLES. Could we get that picture?

Mr. PAINE. I think it was beside the point. It was a piece of newspaper showing a fashion ad, I think. I think his job was——

Mr. DULLES. Nothing to do with politics at all, to do with his job. I see.

Mr. PAINE. I asked him what he thought, I wanted to know why he had gone to Russia and why he had then come back. He had told me he had become a Marxist in this country without ever having met a Communist, by reading books and then he got to Russia, and——

Mr. LIEBELER. Did he tell you why he went to Russia?

Mr. PAINE. He said he wanted to go to Russia. He had chosen to go to Russia.

Mr. LIEBELER. He didn't elaborate on it?

Mr. PAINE. No; I gathered he had had an interest in going to Russia for a number of years prior to the time he got there and decided that that was the paradise of the world and through fortunate relations between this country and Russia at the time, I would have to remember history to know whether that was a warm, a friendly time or not, but he indicated both his going and his coming were fortunate times in history or something that made it possible for him to do these.

Mr. DULLES. Fortunate times?

Mr. PAINE. Fortunate times, this was sort of an accident in history. This is what I gathered from his conversation.

Representative FORD. Fortunate that he could leave at the time and fortunate that he could come back.

Mr. PAINE. Fortunate that he could be accepted to emigrate to Russia. He told me that he had—so he went to Russia and he tried to surrender his passport to the Russians but the State Department would not give it to him, or the consul in Moscow, which was—which proved to be fortunate because then a few years later when he wanted to return it would not have been possible, except if they still had his passport. He had not legally surrendered it.

Mr. LIEBELER. Did he indicate that was a fortunate circumstance?

Mr. PAINE. I think he smiled, he indicated to me he genuinely had wanted to become a Russian citizen and to surrender it. He wanted to renounce his American citizenship. He tried to, and the Russians, he told me, had accepted his bona fide intentions and tried to get the passport away from the Americans.

Representative FORD. Was the failure to get his passport a determining factor in their not accepting his desires?

Mr. PAINE. No. He told me that they did accept his desires despite his inability to get the passport and give it to them.

Representative FORD. Despite his inability?

Mr. PAINE. Yes.

Mr. LIEBELER. "They" being the Russians?

Mr. PAINE. Yes; they being the Russians and they issued to him, he told me, the standard kind of temporary citizenship paper which is given to all emigres to Russia, and there are some——

Mr. DULLES. Was it citizenship paper he said or something else, citizenship paper?

Mr. PAINE. Now, I suppose there was a regular paper and everybody would know of it.

Mr. DULLES. Domicile paper or something allowing domicile.

Mr. PAINE. I had thought, my impression was, that it was kind of probationary citizenship. It is a kind of paper issued for a year to somebody who is seeking citizenship. That was my impression at the time.

Mr. DULLES. Could it have been a probationary residence permit or something of that sort. He said citizenship, did he?

Mr. PAINE. That was my impression. That it was the commencement of a citizenship paper.

Mr. DULLES. Did he tell you about any difficulties he had in getting permission to stay on in Russia?

Mr. PAINE. Well, this was a question. I asked him how was it they so readily accepted—you know other Americans have a hard time staying more than 30 days there. "How was it that you were so readily accepted into the bosom of Soviet Society?" And to that he answered, "well, it was just a fortunate mood between the countries or something to that effect," is something that I gathered.

I didn't remember the history and I thought it would be—he smiled a little bit. I can't remember whether he smiled a little bit when I then asked him how did he manage to get out, at one time, but at one time I do remember he smiled as though there were a story there, and I didn't—I supposed the story would be too intricate, not interesting enough to try to get him to relate it.

Mr. LIEBELER. You did not ask him to relate the story?

Mr. PAINE. No; I did not.

Mr. LIEBELER. Did you ever learn the circumstances under which he left Russia, from him?

Mr. PAINE. As he told me at that same half hour before we came back to our house on Fifth Street.——

Mr. DULLES. Was this the first time you had seen him?

Mr. PAINE. All this happened in the first half hour.

Mr. DULLES. The first time you had ever seen him?

Mr. PAINE. The first time I had seen him or at least that first night.

He told me he had decided, that he had wanted, to come back to this country and it was through the fortunate circumstance of the Embassy still having his passport which was a legal loophole that made it legally possible, and I asked him—at sometime I thought this was rather nice that the State Department, I think this was a little later in the same evening, the State Department had forewarned him, had granted him money also, to come back.

Mr. LIEBELER. Did he tell you that?

Mr. PAINE. He told me that and I was rather proud of the State Department for its generous behavior toward such a wayward citizen. He actually had spoken—I had mentioned this because he had spoken abusively of the American Government.

Mr. LIEBELER. At this time, during the first meeting?

Mr. PAINE. Not just the American Government—yes; at this same meeting. He had spoken with abuse of, sort of resentment that they didn't let him have his passport and I thought, well now, that was just kind of a nice trick, by having a consular official there that he knew, this man wanted to change his mind, this little legal dodge of not wanting to give him his passport which I think is illegal if the man wants it, it would be the thing to permit him to come back.

Mr. LIEBELER. Did you point that out to Lee Oswald?

Mr. PAINE. Yes; I did.

Mr. LIEBELER. What did he say?

Mr. PAINE. I don't think he responded to it.

Mr. DULLES. He talked about surrendering the passport rather than surrendering citizenship, did he?

Mr. PAINE. The two were synonymous, I thought, that if you surrendered your passport and with the intention of adopting another one that was renouncing American citizenship.

Mr. DULLES. I see.

Mr. PAINE. Which he wanted, he told me he wanted to renounce his American citizenship. He said that quite flatly.

Mr. LIEBELER. Do you remember anything else about this conversation concerning his trip back and his attitude toward the State Department and the United States that he discussed during this first meeting?

Mr. PAINE. I don't believe so. I think I have got it a little confused with Marguerite Oswald what she said at the time of the assassination, at the time of the night of the 22d. She was resentful of the State Department, thinking it had been remiss in taking so long in getting him back. I don't remember whether he had voiced the same—I am confused, I don't know whether it was he or she who had voiced this resentment. I thought to the contrary it was very generous.

Mr. LIEBELER. Do you remember whether or not Oswald himself voiced resentment against the Government of the United States in this connection?

Mr. PAINE. Yes; I do remember that. That was the thing that prompted me to say that it was actually rather nice of them to have been illegal just for this——

Mr. DULLES. I didn't catch the last. Nice of them to have been what?

Mr. PAINE. I though it probably was illegal of the embassy official not to hand over his passport when he demanded it in order to surrender it to the Soviet Union.

Mr. LIEBELER. But you don't remember Oswald responding to that when you made that answer to him?

Mr. PAINE. I don't remember his response.

The CHAIRMAN. You also said you thought it was rather nice of the State Department to do that in order to make it possible for him to return if he wanted to?

Mr. PAINE. Yes; I said both of these things. They had given him money. They had held, a peccadillo to hold, the passport out of the knowledge that he might, such people might, want to return, change their mind, and then to provide him money moreover to come back, this all seemed to me rather nice even though it had taken 2 more months than when he originally wanted to come back.

I had said, this in response to his, some kind of expression on his part of criticism of the State Department or the foreign embassy or whatever it is.

Mr. LIEBELER. Do you remember why he was critical? Was he critical because they had not given him his passport when he went to Russia or was he critical because in his opinion they had taken so long to arrange his return?

Mr. PAINE. I think he was critical when he first mentioned it, he seemed to have the critical attitude—some of this critical attitude may have been facial expressions or way of speaking, which was somewhat common with him. Therefore, I can't remember for sure whether it was in the words or in his attitude.

He was critical, though, certainly of the first, of the State Department not relinquishing his passport.

Mr. DULLES. Was he critical at this latter time?

Mr. PAINE. He was critical of that as he was relating to his desire to go to the Soviet Union. He was relating the story to me, and then he had spoken of the State Department as though they were a bunch of bastards, wouldn't—or illegal or something. Anyway, he was unfavorable.

Mr. DULLES. But did you indicate he was rather glad that they had later taken this position so that he could get his passport back or did I misunderstand you on that?

Mr. PAINE. Well, I pointed out to him that or said "it was kind of fortunate that they had held your passport," and I think he nodded his assent to that.

Mr. LIEBELER. Did he tell you why he decided to return to the United States from Russia?

Mr. PAINE. Most of this conversation, I think, was when we had first met and I wasn't sure whether he was speaking derogatively of the Soviet Union in order to win my good graces or thinking he could win my friendship that way.

However, he spoke more with disfavor of the Soviet Union during this first meeting than was quite comprehensible to someone who had gone there.

Mr. LIEBELER. What did he say?

Mr. PAINE. But chiefly what he said was that he didn't have choice of where he could live, you were assigned, he spoke with a certain amount of derision, scorn of the fact that you were assigned jobs, and he thought the food was boring, I think, to use his word. He had mentioned that he liked to—he had gone hunting with some friends, that was the only thing he mentioned about the Soviet Union in which I sensed that he had been with people except for also mentioning that he had been the center of interest as an American who couldn't drive a car.

But apparently he had relished going hunting. He had also said with resentment, a Soviet citizen could not own a rifle. They could own shotguns but not a rifle, and that you could shoot a rifle only by joining a rifle club which he said was a paramilitary organization.

Again, this was with a degree of scorn in his voice or his attitude. I had assumed that he at least tried the paramilitary organization, the rifle club, so he could speak with such scorn, with knowledge of what he was speaking about.

Mr. LIEBELER. Did he tell you that he had joined an organization in which he was permitted to shoot a rifle?

Mr. PAINE. No; he did not. I don't know that for a fact. I had assumed from his conversation that he had tried it but I gather that he did not like this organization.

Mr. DULLES. Did he say anything about having to leave the rifle at the club, that you couldn't take the rifle away from the club, or anything of that kind?

Mr. PAINE. I assume that was true. He didn't mention it, he mentioned that a Soviet citizen could not possess a rifle.

Mr. LIEBELER. Did he speak of any training that he might have received in connection with either a rifle or a shotgun while he was in the Soviet Union?

Mr. PAINE. No; he didn't.

Mr. LIEBELER. Did he indicate to you the degree of facility with which he used either of these weapons while he was in the Soviet Union?

Mr. PAINE. No; he did not.

Mr. LIEBELER. He—is there anything else he told you about this hunting club or this rifle or shotgun that you can remember now?

Mr. PAINE. No; I am not particularly interested in rifles and hunting so that I didn't—it was an ideal opportunity—I think he did love hunting so I think it would have been an ideal way to reach him in a somewhat human way.

Mr. DULLES. You got no idea of how much time he was at the rifle club or what? Did it seem to be a frequent occupation?

Mr. PAINE. No; I can't say I had any fruitful idea of whether he was a member of it. I assumed he was a member of it. He didn't say he was a member of it. I assumed he spoke with authority saying it was a paramilitary organization and somehow conveying the idea that he didn't like that aspect of it and, therefore, I assumed he didn't like it. He spoke only with pleasure of his hunting trip. He mentioned a hunting trip, I don't think he mentioned them in plural, which he had taken with some friends.

Mr. LIEBELER. Do you remember any more details about that hunting trip?

Mr. PAINE. We talked, this was within the first half hour, the talk was very brief.

Mr. LIEBELER. Did he ever mention to you this hunting trip or anything relating to a rifle or shotgun in the Soviet Union at any later time?

Mr. PAINE. No; I didn't know what time he was referring to.

Mr. LIEBELER. I mean at any other time after the first meeting with you did he refer again to his activities in the Soviet Union?

Mr. PAINE. I see.

Mr. LIEBELER. In connection with this rifle?

Mr. PAINE. No; that subject never came up again.

Mr. LIEBELER. Did he tell you at this first meeting about his work in the Soviet Union?

Mr. PAINE. I had gathered he worked somewhere in a television factory.

Mr. LIEBELER. Did he tell you that?

Mr. PAINE. Yes; I can't remember whether it was television, it was electronics of some sort.

Mr. LIEBELER. Did he tell you the nature of his work?

Mr. PAINE. He did not tell me. I thought to myself that if he was in a very honorable position there he would have mentioned it. So, I thought he was probably just a mechanic of some sort, wiring it together.

Mr. LIEBELER. Did he tell you how much he was paid?

Mr. PAINE. I can't remember, I think he did but I don't remember what he said.

Mr. LIEBELER. Did he indicate that he received any income other than from his work?

Mr. PAINE. No; I don't believe he told me anything about that.

Mr. LIEBELER. We have been referring primarily here in our questioning to the first meeting that you had with him, but do you remember any subsequent conversation with Oswald about his work, his pay, and his income in the Soviet Union after this first meeting?

Mr. PAINE. I think he thought it was too low. He thought the standard of living, he recognized the standard of living was low, and they were restricted therefore in their—just too confined, told where to live. The food was boring and there was nothing to do. I didn't get the idea it was lack of money. He did not say anything about lack of money.

Mr. DULLES. I wonder if we could get for our guidance the approximate number of times he saw Lee Oswald?

Mr. PAINE. It was about four times that we had lengthy conversations.

Mr. DULLES. Four times, that is four times prior to the date of the assassination.

Mr. PAINE. That is correct.

Mr. DULLES. Or that includes all the times?

Mr. PAINE. I didn't see him again after the assassination.

Mr. DULLES. You didn't see him after the assassination. Four times prior to the assassination including this one time you have already described?

Mr. PAINE. Yes. This is the first meeting before he went to New Orleans and then about three weekends after he came back——

Mr. DULLES. I think that will be taken up. I just wanted to get in my mind approximately how many times in all you saw him.

Mr. LIEBELER. Did Oswald at any time indicate to you that he was treated by the Russian authorities in any way different from ordinary Russian citizens who occupied a similar status in the Soviet Union?

Mr. PAINE. No; I wasn't aware of that.

Mr. LIEBELER. Did he tell you about any special training that he had?

Mr. PAINE. No; he did not.

Mr. LIEBELER. Did he mention his living accommodations?

Mr. PAINE. Well, with some kind of resentment he did, that it was assigned, and I think that is about all he said.

Mr. DULLES. May I ask whether these questions relate to all the four times or just to the first time, are we still on the first?

Mr. LIEBELER. Basically on the first time, sir, unless we specify to the contrary.

Mr. DULLES. Yes.

Mr. LIEBELER. Tell us what else you and Oswald discussed during this first meeting that you had?

Mr. PAINE. Unfortunately that first meeting was the clearest one. I was asking him questions, taking his answers. I had hoped when I met this man to have insights into Russia, both meeting him and meeting his wife, and interesting talks about the differences between the Russian system and the American, the western system.

Then I found that he was—some questions, later in the evening, the conversation was translated into Russian also so that Marina could follow along.

Mr. DULLES. You mean after the first half hour when you were preparing——

Mr. PAINE. That is right, when we came back after dinner to our house.

Mr. DULLES. Your house. So this went on?

Mr. PAINE. What you have heard now occurred mostly in the first half hour when I was speaking directly to him when I met him.

Mr. LIEBELER. Then you returned to Irving to your house and had dinner and had the additional conversation?

Mr. PAINE. Yes. Now, in all the subsequent conversations, you are going to get less information in what he said.

Mr. DULLES. In the first part of this meeting you were alone and in the second part of the meeting there were other people there?

Mr. PAINE. My wife and Marina was able to join us. At this time Marina was packing things for Junie and I noticed that he was speaking very harshly to her. He was telling her what bag or satchel to take. I gathered from it, of course, it was in Russian, and I thought to myself, here is a little fellow who certainly insists on wearing the pants.

Mr. DULLES. You don't understand Russian yourself?

Mr. PAINE. No. So he spoke loudly to her, and didn't rise from his seat. But spoke surprisingly harshly especially in front of a guest.

Mr. DULLES. How did she take this?

Mr. PAINE. With a bit of umbrage. She didn't like it. It rankled her.

Representative FORD. In other words, this half hour conversation took place in their apartment?

Mr. PAINE. Yes.

Representative FORD. While she was packing the bags to go to your home?

Mr. PAINE. That is right.

Mr. DULLES. Was she packing the bags for some days or was this——

Mr. PAINE. No; just bottles, diapers, clothing, something.

Mr. DULLES. For a weekend?

Mr. PAINE. Just for the evening.

Mr. DULLES. Just for an evening?

Mr. PAINE. I don't know why it took so long but it did. I guess they weren't quite ready when I arrived.

Mr. LIEBELER. What else did you and Oswald speak about during this evening, do you remember?

Mr. PAINE. After supper the conversation was translated into Russian, and I wanted to gather Marina's or get Marina's corroboration of certain things he said about Russia and there we found when she had differing opinions from him that he would not let her, he would slap her down verbally, and not let her express them or say—Ruth told me later, he was calling her a fool, "You don't know anything."

When I encountered this, I actually trusted Marina to know—the questions I was asking, it seemed to me could be better answered by Marina, so I wasn't paying very close attention to what he had said about that.

Mr. DULLES. Could you indicate on what points they seemed to differ or what points that he raised that irritated her or vice versa in their discussion about

Russia? You said he slapped her down. I was wondering on what kind of points he slapped her down.

Mr. PAINE. I have unfortunately tried to remember those points myself wishing, wondering whether hypnosis would bring it out of me as a tape recorder, or something. I was interested to know whether the Russians were happy with their system, whether they felt the presence of the Secret Police, these are questions, I don't remember asking them, these are questions that I would have been interested in.

Mr. LIEBELER. Do you remember any response either from Marina or from Oswald on these points?

Mr. PAINE. And I don't remember anything specific here. I just remember that I encountered too many points where they apparently differed and, therefore, I had in mind I will just wait until she can learn English and we will get it from the horse's mouth.

Mr. LIEBELER. Did you speak with Oswald during this first meeting of the circumstances under which he met Marina and married her in Russia?

Mr. PAINE. I don't remember when I learned that. I think I learned it from Ruth, who had spoken to Marina on this subject.

Mr. LIEBELER. What did you learn?

Mr. PAINE. It may have been—I don't remember when it occurred, it may have been after the assassination, I may have read it in the paper or something.

Mr. LIEBELER. You don't remember any specific conversations with Oswald on that subject?

Mr. PAINE. No; I don't.

Mr. LIEBELER. Did Lee Oswald ever speak to you about his experience in the United States Marine Corps?

Mr. PAINE. He mentioned that his brother went in the Marine Corps and apparently enjoyed it and he had then, I think he said he had left school early to join it and I gathered, I thought to myself, he is expecting to find the joy his brother found there and he did not find it. He did not like the Marine Corps.

Mr. LIEBELER. Did he tell you anything—pardon me.

Mr. PAINE. He did not mention that I can recall his exit from the Marine Corps.

Mr. LIEBELER. Did he ever mention the name of Governor Connally in connection with his experiences in the Marines?

Mr. PAINE. Not that I remember.

Mr. DULLES. Did he ever mention the President in this or any other conversations?

Mr. PAINE. He mentioned the President only once that I can remember specifically; at the ACLU meeting I think.

Mr. DULLES. At the which?

Mr. PAINE. At the ACLU meeting I took him to. He had mentioned, he thought President Kennedy was doing quite a good job in civil rights, which was high praise coming from Lee.

Mr. LIEBELER. Did you have any discussion during this first meeting other than the discussion you have already mentioned concerning Oswald's political beliefs?

Mr. PAINE. There, of course, I was interested in that subject, found we differed, and then in order to not wrestle with concepts or arguments that were unmanageably large, I tried to bring it down to more specific instances of how he would like to see the world be.

Mr. LIEBELER. How did you become aware of the fact that you differed, do you remember?

Mr. PAINE. I don't remember him making any bones about it the very first meeting. He told me he had become a Marxist, in his own apartment there, that he had become a Marxist by reading books and never having met a Communist in this country.

And he also then told me with a certain sadness or regret that he couldn't speak about political and economic subjects with his people, and fellows at work.

(At this point Senator Cooper entered the hearing room.)

Mr. LIEBELER. You were going to mention specific areas of political discussion that you had with him.

Mr. PAINE. One other thing happened in this first half hour, the most fruitful half hour I had ever had with him. He had mentioned his employer. I probably asked him why did he leave this country to go to the Soviet Union, and his supreme theme in this regard is the exploitation of man by man, by which he means one man making a profit out of another man's labor, which is the normal employment situation in this country and to which he found—took, felt great resentment.

He was aware that his employer made—he made more money for his employer than he was paid and specifically he mentioned how his employer of the engraving company goods and chattels that he had, that Oswald didn't have, and with some specific resentment toward this employer, and I thought privately to myself that this resentment must show through if he ever meets his employer, it must sort of show through and that his employer wouldn't find that man very attractive. So this was his guiding theme.

The reason it appears that this country, the system in this country had to go, had to be changed, was because of this supreme immoral way of managing affairs here, the exploitation of man by man which occurs in this country.

We discussed about it occurring in the Soviet Union, the taxation of a man's labor, it occurs there also, and it appeared that only, he seemed to agree or sometimes I had to feed him, this conversation now is a later one, when we were talking about the specifics of exploitation of man by man, he agreed that the only difference was that in the Soviet Union it is a choice which is impersonal.

The person who decides the man's wages and labor does not stand to gain by it whereas in this country the man who decides stands to gain by it.

Mr. DULLES. The man who decides what, to employ the other man?

Mr. PAINE. No; what wage to pay him.

Mr. DULLES. What wage to pay him?

Mr. PAINE. Or what his return shall be. So that was the only—the most important, by far economic and political almost, let's call it economic doctrine he held.

Mr. LIEBELER. Did he translate that economic doctrine to specific policies that he thought should be adopted or specific changes that should be made in the structure of this country?

Mr. PAINE. I had never, to my satisfaction, uncovered an area of progessive change that he would advocate. I asked him how did he think this change was going to come about, and he never answered that.

And it seemed to me he was critical of almost everything that occurs in this country. So that he did not—I did not come to—did not know of anything in which he could see a progressive evolutionary change or policies that could be pushed in order to promote his ideals.

Representative FORD. Did he react academically, intellectually, violently or in what way did he express these views?

Mr. PAINE. Well, he was quite dogmatic. First he wanted to put me in a category. In one of the later talks—when we first met he talked very freely and then I think as we made, in later conversations, I had to do more and more of it—make more and more effort to draw something out of him.

In his later conversations, Ruth found him so bothersome.

Mr. DULLES. What was that word?

Mr. PAINE. Bothersome, that she couldn't join the conversations. He would get too angry or too——

Representative FORD. He resented the probing or the questioning?

Mr. PAINE. No; he did not really resent the probing. For instance, take this issue of the exploitation of man by man. When we had boiled it down to this rather fine difference or technical difference that one was done by an impersonal body and one was done personal.

Mr. DULLES. The Soviet being the first and the American being the second?

Mr. PAINE. That is correct. That being then the crux of the matter and the reason this is the matter to be changed, if we were to follow the logic of the discussion, many arguments seemed to approach at that kind of a point where it

400

is just logic or reason just didn't seem to work or hold water in this case, and we were left then with the starkness of his statement that this was an unforgivable moral sin, and he called it a moral sin or I questioned him to that effect, and so he thought it was a moral sin and he thought he was moral by adhering to that doctrine.

Representative FORD. Did he appear to enjoy these give and takes between you and himself or did he resent them as you proceeded in your discussions?

Mr. PAINE. I don't think he resented them. I noticed at times he got quite hot under the collar and I noticed that he was holding his, staying on a steady keel even better than I was, as though he had had considerable practice in sticking to, controlling himself, holding his position and not getting ruffled.

Representative FORD. But in this process over a period of time during these four discussions he never deviated from his basic thesis?

Mr. PAINE. Yes. Of course, as I said to the others, I don't believe whether you were here, we only had about four talks altogether, and I later came to realize that if he were to have abandoned any one of these or have abandoned that one in particular, that would have undermined his whole philosophy, would humanly itself quite unreasonable to expect a fundamental exchange within an evening, just because of a logical compulsion or logical argument or something.

Mr. DULLES. Did you get the impression that he felt both systems, the American system and the Soviet system involved the exploitation of man by man except it was a different exploiter?

Mr. PAINE. I gathered—I was irked because it seemed to me the difference that he accepted as a sufficient difference, the one in the Soviet Union was impersonal, that he was not, in other words—he admitted in the Soviet Union that the tax rate which was a general term then for the amount of money or reward that is not returned of what a man makes, was higher in the Soviet Union. He agreed that that could be true, and didn't seem to be dismayed at that. So I did not find criticism of the Soviet Union on that score.

And in fact he didn't—I didn't discover in what ways he would like to try to change the Soviet Union except he didn't like the restrictions on his freedom there. Neither did he see there was any connection between the restrictions on freedom there and the freedom we have here without control of how the relationship between men would be governed.

Mr. DULLES. Did he ever go into the question of the relative position of labor in the United States from the point of view of its freedom of bargaining and the control of labor in the Soviet Union? Did that ever come up?

Mr. PAINE. No. I think, I can't remember whether it was a conversation I had directly with him or immediately after, I was following this idea that here we feel we have quite a different attitude about exploitation. Somebody—he felt exploited and he thought all the working class was exploited, and he also thought they were brainwashed, and he also thought that churches were all alike, all the religious sects were the same and they were all apparatus of the power structure to maintain itself in power.

When I pointed out that our church was financed by people like myself, when I contribute so many dollars to the church, he just shrugged his shoulders. It didn't—his views still stood and it also permitted him, I think, gave him the moral ground to dismiss my arguments because I was here just a product of my environment and I didn't know better and he had the word from the enlightenment, that he knew the truth and therefore I was just spouting the line that was fed to me by the power structure.

Mr. LIEBELER. I think you mentioned before that he had wanted to put you in a category, categorize you. Did he indicate to you during that first conversation that he had concluded what category?

Mr. PAINE. No; it was over several conversations, I suppose it was the last conversation we had, he couldn't put me in a category and he named about seven or eight categories.

Mr. LIEBELER. What were they?

Mr. PAINE. I wasn't a Bircher, I wasn't a liberal, a Communist, a Socialist, probably something to do with religion, something like that, atheist.

Mr. DULLES. He didn't say whether you were a Republican or Democrat?

Mr. PAINE. I don't believe he was concerned about that.

(Laughter.)

Mr. PAINE. No; I am sure he would see no distinction between the two parties.

Mr. LIEBELER. So he concluded that he was unable to categorize you?

Mr. PAINE. Yes. And I also felt as soon as he had realized that that he could then dismiss me as not something that functions in this world, not one of the forces or the opposing camps he has to contend with.

Mr. LIEBELER. You mentioned that your wife became bothered or Oswald proved bothersome to your wife. Could you tell us in what way Oswald was bothersome to Mrs. Paine?

Mr. PAINE. Well, I think one of the most outstanding was in this discussion of religions and I was trying to suggest that religions did embody many of the values of many people and so the conversation was trying to talk about those values quite apart from—I think the Russian, I think Marina's view of religion is quite primitive—never mind Marina. Ruth was bothered by his logic or argument being of no avail. She would be content, you know if he had followed the laws of debate or something, you present evidence and he presents opposite evidence and you try to answer, let one answer the other. But when he couldn't answer he would just state his belief and there he followed the Communist line.

He talked something about feudalism, or the church being more powerful in feudalism than it was today and he tried to explain why that was.

I had then suggested that maybe science was instrumental as an alternative explanation to his explanation but instead of supporting further his view, which just didn't make sense to me, he just restated it. Well, this kind of thing.

Mr. LIEBELER. Upset your wife?

Mr. PAINE. Yes; you just couldn't enter the conversation deeper.

Mr. LIEBELER. Do you remember any other conversation you and Oswald had during this first evening that you met?

The CHAIRMAN. From the first day, are you going back to?

Mr. LIEBELER. Yes.

Mr. PAINE. I think we probably spoke, I was trying still to find common ground with him, and I think we probably spoke critically of the far right. It even seems to me we may have mentioned Walker.

I had been bothered at the time that Walker had—I guess it doesn't do any good to enter into the matter because I don't remember his response.

Mr. LIEBELER. Did you mention Walker's name during the first meeting?

Mr. PAINE. My memory is very foggy. But I would take it as—this was an impression.

Mr. LIEBELER. Give us your best recollection, and I want to ask you again this was in early April 1963, that you had this conversation, is that correct?

Mr. PAINE. It was that first meeting when we had them over to dinner and Ruth can give you the date of that.

Mr. LIEBELER. For the benefit of the Commission the record indicates it was about April 2, 1963, that that occurred. Tell us to the best of your recollection what the conversation about General Walker was at that time?

Mr. PAINE. I think he had mentioned, a friend of ours had a German wife and she just achieved her citizenship papers, and this had been done at the ceremony and General Walker had been invited to lead the singing, conducted by June Davis who is somewhat old and slipped into error of calling him Judge Walker every once in a while, and it somewhat offended this friend of ours who was aware of why she liked this country, freedoms, and liberties and values that are expressed here. And she was rather sorry that Walker should take it upon himself to define, to these stupid foreigners or these ignorant foreigners, what this country stands for. So I think I mentioned this episode to him.

Representative FORD. Him being Oswald?

Mr. PAINE. Oswald, and I think he smiled and nodded his assent. I don't think he said any—I don't think he made any important remarks about Walker.

Mr. LIEBELER. Do you remember anything that he said about Walker at all?

Mr. PAINE. I think that is the only time, probably the only time we mentioned Walker.

Mr. DULLES. To refresh my recollection, there was about 2 days or——

Mr. LIEBELER. 8 days before.

Mr. RANKIN. It was on the 10th.

Senator COOPER. Did he indicate in any way that he knew about General Walker at that time?

Mr. PAINE. We seemed to agree at least superficially that in thinking the far right was unfortunate in its thoughts.

Mr. LIEBELER. Did he say anything or do anything that would lead you to believe that he planned an attack on General Walker?

Mr. PAINE. Absolutely not.

Senator COOPER. Did he indicate in any way that he knew about General Walker's activities and beliefs and position on public affairs?

Mr. PAINE. When I went to the ACLU meeting he then got up, stood up and reported what had happened at the meeting of the far right which had occurred at convention hall the day before, U.N. Day, they called it U.S. Day, and I think Walker had spoken then.

From this I gathered that he was doing more or less the same thing— I thought he was, I didn't inquire how he spent his free time but I supposed he was going around to right wing groups being familiarizing himself for whatever his purposes were as I was.

Senator COOPER. Is that prior to the conversation you have talked about?

Mr. PAINE. No; this is after this conversation.

Senator COOPER. What?

Mr. PAINE. This is after this conversation and I only had this, this was the only concrete evidence I had of how he spent, might have spent some of his time. It happened in the ACLU meeting in late October. I suppose he was familiar with the right-wing groups and activities, and movements. And certainly familiar with Walker; yes.

Mr. LIEBELER. Confining the Senator's question to the meeting in April, he didn't indicate in any way that he was familiar with Walker's attitude or activities?

Mr. PAINE. He was familiar with Walker. He knew who Walker was, there was no doubt about that. We were talking about Walker.

Representative FORD. To find some common ground.

Mr. DULLES. He didn't say he knew where Walker lived or anything of that kind. That didn't come up?

Mr. LIEBELER. Did he indicate any understanding to you at that April meeting of Walker's attitude?

Mr. PAINE. I don't think he singled out Walker as—I had the impression that he was quite familiar with Walker and probably familiar with the names of various right-wing groups, shall we say, the Christian Science, not the Christian Science, I have forgotten the names of various organizations.

Mr. LIEBELER. Did you relate to Oswald this story about Walker speaking at the meeting or the ceremony at which the immigrants were given their citizenship?

Mr. PAINE. I believe I did; yes. I believe that is what I said about Walker at the time.

Mr. LIEBELER. What was his response to that?

Mr. PAINE. And I think he didn't say much. I think he smiled and nodded his head and did that kind of thing. He may have said just a few words.

Mr. LIEBELER. Did you take it that Oswald agreed with the views that you expressed?

Mr. PAINE. Yes; I did.

Mr. LIEBELER. Now, after this first meeting——

Senator COOPER. May I interrupt you again, I don't want to interrupt your train too much but I think you had said that during this conversation that you did have some discussion about right-wing groups.

Mr. PAINE. Yes.

Senator COOPER. And their position and activities, and so forth. In that discussion were individuals named or members assumed to be members of that group?

(At this point Representative Ford left the hearing room.)

Mr. PAINE. It is possible we would have mentioned Welch. I don't think I would have mentioned Welch, I didn't know anything specifically about the John Birch Society at the time.

Senator COOPER. Was Walker, he was talking about Walker?

Mr. PAINE. He was the only one whose name was mentioned.

Senator COOPER. Are you sure whether or not Oswald made any comment at any time during this conversation about Walker?

Mr. PAINE. I don't remember, as I say, I remember it very vaguely but I remember telling that instance of his conducting that ceremony. But—and Walker was known, I knew that Walker was known to Lee. And at least it achieved a certain feeling of similarity there, even though the similarity was only superficial in our views and feelings about it. I don't think he went on to describe any—it was mostly a ploy on my part to curry him or make him feel more at ease.

Mr. LIEBELER. It was clear to you at that time that both you and Mr. Oswald had an adverse view of General Walker and did not think favorably of him, is that correct?

Mr. PAINE. That is correct.

Mr. LIEBELER. Had you heard of Lee Oswald before you had occasion to go and pick him up that time and bring him to your house for dinner?

Mr. PAINE. Yes; I heard about him as soon as Ruth had been invited to this party back in February, whenever it was.

Mr. LIEBELER. What was the basis of your wife's interest in the Oswalds and of your interest in the Oswalds?

Mr. PAINE. Everett Glover invited us knowing that Ruth was studying Russian and that—asked us if we would be interested in meeting this—they were presented to us as an American who had defected to Russia and decided he didn't like it and came back and brought a Russian wife with him. Would we like to meet these people? Yes, that sounded interesting.

Mr. DULLES. Was this the Fort Worth group?

Mr. PAINE. No; this is in Dallas.

Mr. DULLES. Dallas.

Mr. LIEBELER. After this first meeting with Lee Oswald when was the next time that you saw him?

Mr. PAINE. That would be after he returned, when Marina was living with us, when he returned, we thought he returned from looking for work from Houston but apparently it had been his trip to Mexico.

Mr. LIEBELER. Tell us the circumstances of how you met him and what happened at that time?

Mr. DULLES. Could we have the date of this?

Mr. LIEBELER. This would have been what, early October or late September of 1963?

Mr. PAINE. I think Marina was there about a week, at least a week before he came, if she came the 24th of September, which comes to my mind, it would be in the early part of October. I would normally appear at the house on Fridays, sometimes occasionally on Sundays, I would come on Friday evening, and——

Mr. LIEBELER. You were separated from your wife at this time?

Mr. PAINE. That is correct.

Mr. LIEBELER. And you had your own apartment at Arlington, Tex.?

Mr. PAINE. Grand Prairie.

Mr. LIEBELER. Grand Prairie.

Mr. PAINE. I don't particularly remember, the occasions don't stand out one from another. The first two meetings, I think were before he found work, and at first I talked a little bit about the problem of finding work with him.

Mr. DULLES. These were the first two meetings after the preliminary meeting?

Mr. PAINE. Yes. While Marina was staying with us.

Mr. LIEBELER. Go through your testimony, Mr. Paine and tell us as best you can recall how many times you saw Oswald after his return from New Orleans, up until the time of his assassination?

Mr. PAINE. I think I saw him every weekend on Friday; I think he was there except for the weekend, before the assassination, exceptional.

I would arrive on Tuesday or Wednesdays and, of course, he was not there and there was Ruth and Marina. I would simply come in on Sunday when he was generally there.

Also, I quite specifically remember on the long holiday he had some period there, I don't remember, what celebration it is, when Bell did not have that day off and he did, so he was there that morning, a Monday morning on that date of that holiday, perhaps you can feed me the date.

Mr. LIEBELER. Would that be November 8th, 9th and 10th, 1963?

Mr. PAINE. I think that is right.

Mr. LIEBELER. Was that the last time you saw him?

Mr. PAINE. That would be correct; yes.

Mr. LIEBELER. Now, tell us the circumstances about how Oswald arrived in Irving upon his return from New Orleans as best you can recall it, what happened, what was said.

Mr. PAINE. I must not have been there when the phone call arrived but I think Ruth reported it to me so that Ruth said that Marina was very pleased, very happy to receive this call, a surprise or something. I think I had at one or two times seen her answer a call from him, and I observed she was glad to have this call from him but I wasn't there when he first called, I don't believe.

Mr. DULLES. Was that the call from New Orleans to Irving?

Mr. PAINE. No; that is the call from somewhere in Dallas to Irving asking if he could come out. I don't know of a call from New Orleans to Irving.

Mr. LIEBELER. Did he subsequently come out to the house in Irving that weekend?

Mr. PAINE. Then he came out that weekend. I suppose he came out on a Friday and it was probably before I got over there, I arrived about six.

Mr. LIEBELER. Do you remember if he was there when you arrived home that weekend?

Mr. PAINE. I don't remember that. I think he was there; yes. I think he was there because otherwise I would have seen that meeting. I did not see them first embrace each other.

Mr. LIEBELER. Did he say anything to you about where he had been?

Mr. PAINE. No; I thought I knew where he had been. Ruth had told me he was looking for work in Houston.

Mr. LIEBELER. Ruth had told you that before this date?

Mr. PAINE. I don't know.

Mr. LIEBELER. There was no conversation among any one at that time about Oswald having been in Mexico.

Mr. PAINE. No; it was a complete surprise to Ruth and myself. When we saw this letter where he mentioned having been to Mexico, Ruth took it as an example of his colossal lying.

Mr. LIEBELER. Tell us about this letter, what were the circumstances surrounding that?

Mr. PAINE. He had written a letter using her typewriter and her desk to a party I don't know.

Mr. DULLES. That is Ruth's typewriter and desk?

Mr. PAINE. Ruth's typewriter and he left the rough draft of the letter on her desk, not folded, just out there on her desk, in English. Ruth had given me the impression it was there for a couple of days. Actually it was there for a day and a half or so. I think he wrote it on Saturday and we then moved the furniture on Sunday night.

Mr. DULLES. This would be Saturday, November what?

Mr. PAINE. This might be that holiday November. I don't remember for sure about that.

Mr. LIEBELER. Mr. Paine, you and I discussed this question yesterday and I asked you whether you recalled seeing Oswald again after you had discussed this letter with your wife. What did you tell me?

Mr. PAINE. I thought probably not but we figured out the dates from my probable reaction that I read that letter and then had I encountered him again I would have had a different, I would have had questions or feelings or something in response to this letter and since I didn't encounter him with those feelings I must not have seen him again.

Mr. LIEBELER. So that would place the date of your seeing this letter as approximately shortly after the weekend of November 8, 9, and 10?

Mr. PAINE. That is correct.

Mr. LIEBELER. I show you Commission Exhibit 103 and ask you if you ever saw the original of this letter and if you did to tell us the circumstances surrounding that event.

Mr. PAINE. Yes; I saw this letter. I remembered most of the contents. I apparently didn't remember that he didn't use his real name, I was reading something else at the time and Ruth handed me this letter and it took a while—I didn't read it as thoroughly as I could have.

Mr. DULLES. Could you tell us just briefly the contents of this letter just for the record?

Mr. LIEBELER. Yes, sir; apparently it is a draft of a letter that Oswald wrote in his own hand. The Commission does have a copy of the actual letter, and it was a letter to the Russian Embassy, I believe in Washington.

Mr. DULLES. The Russian Embassy in Washington?

Mr. LIEBELER. Yes, sir; in which he tells them about his trip to Mexico and his political activity on behalf of the Fair Play for Cuba Committee. I believe it includes the words "notorious FBI," which is no longer interested in his political activity in Texas.

Mr. DULLES. Was this letter ever sent?

Mr. LIEBELER. I believe it was.

Mr. DULLES. There was a letter sent like this? You said you had the original?

Mr. RANKIN. It is in evidence.

Mr. DULLES. What was sent, a letter like this?

Mr. RANKIN. A redraft.

Mr. DULLES. A redraft.

Mr. PAINE. Typewritten copy.

Mr. LIEBELER. This letter refers to the fact that Oswald had been in Mexico, does it not?

Mr. PAINE. Yes; it tells of his visit to the Cuban Consul and the Soviet Embassy there.

Mr. LIEBELER. Did your wife call that to your attention when she showed you this letter?

Mr. PAINE. We took it, she took it, and I likewise took it as somewhat of a fabricated story, I didn't suppose he had been down to Mexico. I read "Dear Sirs" there, I read "Dear Lisa." I thought he was writing to a friend, and Ruth pointed out to me after I had given the letter back to her, Ruth was somewhat irked that I didn't take more interest in the thing. I think I might have—no, I don't know as I might have since I might have dismissed it as a lie but anyway Ruth was irked and didn't show it to me again and I asked her now what was in that letter that I didn't see and she didn't tell me.

Mr. LIEBELER. This was all prior to the assassination?

Mr. PAINE. Yes.

Mr. LIEBELER. What did she say to you?

Mr. PAINE. Ruth was quite bothered by that letter, and apparently had—apparently I hadn't really taken it in. I said, "The heck with it. Yes; it is a fantastic lie, isn't that amazing that he will fabricate such stories here."

Mr. LIEBELER. What did she say?

Mr. PAINE. No; she said—she approached me and said, "I never realized how much he could lie" or that he was a liar or something like that, and "I want you to read this letter." So I put aside the thing I was reading in which I was more interested and read most of the letter, not the latter part about having used another name.

And then I thought it was too personal, "Dear Lisa," so I thought he was telling her, being rather braggadocio telling about his exploits which were rather imaginary and I put it out of my mind. Then later Ruth asked me what did I think about it——

Mr. LIEBELER. This was before the assassination that she asked you this?

Mr. PAINE. I think so.

Mr. LIEBELER. Was it later the same day?

Mr. PAINE. No; I think it probably was another day but I don't remember.

Mr. LIEBELER. What did she say?

Mr. PAINE. Well, she was—I think I said, "Let me see that letter again," and she said, "No; if you didn't absorb it, never mind." So, heck, if she felt that way, I wasn't going to bother. My first impulse was to throw it aside and pay no attention to it. If she felt that way I continued to do it.

Mr. LIEBELER. Who brought the letter up the second time, did Ruth bring it up?

Mr. PAINE. Yes; Ruth brought it up.

Mr. LIEBELER. Do you remember whether there was any event that caused her to bring it up or did she bring it up out of the clear blue sky or what?

Mr. PAINE. I don't remember having slept with her but I have the impression she brought it up while I was in bed anyway. So it might have been, just be, I was staying late that night also, I don't know.

Mr. LIEBELER. Did you know that Oswald had given Marina a charm made out of a Mexican peso at the time that you read this letter?

Mr. PAINE. No; I didn't.

Mr. LIEBELER. Did you learn about that at any time prior to the assassination?

Mr. PAINE. Not that I remember.

Mr. LIEBELER. Did you note the fact that Oswald had a record of Mexican music in your home prior to the assassination?

Mr. PAINE. I didn't know that.

Mr. LIEBELER. Did you subsequently learn that Oswald had given Marina this charm made from a Mexican peso?

Mr. PAINE. Yes; I did.

Mr. LIEBELER. Under what circumstances?

Mr. PAINE. The FBI came out and they were wondering whether Oswald had used my shop to mount his sight so we went out to look at the shop and tools and we looked at the threading tap and what not, the threading tap looked as though it hadn't been used but the drill press seemed to have little chips of metal on it and then Ruth remembered that he had gone in there and used the drill press to have drilled out this coin which Marina put around her neck, and I think she then mentioned it was a peso. But it hadn't sunk into Ruth with significance of its being a peso, hadn't impressed itself upon her prior to the assassination.

Mr. LIEBELER. So that neither you nor your wife believed that Oswald had been in Mexico prior to the assassination?

Mr. PAINE. You will have to ask Ruth about that. That was my impression he hadn't been there.

Mr. LIEBELER. Your wife hadn't said anything to you that indicated that she believed it?

Mr. PAINE. No.

Mr. LIEBELER. Now, you mentioned before the fact that you had gone with Oswald to a meeting of the American Civil Liberties Union, is that correct?

Mr. PAINE. That is correct.

Mr. LIEBELER. When did you do that?

Mr. PAINE. That was the day after Stevenson had been stoned.

Mr. LIEBELER. Would you tell us the circumstances of that event?

Mr. PAINE. That was a Friday I had intended to go, I had also invited Frank Krystinik for his first visit, I had been telling him about the ACLU. So I invited Lee to come thinking it might be part—I was not really talking to him very much, but just being civil but I thought it might be helpful for him to see something in which I was interested, that I might find some way that he might find an interest, something constructive to do.

So, I took him in my car, he and I alone, and on the way, which takes about 35 minutes, described the ACLU to him, and he didn't know about it, and described its purpose. Then we went to the meeting which was a meeting, first we saw a movie called "Suspect," I think it was showing how a candidate lost, who had won handily in a previous election, lost after a smear campaign in Washington State, which it had been brought out that his wife had once been a Communist Party member.

I didn't think the movie showed very much, but the meeting, the discussion following the movie, there were two people who gave little talks about the movie and the principles involved afterward, this—do you want to break?

Mr. LIEBELER. Who went with you in the car to the meeting, just you and Mr. Oswald or was Mr. Krystinik with you?

Mr. PAINE. No; Krystinik came in his own car, so just Lee and myself.

Mr. LIEBELER. Go ahead with your story.

Mr. PAINE. I thought the meeting was conducted in a manner that illustrated its own beliefs. One of the things said was that the Birchers must not be considered anti-Semitic, anti-Semites because they are also Birchers.

Lee at this point got up, speaking loud and clear and coherently, saying that, reporting that, he had been to this meeting of the right-wing group the night before or two nights before and he refuted this statement, saying names and saying how that people on the platform speaking for the Birch Society had said anti-Semitic things and also anti-Catholic statements or spoke against the Pope or something.

Mr. LIEBELER. Do you remember what Oswald said?

Mr. PAINE. No; I don't remember. He said something very similar to, "I disagree with what had just been said," and I do remember that it contained both some corroboration of his points of view. There had been some kind of an anti-Semitic statement and criticism of the Pope.

Mr. LIEBELER. Oswald seemed to make a convincing argument and seemed to make sense?

Mr. PAINE. That was good speaking. It was out of keeping with the mood of the meeting and nobody followed it up in a similar manner but I think it was accepted as—it made sense; yes.

Mr. LIEBELER. Did anybody else say anything in response to Oswald's remarks?

Mr. PAINE. I think not.

Mr. LIEBELER. What happened then later on in the meeting?

Mr. PAINE. Later on in the meeting, when the meeting broke up, people clustered into discussion groups, and Frank, I told Frank, who was a colleague at work, Frank Krystinik, about Lee and 'Marina, and so of course he immediately came to defend free enterprise and what not in opposition to this fellow I told him about, and I left the discussion at that point, thinking I knew the kind of discussion it would be.

It was a discussion between three people, a more elderly man whom I probably thought was a member of the ACLU, and Frank and Lee.

Mr. LIEBELER. Did you hear any part of the discussion?

Mr. PAINE. I didn't hear any part of the discussion.

Mr. LIEBELER. Did you subsequently discuss it with either Oswald or Krystinik?

Mr. PAINE. And in the car going home, Lee asked me if I knew this man he had been talking to, this older man he had been talking to, and I think he said that the man seemed to be friendly to Cuba or rather he said, "Do you think that man is a Communist?" And I said, "No." And then he said something, "I think he is." Then I asked him why and I think he said something in regard to Cuba or sympathy with Cuba, and then I thought to myself, well, that is rather feeble evidence for proving a Communist.

But he seemed to have the attitude of, felt he wanted to meet that man again and was pleased he had met him. I thought to myself if that is the way he has to meet his Communists, he has not yet found the Communist group in Dallas.

Mr. LIEBELER. Was there a Communist group in Dallas, to your knowledge?

Mr. PAINE. Not to my knowledge.

Mr. LIEBELER. Did Oswald ever speak of a Communist group in Dallas?

Mr. PAINE. No; he did not. I had the impression, this I remember clearly that he had not found the group with similar feelings to his. I then asked Frank in regard to, I can't remember when I asked Frank but I asked Frank about the same conversation and whether he thought that this third man was a Communist. And he thought no, he thought the other man was a better—Frank almost got into a fight with Lee, and the other man was more receptive or didn't argue with him, or drew him out better, Frank used the word, I think.

Mr. LIEBELER. Drew Oswald out better?

Mr. PAINE. Drew Oswald out better. But he didn't gather the impression that he was favoring Castro or Cuba.

Mr. LIEBELER. What else did you and Oswald say on the way home after the meeting?

Mr. PAINE. So I was describing to him the purpose of the ACLU, and he said specifically, I can remember this, after I had described it and said that I was a member, that he couldn't join an organization like that, it wasn't political and he said something or responded in some manner, which indicated surprise that I could be concerned about joining an organization simply to defend, whose purpose it is, shall we say, to defend, free speech, free speech, per se, your freedom as well as mine.

He was aware of enjoying his freedom to speak but he didn't seem to be aware of the more general principle of freedom to speak for everyone which has value in itself. And I think it took him by surprise that a person could be concerned about a value like that rather than political objective of some sort, and this was, struck me as a new idea and it struck me that he must never have met people who paid more than lip service, he wasn't familiar with the ways of expressing this value.

Mr. DULLES. Did you say anything to him about the activities of the Civil Liberties Union in connection with the defense of people accused of crimes under certain conditions?

Mr. PAINE. Yes; I am sure I told him that it came to the defense of all people who didn't seem to be receiving adequate help when it seemed to be an issue involving the Bill of Rights. I was then—that was a pang of sorrow that occurred after the assassination when I realized that he had then subsequently, a fortnight later, joined the ACLU, and still didn't quite seem to perceive its purpose, and then I realized—I had also perceived earlier that he was still a young fellow and I had been expecting rather a lot of him, when I first approached meeting him; this man had been to Russia and had been back and I had been—met some others who had been around the world like that and they are powerful people.

Mr. LIEBELER. Did Oswald impress you that way?

Mr. PAINE. And he did not impress me that way; no.

Mr. LIEBELER. Did Oswald respond to your, or did you request Oswald or did you suggest to him that he join the ACLU?

Mr. PAINE. No; I don't think I was eager to have him join until he knew what was what about it.

Mr. LIEBELER. During the time after the ACLU meeting did Oswald say anything about his discussion with Mr. Krystinik?

Mr. PAINE. No; I don't believe so.

Mr. LIEBELER. Did you subsequently discuss that with Mr. Krystinik?

Mr. PAINE. Yes; I did.

Mr. LIEBELER. What did you say and what did he say?

Mr. PAINE. He told me how he had argued, that he had pointed out that he had employed a few people himself, he works at Bell but on the side, at night he had done a little extra business and had employed other people, and had to receive from them more than he paid them, that he received from their labor, for their product, more than he paid them but that he created work and jobs, and he was fully—and he was ready to defend his way of that activity and was presenting that against Lee's criticism and apparently encountered the same kind of nonsequitur response or no response from him or Lee's response didn't— Lee presented his opposing view against it without any issue.

Mr. LIEBELER. You mentioned that Krystinik and Oswald had almost gotten into a fight, did Krystinik tell you that?

Mr. PAINE. I think it was Frank who told me that.

Mr. LIEBELER. Can you tell us more about that?

Mr. PAINE. I am sure Frank would not haul off and slug him, but just Frank said he got pretty mad at this. I think Frank was using that expression to me only, you know, saying how irked he was at Lee.

Mr. LIEBELER. He didn't indicate that Oswald had threatened any physical violence toward him in connection with the argument, did he?

Mr. PAINE. Oh, no; I think Lee knows how to keep his temper, knows how to control himself,

Senator COOPER. Might I ask a question at this time?

Earlier you talked about your, I think your, first meeting with Oswald and your conversation with him?

Mr. PAINE. Yes.

Senator COOPER. You said, you talked about, the fact that subsequently your wife was bothered by his attitude?

Mr. PAINE. She was bothered by——

Senator COOPER. I am not going into that.

Now, you have talked about this conversation with Mr. Krystinik?

Mr. PAINE. Krystinik.

Senator COOPER. In which they reached some point in which further discussion was not, if not impossible, was at least difficult between them?

From these experiences you had was there a situation, that after some arguments or discussion of economic or political issues, he would reach a point in which he relied upon certain fixed positions that he held about which he would not admit of any further discussion or argument?

Mr. PAINE. That is correct. He would just present his dogmatic view and then one was at loss to find any way to get off that impasse.

Senator COOPER. When he was questioned about that view or when an attempt was made to argue that view with him, would he then become angry or disturbed in any way?

Mr. PAINE. The time that I reported I was angry and I noticed he was holding his temper pretty well and I wasn't going to let him hold his temper better than mine.

Senator COOPER. Did you see indication——

Mr. PAINE. I saw he was angry, his hands trembled a little bit.

Senator COOPER. All right.

Mr. PAINE. But he was dogged, I think he was practiced or skilled or took pride in this was a kind of struggle or fight that he would do this, and he would do it for a long time.

Mr. LIEBELER. Clench his fists and put them together?

Mr. PAINE. No; it was expressing this as a mood.

Mr. LIEBELER. He would hold himself back?

Mr. PAINE. He would oppose himself to you steadily, and it seemed to me he liked to put himself in a position of belligerence or opposition, and he would just hold his ground or something, was accustomed to doing that and expected to stick it out. It reminded me a little bit of Lawrence of Arabia when Lawrence held the match that burned down to his finger and the fellows asked him what is the trick? He said no trick you just learn how to stand the pain.

Senator COOPER. I have to go and I would like to ask a few questions.

I ask these questions to get a certain background of his views which you have said he finally came to some fixed position which he would hold and would not move and there was no brooking of real argument on that position.

You said earlier in response to a question by counsel that he did not believe there was any possibility of any evolutionary progress in this country, at least upon this issue of economic change.

Mr. PAINE. This he never said that specifically. But I would ask him what policy should we take or I was trying to find if he didn't have some avenue of following a policy in this country.

Senator COOPER. Did you direct questions to him which showed some evolution in our own economic ideas and theories which he either refused to accept——

Mr. PAINE. Yes; I did. I mean I tried to show him how labor and management, first labor had a right, I was criticizing labor for the rigid position it is getting us into now——

Senator COOPER. He would not accept that idea of evolution?

Mr. PAINE. I think he did not accept it; yes.

He didn't have patience with it.

Senator COOPER. Is that also a tenet of the Communist dogma, do you know?

Mr. PAINE. I don't believe. I don't know whether you can say there is a single Communist dogma of that sort. I suppose there are some groups that feel that way and others don't.

Senator COOPER. Did he indicate any other way in which he thought that economic change might come about in the United States?

Mr. PAINE. He did not indicate or reveal to me how he thought it would come about and I on several occasions felt by his, perceived from his attitude or felt impelled by his attitude to say that the values that I held dear were diminished in a situation of violence, to which he remained silent and I took it as disagreement. But I don't remember if he had said that.

Senator COOPER. He remained silent when you spoke about that?

Mr. PAINE. When I said I was opposed to violence or said, why, when I said that he remained silent and I took it——

Senator COOPER. You took it that he disagreed in any way by your statement?

Mr. PAINE. Well, just by the way he would sort of withdraw.

Senator COOPER. He did not agree with your position?

Mr. PAINE. He did not agree; no.

Senator COOPER. That violence was unacceptable as a means of change?

Mr. PAINE. That is right, and I don't think he perceived also, was a war of the kind of values that I am—tolerance, for instance seems to me disappears when strained situations——

Senator COOPER. Did you discuss at least the kind of economic changes that had occurred in Russia by means of violence?

Mr. PAINE. No; I was trying to find out whether he thought it was going to come by revolution or not and he never did say, I never got an answer as to how he thought this change was going to come. He did not reveal constructive, or from my point of view, constructive effort to make.

Senator COOPER. Did he ever discuss the revolution in Russia where by means of violence the change had come about?

Mr. PAINE. He did not. That would have been the kind of argument I would have accepted, a normal kind that you would have accepted it as evidence here is the normal way to produce it, but he never said that.

Senator COOPER. Did he ever say any way in which he was expecting Russia or any other country to indicate that he felt the use of violence had produced good?

Mr. PAINE. No. As I say he did not—I would have accepted that argument as a debating argument but he didn't bring it up.

Senator COOPER. That is all.

Mr. DULLES. Did he say or did you get the impression that he felt that violence was the only way to improve things, let's say, in the United States?

Mr. PAINE. I felt he was so disgusted with the whole system that he didn't see a way that was worthwhile fussing around trying to modify the situation.

Mr. DULLES. Other than violence or he didn't go that far?

Mr. PAINE. He didn't mention advocating violence or didn't say anything in regard to violence but he did seem to me he didn't see dismissed as trivial, no difference between the parties so why join one party or another. They were all the same.

Churches—there is no avenue out that way. Education—there is nothing there. So that he never revealed to me any constructive way that wasn't violent.

Mr. DULLES. Did he think that communism was different from capitalism in this respect?

(Short recess.)

The CHAIRMAN. All right, gentlemen, the Commission will be in order.

Mr. DULLES. What I was getting at with my question was as to whether he thought that probably violence was necessary with respect to both systems to achieve the millennium that he sought or did he think it was just necessary with regard to the American system.

Mr. PAINE. He didn't reveal to me to my satisfaction what criticism he found of the Soviet Union. He had indicated he didn't like it. But I wasn't aware that he was proposing to change that system also in some way. Neither did he ever speak, he never spoke to me, in a way that I could see a paradise, see his paradise. He spoke only, he was opposed to exploitation of man by man. That was his motivating power.

(At this point Senator Cooper left the hearing room.)

Mr. LIEBELER. Did Oswald indicate to you in any way that he had been present at the right-wing rally that was held in Dallas the night before Stevenson appeared in Dallas?

Mr. PAINE. He indicated that at the ACLU meeting.

Mr. LIEBELER. Did he say he had met anybody there?

Mr. PAINE. Not that I recall, no.

Mr. LIEBELER. Did he mention speaking to anyone at that meeting?

Mr. PAINE. No.

Mr. LIEBELER. Did he tell you whether or not he was at the Stevenson meeting itself?

Mr. PAINE. I guess I didn't ask him that. I remember asking myself subsequently what was the answer to that question and I couldn't answer it then and I can't answer it now.

Mr. LIEBELER. You have no recollection of his mentioning it at all?

Mr. PAINE. No, I don't remember what—I think I assumed that he had but——

Mr. LIEBELER. You assumed that he had been at the Stevenson affair?

Mr. PAINE. I think I assumed that.

Mr. LIEBELER. Do you have any basis for that assumption?

Mr. PAINE. There had been some discussion in the ACLU, some other people had gotten up and had spoken of that awful last night, I guess, this was the previous night, that awful time and I think he seemed to nod his assent. That was my——

Mr. LIEBELER. You inferred from that that he had possibly been present at the Stevenson meeting?

Mr. PAINE. Yes.

Mr. LIEBELER. There was no other basis for your assumption in that regard?

Mr. PAINE. That is right.

Mr. LIEBELER. On the weekend of November 8, 9, and 10, do you recall when you came to your house in Irving?

Mr. PAINE. Well, I would come out regularly on Friday after cashing my check at the bank.

Mr. LIEBELER. Do you remember coming on Friday evening on the 8th of November?

Mr. PAINE. I don't remember any break in that habit.

Mr. LIEBELER. Do you recall whether or not Oswald was present at your home on the Friday evening November 8, 1963?

Mr. PAINE. No; I don't specifically remember that.

Mr. LIEBELER. You don't remember one way or the other?

Mr. PAINE. That is right.

Mr. LIEBELER. Were you at the house on Saturday? November 9th?

Mr. PAINE. I was at the house probably on Saturday and certainly on Sunday. I think that weekend I remember stepping over him as he sat in front of the TV, stepping past, one of these things laying on the floor and thinking to myself for a person who has a business to do he certainly can waste the time. By business I mean some kind of activity and keeping track of right-wing causes and left-wing causes or something. I supposed that he spent his time as I would be inclined to spend more of my time if I had it, trying to sense the pulse of various groups in the Dallas area.

Mr. LIEBELER. Do you know what Oswald did on Saturday morning, November 9, 1963?

Mr. PAINE. No.

Mr. LIEBELER. Did you know that he was taken by your wife to apply for a driver's license and take a driver's license test on that morning?

Mr. PAINE. She told me sometime subsequently that she had taken him for—wait. I remember the incident that he had arrived on a Saturday morning at the drivers' license bureau, stood in line for a long time but they cut off the line at 12 o'clock and he did not stay there long enough for him to get his driver's license student permit.

Mr. LIEBELER. Was this at this time or would that have been another time. Let me help you.

Mr. PAINE. I don't remember that.

Mr. LIEBELER. Would it help to refresh your recollection if I suggested that November 9th was a local election day in Dallas, I believe?

Mr. PAINE. I think that is an election that I have forgotten.

Mr. LIEBELER. You have no knowledge of Oswald's activities on that day, no direct personal knowledge?

Mr. PAINE. It doesn't, it didn't cue me in, so I don't——

Mr. LIEBELER. Did you ever see Oswald drive a car?

Mr. PAINE. No; I did not.

Mr. LIEBELER. Did you ever discuss with him driving an automobile or obtaining a driver's license?

Mr. PAINE. I probably said it would be well to get a driver's license. It would be well—I probably said, "You probably need a car to get around here." In other words, effectively; no.

Mr. LIEBELER. Did he ever indicate to you that he planned to purchase an automobile?

Mr. PAINE. I bought this second-hand car for $200.

Mr. LIEBELER. What kind of a car is that?

Mr. PAINE. That is a 1956 Oldsmobile.

Mr. LIEBELER. When did you buy it?

Mr. PAINE. I bought it while they were there, while Marina was staying with us, which was sometime in November. Either October or November, probably the early part of November. They went out to admire the car. $200, I suppose, didn't seem out of their reach then.

Mr. LIEBELER. Did he indicate to you that he was thinking——

Mr. PAINE. Therefore, I think Ruth, they went out to admire the car and, of course, I was thinking that it, this might make it appear to them that the car was within reach, and driving was something to be sought.

Mr. LIEBELER. In addition to the Oldsmobile that you mentioned, you personally own a Citroen automobile and your wife owns a station wagon, is that correct?

Mr. PAINE. That is correct.

Mr. LIEBELER. You never saw Oswald drive any of those cars at any time?

Mr. PAINE. That is correct. I had keys to both of my cars so he could not have driven them without——

Mr. LIEBELER. Without your knowldege?

Mr. PAINE. Or else somehow getting another. He would have to—you can, I have driven my car when I have broken the key.

Mr. LIEBELER. But you never saw him drive it?

Mr. PAINE. I never saw him drive it.

Mr. LIEBELER. Did your wife ever tell you that she had seen Oswald driving a car or she was trying to teach him how to drive a car?

Mr. PAINE. Yes; she did.

Mr. LIEBELER. Did she indicate what proficiency he had at operating an automobile?

Mr. PAINE. She thought he was, she observed how much one has to learn in order to drive a car. He had a difficulty in some manner, perhaps it was in judging when to turn the wheel when parking. And I think she said he over controlled it, turned too far.

Mr. LIEBELER. Looking back now on all your conversations with Oswald, after his return from New Orleans, did you have any discussions with him other than the ones you have already mentioned in your previous testimony?

Mr. DULLES. Could I ask a question before you answer this question. About the car, did you get any idea as to why he didn't want to drive a car or to have a car, did he think this would make him a capitalist or anything of that kind? Did anything come up in the conversations with regard to his not having a car or not driving a car?

Mr. PAINE. No. I gathered that was slightly embarrassing not to be able to drive a car.

Mr. DULLES. All right. Thank you.

Mr. LIEBELER. Can you recall any conversations that you had with Oswald

413

that you think would be helpful for us to know other than the ones you have already mentioned?

Mr. PAINE. I don't recall one now.

Mr. LIEBELER. Did he ever indicate to you any specific hostility toward President Kennedy?

Mr. PAINE. I think at this ACLU meeting he mentioned this specifically that he thought Kennedy had done a good job in civil rights. That was it—generally my impression was that he liked—he didn't like anybody, but he disliked Kennedy least as you might go right from Kennedy.

Mr. LIEBELER. To the best of your recollection, was that the only time he mentioned President Kennedy specifically?

Mr. PAINE. Yes.

Mr. LIEBELER. Did he ever mention Governor Connally?

Mr. PAINE. Not to my knowledge.

Mr. LIEBELER. Did he ever indicate any hostility toward the United States other than the hostility that you have previously testified to after his return from the Soviet Union and his general dislikes of the American system?

Mr. PAINE. That is right. Just his general dislike.

Mr. LIEBELER. Did he ever indicate to you a desire to return to the Soviet Union?

Mr. PAINE. No; I think when I learned, I don't know when it was that he had planned to go back there that it was a surprise to me.

Mr. LIEBELER. When did you learn that he planned to go back there?

Mr. PAINE. That was probably subsequent; yes, that was certainly subsequent to November 22.

Mr. DULLES. Or to go to Cuba?

Mr. PAINE. Or to go to Cuba, yes.

Mr. LIEBELER. When that was spoken——

Mr. PAINE. I remember now, first it was mentioned could he be connected with a Communist plot and there I thought of Russian Communists and that didn't seem to ring a bell.

Mr. LIEBELER. When was that mentioned?

Mr. PAINE. This was after the assassination, a day or two later. Then when the Fair Play for Cuba Committee was mentioned, that was the first I had heard of it except for his mentioning Cuba to this man at the ACLU meeting referring to it in the car to me.

Mr. LIEBELER. He never told you that he had been active in the Fair Play for Cuba Committee?

Mr. PAINE. That is correct, that was the only recollection I could remember his ever having mentioned Cuba.

Mr. LIEBELER. Now yesterday, we asked you about an incident or spoke to you about an incident that happened in September of 1963 when you went into your garage to use some tools, your garage in Irving, Tex. Would you tell us about that?

Mr. PAINE. I don't remember whether the date was September. I remember that was the date they came back from New Orleans and I do remember that my wife asked me to unpack some of their heavy things from their car. I only recall unpacking duffelbags but any other package, that was the heaviest thing there and they were easy also.

Mr. LIEBELER. You must have moved the duffelbags from the station wagon into the garage?

Mr. PAINE. That is right. I unpacked whatever was remaining in the station wagon to the garage.

So sometime later, I do remember moving about this package which, let's say, was a rifle, anyway it was a package wrapped in a blanket. The garage was kind of crowded and I did have my tools in there and I had to move this package several times in order to make space to work, and the final time I put it on the floor underneath the saw where the bandsaw would be casting dust on it and I was a little embarrassed to be putting his goods on the floor, but I didn't suppose, the first time I picked it up I thought it was camping equipment. I said to myself they don't make camping equipment of iron pipes any more.

Mr. LIEBELER. Why did you say that to yourself when you picked up the package?

Mr. PAINE. I had, my experience had been, my earliest camping equipment had been a tent of iron pipes. This somehow reminded me of that. I felt a pipe with my right hand and it was iron, that is to say it was not aluminum.

Mr. LIEBELER. How did you make that distinction?

Mr. PAINE. By the weight of it, and by the, I suppose the moment of inertia, you could have an aluminum tube with a total weight massed in the center somehow but that would not have had the inertia this way.

Mr. DULLES. You were just feeling this through the blanket though?

Mr. PAINE. I was also aware as I was moving his goods around, of his rights to privacy. So I did not feel—I had to move this object, I wasn't thinking very much about it but it happens that I did think a little bit about it or before I get on to the working with my tools I thought, an image came to mind.

Mr. LIEBELER. Did you think there was more than one tent pole in the package or just one tent pole?

Mr. PAINE. As I say, I moved it several times, and I think I thought progressively each time. I moved it twice. It had three occasions. And the first one was an iron, thought of an iron pipe and then I have drawn, I drew yesterday, a picture of the thing I had in mind. Then in order to fill out the package I had to add another object to it and there I added again I was thinking of camping equipment, and I added a folding shovel such as I had seen in the Army, a little spade where the blade folds back over the handle. This has the trouble that this blade was too symmetrical I disposed to the handle and to fit the package the blade had to be off center, eccentric to the handle. Also, I had my vision of the pipe. It had an iron pipe about 30 inches long with a short section of pipe going off 45 degrees. No words here, it just happened that I did have this image in my mind of trying to fill up that package in the back burner of my mind.

Mr. LIEBELER. The witness yesterday did draw a picture of what he visualized as being in the blanket, and I will offer it in evidence later on in the hearing.

How long was this package in your estimation?

Mr. PAINE. Well, yesterday we measured the distance that I indicated with my hand, I think it came to 37 inches.

Mr. LIEBELER. Approximately how thick would you say it was?

Mr. PAINE. I picked it up each time and I put it in a position and then I would recover it from that position, so each time I moved it with the same position with my hands in the same position. My right hand, the thumb and forefinger could go around the pipe, and my left hand grabbed something which was an inch and a half inside the blanket or something thick.

Mr. LIEBELER. Did it occur to you at that time that there was a rifle in the package?

Mr. PAINE. That did not occur to me.

Mr. LIEBELER. You never at any time looked inside the package?

Mr. PAINE. That is correct. I could easily have felt the package but I was aware that of respecting his privacy of his possessions.

Mr. LIEBELER. Were you subsequently advised of the probability or the possibility that there had been a rifle wrapped in that package?

Mr. PAINE. When I arrived on Friday afternoon we went into the garage, I think Ruth, Marina and the policeman, and I am not sure it was the first time, but there we saw this blanket was on the floor below the bandsaw——

(At this point Representative Ford entered the hearing room.)

Mr. PAINE. And a rifle was mentioned and then it rang a bell, the rifle answered, fitted the package that I had been trying to fit these unsuccessfully. It had never resolved itself, this shovel and pipe didn't fit in there.

Mr. LIEBELER. And it seemed to you likely that there had in fact been a rifle in the package?

Mr. PAINE. That answered it.

Mr. LIEBELER. Can you tell us when the last time was that you saw that package in the garage prior to the assassination?

Mr. PAINE. No; I am afraid I can't.

Mr. DULLES. Do we have the date of the first time in the record?

Mr. LIEBELER. Yes; I think the witness testified it was either late September or early October of 1963.

I show you a blanket which has been marked as Commission Exhibit 140 and ask you if that is the blanket you saw in the garage?

Mr. PAINE. This looks a little cleaner, of course. I was there in the night, and I also put the thing on the floor thinking it was rustic equipment and that sawdust wouldn't hurt it.

I also was concerned with moisture. This is very close to what I remember. Yesterday in my testimony I had a desire to add blue to the colors of brown and green. Last night I remembered that Thanksgiving weekend I had bought another rustic blanket of a similar nature which had blue in it, which is why I tried to get blue into the blanket.

Mr. LIEBELER. Are you able to say at this time positively that this was the blanket that you saw in your garage and that you moved on various occasions in October and possibly November of 1963?

Mr. PAINE. I didn't notice the particular design so I can't—it is a very good representative of what I remember.

Mr. LIEBELER. Do you remember the texture of the blanket?

Mr. PAINE. The texture. I felt it, of course, these several times and the texture is the same.

Mr. LIEBELER. Was the package wrapped securely when it was in your garage?

Mr. PAINE. I had the impression—yes, it was. The whole package was stiff. There was no shaking of the parts, and I had the impression it was wrapped with about two strings.

Mr. LIEBELER. I now show you Commission Exhibit 139, which is a rifle that was found in the Texas School Book Depository Building, and ask you if you at any time ever saw this rifle prior to November 22, 1963?

Mr. PAINE. I did not.

Mr. LIEBELER. Have you seen it since that time and prior to yesterday?

Mr. PAINE. I saw a rifle being shown to Marina in an adjoining cubicle with a glass wall between us.

Mr. LIEBELER. When was that?

Mr. PAINE. That was the night of the 22d.

Mr. LIEBELER. Have you ever seen this leather strap that is attached to the rifle.

Mr. PAINE. I have not seen that strap.

Mr. LIEBELER. Have you ever seen a strap like this strap?

Mr. PAINE. Or anything like it.

Mr. LIEBELER. Have you any idea where this strap could have come from?

Mr. PAINE. I don't.

Mr. DULLES. May I ask in that connection, was this just loosely wound up in that blanket or was there some string around it or——

Mr. PAINE. I had the impression there were about two strings on the thing. It wouldn't—also, I didn't think you could look into the package readily.

Mr. DULLES. You would have to take something off, some string or something in order to get into the package?

Mr. PAINE. Yes.

Mr. LIEBELER. I now show you Commission Exhibit 364 which is a replica of a sack which was prepared by authorities in Dallas, and I also show you another sack which is Commission Exhibit 142, and ask you if you have ever seen in or around your garage in Irving, Tex., any sacks similar to those?

Mr. PAINE. No; I haven't.

Mr. LIEBELER. Have you seen any paper in your garage in Irving prior to November 22, 1963, or at any other place, at your home in Irving, Tex., that is similar to the paper of which those sacks are made?

Mr. PAINE. No, I haven't; we have some rugs, most of them are wrapped in polyethylene. I couldn't be sure that one of the smaller ones wasn't wrapped in paper. To my knowledge, we had no free kraft paper of that size.

Mr. LIEBELER. Will you examine the tape on the sacks and tell me whether you have any tape similar to that or whether you have seen any tape similar to that in your garage before November 22, 1963?

Mr. PAINE. We have some tape in a drawer of my desk at the house, my recollection is that the tape is a 2-inch tape, gum tape.

Mr. LIEBELER. And the tape on the sack appears to be three?

Mr. PAINE. This is 3-inch.

Mr. LIEBELER. Did you ever observe in your garage any scraps of paper or scraps of tape similar to the materials used to construct those sacks?

Mr. PAINE. No, I did not.

Mr. LIEBELER. Either before November 22, 1963, or afterwards?

Mr. PAINE. That is correct.

Mr. LIEBELER. When you moved the sacks, the blanket, the package that was wrapped in the blanket in your garage, were you able to determine whether or not the object inside the sack was also wrapped in paper?

Mr. PAINE. I would have said that it was not. When we practiced wrapping that rifle yesterday I would have guessed that any paper around the barrel in there, which I could feel with some clarity, would have crinkled.

Mr. LIEBELER. And to your recollection there was no crinkling in the package wrapped with the blanket?

Mr. PAINE. Yes. It was a very quiet package.

Mr. LIEBELER. Yesterday we did try to and did wrap the rifle previously referred to in our testimony in the blanket which you have just examined. Would you tell the Commission about that?

Mr. PAINE. I tried wrapping it to the shape and size and bulk that I remembered the package. I had a little difficulty, it got quite close to the right shape by wrapping it at an angle. The rifle was laid in the blanket somewhat on a bias to the rectangle blanket form. Then there was a small end of the barrel. I didn't discover how you could fold that over to tie it with string without making it bulkier than I remember. But the package came quite close to what I remembered.

Mr. LIEBELER. Now on the basis of wrapping that rifle in the blanket, would you say that it was probable, that the package that was in your garage was in fact that rifle wrapped in that blanket?

Mr. PAINE. Yes, I think it was or a rifle of that size.

Mr. LIEBELER. You said just a moment ago that you saw the rifle we have had here this morning or a similar rifle shown to Marina Oswald sometime shortly after the assassination. Would you tell us the circumstances surrounding that event?

Mr. PAINE. We went to the police station that evening, and probably about 9 o'clock, I saw the rifle being shown to Marina.

Mr. LIEBELER. This was at the Dallas police station?

Mr. PAINE. Dallas police station. Ruth was present, and Mamantov was present.

Representative FORD. Who was the last one?

Mr. PAINE. Ilya Mamantov, I think Ilya is the first name, but Mr. Mamantov. He teaches parttime, parttime teaching in Russian, was familiar to Ruth as the son-in-law of her tutor.

Mr. LIEBELER. Did you hear any of the conversation that was going on in the room in which Marina was being shown this rifle?

Mr. PAINE. No, no.

Mr. LIEBELER. Do you know whether or not your wife heard them?

Mr. PAINE. My wife, of course, was right there. And heard the whole thing.

Mr. LIEBELER. Did she subsequently tell you what occurred?

Mr. PAINE. Yes, she did.

Mr. LIEBELER. What did she tell you?

Mr. PAINE. She told me that Marina wasn't able to identify that rifle as the one that Lee had. She knew that Lee had a rifle, and I think she knew it was wrapped in a package like this. I think Ruth reported that she had, Marina had, opened up a corner of the blanket and looked in and seen part of the butt, and hadn't liked the idea of rifles, the rifles made her a little uncomfortable and hadn't looked at it further.

Mr. LIEBELER. This was at the time the rifle was presumably wrapped in the blanket in your garage, correct?

Mr. PAINE. I assumed that. I didn't ask that question.

Mr. LIEBELER. Did your wife tell you anything more about what happened at that time?

Mr. PAINE. You will have to jog my memory if you have any specific questions. I don't recall.

Mr. LIEBELER. That is the best of your recollection now that you have given us?

Mr. PAINE. Yes.

Mr. LIEBELER. How much would you say that the package that you saw in your garage weighed?

Mr. PAINE. I reported earlier to the FBI 7 or 8 pounds. I never at the time thought of the weight of it as I was moving it around.

Mr. LIEBELER. In your previous discussions or conversations with the FBI did you ever tell them in word or substance that if there had been a rifle in the package that was located in your garage that you did not think it could have a telescopic sight mounted on it?

Mr. PAINE. I don't recall having said that. I don't believe I would have known that.

Mr. LIEBELER. Do you recall any discussions of that sort with the FBI at all. Did they ask you about that?

Mr. PAINE. Yes, I think they asked me coming out to find out when and where and how the sight may have been put on but I never felt the package in the center. I always grabbed it at these two ends.

Mr. LIEBELER. To the best of your recollection you never told the FBI that you didn't think the package contained a rifle with a telescopic sight?

Mr. PAINE. That is correct.

Mr. LIEBELER. Did you ever observe or hear prior to the assassination that Lee Oswald had been practicing with a rifle?

Mr. PAINE. No, I didn't know prior to the assassination, we didn't know he had a rifle. I had supposed from my conversation with him back on Neely Street that he would like to have a rifle but I didn't gather that he did.

Mr. LIEBELER. Aside from whether or not you knew that he had a rifle, did you ever hear or observe him practicing with a rifle?

Mr. PAINE. No, I did not.

Mr. LIEBELER. Are you familiar with the Sport's Drome Rifle Range in Grand Prairie, Tex?

Mr. PAINE. I think I know about where it is. No, I don't even know where it is. I know the race track is there.

Mr. LIEBELER. Have you ever been there?

Mr PAINE. No.

Mr. LIEBELER. Did you know that Oswald received mail at your house from Irving, Tex?

Mr. PAINE. Yes.

Mr. LIEBELER. Do you know what kind of mail he received?

Mr. PAINE. I suppose he used it as the mailing address for most of his mail until he would receive, get a permanent address, so he received the Daily Worker there, or The Worker, and also, I didn't see it come, I don't generally see the mail that arrives there. Most of my mail would arrive at that address even though I was living somewhere else because I also didn't feel permanent in my other addresses, so Ruth would collect the mail and separated mine into a separate pile. I didn't see the Militant arrive. I did see various Russian magazines, Agitateur, maybe a very large one. A very large one and the Daily Worker, The Worker.

Mr. LIEBELER. Did you ever discuss these publications with Oswald?

Mr. PAINE. Yes, we talked with regard to the Daily Worker. He said that, he told me, that you could tell what they wanted you to do, they, a word I dislike, what they wanted you to do by reading between the lines, reading the thing and doing a little reading between the lines. He then gave me an issue to look and see. I wanted to see if I could read between the lines and see what they wanted you to do.

Mr. LIEBELER. Did you read the particular issue that he referred to?

Mr. PAINE. I tried to. I don't think I had very much patience to go through it.

418

Mr. LIEBELER. Do you remember what particular issue it was?

Mr. PAINE. No, I didn't notice.

Mr. LIEBELER. Can you set the date of this discussion that you had with Oswald?

Mr. PAINE. That was fairly soon after his coming back. So let's say the middle of October.

Mr. LIEBELER. Did he discuss with you, your ability or inability to determine what they wanted you to do by reading between the lines after you had read the publication?

Mr. PAINE. No, I just handed it back to him.

Mr. LIEBELER. Was there anything else said between you at that time on that subject?

Mr. PAINE. He asked me how did I like it.

Mr. LIEBELER. What did you say?

Mr. PAINE. And I tried to be polite. I said it was awful extreme, I thought.

Mr. LIEBELER. Did he respond to that?

Mr. PAINE. I think that was the end of it.

Mr. DULLES. Do I understand that this was, this Daily Worker was, mailed——

Mr. PAINE. To 515.

Mr. DULLES. To your address in Irving?

Mr PAINE. That is right. Or Ruth's address.

Mr. DULLES. It wasn't readdressed but it was directly sent?

Mr. PAINE. That is correct.

Mr. DULLES. He gave your address for The Worker to come to?

Mr. PAINE. That is right.

Representative FORD. What prompted him to hand you The Worker? Was there any preface to the actual handing of it to you?

Mr. PAINE. Yes. I think I was asking him, I would like to, I wanted to see some literature or what he liked to read or something like that. I think it was as a response to some question or inquiry of mine.

Mr. DULLES. Do you know whether this was addressed to him in care of you or Ruth Paine or was it just sent at the Paine address?

Mr. PAINE. I don't remember for certain. I would think it would have just been Oswald at that address but I don't remember. It may have been. There were enough of those packages but I just don't remember.

Mr. LIEBELER. Did you draw any inference at the time as a result of this conversation with Oswald about his statement that you could tell what they wanted you to do by reading between the lines?

Mr. PAINE. Well, it made me realize that he would like to be active in some kind of—activist. It made me also feel that he wasn't very well connected with a group or he wouldn't have such a tenuous way of communication, and I thought it was rather childish to someone like Dick Tracy, attract a child to Dick Tracy, to think that that was his bona fide way of being communicated or being a member of this Communist cause or something.

Mr. LIEBELER. Did you ever have any other discussions with him about literature that he received?

Mr. PAINE. I didn't know. Other literature. I was somewhat interested in what the Russian publications were saying but I didn't take it up with him. I wanted Ruth to translate those.

Mr. LIEBELER. Did you ever observe any Cuban literature?

Mr. PAINE. No, I didn't.

Mr. LIEBELER. Did you ever know that he ever received any such literature?

Mr. PAINE. No, I never, until after the assassination, I had never thought of Cuba either in connection with Oswald or in connection with the Communists or the Communist Party.

Mr. LIEBELER. I show you Commission Exhibit 128 which is ENCO Map of the Dallas-Fort Worth area, and ask you if you recognize that map.

Mr. PAINE. This is the kind of map that I always used, stopping in stations when I am out of one so I always have one in my car, and when the FBI showed me this particular map, which I trust is the same one I looked at before.

I found on the back side a mark where it shows the whole map of the whole area, the Dallas-Fort Worth area, a little mark where our house is, that is the kind of mark that I would make when I was trying to buy some land earlier and had in mind for a long time and I wanted to find the location that was accessible to the places I would then want to go.

Mr. LIEBELER. Can you tell us——

Mr. PAINE. This mark is still here.

Representative FORD. This is the mark or can you identify that mark that you placed on this map?

Mr. PAINE. Yes, I think I see a mark here of the sort which looks reasonable to me. I think it is the only mark on this side of the map.

Generally, I didn't make marks on the other side of the map.

Mr. LIEBELER. In your statement referring to one side of the map you were referring to the side that shows a map of the entire Fort Worth-Dallas area, is that correct?

Mr. PAINE. That is correct.

Mr. LIEBELER. And you say as best you can see there is only one mark on this side of the map?

Mr. PAINE. That is the only one that is here, that I remember having found. I don't remember finding another one.

Mr. LIEBELER. Do you remember putting that mark on the map?

Mr. PAINE. I remember putting—I think I put this kind of mark on more than one map. That is our house. It then helps locate it with regard to all the arteries and what not that lead to various places.

Mr. LIEBELER. You do think then it is probable that you did place the mark on the map that indicates the location of your house in Irving, Tex.; is that correct?

Mr. PAINE. Yes, I think that is correct.

Mr. LIEBELER. Do you know whether or not Oswald ever came into possession of this map?

Mr. PAINE. And Ruth gave Oswald a map to—she told me she gave him a map, and this is the kind we have around the house, the best one she could get in the service station, to help him find a job, or help him when he was searching for a job.

Mr. LIEBELER. Do you remember any other conversations with your wife about the map before the assassination?

Mr. PAINE. No, I don't believe she told me she had given him the map. I don't believe we discussed it at all.

Mr. LIEBELER. Would you open the map to the portion that shows the area of Dallas. I call your attention to a mark at the intersection of Boll Street and San Jacinto, and ask you if you have any recollection of placing that mark on the map?

Mr. PAINE. No, I don't have any recollection of placing that mark on the map.

Mr. LIEBELER. Do you remember any circumstances that might make it likely that you placed that mark on the map?

Mr. PAINE. I could have placed that mark on the map when I was looking for properties. I went down to the courthouse to get plats of the areas that I was thinking of buying, and they had a copy of the plat, and so they sent it out late on Saturday, short of 12 o'clock, and just short of closing, and it was a reproduction company at that address or near that address.

Mr. LIEBELER. Is that the L. L. Ridgway Co.?

Mr. PAINE. Yes. That is the company that I am referring to. I don't know exactly.

Mr. LIEBELER. But it is near the intersection we have just referred to?

Mr. PAINE. I will take your word for that.

Mr. LIEBELER. Do you know that it is?

Mr. PAINE. No, I don't know. I think the FBI man said it was. I hadn't looked into it and didn't check it.

Mr. LIEBELER. You haven't any knowledge at this point whether the Ridgway company is in this intersection or not?

Mr. PAINE. I remember it is right beside the expressway and in about that area. I don't remember the names of the roads.

Mr. LIEBELER. Do you think it is probable or improbable that you placed the mark on the map, the one we have just been talking about, at Boll and San Jacinto Streets?

Mr. PAINE. I remember in asking the clerk where it was, and I had a map of this sort, that was also in August when I was looking for places. I would have guessed I would not. I would have been able to see where it was and know in my mind where I wanted to go.

Mr. DULLES. Is that the same kind of a mark or a different kind of mark that is on the other side of the map to which we have just referred, the area map?

Mr. PAINE. It is a different mark. That mark that is on the other side of the map to which we have just referred, the area map, was our house. So I made a little square that I can see and indicate a house rather than—generally I don't make marks on maps. I look up where I want to go and I go.

Mr. LIEBELER. Did your wife tell you when she had given this map to Oswald?

Mr. PAINE. I suppose she gave it very soon after he came back and started looking for work.

Mr. LIEBELER. And you said it was August of 1963 when you were looking to find this reproduction place; is that correct?

Mr. PAINE. That is correct.

Mr. LIEBELER. I call your attention to a mark on Hillcrest and Asbury, and I ask you if you put that mark on the map?

Mr. PAINE. I don't recall making that mark. I think it is different from the other mark, and it is—if I were to make a mark that is more the way I would make a mark. It also happens to be the cafeteria where I like to eat, where you can get all you want for a dollar there, and it is a very good meal. So I would be interested in that, in locating it. Here is one of the places where I was thinking of buying property.

Mr. DULLES. Is there a mark there at that place where you were interested in buying property?

Mr. PAINE. I don't think there is. I almost guessed that I didn't have that map at that time. Also I was not living—I would guess for a further reason that I would not have this map on the time of that August date was because I hadn't been living—I had been living in this apartment, and I had a map over there, and I probably didn't have the same map that Ruth had around her house.

Mr. LIEBELER. So you think it is probably likely you didn't place any marks on that map other than the one indicating your home?

Mr. PAINE. That is correct. In other words, I think that mark was placed there quite a long time back, because I have been interested in this locating of property for several years.

Mr. LIEBELER. Is the mark at the Hillcrest Avenue spot, a mark of the type that you usually make?

Mr. PAINE. And, as I say, I don't usually make a mark, but I think I might more likely have made that kind of mark, more than some of the others—somebody else has put marks here with a ball-point pen which are not the kind I would make.

Mr. LIEBELER. In reviewing this map with the FBI, were there any other marks on the map that it was developed that you possibly put on the map other than the ones we have discussed?

Mr. PAINE. I don't now remember any others. This one of the cafeteria there is not exactly at the right spot.

Mr. LIEBELER. The mark at Hillcrest Avenue?

Mr. PAINE. That is right.

Mr. LIEBELER. As you look at the map now do you see any other marks which you think you might have put on the map?

Mr. PAINE. No. We went over it at mealtime in considerable detail, he having located most of the marks he could find on the map—no, I guess it was still marked up like this. We didn't find anything that I can remember there that I might have put on there.

Mr. LIEBELER. Now, on the basis of your knowledge of Oswald and your meeting with him, and your familiarity with him prior to the time of the assassination, did you form an opinion about him as to whether or not he would be likely to commit an act such as this, or whether he would be likely to take the life of any human being?

Mr. PAINE. It was a question we had to consider when we considered having Marina at our house. So Ruth and I discussed that, whether he was a dangerous person, and he didn't seem to be dangerous. Of course, I also felt that I wasn't a particular opponent or foe of his. Helping his family we were quite free and would let him, roughly, think of our arguments. I talked about getting angry, but, for the most part, it was a cordial relationship, so I didn't sense—he didn't display hostility to me or to Ruth, and he was nice with the children, and while they were living with us, he was nice to Marina also. He was during this time when he returned from Mexico, he was quite a reasonable person. He was only unreasonable the first time I had met him.

Mr. LIEBELER. When did you have this discussion with your wife concerning whether or not you should let Marina live with you? Was that before they came back from New Orleans?

Mr. PAINE. Yes, it was.

Mr. LIEBELER. And you concluded at that time there was no reason why Marina should not come there; is that right?

Mr. PAINE. That is right. Of course, Ruth went in and sounded them out rather cautiously and reported to me also his facial expressions and what-not when she was suggesting this, and he seemed to be glad of that rather than worried.

Mr. LIEBELER. Now, after Marina came and lived at your house, Oswald was there during parts of the months October and November. Did you change your opinion in this respect or was it reinforced. on the basis of his activities and your observation of him during that period?

Mr. PAINE. It was reinforced.

Mr. LIEBELER. You did not think him to be a violent person or one who would be likely to commit an act such as assassinating the President?

Mr. PAINE. I didn't—I saw he was a bitter person, he was bitter and quite a lot of very negative views of people in the world around him, very little charity in his view toward anybody, but I thought he was harmless.

, Representative FORD. Was this a different reaction from the one you had had at your first meeting or your first acquaintance?

Mr. PAINE. When we first became acquainted I was somewhat shocked, especially that he would speak so harshly to his wife in front of a complete stranger, and it was at that point, or at that time, that I was persuaded I would like to free Marina from her bondage and servitude to this man. He seemed to me he was keeping her, not helping her to learn the language, keeping her vassal to him, and this offended me, so at that point I became interested in helping her escape from him. Of course, I was not going to try to force that. I didn't want to be separating a family that could get along.

Mr. LIEBELER. This bitterness that you detected following his return from Mexico, was that a new reaction?

Mr. PAINE. No. That bitterness had existed all along. He also had been disagreeable to his wife, cruel to her.

Mr. LIEBELER. I see.

Mr. PAINE. Not allowing her any personality, a mind of her own, and making sharp jibes at her.

Mr. DULLES. And that continued awhile?

Mr. PAINE. That only existed that first night in March or April.

Mr. DULLES. It did not continue when Marina was at your house in Irving?

Mr. PAINE. When Marina came to our house she gained in health and weight. She started to look better and it looked to me as if the strain was off the family relationship. They were not quarreling. They billed and cooed. She sat on his lap and be said sweet nothings in her ear.

Mr. DULLES. Did you get any information from any source with regard to the situation while they were living in New Orleans that she wanted to get away from him?

Mr. PAINE. Oh, yes; well, Ruth had told me when she came back from delivering Marina to New Orleans, she had gone down there expecting to spend a week, seeing New Orleans, and it was a pretty long trip, and found the household, she reported to me, so uncomfortable living there. They were fighting, I mean, so difficult. She wanted to leave right away, and she left in a few days, left a lot sooner than she had expected to leave.

Mr. DULLES. Then your wife took her back, as you recall?

Mr. PAINE. Then, my wife came home, and then she went back to Naushon, Mass., for a couple of months in the summer, and on her way back to Texas stopped in New Orleans, found him out of work, and invited Marina to come back with her right then.

Mr. DULLES. What did she learn at that time about Oswald? What did she learn about Lee Oswald's treatment of Marina, anything new or different at the time she stopped by New Orleans, and then went back?

Mr. PAINE. She, perhaps, saw he loved her because she said that the parting, he genuinely seemed so happy to have Ruth take her back. In other words, he seemed to be exhibiting some concern for Marina, who was with child, and the child would be adequately taken care of, and sorry—it was a cheerful parting or something. She saw human qualities in him at that time.

Mr. LEIBELER. Did she say after Marina returned to your home in Irving, and after Oswald came back to Dallas that their relationship improved even more, and Oswald seemed to be under less strain than he had been prior to that time; is that correct?

Mr. PAINE. Well, I don't—I only know two times, at the time in April when they came to dinner with us, and he was rough, crude, uncivil to her, and Ruth's report of how they were while she was trying to live in this house in New Orleans, when she just moved in.

She also reported to me, and she will tell you this though that apparently Lee had wanted to make her happy in this house, had liked the house, said it was in the old famous quarter of New Orleans, and Ruth could see that Marina was unhappy. She thought it was uncomfortable in this darkness, and Ruth thought it was a tragedy. Both points of view were valid depending on which way you looked at it, so she saw that Lee apparently had wanted to make her happy, wanted her to like the house when she arrived in New Orleans, and had called her out there. She had also been eager to go out.

Apparently Ruth reported to me when he called from New Orleans, saying he had a job and "come live with me, come back with me," Marina had been very happy.

Mr. LIEBELER. Did you specifically consider the question before you let Marina move into your home as to whether Oswald was a violent person?

Mr. PAINE. Yes, specifically. I talked it over with Frank. Frank raised the question also. So I talked it over with Ruth several times, and Frank brought up the question, and I thought of it myself.

Mr. LIEBELER. And you concluded on the basis of these discussions and your knowledge of Oswald, your collective knowledge of Oswald, at that time that he was not a violent person; is that correct?

Mr. PAINE. That he wasn't going to stab Ruth or Marina.

Mr. LIEBELER. That he wasn't going to exhibit any violence to any of you people?

Mr. PAINE. That is right. He wouldn't be a danger to Ruth. That was partly based, first, on the fact that we were not—we were careful to avoid putting him in a position that he felt offended.

Mr. LIEBELER. You didn't consider at the time that you were considering Oswald's possible violence toward you and your group whether he might exhibit violence to some other person?

Mr. PAINE. That is correct; yes.

Mr. LIEBELER. You formed no judgment about that one way or the other?

Mr. PAINE. That is correct. We assumed or felt that—if we handled him with a gentle or considerate manner that he wouldn't be a danger to us.

Mr. DULLES. In the light of subsequent information and developments, and the information which is publicly available, have you reached any other conclusions as to or any conclusions as to whether or not Lee Oswald was the assassin of the President?

Mr. PAINE. When the police first asked me did I think he had done it, my dubiousness in my mind arose from not seeing how this could fit, how this could help his cause, and I didn't think he was irrational. It did not seem to me that he could shoot a man as he would shoot a tin can. Difficulty of a person shooting another person was not the reason for my doubting, and the circumstantial evidence seemed quite powerful to me.

Mr. LIEBELER. Seemed quite powerful?

Mr. PAINE. Yes. But then I realized with subsequent people calling from all over the country, somebody had said it is only a single-shot rifle, and I recognize one little fact like that could alter my thinking entirely. Somebody else said there was a shot through the windshield of the car. We went down to the place and looked around, and he thought that—he had a theory that the man had been shot from a manhole in the street, so I recognized that my views could change with evidence.

Mr. LIEBELER. Do you have a view on Oswald's guilt at this time?

Mr. PAINE. Most of these other things have proved to be false. It seems to be a clip-fed rifle. The man who thought it was shot from the place, I went down and saw the diagram drawn by Life seemed to be quite accurate so far as I could reconstruct the thing, and there was confusion about the number of bullets. I never did discover—it didn't quite make sense, but for the most part, I accept it, the common view that he did it.

Mr. LIEBELER. Where were you on the morning of November 22, 1963?

Mr. PAINE. I was having, at the time of the assassination I was at work, of course, but at the time of the assassination I was in the cafeteria associated with the bowling alley having lunch.

Mr. LIEBELER. Who was with you?

Mr. PAINE. A student, a co-op student called Dave Noel happened to be with me. We happened to be talking about the character of assassins at that lunchtime, of all things.

Mr. LIEBELER. Prior to the time you heard of the assassination?

Mr. PAINE. That is right. When we first sat down at the meal we were discussing it, beside the point, except unless you believe in extrasensory perception, but we happened to just—we didn't have enough historical knowledge to explore it, but I just raised the question and tried to pursue it, and then dropped it, and then a waitress came and said the President had been shot, and I thought she was cracking a nasty joke, and went over to a cluster of people listening around a transistor set, and heard there was some commotion of this sort from the tone of the voice of the transistor set, and we went back to the lab where there is a good radio, and followed the news from there.

When it was mentioned, the Texas School Book Depository Building was mentioned, then I told Frank Krystinik that that was where Lee Oswald worked, and then in a few minutes he came back and said, he asked me, didn't I think I had better call the FBI and tell them.

So over a period of about 20 minutes, I trying to carry on work in a foolish way, or talking or discussing other things or something, we were discussing this problem, and I thought, I said to myself, or said to him, that the FBI already knew he worked there. Everybody would know he was a black sheep, and I didn't want to—a friend or one of the few friends in position of friendship to him, I didn't want to—join the mob barking at his heels or join in his harassment, so I declined. I didn't tell Frank that he couldn't call the FBI, but I said I wasn't going to do it, so I didn't.

I called Ruth immediately after getting back just to see that she would turn on the radio and be clued in with the news, but this was before the Texas School Book Depository Building was mentioned, to my knowledge, and she was already watching the news. So we communicated nothing at that time.

Mr. DULLES. Do you know whether your luncheon companion did or did not telephone the FBI?

Mr. PAINE. This is not the luncheon companion. This is Dave Noel. Frank Krystinik brings his lunch, and he eats his lunch at the lab.

Mr. DULLES. At the lab?

Mr. PAINE. Yes.

Mr. LIEBELER. Mr. Paine, would you give us the nature of the conversation you were having concerning assassination prior to the assassination. First let me ask you was anybody else present beside you and your companion at the time of the conversation?

Mr. PAINE. No, just he and I.

Mr. LIEBELER. Tell us the general essence of the conversation as best you can recall.

Mr. PAINE. There had been talk, of course, people, I don't get a newspaper, but I do listen to the radio. I know what my news source is, it is mostly magazines. So there was some anxiety about the President coming to Dallas-Fort Worth, and it appeared that this thought was in the minds of several others, I was not singular in this way. It had been expected, of course, that trouble would come from the right-wing, and I was wondering whether there was any danger, I suppose, that is somebody who could be drummed up by local feeling. The number of anti-Kennedy jokes cracked was quite large in Texas, and so I was wondering, you know, what kind of a person would kill a President, and I don't think Dave Noel knew anything about it, so it was just musing or conjecturing on my part. I certainly didn't think of Lee Oswald. I didn't expect it from that cause, from that end of the spectrum.

Mr. LIEBELER. When did you first think of Lee Oswald in connection with the assassination?

Mr. PAINE. As soon as I heard the Texas School Book Depository Building mentioned. Now, I did not know that—it never occurred to me, I didn't realize, there was a building there on his route. I had seen this warehouse building from the expressway, you can see the name written in large letters, but that is the way from any main thoroughfare. So I had supposed, I never put—except when it was mentioned that that was the building he shot from or was the building that the shot was fired from, then I realized I did know where he worked.

Mr. DULLES. You had not been at Irving that previous night?

Mr. PAINE. No, I had not.

Mr. LIEBELER. You knew Oswald worked at the Texas School Book Depository Building?

Mr. PAINE. Yes, I did.

Mr. LIEBELER. As soon as you heard that that building was involved in the assassination, you thought of Oswald, did you not?

Mr. PAINE. Yes.

Mr. LIEBELER. What did you think?

Mr. PAINE. Wondering whether Oswald would do it. And the argument against it, the only argument against it, was just I didn't think he was irrational, or it seemed to me to be irrational.

Mr. LIEBELER. And you asked yourself the question of whether or not Oswald would do it solely on the basis of your knowledge that he worked in that building, is that correct?

Mr. PAINE. Yes. Well, I didn't realize he worked in that building, but then I realized I didn't know—I knew he worked at that organization. I didn't realize there was a building on Elm Street there.

Mr. LIEBELER. Did you talk to your wife after you heard that the Texas School Book Depository Building was involved in the shooting, and before you subsequently heard that Oswald had been arrested in connection with the assassination?

Mr. PAINE. I don't believe so. I think I called her only once to see that she was listening to the news, and then I assumed she would know all that I knew, and as soon as she heard that I supposed she would be wondering the same thing. It wasn't many minutes later though, it seemed to me, that the name Lee Oswald was mentioned—in the theater. The newsmen didn't connect it up at all, but that is all I needed to send me home.

Mr. LIEBELER. So then you left for your home in Irving?

Mr. PAINE. Yes.

Mr. LIEBELER. You left for home before there had been any public connection made between Oswald and the assassination, is that correct?

Mr. PAINE. Well, of course, the police were reporting they had suspects here and suspects there, were chasing suspects over here, and here was a man who had shot Officer Tippit. They didn't even mention him as a suspect, but there was another murder coincident in time.

Mr. LIEBELER. So the news broadcast connected Oswald with Officer Tippit?

Mr. PAINE. That is right.

Mr. LIEBELER. Did you then consider again whether or not Oswald had been involved in the assassination?

Mr. PAINE. Well, that was too much to have his name mentioned away from his place of work as having killed somebody; the stew was too thick to stay at work, and I was shaken too much, anyway.

Mr. LIEBELER. So your testimony is that you first thought of Oswald after you heard of the Texas School Book Depository Building being involved in the assassination, but you concluded at that time that Oswald was probably not involved in the assassination; is that correct?

Mr. PAINE. That is correct.

Mr. LIEBELER. Is there any other reason other than the fact Oswald was at that building that made you think of him when you heard that building mentioned in connection with the assassination?

Mr. PAINE. Well, yes; Oswald, of course, stands—he is a black sheep in society; I mean he is, if you were to pick out the singular person among the employees there, he is the one, or he is probably the one. I don't happen to know the people who worked there. I gather from him there were about 30 people working there in a fairly large building.

Mr. LIEBELER. What was your state of mind when you heard that the Texas School Book Depository Building was involved in the shooting, did you deeply suspect Oswald had been involved, or was it just a passing thought? Tell us some more about that if you can, recreate your state of mind.

Mr. PAINE. I think I was nervous. I know I was trying to assemble a vibration meter and could not put in the screws or I kept making mistakes. I was preoccupied. Of course, the darn fools, we should have all stopped to mourn the President, but it is kind of a habit, I wasn't accustomed, habit drove us on, very unhappy or unresolved emotional time. I thought, firstly, Frank was quite insistent, he didn't just ask me once, but several times, whether I didn't think I should call the FBI.

Mr. LIEBELER. Did he tell you why he thought you should call the FBI?

Mr. PAINE. Well, he would have, but he is of that nature. At one time he had seen someone taking pictures of Hensley Field, which has signs on the outside "No Photographs Allowed," and I said I believe more in freedom. It seems to me if the field doesn't want the pictures taken, they had better put up a big fence. But he had gone ahead and called up the base commander, and the base commander knew the man. That was his normal mode of behavior, whereas my normal defense is of the individual, and I didn't think—I would not like to, if Lee is falsely accused, I wouldn't want to be jumping on him with the mob. If he is properly, if he is guilty, he will be found. They know he works there, he is connected to us. I couldn't contribute to his capture, so that my withholding information wouldn't harm the search for the right man, and having jumped on him unfairly I might be ashamed of that later on. So that was my feeling in regard to whether I should call the FBI. I think I just kind of felt cold sweats or something like that in regard to the question could he have done that thing. I don't think I went much beyond that, could he, could he.

Mr. LIEBELER. Did Krystinik indicate to you any reason for his desire to call the FBI? Did he suspect Oswald had done this on the basis of his knowledge of Oswald?

Mr. PAINE. It seemed to me very reasonable that he should think so. Of course, I don't think the others were so sharply aware, the others in the lab were so sharply aware that we were wrestling with this problem.

The CHAIRMAN. He didn't say anything to you, he didn't tell you any other reason?

Mr. PAINE. No, he didn't; but his reaction seemed perfectly reasonable to me.

The CHAIRMAN. Yes.

Mr. PAINE. I felt the same one—if you were to pick out somebody in that building, it was a rather singular coincidence we knew this man who was so

426

negative to our society and not an ingratiating person, not a person with compassion or something.

Mr. LIEBELER. What time did you arrive at your home in Irving?

Mr. PAINE. I would guess about 3 or 3:30, somewhere in that neighborhood.

Mr. LIEBELER. Who was there when you arrived?

Mr. PAINE. The police, the Dallas police mostly were there.

Mr. LIEBELER. Your wife was there?

Mr. PAINE. My wife and Marina.

Mr. LIEBELER. Do you remember what you said when you arrived?

Mr. PAINE. I don't know. No, I don't remember what I said.

Mr. LIEBELER. Did you say in words or substance, "I came right home as soon as I heard the shots were fired from the Texas School Book Depository Building?"

Mr. PAINE. No, I came right home as soon as I heard Lee Oswald mentioned. I did not come home.

Mr. LIEBELER. Do you remember saying that you came right home as soon as you heard that Oswald was involved?

Mr. PAINE. Yes, I think I said something like that. Ruth asked me.

Mr. LIEBELER. Now, you mentioned before that after you arrived home you went into the garage when the police officers went into your garage. Was there any indication to you at that time that the garage had been previously searched by the police or anyone else?

Mr. PAINE. This I don't remember very well. But, as I remember, this was not the first time we had gone in there. I think, perhaps, they went into—I don't remember, but I don't think it was the first time they had gone in.

Mr. LIEBELER. You said when you did go into the garage, however, the blanket was there in the garage?

Mr. PAINE. I think it was. It was still there.

Mr. LIEBELER. Tell us, to the best of your recollection, what was said in respect of the blanket and search of the garage, as you say. Before you answer that question, let me ask you, did your wife go with you into the garage with the police officers?

Mr. PAINE. I think they were further in in the garage. I think I stayed—the band saw is fairly close to—there is an overhead door to the garage, and close to the under edge of that when it is pulled up. In other words, it is fairly close to the outside in the garage, and I think I stayed somewhat near the door entering the garage, which is the inside end of the garage.

Mr. LIEBELER. And your wife was with the police officers further in?

Mr. PAINE. Yes, I think she was.

Mr. LIEBELER. Was Marina Oswald there?

Mr. PAINE. Failure of recollection, I would say, yes. But it is a very fuzzy recollection.

Mr. LIEBELER. Can you tell us where the blanket was found?

Mr. PAINE. It doesn't really make sense as to why they would still leave the blanket there, and these things would have been discussed at that time, but I kind of remember a kind of silhouette situation, a police officer either lifted up or kicked this blanket, which was in exactly the same location that the rifle, the package had been, underneath the saw and somewhat in the sawdust. And I think he put it back there. He may have asked me at that time, "Did you know what was in this?"

Mr. LIEBELER. Do you remember that?

Mr. PAINE. And that is why I think they asked me, it may have been as early as that, whether it was a rifle, "Do you think it could have been a rifle?" I don't remember how it was posed, but I probably answered when it was suggested, it was a rifle, and there they suggested it was a rifle, because they had already learned from Marina that he had had a rifle, and it had been, perhaps, had learned it had been in that blanket.

Mr. LIEBELER. Do you know they had previously asked Marina about that?

Mr. PAINE. No; but I think—I'm just telling you my impressions here, very fuzzy impressions.

Mr. LIEBELER. Go ahead.

Mr. PAINE. My impression was that they asked me if I knew what was in this blanket, or he asked me, and then he asked me if it could be a rifle, and

I probably responded, yes. It didn't take long once the rifle was suggested as the object to fit this puzzle together, this puzzle of the pieces that I had been trying to assemble in the package.

Mr. LIEBELER. What else happened?

Mr. PAINE. We went out of the garage, I don't think he took the blanket then even.

Mr. LIEBELER. This is the Dallas police officer?

Mr. PAINE. Yes, plainclothesman, wearing black hats; one of them had one of those Texas hats. He collected all the useless stuff in our house, he went around and collected all the files of Ruth, and a drawer of cameras, mostly belonging to me. I tried to tell him one of the files contained our music or something like that, and the more I suggested it, that he not bother taking those, the more insistent he was in taking those objects.

So with the various boxes and piles of stuff, mostly of our stuff, we got in the car and went off, and he was quite irked that we had wasted quite enough time around there, he said, and Ruth was irked, and everybody was irked by it. He wouldn't let us be helpful, and thought we were—he became angry when we tried to be helpful or something that we would suggest that he should do.

Mr. LIEBELER. Did they tell you how they happened to come to your house?

Mr. PAINE. No. I don't remember. I think I may have asked it, "You found us pretty quickly," or somebody said this, but I don't remember.

Mr. LIEBELER. Do you remember any other conversations about this blanket?

Mr. PAINE. No.

Mr. LIEBELER. Did anyone notice any scraps of paper or tape similar to the ones of which these sacks were constructed that we previously identified, particularly Commission 142?

Mr. PAINE. Not that I remember.

Mr. LIEBELER. Is there anything else that happened during this period prior to the time the police left that you think would be significant or that we ought to know about?

Mr. PAINE. No; very little happened. We just bundled up and went. Marina was—whimpered a little bit, but mostly it was dry.

Mr. LIEBELER. You went with the police?

Mr. PAINE. We went with the police in several cars and didn't come back until quite a lot later that night, didn't go into the garage again; didn't want the Life reporters to take photographs, so I don't think they went in the garage to take photographs. Several—their possessions were searched by various waves of succeeding policemen, Dallas, and Irving and FBI, and what not.

Mr. LIEBELER. Now, there has been a report that on November 23, 1963, there was a telephone call between a man and a woman, between the numbers of your residence and the number of your office, in which the man was reported to have said in words or substance, "We both know who is responsible for the assassination." Have you been asked about this before?

Mr. PAINE. I had heard that—I didn't know it was associated with our numbers. I had heard a report that some telephone operator had listened in on a conversation somewhere, I don't know where it was. I thought it was some other part of the country.

Mr. LIEBELER. Did you talk to your wife on the telephone at any time during Saturday, November 23, on the telephone?

Mr. PAINE. I was in the police station again, and I think I called her from there.

Mr. LIEBELER. Did you make any remark to the effect that you knew who was responsible?

Mr. PAINE. And I don't know who the assassin is or was; no, so I did not.

Mr. LIEBELER. You are positive in your recollection that you made no such remark?

Mr. PAINE. Yes.

Mr. LIEBELER. Would you tell us your impression and your opinion of the relationship that had developed between Marina Oswald and your wife during the period that they knew each other up to the time of the assassination and subsequent to the assassination when, as we discussed briefly yesterday, there came to be a cooling off between them or a disenchantment.

Mr. PAINE. Ruth was mostly learning the language, so she was limited in her vocabulary and couldn't talk about—she explained to me she couldn't talk about—political or economic subjects. It was a topic on which her vocabulary didn't serve her, but it did appear she had spoken of quite a number of things. Marina had told her about movies she had seen in the Soviet Union, but I thought that the knowledge, Ruth's knowledge, I suppose Ruth's knowledge of Marina was fairly shallow. And Marina was quite reserved. Now, it may have been more so when I was in the house that she was not as much at ease as she was, perhaps, with Ruth herself.

Of course, Marina was in a position where she always had to be polite. Ruth is easy to get along with, however, so I didn't expect Marina to have difficulty. But I didn't think Ruth and Marina were bosom friends or buddies, but neither, of course, I didn't mean to suggest the opposite.

Ruth was enjoying Marina's company and I was glad to have Marina staying with Ruth. It actually reduced the cost. Ruth saved money. The bills were less while Marina was there, and Ruth, in general, was happier.

Mr. LIEBELER. Did you learn——

Mr. PAINE. I didn't think Ruth knew Marina very well, but I don't know how well she knew her.

Mr. LIEBELER. Did you learn subsequently or are you aware that subsequent to the assassination there has been a disenchantment or some strain between Marina and Ruth?

Mr. PAINE. Several things happened. Ruth was put out when she learned Marina knew afterward that Oswald had taken a shot at Walker, if that were true. She thought that was quite morally remiss on Marina's part, and so we talked about that thing.

Mr. DULLES. When did she learn that?

Mr. PAINE. This was in the newspaper report.

Mr. DULLES. She only learned it through the newspaper?

Mr. PAINE. That is correct. So we discussed the mitigating circumstances of Marina not knowing the language and not knowing who she could go to if she wanted to stay in this country and, perhaps—we believe there were extenuating circumstances which would, perhaps, excuse Marina. Ruth was troubled about that, and so she wrote a series of quite a number of letters, each one referring to previous letters, trying to discover whether they were being withheld, thinking Marina was a responsible person or normally civil person, she would normally respond to or at least acknowledge receipt of them.

So Ruth didn't know whether she was receiving them or not, and had another—some encounters with Martin and Thorne which didn't put her at ease. She still didn't know whether Marina was receiving them. She saw only some of the checks had been signed by Thorne rather than Marina. Thorne had said that Marina didn't say he had power of attorney, and Marina was trying to do everything that she could which, at least, she could sign her checks, checks or gifts.

So there were these indications. Ruth was very much in the dark, not knowing why she had received no communication from Marina, and having conflicting reports from Martin. Martin said she had a phone right beside her if she wanted to call.

Mr. DULLES. How did she receive these checks?

Mr. PAINE. I guess Ruth—some of the checks came to Ruth as gifts to her, and Ruth would write her own check so she got her own stub back.

Mr. DULLES. I see.

Mr. PAINE. Therefore, Ruth had this question of whether she had offended Marina or whether Marina had done something that offended Ruth or whether Marina didn't like Ruth and had never let on. This would be a great blow to her ego. It had Ruth in great periods of depression and anxiety.

Mr. DULLES. Did either you or your wife, to your knowledge, know Robert Oswald?

Mr. PAINE. We only met him for the first time on the night of the assassination. We both liked him at that time.

Mr. LIEBELER. Mr. Paine, is there any other subject that we haven't covered in the testimony that you think the Commission ought to know about in connection with this assassination?

Mr. PAINE. I don't believe there is anything else that I know.

Mr. LIEBELER. I have no more questions.

The CHAIRMAN. Do you have any questions, Mr. Dulles?

Mr. DULLES. The only question I have in mind is as to what took place as far as Mr. Paine is concerned on the night of the assassination. Were you in the police station?

Mr. PAINE. We went down to the police and stayed there until about 8 or 9 o'clock. Then Marguerite came home with us and spent the night.

Mr. DULLES. You didn't see Lee Harvey at that time, did you?

Mr. PAINE. They asked me and I declined to see him at that time. I changed my mind. When they immediately asked me, I declined. I did not know what he would ask me, so I did not see him.

Mr. DULLES. You did not see him?

Mr. PAINE. No.

Mr. DULLES. Did your wife see him?

Mr. PAINE. I think no one saw him. Marina went in the next morning hoping to see him.

Mr. DULLES. There were no conversations that took place that evening that are pertinent to our investigation so far as you know?

Mr. PAINE. Quite soon I called the ACLU. There were reports, yes, I think at that time, that Friday night, Marguerite was saying he wasn't receiving counsel, and so I called the ACLU to see if there was anybody there checking to see if this was true, and apparently a delegation, this was Saturday morning, and apparently a delegation had been sent.

Mr. DULLES. But to your knowledge neither you nor your wife had any conversations with Marina or Robert that would throw any light on this apparent coolness?

Mr. PAINE. Ruth apparently saw Marina this last week-end. We have some indications that people had gone between, chiefly Levine.

Mr. DULLES. You think money considerations had anything to do with this?

Mr. PAINE. I think quite a lot—it will be borne out, between Ruth and Marina subsequently, I think they will find the difficulties. I think Thorne——

Mr. DULLES. What I have in mind is as to whether some of these other people thought that you and Ruth might intervene in as business manager or something of that kind between them, and the monetary considerations that were coming in to Marina.

Mr. PAINE. We didn't know why. We have the feeling that Thorne was advising her not to speak to Ruth. Ruth is not interested in the money, but is interested in protecting her from the wolves, and so she thought, we both thought, there were some false stories being told to Marina in regard to Ruth.

Mr. DULLES. That is all.

The CHAIRMAN. Thank you very much, Mr. Paine.

Mr. PAINE. Thank you, sir.

The CHAIRMAN. We will examine Mrs. Paine this afternoon at 2 o'clock.

(Whereupon, at 1:05 p.m., the President's Commission recessed.)

Afternoon Session

TESTIMONY OF RUTH HYDE PAINE

The President's Commission reconvened at 2:20 p.m.

Mr. McCLOY. Before I ask you to be sworn, Mrs. Paine. I will give you a little general indication of what our testimony is apt to cover.

We have heard that you and your husband made the acquaintance of the Oswalds somewhere during 1963, and that Mrs. Marina Oswald lived in your home from late September 1963, I believe, to the time of the assassination.

Since we are inquiring under our mandate into the background and the possible motives of the assassination by Lee Harvey Oswald, the alleged assassin, we will question you regarding your association with Mr. Oswald and try to glean from you any other facts that may bear upon the assassination or its motivation.

I believe you have been furnished with a copy of the executive order under which we are operating as well as the Congressional resolution?

Mrs. PAINE. Yes.

Mr. McCLOY. Now if you will please stand, I will swear you.

Mrs. PAINE. I would like to affirm.

Mr. McCLOY. Do you solemnly affirm that the evidence you will give in this investigation will be the truth, the whole truth, and nothing but the truth?

Mrs. PAINE. Yes; I do.

Mr. McCLOY. Will you state your full name for the record and your address?

Mrs. PAINE. I am Ruth Hyde Paine. I live at 2515 West Fifth Street, in Irving, Tex.

Mr. McCLOY. Mr. Jenner is going to conduct the examination.

Mr. JENNER. Your maiden name?

Mrs. PAINE. Is Hyde.

Mr. JENNER. Ruth Avery Hyde.

Mrs. PAINE. Right.

Mr. JENNER. You are wife of Michael Ralph Paine?

Mrs. PAINE. Yes.

Mr. JENNER. And you were born September 3, 1932?

Mrs. PAINE. Yes.

Mr. JENNER. You are almost 34 years old.

Mrs. PAINE. Almost 32. I will be 32 in September.

Mr. JENNER. Pretty bad arithmetic. Just a little bit of your background, Mrs. Paine, very little. Your mother and father are living?

Mrs. PAINE. That is right.

Mr. JENNER. And your mother is an Unitarian Minister ordained in the Unitarian Church at the moment?

Mrs. PAINE. Yes; she is.

Mr. JENNER. And received her degree in theology last summer I believe, is that correct?

Mrs. PAINE. No, she has completed her work for a Bachelor of Divinity Degree from Oberlin College and she will receive it in the spring. They don't give them in mid-year. She completed just the first of February.

Mr. JENNER. You yourself are a college graduate?

Mrs. PAINE. Yes.

Mr. JENNER. Antioch College?

Mrs. PAINE. Yellow Springs.

Mr. JENNER. Yellow Springs, Ohio?

Mrs. PAINE. Right.

Mr. JENNER. You have a brother and sister.

Mrs. PAINE. Yes.

Mr. JENNER. And your mother, your father, yourself, your brother, and your sister are your entire family.

Mrs. PAINE. My immediate family.

Mr. JENNER. Your brother is a graduate of Antioch also, he and your sister. Are they older than you?

Mrs. PAINE. Yes, they are.

Mr. JENNER. Which is the elder of the two?

Mrs. PAINE. My brother is the oldest.

Mr. JENNER. And your brother is a professional man, is he?

Mrs. PAINE. He is a doctor, general practitioner.

Mr. JENNER. A general physician, and he practices in Yellow Springs, Ohio?

Mrs. PAINE. That is right.

Mr. JENNER. Would you tell us where Yellow Springs is?

Mrs. PAINE. It is about 60 miles south and west from Columbus, Ohio, the capital, which is more or less in the middle of the State, and just a little bit east of Dayton.

Mr. JENNER. Is your brother married.

Mrs. PAINE. Yes, he is.

Mr. JENNER. Does he have a family?

Mrs. PAINE. He has four children.

Mr. JENNER. And is your sister married?

Mrs. PAINE. Yes; she is.

Mr. JENNER. Does she have a family?

Mrs. PAINE. She has four children.

Mr. JENNER. And each of your brothers and your sister, it is their first marriage?

Mrs. PAINE. That is right.

Mr. JENNER. Now you were married to Mr. Paine December 28, 1957, is that correct?

Mrs. PAINE. Yes; I believe so.

Mr. JENNER. And you were married where, in Philadelphia?

Mrs. PAINE. It was suburban Philadelphia. Friends meeting in Media, Pa.

Mr. JENNER. Would you tell us what the Friends meeting is which you have mentioned?

Mrs. PAINE. I am a member of the Society of Friends often known as Quakers.

Mr. JENNER. You are a Quaker?

Mrs. PAINE. I am.

Mr. JENNER. When did you embrace that faith?

Mrs. PAINE. I joined in early 1951, I believe.

Mr. JENNER. Has any other member of your family embraced the Quaker faith?

Mrs. PAINE. Yes; my brother is also a Quaker.

Mr. JENNER. When did he embrace that faith.

Mrs. PAINE. Similar in time. a year or two one way or the other. I don't recall exactly.

Mr. JENNER. I am afraid I might have been inattentive. When did you say that occurred?

Mrs. PAINE. Similar in time. I don't remember just when exactly he joined.

Mr. JENNER. I was thinking more as to when you said you did.

Mrs. PAINE. In early '51, I think: I am quite certain it was winter of '51.

Mr. JENNER. You were then in college?

Mrs. PAINE. That was the year out. I went to Antioch one year and then I took a year out and I joined my home meeting in Columbus which I had already attended perhaps 2 years.

Mr. JENNER. And from the time you joined the Quaker church you have been a member of that church?

Mrs. PAINE. Yes.

Mr. JENNER. Or that faith?

Mrs. PAINE. Or church; yes.

Mr. JENNER. Ever since?

Mrs. PAINE. Yes.

Mr. JENNER. Now you and Mr. Paine, did you take up a residence in Philadelphia as soon as you married?

Mrs. PAINE. I had been living in Philadelphia working there, and then when we married I moved to suburban Philadelphia where Michael was living, Paoli, Pa.

Mr. JENNER. His folks live in Paoli, also, do they not?

Mrs. PAINE. His mother and stepfather.

Mr. JENNER. And you remained in Paoli until when?

Mrs. PAINE. Well, it was summer of '59 we were in the process of moving, didn't complete it until fall of '59.

Mr. JENNER. I see. You moved to where?

Mrs. PAINE. To Irving, where we are now, to the present address.

Mr. JENNER. To your present home? And that was in the summer of 1959?

Mrs. PAINE. Yes.

Mr. JENNER. At some later stage we will go into what occurred. In the meantime we have you now in Irving, Tex. Is that a suburb of Dallas?

Mrs. PAINE. Yes.

Mr. JENNER. You and your husband purchased the home you have there before you went down.

Mrs. PAINE. Oh, no; we stayed at a small apartment for several weeks looking around and then rented for a year, and then we purchased the house we have been renting.

Mr. JENNER. So you purchased that and moved in in 1960, is that about right?

Mrs. PAINE. We first moved into it in the fall of '59.

Mr. JENNER. You rented it and then purchased it.

Mrs. PAINE. The same house; yes.

Mr. JENNER. All right, thank you. You have two children?

Mrs. PAINE. That is right.

Mr. JENNER. A boy and a girl?

Mrs. PAINE. A girl and a boy.

Mr. JENNER. Would you name the oldest of the two.

Mrs. PAINE. Sylvia Lynn and the boy—she is now 4. The boy is Christopher and he is 3.

Mr. JENNER. The point I was getting at, your daughter, Sylvia, was born after you reached Texas?

Mrs. PAINE. Yes.

Mr. JENNER. And what was her birth?

Mrs. PAINE. She was born on November 17, '59.

Mr. JENNER. 1959. Now you are acquainted, became acquainted with Marina Oswald, did you not, in due course in Irving, Tex.?

Mrs. PAINE. No. I first met her and her husband at a gathering of people in Dallas at the home of Everett Glover.

Mr. JENNER. I will get to that in a moment.

Mrs. PAINE. Okay. I had not met her before that.

Mr. JENNER. At this time you and your husband were living in your present home in Irving, Tex.?

Mrs. PAINE. In '59.

Mr. JENNER. At the time that you met Marina Oswald?

Mrs. PAINE. No. Michael moved to an apartment in September of 1962.

Mr. JENNER. There had been some strained relations or difficulties between yourself and your husband Michael. When we shake our heads we don't get it on the record.

The answer to that is "Yes"?

Mrs. PAINE. Is "No." I had not met her when there had been some strained relations between me and my husband. It is just we are having difficulties with words.

Mr. JENNER. What I was getting at—there had been some strained relations, is that correct?

Mrs. PAINE. Yes.

Mr. JENNER. And Mr. Paine had moved to separate quarters. This was in September of 1962, correct.

Mrs. PAINE. Right.

Mr. JENNER. You met Marina for the first time when.

Mrs. PAINE. I judge it was the last of February, towards the end of February of 1963.

Mr. JENNER. You were then living with your children in your home at 2515.

Mrs. PAINE. West Fifth.

Mr. JENNER. West Fifth Street in Irving, Tex. Now would you please relate the circumstances under which the meeting between yourself and Marina Oswald first occurred in February of 1963.

Mrs. PAINE. I was invited to come to the home of Everett Glover to meet a few friends of his, and I judge that was on the 22d of February looking back at my calendar.

Mr. JENNER. Would you please tell us who Mr. Everett Glover was and how you became acquainted with him.

What was the milieu?

Mrs. PAINE. I met Mr. Glover at a group gathered to sing madrigals together. These are old English songs where each part has a melody and it was for the enjoyment of reading the music and in harmony, and we often had coffee afterward and would talk.

Mr. JENNER. This included your husband, however, did it not?

Mrs. PAINE. Yes indeed.

Mr. JENNER. You had a common interest in this?

Mrs. PAINE. Madrigal singing?

Mr. JENNER. Madrigal singing?

Mrs. PAINE. Yes. And went together.

Mr. JENNER. Proceed.

Mrs. PAINE. And then Everett knew that I was interested in learning Russian well enough to teach it, and since this gathering was to include some people who spoke Russian, he invited me and he invited Michael also to attend. Michael caught a bad cold and wasn't able to go.

I went.

Mr. JENNER. Excuse me, could I interrupt you a moment here. Though your husband was living in his own quarters, the relations between you, however, were not so disruptive but what you were friendly, and you were attending these singing groups?

Mrs. PAINE. That is right. I saw him perhaps once or twice a week for dinner at my house, and we went out to rather more movies than some of my married friends.

Mr. JENNER. There was reasonable cordiality?

Mrs. PAINE. Yes.

Mr. JENNER. Yes. I don't wish to pry into your private life.

Mrs. PAINE. If it is pertinent, go ahead.

Mr. JENNER. Mrs. Paine, there is some necessity. We might touch a little on your private life if you will forgive me for doing it. Mr. Glover, is he a single person?

Mrs. PAINE. He was at the time of the party. He has been divorced from his wife. He is now remarried.

Mr. JENNER. Now I interrupted you at the point at which you were relating that Mr. Glover had raised with you, I assume this was a telephone call, that he was going to have some guests. He knew of your interest in the study and the learning of the Russian language and its use?

Mrs. PAINE. Yes.

Mr. JENNER. Do I correctly summarize it up to the moment?

Mrs. PAINE. Yes.

Mr. JENNER. You have an entry in your calendar as I recall on this subject. There is a question mark.

Mrs. PAINE. I recall it says "Everett?"

Mr. JENNER. May I hand the witness the document?

Mr. McCLOY. You may.

Mr. JENNER. This will be Commission Exhibit No. 401. Gentlemen for the purpose of identification of the exhibit, it is Mrs. Paine's calendar which she used in part as a diary and part to record prospective appointments and she surrendered it to the FBI. This is not merely a photostat, it is a picture taken with a camera of that calendar.

(Commission Exhibit No. 401 was marked for identification.)

Mr. JENNER. May I ask you a question or two about it Mrs. Paine. Did you not go through each of the pages of that calendar with me this morning?

Mrs. PAINE. Yes, I did.

Mr. JENNER. And I asked you, did I not, whether it was all in your handwriting?

Mrs. PAINE. You did.

Mr. JENNER. Except for the identification on the front, the officer who received it from you—he made a notation of the date of receipt—it is all in your handwriting?

Mrs. PAINE. That is correct.

Mr. JENNER. And it is in the same condition now, isn't it, as it was when you surrendered it?

Mrs. PAINE. It is.

Mr. JENNER. Would you turn to the diary page to which I have reference in connection with the first meeting with Marina Oswald, and that is what month and what page and what date?

Mrs. PAINE. It is on the page for February, and the only thing I can——

Mr. McCLOY. February what year?

Mrs. PAINE. February 1963.

Mr. JENNER. And the day please?

Mrs. PAINE. There is a notation on the 22d of February.

Mr. JENNER. Excuse me, there is a square with the figure 22 in it indicating February 22, 1963. Do you have something written in there?

Mrs. PAINE. Yes.

Mr. JENNER. What is written in there?

Mrs. PAINE. It says "Everett's?"

Mr. JENNER. Is that all there is in that square?

Mrs. PAINE. That is all.

Mr. JENNER. Would you explain that and how it related to what you are now telling us?

Mrs. PAINE. I believe it refers to the invitation to come to his home. As I recall, he telephoned me twice, first to say that they might get together a group of people, hence the question mark. Then he called again to say they were going to have a party, and to make the invitation definite.

Mr. JENNER. Now you used the expression "I believe." Is that your best recollection at the moment?

Mrs. PAINE. That is my best recollection.

Mr. JENNER. And I went over this with you this morning and you gave me the same explanation, did you not?

Mrs. PAINE. Yes.

Mr. JENNER. Now did that event take place?

Mrs. PAINE. Yes.

Mr. JENNER. And what is your best recollection as to the day of the month it took place?

Mrs. PAINE. I have no other way of guessing when it was except to assume that this notation means it was on the 22d of February.

Mr. JENNER. And that does represent your present best recollection refreshed to the extent it is refreshed by the memorandum before you?

Mrs. PAINE. That is right, and of course this first——

Mr. JENNER. What day of the week was that?

Mrs. PAINE. That was a Friday.

Mr. JENNER. Friday night. You attended the party did you not?

Mrs. PAINE. Yes, I did.

Mr. McCLOY. I believe you used the word Friday. I don't believe she did, Friday night. You said Friday night.

Mrs. PAINE. It was Friday evening.

Mr. JENNER. Friday evening?

Mrs. PAINE. The 22d was Friday. I don't recall.

Mr. McCLOY. You used the word "evening"?

Mrs. PAINE. It was an evening party.

Mr. JENNER. It was held in Mr. Glover's home was it?

Mrs. PAINE. Yes, it was.

Mr. JENNER. Where is his home?

Mrs. PAINE. At that time he was living in the Highland Park section of Dallas.

Mr. JENNER. How far from your home is that?

Mrs. PAINE. Half hour drive.

Mr. JENNER. By what means did you get to Mr. Glover's home?

Mrs. PAINE. I drove.

Mr. JENNER. You owned or then had, or maybe you still have a station wagon?

Mrs. PAINE. That is right.

Mr. JENNER. Is it the same car still?

Mrs. PAINE. It is the same car.

Mr. JENNER. And when you arrived, were either of the Oswalds present?

435

Mrs. PAINE. I am not sure I recall accurately. I think they came a little after I arrived.

Mr. JENNER. Would you give us your best recollection of all the people, couples if you can remember them that way, and then single persons or persons there without their wives or husbands, as the case may be, that evening?

Mrs. PAINE. Well, I will try. The Oswalds, two were there, Marina and Lee, Everett Glover, the host, Mr. and Mrs. De Mohrenschildt who were the friendship link between the Oswalds and Glover.

Mr. JENNER. Could I interrupt you there? Had you known the De Mohrenschildts?

Mrs. PAINE. I had never met them. I have not met them since.

Mr. JENNER. That is the only occasion?

Mrs. PAINE. That is right.

Mr. JENNER. That you ever saw either Mr. or Mrs. De Mohrenschildt?

Mrs. PAINE. That is right.

Mr. JENNER. You had no conversations, no letters, no contact whatsoever with them either before or after this party?

Mrs. PAINE. That is correct, no contact whatsoever before or after. There was a roommate of Everett's. Dirk, I think, I forget the name.

Mr. JENNER. Are you attempting to recall his first name or his last name?

Mrs. PAINE. His first name. I may be wrong. It was a young German fellow.

Mr. JENNER. Schmidt?

Mrs. PAINE. Do you know the first name?

Mr. JENNER. No, I don't recall the first name.

Mrs. PAINE. And he had two roommates, so that is two other single men, and I don't recall their names.

Mr. JENNER. Was each of them there?

Mrs. PAINE. They were both there.

Mr. JENNER. There were two roommates.

Mrs. PAINE. Two roommates and they were both present at the party. I should remember their names but I don't.

Mr. JENNER. All right.

Mrs. PAINE. And there was a couple who lived in Irving; again I don't recall the name. I don't believe I have seen any of these people since with the exception of one of the roommates once, and again I don't recall the name.

Mr. JENNER. Did you see the roommate the second——

Mrs. PAINE. I may have seen him since. All these people were new to me when I came to the party with the exception of Everett.

Mr. JENNER. Did you see the roommate the second time before or after November 22, 1963?

Mrs. PAINE. Oh, it was before.

Mr. JENNER. But it is a fact that none of these people who were at the party other than Mr. Glover had you seen or heard of?

Mrs. PAINE. Before.

Mr. JENNER. Up to the time that the party was held.

Mrs. PAINE. That is right.

Mr. JENNER. Have you exhausted your present recollection as to the people who were present on that occasion.

Mrs. PAINE. I can't get a name. The couple were living in Irving, I recall that, but I don't—I have forgotten their name.

Mr. JENNER. Now the Oswalds arrived shortly after the party began or at least after you arrived?

Mrs. PAINE. I believe they came with the De Mohrenschildts.

Mr. JENNER. And you were introduced, were you?

Mrs. PAINE. Yes, I was introduced.

Mr. JENNER. By whom?

Mrs. PAINE. I don't recall. It was a very informal gathering. Marina was wearing slacks and Mrs. De Mohrenschildt also was. I doubt pains were taken with the introductions.

Mr. JENNER. Excuse me.

Mrs. PAINE. I doubt any pains were taken with the introductions.

Mr. JENNER. How long did the party proceed?

Mrs. PAINE. It must have started something after 8 o'clock and went until towards midnight.

Mr. JENNER. You have an interest in square dancing and that sort of thing also. Did you do any of that then?

Mrs. PAINE. No. We talked and ate.

Mr. JENNER. Did you do any madrigal singing?

Mrs. PAINE. No.

Mr. JENNER. No singing that evening?

Mrs. PAINE. No.

Mr. JENNER. Now before I get to any specificity with respect to Marina and Lee Oswald, was Russian spoken that night by anybody?

Mrs. PAINE. Yes.

Mr. JENNER. Did you speak Russian?

Mrs. PAINE. Yes.

Mr. JENNER. Who else at the party had some facility with Russian in addition to Lee Oswald and Marina Oswald?

Mrs. PAINE. Just the De Mohrenschildts, both of them, and myself.

Mr. JENNER. And yourself. Did you mention that Mr. Glover had some interest in the Russian language?

Mrs. PAINE. No, I don't believe he does.

Mr. JENNER. He did not, all right. Were the Oswalds really the center of attention that evening?

Mrs. PAINE. I think so, yes, although you can't say that there was a single center for the entire evening. It wasn't like being invited to hear what he had to say. It was much more informal than that.

Mr. JENNER. Did you speak with Marina?

Mrs. PAINE. Yes, I did.

Mr. JENNER. Did you converse with her during the course of the evening?

Mrs. PAINE. Very briefly. She spent the first part of the evening trying to get June to go to sleep.

Mr. JENNER. June is her daughter?

Mrs. PAINE. The little girl with her.

Mr. JENNER. She brought her daughter with her did she?

Mrs. PAINE. Yes, and then we talked some in the kitchen with Mrs. De Mohrenschildt, Marina and I.

Mr. JENNER. And what subject did you ladies pursue?

Mrs. PAINE. I really can't remember. The actual conversation with Marina didn't cover much time at all. I saw very little of her that evening.

Mr. JENNER. That evening?

Mrs. PAINE. That is right.

Mr. JENNER. Can you remember any subject you talked to her about in the kitchen?

Mrs. PAINE. No.

Mr. JENNER. What subjects were discussed, I assume in the living room or—where everybody was gathered? Do you recall what was being pursued there in the way of conversation.

Mrs. PAINE. Part of the time Lee talked with people who were asking him about his trip to Russia. I believe Everett had told me that he had been, so I knew that when I arrived. And the fact that he had gone intending to become a citizen in the Soviet Union. He talked freely and with considerable interest in his subject to the three or four people around him.

Mr. JENNER. Were you gathered in that group?

Mrs. PAINE. Part of the time at least I was listening to that. He spoke of the things about the Soviet Union that had displeased him, as for instance the censorship. He knew that it had been going on regarding his letters.

Mr. JENNER. Mrs. Paine, when you talk in terms of conclusion, we have a little trouble testifying. If you will give us examples such as you just gave us about censorship, could we go back a moment to the conversation about his going to Russia. During the course of that subject, in questions put to him, was anything he listed as to why he went to Russia? May I have a yes or no first?

Do you recall anything like that?

Mrs. PAINE. I can't be certain that this is when I first got an idea about why he wanted to go or whether I learned this later.

Mr. JENNER. Does your memory serve you enough so that there is a fair possibility that—it is important to us—was the subject discussed at that gathering?

Mrs. PAINE. I think so.

Mr. JENNER. And that is your best recollection?

Mrs. PAINE. Yes.

Mr. JENNER. Now would you give us your best recollection of what he said or what Marina said, but primarily what Mr. Oswald said on that subject. Why did he go to Russia?

Mrs. PAINE. I carry the impression, and I think it is recalled from this evening——

Mr. JENNER. Excuse me. When you say you carry the impression you are saying "It is my present recollection."

Mrs. PAINE. All right. That he spoke of himself as a Marxist that evening, that he had read certain Marxist books and thought that the Soviet economic system was superior to ours, and wanted to go to the Soviet Union and live there.

Mr. JENNER. What response was elicited from others at the meeting, agreement?

Mrs. PAINE. No; I would not say there was any agreement. People were interested. This is an unusual thing to do. And they were interested in hearing how he found Soviet life, what he thought of it, whether he was pleased or disappointed.

Mr. JENNER. Would you be good enough to tell the members of the Commission what Mr. Oswald said in those respects, to the best of your recollection?

Mrs. PAINE. He mentioned that he was displeased with the censorship, or at least he commented on it in a way that I took as unfavorable.

Mr. JENNER. Thank you, Ma'am.

Did he say he was——

Mrs. PAINE. What had happened, yes.

Mr. JENNER. What censorship is he talking about?

Mrs. PAINE. He referred to a letter that had been sent to him by Robert Oswald that he later learned, after he had come back to the United States, had been sent. He had not received it. He judged that they had simply stopped it, and he commented that they are more apt to just take a letter than take out a piece of it and then send it on, and that censorship is more obvious.

Mr. JENNER. All right, go on.

Mrs. PAINE. I wondered, listening to him, whether he really was——

Mr. JENNER. Excuse me, please. Before we get to what you wondered about, exhaust your recollection as to what he said, what others might have said on the subjects in his presence about which he talked.

Mrs. PAINE. That is all I can think of.

Mr. JENNER. You mentioned, also, Mrs. Paine, that there was discussed that evening the subject of his return to America.

Mrs. PAINE. Obviously, yes.

Mr. JENNER. Why he returned, was that subject discussed?

Mrs. PAINE. Not very much, no. I can't recall any specifics relating to that.

Mr. JENNER. All you can recall, I take it, at the moment, is that there was an allusion to the subject?

Mrs. PAINE. Well, he was clearly here, yes. He had come back, and—well, I have to put it in terms of what I guess or what I feel was his reaction. I can't give you a specific recall.

Mr. JENNER. We have no objection to your doing that. We would like to have you first state all you can recall as to what specifically happened in this instance. How did Mr. Oswald treat or regard—what relationship did you gather existed between Marina and her husband, a cordial one as of that occasion, separating from what you learned afterward, but just this initial instance. What impression did you have?

Mrs. PAINE. Almost none. There was very little contact between them during the evening. He spoke English to those that were asking them questions. She was either in the bedroom by herself trying to get the little baby to go to sleep, or in the kitchen speaking Russian to the De Mohrenschildts. I listened more than I spoke in that situation.

Mr. JENNER. When Mr. Oswald was in the living room with you ladies and gentlemen, the conversation was in English, was it not?

Mrs. PAINE. Yes.

Mr. JENNER. I take it, then, that when Marina returned to the room Russian was spoken, at least by those who had command of the Russian language.

Mrs. PAINE. When she was in the same room, there was more than one conversation going on, and in two languages.

Mr. JENNER. When anybody spoke to Marina——

Mrs. PAINE. It was in Russian.

Mr. JENNER. It was in Russian. When people spoke with each other other than with Marina, it was in English, is that correct?

Mrs. PAINE. That is my best recollection.

Mr. JENNER. Now, in very short compass what was your impression of Mr. Oswald at that initial party?

Mrs. PAINE. I thought he was pleased to be interesting to this group of people and glad to tell them about his experience, to answer their questions. He seemed open and forthright. I did wonder as he was talking about it whether he had come to the conclusion after being in the Soviet Union that their system was inferior.

Mr. JENNER. Inferior to ours?

Mrs. PAINE. To ours, or whether he still thought that the Soviet system was a better one. His discussion of the censorship made me feel that he wanted his listeners to know that he was not blind to the defects of the Soviet system, but it did not convince me that he was in favor of the American system. I was left wondering which country he thought conducted itself better.

Mr. JENNER. Did you have an interest in the Oswalds at this moment wholly apart from your interest in the Russian language?

Mrs. PAINE. No.

Mr. JENNER. Were you intellectually curious about them is all I meant.

Mrs. PAINE. Oh, yes. Well, it is most unusual to take such a step as he took.

Mr. JENNER. Had you had some notice in advance of this meeting, Mrs. Paine, of the fact that Mr. Oswald was at least—there had been publications of his having been a defector?

Mrs. PAINE. No; I wasn't aware of that.

Mr. JENNER. When did you first learn of that?

Mrs. PAINE. Well, a name is always given to someone who goes to the Soviet Union and wants to have citizenship there, isn't it, so I could well have assumed that there had been such, but I really didn't learn about it until after the assassination. I guess. No; I take it back.

There was a reference now.

Mr. JENNER. That evening?

Mrs. PAINE. Specific recall. It is coming. The content of Robert's letter to him, as I recall, included a clipping from the Fort Worth newspapers relative to his defection.

Mr. JENNER. Excuse me, Mrs. Paine, you are talking about a letter of Robert Oswald's?

Mrs. PAINE. A letter from Robert to Lee which Lee never got but heard about when he came back to the States.

Mr. JENNER. And that was the subject of discussion that evening?

Mrs. PAINE. That came up, so, therefore, I did know that he had been called a defector.

Mr. JENNER. Did Robert refer to this letter or did someone in the meeting refer to the letter?

Mrs. PAINE. Lee referred to the letter in discussion of censorship.

Mr. JENNER. But up until that moment, you had not had any prior impression with respect to whether he had been a defector or an attempted defector?

Mrs. PAINE. Well, I think, yes; I had some impression of that sort, but it came directly from Lee. He said he went to the Soviet Union and tried to give up his American citizenship, and as I recall, he said that the American embassy did not relinquish his passport, and, therefore, he was not eligible to get Soviet citizenship.

Mr. JENNER. You are remembering more now.

Mrs. PAINE. I am.

Mr. JENNER. I am pleased that you are, Mrs. Paine. He did discuss his attempts to obtain——

Mrs. PAINE. Yes.

Mr. JENNER. To surrender his passport and to accomplish his Soviet citizenship?

Mrs. PAINE. Yes.

Mr. JENNER. And that was openly discussed in this gathering?

Mrs. PAINE. Yes.

Mr. McCLOY. This is Senator Cooper, a member of the Commission, Mrs. Paine.

Mrs. PAINE. How do you do?

Mr. JENNER. This party, I gather, lasted approximately from 7 to 12, did you say?

Mrs. PAINE. Eight to eleven-thirty or twelve.

Mr. JENNER. And the party broke up, and you went home?

Mrs. PAINE. Yes.

Mr. JENNER. What was your overall impression of Marina Oswald?

Mrs. PAINE. I had very little impression altogether. I did ask for her address.

Mr. JENNER. Why did you do that?

Mr. PAINE. And I asked if I could write her. I wanted to go visit her at her home.

Mr. JENNER. Why?

Mrs. PAINE. To talk Russian. She is very hard to find, a person speaking modern Russian, and in fact I know of no other, and this was an opportunity for me to again practice in the language, a rather unusual opportunity, and I was interested in meeting her and getting to know her.

Mr. JENNER. Mr. Chairman, I will go back and develop this lady's interest in the Russian language during the course of the examination, and her prior study of the language up to this point. She did have an abiding interest in the language at this particular point, but I wanted to get at the initial meeting first before anything further.

Mr. McCLOY. Very well.

Mr. JENNER. You say modern Russian, that Marina Oswald had a command of modern Russian. Would you please explain to us what you mean by that?

Mrs. PAINE. Well, I am not in a position to judge a person, whether a person is speaking modern Russian or not. My language is not that good, but she talked with—this was later, I only assumed that she had—I hoped that she spoke good Russian. I didn't know at that time whether she spoke educated Russian or not. Shall I jump ahead?

Mr. JENNER. Well, I wish you wouldn't. You meant, then, by your expression that you hoped to find that she did speak educated Russian?

Mrs. PAINE. Yes; right.

Mr. JENNER. And if she did, that then you might profit or learn from her educated Russian to a greater degree than you knew it as of that time? That was your main interest at the moment?

Mrs. PAINE. Yes.

Mr. JENNER. Aside from interests in another lady or human being under those circumstances?

Mrs. PAINE. Well, until I then got to know her it was my only interest.

Mr. JENNER. Yes. That is the point I was seeking to make. Did you become better acquainted with the Oswalds thereafter?

Mrs. PAINE. I met——

Mr. JENNER. Did you, first, yes or no?

Mrs. PAINE. I became better acquainted with Marina.

Mr. JENNER. Mr. Chairman, if members of the Commission—I am going to pass from this initial event—if you have any questions you would like to put to the witness now rather than my deferring it.

Mr. McCLOY. Are there any questions?

The CHAIRMAN. Not for me.

Representative FORD. Not at this point.

Senator COOPER. No.

Mr. McCLOY. May I ask one? Did Oswald, Lee Oswald on this occasion express any dislike for any elements or aspects of American society?

Mrs. PAINE. I can't recall anything specific that was said.

Mr. McCLOY. He did not indicate to this group why it was that he left the United States to go to Russia originally?

Mrs. PAINE. It is hard to say how I formed this opinion, but I gathered that he disapproved of the economic system.

Mr. McCLOY. Was there anything more specific than that that he referred to? Did he refer, for example, to any dislike of individuals?

Mrs. PAINE. Individuals? No; I am certain there was none.

Mr. McCLOY. In government or out of government?

Mrs. PAINE. No.

Mr. McCLOY. Your impression was that he was motivated to go to the Soviet Union because he didn't like the capitalist system?

Mrs. PAINE. Right.

Mr. McCLOY. And had an affinity for what might be called the Marxist system, is that right?

Mrs. PAINE. Right.

Mr. McCLOY. That is all the questions that I have.

Mr. JENNER. Along those lines, Mrs. Paine, did he make any remarks with respect to workers in Russia as compared with the position, the economic position of workers in America? Did he refer to workers as a subject?

Mrs. PAINE. I don't remember.

Mr. JENNER. I am trying to refresh your recollection. You said economics, he thought that the economic situation was superior in Russia. I wonder whether he related it to the ordinary worker rather than the overall system.

Mrs. PAINE. I don't remember.

Representative FORD. How well did Marina speak English at the time you made the first acquaintance or first contact?

Mrs. PAINE. I was under the impression she spoke no English at all.

Representative FORD. Did she appear to understand any English at that time?

Mrs. PAINE. I don't believe she understood much of anything.

Mr. JENNER. That was your definite impression?

Mrs. PAINE. Yes.

Mr. JENNER. Did you hear her speak any English words that evening?

Mrs. PAINE. No.

Mr. JENNER. None whatsoever?

Mrs. PAINE. No.

Mr. McCLOY. Senator Cooper?

Senator COOPER. I believe you said a few minutes ago that you were interested in knowing why Lee Oswald left the United States and went to Russia. Did you say that?

Mrs. PAINE. Well, I don't recall saying it. I suppose I was curious.

Mr. McCLOY. I don't recall that she actually said that. She said it was an interesting situation.

Mrs. PAINE. It was unusual, I think I probably said.

Mr. McCLOY. She used the word unusual.

Mrs. PAINE. An unusual thing to do, certainly.

Senator COOPER. I don't want to say that you said something you didn't, but I got the impression that one of the reasons you were interested in meeting this family was in fact that this man had left the United States and gone to Russia.

Mrs. PAINE. No.

Senator COOPER. In some sense?

Mrs. PAINE. Not in any sense whatever.

Mr. McCloy. As I recall it she did say that this was an unusual situation, and that to some extent developed your interest. This is Mr. Dulles, a member of the Commission.

Senator Cooper. Maybe I could put it this way. Perhaps we could read back and find out, but I thought that you intimated or indicated that you were interested in the fact that this man had gone to Russia.

Mrs. Paine. Perhaps I can answer your question——

Senator Cooper. And it provoked your interest.

Mrs. Paine. I can answer it this way. I was interested at the party to hear something of what he had to say. I was hopeful when I wrote and inquired if I could see Marina where they lived; and knowing that he would be at work, that I would try to go during the week when I would have a chance simply to talk with her.

Senator Cooper. That night he did say that he did not like the capitalist system?

Mrs. Paine. That is my best recollection.

Senator Cooper. Were you interested, then, in finding out what it was about it he didn't like?

Mrs. Paine. No.

Senator Cooper. In reference to his experience in Russia or for any other reason?

Mrs. Paine. No.

Senator Cooper. You didn't inquire further to have him elaborate on his reasons for not liking the capitalist system?

Mrs. Paine. No. Of course, it is a rather short space of time we are talking about, perhaps 45 minutes or so or less. People were inquiring of him.

Mr. Jenner. But others did inquire on these subjects?

Mrs. Paine. For the most part the other people asked questions, yes.

Mr. Jenner. On the subject that Senator Cooper has inquired about, is that true?

Mrs. Paine. I don't recall.

Mr. Jenner. Now perhaps to help your recollection a little bit on that, was this roommate of whom you speak named Volkmar Schmidt?

Mrs. Paine. Volkmar sounds familiar.

Mr. Jenner. Do you recall a couple by the name of Richard Pierce, or a gentleman at least by the name of Richard Pierce who attended that meeting?

Mrs. Paine. Yes; that would be the other roommate, not a couple, he was single, Richard Pierce.

Mr. Jenner. Was there not present a Miss Betty MacDonald?

Mrs. Paine. Which I had completely forgotten about, yes: there was.

Mr. Jenner. And you still are unable to recall the name of the other couple?

Mrs. Paine. I am unable to. Betty MacDonald I do recall lives in the same apartment building as this couple, and it is a long German sort of name, I think.

Mr. Jenner. Had you become acquainted with Mr. Glover through your husband?

Mrs. Paine. Well, you might say so. We both became interested in going to madrigal sings at the same time. My interest in madrigals was developed by Michael, but that was before we ever moved to Texas.

Mr. Jenner. Were you teaching Russian at this time?

Mrs. Paine. No.

Mr. Jenner. You were not? Had you done any teaching of Russian prior to this occasion?

Mrs. Paine. No.

Mr. Jenner. You subsequently did some teaching; have you done some teaching of Russian?

Mrs. Paine. Just this past summer.

Mr. Jenner. Yes. I will get to that in due course. Did you do some translating that evening for Marina?

Mrs. Paine. No.

Mr. Jenner. You did not?

Mrs. Paine. I spoke to her very little. I was embarrassed to.

Mr. Jenner. Why was that?

Mrs. PAINE. Because my Russian was so poor, and the De Mohrenschildts could both do it all so much better.

Mr. JENNER. Was Mr. Oswald's command of Russian very good, also?

Mrs. PAINE. I didn't hear him speak Russian that night at all.

Mr. JENNER. Oh, is that so?

Mrs. PAINE. He may have, but I don't recall.

Mr. JENNER. He did no translating?

Mrs. PAINE. No. For her, no.

Mr. JENNER. For Marina. And on no occasion—he sat there and on none of the occasions did he translate, but, rather, Mr. De Mohrenschildt did the translating?

Mrs. PAINE. I don't even believe that was translating. They would address themselves to her in a separate conversation from what was going on from these three or four around him.

Mr. JENNER. So that those who did not understand Russian got nothing from it?

Mrs. PAINE. Those who did not understand English got nothing from what he was saying—is that what you mean, or do you mean the other way?

Mr. JENNER. If no one interpreted her in English, translated for her.

Mrs. PAINE. No one understood it; yes.

Mr. JENNER. Then whose who didn't understand Russian——

Mrs. PAINE. That is right.

Mr. JENNER. Did not understand what she was saying?

Mrs. PAINE. That is right.

Mr. JENNER. And that went on through the entire evening?

Mrs. PAINE. You must understand she was not present for, I would say, more than half of the evening. She was just with her child.

Mr. JENNER. But while she was present.

Mrs. PAINE. There was no translation done for her benefit.

Mr. JENNER. Or for the benefit of anybody else who did not understand Russian?

Mrs. PAINE. The other way; no. It is a long time ago.

Mr. JENNER. Oh, yes. Was anything the subject that evening of Mrs. Oswald's family background? Was that discussed?

Mrs. PAINE. Of Marina's?

Mr. JENNER. Yes.

Mrs. PAINE. No; nothing.

Mr. JENNER. It was not discussed at anytime during that evening, the fact that she was in Russia, she had been educated as, and was, a pharmacist?

Mrs. PAINE. That might have been said. I don't recall.

Mr. JENNER. What was your reaction to the De Mohrenschildts that evening?

Mrs. PAINE. I had heard from Everett that they were interesting people, that they had gone on a hiking tour through Mexico taking pictures as they went. I learned or had known from Everett, also, in this one telephone conversation, that he was a geologist, a free lancer.

Mrs. De Mohrenschildt seemed somewhat protective toward Marina in the sense of wanting her to understand what was——wanting to talk with her, to include her. Mr. De Mohrenschildt talked about his past life some in English.

Mr. JENNER. His speaking of his past life was in English?

Mrs. PAINE. Was in English. I recalled to him his first wife who was also a Quaker. I remember he said that.

Mr. JENNER. When was your next contact with either Marina Oswald or Lee Oswald?

Mrs. PAINE. I wrote a letter, a note to Marina at the address I had been given, and got a note back saying, "We have moved. This is the new address. Come in perhaps a week." From that time. She wanted to get the house cleaned up before I came.

Mr. JENNER. They lived in Dallas, did they not?

Mrs. PAINE. That was in Dallas; yes.

Mr. JENNER. On this February 22 occasion they were then living on Neely Street in Dallas?

Mrs. PAINE. I believe they moved just in that period that I had the previous address, and as soon as I wrote, the first letter I got back gave the Neely Street address.

Mr. JENNER. You have recorded that, have you not, in your address book?

Mrs. PAINE. Yes.

Mr. JENNER. Which I will follow up in a moment. Do you have a copy of the letter that you wrote to Marina?

Mrs. PAINE. No. That initial letter asking if I could come over? I don't believe I do.

Mr. JENNER. Not having——

Mrs. PAINE. I have her reply.

Mr. JENNER. You do have a reply?

Mrs. PAINE. I have her reply.

Mr. JENNER. Do you have it with you?

Mrs. PAINE. She drew a map. Yes.

Mr. JENNER. May I have it, please?

Mrs. PAINE. Do you want it right now?

Mr. JENNER. Yes.

Mrs. PAINE. All right. Wait—no; perhaps I have it at the hotel. I don't think it is here. I didn't think I would be before the Commission today at all.

Mr. JENNER. We will pass that. You can get it tonight.

Mrs. PAINE. Yes; I am certain I have it.

Mr. DULLES. That was written in Russian, I assume.

Mrs. PAINE. Oh, yes; in my letter to her, bad Russian.

Mr. JENNER. As long as you have the letter I don't want you to attempt to summarize it then, but you did write her a note in which you sought to come see her. She responded advising you of a change of address. There would be some delay, I gather, because she wished to get her home in order, having just moved. And this exchange of letters took place approximately when?

Mrs. PAINE. It was early March some time.

Mr. JENNER. 1963?

Mrs. PAINE. I think her letter is postmarked the 8th of March.

Mr. JENNER. 1963?

Mrs. PAINE. Yes.

Mr. JENNER. After that exchange of letters, did you see Marina Oswald?

Mrs. PAINE. Yes.

Mr. JENNER. Did you go to her home or did she come to yours?

Mrs. PAINE. I drove to her home. There would be no way for her to come.

Mr. JENNER. Had you had another exchange of letters before you went to her home?

Mrs. PAINE. I don't believe so.

Mr. JENNER. You just waited a few days, guessed how long it would take her to have her home in order, and you visited her, am I correct in my summary?

Mrs. PAINE. She suggested Tuesday, as I recall in her letter, but what Tuesday I don't know. If it was written the 8th that would be Tuesday the 12th. There is no notation on my calendar.

Mr. JENNER. But you do have her response to your letter?

Mrs. PAINE. Yes; that is what I have.

Mr. JENNER. In the hotel. We will get that this evening. Was Mr. Oswald home when you visited her?

Mrs. PAINE. No.

Mr. JENNER. On the next occasion?

Mrs. PAINE. He was not.

Mr. JENNER. Did you make a description in your calendar with respect to this visit?

Mrs. PAINE. I judge not.

Mr. JENNER. Do you find any in your calendar?

Mrs. PAINE. With respect to this visit?

Mr. JENNER. Yes.

Mrs. PAINE. I don't believe so.

Mr. JENNER. By the way, that calendar is all in your handwriting, isn't it?

Mrs. PAINE. It is.

Mr. JENNER. Mr. Chairman, I offer in evidence as Exhibit No. 401 the document that has been given that exhibit number.

Mr. McCLOY. It may be admitted.

(The document heretofore marked for identification as Commission Exhibit No. 401, was received in evidence.)

Representative FORD. What time of day was this visit, Mrs. Paine?

Mrs. PAINE. It was midmorning, up to lunchtime. She had hoped I could stay through lunch but I wanted to get back so my children could have naps.

Mr. JENNER. Was there anybody at home to care for your children when you made this visit?

Mrs. PAINE. I took them.

Mr. JENNER. Oh, you took them.

Mrs. PAINE. Therefore, I wanted to get them home to take naps.

Mr. JENNER. What is the driving time from your home in Irving——

Mrs. PAINE. Thirty-five to forty minutes.

Mr. JENNER. To the Neely Street address of the Oswalds?

Mrs. PAINE. Yes. .

Mr. JENNER. I take it—or was Mr. Oswald home?

Mrs. PAINE. No.

Mr. JENNER. Just Marina? And that visit—tell us about that visit, please.

Mrs. PAINE. I fear my recollection may meld one or two visits that occurred in March.

Mr. JENNER. It might be a good idea, then,—go ahead and tell us about them in a melded form.

Mrs. PAINE. All right. I recall we walked out to a nearby park.

Mr. DULLES. In both cases?

Mrs. PAINE. I am not sure.

Mr. DULLES. You think so?

Mrs. PAINE. Anyway, I recall walking to the park, and I think this was the first visit, and we sat and talked. It was warm weather, March, in Dallas. And the children played on the park equipment, and we talked, and she told me that she was expecting a baby, and asked me not to talk about it among the Russian community.

Mr. JENNER. Excuse me. Had anything been said on that subject when you first met Marina Oswald the night of February 22?

Mrs. PAINE. No.

Mr. JENNER. Nothing? This was your first notice of that?

Mrs. PAINE. Yes.

Mr. JENNER. And she told you not—would you repeat that, please?

Mrs. PAINE. She told me that she was expecting a child.

Mr. JENNER. She told you not to do what?

Mrs. PAINE. Not to tell members of the Russian-speaking community in Dallas. She preferred for it not to be publicly known, so to speak.

Mr. JENNER. Were you in contact with the Russian-speaking community in Dallas?

Mrs. PAINE. No.

Mr. JENNER. Did you say that to her on that occasion?

Mrs. PAINE. Well, it is a contact I could have had. It was reasonable for her to assume I might be.

Mr. JENNER. But you said nothing in response to that. Did you reassure her?

Mrs. PAINE. I just said I wouldn't talk about it, that it was up to her to make such an announcement when she felt like it.

Mr McCLOY. May I ask a question at this point?

You said Lee Oswald was not there. A little earlier in your testimony you said you hoped he would not be there.

Mrs. PAINE. That is correct.

Mr. McCLOY. Why did you say that? Was it because you took any dislike to his being there or was it merely because you wanted exclusive contact with Marina, or both?

Mrs. PAINE. I certainly wanted to make the contact with Marina. She had not appeared as a person at all at the party. I couldn't tell what sort of person she was, and I felt meeting alone with her would make an opportunity both to speak the language and to find out what sort of person she was.

Mr. McCloy. Go on. Did you have any further motivation for that wish? Did you take any dislike to him?

Mrs. Paine. Not an active dislike, but I didn't like him. I think we can say that.

Mr. Jenner. And you gathered that impression the evening of February 22?

Mrs. Paine. It is very hard to know whether I gathered it then or in terms of things she told me then after we met, and I will outline them.

Mr. Jenner. Yes; we will get into those.

Mrs. Paine. I would say it was more formed later.

Mr. Jenner. And in your responding to Mr. McCloy's question you were attempting to transport yourself back to that particular occasion and not be affected by the course of events that had taken place in the meantime, am I correct about that?

Mrs. Paine. I tried to

Mr. Jenner. To the best of your ability. Tell us a little more, then, to the extent you have a recollection what occurred and what was said in the park on that occasion.

Mrs. Paine. Well, I recall that we talked, and, as I said, it may be the first visit or it may have been the first and the second melded in my mind. She said that she was expecting a baby. She said that Lee didn't want her to learn English. He was not encouraging her to learn English or helping her with it, that he spoke only Russian to her and to their baby June. And she told me— now, let me say that my calendar does show a notation on the 20th of March, it says, "Marina" and I judge I went again to see her at her home on that day, or brought her to my house, I am not certain which. But I judge, also, that this was the second visit.

Mr. Jenner. I suggest that you might have melded these a moment ago. Now I wish you would keep these apart for the moment.

Mrs. Paine. So far as I can.

Mr. Jenner. And stick with the occasion in the park first and exhaust your recollection.

Mrs. Paine. Well, I was impressed, talking with her in the park, with what I felt to be her need to have a friend. This was virtually our first meeting, but she confided to me something that she didn't want generally known among the Russian segment.

Mr. Jenner. That was her pregnancy?

Mrs. Paine. Of Dallas. She inquired of me, a young woman, about birth control methods, and she said that she felt—well, clearly this pregnancy had surprised her, but she said that she didn't believe in abortion, and didn't want to consider such a course.

Mr. Jenner. Have you exhausted your recollection?

Mrs. Paine. That is all I recall; yes.

I do not recall whether it was this time or the next time, it may well have been the next time, that she told me that——

Mr. Jenner. Excuse me, please.

Mrs. Paine. All right, sir.

Mr. Jenner. I would like to stick with this. When Mrs. Oswald, this is your first visit, she related to you and said that her husband did not wish her to acquire any command of the English language, what did you say? Did you express yourself in some fashion as to why? Didn't that seem curious to you?

Mrs. Paine. I likely said that——

Mr. Jenner. Excuse me?

Mrs. Paine. I don't recall.

Mr. Jenner. It is best you don't guess.

Give us your best recollection.

Mrs. Paine. My best recollection is that she did most of the talking because she could. My Russian was bad enough that if she talked I was happy.

Mr. Jenner. Did you feel any embarrassment because you were——

Mrs. Paine. Oh, a terrible embarrassment.

Mr. JENNER. You did?

Mrs. PAINE. It is a terrible impediment to talking and to friendship.

Mr. JENNER. I wish you would elaborate on that because I am sure the members of the Commission would like to have your mental reaction to what you thought was your limited command of the Russian language and whether it interfered with communication between you.

Mrs. PAINE. It interfered very markedly.

Mr. JENNER. Would you elaborate?

Mrs. PAINE. I could think of many more things to say than I could think of the words to use in order to say it in Russian. I want to keep jumping ahead to illustrate this. But just it was very difficult for me to communicate.

I understand much more readily than I speak, so that I could understand what she was saying to me easily, especially as she took care to see that she used small words and made herself understood.

But it was very difficult for me just to speak. I could not possibly have reacted to her as I would to someone else in English, as I would if she had been speaking English.

Mr. DULLES. At this time you felt that she could not gain very much if you talked to her in English?

Mrs. PAINE. I was certain of that, yes.

Mr. DULLES. But later she had improved, apparently?

Mrs. PAINE. After the assassination, to my knowledge.

Mr. DULLES. That was after the assassination?

Mrs. PAINE. Yes. I never knew her to speak English at all.

Mr. DULLES. Or to understand?

I wasn't speaking of just speaking, but about the comprehension of it.

Mrs. PAINE. Well, she said to me in November that she has changed from never listening to an English conversation to giving it some of her attention because she is able to pick up some words. You know how if you don't understand anything there is no point even——

Mr. DULLES. I personally got the impression when she was here that she understood a good deal of English.

Mrs. PAINE. I believe she does, yes.

Mr. DULLES. But this time she did not have that facility at all?

Mrs. PAINE. No.

Mr. JENNER. Did you not think it was curious that her husband was adverse to her acquiring some facility with the English language?

Mrs. PAINE. I thought it was distinctly thoughtless on his part, even cruel.

Mr. JENNER. Did you discuss it with her to the extent that you could in your limited command of Russian?

Mrs. PAINE. I think the easiest thing was to agree with what she was saying about it, agree with what she was saying.

Mr. JENNER. Which was what?

Mrs. PAINE. Which is that this wasn't the way it should be and I certainly agreed.

Mr. JENNER. She complained, did she?

Mrs. PAINE. She complained, yes.

Mr. JENNER. I see. Did she express an interest, then, in acquiring some facility?

Mrs. PAINE. Not against his wishes, no. She didn't express an interest. In learning English through me, for instance.

Mr. JENNER. Yes. She showed no interest unlike the interest you had in her helping you with Russian, she showed no interest at that moment in learning from you some command of the English language?

Mrs. PAINE. No.

Mr. JENNER. Now you think the second occasion occurring in your calendar entry there was possibly March 20?

Mr. JENNER. And what is the entry?

Mrs. PAINE. It says, "Marina".

Mr. JENNER. And that is the only word?

Mrs. PAINE. That is all it says.

Mr. JENNER. In that square?

Mrs. PAINE. Probably I went again to her home.

Mr. JENNER. Excuse me. Does that refresh your recollection as to anything on that occasion?

Mrs. PAINE. No.

Mr. JENNER. It does not?

Mrs. PAINE. I am guessing, again, that this was the second meeting. I think I went to her home twice before I carried her from her place to my home, which was considerably more of an event, since it was 35 or 40 minutes each way, going twice in one day.

Mr. JENNER. You say carry?

Mrs. PAINE. Carry, that is a good Texas term for driving a person in a car.

Senator COOPER. I must say there, that is an old term even in Kentucky. You take some person some place you carry them.

Mrs. PAINE. You carry them; yes.

Mr. JENNER. It is an odd expression to me.

Mrs. PAINE. I have been in Texas longer than I think.

Mr. JENNER. I take it then there were two occasions when you visited her.

Mrs. PAINE. I believe there were two down there, and then I asked her, went to pick her up and brought her to my home and we spent a portion of the day at my home, and I then took her back.

Mr. JENNER. This was at your invitation?

Mrs. PAINE. Yes; surely.

Mr. JENNER. Had you by this time—let us take the March 20 affair, occasion—had you some feeling of affinity or liking for Marina?

Mrs. PAINE. Yes.

Mr. JENNER. As a person?

Mrs. PAINE. I did feel that she was in a difficult position from the first I met her.

Mr. JENNER. Now, chronologically, would you in your own words, so that I don't suggest anything to you, what was the next occasion?

The next time it was under circumstances in which you went to her home in your station wagon, picked her up and brought her to your home?

Mrs. PAINE. It was probably then that she mentioned to me that Lee wanted her to go back to the Soviet Union, was asking her to go back.

Mr. JENNER. He mentioned this subject as early as that, did he not?

Mrs. PAINE. This was still in March.

Mr. JENNER. She did?

Mrs. PAINE. She did, yes; and said that she didn't want to go.

Mr. JENNER. The Commission is interested in that. Would you please relate it?

Mrs. PAINE. She said she did not want to go back, that he asked her to go back, told her, perhaps, to go back.

Mr. JENNER. State just as accurately——

Mrs. PAINE. As she described it I felt——

Mr. JENNER. Just what she said now, please.

Mrs. PAINE. He told her he wanted to send her back with June.

Mr. JENNER. Alone?

Mrs. PAINE. To the Soviet Union. As she described it, I judged that meant——

Mr. JENNER. Please——

Mrs. PAINE. A divorce——

Mr. JENNER. Instead of saying as she described it tell us what she said, if you can.

Mrs. PAINE. She said that she had written to the Soviet Embassy to ask about papers to go back, and received a reply from them saying, "Why do you want to go back?" And she said she just didn't answer that letter because she didn't want to go back, and that that was where the matter stood at that time.

Mr. JENNER. She had not answered the letter?

Mrs. PAINE. The inquiry from the Embassy. She did not answer it.

Mr. DULLES. Did she say whether or not she showed that answer from the Soviet Embassy to her husband?

Mrs. PAINE. No; she didn't say.

Mr. JENNER. Did I understand you to say that Marina said to you that she thought that meant a divorce?

Mrs. PAINE. I will state again that she felt she was being sent back to stay back, that he would stay here, that this amounted to the end of the marriage for them, but not legally done.

Mr. JENNER. I see. And did she express any opinion of opposition to that?

Mrs. PAINE. She particularly was opposed to going back. It was leaving the United States that she was opposed to.

Mr. JENNER. She wanted to stay here, did she?

Mrs. PAINE. Yes; very much so.

Mr. JENNER. I ask you this general question, then, Mrs. Paine: During all of your contact with Marina Oswald, did she ever express any view other than that one of wanting to remain in America?

Mrs. PAINE. No: she did not.

Mr. JENNER. What did she? Was she affirmative about it?

Mrs. PAINE. Very.

Mr. JENNER. Of wanting to stay in this country?

Mrs. PAINE. Yes.

Mr. JENNER. Now, what did you say when she related that her husband wanted her to return to Russia, and she thought to remain in Russia. Did it elicit some curiosity from you?

Mrs. PAINE. Curiosity? It elicited anger at Lee that he would presume to drop his responsibilities so preemptorily.

Mr. JENNER. Did you discuss it with her?

Mrs. PAINE. I wrote a letter to her in an effort to gather my words. I couldn't just discuss it with her. My language was not that good. What I wanted to do was offer her an alternative to being sent back, an economic alternative, and I thought for some time and thought over a week about inviting her to live with me. I was alone with my two children at the time, as an alternative to being sent back. If he thought he couldn't support her or didn't care to or whatever reason he had, I simply wanted to say there was an alternative to her going back, that she could stay and live with me if she wanted to. I wrote such a letter, really, to gather——

Mr. JENNER. Do you have it?

Mrs. PAINE. Yes; I do. This letter was never sent.

Mr. JENNER. Is that also at the hotel?

Mrs. PAINE. I don't know. It may be here. I can look if you want. This letter was never sent and never mentioned to her. I wrote it so that I would have the words before me to use if it seemed appropriate to me to make the invitation, you see, a way of gathering enough of the language, enough Russian, and to say what I wanted to say. And this letter is dated the 7th of April.

Mr. JENNER. The 7th of April?

Mrs. PAINE. And I know I spent at least a week thinking about it. I talked it over with Michael before I wrote it, and it is plainly marked "never sent" on the letter. I carried it with me, as I recall I carried it once to the apartment so that if——

Mr. JENNER. To what apartment?

Mrs. PAINE. To their apartment on Neely Street, so that if it seemed appropriate I could hand it to her, you see. I could make this invitation at home with time and a dictionary in hand, and then let her read it. It was ever so much easier than just trying to say it.

Mr. McCLOY. Though you never delivered it, did you ever speak from it to her?

Mrs. PAINE. When she was staying with me the last few days of April and the first week of May, I made, yes, a verbal invitation of that sort, and in the April 7 letter, I have just gone over this correspondence or I wouldn't recall what it said, but——

Mr. JENNER. Excuse me, Mrs. Paine. I think we can take the time to see if you have the letter in your bag.

Mrs. PAINE. I am sorry that I feel precipitated into a discussion of this correspondence, and I would rather—no, it is not here—go at it—there are several things I want to say about it. I began to mention it to Mr. Jenner this morning and thought we would have a whole afternoon to talk more.

Mr. JENNER. We will have time tonight, Mrs. Paine.

Mrs. PAINE. You will have time tonight?

Mr. JENNER. I thought Mr. Redlich might look at the letter. I didn't want to delay the Commission. You do have it at hand?

Mrs. PAINE. It is not here. It is at the hotel.

Mr. JENNER. I would like to return to something else for the moment, then, first.

What reasons did Marina give, if she gave any, as to why her husband wished her to return to Russia? What did she say on that subject?

Mrs. PAINE. She didn't say.

Mr. JENNER. Nothing at all?

Mrs. PAINE. No.

Mr. JENNER. No explanation?

Mrs. PAINE. No.

Mr. JENNER. On that occasion?

Mrs. PAINE. No.

Mr. JENNER. I meant by that last question to imply that there might have been another occasion subsequently in which the subject was discussed again in which she did state what Mr. Oswald's reasons were, if any?

Mrs. PAINE. She never stated any reasons.

Mr. JENNER. Never?

Mrs. PAINE. She implied that it was because he didn't want her.

Mr. JENNER. He didn't what?

Mrs. PAINE. Want her.

Mr. JENNER. What is the date of this letter, April 7?

Mrs. PAINE. Yes.

Mr. McCLOY. We will take a brief recess.

(Brief recess.)

Mr. JENNER. Now, would you turn to your calendar, please. What is the next day, date, in your calendar, in which you have an entry?

Mrs. PAINE. Regarding the Oswalds?

Mr. JENNER. Regarding the Oswalds.

Mrs. PAINE. It is April 2, Tuesday.

Mr. JENNER. What is the entry?

Mrs. PAINE. "Marina and Lee dinner."

Mr. JENNER. All right. Now, I take it that by this time, that is, up to April 2 you had had several visits with Marina and you had reached the point at which you invited them to your home for dinner?

Mrs. PAINE. Yes. Now, Michael had never met either. By this time I had talked to him. I had indeed invited them to stay indefinitely.

Mr. JENNER. Yes.

Mrs. PAINE. And so I wanted him to meet them and invited them both to come to dinner.

Mr. JENNER. Excuse me, Mrs. Paine, if I seem presumptuous.

Mrs. PAINE. Yes.

Mr. JENNER. But you have stated several times, and now you state you inquired of your husband as to whether you could invite Marina to stay with you. Didn't you think that was a little presumptuous on your part to invite a man's wife to come to live with you?

Mrs. PAINE. Well, toward Lee it was presumptuous.

Mr. JENNER. Beg pardon?

Mrs. PAINE. Presumptuous in relation to Lee.

Mr. JENNER. In relation to Lee?

Mrs. PAINE. Indeed it is. Well, I will have to refer again to the letter of April 7 where I said I didn't want to hurt Lee by such an invitation, but that if they were unhappy, if their marital situation was similar to mine, and this is not specifically in the letter, but if he just did not want to live with her, that I would have offered this as an alternative, really to both of them. I didn't want to get into a position of competition with Lee for his wife. I thought about that, and thought he might be very offended.

Mr. JENNER. It is possible he might very well be.

Mrs. PAINE. Yes, it is possible he even might have been violent, but I didn't think anything about that.

Mr. JENNER. Did you have any impression of him up to this moment on this score?

Mrs. PAINE. No.

Mr. JENNER. As a man of temper?

Mrs. PAINE. No.

Mr. JENNER. Violence?

Mrs. PAINE. No.

Mr. JENNER. None of that?

Mrs. PAINE. No. I had met him once.

Mr. JENNER. You invited the Oswalds to dinner on the evening of April 2?

Mrs. PAINE. Yes.

Mr. JENNER. What day of the week was that?

Mrs. PAINE. Tuesday.

Mr. JENNER. Did anything occur that evening?

Mrs. PAINE. Well, Michael picked them up.

Mr. JENNER. Who did?

Mrs. PAINE. Michael picked them up.

Mr. JENNER. Your husband?

Mrs. PAINE. At the Neely Street address. Has he talked about that? It didn't come up?

Mr. JENNER. I don't know. I haven't the slightest notion. I was talking with you.

Mrs. PAINE. Should I go ahead? I just want to get this first impression into the record somewhere if he hasn't already.

Representative FORD. I think it would be helpful if you gave your impression of his impression.

Mr. JENNER. Of his impression.

Mrs. PAINE. All right. This I have learned since the assassination, he didn't give me this impression as at the time we didn't talk that much.

Mr. JENNER. Please, you are not giving us your impression of his impression on this occasion, but rather your impression of what he said to you after the assassination.

Mrs. PAINE. You still want it?

Representative FORD. I think it is important.

Mr. DULLES. Let us hear it.

Mrs. PAINE. He said—you must understand, that not living together we talked together very little. I am sure he would have given me his impression if we had been having dinner together the next day afterwards, you see. He went over and Marina was not yet ready. He thought that Lee was somewhat thoughtless. While doing absolutely nothing to help her get ready, get the baby's things together, prepare himself, he was quite impatient, thought she should be ready, and gave orders while he himself sat down and talked to Michael, and Michael carried the impression that Lee was somewhat thoughtless.

Mr. DULLES. What did you do? That was about a half hour—what did you do during that period?

Mrs. PAINE. I was at the house preparing the dinner.

Mr. DULLES. You were at home?

Mrs. PAINE. Yes. It has to be my impression of his impressions. I don't recall the evening too well, the evening of the second. I do recall we certainly had dinner together. I can't recall what the predominant language was. Lee and Michael, of course, talked in English. Not wanting to exclude her entirely from the conversation, I made opportunity to talk with her in Russian after the meal was over. She and I did the dishes and talked in Russian, and we were in the kitchen while Michael was talking to Lee in English in the living room, so I do not know what was said then between the two of them.

Mr. JENNER. How did your husband get along with Lee Oswald?

Mrs. PAINE. Well, you probably have something on that.

Mr. JENNER. What was your impression? I want your impression of how your husband got along.

Mrs. PAINE. Okay. He was initially very interested in learning what sort of man this was who had taken such a dramatic and unusual step to go to the Soviet Union and attempt to renounce his citizenship. He thought here is a person that must have thought things out for himself, a very individualistic person, not a follower of the masses, and he wanted to hear what the ideology was that led Lee to this step.

Michael has told me that he very soon felt that there wasn't much ideology or thought, foundation. That Michael had thought he might be able to learn from this man something and find at least good thinking going on or inquiry, but he didn't find it. He rather found very rigid adherence to a few principles such as the principle of the capitalist exploiting the worker, and that this was a great moral failing of the capitalistic society. Michael's own feeling was that Lee's view of morality was very different from Michael's.

Mr. JENNER. In what respect, Mrs. Paine?

Mrs. PAINE. Michael recalls having—now, this is later. This is not that evening. Did you expect it was? This is answering your question of Michael's impression of Lee.

Mr. JENNER. I wanted his initial impression.

Mrs. PAINE. All initial impressions. Well, I have passed that. I have gone considerably past it, in fact.

Mr. JENNER. I see. How many times had you seen Marina up to this moment, that is, up to April 2?

Mrs. PAINE. It was two or three times besides the initial party in February.

Mr. JENNER. And your best recollection is that this was a nice, pleasant evening, and that was about all?

Mrs. PAINE. Yes.

Mr. JENNER. Did your husband take the Oswald's home that evening?

Mrs. PAINE. Yes.

Mr. JENNER. This is the second. When was the next occasion that you had contact with either of the Oswalds?

Mrs. PAINE. There is a notation of the eighth of April. I am looking on my calendar, I have no other way of knowing, and one also on the tenth which has an arrow going to the eleventh.

Mr. JENNER. I would like to ask you a little bit about that before you go into it. Would you describe for the Commission now the condition, the physical condition, of your calendar there?

Mrs. PAINE. Physical?

Mr. JENNER. Yes. There is a square, and in the square there is written something.

Mrs. PAINE. "Marina" is written this time in Russian. I am improving, it seems.

Mr. JENNER. In Russian. It is in the square dated April 10.

Mrs. PAINE. I am talking now about the square on April 8. There is a notation "Marina".

Mr. JENNER. Is that all there is in that square?

Mrs. PAINE. That is all that is in that square.

Mr. JENNER. Yes.

Mrs. PAINE. Then the only thing that appears in the square for April 10 is the name "Marina" in Russian, and an arrow pointing, an arrow from it pointing, to April 11.

Mr. JENNER. Now, go back, if you will, to April 8.

Mrs. PAINE. Yes.

Mr. JENNER. Does that refresh your recollection or stimulate you as to whether you had any contact with Marina on that day or whether it was prearranged and what the occasion was?

Mrs. PAINE. Certainly, it says that there had been an arrangement to get together. Whether we did I don't know.

Mr. JENNER. I thought you had read everything that appeared in that square. Is there more than just the word "Marina" in the square?

Mrs. PAINE. No.

Mr. JENNER. That is my recollection. But that refreshes your recollection in turning that, that was a prearranged meeting?

Mrs. PAINE. Well, all of these were, since there was no way over the telephone.

Mr. JENNER. Is your recollection sufficiently refreshed to state whether the meeting was a visit by you to her or she to you?

Mrs. PAINE. No; I don't recall.

Mr. JENNER. Does it have a relation to the letter that you say that you prepared dated April 7, which is the day before?

Mrs. PAINE. I might have taken it that day, I don't know. Yes; it is entirely possible. I hadn't thought about it.

Mr. JENNER. But anyhow my mentioning those two events together, does that refresh your recollection or stimulate it more specifically on the subject?

Mrs. PAINE. No.

Mr. JENNER. It does not. You have no recollection beyond the fact that on April 8 you have an entry with the word "Marina." Is that written in Russian?

Mrs. PAINE. Yes.

Mr. JENNER. The word "Marina" in Russian, it doesn't stimulate you in any respect, does not stimulate your recollection?

Representative FORD. At the time of the dinner at your home on April 2, following that or during that time, do you recollect any discussion about General Walker between your husband and Lee Harvey Oswald?

Mrs. PAINE. No; I don't recollect any such discussion.

Representative FORD. That night?

Mrs. PAINE. If there was any it would have had to have been in the living room while I was talking to Marina in Russian in the kitchen. I didn't hear any reference to it.

Representative FORD. You didn't hear any discussion that evening between your husband and Lee Oswald about General Walker?

Mrs. PAINE. No.

Representative FORD. Did your husband ever tell you subsequently of any such discussion?

Mrs. PAINE. I don't recall it. There was one reference, but that was later.

Representative FORD. That was later. Do you recall when?

Mrs. PAINE. Yes. It would be the Friday after U.N. Day, October the 4th.

Representative FORD. That was October 1963?

Mrs. PAINE. Yes.

Representative FORD. And this was April 2d?

Mrs. PAINE. 1963.

Representative FORD. 1963.

Mr. JENNER. Do you recall any discussion of General Walker at all with Marina or in the presence of Marina or with Lee Oswald or in his presence in your home or their home or even out in the parkway on the subject of General Walker up to April 11, 1963?

Mrs. PAINE. No.

Mr. JENNER. None whatsoever?

Mrs. PAINE. No.

Mr. JENNER. Any discussion between yourself and your husband on that day?

Mrs. PAINE. No; none that I recall.

Mr. JENNER. Do you subscribe to a newspaper?

Mrs. PAINE. At that time I subscribed to the Irving local paper.

Mr. JENNER. Is that an evening or a morning paper?

Mrs. PAINE. At that time it was a morning paper.

Mr. JENNER. Morning paper. Do you have a recollection of being aware in the edition of April 11 of an attack on General Walker the night before?

Mrs. PAINE. It is more likely that I heard it on television. I think I must have heard it.

Mr. JENNER. You have a television and a radio?

Mrs. PAINE. We get news from the television.

Mr. JENNER. And you were aware of the attack on General Walker the evening of April 10. Did you see Marina Oswald on the 11th?

Mrs. PAINE. I can only guess so judging from these marks on my calendar.

Mr. JENNER. We would like your very best recollection, please, Mrs. Paine?

Mrs. PAINE. I don't recall; I just don't recall.

Mr. JENNER. You just don't have any present recollection that you did see her on the 11th or you didn't? You just have no—you are blank?

Mrs. PAINE. I can only guess from the calendar, that is all.

Mr. JENNER. Other than that entry you have no recollection whatsoever?

Mrs. PAINE. That is right.

Mr. DULLES. If you had seen her would it have been at her house, at her apartment?

Mrs. PAINE. I don't even know that.

Mr. DULLES. Wouldn't you have remembered four trips back and forth?

Mrs. PAINE. I remember that I made such trips, but which day it is, it is very difficult to know.

Mr. DULLES. I see. But you think—have you had a recollection about seeing her at this time, without pinpointing it?

Mrs. PAINE. Yes.

Mr. JENNER. Was there any discussion between you and Marina on the subject of the General Walker incident?

Mrs. PAINE. No.

Mr. JENNER. None whatsoever?

Mrs. PAINE. I am trying to recall now when she first told me that Lee was out of work. The next note I have of having seen them, and you must understand this calendar by no means tells everything I have done or would even be accurate about what I have done on account of what has happened, but at some point she told me that he was out of work.

Mr. JENNER. Was it some point near the time we are now discussing?

Mrs. PAINE. Near the time we are now discussing. I am trying to get some content in order to answer the question of what happened, did I see her, what happened. The next date I have down for seeing her is a picnic on the 20th of April.

Mr. JENNER. Had she told you——

Mrs. PAINE. I don't recall it having been that long, but it probably was, between the 11th and the picnic. It was before the picnic she told that he was out of work and had been for a few days before he told her.

Now, you probably know when he was out of work, but I don't, when he lost his job. So I am judging that possibly this was mentioned on the 11th that he was out of work, because we did plan to have a picnic on the 20th which included Lee, but it could have been even that day that she told me that he was out of work and had been for some time.

Mr. JENNER. Was there any day on or about this time, the 10th or 11th or 12th, within those 3 days, that you saw Marina, where your attention was arrested by her being upset or disturbed?

Mrs. PAINE. No.

Mr. JENNER. In any fashion?

Mrs. PAINE. No.

Mr. JENNER. Now, I notice in your calendar and entry April 16. "St. Marks open again 12 noon." Is that the school your children attend?

Mrs. PAINE. No, they are both preschool age. It must have been an Easter— my children are preschool age.

Mr. JENNER. What was the occasion of your making that entry?

Mrs. PAINE. I probably wanted to visit the class.

Mrs. JENNER. What class?

Mrs. PAINE. A language class. This is a school at which I subsequently taught. Last summer I taught at St. Marks School.

Mr. JENNER. You were visiting the class in advance of your teaching?

Mrs. PAINE. So I probably wanted to visit—no, just any language class there, and inquired, I judge, you see, you will find on Good Friday no school, too, the 12th. So I was marking when the Easter vacation was for St. Marks in order to make plans sometime later to go and visit.

Mr. JENNER. All right. Would you return to April 2, that dinner. Is that entry "dinner at 8"? I couldn't quite figure out——

Mrs. PAINE. I believe that is the 7.

Mr. JENNER. Seven. Was anything said that night about Lee Oswald's work?

Mrs. PAINE. No; nothing.

Mr. JENNER. About his job?

Mrs. PAINE. Well, I asked him how could I reach them if I had to call off a get-together. I had no way of telephoning Marina. If the child got sick how would I tell her I am not coming. So I said could I have his telephone at work in order to reach them through him if I felt it necessary some time, and he wrote down for me the address and telephone number of the place where he worked. This was on the 2d of April.

Mr. JENNER. And that, I will turn to that, if I might, and that will be Commission Exhibit 402, and we have a like photograph of the exhibit. Is all of that exhibit in your handwriting?

Mrs. PAINE. Well, I have just said he wrote down Jaggars-Chiles-Stovall.

Mr. JENNER. There is one entry that is in his handwriting?

Mrs. PAINE. That is right.

Mr. JENNER. Give us the letter page of that, will you?

Mrs. PAINE. The letter page, "O" for Oswald.

Mr. JENNER. "O" for Oswald. The entry Jaggars-Chiles-Stovall was written by Mr. Oswald; all other entries on that page are in your handwriting; is that correct?

Mrs. PAINE. That is correct.

Mr. JENNER. Are all other entries in the entire address book in your handwriting?

Mrs. PAINE. Did we go over it? What did I say?

Mr. JENNER. Yes, we did this morning.

Mrs. PAINE. I would guess so. I don't recall. Did we say so this morning? I will have to look it over again.

Mr. JENNER. I am not permitted to testify, Mrs. Paine.

Mrs. PAINE. All right. You want me to look right now? I usually write the addresses down myself, so it would be quite unusual for someone else to.

Mr. JENNER. Is this address book in the same condition now as it was when you gave it to the police?

Mrs. PAINE. I did not give it to the police, they took it, and I didn't know it was gone until later that day. It is in the same condition except it has been through the finger-printing process.

Mr. JENNER. I am particularly interested——

Mrs. PAINE. Yes; it is all in my handwriting.

Mr. JENNER. I am particularly interested in the entries on the page lettered "O," and I want to especially ask you whether that page is in the same condition now as it was when it was——

Mrs. PAINE. Yes; it is.

Mr. DULLES. Could I ask the witness why there are certain lines half horizontal, half perpendicular there, certain of these?

Mrs. PAINE. It means it is an old address, no longer applicable.

Mr. DULLES. I see.

Mr. JENNER. Mr. Dulles, you were referring to the page lettered "O"?

Mr. DULLES. That is correct; yes.

Mr. JENNER. I had digressed or interrupted at that point because you, for the first time, made reference to an entry in your address book made by Mr. Oswald.

Mr. Chairman, I offer in evidence the document identified as Exhibit 401.

Mr. McCLOY. Where is that——

Mr. JENNER. 402 rather. That is the address book.

Mr. McCLOY. It may be admitted.

(Commission Exhibit No. 402 was received in evidence.)

Mr. JENNER. And you were relating that you inquired as to how you could reach them if you had to reach them, and Mr. Lee Oswald wrote——

Mrs. PAINE. His work, the name of the company and the telephone number.

Mr. JENNER. I take it they did not have a telephone?

Mrs. PAINE. They did not; no.

Mr. JENNER. Did they ever have a telephone even when they were in New Orleans?

Mrs. PAINE. No; they did not.

Mr. JENNER. When they came back again to Dallas, they did not?

Mrs. PAINE. They did not.

(At this point in the proceedings Senator Cooper left the Commission hearing room.)

Mr. JENNER. Now, was the April 2d occasion the second time that you had seen Lee——

Mrs. PAINE. Yes, sir.

Mr. JENNER. Oswald? You had not seen him in the interim?

Mrs. PAINE. That is right.

Mr. JENNER. When next did you see him?

Mrs. PAINE. I next saw him on the 20th of April at a picnic at a park near where they lived on Neely Street.

Mr. JENNER. In between certainly the 2d of April and, possibly, in that period from the 8th, 9th, 10th and 11th, let us take that period up, until the time of the 20th, did you see Marina Oswald in between?

Mrs. PAINE. Did you say between the 2d——

Mr. JENNER. Between the 8th and 10th through the 20th.

Mrs. PAINE. I guess not : between the 11th or so and the 20th.

Mr. JENNER. Is that your best recollection?

Mrs. PAINE. So far as I know, no.

Mr. JENNER. How did you communicate with her about the picnic?

Mrs. PAINE. Probably by letter.

Mr. JENNER. By a letter. Do you have that letter?

Mrs. PAINE. I have—I don't know if I have it. I have a letter that closes "October 20th" in my hand, a scratch note.

Mr. JENNER. Could I look at that correspondence this evening?

Mrs. PAINE. At the same time.

Mr. JENNER. Thank you.

Then the next occasion was when you had the picnic on the 20th, is that right?

Mrs. PAINE. Yes.

Mr. JENNER. I notice in that entry what looks to me like "Miss Mary 7:15." What is the significance of that?

Mrs. PAINE. That is probably going out in the evening. It had no relationship with the picnic at all. It has a relationship with a dinner group which is at the time, you see the line "dinner group—7:15 Miss Mary," who is a babysitter.

Mr. JENNER. That entry has nothing to do with the Oswalds?

Mrs. PAINE. No.

Mr. JENNER. Without elaborating, please, Mrs. Paine, what would the subjects of discussion between you and Marina and Mr. Oswald have been at the picnic?

Mrs. PAINE. At the picnic?

Mr. JENNER. Yes.

Mrs. PAINE. He spent most of his time fishing. We saw almost nothing of him and heard virtually nothing from him. I was impressed with his unwillingness to be sociable really in this situation. He came to eat when it was time to, and complained about the food.

Mr. JENNER. Did he complain about the food?

Mrs. PAINE. Yes.

Mr. JENNER. Was your husband present at this picnic?

Mrs. PAINE. No ; he was not.

Mr. DULLES. Did you supply the food?

Mrs. PAINE. No ; Marina had cooked it. He complained about it. He caught a fish, as I recall, and took it home to be cleaned. I hardly know who would clean it.

Representative FORD. Who did clean it?

Mrs. PAINE. I don't know. I left about that time.

Mr. JENNER. What discussion occurred between you and Lee Oswald, if any, with respect to his life in Russia on that occasion?

Mrs. PAINE. None.

Mr. JENNER. Did you have any conversation with him other than some pleasantries?

Mrs. PAINE. I don't believe so. I can't even think of the pleasantry.

Mr. DULLES. As I understand it, as you were sitting there, the picnic took place in the park——

Mrs. PAINE. Yes.

Mr. DULLES. What was he doing?

Mrs. PAINE. He was way over at the lake fishing.

Mr. DULLES. He was over fishing at the lake?

Mrs. PAINE. Yes.

Mr. JENNER. Did any further discussion occur between you and Marina on that occasion, or on any interim occasion, of Mr. Oswald's desire to have her return to Russia or the fact that she did not wish the Russian emigré group to know she was pregnant and was about to have a child?

Mrs. PAINE. I don't recall specifically. I did feel that it wasn't a particularly happy occasion. I don't recall it with lightness.

Mr. JENNER. Was he out of work at that time or not?

Mrs. PAINE. Yes; he was out of work. I knew at that time he was out of work. Whether I found out that morning or the previous time I had seen her I don't recall. I only recall when she said he was out of work she also said he had been out of work for a week or a few days before he told her.

Mr. JENNER. I would like to have you draw on your recollection as closely as you can. Did you learn of his being out of work from him or from Marina?

Mrs. PAINE. From her.

Mr. JENNER. What did she say on that subject as to whether he was discharged or whether he had left his employment, or did she say anything in that area?

Mrs. PAINE. I judged he had been discharged.

Mr. JENNER. Give me your best recollection of what she said.

Mrs. PAINE. Do you want something else?

Mr. JENNER. Give me your best recollection of what she said, Mrs. Paine.

Mrs. PAINE. I can't recall it that closely.

Mr. JENNER. You next have an entry on April 24 reading "Lee and Marina." Do you find it?

Mrs. PAINE. Yes.

Mr. JENNER. Was that a meeting with Lee Harvey Oswald and his wife, Marina?

Mrs. PAINE. Yes.

Mr. JENNER. Where was that held?

Mrs. PAINE. That was to be a visit at the apartment on Neely Street.

Mr. JENNER. At their apartment?

Mrs. PAINE. Yes.

Mr. JENNER. Did it take place?

Mrs. PAINE. I arrived and found that he was packed to go to New Orleans.

Mr. JENNER. Was this a surprise to you?

Mrs. PAINE. This was a distinct surprise.

Mr. JENNER. Had there been some communication between you and the Oswalds about your visiting them on the 24th of April?

Mrs. PAINE. It had been arranged that I would come over to visit as much as these other visits had been arranged, just with Marina to talk.

Mr. JENNER. Had you had any visit with Marina between the 20th of April and the 24th?

Mrs. PAINE. No.

Mr. JENNER. None whatsoever?

Mrs. PAINE. None.

Mr. JENNER. Had you arranged on the 20th to visit on the 24th?

Mrs. PAINE. Probably.

Mr. JENNER. That is your best recollection?

Mrs. PAINE. Yes.

Mr. JENNER. What time of day did you arrive, or night?

Mrs. PAINE. Mid-morning, perhaps around 10.

Mr. JENNER. And then you found him packed or packing to leave?

Mrs. PAINE. He was fully packed. I was evidently expected. I and my car, because he asked if I could take these bags and duffel bags, suitcases, to the bus station for him.

Mr. JENNER. Yes.

457

Mrs. PAINE. Where he would buy a ticket to go to New Orleans, and he said he had not been able to——

Mr. JENNER. What he said to you is what I am interested in.

Mrs. PAINE. That he said——

Mr. JENNER. Yes.

Mrs. PAINE. He said he had not been able to find work in Dallas, around Dallas, and Marina suggested going to New Orleans, which is where he had been born.

Mr. DULLES. He said she had suggested?

Mrs. PAINE. Yes. That is my best recollection.

Mr. JENNER. Was Marina present now while he is relating this to you?

Mrs. PAINE. Yes; I think so.

Mr. JENNER. She was present. Was he speaking in Russian or in English?

Mrs. PAINE. I think he must have been speaking in English when he asked me to take the things to the bus station and explained that he was going to look for work.

Mr. JENNER. Your best recollection is that this was in English?

Mrs. PAINE. I don't recall. It could well have been in Russian also. He didn't like to speak English to me. He preferred to speak Russian.

The CHAIRMAN. To you?

Mrs. PAINE. To me; yes.

Representative FORD. Did he ever indicate why?

Mrs. PAINE. No.

Mr. JENNER. I think you said to me this morning, and please correct me if my recollection is not good, that he always spoke to you in Russian.

Mrs. PAINE. With, perhaps, a couple of rare exceptions, yes, he spoke to me in Russian. When I tried to teach him to drive I tried to explain to him, proceeded to explain to him in English.

Mr. JENNER. Excuse me, you tried to teach him to do what?

Mrs. PAINE. To drive. This is later.

Mr. JENNER. Drive, yes.

Mrs. PAINE. But he would answer me in Russian, which is a way of getting the person to go back to Russian. But I couldn't explain driving in Russian, so I did it in English.

Mr. JENNER. That incident, Mrs. Paine, is very important, and we will get to that at a later stage as to your efforts to teach him to drive.

Going back to this 24th of April, there was here, this was, a complete surprise to you. You arrived at the home and this man was all packed to go to New Orleans.

Mrs. PAINE. Yes.

Mr. JENNER. Had you had any discussion with Marina about her coming to live with you of which she was aware prior to this occasion on April 24?

Mrs. PAINE. I had discussed with her the possibility of her coming at the time the baby was expected.

Mr. JENNER. When was the baby expected?

Mrs. PAINE. Mid-October.

Mr. JENNER. But there had been no discussion up to April 24, to your recollection, even about your inviting Marina to come to live with you?

Mrs. PAINE. You mean on a more permanent basis, other than to stay when the baby was due?

Mr. JENNER. Yes; which would be in the fall of the year.

Mrs. PAINE. That is right. There was none.

Mr. JENNER. There was no discussion about her coming to live with you in the spring around about this time?

Mrs. PAINE. I remember feeling when I arrived that they were, and probably appropriately, making their own plans, and wondering whether I should have already made this invitation, but I had not.

Mr. JENNER. You say they were already making their own plans; are you seeking to imply that they had some notion she might join you?

Mrs. PAINE. No; I don't think there was any notion. I am trying to say I recall that I hadn't made that invitation at that time.

Mr. JENNER. To the best of your recollection it is now that you had not discussed the subject with Marina up to this occasion?

Mrs. PAINE. Not the subject of staying on with me as an alternative to going back to Russia.

Mr. JENNER. Only staying with you in the fall?

Mrs. PAINE. Yes.

Mr. JENNER. When the baby came?

Mrs. PAINE. Yes.

Mr. JENNER. What did you say, Mrs. Paine—excuse me. First, have you exhausted your recollection of everything that Lee Oswald said on that occasion when you arrived there?

Mrs. PAINE. Yes.

Mr. JENNER. What did you say?

Mrs. PAINE. I said, yes, I would take his bags to the station if he wanted me to.

Mr. JENNER. All right.

Mrs. PAINE. And we then did.

Mr. JENNER. You just left?

Mrs. PAINE. Take them to the bus station to be checked.

Mr. JENNER. Did Marina accompany you?

Mrs. PAINE. Marina went, and he checked the baggage. It was rather more than he could have carried on the city bus, and I am sure he preferred me to a taxi because I don't cost as much.

Mr. JENNER. You didn't cost anything?

Mrs. PAINE. That is right. And he then bought a ticket, he bought a ticket for Marina, I mean I was thinking, while he was in the bus station, and suggested that it would be a very difficult thing for a pregnant woman with a small child to take a 12-hour, 13-hour bus trip to New Orleans, and suggested that I drive her down with June.

Mr. JENNER. You volunteered this?

Mrs. PAINE. I volunteered this, and suggested further that instead of her staying at her—at the apartment, as was planned at that time, while waiting to hear from him, that she come and stay at my house where he would reach us by phone, and where she would have someone else with her while she waited to hear if he got work.

Mr. JENNER. This was the conversation between you and Lee Harvey Oswald? Was it in English or in Russian?

Mrs. PAINE. Probably in Russian. I would think so, because I wanted her to understand.

Mr. JENNER. Was Marina along?

Mrs. PAINE. She was present.

Mr. JENNER. She was present; I see.

Representative FORD. This took place where, in the car?

Mrs. PAINE. Probably in the bus station—in the car near the bus station. He then took the bus ticket back, returned it, and got the money.

The CHAIRMAN. Ticket for her?

Mrs. PAINE. Ticket for her.

Mr. DULLES. Her bus ticket?

Mrs. PAINE. Yes; and he left some money for her for buying things in the next few days before she could join him.

Mr. JENNER. Did he get on the bus then and depart?

Mrs. PAINE. No; the bus left in the evening. We all drove back to the apartment after he had checked the baggage, and he helped load the baby things and things that Marina would need during the next few days into my car, and we emptied what was left there of the things that were in the apartment, and which belonged to them, and then drove, I drove with Marina and June and my two children back to my house, and he stayed at the apartment. He was scheduled to leave by bus, city bus, and an interstate bus that evening.

Mr. JENNER. I take it then, Mrs. Paine, that your impression was that it was contemplated, when you arrived at the Oswalds that morning, that Mrs. Oswald, Marina, and her child June, and her husband, Lee, were contemplating going to New Orleans together that day?

Mrs. PAINE. No.

Mr. JENNER. Am I wrong?

Mrs. PAINE. That is wrong. She was to have stayed in the apartment.

Mr. JENNER. I see.

Mrs. PAINE. And wait to hear from him.

Mr. JENNER. Yes.

Mrs. PAINE. If they had been going together that would not have been the hardship on her, but that traveling alone was, I felt.

Representative FORD. Why did he buy the ticket for her at the——

Mrs. PAINE. To leave with her so that she could follow him when he called, to leave the ticket in her hand as a means of her following him. I haven't been clear.

Mr. JENNER. It was a little indefinite.

Mr. DULLES. I thought the ticket had been redeemed; then he bought another ticket?

Mrs. PAINE. He bought a ticket for himself and a ticket for her.

Mr. DULLES. You said, "I will take her," and then he redeemed the ticket for her, and gave her the cash?

Mr. JENNER. Gave her some money?

Mrs. PAINE. Yes.

The CHAIRMAN. But the ticket that he did buy for her——

Mrs. PAINE. Was to have been left with her.

The CHAIRMAN. Was for a subsequent date?

Mrs. PAINE. For a subsequent date following.

The CHAIRMAN. Yes.

Mrs. PAINE. That is it.

Mr. JENNER. That was clear to you on that occasion?

Mrs. PAINE. That was clear.

Mr. JENNER. She was scheduled to join him subsequently?

Mrs. PAINE. She was scheduled to join him subsequently if he did find work. If he found no work there would have been no point to her making the trip.

Mr. JENNER. Is this a discussion or is it your rationalization?

Mrs. PAINE. It was clearly said she would stay.

Mr. DULLES. I am puzzled. I am puzzled, Mr. Jenner, about this ticket business.

Mr. JENNER. I am, too.

Mr. DULLES. A ticket was bought for her on the theory that she was going with him first.

Mr. McCLOY. No.

Mr. DULLES. That is where I got off the track. He bought two tickets, then why was the ticket redeemed?

Mr. McCLOY. Because it was made clear by Mrs. Paine that she was going to take Marina down in her own car.

Mr. DULLES. But only going to stay with you during the period until he got work, hence she wouldn't need a ticket. You were going to drive her down?

Mrs. PAINE. Yes.

Mr. JENNER. You would drive her down all the way to New Orleans?

Mrs. PAINE. In either case it was planned to delay going.

Mr. DULLES. She would go down if he got work, but she would not need a ticket if she stayed with you. Therefore, the ticket was redeemed.

Mrs. PAINE. Yes. But I did not think of this or suggest it until after he had already bought the ticket.

Representative FORD. May I ask this, Mrs. Paine? In the things that were packed when you arrived, or things that were packed while you were present——

Mrs. PAINE. Nothing was packed while I was present. It was already packed.

Representative FORD. Everything was already packed by the time you got there?

Mrs. PAINE. Yes.

Representative FORD. Were any of the things for Marina or Lee packed?

Mrs. PAINE. They were all packed. I don't understand your question. All of the things he wanted to take with him to the bus station were already packed.

Representative Ford. Well, in that group of things which were so packed, were there things for Marina and Lee?

Mrs. Paine. Yes.

Representative Ford. I mean Marina and June, excuse me?

Mrs. Paine. Yes. Some of their things were among those things, yes, I judge so, clothing. The things that remained were a crib, playpen, baby stroller, some dishes, some clothing.

Representative Ford. The things you would not ordinarily take on a bus, however.

Mrs. Paine. Yes; it would be very difficult. That was another one of the things that motivated me to suggest driving her down. I thought sending these by train, with the risk of their getting strayed or—it would be difficult, trying, for her to try to handle them, or convey them with her by bus—that would have been worse.

Representative Ford. But there were some things that were packed in the things that Lee was going to take with him that would include things——

Mrs. Paine. That belonged to——

Representative Ford. To—to Marina and to June?

Mrs. Paine. I would judge so simply by what remained. Surely it was not the total sum of her clothing and June's clothing.

Representative Ford. Which could lead a person to the conclusion that at one stage of their discussion Marina was going to accompany Lee to New Orleans.

Mrs. Paine. Not from the time I arrived.

Representative Ford. From the station.

Mrs. Paine. It was clear she would stay up in the apartment.

Mr. Jenner. Up to that time it appeared to you from what was in the duffel-bag——

Mrs. Paine. I think he was carrying all he could to lighten her burden. In other words, if and when she followed, he was carrying all he could.

Mr. Jenner. Representative Ford is interested in this, Mrs. Paine——

Mr. Dulles. I am puzzled, too.

Mr. Jenner. When you arrived at the Oswald apartment that morning, Lee Oswald had duffelbags packed and some——

Mrs. Paine. Suitcases.

Mr. Jenner. Suitcases. He had in those suitcases and in the duffelbag some of the apparel for Mrs.—Marina?

Mrs. Paine. Of course, I did not see it. I have to guess what was in it.

Mr. Jenner. But, from your knowledge of the household and afterwards, this was at least your impression?

Mrs. Paine. That they must have included some of her things.

Mr. Jenner. Yes. Which, in turn, might lead to the inference that, therefore, they contemplated at that moment from what he was taking that Marina was ultimately to join him in New Orleans.

Mrs. Paine. Oh, yes; absolutely.

Mr. Jenner. Is that correct?

Mrs. Paine. Yes. Was that your question?

Representative Ford. Or even at one point in the process of packing, she and June were going to accompany him to New Orleans on the bus.

Mrs. Paine. I didn't have that impression, no. No, he was going and happened to stay with an aunt and uncle where he could live without much charge. For her to come would have been quite a greater expense, and a risky one without a job, nothing coming in, so he was hoping that he could stay with the aunt and uncle while he looked, and then if he got remunerative work, get an apartment and call her to come, too.

Representative Ford. If that is so, and let us assume that is so——

Mrs. Paine. Yes.

Representative Ford. It puzzles me that he went into the bus station and bought two tickets, one for himself and one for her.

Mrs. Paine. How would she get there?

Representative Ford. Well, eventually she might have to go by bus. But why should he at this time make an investment in a bus ticket when there was no certainty——

461

Mrs. PAINE. Oh, yes.

Representative FORD. When she might follow? This is what puzzles me.

Mrs. PAINE. Yes. Well, I can only guess about this. I judge from his having done this that he certainly intended for her to follow, and it is also possible she couldn't have asked for a bus ticket herself. If he had written her and said, "Don't come to New Orleans, come to Nashville," and he had said, "That is where I have got my job," he might have felt she would not know how to go and get such a bus ticket.

Mr. DULLES. Is it also possible he may not have wanted to leave that amount of money with her to buy a ticket and preferred to leave her a ticket rather than cash?

Mrs. PAINE. This is possible, this is possible.

Mr. JENNER. All right.

Now, Mrs. Paine, in light of that speculation, tell us what discussion there was on the subject.

Mrs. PAINE. I think I have, that while he was in the bus station I thought how difficult it would be for her to travel alone with the baby, and all the things——

Mr. JENNER. And you raised that yourself for the first time at that point?

Mrs. PAINE. Then I said she might stay with me while waiting to hear from him, and that I would drive her down if we did hear that he had gotten work.

Mr. JENNER. Had there been prior discussion that it was contemplated that, if he obtained a position, she would join him in New Orleans, or wherever he obtained a position.

Mrs. PAINE. Yes. We had already talked about that at the apartment.

Mr. JENNER. And that had been discussed with her present?

Mrs. PAINE. Yes.

Mr. JENNER. And discussed in Russian so that she could have understood the discussion?

Mrs. PAINE. To the best of my recollection, yes.

Mr. JENNER. Now, Mrs. Paine, the staff is interested in Lee Harvey Oswald's luggage.

Mrs. PAINE. What?

Mr. JENNER. His luggage.

Mrs. PAINE. Luggage.

Mr. JENNER. Would you please, to the best of your recollection, tell us what pieces of luggage he had on that occasion, what they looked like, their shape and form?

Mrs. PAINE. Yes. He had two large marine duffelbags with his name on them, and probably his Marine serial number. It was marked with a good deal of white paint. It stood quite high.

Mr. JENNER. Were they up-ended when you say high? You mean standing on end, they were high?

Mrs. PAINE. Standing on their end they would come well above this table.

Mr. JENNER. I see. About 40 inches?

Mrs. PAINE. Something like that; I would guess so.

Mr. JENNER. Excuse me, I am interested in just that. Would you go over to the drawing board and move your hand, judge from the floor, and stop right there? We will measure that later.

Mrs. PAINE. Understand I saw those two later in my garage.

Mr. JENNER. I understand, and I will get to that. That is just about 45 inches, and there were two of them.

Mrs. PAINE. There were two of them. Do you want anything about the rest of the luggage? Does that interest you the most?

Mr. JENNER. Yes, I am interested, and I would like to stick with the duffelbags for a moment. Was there any appearance as to either duffelbag, which, to you, would indicate some long, slim, hard——

Mrs. PAINE. I assume them to be both full of clothes, very rounded.

Mr. JENNER. I don't wish to be persistent, but was there anything that you saw about the duffelbags that lead you at that time to even think for an instant that there was anything long, slim and hard like a pole?

Mrs. PAINE. No.

Mr. Jenner. Or a gun, a rifle?

Mrs. Paine. No.

Mr. Jenner. No? Nothing?

Mrs. Paine. Nothing. I did not move these bags.

Mr. Jenner. To the extent you saw them is all I am inquiring about. You did not touch them, you did not lift them, but you saw them.

Mrs. Paine. I did.

Mr. Jenner. There appeared—the entire circumference of these bags which you could see was smooth?

Mrs. Paine. Well, smooth, bumpy, but irregular.

Mr. Jenner. But no stick, no hard surface. Now, what about the diameter of these bags, these duffelbags, what would you say it was?

Mrs. Paine. About like this, 15, 18, 20 inches across.

Mr. Jenner. Eighteen, twenty inches across?

Mrs. Paine. Probably more than that.

Mr. Jenner. This is 15 inches.

Mrs. Paine. About like this; a little more than 15, probably.

Mr. Jenner. About 18 inches. Now, how many pieces of luggage in addition to the two duffelbags?

Mrs. Paine. Quite a few. There were probably three suitcases.

Mr. Jenner. Three suitcases?

Mrs. Paine. Or more. A small radio bought in Russia.

Mr. Jenner. I want to stick with the luggage.

Mrs. Paine. All right.

Mr. Jenner. Three suitcases?

Mrs. Paine. I think so, two or three, and a large softsided suitcase, I don't know what to call it. It zips around the side.

Mr. Jenner. Zipper case?

Mrs. Paine. Yes, made of canvas.

Mr. Jenner. We would like to have you describe that zipper case.

Mrs. Paine. It is green——

Mr. Jenner. I am interrupting you, I am sorry. Were there any other pieces of luggage, first?

Mrs. Paine. I don't recall.

Mr. Jenner. So there were two or three or possibly four, is that true, suitcases?

Mrs. Paine. Yes.

Mr. Jenner. And there was a zipper case?

Mrs. Paine. Yes.

Mr. Jenner. Describe this zipper case to us first.

Mrs. Paine. It stood about so high [indicating].

Mr. Jenner. So high is 15 inches, about 30 inches long?

Mrs. Paine. Not quite, about that long [indicating].

Mr. Jenner. It was a generous sized zipper case?

Mrs. Paine. Yes. With generally green canvas and leather, dark-colored leather.

Mr. Jenner. Black or brown—do you remember the color?

Mrs. Paine. Dark brown, I guess, or black, certainly very dark.

Mr. Jenner. It was a generous sized one, was it not?

Mrs. Paine. Yes.

Mr. Jenner. Did it appear to be well packed?

Mrs. Paine. Yes.

Mr. Jenner. Would you describe each of the three suitcases now, with particular reference to the staff being interested in whether they were rectangular, whether they were hard boarded types of things, or whether they were canvas or soft?

Mrs. Paine. I don't remember how many there were. I recall they had a hard composition kind of suitcase such as you don't buy here, and I judge they were bought in the Soviet Union. I think there may have been two of those.

Mr. Jenner. Was any one of them rectangular in shape?

Mrs. Paine. Yes. That was rectangular.

Mr. JENNER. The one you specifically have in mind, he did have a rectangular one?

Mrs. PAINE. Yes.

Mr. JENNER. And what color was it?

Mrs. PAINE. Dark, blackish green, or dark brown, something of this nature.

Mr. JENNER. Anything else you can think about it in the way of description?

Mrs. PAINE. I think it had—it was reinforced, corners, with rivets, or bolts, of something to hold it, hold the corners on it.

Mr. DULLES. How long was this rectangular suitcase?

Mrs. PAINE. I don't recall. In fact, I can't recall whether it was one or two, but something like that, normal suitcases.

Mr. JENNER. Mr. Chairman, may I have your permission to approach the witness?

Mr. McCLOY. And take the measurements?

Mrs. PAINE. And take the measurements.

Mr. McCLOY. The witness may be approached.

Mrs. PAINE. That or larger, I would say.

Mr. JENNER. You are now describing the length of the rectangular suitcase, is that correct?

Mrs. PAINE. Yes.

Mr. JENNER. And that would be 21½ inches?

Mrs. PAINE. Yes.

Mr. JENNER. That is your best recollection?

Mrs. PAINE. I am brief in my recollection, a normal rectangular shape here.

Mr. JENNER. Width, that is the side, you mean?

Mrs. PAINE. That is the whole thing. That is looking at the top. How high it is.

Mr. JENNER. No; wide.

Mrs. PAINE. I am filling it out. This would be the width then from here to here, possibly more.

Mr. JENNER. Fourteen inches?

Mrs. PAINE. I am not sure I am recalling one or two at the same time. I have to be under oath, and giving you details on things I don't recall that well.

Mr. JENNER. All we are seeking is your best recollection.

Mrs. PAINE. All right, that is my best recollection.

Mr. JENNER. Twenty-one and a half times fourteen, and how high was it?

Mrs. PAINE. About so, 6, about 6.

Mr. JENNER. I said high. Was this lying flat on its side when you saw it?

Mrs. PAINE. Well, all these things again I saw in the fall, so it is a mixed recollection.

Mr. JENNER. I am going to get as to what you saw in the fall, but it is important to us as to what you saw on this occasion.

Mrs. PAINE. Well, I particularly recall the duffels because they are unusual, and I recall this bag being, I judge Russian make rather than American, it was a large zipper bag.

Mr. JENNER. And Mrs. Paine, you do recall that zipper bag on this occasion?

Mrs. PAINE. I believe so.

Mr. JENNER. And there was at least one, if not more than one, rectangular——

Mrs. PAINE. I can't be certain of the zipper bag.

Mr. JENNER. Hard-sided suitcase?

Mrs. PAINE. Yes; hard-sided suitcase. I can't be certain, absolutely certain, of the zipper bag. I recall seeing so much of it since, tripped over it numerous times, that it may be just that I recalled it. I didn't move this luggage at all.

Mr. JENNER. I am not suggesting that you did.

Mrs. PAINE. I am sorry I can't remember it better.

Mr. JENNER. Were all of these suitcases about the same size and shape?

Mrs. PAINE. No.

Mr. JENNER. You have described the rectangular one. Would you now describe the second, the second in order of your recollection?

Mrs. PAINE. Well, there was at least another rectangular one.

Mr. JENNER. Hard-sided?

Mrs. PAINE. Yes.

Mr. JENNER. Was it larger or smaller than the one you have described?

Mrs. PAINE. I don't recall with certainty.

Mr. JENNER. Was there a third?

Mrs. PAINE. There may have been a third. I certainly recall this radio that was unusual. The others I don't.

Mr. JENNER. It is possible you might be confused between the radio case and a suitcase.

Mrs. PAINE. No, no; no possibility of that.

Mr. JENNER. All right. He checked all these articles, checked them into the bus station?

Mrs. PAINE. Yes.

Mr. JENNER. And did you and Lee and Marina return to their home?

Mrs. PAINE. That is right.

Mr. JENNER. Did you remain there?

Mrs. PAINE. No. He then helped pack up the remaining things, the playpen, the bed, and then we left there midafternoon, perhaps 4, all of this must have taken quite a long time, because——

Mr. JENNER. They removed everything from their home?

Mrs. PAINE. They removed everything that remained to them.

Mr. JENNER. Put it in the station wagon?

Mrs. PAINE. Put it in the station wagon and went with Lee and Marina.

Mr. JENNER. Your station wagon was big enough to hold everything in the house, is that correct?

Mrs. PAINE. Well, they had no furniture, but it held all the rest of their things; yes.

Mr. JENNER. Did he do the packing?

Mrs. PAINE. Yes.

Mr. JENNER. What were you doing in the meantime?

Mrs. PAINE. Packing was haphazard, this packing was haphazard; put the dishes in a box and carried it out to the car.

Mr. JENNER. It was in the open so you could see what went into your car?

Mrs. PAINE. I think so. I certainly then repacked it to go to New Orleans.

Mr. JENNER. Well, I want to stick with this occasion, please.

Mrs. PAINE. All right.

Mr. JENNER. Was there a rifle packed in the back of the car?

Mrs. PAINE. No.

Mr. JENNER. You didn't see any kind of weapon?

Mrs. PAINE. No.

Mr. JENNER. Firearm, rifle, pistol, or otherwise?

Mrs. PAINE. No; I saw nothing of that nature.

Mr. JENNER. Did you drive them to your home?

Mrs. PAINE. Yes.

Mr. JENNER. Were the materials and things in your station wagon unpacked and placed in your home?

Mrs. PAINE. Yes; immediately.

Mr. JENNER. Did you see that being done, were you present?

Mrs. PAINE. I helped do it; yes.

Mr. JENNER. Did you see any weapon on that occasion?

Mrs. PAINE. No.

Mr. JENNER. Whether a rifle, pistol or——

Mrs. PAINE. No.

Mr. JENNER. Or any covering, any package, that looked as though it might have a weapon, pistol, or firearm?

Mrs. PAINE. No.

Mr. JENNER. Up to this moment, Mrs. Paine, had there been any discussion with Marina or with Lee Harvey Oswald in connection with his life in Russia with the use of a firearm or his right to use one in Russia?

Mrs. PAINE. I never heard him mention anything of this sort. Michael told me later he mentioned it to Michael.

Mr. McCLOY. State that, please.

Mrs. PAINE. Michael told me later that Lee had complained in Michael's hearing that they did not permit a private individual to have a gun, but I didn't

465

hear that when it was said. So there was no discussion at any time that mentioned guns, nothing brought up by Marina or Lee.

Mr. JENNER. I will broaden my question. Up to—now up to, and not including, up to November 22, 1963, had there ever been any discussion between you and Lee Harvey Oswald or between you and Marina or any discussion in the presence of either of them by anybody, including yourself, about the use of a firearm by Lee Harvey Oswald?

Mrs. PAINE. Yes. Marina told me that he had been hunting in the Soviet Union.

Mr. JENNER. Now, please, to the best of your recollection when did that occur?

Mrs. PAINE. When did she tell me?

Mr. JENNER. Yes.

Mrs. PAINE. It might have been as long ago as May, when she was first staying at my house. She quoted a proverb to the effect that you go hunting in the Soviet Union and you catch a bottle of vodka, so I judge it was a social occasion more than shooting being the prime object.

Mr. JENNER. That was in this period when she was living with you in the spring of 1963?

Mrs. PAINE. It could have been there. It might have been in October, but I would guess it was in May.

Mr. JENNER. I wish you would elaborate on that.

Mrs. PAINE. I wish I wouldn't guess, I know.

Mr. JENNER. Did she say that Lee Harvey Oswald had some kind of a firearm in Russia?

Mrs. PAINE. That he had gone hunting with a group, in other words, in Russia.

Mr. JENNER. What was the occasion——

Mrs. PAINE. And she quoted this proverb.

Mr. JENNER. Can you remember the circumstance in which she made that utterance?

Mrs. PAINE. No.

Mr. JENNER. Anything that provoked it or brought it about?

Mrs. PAINE. I think she was probably recalling something of their life in Russia.

Mr. JENNER. In a discussion between you and Marina as to their life in Russia?

Mrs. PAINE. Yes.

Mr. JENNER. Any other occasion in which a discussion occurred between you and either of them or in their presence while you were present on the subject of a firearm prior to November 22?

Mrs. PAINE. On one occasion around the middle of November I said to Marina that——

Mr. JENNER. Was Lee Harvey Oswald present?

Mrs. PAINE. He was not present.

Mr. JENNER. Just Marina and you?

Mrs. PAINE. Just Marina and I.

Mr. JENNER. Was it in your home?

Mrs. PAINE. Yes. I said to her that I did not want to buy toy guns for my children, and that this view of things was shared with a German friend of mine who had been a young girl at the time of the last World War in Germany, and she didn't wish to buy guns for her children to play with, and I said too few people think about this. She said nothing in reply.

Mr. JENNER. She didn't say anything at all in response to that. Does that exhaust your recollection of all discussion of firearms?

Mrs. PAINE. Yes; it does.

Mr. JENNER. That occurred in your presence?

Mrs. PAINE. Yes.

Mr. JENNER. Up to November 22, 1963?

Mrs. PAINE. Up to, that is right.

Mr. McCLOY. There was no suggestion of Lee's using a firearm for hunting purposes in the United States?

Mrs. PAINE. None; nor that he might have had any gun.

Mr. McCloy. Nor that he might have had any gun.

Mr. Jenner. After Marina's things and the baby's things had been placed in your home then what occurred in the evening, was this late in the day of the 24th?

Mrs. Paine. It was close to supper. I am sure we then ate and put our children to bed, possibly talked a short time. I no doubt explained to her quite soon that I was to go away for the weekend. Indeed, this invitation was made quite on the spur of the moment. You don't normally invite someone to come and stay with you when you are about to go away, but I was to go to a folk-dance camp with Michael that weekend, and you see on the calendar "FDC" which stands for folk-dance camp, arrow San Antonio. That is the 26th, 27th and 28th.

Mr. Jenner. Yes; I noticed that.

Mrs. Paine. And I left her in the house with the telephone number of my Russian tutor to call, and I believe they talked, in fact, before I left.

Mr. Jenner. Would you tell us the name of your Russian tutor.

Mr. Dulles. Could I ask one question that we passed by?

Mr. Jenner. Yes.

Mr. Dulles. When you unloaded Marina's things and the baby's things, did this subtract one suitcase from this number you have indicated? Was one of the suitcases delegated to her things or were they just loose in the car?

Mrs. Paine. Insofar as I remember, I believe they were loose.

Mr. Dulles. They were loose. So that the number of suitcases you have indicated were those that were eventually checked and taken by Lee Harvey Oswald to New Orleans.

Mrs. Paine. Well, that is the way I remember it. It does not seem reasonable that he would go off without leaving her a suitcase to put her things in, so I would guess there was something for her in the nature, perhaps, of a small bag.

Mr. Dulles. So that one of these bags may have been unloaded at your house?

Mrs. Paine. Yes.

Mr. McCloy. You testified, I believe, you started to testify, that there was also a radio that had been presumably purchased in Russia. Did he take that with him?

Mrs. Paine. He took that.

Mr. McCloy. He took that with him. He didn't return that to her.

Mr. Jenner. Mrs. Paine, I don't want to speculate, but I thought you had testified in response to my questions that the two or three pieces of luggage, that is, the suitcases, plus the two duffel bags, plus the zipper bag, plus the radio, had been checked into the bus station.

Mrs. Paine. Yes; that is right.

Mr. Jenner. All of those pieces of luggage were actually checked in, and when you left the bus station none of the pieces of luggage or the radio or the duffel bags had been placed back in your car.

Mrs. Paine. I don't recall it, but it seems to me unreasonable——

Mr. Jenner. Now, please, I don't want you to rationalize. I want your best recollection.

Mrs. Paine. I cannot recall. I mean the suitcases that came to my house——

Mr. Jenner. You don't recall having taken one of the pieces of luggage and placed that piece back in your station wagon?

Mrs. Paine. Oh, no, no, that is definite. All that went to the bus station.

Mr. Jenner. Remained there.

Mrs. Paine. Remained there.

Mr. Jenner. I see.

Mr. Dulles. At what stage did they go to the bus station? Did you go from their apartment to your house and then to the bus station or did you go to the bus station first?

Mrs. Paine. Directly to the bus station.

Mr. Dulles. And then went to your house?

Mrs. Paine. Directly to the bus station from their apartment, back to their apartment and picked up the rest of the things.

Mr. Dulles. I see.

Mrs. PAINE. The baby things and her clothing and then went to my house.

Mr. DULLES. I see.

Mr. JENNER. Mrs. Paine, apart from your rationalization, do you have the recollection that there was any luggage at all in the Oswald home when you got back?

Mrs. PAINE. No; I have no such recollection.

Mr. JENNER. So that in response to Mr. Dulles' questions when you talked about the possibility of some luggage, you were rationalizing?

Mrs. PAINE. That is right.

Mr. JENNER. You are not drawing on your recollection?

Mrs. PAINE. That is right.

Mr. JENNER. I take it your best recollection, in fact, is that there was no luggage remaining at the Oswald home when you got back?

Mrs. PAINE. There was nothing packed when we got back.

Mr. JENNER. Do you recall undertaking to pack anything when you got back in order to remove what they had there remaining to your home?

Mrs. PAINE. You mean was there a suitcase into which I could pack anything?

Mr. JENNER. That is it.

Mrs. PAINE. I don't recall.

Mr. JENNER. All right. Now, you have related to us that you went away for the weekend.

Mrs. PAINE. Yes.

Mr. JENNER. With your husband.

Mrs. PAINE. Right.

Mr. JENNER. Now, you have an entry in your diary, and I quote it on the 24th of April, 1963: "Lee and Marina."

Mrs. PAINE. Yes.

Mr. JENNER. Was that an entry made after the fact?

Mrs. PAINE. No; I judge that was——

Mr. JENNER. Now, please give me your best recollection.

Mrs. PAINE. That was the plan to meet, knowing Lee was no longer working; it was there for not only a meeting with Marina, but I expected to see them both at the apartment.

Mr. JENNER. So that is confined to the meeting you expected to have with Lee and Marina that morning when you went there and, to your surprise, you found that Mr. Oswald was all packed to go to New Orleans.

Mrs. PAINE. All packed and looking for a cab; yes.

Mr. JENNER. How long did Marina remain in your home on that occasion?

Mrs. PAINE. She stayed then until May 9—well, excuse me, she stayed until the 10th of May.

Mr. JENNER. You have an entry, do you not, in your diary as to the May 9th or 10th.

Mrs. PAINE. Yes.

Mr. JENNER. Read it.

Mrs. PAINE. It says now going over to the 11th "New Orleans."

Mr. JENNER. And you have written across then "May 10 and May 11," is that right?

Mrs. PAINE. Yes.

Mr. JENNER. What does the "New Orleans" signify, please?

Mrs. PAINE. Lee called on the evening of the 9th to say he had work.

Mr. JENNER. You recall that?

Mrs. PAINE. I recall that definitely. Marina says, "Papa naslubet," "Father loves us," "Daddy loves us, he got work and he wanted us to come." She was very elated.

Mr. JENNER. This is Marina talking to you?

Mrs. PAINE. I could see as she talked on the phone.

Mr. JENNER. You overheard this conversation?

Mrs. PAINE. Afterward. She said over and over, "Papa naslubet," "Daddy loves us," "Daddy loves us."

Mr. JENNER. She was elated?

Mrs. PAINE. She was elated and, let's see, we tried to think when we could leave, and first said over the phone that we would leave on the morning of the

11th. But I thought it would be too long to do all this in one day, and we accelerated our preparations and left midday on the 10th which got us to Shreveport.

Mr. JENNER. Before we get into this, and I would like to cover this interim period before any adjournment today; there was a 16-day period now, approximately, maybe we will limit it to 15 days, that Marina stayed with you in your home.

Mrs. PAINE. That is right.

Mr. JENNER. Did you have conversations with her about her husband?

Mrs. PAINE. Yes.

Mr. JENNER. About their life in Russia?

Mrs. PAINE. Well, even going so far as to wonder——

Mr. JENNER. During this 15-day period?

Mrs. PAINE. Yes. We had such conversations.

Mr. JENNER. Would you please relate to us your discussions with Marina with respect to her husband Lee Harvey Oswald?

Mrs. PAINE. Well, she wondered if he did, in fact, love her.

Mr. JENNER. What did she say?

Mrs. PAINE. She said she supposed most couples had at some time wondered about this. She wondered herself whether she loved him truly. She talked some of her few months of dating that she had in Minsk, and of living there.

Mr. JENNER. That is before her marriage to Lee Harvey?

Mrs. PAINE. Yes. At some point, and I want to tell you this, whether it is appropriate or whether it happened later in October, I can't be certain, but I think in May she told me that she had written a letter to a previous boyfriend, and that this letter had come back because she had put insufficient postage on it, and Lee had found it at the door coming back through the mail, and had been very angry.

Mr. JENNER. Did she go beyond that?

Mrs. PAINE. She did not. To tell me what was in the letter, you mean?

Mr. JENNER. I am not thinking so much within the letter. Did she go beyond stating that he was merely only angry? Was there any discussion about his having struck her?

Mr. PAINE. No; none. No; none. She never mentioned to me ever that Lee had struck her.

Mr. JENNER. And during all the visits you ever had with her, all the tete-a-tetes, her living with you on this occasion we now describe as 15½ days, and in the fall, was there any occasion when Marina Oswald related to you any abuse, physical abuse, by her husband, Lee Harvey Oswald, with respect to her?

Mrs. PAINE. There was never any such occasion.

Mr. JENNER. Never any such occasion. And in particular this incident?

Mrs. PAINE. She related this incident, but it did not include anything further than he had been very angry and hurt.

Mr. JENNER. Up to this time, that is, the time she came to you on the 24th, had you ever seen any bruises——

Mrs. PAINE. No; I never saw her——

Mr. JENNER. On her person?

Mrs. PAINE. No; I never saw her bruised.

Mr. JENNER. At no time that you have ever seen her or known her, have you ever seen her bruised?

Mrs. PAINE. At no time.

Mr. JENNER. So that there has been no occasion when you have seen it, or been led to believe, she had been subjected to any physical abuse by her husband?

Mrs. PAINE. That is right.

Mr. JENNER. Was there any discussion during these 15 days of any occasion when Marina had gone off to live with someone else?

Mrs. PAINE. No. I think she told me that in the fall.

Mr. JENNER. I see. As long as I have raised that, would you please give us the time and the occasions and tell us what occurred?

Mrs. PAINE. What she told me?

Mr. JENNER. What she said. When was this?

Mrs. PAINE. This probably was in October. She told me that the previous year she had——

Mr. JENNER. 1962?

Mrs. PAINE. Yes. She had in the fall, she had gone to a friend's home, left Lee. She described his face as she left, as shocked and dismayed and unbelieving.

Mr. JENNER. Unbelieving?

Mrs. PAINE. In a sense that she was truly walking out on him.

Mr. JENNER. Yes. Excuse me. Did she put it in those terms, that she was leaving?

Mrs. PAINE. She was leaving; yes.

Mr. JENNER. She left him?

Mrs. PAINE. Yes; and went to stay with a friend. Then moved to the home——

Mr. JENNER. Did she name the friend?

Mrs. PAINE. She did not name the friend; no. The friend's name came up in another connection, but I had no way of making the connection until after I learned about this to whom she referred.

Mr. JENNER. Do you now recall the name?

Mrs. PAINE. She went to Katya Ford's.

The CHAIRMAN. To the Fords?

Mrs. PAINE. To Katya, being the friend, Mrs. Ford.

The CHAIRMAN. Mrs. Ford.

Mrs. PAINE. And then moved. She did tell me this. She had moved on the weekend to a different home. Then Lee came there, pleaded for her to come back, promised that everything would be different. She went back and she reported—as she reported it to me, things were no different.

Mr. JENNER. Were not different?

Mrs. PAINE. Were not different.

Mr. JENNER. Did you undertake a discussion with her as to what the things were that were disturbing her?

Mrs. PAINE. That offended her that much? No; I did not.

Mr. JENNER. That led her to leave her husband?

Mrs. PAINE. No.

Mr. JENNER. There was no discussion of that?

Mrs. PAINE. No.

Mr. McCLOY. Did you ever witness any altercations?

Mrs. PAINE. Indeed I saw them argue a good deal.

Mr. McCLOY. Sharp arguments?

Mrs. PAINE. Yes.

Mr. DULLES. But no violence of any kind?

Mrs. PAINE. No physical violence.

Mr. McCLOY. Any profanity?

Mrs. PAINE. I am not sure I know Russian profanity. He was very curt and told her to shut up quite a great deal.

Mr. JENNER. In your presence?

Mrs. PAINE. Yes.

Mr. JENNER. In the presence of others?

Mrs. PAINE. Particularly in New Orleans the first time when we went down, when I took her to New Orleans in May, he was very discourteous to her, and they argued most of that weekend. I was very uncomfortable in that situation, and he would tell her to shut up, tell her, "I said it, and that is all the discussion on the subject."

Representative FORD. What were the kinds of discussions that prompted this?

Mrs. PAINE. I can't recall that, and I have already had my brain picked trying to, with other people trying to, to recall what was the difficulty. I do recall feeling that the immediate things they were talking about were insufficient reason for that much feeling being passed back and forth, and I wondered if I wasn't adding to the strain in the situation, and did my best to get back to Texas directly. But the—well, I do recall one thing, yes—we arrived with a big load of blackberries that we bought from a vendor along the street.

Representative Ford. On the way down?

Mrs. Paine. On the way down, on the road, and ate them, and then, he, one morning, started to make blackberry wine, and she bawled him out for it, what a waste of good blackberries, and she said, "What do you think you are doing? Ruining all this." And he proceeded, and argued about it, but thought he should, you know, defend himself. On this occasion she was making the attack in a sense and didn't think he should do it this way, and then, so, under fire and attack, he continued. But then the next day she observed that he had tossed it all out and lost heart after the argument, and decided it wasn't——

Mr. Dulles. He tossed out the wine?

Mrs. Paine. He tossed it out; yes.

Mr. Jenner. You detected, then, irritability as between them. Is that a fair statement?

Mrs. Paine. That is accurate.

Mr. Jenner. And anger rose to the surface pretty easily?

Mrs. Paine. Very easily.

Mr. Jenner. What was your impression? Of course he hadn't seen her then for a couple of weeks.

Mrs. Paine. That is right.

Mr. Jenner. Tell us about it—when she came in. Did they embrace?

Mrs. Paine. Yes. We arrived at his uncle's in one section of New Orleans, and had a very friendly half hour or so——

Mr. Jenner. Was he there?

Mrs. Paine. Yes: he was there. He introduced her and little June, and played with June, on his shoulders, perhaps. At any rate, he was very glad to see the baby, and was congenial and outgoing. We talked with the relatives for a short time.

Then the uncle drove them to the apartment—I was following with my children in my car—drove to the apartment he had rented, which was in a different section of the city. And Lee showed her, of course, all the virtues of the apartment that he had rented. He was pleased that there was room enough, it was large enough that he could invite me to stay, and the children, to spend the night there. And he pointed out this little courtyard with grass, and fresh strawberries ready to pick, where June could play. And a screened porch entryway. And quite a large living room. And he was pleased with the furniture and how the landlady had said this was early New Orleans style. And Marina was definitely not as pleased as he had hoped. I think he felt—he wanted to please her. This showed in him.

Mr. Jenner. Tell us what she said. What led you to that conclusion?

Mrs. Paine. She said it is dark, and it is not very clean. She thought the courtyard was nice, a grass spot where June could play, fenced in. But there was very little ventilation. We immediately were aware there were a lot of cockroaches.

Mr. Jenner. Was she aware of this, and did she comment on that?

Mrs. Paine. I don't know as anything was said. He was pretty busy explaining. He was doing his best to get rid of them. But they didn't subside. I remember noticing that he was tender and vulnerable at that point, when she arrived.

Mr. Jenner. He was tender?

Mrs. Paine. Hoping for—particularly vulnerable, hoping for approval from her, which she didn't give. It wasn't a terribly nice apartment. And she had been disappointed, because when we first arrived she thought that the home we were going to was the apartment.

Mr. Jenner. She thought the Murrets' home?

Mrs. Paine. Yes. So when we came up to the Murrets' home, she said, "This is lovely, how pleased I am." So that she was in—disappointed by contrast with the apartment that she really had to live in.

Representative Ford. She expressed this?

Mrs. Paine. She expressed her disappointment; yes; and didn't meet his hopes to be pleased with it.

Mr. Dulles. As compared with their previous place of residence, how was the New Orleans apartment? It was bigger, I gather.

Mrs. PAINE. It was larger. It was darker, less well ventilated. It was on the first floor, the other was upstairs. I would say they were comparable in cost and in attractiveness.

Mr. JENNER. What about vermin?

Mrs. PAINE. I didn't see any vermin at the first place. But then I didn't spend the night there.

Mr. JENNER. So the welcoming was cordial?

Mrs. PAINE. The welcoming was cordial.

Mr. JENNER. They seemed to have a fine relationship at that moment?

Mrs. PAINE. Yes.

Mr. JENNER. But as the weekend progressed, and she saw the new apartment, all the time you were there, you were aware of friction and irritability?

Mrs. PAINE. Yes.

Mr. JENNER. Going back to the 15 days again, was there any discussion during this period, again, on the subject of Mr.—of Lee Oswald wishing Marina to return to Russia?

Mrs. PAINE. I believe I made definite, but only verbal, an invitation for her to stay on with me, past the time of the baby's birth, if she wished to.

Mr. JENNER. I take it—I will get into that. But I take it your answer to my question first is yes.

Mrs. PAINE. Yes.

Mr. JENNER. Now, tell us what that discussion was.

Mrs. PAINE. Well——

Mr. JENNER. And how it arose.

Mrs. PAINE. Well, we still discussed the possibility of her coming back to have the baby here—although by no means a definite—definitely planned.

Mr. JENNER. Excuse me. I am a little confused. When you say coming back to have the baby here——

Mrs. PAINE. It was assumed she would go to New Orleans when he called, but we talked about the possibility of her coming back to Dallas. I said she was still welcome to if she wants to, if it seems appropriate, to come here to have the baby.

Mr. DULLES. That was to your house, you mean?

Mrs. PAINE. Yes; to stay at my house before, or especially right after the baby's birth, where I could look after June while she was in the hospital and later. June didn't take readily to strangers. She did like me and was comfortable with me, so I felt she might want to have someone she knew and got along with.

Mr. JENNER. But in this connection, was there a discussion between you and Marina Oswald subject to her husband wishing her to return to Russia?

Mrs. PAINE. I don't believe she again said that he was after her to return.

Mr. JENNER. Well, then, on the whole, your answer to my question would be no.

Mrs. PAINE. That is right. As far as I recall, it came up only once in our discussions prior to New Orleans.

Mr. JENNER. Which you have already related?

Mrs. PAINE. Right.

Mr. JENNER. Was there any discussion during the 15-day period on the subject of her acquiring greater facility with the English language?

Mrs. PAINE. Yes.

Mr. JENNER. And his attitude toward that?

Mrs. PAINE. His attitude had already been discussed, and I don't believe it was particularly discussed further. But she did indicate that she was going to try to learn some anyway.

Mr. JENNER. Despite that?

Mrs. PAINE. I judged so. I asked if she had a book written in Russian entitled "The Self Teacher in the English Language." She did not. And I ordered it. And I think I gave it to her even then. I am quite certain of that. This turned out to be not much help. At least she was interested in trying to learn English.

Mr. JENNER. Was there any discussion of the subject of it being disclosed to the Russian emigré group that she was pregnant.

Mrs. PAINE. No; she continued to ask me not to mention that. We did, however, meet someone in the Russian emigré group in Fort Worth after she had the first day put on maternity clothes—and so she was sorry that that meeting had occurred. She judged how people would know.

Mr. JENNER. All right. Did anything else occur in the way of discussions during that 15-day period on the subject of life in Russia, his political philosophy, how they got along, his general disposition, her reaction to America?

Mrs. PAINE. She discussed her reaction to America. She was very impressed with the variety of goods available in the stores. She thought the quality was better here than in Russia. Then there was more of that later in October.

Mr. JENNER. I will get to that, in October. Have we pretty well exhausted this 15-day interim period, then?

Mrs. PAINE. Yes, sir.

Representative FORD. Mr. Jenner, may I ask a question there? During this 15-day period, did any individual, male or female, come and visit you at your home?

Mrs. PAINE. You mean particularly to see her? I am sure there are people coming and going at my house. There must have been. For instance, May 1, Mary—this is again Miss Mary referred to previously, a babysitter, "8:15. War and Peace." Mary came and stayed with my children, and Marina and June and I went to see War and Peace. Miss Mary recalls that meeting.

Mr. JENNER. Is that a play or the movie?

Mrs. PAINE. This is the movie, War and Peace, in English. But, of course, she knew the story, so she could enjoy seeing it. "Ed tennis confirm." I went over to play tennis. On the fourth of May, Craig's children—they came here.

Representative FORD. Into your home?

Mrs. PAINE. Probably.

Mr. JENNER. Who is Craig?

Mrs. PAINE. Craig is this young German woman who didn't want to buy guns for her children either, that I mentioned. And we exchanged children often.

Mr. JENNER. Does she speak Russian?

Mrs. PAINE. No; German only, and English. And, mow the lawn, it says on the third, but that is not me, it is a neighbor who mows the lawn. And May 9 in the morning, "Ilse"—means Mrs. Craig again—kept my children while I went at 8:10 to Saint Marks for an interview. So there was a normal flow. And I told my immediate neighbor, Mrs. Roberts, who figures later, that Marina was there over the weekend, that I wouldn't be there, and introduced them, so Marina could go to Mrs. Roberts and make signs or symbols if she had to get a message through to someone.

Mr. JENNER. Mrs. Roberts is your next door neighbor?

Mrs. PAINE. That is right.

Mr. JENNER. Then your response to Representative Ford's question is that——

Mrs. PAINE. A normal flow to my house.

Mr. JENNER. But there wasn't anybody that came specifically to see her from the Russian emigré group, is that correct?

Mrs. PAINE. No.

Representative FORD. Were there any telephone calls to her from anybody of this group, or any other group?

Mrs. PAINE. No. I made the contact for her with my tutor, got her to call. But that is all.

Mr. DULLES. She probably could not operate the telephone.

Mrs. PAINE. She could. That was the first I knew. I wasn't certain. But she knew how to operate the telephone.

Mr. JENNER. I am pleased you raised that, sir.

She could dial. Did you have the dial system in effect at that time?

Mrs. PAINE. Way out in Irving; yes.

Mr. JENNER. And she could dial the number if she wished?

Mrs. PAINE. Yes; she knew how to do that.

Mr. McCLOY. Did you at any time get any evidence to indicate that she was in touch with any Soviet officials at all, the consul general? Did she ever talk of going to the Soviet Embassy or the Soviet Consulate in regard to her problems?

Mrs. PAINE. No. The only thing ever mentioned was this that I have already

473

mentioned for the record—that she had written to the Soviet Embassy inquiring about papers to go back.

Mr. McCloy. Did you think she did that on her own initiative?

Mrs. Paine. No; because he was insisting.

Mr. Dulles. We have a copy of that letter, have we not?

Mr. McCloy. Did she ever tell you why she didn't want to return to the Soviet Union?

Mrs. Paine. She said she liked America better.

Mr. McCloy. And she rather liked the conditions here better than she had experienced them in the Soviet Union?

Mrs. Paine. Yes.

Mr. McCloy. And that you think was her fundamental motivation for staying here?

Mrs. Paine. Yes.

Mr. McCloy. Wanting to stay here? When you were in contact with her at all did any—when she was staying with you, was there any unidentified characters or people that called to see her?

Mrs. Paine. No; there was no one at all that called to see her.

Mr. Jenner. Were there any telephone calls received during that period when you answered the phone that someone asked for Marina?

Mrs. Paine. Only that from Lee on the night.

Mr. Jenner. Only from Lee?

Mrs. Paine. Only from Lee.

Mr. Jenner. No other calls to her?

Mrs. Paine. That is right.

Mr. Jenner. And no other callers—that is persons who came to your home?

Mrs. Paine. None.

Mr. McCloy. What was the name of these—De Mohrenschildts. Did they communicate with her when she was with you?

Mrs. Paine. No; my impression is they were already out of the country.

Mr. Jenner. Was there any mail received or delivered to your home during this period for her?

Mrs. Paine. No; I don't think so. It is possible that Lee wrote once. I think it is more likely she wrote him.

Mr. Jenner. In the household goods and paraphernalia transferred to your house, were there any books, pamphlets, literature?

Mrs. Paine. I didn't see any.

Mr. Jenner. You did not see any?

Mrs. Paine. I did not.

Mr. McCloy. Did you ever engage in any discussion or dialectics with Lee about the respective merits of the capitalist system or the Soviet system? Did you engage in any debates with him on political philosophy?

Mrs. Paine. I once listened to such a debate between Lee and my husband, in October.

Mr. Dulles. You kept out of the debate?

Mrs. Paine. I tried hard. I felt it was not going anywhere, and that he was not a man that could be approached by logic, and that there was no point to arguing with him. I disagreed with him quite strongly, and I didn't see how it would help in any way to say so, or to try to change—certainly it would not have helped to try to change his views. He, for instance, was of the opinion that all churches were an arm of the state, intent upon blinding the people. I thought his thinking was extremely erroneous, and not open to introduction of other facts, anything contradictory to his own view.

Mr. McCloy. Did he become intemperate in argument?

Mrs. Paine. No; he did not.

Mr. McCloy. But in the course of his discussions with your husband, did he assert adherence to the element of violence as a factor——

Mrs. Paine. Michael tells me he did. I didn't hear that particular discussion.

Representative Ford. In response to Mr. McCloy, you told of this argument that your husband and Lee Oswald had. You said it was October. This is October 1963?

Mrs. Paine. Yes.

Mr. McCloy. Do you have any more questions? We are going to resume in the morning at 9 o'clock.

The Chairman. Will you be here?

Mr. McCloy. Yes; I will be here.

The Chairman. Then you continue to preside throughout her testimony. I will be here, though.

Mr. Dulles. I have no questions.

Mr. McCloy. Do you want to close?

Mr. Jenner. I would just as soon adjourn now, if it suits your convenience.

Mr. McCloy. All right. We will excuse you. Thank you for your cooperation.

(Whereupon, at 5:20 p.m., the President's Commission recessed.)

Thursday, March 19, 1964

TESTIMONY OF RUTH HYDE PAINE RESUMED

The President's Commission met at 9:05 a.m. on March 19, 1964, at 200 Maryland Avenue NE., Washington, D.C.

Present were Chief Justice Earl Warren, Chairman; Senator John Sherman Cooper, Representative Hale Boggs, Representative Gerald R. Ford, John J. McCloy, and Allen W. Dulles, members.

Also present were Albert E. Jenner, Jr., assistant counsel; and Wesley J. Liebeler, assistant counsel.

Mr. McCloy. Mrs. Paine, I must remind you that you are still under affirmation. We don't take a new affirmation with each hearing.

Mr. Jenner. We had concluded, if you recall, the 15-day period in May that Mrs. Oswald resided at the home of Mrs. Paine.

Would you please describe for us the items of household furniture, or whatever the articles were, that were packed in your station wagon when you took Mrs. Oswald to New Orleans?

Mrs. Paine. We packed in a play pen and crib. I recall a stroller, some kitchen utensils, and personal clothing for herself and the baby.

Mr. Jenner. Was there any luggage of any character?

Mrs. Paine. There may have been a small suitcase but I don't recall it specifically.

Mr. Jenner. You do not?

Mrs. Paine. I am just guessing.

Mr. Jenner. As I recall you have told us yesterday that when you arrived in New Orleans, you went by the Murrets' home first?

Mrs. Paine. That is right.

Mr. Jenner. And then from the Murrets' home to the apartment at, what was that address on Magazine Street?

Mrs. Paine. 4907.

Mr. Jenner. That was 4907 rather than 4905.

Mrs. Paine. Yes.

Mr. Jenner. Mrs. Paine, there has been a touch of testimony, at least of the possibility that Mr. Oswald may have dry-fired or dry-sighted any rifle in the courtyard or garden space at 4907?

Would you be good enough to draw for us free hand the layout, at least the ground layout of the 4907 premises on Magazine Street in New Orleans?

Mrs. Paine. Now, shall I describe this?

Mr. Jenner. Could I first show the diagram. I have marked the diagram the witness has drawn as Commission Exhibit No. 403.

(The diagram referred to was marked Commission Exhibit No. 403 for identification.)

Mr. JENNER. Mr. Chairman, might it be helpful and permissible if I had the witness stand to your rear and point to the diagram so that you might follow her testimony?

Mr. McCLOY. Very well.

Mrs. PAINE. This street is Magazine Street; it is a corner house.

Mr. JENNER. Excuse me, Mrs. Paine, left on your plot is east and west and up and down are north and south?

Mrs. PAINE. Yes; that is the way I recall it. This is a corner house and there was room enough——

Mr. JENNER. Excuse me, I have to keep the record. You are referring now to a square on the right-hand margin of your outline.

Mrs. PAINE. Between this house, and the courtyard and house where the Oswalds were staying, there was room enough to drive a car.

Mr. JENNER. Have you marked the courtyard with that word?

Mrs. PAINE. No.

Mr. JENNER. Now, you have written "courtyard" in the sort of an "L" shaped space that you have indicated on the plot, is that right?

Mrs. PAINE. This is a square space cut by a walk.

Mr. JENNER. All right.

Mrs. PAINE. This was a low fence.

Mr. JENNER. When you say this, it does not help us on the record; what is this to which you have pointed—you have written something across it?

Mrs. PAINE. Around this courtyard and in front of the house was a low metal picket fence.

Mr. JENNER. That you have so designated?

Mrs. PAINE. Correct.

Mr. JENNER. Thank you.

Mrs. PAINE. There was grass within this small courtyard or walk, steps——

Mr. JENNER. Which you have also marked "walk"?

Mrs. PAINE. Yes. Steps going up.

Mr. JENNER. Which you have likewise so marked?

Mrs. PAINE. To a screened porch.

Mr. JENNER. Likewise so marked?

Mrs. PAINE. And then the doorway from the porch goes into the living room.

Mr. JENNER. And the living room is marked "Living room." Would you use those names and those designations as you testify?

Mrs. PAINE. All right.

Mr. JENNER. Now, would you please indicate the courtyard or square or oblong portion you have marked, rectangular portion, that was open space, was it, it was not roofed?

Mrs. PAINE. It was fully open.

Mr. JENNER. It was fully open, and it faced out on Magazine Street?

Mrs. PAINE. That is right.

Mr. JENNER. And was there open space to the east, that would be toward the building, which you have merely designated as an empty square?

Mrs. PAINE. I will write in here "driveway;" this was open here as a driveway.

Mr. JENNER. Mrs. Paine, is that what you have now marked a building, a dwelling?

Mrs. PAINE. It was a dwelling.

Mr. JENNER. Were there dwellings to the south of Magazine Street and on the opposite side of the street?

Mrs. PAINE. That so far as I recall, that is my best recollection.

Mr. JENNER. What was to the east in the way of dwellings or buildings?

Mrs. PAINE. The rest of the house; they lived in a portion; entered from the side door of a large house; I assume it was once a one-family dwelling.

Mr. JENNER. Then for our purpose here as far as the courtyard is concerned on the east it was—there was a walk?

Mrs. PAINE. A building.

Mr. JENNER. West, I am sorry. On the west line of the courtyard there was a walk?

Mrs. PAINE. Right.

470

Mr. JENNER. On the north of the courtyard there was the screened porch and to the east, but with intervening driveway there was a dwelling house?

Mrs. PAINE. Yes.

Mr. JENNER. Then the courtyard was open on Magazine Street?

Mrs. PAINE. Yes.

Mr. JENNER. Does your recollection serve you that anybody standing in the courtyard and dry-sighting a rifle would be visible to people who just happened by, or who would be looking out a window on the south side of Magazine Street, or in the home or in the dwelling house to the east of the courtyard?

Mrs. PAINE. He would have been very visible. Would have collected a clutch of small boys.

Mr. JENNER. This was a neighborhood, then, in which there were small children?

Mrs. PAINE. Yes.

Mr. JENNER. Was it a reasonably busy street?

Mrs. PAINE. Very busy street.

Mr. JENNER. What were the days of the week that you were there when you returned, when you brought Mrs. Oswald to New Orleans?

Mrs. PAINE. When we first went down, we arrived on Saturday, I was there Sunday and Monday and left Tuesday morning.

Mr. JENNER. All right.

Does your recollection serve so that you can state that the days you were there you observed during the daytime, at least many or a reasonable number of small children and mothers and fathers, in and about the neighborhood?

Mrs. PAINE. A good many small children and adults.

Mr. JENNER. Was that likewise true when you returned in September about which you will testify in a few moments?

Mrs. PAINE. That was certainly true in September.

Mr. JENNER. Mr. Chairman, I offer in evidence as Commission Exhibit No. 403, a plot which Mrs. Paine has just drawn and which is so marked.

Mr. McCLOY. So received.

(The diagram referred to heretofore, marked Commission Exhibit No. 403 for identification, was received in evidence.)

(At this point, Mr. Dulles entered the hearing room.)

Mr. JENNER. Was the dwelling in which the Oswalds were residing, 4907 Magazine Street, a single level or a double level house?

Mrs. PAINE. It was all on the ground floor.

Mr. JENNER. It was a one-story house, one story high?

Mrs. PAINE. It was a segment of a house that probably had two stories to it. I don't recall. But the segment they had was all on one level.

Mr. JENNER. And that was the ground level?

Mrs. PAINE. Yes.

Mr. JENNER. Directing your attention to Exhibit No. 403, and Mr. Dulles, would you favor me by handing her the exhibit, and with particular reference to the screen porch, the screen porch likewise opened up on Magazine Street, did it?

Mrs. PAINE. Well, it was set back a short space from the street, but the door opened up toward Magazine.

Mr. JENNER. The screened portion, that is, that faced on Magazine Street?

Mrs. PAINE. Yes.

Mr. JENNER. If anyone were on the screen porch, let us say, dry-sighting a rifle or some other firearm, would he be, would that person be observable from Magazine Street, and from the east?

Mrs. PAINE. I doubt he would have been noticed from Magazine Street. A small boy passing in the driveway could have looked through the screen, up to the——

Mr. JENNER. That is to the east?

Mrs. PAINE. I will mark "screen" on the south and east side so you know it is screened on both sides.

Mr. JENNER. Yes.

Mrs. PAINE. I don't recall for certainty but there may have been a kind of shade that could have been put down. It was not when I was there, down, but there may have been some means of——

Mr. JENNER. Lattice shade?

Mrs. PAINE. Putting down a lattice blind.

Mr. JENNER. A blind or something?

Mrs. PAINE. Yes.

Mr. JENNER. Of course, if the blind were down no one could see it. Did you have occasion when you were there, Mrs. Paine, on either of your two trips to be on the screen porch?

Mrs. PAINE. Oh, yes.

Mr. JENNER. And looking out?

Mrs. PAINE. Yes.

Mr. JENNER. And was there any impediment to your view?

Mrs. PAINE. No, I could see the street very well.

Mr. JENNER. Did you have occasion there on either of those occasions to be out in the courtyard or on the street to be looking into the porch area.

Mrs. PAINE. Yes; I did.

Mr. JENNER. Could you see the persons, from the courtyard, could you see persons behind the screen?

Mrs. PAINE. From the courtyard you could see persons behind the screen.

Mr. JENNER. Do I take it then by your emphasis on courtyard, do you mean by that if you were on Magazine Street itself, that is the sidewalk in front of the home it would be difficult to see in?

Mrs. PAINE. Looking directly in you would notice someone but just passing by you would not have been apt to see them.

Mr. JENNER. But if you looked directly you could see in on the porch?

Mrs. PAINE. I think so; yes.

Mr. JENNER. You mentioned yesterday a series of letters and correspondence and you spent some time with me last night and we went over all that, do you recall?

Mrs. PAINE. Yes.

Mr. JENNER. Do you have your summary we worked with last night at hand to assist you?

Mrs. PAINE. Yes; I do.

Mr. JENNER. Would you mind taking that out, please?

You mentioned yesterday in your testimony a note that you had sent to Marina Oswald shortly after your initial acquaintance with her in February of 1963. Did you receive a response to that note?

Mrs. PAINE. I did; and I have that response.

Mr. JENNER. I have here a document which we will mark as Commission Exhibit No. 404, including its envelope as 404A.

Is that the document or note you received from Mrs. Oswald and the envelope?

(The document and envelope referred to were marked Commission Exhibits Nos. 404 and 404A, respectively, for identification.)

Mrs. PAINE. Yes; it is.

Mr. JENNER. Did that reach you in the ordinary course of its posting by mail?

Mrs. PAINE. Yes.

Mr. JENNER. Are you familiar with the handwriting of Marina Oswald?

Mrs. PAINE. I am now.

Mr. JENNER. Is that—do you identify the handwriting in that document 404?

Mrs. PAINE. That is her handwriting.

Mr. JENNER. That is hers.

Mrs. PAINE. Yes.

Mr. JENNER. And is it in the same condition now as it was when you received it?

Mrs. PAINE. Yes; it is.

Mr. JENNER. And that is her response to your note?

Mrs. PAINE. Yes.

Mr. JENNER. I offer in evidence as Exhibit No. 404 the document now so marked.

Mr. McCLOY. It may be admitted.

(The letter and envelope referred to, heretofore marked for identification as Commission Exhibits Nos. 404 and 404-A, were received in evidence.)

Mr. JENNER. Now, that is in what language?

Mrs. PAINE. That is in Russian. Except for the address on the outside.

Mr. JENNER. Yes.

Have you made a translation of that note?

Mrs PAINE. I have.

Mr. JENNER. And is it the translation on the notes that you exhibited to me last night which we have marked as No. 1?

Mrs. PAINE. It is.

Mr. JENNER. May I inquire, Mr. Chairman, if you would prefer that I read the translation in evidence or may we have it——

Mr. McCLOY. It is a short note?

Mr. JENNER. It is a short note. Others are a little longer, however, and if I have your permission, to save you time, I would read that into the record during the noon recess or something of that character.

Mr. McCLOY. Very well.

Mr. JENNER. Is that acceptable.

Now, did you thereafter—you wrote Mrs. Oswald at or about that time in response to that note of yours, did you not?

Mrs. PAINE. No. Let's see—I don't recall whether I did or not or whether I arrived on the Tuesday that she had suggested.

Mr. JENNER. I have a little difficulty in handling these, Mr. Chairman, because they are in Russian, and I don't immediately have a vision of it.

(At this point, Representative Ford entered the hearing room.)

Mr. JENNER. I am handing you a document which I have numbered as No. 2. Would you locate that for me on your summary?

Mrs. PAINE. I have it.

Mr. JENNER. Is that the second page?

Mrs. PAINE. Yes.

Mr. JENNER. That note also in Russian but in whose handwriting?

Mrs. PAINE. In my handwriting.

Mr. JENNER. And that is a draft, I take it, of a letter or note that you transmitted to Mrs. Oswald.

Would you identify in your sheaf of notes the point at which you made a translation of that note?

Mrs. PAINE. When did I make a translation of it? I didn't understand your question.

Mr. JENNER. Would you point out in your notes the translation of the document? Is that the center of the page on page 2?

Mrs. PAINE. Yes.

Mr. JENNER. Is the document which I will have marked as Commission Exhibit No. 405 in your handwriting?

(The document referred to was marked Commission Exhibit No. 405 for identification.)

Mrs. PAINE. Yes; it is.

Mr. JENNER. Is it in the same condition now as it was when you completed it?

Mrs. PAINE. Yes; being, of course, a rough draft of what I sent and not what I sent.

Mr. JENNER. You do not have the original of that because you sent it to Marina Oswald, is that correct?

Mrs. PAINE. That is right.

Mr. JENNER. But it does represent your present best recollection of the note as you transmitted it to her?

Mrs. PAINE. That is right. This note is without a date. Shall I give my recollection of when I think it was written?

Mr. JENNER. Yes; please.

Mrs. PAINE. I think it was written in March and referred to—it closes, "Until the 20th." I believe that referred to Wednesday, March 20, which is what appears here with the name Marina.

Mr. JENNER. Which is what you testified to yesterday, and when you say "appears here" you meant Exhibit 401?

Mrs. PAINE. Yes.

Mr. JENNER. I offer in evidence the original document which has now been identified as Commission Exhibit No. 405.

Mr. McCLOY. It may be admitted.

(The document referred to heretofore marked Commission Exhibit No. 405 for identification, was received in evidence.)

Mr. JENNER. I will read the translation in the record during the noon recess. You shortly transmitted another letter of your own to Mrs. Oswald, did you not?

Mrs. PAINE. Yes.

Mr. JENNER. And I have here a document which I have marked Commission Exhibit No. 406. Is this a draft of the letter in your handwriting?

(The document referred to was marked Commission Exhibit No. 406 for identification.)

Mrs. PAINE. Yes; it is.

Mr. JENNER. And did you shortly after the completion of that draft retranscribe it and transmit the letter to Marina Oswald?

Mrs. PAINE. Yes.

Mr. JENNER. Have you made a translation of that letter?

Mrs. PAINE. Yes; I have.

Mr. JENNER. Is the draft of that document in the same condition now as it was when you completed it?

Mrs. PAINE. Yes.

Mr. JENNER. Where is that document transcribed on your notes?

Mrs. PAINE. That is at the top of page 2.

Mr. JENNER. That is what we call No. 3, is it not?

Mrs. PAINE. And dated March 26.

Mr. JENNER. This, Mr. Chairman, is her note to which she testified yesterday was an invitation to the Oswalds to dinner at her home on April 2.

Mrs. PAINE. It appears—the following invitation is a full explanation of it. I believe I had made the explanation in person. This letter was to say that Michael would come and pick them up.

Mr. JENNER. This was confirmation of your original invitation?

Mrs. PAINE. Yes; this was that Michael could pick them up.

Mr. JENNER. I offer in evidence a document marked Commission Exhibit No. 406.

Mr. McCLOY. It may be admitted.

(The document referred to, heretofore marked Commission Exhibit No. 406 for identification, was received in evidence.)

Mr. JENNER. Did you receive from Marina herself a note with respect to your invitation to have her and her husband join you?

Mrs. PAINE. I have a note which I take to be a reply to that invitation, saying that that date, Tuesday, would be fine.

Mr. JENNER. And I hand you Commission Document No. 407.

Is that the note you received from Marina Oswald?

Mrs. PAINE. Yes; it is.

(The document referred to was marked Commission Exhibit No. 407 for identification.)

Mr. JENNER. Have you made—is it in the same condition now as it was when you received it?

Mrs. PAINE. I have no envelope anymore. I don't know what happened to it.

Mr. JENNER. Is the note itself in the same condition as it was at the time you received it?

Mrs. PAINE. No. I have written on it in my hand to help me understand the meaning of it, some pen notations, translation of the Russian words.

Mr. JENNER. I am interested in that, Mrs. Paine.

Did you also—are there some additions in your handwriting on the first page of the note?

Mrs. PAINE. Yes, marked one, two, three, four and clearly taken from a dictionary.

Mr. JENNER. Why did you do that?

Mrs. PAINE. To explain to myself the meaning of these particular words. I had to look them up.

Mr. JENNER. Is it a fair statement, Mrs. Paine, that your command of the Russian language was not facile enough for you to read the total letter freehand, as soon as you received it, but you wrote on the letter definitions of words and of phrases to assist you in interpreting it?

Mrs. PAINE. That is a fair statement.

Mr. JENNER. Were all the notations you have now identified placed by you on that letter shortly after you received it, or in the course of your effort to interpret it?

Mrs. PAINE. That is correct.

Mr. JENNER. Now, save for those additions of yours, is the document in the same condition now as it was when you received it?

Mrs. PAINE. Yes.

Mr. JENNER. And is it otherwise in the same condition as it was when you placed those notes on it?

In other words, there have been no notes of your own placed on the document subsequent to, at, or about the time you received it when you were attempting to interpret it?

Mrs. PAINE. Well, you first said, or when I was translating it.

Mr. JENNER. Yes.

Mrs. PAINE. I translated it immediately for myself at the time, and then when I made a written translation I made a more careful one so that some of these notes were done a week ago.

Mr. JENNER. That is what I was getting at.

Would you please, for the Commission identify the particular notes that you placed on there at the time you were seeking to interpret it when you first received it, and the notes you placed on there about a week ago, and indicate the pages.

Mrs. PAINE. I can easily answer that.

There is only one that was placed more recently. That is an underline on the inside.

Mr. JENNER. Right-hand inside page?

Mrs. PAINE. Right-hand side.

Mr. JENNER. Is it merely an underlining?

Mrs. PAINE. Underline and a question mark.

Mr. JENNER. And would you interpret that for us, please?

Mrs. PAINE. I couldn't read her handwriting, but later realized the word to be "if."

Mr. JENNER. When you were seeking to interpret it a week ago to translate it, you placed a question mark over that word because you couldn't quite figure it out?

Mrs. PAINE. And then later realized what it was.

Mr. JENNER. As being the word "if"?

Mrs. PAINE. That is correct.

Mr. JENNER. Other than that, Mrs. Paine, is the document in the condition it was when you received it and when you initially placed notations on it?

Mrs. PAINE. Yes; it is.

Mr. JENNER. Do you recognize that handwriting?

Mrs. PAINE. Yes, that is Marina Oswald's handwriting.

Mr. JENNER. Have you made a translation for the Commission of that letter?

Mrs. PAINE. Yes; I have.

Mr. JENNER. And that appears in your notes at page what?

Mrs. PAINE. The first page at the bottom.

Mr. JENNER. Which I have marked No. 4, I believe, is that correct?

Mrs. PAINE. Beginning "For Ruth and Michael Paine."

Mr. JENNER. Does you interpretation or translation of the letter represent your impressions of the letter when you read it?

Mrs. PAINE. Yes.

Mr. JENNER. And that is true, is it, of the other translations which we will introduce through you today? Is that true of all your translations?

Mrs. PAINE. I am not sure of what you are inquiring.

481

Mr. JENNER. What I am inquiring about, others—as you related to me last night—other persons with the command of the Russian language.

Mrs. PAINE. I had no help with the translations.

Mr. JENNER. Yes.

Other persons with their command of the Russian language might read one of Marina's letters and have at least, as to some words, an interpretation different from yours. What I am saying——

Mrs. PAINE. In a minor regard, yes.

Mr. JENNER. It may be?

Mrs. PAINE. But I believe the meaning would have been the same.

Mr. JENNER. But it is important to get your impressions, Mrs. Paine, of Marina's letters to you, despite what interpretations some other people might give to the same letter, and what I am seeking to emphasize is whether your translations are your impressions of those letters?

Mrs. PAINE. Yes; but they are good translations.

Mr. JENNER. I don't mean to question that. We seek the impact of these notes upon you.

Mrs. PAINE. I see. This is exactly what I understood them to mean, of course.

Mr. JENNER. That is fine.

Now, you received in May or on or about May, or shortly after May 25, 1963, another note from Marina Oswald, did you not?

Mrs. PAINE. This was postmarked May 25.

Mr. JENNER. After you had taken her to New Orleans?

Mrs. PAINE. That is correct. This was the first letter I received from her from New Orleans.

Mr. JENNER. And you have kindly produced the original of that letter for the Commission, have you not?

Mrs. PAINE. Yes.

Mr. JENNER. Is that correct?

Mrs. PAINE. Yes; it is.

Mr. JENNER. I am sorry, I have to have your answer aloud or I can't get it on the record.

The document you have produced is marked Commission Exhibit 408.

Do you recognize the handwriting of that note and of that envelope?

(The document referred to was marked Commission Exhibit No. 408 for identification.)

Mrs. PAINE. This is the handwriting of Marina Oswald.

Mr. JENNER. Both documents?

Mrs. PAINE. On both.

Mr. JENNER. Did you receive—that is a letter, is it not?

Mrs. PAINE. That is a letter.

Mr. JENNER. Did you receive it?

Mrs. PAINE. Yes; I did.

Mr. JENNER. Is it on or about, did you receive it on or about the date it is postmarked?

Mrs. PAINE. Shortly after, I would guess.

Mr. JENNER. I can see some handwriting written horizontally on the back of the envelope, is that handwriting yours or Marina's?

Mrs. PAINE. That is mine.

Mr. JENNER. When did you place that handwriting on the reverse side?

Mrs. PAINE. When I first read the letter and sought to understand it.

Mr. JENNER. I see.

And those notations are in Russian or in English?

Mrs. PAINE. A word is given in Russian followed by a translation in English.

Mr. JENNER. As in the case of one of the earlier exhibits, did you place those notations on the reverse side of the envelope at the time you received the letter in the course of your attempting to interpret the letter?

Mrs. PAINE. Yes; I did.

Mr. JENNER. And those notations were in the course of your doing that. Except for the notations on the reverse side of the envelope, is the letter and is the envelope, each in the same condition now as when you received it?

Mrs. PAINE. No; I have made a few underlinings.

Mr. JENNER. Would you identify any additions you placed on the original document, indicating the page, front or reverse side?

Mrs. PAINE. I have marked "bind"——

Mr. JENNER. Is that b-i-n-d?

Mrs. PAINE. Over one word.

Mr. JENNER. Have you written the word "bind"? Is that what you mean?

Mrs. PAINE. B-i-n-d.

Mr. JENNER. And that is an interpretation, I take it of a word written in Russian underneath it.

Mrs. PAINE. Yes.

Mr. JENNER. And that word then to you in English was "bind", b-i-n-d.

Mrs. PAINE. Yes.

Mr. JENNER. Anything else?

Mrs. PAINE. I have written the word "thaw" and crossed it out; that was wrong.

Mr. JENNER. Meaning what, Mrs. Paine?

Mrs. PAINE. I had the wrong translation for that word. I realized it later.

Mr. JENNER. What was the word rather than——

Mrs. PAINE. The meaning was "insists"; the rest of the markings by me are underlinings.

Mr. JENNER. I will cover those by asking you this. Were there any underlinings on the letter placed there by Marina Oswald at the time you received the letter?

Mrs. PAINE. Only one, under this word here.

Mr. JENNER. That is on the reverse side of the second page of the letter?

Mrs. PAINE. It is on the last page. The second page; yes.

Mr. JENNER. It is the reverse side of the second sheet of paper?

Mrs. PAINE. Right.

Mr. JENNER. And it looks to help from her as though it is an arrow, is that correct?

Mrs. PAINE. There is an underline and then from the underlined word is an arrow.

Mr. JENNER. I offer in evidence as Commission Exhibits Nos. 407 and 408 the documents now so marked and identified by the witness.

Mr. McCLOY. They may be admitted.

(The documents referred to, heretofore marked for identification as Commission Exhibits Nos. 407 and 408, were received in evidence.)

Mr. JENNER. Would you retain that for a moment, please?

Mr. DULLES. May I ask, is the envelope 408A attached?

Mr. JENNER. Yes; and in the case of the earlier exhibit the envelope——

Mrs. PAINE. It is only the second envelope we have had.

Mr. JENNER. The envelope accompanying Exhibit 404 was marked 404A, and the envelope now accompanying 408 is marked 408A.

Mr. McCLOY. Is it so marked now?

Mr. DULLES. Do you wish me to mark it?

(The enevelope was marked Commission Exhibit 408A for identification and received in evidence.)

Mr. JENNER. Have you supplied the Commission, Mrs. Paine, with your translation of that letter?

Mrs. PAINE. Yes, I have.

Mr. JENNER. And your interpretation and the effect or the impression that you had of that letter when you received it and as you read it?

Mrs. PAINE. Yes.

Mr. JENNER. Now, turning to the first page, I would like to direct attention——

Mr. DULLES. Do you wish this back?

Mrs. PAINE. No; I will look at the translation.

Mr. JENNER. She has supplied me with an interpretation. In the first paragraph it reads and I quote, and you follow me, please. I will read the whole paragraph:

"Here it is already a week since I received your letter. I can't produce any excuses as there are no valid reasons. I am ashamed to confess that I am a person of moods and my mood currently is such that I don't feel much like anything. As soon as you left all love stopped and I am very hurt that Lee's attitude toward me is such that I feel each minute that I bind him. He insists that I leave America which I don't want to do at all. I like America very much and I think that even without Lee I would not be lost here. What do you think?"

Had you had any discussion with Marina when you were in New Orleans on the subject matters which I have just read to you from the first paragraph of her letter, Commission Exhibit No. 408?

Mrs. PAINE. There was no such discussion in New Orleans.

Mr. JENNER. What impact did this have on you, Mrs. Paine, when you received this letter and read that first paragraph?

Mrs. PAINE. It was a repetition, or similar to something she had told me late in March, which I have already put on the record yesterday, saying basically that he wanted her to go back, wanted to send her back to the Soviet Union.

Mr. JENNER. And to send her back alone, is that correct?

Mrs. PAINE. That was the impression I carried.

Mr. JENNER. Was there ever any occassion, during all your acquaintance with the Oswalds, when there was any suggestion or implication that if she returned to Russia, at his request, that he would accompany her?

Mrs. PAINE. There was no such suggestion.

Mr. JENNER. Was it always that she was to go to Russia alone?

Mrs. PAINE. As she described it, it carried from her the feeling that she was being sent away.

Mr. JENNER. What about the little child, June?

Mrs. PAINE. June with her.

Mr. JENNER. Was to accompany her to Russia. Now, the second paragraph, if I may:

"This is the basic question which doesn't leave me day or night. And again Lee has said to me that he doesn't love me. So you see we came to mistaken conclusions. It is hard for you and me to live without a return of our love interest gone. How would it all end?"

Had there been discussions between you and Marina Oswald on the subject of whether or not her husband had love for her, and in that area?

Mrs. PAINE. What I particularly recall is what I mentioned yesterday, when he telephoned her and said he had found a job and wanted her to come——

Mr. JENNER. This was just before going to New Orleans?

Mrs. PAINE. Just before going to New Orleans.

Mr. JENNER. In the spring?

Mrs. PAINE. Right. She said "Papa loves us," as I have testified. She had wondered to me during the 2 weeks previous whether he did, whether she loved him. But was clearly elated by his call and gradually came to her own conclusions. Really, I had no ground upon which to make a conclusion.

Mr. DULLES. She was speaking in Russian then to you?

Mrs. PAINE. Yes.

Mr. JENNER. Now, were you impressed that this paragraph, however, was not consistent with her immediate response at the time that telephone call had been made to her?

Mrs. PAINE. It showed me there was not as much change as she had hoped.

Mr. JENNER. Did you have any discussion with her on this subject when you were in New Orleans, and when you took her or when you were taking her from Irving, Tex., to New Orleans?

Mrs. PAINE. No.

Mr. JENNER. None whatsoever. When you were in New Orleans, Mrs. Paine, did you tour any night clubs?

Mrs. PAINE. No.

Mr. JENNER. Did you or Marina ever evidence any interest in touring Bourbon Street, for example?

Mrs. PAINE. You are talking about the spring visit?

Mr. JENNER. Yes; I am.

Mrs. PAINE. We went to the French Quarter during the day.

Mr. JENNER. Please identify whom you include when you say "we."

Mrs. PAINE. Lee, Marina, I, and three children.

Mr. JENNER. Did all of you, including Lee, go to the French Quarter?

Mrs. PAINE. Yes; we did.

Mr. JENNER. Did you tour the Bourbon Street areas, Royal Street, and the other areas?

Mrs. PAINE. No; we did not.

Mr. JENNER. Will you tell us without any length—you did not. This was a tourist visit of the French Quarter, is that right?

Mrs. PAINE. Yes.

Mr. JENNER. In the day?

Mrs. PAINE. Yes.

Mr. JENNER. With the children?

Mrs. PAINE. Yes.

Mr. JENNER. Was anything said during the course of that tourist visit about visiting Bourbon Street at night rather than in the daytime?

Mrs. PAINE. I don't recall that there was anything said.

Mr. JENNER. Was there any discussion about Lee Oswald visiting or frequenting night clubs?

Mrs. PAINE. None.

Mr. JENNER. Either in Dallas, or in New Orleans or in Irving, Tex.?

Mrs. PAINE. None; at any time.

Mr. JENNER. Did any one of you tour Bourbon Street at night during that spring visit?

Mrs. PAINE. No.

Mr. JENNER. Any discussion of the subject?

Mrs. PAINE. Not to my recollection.

Mr. JENNER. Was there a subsequent occasion when you did visit Bourbon Street at night?

Mrs. PAINE. In September, when I visited again in New Orleans. Shall I tell that?

Mr. JENNER. Yes; please, because there is a measure of contrast to that I would like to bring out.

Mrs. PAINE. Marina and I and our three small children went down in the early evening and walked along the street.

Mr. JENNER. Would you tell us how that came about, whether Lee Oswald accompanied you?

Mrs. PAINE. He did not accompany us. He was asked if he wanted to go, and he said he did not. Marina was interested in my seeing Bourbon Street at night simply as a tourist attraction.

Mr. JENNER. And you two girls took your children?

Mrs. PAINE. Yes.

Mr. JENNER. Did she take June?

Mrs. PAINE. Yes.

Mr. JENNER. You two girls walked down Bourbon Street?

Mrs. PAINE. And one of us very pregnant.

Mr. JENNER. And observed everything from the outside. You didn't go inside any night clubs?

Mrs. PAINE. No. In fact, when I realized we weren't permitted, we went on.

Mr. JENNER. You had small children?

Mrs. PAINE. Yes.

Mr. JENNER. Was there any discussion with Mr. Oswald at that time or with Marina which led you to form a judgment as to whether he was a man who might or would, or had frequented night clubs?

Mrs. PAINE. I judged he was not such a person.

Mr. JENNER. In all your experiences with the Oswalds from February, sometime in February 1963, even to the present date, had any mention been made of Lee Oswald frequenting night clubs?

Mrs. PAINE. None.

Mr. JENNER. Or of Marina at any time?

Mrs. PAINE. No mention of her.

Mr. DULLES. Did you get the impression when you made this trip that Marina had previously made the trip herself, that she seemed to know the surroundings?

Mrs. PAINE. This occurs in the next paragraph of the letter she wrote in May, so I knew she had been herself.

Mr. DULLES. She had been there before?

Mrs. PAINE. Yes. From the letter I judge with Lee accompanying her.

Mr. JENNER. Mrs. Paine, if you will pardon me. Mr. Reporter, will you read the question?

(Question read.)

Mr. JENNER. Would you answer just that question?

Mrs. PAINE. Yes.

Mr. McCLOY. She did answer it.

Mr. JENNER. I didn't think she did.

Mr. DULLES. I think she said "yes."

Mr. JENNER. Now the letter of May 25th to you does make reference to visits to the French Quarter, is that correct?

Mrs. PAINE. Yes.

Mr. JENNER. Gentlemen of the Commission, that portion of the letter reads as follows:

"Now a bit about the impressions I have received this week. Last Saturday we went to Aunt Lillian's"—Aunt Lillian, Mrs. Paine, is Lee Oswald's aunt?

Mrs. PAINE. Yes.

Mr. JENNER. Mrs. Murret?

Mrs. PAINE. Mrs. Murret.

Mr. JENNER. "And leaving June with her we are at the lake. Lee wanted to catch crabs but caught nothing. I have a very high opinion of his relatives."

By the way, what was your opinion of his relatives?

Mrs. PAINE. I met them only once. I thought them to be very nice.

Mr. JENNER. "Straightforward and kind people. To me they are very attentive. I like them. We have been to the French Quarter in the evening. It is a shame you didn't manage to get there in the evening. For me it was especially interesting as it was the first time in my life I had seen such. There were many night clubs there. Through the open doors were visible barrel covered dancing girls (so as not to say entirely unclothed). Most of them had really very pretty, rare figures and if one doesn't think about too many things then one can like them very much. There were a great many tourists there. For the most part very rich. We have been to the near park again."

That is all of that paragraph dealing with the nightclubs. Now, did you ever know a man or person by the name of Jack Rubinstein or Jack Ruby?

Mrs. PAINE. No.

Mr. JENNER. Prior to November 24, 1963?

Mrs. PAINE. No.

Mr. JENNER. Did you ever hear of any such individual?

Mrs. PAINE. No, I did not.

Mr. JENNER. Had you frequented a nightclub in Irving or in Dallas prior to November 24, 1963?

Mrs. PAINE. Not at any time. In either town.

Mr. JENNER. You and your husband Michael were not in the habit of visiting, frequenting nightclubs?

Mrs. PAINE. No.

Mr. JENNER. It is a fact, is it not, Mrs. Paine that neither you nor Mr. Paine attended nightclubs at all?

Mrs. PAINE. That is correct.

Mr. JENNER. Is this true prior to your moving to Irving?

Mrs. PAINE. Yes.

Mr. JENNER. Was there anything that occurred during all these months of your acquaintance with the Oswalds that did or might have led you to any opinion as to Lee's frequenting of nightclubs or his acquaintance with nightclubs or his being intimate with nightclub people?

Mrs. PAINE. During the entire time, is that your question?

Mr. JENNER. Yes. Let us end the day for you for this purpose at November 22, 1963?

Mrs. PAINE. He was, I would say, actively disinterested in going down to Bourbon Street in the last weekend in September.

Mr. JENNER. But even prior to that time?

Mrs. PAINE. It was the 21st.

Mr. JENNER. Had anything occurred by way of a remark at all that made an impression on you in the area of his being acquainted possibly with any nightclub people, any entertainers?

Mrs. PAINE. There had been no hint of any sort that he was acquainted with nightclub people?

Mr. McCLOY. Whether in Dallas, New Orleans or Irving?

Mrs. PAINE. That is right. Of course, I had not talked to him a great deal up to the New Orleans trip. Then after that time there was also no hint or mention of any nightclub people. After that time in New Orleans he did refuse table wine at my home, so I got the impression of him as a person who didn't like to drink.

Mr. JENNER. During all your acquaintance with Lee Harvey Oswald, did you ever see him take a drink of spirits, intoxicating spirits?

Mrs. PAINE. It is possible he had beer at the initial party on the 22d of February, that is as far as I can remember.

Mr. JENNER. What impression did you have of him as a man of temperance?

Mrs. PAINE. He teased Marina about liking wine as if it displeased him mildly.

Mr. JENNER. Excuse me, Mrs. Paine. You are talking in terms of conclusions which is all right with me if you will give me the specifics also. Could you give us an example or an occasion of what you have in mind?

Mrs. PAINE. Well, at the same occasion when he refused the wine, she had some.

Mr. JENNER. I see. Did he say something that led you to say he was teasing her?

Mrs. PAINE. Yes.

Mr. JENNER. Would you describe what that was?

Mrs. PAINE. Indicating a mild disapproval.

Mr. JENNER. Would you please relate to the Commission your impression of Marina Oswald as a temperate person?

Mrs. PAINE. She did not like liquors.

Mr. JENNER. What we would call hard liquor?

Mrs. PAINE. Strong spirits.

Mr. JENNER. Strong spirits.

Mrs. PAINE. But she did drink beer at my home, and did occasionally have wine.

Mr. JENNER. She occasionally had a bit of wine and she occasionally had some beer?

Mrs. PAINE. Yes.

Mr. JENNER. Is that the extent of, as far as your personal knowledge is concerned, her indulgence in intoxicating spirits?

Mrs. PAINE. That is right.

Mr. JENNER. Does that likewise describe your indulgence or do you——

Mrs. PAINE. I would also drink a cocktail on occasion.

Mr. JENNER. But very limited and just an occasional drink?

Mrs. PAINE. Yes.

Mr. JENNER. Is that likewise true of your husband, Michael?

Mrs. PAINE. Yes.

Representative FORD. Did Marina ever drink to excess?

Mrs. PAINE. Certainly not that I ever heard about or saw.

Mr. JENNER. Not that you ever heard about or that you saw?

Mrs. PAINE. Or saw.

Mr. JENNER. From your testimony that is certainly true with Lee Harvey Oswald?

Mrs. PAINE. It is certainly true of him also.

Mr. JENNER. As far as you are concerned?

Mrs. PAINE. As far as I am concerned.

Mr. JENNER. Now, I think you testified yesterday that Marina would assist you in your becoming more proficient in the Russian language by returning letters that you had written her, upon which she would place her comments of instruction or criticism or suggestion?

Mrs. PAINE. Before she left for New Orleans in May, she offered to correct and send back any letters I wrote to her. In the correspondence which included some four letters with her altogether, there was only one of mine that was actually corrected and sent back and you have that.

Mr. JENNER. I have marked a three-page document as Commission Exhibit 409, and the envelope as Commission Exhibit 409A, the envelope being postmarked at New Orleans on June 6, 1963, and being addressed to Mrs. Ruth Paine.

Mrs. PAINE. Do you want to make a separate designation for my return letter? You are looking at the letter which accompanied her letter.

Mr. JENNER. That document I will mark as Commission Exhibit——may I have permission, Mr. Chairman, to mark this document in my own hand because the sticker, I am afraid, will obliterate some of the letter.

Mr. McCLOY. You may.

Mr. JENNER. I will mark this as 409B.

Now, Mrs. Paine, would you be good enough to identify 409, 409A, and 409B, the sequence in which they passed back and forth between you and Mrs. Oswald?

Mrs. PAINE. It includes, No. 409 is my letter to her dated the 1st of June, which she——

Mr. JENNER. 1963?

Mrs. PAINE. 1963.

Mr. JENNER. Is that document, or do you recognize the handwriting on that document?

Mrs. PAINE. That is my hand.

Mr. JENNER. Would you turn to the reverse side of the second page, third page. I see there is something on that in red crayon.

Mrs. PAINE. All the red marks and the little bit in ballpoint pen are made by her.

Mr. JENNER. That is what I was seeking to bring out.

Mrs. PAINE. At the end it includes a note of comments.

Mr. JENNER. Now, Mrs. Paine, the portion of the letter in blue ink in longhand is in whose handwriting?

Mrs. PAINE. In my handwriting.

Mr. JENNER. And the portion of the letter in red crayon on the reverse side of the third page is in whose handwriting?

Mrs. PAINE. Is in her handwriting.

Mr. JENNER. On the first page is there any of her handwriting?

Mrs. PAINE. On the first page in blue ink, ballpoint pen there is some handwriting which is hers at the top.

Mr. JENNER. Those are notations in between the lines or in the margin?

Mrs. PAINE. Above my writing. Yes, sir.

Mr. JENNER. They are comments of hers on your letter?

Mrs. PAINE. And my spelling.

Mr. JENNER. Of your spelling?

Mrs. PAINE. Yes.

Mr. JENNER. Do any of those markings appear other than on the face of the first sheet?

Mrs. PAINE. In blue ink you are asking?

Mr. JENNER. Yes, I am.

Mrs. PAINE. No. The rest is all in red.

Mr. JENNER. That then was a letter that you had sent to her?

Mrs. PAINE. That is right.

Mr. JENNER. Was it returned to you?

Mrs. PAINE. Yes.

Mr. JENNER. Did some document which you now have before you accompany the letter on its return?

Mrs. PAINE. Her letter dated June 5th.

Mr. JENNER. Which has been marked Commission Exhibit 409B?

Mrs. PAINE. Yes.

Mr. JENNER. And you do recognize that handwriting as having been hers?

Mrs. PAINE. Yes; I do.

Mr. JENNER. Of the two documents you have now identified, 409 and 409B, were they enclosed in an envelope?

Mrs. PAINE. Yes; they were.

Mr. JENNER. Is that envelope before you?

Mrs. PAINE. Yes.

Mr. JENNER. It is marked Commission Exhibit 409A?

Mrs. PAINE. Yes.

Mr. JENNER. Are all those conditions of documents in the condition which they were in when you received them?

Mrs. PAINE. I have again added in my hand on her letter.

Mr. JENNER. That is 409B?

Mrs. PAINE. Translations of certain of the words.

Mr. JENNER. Would you please, for the purpose of the record, identify what your handwriting is, on the letter 409B.

Mrs. PAINE. It is above her words. Most of it is in English.

Mr. JENNER. That is in your hand?

Mrs. PAINE. Yes.

Mr. JENNER. Other than that, are the documents in the condition they were when you received them?

Mrs. PAINE. Yes.

Mr. JENNER. There is one interesting thing to me, Mrs. Paine, to which I would like to draw the attention of the Commission. And I direct your attention in this respect to Exhibits 404, 404A, 408, 408A, 409, and 409A. Each has an envelope addressed to you, and each is addressed written in English.

Is the handwriting on each of those envelopes Marina Oswald's?

Mrs. PAINE. It is.

Mr. JENNER. She was then able to write some English, is that so?

Mrs. PAINE. Yes.

Mr. JENNER. Would you please——

Mrs. PAINE. She learned her own address.

Mr. JENNER. Did her command of the use of the English language, at least from the writing standpoint, extend beyond those examples?

Mrs. PAINE. Not to my knowledge. I knew that she looked at signs and had learned the sound value of the English letters. That she looked at the Thursday supplement to the newspaper for the ads on vegetables and things with pictures on a can or something that showed the English of what it was, to try to determine what this word was and pronounce it.

Mr. JENNER. So she did acquire some command of English with respect to reading newspapers?

Mrs. PAINE. It was not my impression that she could read a newspaper. She could pick out the sound values. It was not until October that I read with her a portion from Time magazine regarding Madam Nhu, whenever that was news, she asked me to read this to her and translate it. I read it.

Mr. JENNER. Did you read it in English first?

Mrs. PAINE. I read it in English, giving translation of some of the words.

Mr. JENNER. As you went along?

Mrs. PAINE. As I went along.

Mr. JENNER. All right.

Mrs. PAINE. But many of the words, English words, were words she understood, because they were either similar to the Russian or because she had learned them.

I was surprised at how much she understood when I pronounced it and read it to her.

Representative FORD. In English?

Mrs. PAINE. In English. Because she was very hesitant to speak English with me, fearful that her pronunciation would not be correct. She would ask me several times, "How do I pronounce this," although she didn't think she was doing very well with the pronunciation, although she did well.

Mr. JENNER. She was sensitive in this respect, Mrs. Paine, she was hesitant to use the English language in the presence, say, of Americans or even the Russian emigré groups?

489

Mrs. PAINE. I think most people are sensitive about using a language when the person they are with can understand them in the language they use better. She also talked with my immediate neighbor for a short time, when only she and the neighbor were present. I went to see about a child.

Mr. JENNER. Could your neighbor understand Russian?

Mrs. PAINE. No.

Mr. JENNER. But there was a measure of communication?

Mrs. PAINE. There was some communication, not a great deal. My neighbor told me after she saw Marina on television in January, whatever it was, "that girl has learned a great deal of English." She was amazed at the change.

Representative FORD. The improvement from October to January?

Mrs. PAINE. Yes.

Mr. DULLES. How would you appraise her general intelligence, her level of intelligence for a girl of that age in the early twenties?

Mrs. PAINE. I think she certainly had above average intelligence.

Representative FORD. What prompted her, if you know, to ask about Madam Nhu?

Mrs. PAINE. She was interested in the family. She was worried about what Madam Nhu would do. Madam Nhu and the children still in her country. She wanted to know were these children going to come out either in Paris or the United States. She was concerned, and her concern for world affairs seemed to go this way, of what is this mother and children going to do.

Mr. JENNER. Was she concerned about the conflict between the North Vietnamese and the South Vietnamese?

Mrs. PAINE. No; this didn't interest her, it didn't appear to.

Mr. JENNER. It was the human side rather than the political side?

Mrs. PAINE. Strictly that.

Mr. JENNER. Thank you; that is what I wanted to bring out. I offer in evidence, Mr. Chairman, as Exhibits with those numbers, the documents marked Commission Exhibits 409, 409-A, and 409-B.

Mr. McCLOY. It may be admitted.

(The documents referred to previously, marked Commission Exhibits Nos. 409, 409-A, and 409-B, were received in evidence.)

(At this point, Representative Boggs entered the hearing room.)

Mr. JENNER. Now, Mrs. Paine, turning to this series of correspondence which has now been admitted in evidence, have you made an interpretation for the Commission of Exhibit 409-B?

Mrs. PAINE. Yes; I have.

Mr. JENNER. Where does that appear on your summary you furnished to me last evening?

Mrs. PAINE. That begins in the middle of page 6, marked second letter from New Orleans.

Mr. JENNER. All right. Your interpretation of the letter dealing with the night club visit of the Oswalds, you have interpreted that for the Commission, and that appears on page what of your summary?

Mrs. PAINE. That appears on page 3 marked first letter from New Orleans.

Mr. JENNER. All right. Were you concerned about Mrs. Oswald, about Marina's condition and her receiving proper medical attention?

Mrs. PAINE. I was very concerned about it.

Mr. JENNER. Did you write her at any time about it?

Mrs. PAINE. I would like to refer you to my letter of June 1st which was returned in the document you just admitted in evidence.

Mr. JENNER. You did write her about it?

Mrs. PAINE. I wrote particularly in that letter to Lee.

Mr. JENNER. You wrote both Lee and Marina?

Mrs. PAINE. In this letter I addressed each, and a particular portion of that letter is in English.

Mr. JENNER. And that is Commission Exhibit No. 409?

Mrs. PAINE. That was to Lee, that particular portion.

Mr. JENNER. You incorporated, did you not, in that letter, a direct communication to Lee Oswald?

Mrs. PAINE. I say in Russian a few words to Lee now about hospital and money.

Mr. JENNER. But incorporated in your note in that letter to Lee Oswald you used the English rather than the Russian language, did you not?

Mrs. PAINE. I wanted to speak of things I couldn't say in Russian. I didn't have the vocabulary to do it with any ease in Russian.

Mr. JENNER. I see.

Mrs. PAINE. And further I particularly wanted to tell him I thought it important she get to a doctor and have prenatal care and felt he would be the one who actually got her there. It was his concern that would produce a visit to the doctor.

Mr. JENNER. I see. That explains that portion of the letter which is Commission Exhibit No. 409.

Mrs. PAINE. 409.

Mr. JENNER. I won't go into the details, Mr. Chairman, because these are recommendations of Mrs. Paine for medical care of Marina Oswald.

Mr. McCLOY. Do I understand you are going to read all of these into the record at the noon hour?

Mr. JENNER. At the noon hour I will read all of these into the record rather than do it now. Now you, last night, Mrs Paine, suggested to me you would like to make an explanation of this series of letters, and I direct your attention to page 7 of your notes.

Mrs. PAINE. Well, the commentary on page 7 by me is——

Mr. JENNER. Refreshing your recollection from having read it, you would like to make a statement to the Commission and you may proceed to do so.

Mrs. PAINE. It doesn't refresh me enough. I could say this. That when I received 409–B, her letter, I read it through. I glanced at 409, her corrected—my letter which she had corrected, and at the note at the back which began, "You write well" and assumed this to be commentary on my letter; it was not until I sat down nearly a month later to write a proper reply to her, I read this through more carefully and found in the middle of the paragraph discussing my writing a comment by her saying, "Very likely I will have to go back to Russia after all."

Mr. JENNER. For the purpose of the record there appears the red crayon to which I earlier drew your attention on the back of page 3.

Would you read that entire notation of hers so that the Commission may now know that to which you are now directing your attention?

Mrs. PAINE. In the back of my letter she writes in red pencil, "You write well, when will I write that way in English. I think never. Very likely I will have to go back to Russia after all. A pity."

Mr. DULLES. What was the last?

Mrs. PAINE. "A pity."

Mr. JENNER. I take it when you first read that notation on the back of the third page of the letter you had not noticed the sentence, "Very likely I will have to go to Russia after all. A pity."

Mrs. PAINE. Yes.

Mr. JENNER. Would you proceed with your comment?

Mrs. PAINE. This was early July when I read this letter more carefully and I was shocked that I hadn't noticed this. That my poor Russian made a scanning of the letter not adequate to picking that up, and I wrote her immediately apologizing for my bad understanding, and I don't have that letter, but I have three which followed it, and——

Mr. JENNER. Excuse me. Do you have a draft, have you produced for the Commission your immediate preceding draft of that letter?

Mrs. PAINE. I have no rough draft of my first letter explaining my shock and my worry at this statement of hers.

Mr. JENNER. I see.

Mrs. PAINE. But I have rough drafts of three letters I wrote subsequently.

Mr. JENNER. Have you ever seen at any time a copy or the original of the letter that you wrote, a draft of which you do not have?

Mrs. PAINE. No; I haven't.

Mr. JENNER. Would you please relate to the Commisson your present recollection of the substance and content of that letter?

Mrs. PAINE. Much what I have said. That I apologized that my poor Russian didn't see this immediately and I inquired after her what she was doing, and asked to hear from her.

Mr. JENNER. You say, that sentence when you finally did read it rather shocked you. Would you rather—would you elaborate on that statement to the Commission? Why did that shock you?

Mrs. PAINE. It seemed more final than anything else that had preceded. She had told me in March that he had asked her to go back, that she had written to the embassy but she didn't reply to the embassy when the embassy inquired why. It looked as though she was able to just say no by not doing anything about it. But this, on the other hand, looked as if she was resigned to the necessity to go back.

Mr. JENNER. Were you aware at this time, Mrs. Paine, that Lee had applied to the State Department for a passport and had obtained one?

Mrs. PAINE. No; I was not aware of that.

Mr. JENNER. When did you first become aware of that, if you ever did?

Mrs. PAINE. It was considerably after the assassination, and I read it in a paper. I still don't remember what time or day it was.

Mr. JENNER. Now, did you write Marina on or about the 11th of July?

Mrs. PAINE. I have a rough draft of that date.

Mr. JENNER. I hand you a document of two pages which has been identified as Commission Exhibit No. 410.

(The document referred to was marked Commission Exhibit No. 410 for identification.)

Would you please tell us what that document is?

Mrs. PAINE. This is the rough draft, to which I just referred, written to Marina.

Mr. JENNER. And you thereupon prepared the final draft and sent it?

Mrs. PAINE. That is correct.

Mr. JENNER. This represents, does it not, your best recollection of the contents of the letter, the letter in its final form as you transmitted it to Marina?

Mrs. PAINE. I think this is probably a very accurate repesentation of the letter in its final form. It was the first time I put on paper an invitation to her to come and stay with me for anything more than a few weeks around the birth of the baby.

Mr. JENNER. Have you supplied the Commission with a translation of your letter?

Mrs. PAINE. Yes; I have.

Mr. JENNER. And that appears at the bottom of page 7 of your notes which you have supplied to me?

Mrs. PAINE. That is correct.

Mr. JENNER. I direct your attention, if I may, and the attention of the Commission as interpreted by Mrs. Paine, the first sentence reads, "Dear Marina, if Lee doesn't wish to live with you any more and prefers that you go to the Soviet Union, think about the possibility of living with me."

You just said is that the portion of your letter which you say this is the first invitation you made to Marina to come to live with you generally?

Mrs. PAINE. This was the first written invitation.

Mr. JENNER. I see.

Mrs. PAINE. I had made an informal invitation face to face when she was staying the first week in May, but felt as I made it that she didn't take this seriously.

Mr. JENNER. Now, you go on in your letter and you make reference, for example, to—let's take the second paragraph of your letter appearing at the top of page 8 of your notes, "You know I have long received from my parents, I live dependent a long time. I would be happy to be an aunt to you and I can. We have sufficient money. Michael will be glad. This I know. He just gave me $500 for the vacation or something necessary. With this money it is possible to pay the doctor and hospital in October when the baby is born, believe God. All will be well for you and the children. I confess that I think that the opportunity for me to know you came from God. Perhaps it is not so but I think and believe so."

492

Had you discussed this matter with your husband?

Mrs. PAINE. Yes; I had.

Mr. JENNER. And you were still living separate and apart at that time?

Mrs. PAINE. Yes. But I felt so long as I was not yet earning, he would be the one, in fact, who was supporting all of us.

Mr. JENNER. I think the Commission might be interested in that. You were not taking this action, either in the earlier stage in the early spring or in the summer of inviting Marina to live with you without discussing that with your husband even though you and your husband at that time were separated?

Mrs. PAINE. That is correct.

Mr. JENNER. Did you do anything, Mrs. Paine, in this connection with respect to keeping Lee Oswald informed of your invitations and your communications in this area with Marina?

Mrs. PAINE. I wrote into the letter that I hoped—well you might just read the last paragraph.

Mr. JENNER. Would you mind reading it?

Mrs. PAINE. I will read it, the last paragraph in the letter, and I might say that the entire letter I wrote with the possibility in mind that he should see this.

Mr. JENNER. Did you desire that he do see it?

Mrs. PAINE. I wanted him to—her to feel free to show it to him. I didn't want her to come to my house if this offended or injured him, if this was in some way——

(At this point, Senator Cooper entered the hearing room.)

Mr. JENNER. Divisive?

Mrs. PAINE. If he did in fact want to keep his family together, I certainly wanted him to, but if the bulk of his feelings lay on the side of wanting to be away, separated from Marina, then I thought it was legitimate for him to have that alternative, although it was not legitimate for him to simply send her back if she didn't want to go.

Mr. JENNER. Send her back where?

Mrs. PAINE. To the Soviet Union, if she didn't want to go. So in this light I will read the last paragraph of Commission Exhibit 410:

"I don't want to hurt Lee with this invitation to you. Only I think that it would be better that you and he do not live together if you do not receive happiness. I understand how Michael feels. He doesn't love me and wants a chance to look for another life and another wife. He must do this, it seems, and so it is better for us not to live together. I don't know how Lee feels. I would like to know. Surely things are hard for him now, too. I hope that he would be glad to see you with me where he can know that you and the children will receive everything that is necessary and he would not need to worry about it. Thus he could start life again."

Mr. JENNER. Mrs. Paine, having all this in mind and what you have testified to up to now, would you please tell the gentlemen of the Commission the factors and motivations you had in inviting Marina to come live with you; first to have her baby, next on a more extended scale, all of the factors that motivated you in your offer, in your own words?

Mrs. PAINE. The first invitation, just to come for a few weeks at the time of the birth is a simpler question, I will answer that first.

I felt that she would need someone simply to take care of her older child for the time that she was in the hospital, and that things would be easier for her if she didn't have to immediately take up the full household chores upon returning from the hospital. This was a very simple offer.

Mr. JENNER. That was all that motivated you at that time?

Mrs. PAINE. Now, in asking her to come and stay for a more extended period, I had many feelings. I was living alone with my children, at that time, had been since the previous fall, nearly a year, at the time this letter is written. I had no idea that my husband might move back to the house. I was tired of living alone and lonely, and here was a woman who was alone and in a sense also, if Lee, in fact didn't want to be with her, and further she was a person I liked. I had lived with her 2 weeks in late April and early May. I enjoyed her company.

Further, being able to talk Russian with her added a wider dimension to my rather small and boring life as a young mother. I didn't want to go out and get a job because I wanted to be home with my children, but on the other hand, I saw a way to, and that is part of what studying Russian altogether is for me, a way to make my daily life more interesting. I also felt when I first heard in March that Lee was wanting to send Marina back, that is how it was presented to me, that it just seemed a shame that our country couldn't be a more hospitable thing for her if she wanted so much to stay, that I thought she should have that opportunity.

I was pleased that she liked America, and thought that she should have a chance to stay here and raise her children here as she wished.

I might say also if I had not been living alone I would not have undertaken such an invitation. My house is small and it wouldn't have gone with married life.

Mr. JENNER. I wanted to afford you that opportunity. Now, you have related all the factors that motivated you?

Mrs. PAINE. Yes.

Mr. JENNER. I offer in evidence as Commission Exhibit No. 410 the document which has been so identified.

Mr. McCLOY. It may be admitted.

(The document referred to, previously marked as Commission Exhibit No. 410 for identification, was received in evidence.)

Mr. McCLOY. We have been going for an hour and a half. If you would like to have a recess you may have it.

Mrs. PAINE. I am all right.

Mr. McCLOY. All right, we will go on then.

Mr. JENNER. You mentioned in the course of your explanation earlier a series of three letters. I hand you a draft of letter dated July 12, 1963, addressed to Dear Marina, consisting of two pages, which we will mark as Commission Exhibit No. 411. And another one-page letter which we will mark as Commission Exhibit No. 412.

In whose handwriting is each of those exhibits?

Mrs. PAINE. Each of these are in my handwriting.

Mr. JENNER. And they are drafts, are they?

Mrs. PAINE. They are.

Mr. JENNER. And you would then, after making those drafts put them in final form?

Mrs. PAINE. That is correct.

Mr. JENNER. Did you transmit the final draft of letter to Marina Oswald?

Mrs. PAINE. I mailed them to her address in New Orleans.

Mr. JENNER. Have you supplied me with your translation of both of those drafts?

Mrs. PAINE. I have.

Mr. JENNER. Each draft is in your handwriting?

Mrs. PAINE. Yes.

Mr. JENNER. And the interpretations appearing at the bottom of page 8 and the bottom of page 9 are the material you supplied me and they consist of your interpretations of those letters or translations, rather?

Mrs. PAINE. That is right. They are dated respectively July 12 and July 14.

Mr. JENNER. I hand you a picture copy rather than a photostatic copy of a two-page letter dated July 14, 1963, and a translation of that letter which we will mark as Commission Exhibits Nos. 413 and 414, respectively.

(The documents referred to were marked Commission Exhibits Nos. 413 and 414 for identification.)

Mr. JENNER. Directing your attention to Exhibit 413, would you tell us what that is?

Mrs. PAINE. This appears to be a photograph of the letter I then wrote from my final draft and sent to Marina, dated the 14th of July.

Mr. JENNER. So that Exhibit No. 413 is the——

Mrs. PAINE. 413, the photograph.

Mr. JENNER. 413 is to the best of your recollection an actual picture of your final draft letter as transmitted to Marina?

Mrs. PAINE. Yes.

Mr. JENNER. Now directing your attention to page 10 of the material that you supplied me, and which you discussed with me last evening, you wished to make a statement to the Commission with respect to this letter, do you?

Mrs. PAINE. Yes.

Mr. JENNER. All right. Would you please proceed to do so?

Mrs. PAINE. I think it would be easier if I read what is here.

Mr. JENNER. Any way you want to handle it, Mrs. Paine.

Mrs. PAINE. Marina stayed with me 2 weeks in the spring as you know, and I realized then what a proud and capable person she is. She was not accustomed to accept help from others, and I knew that her pride and independence would be a stumbling block to her accepting help even though she needed it.

I respected her for this and somehow I wanted to ease such acceptance for her, and to explain that the situation I proposed would be a situation of mutual help. I hoped—now I should say that in Commission Exhibit——

Mr. JENNER. They are to your right on the table.

Mrs. PAINE. Yes; 411 and 412, I mentioned that if she were counted as a dependent on Michael's income tax his yearly payment to the government would be reduced by a certain amount, and that by that amount she—we could very nearly live—her expenses could very nearly come under this, so it would be more a case of breaking even than a case of her accepting so much as she might think from us. But I think that in fact this reference to the tax reduction did not encourage her, as I had hoped.

Mr. JENNER. It wasn't quite correct either, was it, Mrs. Paine?

(Laughter.)

Mrs. PAINE. Did I get a chance to read the second letter as written at 2 a.m. and I was hopeful only more than——

Mr. JENNER. Mrs. Paine, I think the members of the Commission and also you from our talk last night, are interested in your letters which you have now identified suggesting financial arrangements to Mrs. Oswald, since to one who might read them without knowing the background they might seem crass.

Mrs. PAINE. I felt crass in Russian, particularly.

Mr. JENNER. I was not thinking in terms of your difficulty in communicating with her, but you had no selfish or ulterior financial motive, did you, in this connection?

Mrs. PAINE. Did it appear that?

Mr. JENNER. It might.

Mrs. PAINE. Even with such bad arithmetic.

Mr. JENNER. Your arithmetic was all right. Your interpretation of the law was not as good as it might be.

Mr. DULLES. Am I not correct, I understood you were trying to make her feel she was not going to be a burden to you?

Mrs. PAINE. That is right.

Mr. DULLES. And were using certain subterfuges to accomplish that; that is the impression I got from what you said.

Mrs. PAINE. That is absolutely correct. That I hoped, and further I would say in the letters to her I made reference that this money not paid to the government would be therefore available for spending money for her. I had put myself in her position and thought wouldn't it be terrible to have to ask for a nickel for a package of Lifesavers every time you wanted it, and thought I wouldn't want to be in such a situation if she doesn't have her own, something she can count upon as her own money, it would be unbearable to her.

So I tried to cast about both for a way of making her feel that this would not be a burden to us, and a way of getting her petty cash in the pocket that she would not feel was a handout. So that it would be a legitimate possibility for her to consider.

I judge that my effort in this regard, besides the bad understanding of the tax law and the poor arithmetic, didn't help because of her following letter.

Mr. JENNER. That is what I was coming to. Before we get to that, Mrs. Paine, I direct your attention to Commission Exhibit No. 414.

Mrs. PAINE. 414?

Mr. JENNER. That is a translation of your letter, Commission Exhibit No. 413. Have you read that translation?

495

Mrs. PAINE. Yes.

Mr. JENNER. Is there anything in the translation to which you might desire to take exception or at least make a comment?

(At this point Chief Justice Warren left the hearing room.)

Mrs. PAINE. One minute. Yes, it accurately reflects some of my bad Russian.

Mr. JENNER. You take no exception to the translation?

Mrs. PAINE. I think no.

Mr. JENNER. Mr. Chairman, if you please, I offer in evidence, Mr. Dulles, may I have those exhibits——

Mr. McCLOY. They may be admitted.

Mr. JENNER. As Commission Exhibits 411, 412, 413 and 414, the documents that had been so marked?

Mr. McCLOY. They will be admitted.

(The documents referred, previously marked Commission Exhibits Nos. 411, 412, 413, and 414, were received in evidence.)

Mr. JENNER. You did receive a response from Marina, did you not, Mrs. Paine?

Mrs. PAINE. Yes; I did.

Mr. JENNER. And is the response the document now handed to you marked Commission Exhibit No. 415?

Mrs. PAINE. Yes; it is.

Mr. JENNER. And you supplied the Commission with your translation of that letter and that translation——

Mrs. PAINE. 415 is that what you said?

Mr. JENNER. 415. It appears on pages 10, 11, and 12 of the material you supplied me.

Mrs. PAINE. Yes.

Mr. JENNER. You don't have an envelope but you have a letter.

Mrs. PAINE. I don't have an envelope. I don't know what happened to it.

Mr. JENNER. Is the exhibit in Marina Oswald's handwriting?

Mrs. PAINE. Yes; it is.

Mr. JENNER. Is there anything on the exhibit other than that in the handwriting of Marina Oswald?

Mrs. PAINE. There are a few underlinings on the page marked four.

Mr. JENNER. Who placed them there?

Mrs. PAINE. Which are my own.

Mr. JENNER. All right. Anything else?

Mrs. PAINE. Except for the underlining "he does not know" at the very bottom.

Mr. JENNER. "He" refers to whom?

Mrs. PAINE. Lee.

Mr. JENNER. You were about to state to the Commission Marina Oswald's reaction to your series of invitations. Is that correct?

Mrs. PAINE. Yes.

Mr. JENNER. Would you proceed then?

Mrs. PAINE. As reflected in this letter. This was the third letter I received from her after a space of over a month, and I had been very concerned about her. I was much relieved to get it. She said she had been to the doctor and her condition was normal. She responded to this series of four letters of which we have three in rough draft, saying—shall I read in some of the things said?

Mr. JENNER. To the extent that you desire to do so. We will not read the whole letter, it is quite long; that which is pertinent to what you have in mind.

Mrs. PAINE. Well, that for a considerable period Lee has been good to her, she writes. He talks a lot about the coming baby.

Mr. JENNER. Perhaps you might pick out—there are only about four sentences.

Mrs. PAINE. "He has become more attentive and we hardly quarrel".

Mr. JENNER. This indicates a change somewhat in relationship and would you please read that portion of the letter?

Mrs. PAINE. Yes.

Mr. DULLES. Could we have the date of this letter once again?

Mrs. PAINE. The date of the letter. We have no date on the letter. It was written somewhere between July 18 and July 21, which is the date of my reply.

Mr. JENNER. That is how you identify it?

Mrs. PAINE. Yes.

Representative Ford. This is 1963?

Mrs. Paine. Right. Again, "He has become much more attentive and we hardly quarrel. True I have to give in a great deal. It could not be otherwise. But if one wants peace then it is necessary to give in. We went to the doctor, my condition is normal."

And she thanks me for the invitation and thanks Michael also and says:

"I would try to take advantage of it if things really become worse, if Lee becomes coarse with me again and treats me badly."

Mr. Jenner. I direct your attention to the paragraph following that one, Mrs. Paine.

Mrs. Paine. Now another question:

"If as is possible it becomes necessary for me to come to live with you in order to say that I am a dependent of Michael's surely it would be necessary to have an official divorce, isn't that so? But I think Lee would not agree to a divorce, and to go simply from him to become a burden to you that I don't wish. Surely Michael would need to have a paper showing that I am living at his expense but no one would just take his word for it, right?"

And I realized much later that in the Soviet Union you don't do anything without the proper papers, and just having a person under your roof for anyone to see, having them in fact eating at your table is not, would not be, sufficient proof—would not be sufficient there in Russia.

Representative Boggs. It might not be here.

Mrs. Paine. It might not be here. Well, in any case I judged she felt, reading my invitations this was of some importance to me whether Michael counted her as a deduction, and so on, whereas in fact this wasn't the point at all, but that I had hoped to somehow make, if possible, for her to accept such help.

Mr. Jenner. Have you finished your observations?

Representative Boggs. As a matter of fact, there are certain limitations under our law as to how you can claim a dependent.

Mrs. Paine. Well, I asked a few people who didn't know much about it before I wrote it.

Representative Boggs. Yes.

Mr. Jenner. The tenor then of this letter was as I gather from your testimony and as you have related to me last evening whether she would come to live with you in the fall or generally was something which now became subject to reconsideration?

Mrs. Paine. Pardon?

Mr. Jenner. The matter of her coming to live with you, the possibility of her living with you on a more extended basis than——

Mrs. Paine. Was an invitation I had made to her.

Mr. Jenner. And that her response was not acceptance but one that she would now defer?

Mrs. Paine. It was a "thank you" and a refusal basically.

Mr. Jenner. Did you respond to that letter?

Mrs. Paine. Yes; I did. My letter is dated July 12.

Mr. Jenner. Mr. Liebeler will mark that Commission Exhibit 416, which consists of how many pages, Mr. Liebeler, three pages. You have that exhibit. Is that exhibit all in your handwriting?

Mrs. Paine. Yes; it is.

Mr. Jenner. Is that the draft of letter to which you have reference being your response to Marina's letter of——

Mrs. Paine. Undated letter.

Mr. Jenner. Undated letter which would be somewhere just prior to July 21?

Mrs. Paine. Right.

Mr. Jenner. And is that a draft of letter in the same condition now as it was when you completed it?

Mrs. Paine. Yes.

Mr. Jenner. Have you supplied the Commission with a translation of that letter?

Mrs. Paine. I have.

Mr. Jenner. We will mark as Commission Exhibits 417 and 418 two exhibits, the first being a one-page exhibit entitled "Translation from Russian", and the second being a four page photograph of what appears to be a letter dated July 21, 1963. Directing your attention to Exhibit 418.

Mrs. PAINE. Yes.

Mr. JENNER. Do you find it?

Mrs. PAINE. Yes.

Mr. JENNER. Would you please identify that exhibit? It consists of four pages.

Mrs. PAINE. It appears to be a photograph of my letter to her of July 21.

Mr. JENNER. Having observed it and looked at it last night, is it your best recollection at the moment that it is a photograph of the letter that you actually transmitted to Marina?

Mrs. PAINE. Yes.

Mr. JENNER. Directing your attention to the next exhibit which is No. 418——

Mrs. PAINE. 417, you are talking about the translation.

Mr. JENNER. Is that a translation of the letter, of your letter to her?

Mrs. PAINE. That is far from complete.

Representative FORD. It is far from complete?

Mrs. PAINE. Far from complete. It is incomplete.

Mr. JENNER. I would like to have you make then, directing your attention to the translation that has been supplied us.

Mrs. PAINE. It goes as far as two-thirds down on page 2, you must have more somewhere.

Mr. JENNER. No; that is all we have. Would you mark with this red marker pen the point to which Exhibit 417 is a translation?

Mrs. PAINE. Here.

Mr. JENNER. Is the translation accurate up to that point or rather do you have any exceptions to it?

Mrs. PAINE. Yes.

Mr. JENNER. In relation to what?

Mrs. PAINE. "This would" on the next to the last paragraph "this would offend my father very much." "This hurt my father", no subjunctive to it.

Mr. JENNER. Do it this way. Read what is on it, what the interpreter——

Mrs. PAINE. Wait.

Mr. JENNER. Said.

Mrs. PAINE. I guess that is just the interpreter trying to "offer you an alternative". State the question again. You want to know if I take any exception to the translation I have before me, this portion of my July 21 letter? They are all small.

Mr. JENNER. They are small and none of consequence.

Mrs. PAINE. No.

Mr. JENNER. So far as you are concerned. Your translation, however, that you supplied the Commission is as far as you are concerned accurate and what you intend to say, at least?

Mrs. PAINE. Yes; and I think it is what I said.

Mr. JENNER. All right. I offer in evidence, if the Chairman please, the documents that have been marked—may I have them please, Representative Ford?

Mrs. PAINE. These, too?

Mr. JENNER. Documents marked 415, 416, 417, and 418.

Mr. McCLOY. Do I understand there is not a complete translation?

Mrs. PAINE. That is right.

Mr. McCLOY. Of the letter. It is an incomplete translation?

Mrs. PAINE. There is a page 2 somewhere.

Mr. JENNER. That is correct. During the noon hour I will see if that is not a mistake and if I can be supplied with the balance, if there is a balance.

Mr. McCLOY. They may be admitted in this form and then you can advise us after the recess whether there is anything additional to insert at this point.

(The documents referred to, heretofore marked Commission Exhibits Nos. 415, 416, 417, and 418, were received in evidence.)

Mr. JENNER. Now, there is a matter to which I would like to draw your attention in your letter of July 21, which is Commission Exhibit No. 416, the last portion of it, and I direct your attention, in turn, to your own interpretation appearing at page 3. The last paragraph, when you brought Marina to

New Orleans, did you do anything by way of seeking to have people in New Orleans visit her?

Mrs. PAINE. No. I have already testified that after an initial warm greeting with Lee, they quarreled, and I was uncomfortable there, and wanted to get back home. I had thought of making contact for Marina with someone in the Russian speaking community in New Orleans, and later when I didn't hear from her after this note that looks like "I will have to go back to Russia after all," I much regretted that I had not made some contact for her, someone she could talk to, herself. And anxious, not having heard from her a month from the time of this appendage to my corrected letter, I telephoned Ruth Kloepfer who is the clerk of the Quaker Meeting in New Orleans.

Mr. JENNER. Would you spell her name, please?

Mrs. PAINE. She is not someone I know. That is spelled K-L-O-E-P-F-E-R, and I asked her if she knew any Russians in New Orleans. She did not. I then wrote to Mrs. Paul Blanchard.

Mr. JENNER. Excuse me, when you use the pronoun "she" there you asked Marina?

Mrs. PAINE. I asked Mrs. Kloepfer if she knew any Russian-speaking people and described why I was interested in knowing. I must have given her the address of Marina, probably asked that she go and see her. In any case, I have a letter which followed that telephone call, which I wrote to Mrs. Paul Blanchard.

Mr. McCLOY. Pardon me, did you say you telephoned to Mrs. Blanchard or you wrote to Mrs. Blanchard?

Mrs. PAINE. I wrote to Mrs. Blanchard, I had originally telephoned to Mrs. Kloepfer.

Mr. JENNER. Did you make the telephone call when you were in New Orleans?

Mrs. PAINE. No; this was when I was concerned. I had not heard from Marina for a month. I did not know whether she was in good health or had gone back to the Soviet Union.

Mr. JENNER. So you called Mrs. Kloepfer in New Orleans?

Mrs. PAINE. That is correct. After having tried to call the Murrets. I had not had their name accurately.

Representative BOGGS. How did you happen to write to Mrs. Blanchard?

Mrs. PAINE. She is the secretary of the Unitarian Church in New Orleans and I called the Quaker Church in Dallas to find out who was in New Orleans of the Quakers, and then I called the Unitarian Church which my husband belongs to in Dallas to find out who the secretary of the New Orleans Unitarian Church was.

Representative BOGGS. You do not know Mrs. Blanchard?

Mrs. PAINE. I did not know her, and I did not know Mrs. Kloepfer either, and appended to this that I am leaving with the Commission is my carbon of a letter to Mrs. Blanchard of the Unitarian Church, which I sent in carbon to Mrs. Kloepfer so each would know what the other was doing in an effort to find a Russian-speaking person who could be a contact for Marina.

(At this point Representative Ford left the hearing room.)

Mr. JENNER. Mrs. Paine, you have now mentioned a letter that you wrote to Mrs. Blanchard; have you supplied the Commission with a carbon copy of that letter?

Mrs. PAINE. I have.

Mr. JENNER. And it is a two-page document, Mr. Chairman, dated July 18, 1963, now marked as Commission Exhibit 419. That exhibit has now been handed to you, Mrs. Paine. Is that the carbon copy of your letter to Mrs. Blanchard?

Mrs. PAINE. Yes; it is.

Mr. JENNER. You did not know Mrs. Blanchard, had never heard of her prior to the time you wrote the letter?

Mrs. PAINE. That is correct. It begins saying, "Mrs. Philip Harper, the secretary of the Dallas Unitarian Church, suggested I write to you when I told her of the following problem."

Mr. JENNER. Is the document in the same condition now as it was when you prepared the original of which that is a carbon copy?

Mrs. PAINE. Yes.

Mr. JENNER. I offer in evidence as Commission Exhibit No. 419 the document which has been so identified.

Mr. McCLOY. It may be so admitted.

(The document referred to was marked for identification as Commission Exhibit No. 419 and received in evidence.)

Mrs. PAINE. Will there be any difficulty that it starts with typing and then it goes carbon?

Mr. JENNER. Explain that.

Mrs. PAINE. I wrote two carbon paragraphs and then I thought I should write a carbon of this to Mrs. Blanchard and put in a carbon and then in my own copy put in typing.

Mr. JENNER. So that which appears to be a copy is an original and that which follows, what appears to be original, is an actual carbon copy of the letter you actually sent to Mrs. Blanchard?

Mrs. PAINE. With copy stated here to Mrs. Kloepfer.

Mr. JENNER. Did you hear from Marina on that subject at any time?

Mrs. PAINE. Yes. In her succeeding and last letter that I got from her.

Mr. JENNER. Her succeeding letter is dated what?

Mrs. PAINE. It has no date inside. It is postmarked August 11 from New Orleans and sent to me while I was on vacation.

Mr. JENNER. We have marked as Commission Exhibit No. 420 the envelope and attached to 420 is what purports to be a four-page letter in Russian longhand—may we have this as a group exhibit consisting of the envelope and the four-page letter?

Mr. McCLOY. If it is properly attached I guess you can.

Mrs. PAINE. There is no date on the letter, if they separate you don't know what it is.

Mr. JENNER. We have marked the four-page letter as Commission Exhibit 421 in order to avoid any difficulty.

Directing your attention to Exhibit 421, do you recognize the handwriting on that exhibit?

Mrs. PAINE. Yes; that is Marina Oswald's handwriting.

Mr. JENNER. That is a letter to you, is it not?

Mrs. PAINE. Yes; it is.

Mr. JENNER. And you supplied the Commission with your translation of that letter?

Mrs. PAINE. Yes; I have.

Mr. JENNER. That appears at pages 13 and 14 of the materials you furnished me?

Mrs. PAINE. Yes.

Mr. JENNER. Is that letter in the same condition now as it was when you received it?

Mrs. PAINE. Yes; with the exception of an addition in my handwriting on the bottom of unmarked page 3.

Mr. JENNER. Would you read that?

Mrs. PAINE. Which is a translation of one word.

Mr. JENNER. What word is that?

Mrs. PAINE. A word means to grow downcast.

Mr. DULLES. I didn't catch that.

Mrs. PAINE. To grow downcast, to lose courage.

Mr. JENNER. Directing your attention to the envelope which is marked Commission Exhibit 420.

Mrs. PAINE. I want to make one other comment. I underlined the word on the second page that I have translated as "winsome."

Mr. JENNER. W-i-n-s-o-m-e?

Mrs. PAINE. Yes. The other underlinings in her letter are her own.

Mr. JENNER. All right. Directing your attention to the pink envelope which is Commission Exhibit No. 420, was Exhibit 421 enclosed in Exhibit 420?

Mrs. PAINE. Yes; it was.

Mr. JENNER. That also is in English, that is the address?

Mrs. PAINE. The address is in English, addressed to me while on vacation.

Mr. JENNER. And you received those documents in due course?

Mrs. PAINE. Which documents?

Mr. JENNER. You received the documents in due course?

Mrs. PAINE. It was not forwarded. It was addressed to me where I was.

Mr. JENNER. But you received them is all I am asking?

Mrs. PAINE. Oh, yes.

Mr. JENNER. I offer in evidence as Commission Exhibits 420 and 421, the documents which have been so marked.

Mr. McCLOY. They may be so admitted.

(The documents referred to were marked Commission Exhibits Nos. 420 and 421 for identification and received in evidence.)

Mr. JENNER. There is one item in Exhibit 421 to which I wish to direct your attention. On the last page about the third paragraph from the bottom appears the second sentence, "Lee doesn't have work now already three weeks." Do you find that?

Mrs. PAINE. Yes.

Mr. JENNER. Had you had any information prior to the receipt of this letter that Lee Oswald no longer was employed in New Orleans?

Mrs. PAINE. I had no such information.

Mr. JENNER. This was your first information?

Mrs. PAINE. That is right.

Mr. JENNER. Did you respond to that letter?

Mrs. PAINE. I did.

Mr. JENNER. I have a five-page document Mr. Liebeler is identifying as Commission Exhibit No. 422.

Mrs. PAINE. This is not what you want. You want my reply, don't you next?

Mr. JENNER. That is right.

Mrs. PAINE. This is not it. You have my reply but I had had no copy of that.

Mr. JENNER. We will keep that exhibit number. There has been identified as Commission Exhibit 423 an exhibit consisting of four pages, the first three of which are a photograph of a letter, and the last page of which is a photograph of an envelope. Handing you Commission Exhibit No. 423, is that a picture of your letter to Marina Oswald in response to her letter of August 11?

Mrs. PAINE. August 11. Yes; it is dated August 24, 1963.

Mr. JENNER. And you do recognize that as being a picture copy of letter you had written?

Mrs. PAINE. Yes.

Mr. JENNER. And you supplied the Commission with a translation of that letter?

Mrs. PAINE. No; I did not. I did not have this in rough draft. I had no copy of this. You may have a translation but I do not.

Mr. JENNER. All right.

Mrs. PAINE. I supplied you only on this summary that you have with a brief recollection of what it contained.

Mr. JENNER. I now hand you a document, Commission Exhibit No. 424 consisting of two pages which purports to be a translation of Exhibit 423. Did you review that translation with me last evening?

Mrs. PAINE. Briefly.

Mr. JENNER. To the best of your recollection at the moment of what you said last night that the translation is of Exhibit 423?

Mrs. PAINE. It is approximately what I recall writing. I didn't look at the Russian in your pictures.

Mr. JENNER. During the noon recess would you wish to look at that and if you have any exception you wish to take to the translation would you please state it to the Commission?

Mrs. PAINE. Yes.

Mr. McCLOY. May I intervene at this point about Exhibit 422, has that been properly identified?

Mrs. PAINE. No; not yet.

Mr. JENNER. Could we return it to the witness? Exhibit 422 is in whose handwriting?

Mrs. PAINE. It is in my handwriting.

Mr. JENNER. Is that a draft of a letter?

Mrs. PAINE. That is a letter which I wrote but never sent.

Mr. JENNER. You testified about that letter yesterday?

Mrs. PAINE. I did.

Mr. JENNER. Did you not?

Mrs. PAINE. It is dated April 7.

Mr. JENNER. Have you supplied the Commission with a translation, your translation of that letter?

Mrs. PAINE. Yes; I have with appropriate paragraph before it saying that it was not sent, that I wrote it not necessarily to send or give to her but simply to have, I think as I testified yesterday, the words at my command ready in case it seemed appropriate to make such an invitation.

Mr. JENNER. And this was prepared on or about April 7, 1963?

Mrs. PAINE. I would judge on the 7th.

Mr. JENNER. Is that letter in the same condition now as it was when you completed writing it?

Mrs. PAINE. I have added since completing writing, I have added in pencil at the top, "not sent" in English. It is otherwise the same.

Mr. JENNER. I won't go into that further, Mr. Chairman, because the witness did testify about it yesterday other than to offer the document in evidence.

Mr. McCLOY. I simply thought it needed a little elaboration.

Mr. JENNER. You were quite right, sir.

(The document referred to was marked Commission Exhibit No. 422 for identification and received in evidence.)

Mr. JENNER. Where were you in the summer of 1963?

Mrs. PAINE. May I interrupt.

Mr. JENNER. Yes.

Mrs. PAINE. Did you want to make any reference to the reference to Lee's driving in Exhibit 424?

Mr. JENNER. Thank you very much, Mrs. Paine, and I do want to go into it.

Mrs. PAINE. I have it underlined.

Mr. JENNER. Mr. Dulles, would you be good enough to let me have it? This translation which appears as Commission Exhibit 424, the fourth paragraph reads "Lee told me that he learned a little from his Uncle how to drive a car. It would be very useful for him to know how to drive but it is hard to find time for this when he works every day."

Mrs. PAINE. I might make a comment about that.

Mr. JENNER. This is your comment, is it not?

Mrs. PAINE. I might make a comment about that.

Mr. JENNER. This is your comment, is it not?

Mrs. PAINE. I wrote that.

Mr. JENNER. Now, the Commission is very interested in the subject matter of Mr. Oswald, of Lee Oswald being able to drive a car and I think it might be well if we covered the whole subject from the beginning to the end.

Would you give the Commission your full, most accurate recollection of this whole subject? Start at the very beginning.

Mrs. PAINE. I think I learned either in March or April that Lee——

Mr. JENNER. Of 1963?

Mrs. PAINE. 1963.

Mr. JENNER. This would be early in your acquaintance with him?

Mrs. PAINE. Very early. I learned Lee was not able to drive and didn't have a license.

Mr. JENNER. How did you learn he was not able to drive?

Mrs. PAINE. I think it was related to his looking for work the first time in the middle of April, and I had learned he had looked in the Dallas area for work.

Mr. JENNER. How did you learn it?

Mrs. PAINE. We were talking about it.

Mr. JENNER. You were talking with Lee?

Mrs. PAINE. Yes.

Mr. JENNER. Did he tell you that he was not able to drive a car?

Mrs. PAINE. That he had never learned how.

Mr. JENNER. That he had difficulty in getting around?

Mrs. PAINE. Simply he had never learned how.

Mr. JENNER. He said this to you?

Mrs. PAINE. Yes. And I felt immediately that his job opportunities, the jobs to which he could have applied, and the jobs to which he could get himself would be greatly broadened if he were able to drive and said so.

Mr. JENNER. You said that to him?

Mrs. PAINE. And said that to him. Then when we arrived in New Orleans he said to me by way of almost pride that he had been allowed by his uncle to drive his uncle's car.

Mr. JENNER. That is Mr. Murret?

Mrs. PAINE. I don't know whether there was more than one.

Mr. JENNER. But he volunteered the statement to you?

Mrs. PAINE. Yes.

Mr. JENNER. And it was something that had occurred after he had gotten to New Orleans?

Mrs. PAINE. And he was in a sense pleased to report to me that he was getting some experience driving. That his uncle had premitted him to drive the car on the street.

Mr. JENNER. On the street?

Mrs. PAINE. On the street.

Mr. JENNER. Did you have occasion while you were in New Orleans to verify that in any respect whatsoever?

Mrs. PAINE. No.

Mr. JENNER. Or have it verified to you?

Mrs. PAINE. No.

Mr. JENNER. This was confined to a remark that he made to you?

Mrs. PAINE. That is right. Then when I learned in Marina's letter of August 11 that Lee was out of work, I immediately thought it would be well for him to make use of those free weekdays, not only for job hunting but for learning the skill of driving and, therefore, that paragraph—shall we read it?

Mr. JENNER. Haven't I already read it?

Mrs. PAINE. No; I don't think so.

Mr. JENNER. You mean from your letter?

Mrs. PAINE. Did you read that?

Mr. JENNER. The paragraph "Lee told me that he learned a little from his uncle how to drive a car."

Mrs. PAINE. Yes.

Mr. JENNER. Did you read that "It would be very useful for him to know how to drive but it is hard to find time for this when he works every day."

Just to be certain of this, Mrs. Paine, this was a remark made to you by Lee Harvey Oswald when you brought Marina from Irving, Tex., to New Orleans, and——

Mrs. PAINE. The second week in May.

Mr. JENNER. The second week in May of 1963. And then, according to the remark made to you by Lee Harvey Oswald that his uncle had permitted him to drive his uncle's car on the street in New Orleans?

Mrs. PAINE. Yes; and he was proud of this.

Mr. JENNER. Did he ask at that time or any time while you were in New Orleans in the spring to drive your car?

Mrs. PAINE. No.

Mr. JENNER. Was there any discussion at all during—did you have the feeling that he would like to drive the car?

Mrs. PAINE. There was no discussion of it.

Mr. JENNER. Did he demonstrate to you that he could drive?

Mrs. PAINE. There was no discussion of it.

Mr. JENNER. You have given us all that occurred in New Orleans by way of conversation or otherwise on the subject of Lee Harvey Oswald driving an automobile or his ability to drive?

Mrs. PAINE. That is right.

Mr. JENNER. Now, you are telling us the whole story on this subject. So when next——

Senator COOPER. May I ask this one question?

Mr. JENNER. Excuse me.

Senator COOPER. Did Lee Oswald identify the uncle who permitted him to drive his car?

Mrs. PAINE. Senator Cooper, he did not. He just said his uncle. He did not identify his uncle by name.

Senator COOPER. Do you know of your own knowledge who the uncle was?

Mrs. PAINE. I can only assume.

Senator COOPER. What?

Mrs. PAINE. I can only assume it was the uncle he had been staying with. He had been staying at his home.

Mr. JENNER. You had met the uncle at this time?

Mrs. PAINE. Just met him.

Mr. JENNER. So it was the uncle with whom he had been staying just before he obtained the apartment at Magazine?

Mr. McCLOY. What is the uncle's name?

Mr. JENNER. Dutz Murret. This was the relative who had the nice home that Marina first saw when she arrived there and thought maybe that is where she was going to live, is that correct?

Mrs. PAINE. That is correct.

Mr. JENNER. Go ahead, Mrs. Paine.

Mrs. PAINE. You want all other references to driving?

Mr. JENNER. Confining yourself to his ability to drive automobiles, when next, and take it in chronological order as to when you next recall it?

Mrs. PAINE. It came up next after he returned to the Dallas area in October.

Mr. JENNER. When was that?

Mrs. PAINE. After he returned on the 4th, to my knowledge.

Mr. JENNER. The 4th of October?

Mrs. PAINE. That was the first I know.

Mr. JENNER. We will get into the reasons and the circumstances but you stick with the automobile incidents.

Mrs. PAINE. He was looking for work.

Mr. JENNER. In Dallas?

Mrs. PAINE. In the Dallas area and again, of course, I felt that he could find more jobs, be eligible for more if he could drive.

Mr. JENNER. What did you do about it?

Mrs. PAINE. I recalled that I had a copy of the regulations for driving, what you need to know to pass the written test.

Mr. JENNER. In what State?

Mrs. PAINE. In the State of Texas, and I gave him that booklet.

Mr. JENNER. Did you have a discussion with him about your desire, your recommendation, that he qualify to drive an automobile in Texas so it would assist him in connection with his job hunting.

Mrs. PAINE. Probably. We certainly had conversation about it.

Mr. JENNER. Give us the subject of the conversation in terms of recommendations by you, or what did you say?

Mrs. PAINE. I again recommended, as I had in the spring, that he learn to drive.

Mr. JENNER. What did he say?

Mrs. PAINE. He was interested in learning to drive.

Mr. JENNER. Did he say anything to you?

Mrs. PAINE. I would like to offer to the Commission something we didn't get to last night.

Mr. JENNER. I see.

Mrs. PAINE. Which is a letter I wrote to my mother, which she just showed me recently, she just found it recently, which makes reference to the date I first gave him a lesson in driving.

Mr. JENNER. That would be helpful to us. May I have the letter, please?

Mrs. PAINE. Yes. Now only a portion of it is applicable.

Mr. JENNER. Why don't we give it a number?

Mrs. PAINE. Another portion is applicable in another connection, which I would like especially to bring up.

Mr. JENNER. Having that in mind, we will give that document for identification at the moment only, the number Commission Exhibit No. 425.

I won't identify it beyond that for the moment because the witness will be using it to refresh her recollection.

Mrs. PAINE. I will read what applies here.

Mr. JENNER. You are now reading from Commission Exhibit No. 425.

Mrs. PAINE. Which is a letter dated October 14, in my hand, from me to my mother.

Mr. DULLES. Would you give your mother's name?

Mrs. PAINE. Her name is Mrs. Carol Hyde.

Representative BOGGS. Where does she live?

Mrs. PAINE. In Columbus, Ohio. It was likely written to Oberlin, where she was a student at that time.

"If Lee can just find work that will help so much. Meantime I started giving him driving lessons last Sunday (yesterday). If he can drive this will open up more job possibilities and more locations."

Mr. JENNER. Yes.

Mrs. PAINE. I want to comment too on the nature of this lesson.

Mr. JENNER. The Commission will be interested in that but you go ahead.

Mrs. PAINE. Now?

Mr. JENNER. Go right ahead.

Mrs. PAINE. I knew that he had not even a learner's permit to drive. I wasn't interested in his driving on the street with my car until he had such. But on Sunday the parking lot of a neighboring shopping center was empty, and I am quite certain that is where the driving lesson took place.

Mr. JENNER. That is your best present recollection?

Mrs. PAINE. Yes. Now I recall this also, and it is significant. I offered him a lesson and intended to drive him to this area for him to practice. He, however, started the car.

Mr. JENNER. He got in and started the car?

Mrs. PAINE. He got in and started the car so that I know he was able to do that and wanted to drive on the street to the parking lot.

Mr. JENNER. He wanted to?

Mrs. PAINE. He wanted to. I said, "My father is an insurance man and he would never forgive me."

Mr. JENNER. Your father?

Mrs. PAINE. My father. And insisted that he get a learner's permit before he would drive on the street.

Mr. JENNER. At that moment and at that time he acted, in any event in your presence, as though he himself thought——

Mrs. PAINE. That is right.

Mr. JENNER. He would be capable of driving an automobile from your home to the parking area in which you were about to give him a lesson. That was your full impression, was it not?

Mrs. PAINE. Yes. I should add that, as I am recalling, he did drive a portion of the way, he drove in fact, it is about three blocks, to the parking lot. I was embarrassed to just tell him "No, don't." But I did, in effect, on the way there, when he was on the street, driving on the street in my car, when we got there I said, "Now, I am going to drive back." I didn't want him to.

Mr. JENNER. From your home to the parking lot?

Mrs. PAINE. The first time before we had any lesson at all. And at that time I made it clear I didn't want him to drive in the street. Also, it became clear to me in that lesson that he was very unskilled in driving. We practiced a number of the things you need to know, to back up, to turn, right angle turn to come to a stop.

Mr. JENNER. Was this on the parking lot?

Mrs. PAINE. This was all on a parking lot.

Mr. DULLES. Did I understand you to say he drove three blocks, was that all the way to the parking lot? So he drove all the way to the parking lot?

Mrs. PAINE. Perhaps a little longer. But a short distance, whatever it was, to the parking lot, yes. Rather than stopping in midstreet and changing drivers. Going to turn a right angle——

Mr. DULLES. How well did he do on that?

Mr. McCLOY. That is what she is telling.

Mrs. PAINE. No; that is a separate answer.

Mr. JENNER. She is talking about the parking lot.

Mrs. PAINE. I was very nervous while he was doing it and was not at all happy about his doing it. I would say he did modestly well; but no means skilled in coming to a stop and turning a square right angle at a corner.

Mr. JENNER. Was there much traffic?

Mrs. PAINE. No. But then too, I noticed when we got to the parking lot when he attempted to turn in a right angle he made the usual mistake of a beginner of turning too much and then having to correct it. He was not familiar with the delay of the steering wheel in relation to the wheels, actual wheels of the power——

Mr. JENNER. Was it power—

Mrs. PAINE. It was not power steering. But it has no clutch so that makes it a lot easier to drive.

Mr. JENNER. It is an automatic transmission?

Mrs. PAINE. It is an automatic transmission.

Mr. JENNER. Describe your automobile, will you please?

Mrs. PAINE. It is a 1955 Chevrolet station wagon, green, needing paint, which we bought secondhand. It is in my name.

Mr. McCLOY. But automatic transmission?

Mrs. PAINE. Automatic transmission; yes.

Then, in the later lessons, I think there were altogether three with Lee——

Mr. JENNER. Have you finished with this lesson on the Sunday morning, was it?

Mrs. PAINE. No; it was a Sunday afternoon and I drove back to the house.

Mr. JENNER. How long did the lesson take on the parking lot?

Mrs. PAINE. Oh, 20 minutes, perhaps. I will say of him that he set for himself tasks; a good student in the sense that he planned now I am going to back up this way and I am going—one of the problems is to turn around and go the other way on the street. In other words——

Mr. JENNER. U-turn.

Mrs. PAINE. It is not a U-turn, no. It is a narrower one to head in back up and go the other way and he would set this problem for himself, how to do it, back up and do it, and set the problem of backing up, driving, going back, I mean. And set himself a course. I was doing this, too, but I was interested in the eagerness he had and his desire to achieve; desire to do this and do it well.

In helping himself by setting up these course plans, you could almost say,

Mr. JENNER. All right.

Would you refresh my recollection of the date this occurred?

Mrs. PAINE. My letter is dated the 14th. I say, "I taught him yesterday, Sunday."

Mr. JENNER. Fourteenth of October?

Mrs. PAINE. Fourteenth of October. So that would have been——

Mr. JENNER. That would have been October 7?

Mrs. PAINE. Thirteenth.

Senator COOPER. May I ask a question here?

Mr. McCLOY. Senator Cooper has a question.

Mr. JENNER. Yes.

Senator COOPER. On the occasion when you drove with him, did you find it necessary to show him how to turn on the ignition?

Mrs. PAINE. No; I did not.

Senator COOPER. How to take steps to start the car and put it in motion?

Mrs. PAINE. No, indeed; he had started it before I came out or else he wouldn't have been in the driver's seat because I didn't want him to drive on the street. So he had the car ready to go; backed out with a considerable bump.

Mr. JENNER. He backed out of the driveway?

Mrs. PAINE. I am recalling this now, I think so. I recall that he then didn't attempt to go, I didn't let him, but at one point we practiced parking on the street in front of my house.

Mr. JENNER. This was a subsequent occasion?

Mrs. PAINE. This was a subsequent occasion. But when the lesson was done he gradually let me turn the car into the driveway. This is harder and I was glad to do it and he was glad to be relieved of that requirement.

Representative BOGGS. Mr. Chairman, I don't want to interrupt this line of inquiry, but I have to go to a meeting at the Speaker's office and I can't be back this afternoon, and I wonder if I might ask Mrs. Paine several questions?

Mr. McCLOY. By all means.

Representative BOGGS. Not particularly in this line.

Where did you first meet Marina. I know you told us.

Mr. McCLOY. She testified to that yesterday.

Representative BOGGS. Tell me briefly.

Mrs. PAINE. At a party of people at the end of February 1963.

Representative BOGGS. How long was it thereafter that she moved into your home for the first time?

Mrs. PAINE. She first came on the 24th of April.

Representative BOGGS. And she lived there for 2 weeks?

Mrs. PAINE. Yes.

Representative BOGGS. And her husband lived here—her husband was with her?

Mrs. PAINE. No. He had already gone on to New Orleans.

Representative BOGGS. When did she return to your home?

Mrs. PAINE. She came with me from New Orleans, leaving there the 23d of September and arriving in Irving the 24th of September.

Representative BOGGS. And she lived with you in Irving from the 24th of September until the 23d?

Mrs. PAINE. The morning of the 23d.

Representative BOGGS. Of November?

Mrs. PAINE. She left the morning of the 23d, she left expecting to come back.

Representative BOGGS. During that period of time did Lee Oswald live there?

Mrs. PAINE. No.

Representative BOGGS. He visited there on weekends?

Mrs. PAINE. He visited there on weekends.

Representative BOGGS. How well did you know Lee Oswald?

Mrs. PAINE. Insufficiently well.

Representative BOGGS. What do you mean by that?

Mrs. PAINE. Well, I regret, of course, very deeply that I didn't perceive him as a violent man.

Representative BOGGS. You saw no evidence of violence in him at any time?

Mrs. PAINE. No, I didn't. He argued with his wife but he never struck her. I never heard from her of any violence from him.

Representative BOGGS. Did he ever express any hostility toward anyone while he was talking with you?

Mrs. PAINE. Not of a violent or——

Representative BOGGS. Did he ever express any political opinions to you?

Mrs. PAINE. Yes, he called himself a Marxist. He said that on the occasion after Stevenson had been in town in relation to the United Nations Day.

Mr. JENNER. Adlai Stevenson?

Mrs. PAINE. Adlai Stevenson, and Lee had been to a meeting of the National Indignation Committee held another night that week, and he was at our home the following Friday night and commented that he didn't like General Walker. This is the only thing I heard from him on the subject.

Representative BOGGS. Did he ever express any violence toward General Walker?

Mrs. PAINE. No.

Representative BOGGS. Did he ever discuss President Kennedy with you?

Mrs. PAINE. He never mentioned Kennedy at all.

Representative BOGGS. Did you see the rifle that he had in the room in your home?

Mrs. PAINE. In the garage, no.

Representative BOGGS. In the garage, you never saw one?

Mrs. PAINE. I never saw that rifle at all until the police showed it to me in the station on the 22d of November.

Representative BOGGS. Were you at home when the FBI interviewed Marina and Lee?

Mrs. PAINE. The FBI never interviewed Marina and me; I was waiting to hear your question.

Representative BOGGS. At your home?

Mrs. PAINE. The FBI never interviewed Marina and Lee at my home. The FBI was there one afternoon and talked to Marina through me; they never saw Lee Oswald in my home. I told them he would be there on a weekend.

Representative BOGGS. Did you ever discuss politics with Marina?

Mrs. PAINE. As close as we would come, I would say, would be what I have mentioned about Madam Nhu; she was interested in what the family would do. She also said to me that she thought Khrushchev was a rather coarse, country person. She said that she admired Mrs. Kennedy a great deal, and liked, this is all before, liked President Kennedy very much.

Mr. JENNER. This was all before November 22?

Mrs. PAINE. Yes.

Representative BOGGS. Were you aware of the fact that Lee returned to your home the night before the assassination?

Mrs. PAINE. Yes.

Representative BOGGS. Were you curious about that in view of the fact that he seldom came except on weekends?

Mrs. PAINE. It was the first time he had come without asking permission to come. He came after he and his wife had quarreled, and Marina and I said to one another, we took this to be as close as he could come to an apology, and an effort to make up.

Representative BOGGS. That was the reason you thought he had come?

Mrs. PAINE. But I didn't inquire of him.

Representative BOGGS. You did not know that the next morning when he left he had a rifle?

Mrs. PAINE. No.

Representative BOGGS. Did you see him when he left that morning?

Mrs. PAINE. No, I didn't.

Representative BOGGS. Have you been active in politics yourself?

Mrs. PAINE. No; I vote. And I am a member of the League of Women Voters, that is the extent of my activity.

Representative BOGGS. Do you belong to any other political organizations?

Mrs. PAINE. No.

Mr. JENNER. Have you ever belonged?

Mrs. PAINE. No.

Representative BOGGS. Are you, I don't know quite how to state this question, are you a practicing Quaker?

Mrs. PAINE. I am. I am also a pacifist.

Representative BOGGS. You are a pacifist?

Mrs. PAINE. Yes.

Representative BOGGS. You are not a Marxist?

Mrs. PAINE. No; they don't go together, in fact. You can't believe violent overthrow and be a pacifist.

Mr. DULLES. Did you know Norman Thomas quite well?

Mrs. PAINE. When I was 8 I went to a rally of Norman Thomas in New York City. That was my only contact.

Representative BOGGS. Is your feeling towards Marina, shall I say in the Quaker spirit of friendship and hospitality, was that the main objective, plus the intellectual?

Mrs. PAINE. I was interested in the language.

Representative BOGGS. Intellectual stimulation of the language.

Mrs. PAINE. Yes. I found that while living with her, I could say that this day, at least added something to what I knew, what I—I learned a few more words.

Representative BOGGS. You never formed any opinion about Lee Oswald as a person?

Mrs. PAINE. I formed many, and I would like to make that a special area.

Representative BOGGS. Would you just tell me just in a sentence or two, I know you could go into it in greater detail, but was your opinion favorable? Was it unfavorable, or what?

Mrs. PAINE. I disliked him actively in the spring when I thought he just wanted to get rid of his wife and wasn't caring about her, wasn't concerned whether she would go to the doctor. I then found him much nicer, I thought, when I saw him next in New Orleans in late September, and this would be a perfectly good time to admit the rest of the pertinent part of this letter to my mother written October 14, because it shows something that I think should be part of the public record, and I am one of the few people who can give it, that presents Lee Oswald as a human person, a person really rather ordinary, not an ogre that was out to leave his wife, and be harsh and hostile to all that he knew.

But in this brief period during the times that he came out on weekends, I saw him as a person who cared for his wife and his child, tried to make himself helpful in my home, tried to make himself welcome although he really preferred to stay to himself.

He wasn't much to take up a conversation. This says, "Dear Mom," this is from Commission Exhibit No. 425, "Lee Oswald is looking for work in Dallas. Did my last letter say so? Probably not. He arrived a week and a half ago and has been looking for work since. It is a very depressing business for him, I am sure. He spent last weekend and the one before with us here and was a happy addition to our expanded family. He played with Chris"—my 3-year-old, then 2—"watched football on the TV, planed down the doors that wouldn't close, they had shifted and generally added a needed masculine flavor"——

Mr. JENNER. Wait a second.

Mrs. PAINE. "And generally added a needed masculine flavor. From a poor first impression I have come to like him. We saw the doctor at Parkland Hospital last Friday and all seems very healthy" and this refers to Marina. "It appears that charges will be geared to their ability to pay."

Representative BOGGS. Were you——

Mrs. PAINE. May I go on?

Representative BOGGS. Yes: surely. Finish.

Mrs. PAINE. This was an intervening section where he was the most human that I saw him, and, of course, it has been followed by my anger with him, and all the feeling that most of us have about his act. But it seems to me important, very important, to the record that we face the fact that this man was not only human but a rather ordinary one in many respects, and who appeared ordinary.

If we think that this was a man such as we might never meet, a great aberration from the normal, someone who would stand out in a crowd as unusual, then we don't know this man, we have no means of recognizing such a person again in advance of a crime such as he committed.

The important thing, I feel, and the only protection we have is to realize how human he was though he added to it this sudden and great violence beyond——

Representative BOGGS. You have no doubt about the fact that he assassinated President Kennedy?

Mrs. PAINE. I have no present doubt.

Representative BOGGS. Do you have any reason to believe he was associated with anyone else in this act or it was part of a conspiracy?

Mrs. PAINE. I have no reason to believe he was associated with anyone.

Representative BOGGS. Did you ever see him talking with anyone else, in conversation with anybody else or get mail at your home?

Mrs. PAINE. I never saw him talking with anyone else. He received all his mail from home, third class for the most part perhaps one letter from Russia.

Representative BOGGS. Did he have telephone calls at your home of a mysterious nature?

Mrs. PAINE. No.

Mr. JENNER. Excuse me, did he ever have a telephone call at your home mysterious or otherwise?

Mrs. PAINE. No; never.

Representative Boggs. You then would be surprised if he were part of any group?

Mrs. Paine. I would be very surprised. For one thing, I judged, I had to wonder whether this man was a spy or someone dangerous to our Nation. He had been to the Soviet Union and he had come back and he didn't go as a tourist. He went by his own admission intending to become a Soviet citizen and then came back.

Representative Boggs. What about Marina—go ahead and finish.

Mrs. Paine. Then the FBI came, as I thought they well might, interested in this man who had been to the Soviet Union, and I felt that if he had associations this would be very easy for them to know. I didn't see any, but would tend to point to the possibility of his being a spy or subversive. But I didn't see any such and I felt happy that they were charged with the responsibility of knowing about it.

Representative Boggs. Did you see any indication of any connection of Marina with any group that might be considered unusual?

Mrs. Paine. No; no one called her.

Representative Boggs. Did she have any letters?

Mrs. Paine. She received a letter from a friend in the Soviet Union which she showed to me and mentioned to me.

Representative Boggs. Was this just a normal letter?

Mrs. Paine. Girl friend.

Representative Boggs. What is your present relationship with Marina?

Mrs. Paine. I have seen her once since the assassination. That was a week ago Monday. It was the first time since the morning of the 23d when she left my house, both of us expecting she would come back to it that evening. In the intervening period I wrote her a collection of letters trying to determine what her feelings were and whether it was suitable for me to write and see her.

I am presently confused, as I was then, as to how to best be a friend to her. I don't know what is appropriate in this situation.

By that I mean during the time I was writing the letters to her and not getting an answer when she was with Mr. Martin.

Representative Boggs. Was your conversation last Monday friendly?

Mrs. Paine. Yes.

Representative Boggs. Thank you, Mr. Chairman, thank you, Mrs. Paine.

Mr. McCloy. Might I ask one question?

You said that Lee had mentioned General Walker and indicated that he didn't like General Walker. Can you elaborate on that a little bit, to what extent, how violent was he in his expression?

Mrs. Paine. No; it wasn't violent at all. It was more of, oh, well, more not giving him much credit even, but it was done briefly, this was in passing, so my recollection is hazy. But certainly there was no strong expression.

Mr. McCloy. No vehemence about it?

Mrs. Paine. Absolutely not, I would have remembered that. And I recall that Marina said nothing.

Mr. McCloy. Yes.

Mr. Dulles. You mentioned that Lee did not receive any calls at your house. Did he make any telephone calls?

Mrs. Paine. I heard him call what he said was the "Time." You know, he dialed, listened and hung up, and then he told us what time it was. That is all his social contact.

Mr. McCloy. This is only on one occasion that he spoke of General Walker?

Mrs. Paine. Just that one in my hearing, apropos of a discussion that was already begun.

Mr. McCloy. We have rather interrupted the sequence of your questioning.

Mr. Jenner. That is all right.

Representative Boggs. There is one item I might bring out along the line you were inquiring about.

You gave some consideration, did you not, Mrs. Paine, during this period, as to whether Mr. Oswald, Lee Harvey Oswald, could or might have been a Russian agent.

Mrs. PAINE. Yes.

Mr. JENNER. And we discussed this yesterday, as I recall?

Mrs. PAINE. Briefly.

Mr. JENNER. And what conclusions did you come to on that score and why?

Mrs. PAINE. I thought that he was not very intelligent. I saw as far as I could see he had no particular contacts. He was not a person I would have hired for a job of any sort, no more than I would have let him borrow my car.

Mr. JENNER. Did you give consideration in that connection? Did his level of intelligence affect your judgment as to whether the Russian Government would have hired him?

Mrs. PAINE. Yes.

Mr. JENNER. How did it affect you?

Mrs. PAINE. I doubted they would have hired him. I kept my mind open on it to wonder.

Mr. JENNER. And you had doubt why?

Mrs. PAINE. Simply because he had gone to the Soviet Union and announced that he wanted to stay, and then came back, and I wasn't convinced that he liked America.

Mr. JENNER. Did your judgment of him, and as to his level of intelligence, affect your decision ultimately that the Russian Government might not or would not have hired him because he was not a man of capacity to serve in such a way for the Russian Government?

Mrs. PAINE. Yes; that affected my judgment.

Mr. DULLES. Have you any idea as to his motivation in the act, in light of what you have said in the assassination?

Mrs. PAINE. It is conjecture, of course, but I feel he always felt himself to be a small person; and he was right. That he wanted to be greater, or noticed, and Marina had said of him he thinks he is so big and fine, and he should take a more realistic view of himself and not be so conceited.

(At this point, Representative Ford entered the hearing room.)

Mrs. PAINE. And I feel that he acted much more from the emotional pushings within him than from any rational set of ideas, and——

Mr. DULLES. Emotional pushings toward aggrandizement you have in mind is what you said?

Mrs. PAINE. Yes.

Mr. McCLOY. When you testified earlier this morning, Mrs. Paine, about the dry sighting of the rifle, you know what dry sighting is, don't you?

Mrs. PAINE. I found out last night.

Mr. McCLOY. You found that out last night?

Senator COOPER. Tell her to describe it then.

Mrs. PAINE. Shall I try to describe it? See if I know? It involves holding the rifle and as if to fire and pulling the trigger, but without any ammunition in it. Going through the motions and, therefore, wiggling it and having to resight it.

Representative FORD. Going through the motions?

Mrs. PAINE. Of ejecting something.

Senator COOPER. A dry run.

Mr. JENNER. Is that sufficient, Senator?

Mrs. PAINE. Do I understand it?

Mr. McCLOY. That is a pretty good description, it is just as well as I can give.

Representative FORD. You actually saw him doing this?

Mrs. PAINE. No, he showed me last night how it was done.

Mr. McCLOY. We had testimony this morning whether he had an opportunity to dry sight the rifle in his New Orleans house.

Mrs. PAINE. I was just discussing what would be visible in the front of his house.

Mr. JENNER. We were having some testimony, Representative Ford, of Lee Harvey Oswald's dry sighting of the rifle when he was in New Orleans.

Representative FORD. Marina so testified when she was here.

Mr. McCLOY. You don't purport to say it was impossible for him to do it without observation but it was difficult.

Mrs. PAINE. It was difficult.

My then 2-year-old boy found a number of boys with trucks to play with right on that immediate driveway or alley as it is marked on the paper and small boys would have been very interested and they went right by there and Marina complained that Junie couldn't get her nap because there were so many children.

Mr. McCLOY. He could have done it very early in the morning without observation?

Mrs. PAINE. Yes.

Mr. DULLES. Have you any idea generally how Lee Oswald used his time, I mean when you weren't observing him when he wasn't at your house? Did he talk, tell you how he used his time? Did he use it on television? What I am trying to get at is—is there a great deal of time he had available to him that there is no way of knowing what he did. But did he talk about that, did he give you an idea of what he was, how he occupied himself, reading, television?

Mrs. PAINE. Talking just about the time after October 4 when he was——

Mr. DULLES. Yes; let's take it in that period.

Mrs. PAINE. I knew he was occupied with looking for a job.

Mr. DULLES. Yes.

Mrs. PAINE. How much of the day this occupied him, of course, I didn't know. I didn't see him. Then he got the job, and I judge that occupied him more fully. He spoke of one evening meeting he went to, this National Indignation Committee meeting.

Mr. DULLES. What about other evenings? Do you know anything about other evenings when he wasn't with you?

Mrs. PAINE. Except for the one in which he accompanied my husband to a Civil Liberties Union meeting.

Mr. DULLES. All right.

Mr. McCLOY. Did you, at any stage of your life while you were, whether living with your husband or apart from him, did you ever contemplate inviting anyone to come and live with you in anything like the manner in which you did invite Marina?

Mrs. PAINE. My mother completed her studies at Oberlin College in February, and we talked——

Mr. JENNER. February 1963?

Mrs. PAINE. No; just now, February of 1964 and we talked about the possibility as long ago as last summer of 1963, we talked about the possibility of her coming and staying for several months. I said I was tired of living alone. This is not exactly comparable, but it also is a search for a roommate.

Mr. McCLOY. But apart from your mother, there was no one similarly situated to Marina, whom you thought of inviting to live with you?

Mrs. PAINE. No one situated similarly that I knew either.

Mr. McCLOY. No; you didn't invite anyone?

Mrs. PAINE. Didn't make any other such invitation.

Mr. McCLOY. Anyone to live with you.

Mr. JENNER. Before returning to the automobile and somewhat along the tail end at least of Representative Boggs' inquiries of you, did you ever give any consideration, Mrs. Paine, to the possibility that Lee Harvey Oswald might have been employed by some agency of the Government of the United States?

Mrs. PAINE. I never gave that any consideration.

Mr. JENNER. None whatsoever?

Mrs. PAINE. None whatsoever.

Mr. JENNER. It never occurred to you at any time?

Mrs. PAINE. It never occurred to me at any time.

Mr. JENNER. That is all on that.

Was the absence of its occurring to you based on your overall judgment of Lee Harvey Oswald and his lack, as you say, of, not a highly intelligent man?

Mrs. PAINE. Yes.

Mr. JENNER. There was some reason why you gave it no thought, is that correct?

Mrs. PAINE. That, and he was not in a position to know anything of use to either Government. I am questioning myself.

Mr. JENNER. Would you please elaborate?

512

Mrs. PAINE. As regards he might be a Soviet agent, what does this man know that would be of interest to anybody or what could you find out, and you judge he didn't know anything that the Soviets might be interested in, and, as I say, I never gave it any thought of the possibility of his being employed by this Government.

Mr. JENNER. Now, Representative Ford, Mrs. Paine had been relating to us her experiences with Lee Harvey Oswald with respect to his ability to operate an automobile, and she has up to this moment revealed some things to us which we had not known of and it is something that is causing the staff considerable concern. This is his ability to drive which is a proper connection with his visit to Mexico in some one or two instances and also his escape or his attempted escape and other elements.

We interrupted the chronology to have Mrs. Paine state fully everything she knows on this particular subject.

Representative FORD. It is important.

Mr. JENNER. If we can recall just about where you were because I would like to have you pick it up just exactly where you were in this chronology.

Mrs. PAINE. I had about completed the full statement of what I saw of his driving.

I will pick up by repeating when he turned a right angle corner he would turn too far and have to correct. I will complete now by describing my teaching him to park.

Mr. JENNER. Was this on that same Sunday afternoon?

Mrs. PAINE. There were, I think, three altogether, but I am not certain. This is the only particular reference.

Mr. JENNER. Excuse me, but I think, Mr. Chairman, Representative Ford, Mrs. Paine has related to us something we had not known, that this Sunday afternoon——

Mrs. PAINE. October 13.

Mr. JENNER. October 13, when she sought to instruct Lee Harvey Oswald on the local parking lot—was it by a shopping center?

Mrs. PAINE. Yes.

Mr. JENNER. That he had gotten into the car, in the driveway, with the key, and had turned on the motor of the car, had backed it up into the street.

Mrs. PAINE. And then proceeded to drive to the shopping center.

Mr. JENNER. With Mrs. Paine.

Mrs. PAINE. While I complained.

Mr. JENNER. Mrs. Paine complaining because she was concerned; she is the daughter of an insurance actuary.

Mrs. PAINE. In my complaint I simply said that I would drive back, and that I didn't want him to drive on the street, but I didn't insist that he stop at that moment.

Mr. JENNER. Thank you, Mr. Chairman.

Mrs. PAINE. I recall one other afternoon when he practiced just parking directly in front of our house, and when, as I say, after he had done this he wanted me to drive the car into the driveway, that being a little harder to do.

Mr. JENNER. Where did you keep your car ordinarily, in the driveway?

Mrs. PAINE. Always in the driveway in front of our house; the garage itself is too full of many other things.

Mr. JENNER. Did you leave the key in the car?

Mrs. PAINE. I never leave the key in the car; I always lock it.

Mr. JENNER. That was your habit with respect to the ignition key?

Mrs. PAINE. I always lock the car and leave the ignition key in my purse.

Mr. JENNER. You never leave the ignition key around your home?

Mrs. PAINE. Well, my purse was in the home.

Mr. JENNER. So it was not in the open?

Mrs. PAINE. He had to go in the purse, never. Just how he got the car started. I recall my shock that he had. But I must have laid out the key or something because I did not intend for him to start it.

Mr. JENNER. You didn't give him the key on that occasion to go out and start the motor?

Mrs. PAINE. Absolutely not.

Mr. JENNER. But when you came out of the house he had already started the motor and backed the car into the street?

Mrs. PAINE. No, no; I let him back it out.

Mr. JENNER. You did?

Mrs. PAINE. I was deciding what I was going to do.

Mr. DULLES. You were in the car at that time?

Mrs. PAINE. Yes. I had gotten in the car at that time.

Representative FORD. And he was in the driver's seat?

Mrs. PAINE. Yes.

Representative FORD. Yes.

Mr. JENNER. Was he in the driver's seat when you came out of the house?

Mr. PAINE. That is my recollection. Then, referring now to the practice of his parking.

Mr. JENNER. Excuse me, Representative Ford, the witness had also related to us, which we had not known, when she came to New Orleans in the spring to bring Marina from Irving to New Orleans, that Lee Harvey Oswald told her that he had driven his uncle's car, one of the Murrets, in New Orleans on the street.

Go ahead.

Representative FORD. Perhaps I should say that I have been absent for a half hour or so attending a very important committee meeting, so I didn't get this story from the outset and I appreciate being brought up to date on it.

Mrs. PAINE. There were two occasions when we practiced parking, one in the larger parking lot just backing into, pretending there were cars there to back between, as in parallel parking, and another occasion directly in front of my house. On this second occasion directly in front of my house he finally learned how to do it. He had had a bad time, getting his wheels too cramped and not getting in, and getting his wheels straightened out, a beginner's mistakes.

Finally, I got into the car and told him when to start reversing the twist on his wheel and cramp, and he said, so soon. It was a surprise. It didn't feel to him it was time already to start coming out of the turn.

And then he saw that it was when he then got into the parking place correctly, and quite soon got the feel of it but this was clearly his first experience doing it right, and then he practiced doing it right several times, and he learned quite well, I thought.

(At this point, Chief Justice Warren entered the hearing room.)

Representative FORD. On these subsequent occasions did he ask you to help him or did he take the keys and do it on his own initiative?

Mrs. PAINE. No, he never took the keys. I offered to give him—give Lee lessons on Sunday afternoons and we managed to do it a few Sunday afternoons, I think three altogether and there were a couple of weekends when we didn't get the lesson in, something intervened.

Representative FORD. This was in October of 1963?

Mrs. PAINE. October and November. I think the last lesson was November 10, being the last Sunday.

Mr. DULLES. What progress did he make over that period?

Mrs. PAINE. Considerable.

Mr. DULLES. Reasonable progress?

Mrs. PAINE. Very reasonable progress. I thought he learned well, as I have said, both backing and to make a right-angle turn, and really began to understand the feeling of parking.

Representative FORD. Did he indicate to you when he might apply for a driver's license?

Mrs. PAINE. Yes. Oh, yes. Thank you. It is a whole new section.

Mr. JENNER. I was about to go into that.

Mr. DULLES. There was some testimony on that point, I believe.

Mrs. PAINE. Yes.

Representative FORD. Mr. Frazier testified that Oswald mentioned to him that he was going to or had, I am not sure which, and I was wondering whether he mentioned it to you?

Mr. DULLES. Got in line.

Mrs. PAINE. Yes, on November 9, which was election day, Saturday, in Texas.

Mr. JENNER. This was the weekend he was home?

Mrs. PAINE. This was the weekend that he was home, which was the last weekend he was home, don't call it home though.

Mr. JENNER. I am sorry. It was the last weekend that he was at your home?

Mrs. PAINE. That is correct.

Mr. JENNER. And he arrived the previous day, evening or late afternoon?

Mrs. PAINE. That is correct.

Mr. JENNER. Now starting with that Friday afternoon, please relate the course of events?

Mrs. PAINE. Well, I will say that we went Saturday morning to a station in Dallas where you can take the written test and eye test that permits you to get a learner's permit, but when we got there—that is all of us, children, Lee, Marina and myself, driving in my car to Oak Cliff—when we got there it was closed, being election day. I hadn't thought, realized that this would mean it would be closed. So we returned.

The next weekend——

Mr. JENNER. Excuse me, before you reach that.

Mrs. PAINE. Right.

Mr. JENNER. Are you reasonably certain that he came home or came to Irving the previous afternoon?

Mrs. PAINE. Certainly.

Mr. JENNER. Perhaps to refresh your recollection, do you remember a weekend in which Lee Harvey Oswald called from Dallas and said to Marina that he would not be in that Friday afternoon because he was going to do some job hunting the next morning, and that he would come the next day? Could it be that this was that weekend?

Mrs. PAINE. Well, he had already had a job that weekend, didn't he? So he wouldn't have been job hunting. I recall he was there in the morning, Saturday morning.

Mr. JENNER. Looking for another job?

Mrs. PAINE. Oh, well, no.

Mr. JENNER. You don't recall any discussion of his being dissatisfied with the job at the Texas School Book Depository?

Mrs. PAINE. No.

Mr. JENNER. And was undertaking to look for another job?

Mrs. PAINE. No.

Mr. JENNER. There is no discussion?

Mrs. PAINE. There is one Saturday that he came out later but that was still in October. It was the second weekend that he came out, altogether he came out on the weekend of the 4th, so he would have come out on October 12, Saturday. It doesn't check with my recollection.

Mr. JENNER. So just to make sure, it is your present recollection that you can recall no occasion when you were advised by Marina or directly that Lee Harvey Oswald called and said he would not be in on that particular Friday but would come the next day?

Mrs. PAINE. I would be quite certain it was not that weekend. It is possible that this happened, I don't recall any discussion, nor did I have any idea that there had been any occasion when he had to look for a different job.

Mr. JENNER. Never any discussion on that subject?

Mrs. PAINE. Never.

Just to complete the discussion of automobile driving, I will go on to the next weekend then when he did not come out to my house, but I——

Representative FORD. That would be the weekend of the 18th?

Mrs. PAINE. Just prior to the assassination. The 16th I was having a birthday party for my little girl and said I couldn't possibly take him again to this place so he could take a test. But that he didn't need a car. This was news to him. He thought he needed a car for his initial test, learner's permit. I said he could go himself from Dallas.

Mr. JENNER. This was a conversation between you and Lee Oswald?

Mrs. PAINE. Yes.

Mr. JENNER. How did it take place?

515

Mrs. PAINE. It must have been by phone.

Mr. JENNER. Did he call you or did you call him?

Mrs. PAINE. He called to the house nearly every night around 5:30 to talk to Marina. And Marina suggested to him that he wouldn't, shouldn't come out that weekend because I was having a birthday party and it had been a long weekend, the prior weekend. She didn't want him to wear out his welcome, and then I said to him he could still try to get——

Mr. JENNER. You did talk with him on the telephone?

Mrs. PAINE. That is my recollection. I am certain that I talked with him, that he was surprised that he didn't need a car. I had to tell him that he didn't need a car to take with him to take his test.

Mr. JENNER. Take his initial test?

Mrs. PAINE. Take his test, and suggested that he go from Dallas himself to take this test. Then he called us Saturday afternoon of the 16th to say he had been and tried to get his driver's permit but that he had arrived before closing time but still to late to get in because there was a long line ahead of him, the place having been closed both the previous Saturday for election day and the following Monday, the 11th, Veterans Day. There were a lot of people who wanted to get permits and he was advised that it wouldn't pay him to wait in line. He didn't have time to be tested.

Mr. JENNER. Could you help us fix, can you recall as closely as possible the day of the week, this is the weekend of the assassination, was it not?

Mrs. PAINE. The weekend before.

Mr. JENNER. The weekend before, and this conversation you are now relating that you had with him in which he said that he had gone to the driver's license station, when did that conversation with you take place?

Mrs. PAINE. That conversation was with Marina, and she told me about it.

Mr. JENNER. When did she tell you about it?

Mrs. PAINE. He called her, it must have been Saturday afternoon, soon after he had been, he went Saturday morning and they closed at noon.

Mr. JENNER. I see. This was the weekend he did not come out to Irving?

Mrs. PAINE. This was the weekend he did not come out.

Mr. JENNER. The weekend in which you had your birthday party for your son was it?

Mrs. PAINE. It was either that same afternoon or it was possibly Sunday, I don't recall. It is important though. I wish I could recall when his call to her was. Since it relates to the problem of when I dialed his number.

Mr. JENNER. Mr. Chairman, I have marked as Commission Exhibit No. 426 a form or document which purports to be a driver's permit or driver's license permit application by Lee Harvey Oswald. It is a one-page form document on heavy board, or at least heavy paper.

Are you familiar sufficiently with the handwriting or handprinting of Lee Harvey Oswald to be able to tell us whether the writing and handprinting on that document is or is not Lee Harvey Oswald's?

Mrs. PAINE. I am not sufficiently familiar. I can simply compare it with the only other thing I have seen in his printing which is what he wrote down in my diary.

Mr. JENNER. Refreshing your recollection in that respect and looking at the exhibit, if you are able to do so, would you give us your opinion as to whether the exhibit is in the handwriting or handprinting of Lee Harvey Oswald?

Mrs. PAINE. I think it very likely is.

Mr. JENNER. In your short talk with Lee Harvey Oswald on the subject of his having gone to the license application department in Dallas, was anything said about his actually having filled out a driver's license or a learner's permit application?

Mrs. PAINE. No; nothing.

Mr. DULLES. Could we have the date of this document?

Mr. JENNER. If it is dated. My recollection is it is not.

Mrs. PAINE. His birthday is on it only. Picked up at his room on the date of the assassination. I guess it was picked up, I don't know.

Mr. JENNER. Could I review this with you a little bit? Did Lee Harvey Oswald on this occasion tell you in the course of what limited telephone conversation you had with him, that he had gone to the driver's license application bureau?

Mrs. PAINE. No; he told Marina.

Mr. JENNER. And did—he told Marina and then Marina in turn told you?

Mrs. PAINE. Yes.

Mr. JENNER. How near the time of the telephone conversation?

Mrs. PAINE. She told me immediately.

Mr. JENNER. Did Marina tell you?

Mrs. PAINE. Yes.

Mr. JENNER. She just turned from the phone and told you at once?

Mrs. PAINE. That is correct.

Mr. JENNER. This was spontaneous?

Mrs. PAINE. Yes. It may have been while she was still on the phone, I don't recall, but it certainly was immediate.

Mr. JENNER. Mr. Dulles, to answer your question the document is not dated.

Representative FORD. I was just noticing in the upper right-hand corner on the one side he lists his occupation as photographer.

Mr. JENNER. Yes; this is so.

Mrs. PAINE. This is what he wanted to do, not what he was doing.

Mr. JENNER. Would you please relate to the Commission what your impression of what his occupation was or occupation had been during the period of time that you had known him?

Mrs. PAINE. When I first met him he was working at Jaggars-Chiles-Stovall. And had expressed himself as liking his work. I gathered that it was a kind of copying or making up of advertising layout, develop a photographic process.

When we arrived at New Orleans he pointed to a building where he was working. I saw no writing on the outside of the building. He said—no, first on the phone when he first called to say he had a job, he said he was doing work similar to what he had been doing, photographic type of work.

Representative FORD. Work in Dallas?

Mrs. PAINE. He called to us in Dallas from New Orleans to say he was doing such work.

Mr. JENNER. In New Orleans?

Mrs. PAINE. Subsequently, I have heard it is not so, but this is what he told Marina and she told me over the phone. He said, and she told me immediately over the phone, that he was getting $1.50 an hour instead of $1.25 he had been getting, and then in New Orleans he pointed to a building where he was working, somewhere along the river, near the French Quarter, but a big large brick building with no particular designation on it. I don't know what sort of building it was, but he said it was the photo outfit where he was working then.

When he was looking for a job he said, now, in October, early October, he came back to the Dallas area and he was looking for a job, he said he was hopeful of getting similar work again, photographic layout, whatever it was. But that he was pleased to get any job that would produce an income.

Mr. DULLES. For the Commission's information, Mr. Jenner, is this not, that is Exhibit No. 426, a form which Lee Oswald apparently took home, or filled out somewhere, either his home or at the office, but it was never sworn to and is not signed.

Mr. JENNER. That is correct.

Mr. DULLES. It is not a completed document. It has no date on it.

Mr. JENNER. It is my information and there will be testimony and that is why I didn't go into the document, that it was found in his, among his effects in his room on Beckley Street. With permission, I might describe the document possibly a little more in detail in view of the interest and the question. At the top of the document under name there is hand printing on this form, first the form is entitled "Application for Texas Driver's License."

Mrs. PAINE. May I interrupt?

(Whereupon, at 12:45 o'clock the President's Commission recessed.)